MODERNIS...

King Alfred's
Winchester

MODERNIST ISLAM, 1840–1940

A SOURCEBOOK

Edited by CHARLES KURZMAN

UNIVERSITY PRESS

2002

OXFORD
UNIVERSITY PRESS

Oxford New York
Auckland Bangkok Buenos Aires Cape Town Chennai
Dar es Salaam Delhi Hong Kong Istanbul Karachi Kolkata
Kuala Lumpur Madrid Melbourne Mexico City Mumbai Nairobi
São Paulo Taipei Tokyo Toronto

Published by Oxford University Press, Inc.
198 Madison Avenue, New York, New York 10016

www.oup.com

Oxford is a registered trademark of Oxford University Press

Library of Congress Cataloging-in-Publication Data
Modernist Islam, 1840–1940 : a sourcebook, edited by Charles Kurzman.
    p. cm.
Includes bibliographical references and indexes.
ISBN 0-19-515467-3; 0-19-515468-1 (pbk.)
1. Islamic renewal—History—19th century. 2. Islamic renewal—History—20th century.
3. Islamic countries—Intellectual life—19th century. 4. Islamic countries—Intellectual
life—20th century. I. Kurzman, Charles. II. Title.
BP60 .M55 2002
297'.09'04—dc21   2002022046

The editors thank the original copyright holders for permission to re-publish the works in this
anthology. We thank the Noor Research Foundation, the Rockefeller Foundation, and the
University of North Carolina at Chapel Hill for their financial support.
     We thank Ihsan 'Abbas, Edward A. Allworth, Ali Badran, Margot Badran, Niyazi Berkes,
Leon Carl Brown, Kenneth Cragg, Hager El Hadidi, Raghda El Essawi, Howard L. Goodman,
Abu Bakar Hamzah, Achmad Jainuri, Erni Haryanti Kahfi, Nikki R. Keddie, Lathiful Khuluq,
Javed Majeed, Helena Malikyar, Ishaq Masa'ad, Akhmad Minhadji, Natalie Mobini-Kesheh,
Ken Petersen, Samiha Sidhom Peterson, Lisa Pollard, Christopher Shackle, Durlab Singh,
Devin Stewart, Christian W. Troll, and Yektan Türkyılmaz as well as our fellow editors, for
their fine translations.
     We thank Butrus Abu-Manneh, Engin Akarli, Louis Brener, Daniel W. Brown,
Abdelwahab El-Affendi, Carl W. Ernst, Paulo Fernando de Moraes Farias, Thomas
Hinnebusch, Hasan Javadi, Ahmet T. Karamustafa, Enes Karić, Bruce B. Lawrence, Roman
Loimeier, Ma Haiyun, Hossein Modarressi, Ebrahim Moosa, Henry Munson, R. Seán O'Fahey,
Shantanu Phukan, Stefan Reichmuth, Saba Risaluddin, Heba Mostafa Risk, Andrew Robarts,
David W. Robinson, William R. Roff, Holly Shissler, Devin Stewart, Amin Tarzi, Mohamad
Tavakoli-Targhi, Ibrahima Thioub, Ghulam Vahed, John O. Voll, and Muhammad Qasim
Zaman for their kind advice and assistance.

9 8 7 6 5 4 3 2 1

Printed in the United States of America
on acid-free paper

Contents by Region

Contents by Theme

Science and Education

Women's Rights

Section Editors

MODERNIST ISLAM, 1840–1940

FINDING REASONS FOR THE CONSTITUTION IN THE KORAN

(FROM "MULLA NASIR-UD-DIN THE PERSIAN "PUNCH")

Source: Eustache de Lorey and Douglas Sladen, *The Moon of the Fourteenth Night: Being the Private Life of an Unmarried Diplomat in Persia during the Revolution* (London: Hurst & Blackett, 1910), p. 98.

Introduction:
The Modernist Islamic Movement

Edouard Valmont was a French diplomat serving in Tehran, Iran, when a constitutionalist movement erupted and came to power in 1906. This movement, combining religious and secular forces, argued that Islam was compatible with democratic principles. Valmont was bemused. In a ghostwritten memoir, he held that Iranians, even apparently enlightened ones, suffer "the lack of real comprehension of the spirit of the Constitution."[1]

As evidence of the difficulty modern institutions faced in an Islamic country, Valmont's memoir included a cartoon, reproduced at left, showing a clerical figure pointing with one hand to the Qur'an and holding up his other hand to block curious onlookers from peeking. The caption read: "Finding reasons for the constitution in the Koran (from 'Mulla Nasir-ud-din[,'] the Persian 'Punch')." The message seems clear: Muslims may claim that Islam supports constitutionalism, but such claims don't bear close scrutiny.

It is, rather, Valmont's use of this cartoon that doesn't bear scrutiny. The original—published with a slightly different drawing in *Mulla Nasruddin*, the famed satirical journal of Baku, Azerbaijan—had an entirely different caption. It read, in Azeri Turkish: "I cure the ill by writing down verses [from the

Qur'an]."[2] The cartoon said nothing about constitutionalism, but rather mocked an old-fashioned religious practice. Valmont saw an image lampooning an Islamic scholar and inverted its meaning, from antitraditionalism to antimodernism.

Valmont's suspicion of modernist Islam was common among Christians, even among scholars who studied Islam. Duncan Black Macdonald (United States, 1863–1943), for example, wrote in 1903 that Islam does not allow constitutionalism because the caliph "cannot set up beside himself a constitutional assembly and give it rights against himself. He is the successor of Muhammad and must rule, within [divine] limitations, as an absolute monarch."[3] Yet within a few years of that statement, some of the leading scholars of the Islamic world were arguing exactly the contrary. Muhammad 'Abduh (Egypt, 1849–1905; see chapter 3)—the highest-ranking religious official in Egypt—wrote privately in 1904 that he supported a parliamentary democracy.[4] In 1908, Mehmed Cemaleddin Efendi (Turkey, 1848–1917)—the chief religious authority of the Ottoman Empire, appointed

---

2. *Mulla Nasruddin*, September 22, 1906, pp. 4–5. Translation from Azeri by Mahmoud Sadri.

3. Duncan B. Macdonald, *The Development of Moslem Theology, Jurisprudence, and Constitutional Theory* (New York: Charles Scribner's Sons, 1903), p. 58.

4. Malcolm H. Kerr, *Islamic Reform: The Political and Legal Theories of Muhammad 'Abduh and Rashid Rida* (Berkeley: University of California Press, 1966), pp. 147–148.

---

1. Eustache de Lorey and Douglas Sladen, *The Moon of the Fourteenth Night: Being the Private Life of an Unmarried Diplomat in Persia during the Revolution* (London: Hurst & Blackett, 1910), p. 156. "Valmont" was a pseudonym.

directly by the caliph—said that he too supported constitutionalism.[5] Also in 1908, two senior scholars of Shi'i Islam telegraphed their support at a crucial moment in Iran's Constitutional Revolution: "We would like to know if it would be possible to execute Islamic provisions without a constitutional regime!"[6]

Macdonald's blanket statement about the incompatibility of Islam and constitutionalism also ignored, or dismissed, the half-century's crescendo of proposals for Islamic constitutionalism. These proposals formed part of a movement that generated tremendous intellectual ferment throughout the Islamic world in the nineteenth and early twentieth centuries. This movement sought to reconcile Islamic faith and modern values such as constitutionalism, as well as cultural revival, nationalism, freedom of religious interpretation, scientific investigation, modern-style education, women's rights, and a bundle of other themes discussed later in this introduction (see also the Contents by Theme). The authors and activists engaged in this movement saw the tension between Islamic faith and modern values as a historical accident, not an inherent feature of Islam. The modern period both required and permitted this accident to be repaired: the threat of European domination made repair necessary, and the modern values associated with European domination made repair possible. The modernist Islamic movement pioneered the formation or reformation of educational institutions; agitation for political liberalization or decolonization; and the establishment of a periodical press throughout the Islamic world.

One defining characteristic of this movement was the self-conscious adoption of "modern" values— that is, values that authors explicitly associated with the modern world, especially rationality, science, constitutionalism, and certain forms of human equality. Thus this movement was not simply "modern" (a feature of modernity) but also "modernist" (a proponent of modernity). Activists described themselves and their goals by the Arabic terms *jadid* (new) and *mu'asir* (contemporary), the Turkish terms *yeni*

(new) and *genç* (young), and similar words in other languages. (By contrast, *muda*, Malay for young, was initially a pejorative term applied by opponents to the modernist Islamic movement.)[7] A second characteristic involved the usage of a self-consciously Islamic discourse. Activists were not simply Muslims but also wished to preserve and improve Islamic faith in the modern world. This combination of characteristics emerged in the first part of the nineteenth century, as several Islamic states adopted European military and technical organization, and various Muslim travelers to Europe brought back influential tales of progress and enlightenment. We have picked the date 1840 as a rough marker of the emergence of this form of discourse.

Modernism distinguished the modernist Islamic movement from previous Islamic reform movements, which did not identify their values as modern, and from contemporaneous competitors such as traditionalists who rejected modern values. Finally, it distinguished the movement from two of its successors, which supplanted modernist Islam in the middle of the twentieth century: on one hand secularists who downplayed the importance of Islam in the modern world, privileging nationalism, socialism, or other ideologies; on the other hand religious revivalists who espoused modern values (such as social equality, codified law, and mass education) but downplayed their modernity, privileging authenticity and divine mandates. Following one classic study, we have dated the moment of decline at roughly 1940,[8] though modernist Islam continued to spread in several regions after this date. Late in the twentieth century, the combination of modernist and Islamic discourses was revived in a subset of modernist Islam that I have labeled "liberal Islam," which sought to resuscitate the reputation and accomplishments of earlier modernists.[9]

The boundaries of the modernist Islamic movement could be imprecise, but its core was clear: a set

5. Cemaleddin Efendi, *Siyasi Hatıralar, 1908–1913 (Political Memoirs, 1908–1913)* (Istanbul, Turkey: Tercüman, 1978), pp. 43–47; M. Şükrü Hanioğlu, *Preparation for a Revolution: The Young Turks, 1902–1908* (New York: Oxford University Press, 2001), pp. 489–490.

6. Abdul-Hadi Hairi, *Shi'ism and Constitutionalism in Iran* (Leiden, Netherlands: E. J. Brill, 1977), p. 242.

7. William R. Roff, *The Origins of Malay Nationalism*, 2d ed. (Kuala Lumpur, Malaysia: Oxford University Press, 1994), p. 67.

8. Albert Hourani, *Arabic Thought in the Liberal Age, 1798–1939* (London: Oxford University Press, 1962), chapter 13.

9. Charles Kurzman, ed., *Liberal Islam* (New York: Oxford University Press, 1998). Several authors are omitted from the present book because their work was included in this earlier anthology.

of key figures who served as lodestones for Muslim intellectuals of the late nineteenth and twentieth centuries. Three figures in particular were famed throughout the Islamic world: Sayyid Jamal al-Din al-Afghani (Iran, 1838–1897; chapter 11), his student and collaborator 'Abduh, and 'Abduh's student and collaborator Muhammad Rashid Rida (Syria-Egypt, 1865–1935; chapter 6), plus regional pioneers Sayyid Ahmad Khan (North India, 1817–1898; chapter 40), Namık Kemal (Turkey, 1840–1888; chapter 17), and Ismail Bey Gasprinskii (Crimea, 1851–1914; chapter 29). Supporters cited and debated the statements of these figures, especially the periodicals they edited: Afghani and 'Abduh's *al-'Urwa al-Wuthqa* (*The Strongest Link*), published in Paris, 1884; Rida's *al-Manar* (*The Beacon*), published in Cairo, 1898–1935; Sayyid Ahmad Khan's *Tahdhib al-Akhlaq* (*Refinement of Morals*), published in Aligarh, 1870–1896; Namık Kemal's *Hürriyet* (*Liberty*) and *İbret* (*Warning*), published in Paris and Istanbul, 1868–1873; and Gasprinskii's *Tercüman/Perevodchik* (*The Interpreter*), published in Bakhchisaray, Crimea, 1883–1914. Even authors who disagreed with the modernist Islamic project located themselves in relation to these central figures.

The present anthology includes influential writings by these authors. Yet the modernist Islamic movement was not limited to central figures, and this anthology seeks also to highlight the contributions of authors from around the Islamic world who were influential in their regional contexts, from South Africa to East Europe to Southeast Asia,[10] but not so well known to other Muslims or scholars of Islam. The anthology also samples the modernists' varied forms of discourse: journalistic essays, scholarly treatises, and didactic fiction of various sorts, including dialogues, stories, plays, and poems. In addition, the anthology presents a cross section of themes and positions. The modernist Islamic movement was never monolithic, and variation, even deep disagreement, existed on virtually all subjects. Modern values included both state-building and limits on state power; elitism and egalitarianism; discipline and liberty; Europhilism and anti-imperialism. The modernists' Islamic faith encompassed both mysticism and abhorrence of mysticism; strategic use of traditional scholarship and rejection of traditional scholarship; return to a pristine early Islam and updating of early practices in keeping with historical change.

Considerations of influence and diversity guided the selection of authors and works in this anthology. I would like to take this opportunity to thank my colleagues who served as section editors and project advisers, applying their expertise to the selection of succinct, important, relevant, and characteristic contributions from the authors they have chosen. Inevitably, the anthology omits certain important figures for lack of space, and some decisions may be controversial. The Islamic faith of a couple of authors (to be discussed in a moment) may be in question—indeed, opponents charged that 'Abduh and other leading modernists were "irreligious" and even "satanic."[11] The modernism of some authors may be criticized—indeed, modernists criticized one another for going too far, or not far enough, in one direction or another. This is to be expected of any intellectual movement. Readers should note that the editors do not wish to construct a "canon" of modernist Islam but rather to make available in a single volume a representative sampling of major voices in the movement.

What can we learn from these voices? The following sections explore four issues that emerge from the writings of the modernist Islamic movement, each organized around the freedom of speech. I propose that this was the central intellectual issue of the movement: the right to say novel things in an Islamic discourse. In order to defend modern values, modernists had to defend the right to defend modern values. This they did by referring to the particular challenges and opportunities posed by the onslaught of modernity; by arguing that their own, often nontraditional educations qualified them to speak on Islamic issues; by pioneering new forms of discourse; and, finally, by laying out their modernist vision of Islam. These

---

10. The regional classifications are inevitably somewhat arbitrary, as political control and circuits of training reached across geographic boundaries. Much of North Africa, for example, was part of the Ottoman Empire, but it is grouped here with the rest of Africa to provide cross-regional balance.

11. Amal Ghazali, "Sufism, *Ijtihad*, and Modernity: Yusuf al-Nabhani in the Age of 'Abd al-Hamid II," paper presented at the Middle East Studies Association, Chicago, Ill., 1998, pp. 19–20; Yahya Abdoulline, "Histoire et interprétations contemporaines du second réformisme musulman (ou djadidisme)" (Contemporary History and Interpretations of the Second Muslim Reformism, or Jadidism), *Cahiers du monde russe* (*Annals of the Russian World*), volume 37, numbers 1–2, 1996, p. 71.

problematics remain vivid today for Muslims who wish to espouse modern values in an Islamic discourse.

Why Speak Now?

Modernism is hardly the first movement in Islamic history to claim a dire need for reform and revival of the faith. Such calls could be heard already in the eighth and ninth centuries,[12] and revivalist movements recurred up through the eighteenth century, a period whose revivalist activity "created an underlying theme for the modern Islamic experience."[13] Some modernists called upon this and other precedents of reform, in part, it appears, to demonstrate their continuity with Islamic tradition. Rida (chapter 6), among others, cited the *hadith* (saying of the Prophet): "God sends to this nation at the beginning of every century someone who renews its religion."

Yet the modernists faced a challenge that earlier reformers had not, namely the onslaught of modernity. Modernity was not a disembodied set of ideals; it was associated, rather, with the imperialist expansion of Christian Europe, which threatened Islam in at least five registers.

Militarily, modern means of warfare allowed Europe to conquer vast regions of the Islamic world. This trend had begun in the seventeenth century but gained such momentum by the nineteenth century that modernist Muslims worried about the prospect of complete subjugation. "Like a convict, the Muslim world remains everywhere under someone else's control," wrote Musa Jarullah Bigi (Tatarstan, 1875–1949; chapter 35). Even the Ottoman Empire, the most powerful Islamic state, had lost territory and submitted to treaties allowing foreign intervention in the empire's domestic affairs. Namık Kemal (chapter 17), for example, argued that "the [Ottoman] nation is faced with the threat of extinction," and the Ottoman "state will undoubtedly sink" if current

trends continued. He used this dire prediction to justify his call for democratic reform: "every intelligent person realizes that as long as this tyrannical administration prevails in the state, foreign interventions cannot be stopped."

Economically, modernity appeared to generate wealth and commodities that the Islamic world lacked and desired. Muslim visitors to Europe in the early and mid-nineteenth century marveled at the gas street lamps and other indicators of prosperity.[14] Modernist Muslims attributed this prosperity both to European increases in productivity and to exploitation of other regions, including Islamic homelands. A combination of resentment and respect is expressed, for example, by Mahmud Tarzi (Afghanistan, 1865–1933; chapter 14): "European states, by contrast, not only exploit their own mines, but also those of the entire world. In addition to natural resources, they are also capable of industrial production. This is simply because they have the knowledge and we do not."

Cognitively, modern science challenged other worldviews with its dramatic claims of success. Modernist Muslims accepted these claims. Some emphasized the medieval Islamic roots of modern science, while others emphasized the seemingly miraculous advances made in recent years. All, however, recognized science as a challenge to Islamic understandings of the world. Ahmad Khan (chapter 40), for example, identified this threat even as he embraced modern scientific disciplines: "I am certain that as these sciences spread—and their spreading is inevitable and I myself after all, too, help and contribute towards spreading them—there will arise in the hearts of people an uneasiness and carelessness and even a positive disaffection towards Islam as it has been shaped in our time." According to Ahmad Khan, this threat required Muslims to wipe the "black stains" of traditionalism from "the original luminous face of Islam."

Politically, modern institutions of government seemed, according to their proponents, to maintain social peace and build national unity in ways that contemporary Islamic states could not. According to Khayr al-Din (Tunisia, 1822–1890; chapter 2), European "progress in the governance of mankind, which

---

12. Fazlur Rahman, "Revival and Reform in Islam," in P. M. Holt et al., eds., *The Cambridge History of Islam* (Cambridge, England: Cambridge University Press, 1970), volume 2, p. 633; John Obert Voll, "Renewal and Reform in Islamic History," in John L. Esposito, ed., *Voices of Resurgent Islam* (New York: Oxford University Press, 1983), p. 36.

13. John Obert Voll, *Islam: Continuity and Change in the Modern World*, 2d ed. (Syracuse, N.Y.: Syracuse University Press, 1994), p. 30.

14. Nazik Saba Yared, *Arab Travellers and Western Civilization*, trans. Sumayya Damluji Shahbandar (London: Saqi Books, 1996).

has led to the utmost point of prosperity for their countries," relied primarily on respect for personal and political rights, which he identified as "the basis of the great development of knowledge and civilization in the European kingdoms." Rida wrote in 1907, "The greatest benefit that the peoples of the Orient have derived from the Europeans was to learn how real government ought to be, as well as the assimilation of this knowledge." Muslims could not have developed this independently, he continued. "Had you not reflected upon the state of these people [Europeans], you, or others like you, would not have considered this to be part of Islam."[15] *Ayatullah* Muhammad Tabataba'i (Iran, 1843–1921) noted in a speech to the newly founded Iranian parliament: "I've never seen the constitutional countries myself. But I've heard, and those who have seen the constitutional countries have told me, that the constitution is the cause of the security and flourishing of the country."[16]

Culturally, modernity introduced novel patterns of behavior that threatened to displace existing practices. Shaykh al-Amin bin 'Ali al-Mazrui (Kenya, 1890–1947; chapter 7) worried that "every day we see ourselves mimicking whites, and not only in ways that are good and which do not contradict our religion." Muslims adopted alcohol and European garb, but not "their good customs, like their pastimes, their ways of [conducting] meetings, their love of country, their solidarity, and other things like these." Muslim women cut their hair in European styles but ought rather to value "the knowledge European women have in fixing up their houses and making them comfortable and neat, and rearing their children in a healthy way, and with good customs and manners, and the ability they have in [doing] handy work and crafts and cooking."

In sum, the challenges of modernity appeared to threaten the very existence of Islam. In the context of social Darwinist competition, many Muslims worried that Islam would not be able to compete. Khwaja Altaf Hussein Hali (North India, 1837–1914; chapter 38) worried that the "dilapidated hall of the true religion, whose pillars have been tottering for ages, . . . will remain in the world only a few days more." 'Abd al-Rahman al-Kawakibi (Syria, 1854–1902; chapter 19) feared that "danger has come close—may God forbid it—to the heart." A poem published in Iran and Afghanistan suggested that "The black smoke rising from the roof of the fatherland / Is caused by us. / The flames that devour us from left and right / Are caused by us."[17]

Yet these challenges also provided an opportunity, according to modernist Muslims. By realizing modern ideals, in this view, Islamic societies could not only survive but thrive, as well as recover the original ideals of their faith. "All new things are hardly blameworthy. On the contrary, most innovations are praiseworthy," wrote Rifa'a Rafi' al-Tahtawi (Egypt, 1801–1873; chapter 1).[18] According to Şemseddin Sami Frashëri (Albania-Turkey, 1850–1904; chapter 18), "It is a regrettable circumstance that, because today civilization seems to belong exclusively to the Christian nations, ignorant masses of our own nation take it to be a symbol or requisite of Christianity, and thus deem distancing themselves from it and guarding themselves against it to be a religious duty. We can affirm that it is not the religion of Islam which prevents Muslim nations from becoming civilized."

Even colonial dependence had positive implications, some modernists argued. Muhammad Iqbal (North India, 1877–1938; chapter 41), later an apostle of Pakistani independence, argued that the British Empire was "a civilizing factor" in the Islamic world: "England, in fact, is doing one of our own great duties, which unfavorable circumstances did not permit us to perform. It is not the number of Muhammadans which it protects, but the spirit of the British Empire that makes it the greatest Muhammadan Empire in the world." Thomas Ismaël Urbain (France, 1812–1884), a convert to Islam who infuriated French colonizers of North Africa with his criticism of their brutality, nonetheless defended the potential of colonization to develop "an administrative organization favorable to the development of

15. Youssef M. Choueiri, *Islamic Fundamentalism*, rev. ed. (London: Pinter, 1997), p. 46.

16. Fereydun Adamiyat, *Fikr-i dimukrasi-i ijtima'i dar nahzat-i mashrutiyat-i Iran* (*Social Democratic Thought in the Iranian Constitutionalist Movement*) (Tehran, Iran: Intisharat-i Payam, 1975), p. 4.

17. Vartan Gregorian, *The Emergence of Modern Afghanistan: Politics of Reform and Modernization, 1880–1946* (Stanford, Calif.: Stanford University Press, 1969), p. 167.

18. Gilbert Delanoue, *Moralistes et politiques musulmans dans l'Égypte du XIXe siècle (1798–1882)* (*Muslim Moralists and Politicians in Egypt of the 19th Century, 1798–1882*) (Cairo, Egypt: Institut français d'archéologie orientale du Caire, 1982), volume 2, p. 450.

agriculture and commerce . . . an organization of religion and of justice, a large system of public education, and finally various philanthropic institutions."[19] Sayid Syekh al-Hadi (Malaya, 1867–1934), one of the founders of the Singapore reformist journal *al-Imam* (chapter 46), went so far as to praise British colonizers as God's "righteous servants."[20]

Not all modernists fawned so enthusiastically over European civilization. Some distinguished between aspects worthy of adoption and those to be rejected. Rida, for example, concluded that "all that we need to acquire from Europe is its scientific achievements, technical skill and advanced industries. The acquisition of these aspects does not require all this amount of Westernization."[21] Others, such as Ali Suavi (Turkey, 1839–1878; chapter 16), noted the hypocrisy of European ideals in the age of imperialism: "Just look how those Frenchmen talk pretentiously about freedom and equality, all the while seeking world domination like Caesar." Abu'l-Kalam Azad (Bengal-India, 1888–1958; chapter 44) was bitingly critical of the "inequity" of British colonialism, which "cannot possibly countenance any nationalistic awakening or agitation for progress, reform, or justice . . . as such agitation would spell the inevitable downfall of its dominant power." Hadji Agus Salim (Sumatra-Java, 1884–1954; chapter 49) questioned whether the Dutch colonial government was "exercising its power in accordance with the spirit of the times, that is, taking on the responsibility for preparing these people to develop their own independent talents, so that Indonesians can have their own independent country?" 'Abd al-'Aziz al-Tha'alibi (Tunisia, 1879–1944) compared the freedom of the French press with French colonial decrees limiting the Tunisian press and "prohibiting the entry into Tunisia of newspapers and writings published in France and elsewhere."[22] Yet these critics embraced the ideals of modernity, even as they berated Europeans for failing to live up to these ideals.

Some modernists seemed, frankly, conflicted about European civilization. Iqbal (chapter 41), quoted above praising colonialism's "civilizing" mission in 1909, warned Muslims against modernity a few years later:

> But do not seek the glow of Love from the
> knowledge of to-day,
> Do not seek the nature of Truth from this
> infidel's cup!
> Long have I been running to and fro,
> Learning the secrets of the New Knowledge:
> Its gardeners have put me to the trial
> And have made me intimate with their roses.
> Roses! Tulips, rather, that warn one not to
> smell them—
> Like paper roses, a mirage of perfume.
> Since this garden ceased to enthral me
> I have nested on the Paradisal tree.
> Modern knowledge is the greatest blind—
> Idol-worshipping, idol-selling, idol-making![23]

Later in life, Iqbal offered similarly antagonistic opinions. On one hand, for example, he praised Turkey for its drastic Westernizing reforms: "The truth is that among the Muslim nations of today, Turkey alone has shaken off its dogmatic slumber, and attained self-consciousness. She alone has claimed her right of intellectual freedom; she alone has passed from the ideal to the real—a transition which entails keen intellectual and moral struggle."[24] On the other hand, he castigated Turkey for Westernizing:

> The Turk, torn from the self,
> Enravished by the West, drinks from her hand
> A poison sweet; and since the antidote
> He has renounced, what can I say except
> God save him.[25]

19. Charles-Robert Ageron, *Les Algériens musulmans et la France (1871–1919)* (*Muslim Algerians and France, 1871–1919*) (Paris: Presses Universitaires de France, 1968), volume 1, p. 404.

20. Ibrahim bin Abu Bakar, *Islamic Modernism in Malaya: The Life and Thought of Sayid Syekh al-Hadi, 1867–1934* (Kuala Lumpur, Malaysia: University of Malaya Press, 1994), pp. 159–160.

21. Emad Eldin Shahin, *Through Muslim Eyes: M. Rashid Rida and the West* (Herndon, Va.: International Institute of Islamic Thought, 1993), p. 49.

22. Abdelaziz Thaalbi, *La Tunisie martyre* (*Tunisia the*

Martyr*) (Beirut, Lebanon: Dar al-Gharb al-Islami, 1985), p. 29. First published in 1920.

23. *The Secrets of the Self* (*Asrar-i khudi*), trans. Reynold A. Nicholson (Lahore, Pakistan: Shaikh Muhammad Ashraf, 1950), pp. 76–77. First published in 1915.

24. Muhammad Iqbal, *The Reconstruction of Religious Thought in Islam* (Oxford, England: Oxford University Press, 1930), p. 162; also in Kurzman, ed., *Liberal Islam*, p. 262.

25. *Pilgrimage of Eternity* (*Javidnamah*), trans. Shaikh Mahmud Ahmad (Lahore, Pakistan: Institute of Islamic Culture, 1961), p. 167. First published in 1932.

Iqbal's Persian and Urdu poetry denouncing modernity may be at odds with his English-language prose embracing modernity. But this tension represents the challenge of the modernist Islamic movement as a whole. Modernity involved both threat and opportunity, external imposition and internal renovation. Modernists argued that the crisis demanded drastic reform in the Islamic world.

Who Can Speak?

Logically prior to the substance of their arguments, the modernists had to defend their right to make such arguments. They did so by challenging two forms of scholarly authority that stood in their way: the authority of the past and the authority of the credential.

The authority of the past crystallized in the practice of *taqlid*, a term that literally meant to follow established scholars but which modernists ritually denigrated as blind, irrational imitation of tradition.[26] All of the lodestone figures in the modernist movement weighed in on this theme,[27] as did others: "It is better to follow a beast than an imitator," wrote 'Abd al-Qadir al-Jaza'iri (Algeria-Syria, circa 1807–1883; chapter 15). "*Taqlid* and Islam are mutually contradictory," wrote Abdullah Bubi (Tatarstan, 1871–1922; chapter 32). "*Taqlid* of religious leaders who pretend to present true religion is no different from obedience to political tyrants. Either one is a form of idolatry," wrote Muhammad Husayn Na'ini (Iran, 1860–1936; chapter 13).

Rather than follow precedent, the modernists argued that active reinterpretation of Islamic sources was permitted and even necessary under certain circumstances. Some cited revelation and precedent from the early Islamic era in support of this position. Jamal al-Din al-Qasimi (Syria, 1866–1914; chapter 23)—among many others—quoted a *hadith* in which Muhammad sent a companion, Mu'adh ibn Jabal (died 627), to serve as governor of Yemen: "The Prophet said to him, 'How would you act as judge?' He said, 'I would judge by God's book.' The

Prophet then said, 'And if you do not find a ruling in God's book?' He said, 'By the *sunna* [precedent] of God's Messenger.' The Prophet then said, 'And if you do not find it there?' He said, 'I would perform *ijtihad* [rational interpretation] and spare no effort,' and he struck his chest. Muhammad said, 'Praise God to give success to the messenger of the Messenger of God, as he has pleased the Messenger of God.'"

The concept of *ijtihad*, derived from a root meaning "effort" or "struggle," had for centuries been limited to a fairly technical meaning, referring to the intellectual effort of trained Islamic scholars to arrive at legal rulings on matters not covered in the sacred sources.[28] The modernists latched on to the term and broadened its scope to include three distinct usages.[29] First was the right to reach across the several legal schools (*madhhabs*) in which scholars traditionally limited themselves, and draw arguments from any and all of them—Mahmud Shukri al-Alusi (Iraq, 1857–1924; chapter 20) called it "outlandish" to "state that one is obliged to follow the *madhhab* of a particular scholar, and even more outlandish is the opinion of those who state that one is obliged to adopt one of the four *madhhabs*." Second was the right to bypass the *madhhabs* and reach back directly to the sacred sources, namely the Qur'an and the precedent of the Prophet and his Companions—to "put the Qur'an in its rightful place," in the words of Muhammad Akram Khan (Bengal-Pakistan, 1868–1968; chapter 45). Third was the effort to reconcile the sacred sources with human reason, to contend that "Islam is a religion that is compatible with reason; that is, it has no principles that contradict reason," as stated by Muhammad Abdul Khader Maulavi (Malabar, 1873–1932; chapter 42).

This widened door of *ijtihad* should not have been shut in the early centuries of Islam, modernists contended. Syekh Ahmad Surkati (Sudan-Java, 1872–1943; chapter 48) wrote that *taqlid* was not only contrary to reason and revelation, but also "contrary to the instructions of the *imams* [founders of the four main Sunni schools of law] whom those practicing

---

26. N. Calder, "Taklid," in P. J. Bearman et al., eds., *Encyclopedia of Islam*, 2d ed. (Leiden, Netherlands: Brill, 2000), volume 10, pp. 137–138.

27. Kurzman, *Liberal Islam*, p. 8.

28. J. Schacht, "Idjtihad," in Bernard Lewis et al., eds., *Encyclopedia of Islam*, 2d ed. (Leiden, Netherlands: E. J. Brill; London: Luzac, 1971), volume 3, pp. 1026–1027.

29. Muneer Goolam Fareed, *Legal Reform in the Muslim World: The Anatomy of a Scholarly Dispute in the 19th and the Early 20th Centuries on the Usage of Ijtihad as a Legal Tool* (San Francisco, Calif.: Austin & Winfield, 1996), p. 9.

taqlid claim to be imitating." Rizaeddin bin Fakhreddin (Tatarstan, 1858–1936; chapter 33) made a parallel argument about Muslims' veneration of saintly figures, who "would not have approved of such lies and the extravagant praise and miracles attributed to them." Indeed, some modernists suggested that the door of *ijtihad* had never been shut completely, as scholars—even scholars espousing *taqlid*—were forced by changed circumstance to devise novel approaches.[30] Musa Kazım (Turkey, 1858–1920; chapter 22) wrote that "all of the *'ulama'* [religious scholars] in every era wrote books in accordance with the needs of the day.... We have the same need. We must also reform the theological books in accordance with the needs of our era." In a more critical tone, Ahmad Hassan (Singapore-Indonesia, 1888–1958; chapter 50) accused supporters of *taqlid* of adopting the practice only when it suited them: "When these traditionalist religious scholars agree with the actions and words of the Prophet, they go directly to the *hadith* as the source of this agreement. But if they disagree, then they go to their earlier scholars"—that is, they engage in *taqlid*—"on the basis that they themselves are not 'original' scholars and may not use *hadith* directly."

Modernists saw *taqlid* not as a religious requirement but as an instrument of institutional authority designed to suppress challenging views.[31] Indeed, the modernists' polemical denunciation of traditional Islamic thought may have been aimed more at the authority of conservative scholars than at their actual writings, most of which did not conform to the modernists' caricature. Modernists in Damascus, for example, were repeatedly accused by conservatives and interrogated by Ottoman authorities on charges of espousing *ijtihad*,[32] and modernists in Central Asia had to tiptoe around the issue

to avoid trouble.[33] The theme of authority arises time and again in the modernists' works, especially the analogy between religious authority and political authority. Na'ini, quoted above, likened *taqlid* to political tyranny, and both to idolatry. "Islam delivered man from the slavery of priests. It recognized no intermediary between the Creator and the created," wrote Mirza Riza Quli Shari'at-Sangalaji (Iran, 1890–1944).[34] Bubi (chapter 32) called conservative thought "useful only to oppressive rulers and sultans." The Algerian reformist newspaper *al-Muntaqid* (*The Critic*), edited by 'Abd al-Hamid Ibn Badis (Algeria, 1889–1940; chapter 9), directed its opening editorial against the combined tyranny of political and religious authorities who sought "to rule [the community's] political, economic, intellectual, and religious affairs."[35]

Modernists proposed that contemporary scholars are just as qualified as their predecessors to engage in *ijtihad*. "Do not later men study, compose, and see things like earlier men?" Qasimi asked, quoting a tenth century scholar (chapter 23): "If people were limited to the books of the ancients, then a great deal of knowledge would be lost, penetrating minds would go astray, articulate tongues would be blunted, and we would hear nothing but repetition." Even the Prophet's understanding of Islam, according to Khwaja Ahmad Din Amritsari (North India, 1861–1936) of the Ahl-i-Qur'an movement, was not necessarily superior to that of other Muslims.[36] Or perhaps, if one believes in progress, later scholars are more qualified than earlier ones, a theme broached by Bubi (chapter 32): "Since God's creation is progressing day by day, therefore the latest religion, Islam, is the most perfect religion of all the religions. Similarly, it is quite possible and in accordance with

30. Recent scholarship has confirmed this view—see Wael B. Hallaq, *A History of Islamic Legal Theories* (Cambridge, England: Cambridge University Press, 1997), pp. 117–124.

31. Recent scholarship suggests that the original purpose of *taqlid* was enforcement of conformity, or in more flattering terms, the building of legal uniformity and predictability—see Mohammad Fadel, "The Social Logic of *Taqlid* and the Rise of the *Mukhtasar*," *Islamic Law and Society*, volume 3, number 2, 1996, pp. 193–233.

32. David Dean Commins, *Islamic Reform: Politics and Social Change in Late Ottoman Syria* (New York: Oxford University Press, 1990), pp. 51–52, 55–59, 62–63, 114.

33. Ingeborg Baldauf, "Jadidism in Central Asia within Reformism and Modernism in the Muslim World," *Die Welt des Islams* (*The World of Islam*), volume 41, number 1, 2001, p. 77.

34. Yann Richard, "Shari'at Sangalaji: A Reformist Theologian of the Rida Shah Period," in Said Amir Arjomand, ed., *Authority and Political Culture in Shi'ism* (Albany: State University of New York Press, 1988), p. 172.

35. Ali Merad, *Le réformisme musulman en Algérie de 1925 à 1940* (*Muslim Reformism in Algeria from 1925 to 1940*) (Paris: Mouton & Co., 1967), pp. 445–446.

36. Daniel W. Brown, *Rethinking Tradition in Modern Islamic Thought* (Cambridge, England: Cambridge University Press, 1996), p. 68.

God's *sunna* that in our time there might be scholars of the same degree as, or better than, the scholars of the past."

Even if they overcame the hurdle of *taqlid*, modernists faced a second hurdle: many of them lacked the seminary credentials historically required of religious scholars. Educational pioneer Nabawiyah Musa (Egypt, 1886–1951), a teenager prevented by her family from attending school, taught herself to read, memorized the Qur'an, and sought to interpret its verses. A male relative studying at the al-Azhar mosque in Cairo objected to this act as "heretical," and said that even he would not proceed without a mentor.[37] Modernists combated their handicap by arguing that credentialed scholars ought not to monopolize religious interpretation. Several modernists argued, along with al-Jaza'iri (chapter 15), that "the intelligent person must consider the statement rather than the person who is stating it." For Azad, the Qur'anic verse, "Do they not consider the Qur'an?" (Sura 4, Verse 82), legitimated widespread interpretation, since the verse did not limit "they" to a small group.[38] Further, some modernists suggested that all Muslims had a duty to engage in *ijtihad*. Khayr al-Din (chapter 2) and Na'ini (chapter 13)—Sunni and Shi'i, respectively—both cite the precedent of the second caliph, 'Umar ibn al-Khattab (634–644), who invited all Muslims to judge the propriety of his actions. In Khayr al-Din's telling, 'Umar told the Muslims, "O people, let him among you who sees any deviation in me set it right." A man stood up and said, "By God, if we saw in you deviation we would rectify it with our swords." 'Umar replied, "Praise God who created in this *umma* him who would rectify with his sword my deviations." In these precedents, the independent religious judgment of noncredentialed Muslims was deemed praiseworthy.

Some modernists went further and argued that traditional educations had become so sterile and scholastic that they actively *disqualified* their graduates from meaningful intellectual work, leaving the field open to the modern-educated. Afghani (chap-

ter 11) likened traditional scholarship to "a very narrow wick, on top of which is a very small flame that neither lights its surroundings nor gives light to others." Bigi (chapter 35) blamed seminaries for the "widespread stoppage of brains that caused the mind of the Muslim world to remain lifeless and motionless, and therefore to decline." The Singapore newspaper *al-Imam* (chapter 46) excoriated traditional teachers who assigned rote exercises "in order to take up time, lazily believing that [education is like watching] plants grow." The Azerbaijan newspaper *Kaspii* (*The Caspian*) wrote that traditional schools "do not deserve to be called schools."[39]

Education in secular subjects, by contrast, would prepare students properly for the practice and study of Islam. Abdurrauf Fitrat (Bukhara, 1886–1938; chapter 34) made the analogy with trains and steamships, invented by "infidels" but resulting in increased pilgrimages by Muslims: "The question of studying is just the same. Under the old system, women are deprived of learning and most of the men live in illiteracy, and in every generation one or two great scholars appear. Under the new system, because it is easier, both women and men will become learned." The Young Ansar-Ud-Deen Society, founded in Nigeria in 1923, established a series of Western-style schools, arguing, in the words of one its founders, that "by this means alone . . . can Islam be better studied and understood."[40]

This critique emerged from within the seminaries themselves, pioneered by traditionally trained reformists—not necessarily full-fledged modernists—who admired aspects of modern education. They sought to reform the seminaries by incorporating modern discipline—for example, examinations, grades, and prizes at the Deoband seminary in India[41]—and modern disciplines. "A major reason for the decline in the *'ulama*"s influence in the country," wrote a founder of the Nadwat al-'Ulama' seminary in India, "is the popular perception that they have

37. Margot Badran, *Feminists, Islam, and Nation: Gender and the Making of Modern Egypt* (Princeton, N.J.: Princeton University Press, 1995), p. 40.

38. J. M. S. Baljon, *Modern Muslim Koran Interpretation (1880–1960)* (Leiden, Netherlands: E. J. Brill, 1961), p. 16; also Ian Henderson Douglas, *Abul Kalam Azad* (Delhi, India: Oxford University Press, 1988), pp. 127, 198–199.

39. Tadeusz Swietochowski, *Russian Azerbaijan, 1905–1920* (Cambridge, England: Cambridge University Press, 1985), p. 30.

40. Stefan Reichmuth, "Education and the Growth of Religious Associations Among Yoruba Muslims: The Ansar-Ud-Deen Society of Nigeria," *Journal of Religion in Africa*, volume 26, number 4, 1996, p. 373.

41. Barbara Metcalf, *Islamic Revival in British India: Deoband, 1860–1900* (Princeton, N.J.: Princeton University Press, 1982), pp. 104–105.

withdrawn into their cells and know nothing about the state of the world, so that in worldly matters their guidance is entirely unworthy of attention."[42]

Even when they failed in their attempts at institutional reform, leading internal critics served as role models for cadres of modernists. In Bukhara, Shihabuddin Marjani (Tatarstan, 1818–1889) inspired a generation of seminary-trained modernists who considered him comparable to Protestant Reformation leader Martin Luther.[43] At al-Azhar in Cairo, 'Abduh achieved little reform[44]—though as the chief religious official of Egypt he helped to incorporate al-Azhar graduates into a state-run judicial hierarchy.[45] Nonetheless, 'Abduh's plans for al-Azhar fired the imagination of dozens of young religious scholars who came to study with him, even for brief periods. One such student, Džemaluddin Čaušević (Bosnia, 1870–1938; chapter 26), returned to the Balkans as a convinced modernist and called 'Abduh "Respected Teacher" for the rest of his career; another returned to China dedicated to "improved methods" of education.[46] A Tatar seminary in Crimea, attempting comparable reforms, sent a leading student to study at al-Azhar.[47] 'Abduh even inspired Shi'i modernists who never studied in Cairo, such as *Shaykh* Asadullah Mamaqani (Iran, early twentieth century) and Muhammad Rida al-Muzaffar (Iraq, born 1904), who proposed that Shi'i seminaries be reformed on the model of 'Abduh's plans for al-Azhar;[48] and Muhsin Sharara (Lebanon-

Iraq, 1901–1946), who called in 1928 for the coming of a "a Shi'ite Muhammad 'Abduh."[49]

Some seminarians despaired of reforming the seminaries. Munawwar Qari (Turkistan-Uzbekistan, 1878–1931; chapter 30)—trained at the traditional schools of Bukhara—condemned such institutions for limiting themselves to commentaries on commentaries. "Our present schools take four or five years to teach only reading and writing, and our colleges take 15 to 20 years to study introductions [to canonical texts] and the four readings. To hope for them to impart a knowledge of the sciences of the present age is as futile as to expect one to reach out to a bird flying in the sky while standing in a well." Qari founded the first *usul-i jadid* (new principles) school in Tashkent, combining religious and secular coursework. Similar schools emerged throughout the Islamic world, producing graduates who often considered themselves legitimate competitors with seminarians for religious knowledge.

One strain of Islamic modernism went so far in its devaluation of traditional scholarship that its proponents viewed religious training merely as a cover for modern values, without any particular merit in its own right. Mirza Malkum Khan (Iran, 1833–1908; chapter 12), for example, considered his French secondary education as qualifying him to guide the Iranian nation toward "civilization." He told a British audience of his strategic approach to Islamic education: "ideas which were by no means accepted when coming from your agents in Europe, were accepted with great delight when it was proved that they were latent in Islam."[50] Abdullah Cevdet (Turkey, 1869–1932; chapter 21) made similar comments,[51] as did Europeans seeking to inculcate modern values in an

42. Muhammad Qasim Zaman, "Religious Education and the Rhetoric of Reform: The Madrasa in British India and Pakistan," *Comparative Studies in Society and History*, volume 41, number 2, 1999, p. 306.

43. Ahmet Kanlıdere, *Reform within Islam: The Tajdid and Jadid Movements among the Kazan Tatars (1809–1917)* (Istanbul, Turkey: Eren Yayıncılık, 1997), p. 59.

44. A. Chris Eccel, *Egypt, Islam, and Social Change: al-Azhar in Conflict and Accommodation* (Berlin, West Germany: Klaus Schwarz Verlag, 1984), pp. 176–189.

45. Amira El-Azhary Sonbol, *The New Mamluks: Egyptian Society and Modern Feudalism* (Syracuse, N.Y.: Syracuse University Press, 2000), pp. 70–71.

46. Marshall Broomhall, *Islam in China* (London: Morgan and Scott, 1910), pp. 266–268.

47. Hakan Kırımlı, *National Movements and National Identity among the Crimean Tatars (1905–1916)* (Leiden, Netherlands: E. J. Brill, 1996), p. 51.

48. Said Amir Arjomand, "Ideological Revolution in Shi'ism," in Arjomand, ed., *Authority and Political Culture in Shi'ism* (Albany: State University of New York Press,

1988), p. 183; Yitzhak Nakash, *The Shi'is of Iraq* (Princeton, N.J.: Princeton University Press, 1994), pp. 262–268.

49. Sabrina Mervin, "The Clerics of Jabal 'Amil and the Reform of Religious Teaching in Najaf Since the Beginning of the Twentieth Century," in Rainer Brunner and Werner Ende, eds., *The Twelver Shia in Modern Times* (Leiden, Netherlands: E. J. Brill, 2000), p. 82.

50. Hamid Algar, *Mirza Malkum Khan* (Berkeley: University of California Press, 1973), pp. 13–17.

51. M. Şükrü Hanioğlu, *Bir Siyasal Düşünür Olarak Doktor Abdullah Cevdet ve Dönemi (Doctor Abdullah Cevdet: A Political Thinker and His Era)* (Istanbul, Turkey: Üçdal Neşriyat, 1981), pp. 325–341.

Islamic language.[52] This strain shaded into outright secularists, such as Mirza Fath 'Ali Akhundzada (Azerbaijan, 1812–1878), who saw no need for the pretense of Islamic education and doubted that Islam could ever be construed as compatible with modern values.[53]

The modernists' critique of seminary training did not imply complete democratization of the right to engage in Islamic reasoning. Despite the precedents that some modernists cited, urging all Muslims to make independent religious judgments, the modernists generally replaced one form of credentialing with another—just as modernists did outside the Islamic world as well. Suavi (chapter 16) rejected a definition of freedom that permits "saying whatever comes to one's mind," giving the example of a French newspaper that denied the existence of God. 'Abduh (chapter 3) offered a warning from the early centuries of Islamic history, when "every opinion-monger took his stand upon the liberty of thought the Qur'an enjoined," leading to dangerous schisms. Ahmad Khan (chapter 40)—while favoring freedom of speech on the pragmatic grounds that open debate advanced the search for truth[54]—was dismissive of "the opinion or independent judgment of every Tom, Dick, and Harry," and sought to justify his position "not by any traditional argument, nor by any proofs of the *mujtahid*s based on independent judgment, but by nature." Surkati (chapter 48) limited *ijtihad* only to "those who have the capacity and opportunity to understand the proofs of God and His laws."

Other modernists limited *ijtihad* to those who agreed with them. Tahtawi (chapter 1) supported religious freedom "on condition that it adheres to the principles of religion"—meaning the principles that he emphasized. Rida (chapter 6) supported "freedom of religion, opinion, speech, writing, dress, and work," but not for the "horde of heretics" who engage in "chatter, sophistry, audacity in mixing right with wrong, and insolence in criticizing their opponents or critics." Ibn Badis condemned opposing positions as *bid'a* (impermissible innovation),[55] a charge that was often leveled against the modernists themselves. Several authors, though not all, contributed to the polemic between the Sunni and Shi'i sects, considering the other to be disqualified from *ijtihad* by their imperfect faith. And competition within the movement led to other polemics—for example, Rida's resentment at Gasprinskii's leadership of pan-Islamic conference planning in Cairo,[56] or the Calcutta-based challenge to Ahmad Khan's North Indian leadership of the modernist Islamic movement in South Asia.[57]

In sum, the modernists sought to breach the monopoly of traditional religious scholars over Islamic interpretation, and to limit the relativistic damage of this breach, through a single maneuver. They expressed confidence in their own qualifications—seminary training, modern education, or personal virtuosity—as compared both with their scholarly opponents and the "masses." Even when these qualifications were asserted in humble terms, they opened a space for the right to speak, as in Ahmad Khan's statement (chapter 40): "I am an ignorant person, neither a *maulavi* [religious scholar], nor a *mufti* [religious official], nor a *qadi* [judge], nor a preacher. . . . I do not say that whatever I investigated is true. But once I had no other choice but to do whatever

52. Gustave Demorgny, *Essai de reformes et d'enseignement administratifs en Perse* (*Essay on Administrative Reforms and Training in Persia*) (Paris: Ernest Leroux, 1915), p. 7; Christopher Harrison, *France and Islam in West Africa, 1860–1960* (Cambridge, England: Cambridge University Press, 1988), p. 189. Other Europeans considered modernist Islam a threat to colonial control and sided instead with conservative Muslims—for example, see Guy Imart, *Islamic and Slavic Fundamentalisms: Foes or Allies? The Turkestanian Reagent* (Bloomington: Indiana University, Research Institute for Inner Asian Studies, 1987).

53. Mehrdad Kia, "Mirza Fath Ali Akhundzadeh and the Call for the Modernization of the Islamic World," *Middle Eastern Studies*, volume 31, number 3, 1995, pp. 422–448.

54. Mansoor Moaddel and Kamran Talattof, eds., *Contemporary Debates in Islam: An Anthology of Modernist and Fundamentalist Thought* (New York: St. Martin's, 2000), pp. 109–121.

55. Ali Merad, *Le réformisme musulman en Algérie de 1925 à 1940* (*Muslim Reformism in Algeria from 1925 to 1940*) (Paris, France: Mouton, 1967), pp. 231–234.

56. Thomas Kuttner, "Russian *Jadidism* and the Islamic World: Ismail Gasprinskii in Cairo, 1908," *Cahiers du monde russe et soviétique* (*Annals of the Russian and Soviet World*), volume 16, 1975, pp. 383–424; Martin Kramer, *Islam Assembled: The Advent of the Muslim Congresses* (New York: Columbia University Press, 1986), pp. 41–45.

57. Ayesha Jalal, *Self and Sovereignty: Individual and Community in South Asian Islam Since 1850* (New York: Routledge, 2001), pp. 88–90.

could be done by me, then I had certainly to do exactly what I did and what I am still doing. God knows my pure intention."

How to Speak

The novel approaches of modernist Islam frequently found expression in novel forms of discourse. The modernists specified at least three ways in which the literary forms of the past were inadequate.

First, modernists held that long-standing literary themes were insufficiently attuned to the concerns of contemporary Muslims. They sought to replace flowery language, irrelevant fantasy, and crude humor with noble and useful themes. Modernist Islamic poets, for example, adapted traditional poetic forms throughout the Islamic world.[58] One of the most influential exemplars of this adaptation, Hali's "The Flow and Ebb of Islam" (chapter 38), adopted the traditional Urdu structure of the *musadda*s, with its particular rhyme scheme and verse length, but filled the structure with nontraditional content. In an unusually extensive and reflexive introduction to the poem, Hali explained:

> When I beheld the new pattern of the age, my heart became sick of the old poetry, and I began to feel ashamed of stringing together empty fabrications. . . . It is true that much has been written, and continues to be written about this. But no one has yet written poetry, which makes a natural appeal to all, and has been bequeathed to the Muslims as a legacy from the Arabs, for the purpose of awakening the community.[59]

The traditional literary form of debate (*munazara*) was also adopted and infused with modernist content,[60] as in Kawakibi's fictional pan-Islamic assembly (chapter 19) and the startling inversion effected by Fitrat (chapter 34), in which debate between a European and a Bukharan Muslim is staged with the author embodied in the European character. Modernists commandeered the travelogue format, maintaining the positive comparison of Islam with religions of other lands, but also stressing the wonders of modernity—generally focused on Europe, as in books by Tahtawi and Mirza Saleh Shirazi (Iran, circa 1790–1845), but also Iran and India, as described by Siraj al-Din Hakim (Bukhara, 1877–1914), and Japan, as reported by 'Ali Ahmad al-Jarjawi (Egypt, mid-nineteenth–early twentieth century).[61] Theology (*kalam*), long suspect within clerical circles for its rationalist heritage, was revived by Muhammad Shibli Nu'mani (North India, 1857–1914) and İsmail Hakkı İzmirli (Turkey, 1869–1946), among others.[62] Traditional hagiographic literature was transformed into modern biography, as in Fakhreddin's study of the 14th century reformer Ibn Taymiyya, a popular figure among the modernists,[63] in which—according to the author—"every piece of information and fact is examined meticulously, and partisanship is avoided as much as possible" (chapter 33).

A second movement among modernists involved the development of novel forms of religious writing.

---

58. Various articles on "Shi'r," in C. E. Bosworth et al., eds., *The Encyclopedia of Islam*, 2d ed. (Leiden, Netherlands: E. J. Brill, 1997), volume 9, pp. 462–470.

59. Khwaja Altaf Hussein Hali, *Hali's Musaddas: The Flow and Ebb of Islam*, trans. Christopher Shackle and Javed Majeed (Delhi, India: Oxford University Press, 1997), p. 93.

60. E. Wagner, "Munazara," in C. E. Bosworth et al., eds., *The Encyclopedia of Islam*, 2d ed. (Leiden, Netherlands: E. J. Brill, 1993), volume 7, pp. 565–568; Jakob Skovgaard-Petersen, "Portrait of the Intellectual as a Young Man: Rashid Rida's *Muhawarat al-muslih wa-al-muqallid* (1906)," *Islam and Christian-Muslim Relations*, volume 12, number 1, 2001, pp. 93–104.

61. Nadia Abu Zahra, "Al-Tahtawi as Translator of the Culture of Parisian Society," in Ekmeleddin İhsanoğlu, ed., *Transfer of Modern Science & Technology to the Muslim World* (Istanbul, Turkey: Research Centre for Islamic History, Art, and Culture, 1992), pp. 419–424; Monica Ringer, "The Quest for the Secret of Strength in Iranian Nineteenth-Century Travel Literature," in Nikki R. Keddie and Rudi Matthee, eds., *Iran and the Surrounding World* (Seattle: University of Washington Press, 2002), pp. 141–161; Mohamad Tavakoli-Targhi, *Refashioning Iran* (Houndsmills, England: Palgrave, 2001), pp. 35–76; Mirza Siradj ad-Din Hakim, *Souvenirs de voyage pour les gens de Boukhara* (*Travel Memoirs for the People of Bukhara*), trans. Stéphane Dudoignon (Paris: Actes Sud, 1999); Michael F. Laffan, "Making Meiji Muslims: The Travelogue of 'Ali Ahmad al-Jarjawi," *East Asian History*, number 22, 2001, pp. 145–170.

62. Mehr Afroz Murad, *Intellectual Modernism of Shibli Nu'mani* (Lahore, Pakistan: Institute of Islamic Culture, 1976), pp. 4–50; Hilmi Ziya Ülken, *La pensée de l'Islam* (*The Thought of Islam*) (Istanbul, Turkey: Fakülteler Matbaası, 1953), pp. 126–127.

63. Henri Laoust, *Essai sur les doctrines sociales et politiques de Taki-d-Din Ahmad b. Taimiya* (*Essay on the Social and Political Doctrines of Taqi al-Din Ahmad ibn Taimiya*) (Cairo, Egypt: l'Institut français d'archéologie orientale, 1939), pp. 541–575.

The effort to rejuvenate Islam involved an intensive project of outreach and uplift, for which new discursive strategies were deemed necessary. 'Ali Mubarak (Egypt, 1824–1893) made this reasoning explicit in the introduction to one of the first Arab novels:

> I have realized that the readers are inclined to reading epic tales, narrative fiction, and entertaining works, rather than works on pure scientific or practical concerns. The latter works breed boredom and lead the readers to shun them. . . . This persuaded me to write this useful book in a form of attractive narrative to entice the reader to absorb its useful information and instructions, which have been collected from many Arabic and foreign books in arts and sciences.[64]

In an early Urdu novel, *The Repentance of Nasuh*, by Nazir Ahmad (North India, 1836–1912), the title character burns a roomful of old books and identifies the antidote for such "poison" as "books of faith and morality."[65] Similarly, Mahmud Khoja Behbudiy (Samarqand, 1874–1919; chapter 36), author of the first modern play in Central Asia, described theater as "a place for preaching and exhortation."[66] The first plays in the Arab world were adaptations of French works produced in Lebanon in 1847; the first modern Urdu play was performed in 1853; the first modern Turkish play was produced in 1859; and other Islamic regions appear to have followed suit at the end of the nineteenth and beginning of the twentieth centuries.[67]

The third, and perhaps the greatest discursive innovation of the modernist Islamic movement was the periodical press, which it established in virtually every community of the Islamic world. Selections in this anthology include pioneers from Mombasa (chapter 7) to Durban (chapter 8), and from Malabar (chapter 42) to Singapore (chapter 46). The relatively low cost and wide distribution of newspapers, magazines, and journals opened a stream of words that reached a relatively large readership (and listenership, as items were read aloud). The modernist Islamic movement held great hopes for its impact. A 1907 cartoon in *Mulla Nasruddin*, for example, showed a modernist waving a newspaper, causing traditionally garbed religious scholars to run fleeing from the power of the paper.[68] 'Abduh, as a young man, paid homage to the power of the newspaper in a poem, comparing it favorably to the legacy of the Egyptian pyramids: the newspaper is "the nourishment of the spirits," "the tongue of heavenly secrets," and "guidance for those who seek." It "alerts the unattentive" and "has taken it upon itself to spread the sciences among the common people."[69] Later, he admitted a certain skepticism about this power— "These days there are people who believe that the illnesses of nations may be cured with the publication of journals"[70]—but participated in producing the two most influential modernist papers.

An Indian opponent of the modernists mocked their confidence in the medium: "Faced with a gun, bring out a newspaper."[71] Yet conservatives in Malaya feared the power of periodicals of "the new style" enough to try to ban "papers debating the Muhammedan religion" in 1929.[72] Religious conservatives also made use of the same media, founding periodicals such as *Isha'at al-Sunna* (*News of Tradition*) in Lahore (founded 1878), *Din ve Ma'ishat* (*Religion and Life*) in Kazan (1906–1917), and *al-Haqa'iq* (*Truths*) in Damascus (1910–1913).[73] In the 1920s, historian

64. Sabry Hafez, *The Genesis of Arabic Narrative Discourse* (London: Saqi Books, 1993), pp. 130–131.

65. Frances W. Pritchett, *Nets of Awareness: Urdu Poetry and Its Critics* (Berkeley: University of California Press, 1994), p. 186.

66. Adeeb Khalid, *The Politics of Muslim Cultural Reform: Jadidism in Central Asia* (Berkeley: University of California Press, 1998), p. 131.

67. Various articles on "Masrah," in C. E. Bosworth et al., eds., *The Encyclopedia of Islam*, 2d edition (Leiden, Netherlands: E. J. Brill, 1991), volume 6, pp. 746–773.

68. Daniel R. Brower and Edward J. Lazzerini, eds., *Russia's Orient* (Bloomington: Indiana University Press, 1997), p. 192.

69. Jakob Skovgaard-Petersen, *Defining Islam for the Egyptian State: Muftis and Fatwas of the Dar Al-ifta* (Leiden, Netherlands: Brill, 1997), p. 69.

70. Michael F. Laffan, "The Umma Below the Winds: Mecca, Cairo, Reformist Islam, and a Conceptualization of Indonesia," Ph.D. dissertation, University of Sydney, Australia, p. 170.

71. Ralph Russell, *The Pursuit of Urdu Literature* (London: Zed Books, 1992), p. 159.

72. William Roff, "Kaum Muda—Kaum Tua: Innovation and Reaction amongst the Malays, 1900–1941," in K. G. Tregonning, ed., *Papers on Malayan History* (Singapore: Department of History, University of Malaya in Singapore, 1962), p. 178.

73. Jalal, *Self and Sovereignty*, p. 68; Azade-Ayşe Rorlich, *The Volga Tatars* (Stanford, Calif.: Hoover Institution Press, 1986), p. 60; James C. Gelvin, "'Pious' Religious Scholars, 'Overly-Europeanized' Falsifiers, and the Debate about the 'Woman Question' in Early Twentieth-Century Damascus" (paper under review).

'Abd al-Wasi al-Wasi'i (Yemen, died 1959), a supporter of the isolationist Yemeni imamate, credited newspapers as "the great force, the instructive school, the scales for [weighing] the activity of the community and the indicator of its condition, the vigilant overseer of the government."[74] Religious conservatives also published printed books rather than relying exclusively on hand-copied manuscripts.[75]

The press brought news of parallel and competing movements around the world. Like other periodicals of the era, they often reprinted, translated, or summarized articles they found interesting from other periodicals, increasing the density of linkages across regions and language groups. In addition, they trumpeted models of successful modernization. Japanese military victories over Russia in 1904, for example, were carried "live" in the newspapers of the world, offering inspiration. The Malay newspaper *al-Imam* (chapter 46) commented on "the ascent of the Japanese race . . . who defeated the six-foot-tall giants," and referred to writings on Japan by the Egyptian nationalist Mustafa Kamil (Egypt, 1874–1908). The Iranian newspaper *Habl al-matin* (*The Firm Rope*), published in Calcutta, wrote at length on the implications of Japan's success.[76] "We need an independent renewal like that of Japan," Rida wrote years later in Egypt (chapter 6).

The immediacy of the periodical press, especially daily newspapers, expressed in its very form the modernists' view of progress. Each issue presented the latest word, superseding previous statements. A properly informed person had to keep up with breaking news and ongoing debates. The newspaper format exerted pressure toward brevity, glibness, and a minimum of scholarly citations. As a result, newspaper writers were vulnerable to accusations of shallowness. Yet in the competition for religious authority, writers without seminary training may have

preferred to write texts without detailed citations and extended quotations, which seminary-trained writers were more adept at producing.

A similar case could be made for lectures, which eager students or the lecturers themselves sometimes published. Afghani's Calcutta lecture on teaching and learning (chapter 11), for example, was published despite Afghani's complaint that his host "caused this talk to be delivered only in an abbreviated form." Similarly, 'Abd al-Qadir al-Maghribi (Lebanon, 1867–1956; chapter 27) published a lecture in Beirut despite complaining that his host "gave me time only for a phone call. So forgive me if I hasten or if I gloss over certain aspects." These inelegant, ritualized apologies may mask the lack of full scholarly apparatus expected of written work on religious subjects.

In sum, the modernist movement adapted traditional literary forms to modernist purposes and pioneered new forms, especially a periodical press that emphasized the contemporaneity of knowledge and deemphasized scholarly citation.

What to Speak

The substance of the modernist Islamic appeal may be summarized in any number of ways. I choose to emphasize five general topic areas, each of which is deep enough to capture a significant portion of the modernist writings included in this anthology, and wide enough to involve significant differences of opinion within the modernist movement. Religious interpretation has already been covered in this introduction, and we turn now to the other four.

Cultural Revival

The sense that cultural decline had gripped the Islamic world was not limited to modernist authors. Conservatives also pointed to the massive changes they were witnessing, as for example Akbar Allahabadi (North India, 1846–1921):

> The minstrel and the music—both have
>   changed.
> Our sleep has changed, the tale we told has
>   changed.
> The nightingale now sings a different song.
> The color in the cheeks of spring has changed.
> Another kind of rain falls from the sky.

74. Brinkley Messick, *The Calligraphic State: Textual Domination and History in a Muslim* Society (Berkeley: University of California Press, 1993), p. 118.

75. Francis Robinson, "Technology and Religious Change: Islam and the Impact of Print," *Modern Asian Studies*, volume 27, number 1, 1993, pp. 229–251; Muhammad Qasim Zaman, "Commentaries, Print, and Patronage: Hadith and the Madrasas in Modern South Asia," *Bulletin of the School of Oriental and African Studies*, volume 62, number 1, 1999, pp. 60–81.

76. *Habl al-matin* (*The Firm Rope*), August 17, 1906, pp. 12–16.

The grain that grows upon our land has
  changed.
A revolution has brought this about.
In all the realms of nature all has changed.[77]

The distinctiveness of the modernists lay in seeing
modernity as a promising avenue for cultural revival.

Modernists described this revival with a handful
of recurrent metaphors. One set involved light, as in
the European Enlightenment. "Originally, religion
shines, but later it appears to become dull," wrote
Achmad Dachlan (Java, 1868–1923; chapter 47).
"Truly, it is not religion that becomes dull, but the
person who follows the religion." Such imagery was
incorporated into the words for "intellectual":
munawwar al-fikr (enlightened of thought), derived
from *nur* (light), used in Arabic, Ottoman Turkish,
and Persian; and *ziyali* (person associated with *ziya*,
or light), used in Uzbek. A second set of images involved awakening. "Throughout the world a spirit of
awakening has encompassed the Muslims," Ahmed
Aghayev (Azerbaijan, 1865–1939; chapter 31) wrote
in an optimistic moment. Less optimistically, Fitrat
(chapter 34) worried that Muslims "will sleep forever
in the land of dishonor, lowliness, and anonymity."
"Awake ye Arabs and recover," began a poem posted
around Beirut and Damascus in 1880,[78] a motif
adopted in the poetry of Central Asian nationalism:
"Waken, Kazakh!" in 1911;[79] "Awaken, homeland
[Turkestan]" in 1918;[80] and "Awaken! Hey! Uyghur,
it is time to awaken" in the early 1930s.[81] A third set
involved motion, such as the "principle of movement" that Iqbal sought to recover in *The Reconstruction of Religious Thought in Islam.*[82] A fourth set of

images involved rebirth and renewal, often with reference to the Protestant Reformation in Christianity.
"Truly, we are in a dire need for renewal and renewers," wrote Rida (chapter 6). This effort must combine "religious renewal and earthly renewal, the same
way Europe has done with religious reformation and
modernization." Iqbal (chapter 41), in a moment of
respect for the West, drew on parallel imagery:

Germany has witnessed the upheaval of the
  Reformation, which has erased all marks of
  earlier times.
The sanctity of the temple priest has been
  nullified, and the delicate ship of thought has
  embarked on its course.
The French have also seen a revolution, which
  has overturned the world of the Westerners.
The descendants of the Greeks, aged by their
  worship of antiquity, have become youthful
  again with the pleasures of renewal.
The soul of the Muslim has a similar ferment
  today, [but] this is a divine secret which the
  tongue is unable to express.
Let us see what springs from the bottom of this
  ocean; let us see what colors the sky now
  turns.[83]

The modernists disagreed vehemently among
themselves as to the extent to which cultural revival
must erase existing cultural forms. Those who favored almost complete erasure crossed the line from
Islamic modernism to secular modernism, as in the
case of Hasan Taqizada (Iran, 1878–1969), who favored "absolute submission to Europe, and the assimilation of the culture, customs, practices, organization, sciences, arts, life, and the whole attitude of
Europe, without any exception save language."[84]
Islamic modernists, by contrast, justified the erasure
of aspects of recent culture as a recovery of older or
more authentic culture. In the words of Khayr al-Din
(chapter 2), "There is no reason to reject or ignore
something which is correct and demonstrable simply because it comes from others, especially if we had

77. Ralph Russell, *Hidden in the Lute: An Anthology of
Two Centuries of Urdu Literature* (Manchester, England:
Carcanet, 1995), p. 201.

78. A. L. Tibawi, *Arabic and Islamic Themes* (London:
Luzac & Company, 1974), pp. 119, 308.

79. Gulnar Kendirbay, "The National Liberation Movement of the Kazakh Intelligentsia at the Beginning of the 20th
Century," *Central Asian Survey*, volume 16, number 4, 1997,
p. 496.

80. Hamza Hakimzada Niyaziy, *Tola asarlar toplami*
(*Complete Collection of Works*) (Tashkent, Uzbekistan: Fan,
1988–1989), volume 2, p. 145. Translation from Uzbek by
Adeeb Khalid.

81. Justin Jon Rudelson, *Oasis Identities: Uyghur Nationalism Along China's Silk Road* (New York: Columbia
University Press, 1997), p. 148.

82. Iqbal, *The Reconstruction*, pp. 139–170; also in
Kurzman, ed. *Liberal Islam*, pp. 255–269.

83. Muhammad Iqbal, "Masjid-i Qurtuba" (Córdova
Mosque), in *Kulliyat* (*Complete Works*) (Aligarh, India: Educational Book House, 1995), pp. 391–392. First published in
1933. Translation from Urdu by Muhammad Qasim Zaman.

84. Ali Mirsepassi, *Intellectual Discourse and the Politics of Modernization: Negotiating Modernity in Iran* (Cambridge, England: Cambridge University Press, 2000), p. 54.

formerly possessed it and it had been taken from us. On the contrary, there is an obligation to restore it and put it to use." In more provocative language, Halide Edib Adıvar (Turkey, 1882–1964; chapter 28) wrote that "all-round Westernization" reinforced rights that "Islam had already proclaimed . . . a thousand years ago," and expressed the "vital racial instinct" of "the Turkish soul."

Adıvar's reference to race introduces the issue of purportedly biological social hierarchies, which modernists valued along with other "scientific" doctrines of the era. Certainly many Muslims engaged in racial discrimination prior to the modern era, just as Europeans and others did.[85] Arabs such as Kawakibi (chapter 19) objected to Ottoman Turkish "use of the term '*Arab*' for slaves and black animals." Non-Arab Muslims such as Marmaduke Pickthall (England, 1875–1936) detected and detested the tendency among Arab scholars to "think that the Arabs are still 'the patrons', and the non-Arabs their 'freedmen'. . . ."[86] One modernist theme was the erasure of these racialized distinctions, for example the campaign in Southeast Asia to allow female descendants of the Prophet Muhammad to marry Muslim men who did not share this descent.[87] Salim likened this to "the struggle between aristocracy and democracy," and concluded, "It is this spirit of democracy which constitutes one of the main reasons for the spread of Islam in the world. Those who extinguish this spirit belong to those who hamper the development and spread of Islam."[88]

Yet modernists—Muslim, Christian, and otherwise—replaced older forms of racism with a new version based on scientific research into the alleged hierarchy and evolution of human capabilities. It may be unfair to single out a particular author, but Maghribi (chapter 27) is typical of many modernists in mentioning groups at a particular "stage in their social evolution, . . . in Africa or China for example,

constrained by their social situation or the disposition of their temperament to adopt polygamy." A similarly scientized view is evident in Maghribi's discussion of women, whose "weak self-confidence, gullibility, and lack of discipline" are said to justify the lesser value of their courtroom testimony. Similar views have been documented in Egypt and elsewhere.[89]

Modernists also adopted a second form of social hierarchy, that of capitalism. Some modernists favored social-democratic reform—notably Salim (chapter 49), in this anthology, and Muhammad Hifzurrahman Sihvarvi (North India, 1901–1962)[90]—and an Islamic Communist movement emerged to the left of the social democrats in Indonesia in the late 1910s, with figures such as Hadji Mohammad Misbach (Java, circa 1876–1940) criticizing Salim and other Islamic modernists: "To be sure, they perform the precepts of the religion of Islam, but they pick and choose those precepts that suit their desire. Those that do not suit them they throw away. Put bluntly, they oppose or defy the commands of God . . . and rather fear and love the will of Satan—that Satan whose evil influence is apparent in this present age in [the system of] Capitalism."[91] Support of capitalism was indeed the dominant economic theme in the modernist Islamic movement. Khayr al-Din (chapter 2) praised societies in which "the circulation of capital is expanded, profits increase accordingly, and wealth is put into the hands of the most proficient who can cause it to increase." Salah al-Din Khuda Bakhsh (North India, 1877–1931) espoused the right of Muslims "to attend to their religious obligation without sacrificing their worldly prosperity. . . ."[92] Modernists made a moral distinction between rich people who invested in modern economic and cultural enterprises and those who did not, denouncing the latter for their "submersion . . . in luxury and

85. Bernard Lewis, *Race and Slavery in the Middle East* (New York: Oxford University Press, 1990).

86. Peter Clark, *Marmaduke Pickthall: British Muslim* (London: Quartet Books, 1986), p. 64.

87. Natalie Mobini-Kesheh, *The Hadrami Awakening: Community and Identity in the Netherlands East Indies, 1900–1942* (Ithaca, N.Y.: Cornell Southeast Asia Program, 1999), pp. 91–107.

88. Deliar Noer, *The Modernist Muslim Movement in Indonesia, 1900–1942* (Singapore: Oxford University Press, 1973), p. 69.

89. Eve Troutt Powell, *Different Shades of Colonialism: Egypt, Great Britain, and the Mastery of the Sudan, 1865–1925* (Berkeley: University of California Press, 2002), chapter 4.

90. Aziz Ahmad, *Islamic Modernism in India and Pakistan, 1857–1964* (London: Oxford University Press, 1967), pp. 201–204.

91. Takashi Shiraishi, *An Age in Motion: Popular Radicalism in Java, 1912–1926* (Ithaca, N.Y.: Cornell University Press, 1990), p. 285.

92. Wilfred Cantwell Smith, *Modern Islam in India* (London: Victor Gallancz, 1946), p. 32.

carnal appetites, and their avoidance of any kind of glory other than ostentation and wealth," in the words of Kawakibi (chapter 19). It is probably not coincidental, and the matter deserves systematic study, that the modernist movement was bankrolled in part by industrialists and traders promoting international economic linkages, such as Husayn Baybacha, a leading merchant who supported Islamic constitutionalism in eastern Turkistan in the early twentieth century,[93] or H. Z. A. Tagiev and other industrialists who supported cultural reform in Azerbaijan in the late nineteenth and early twentieth centuries.[94]

Some Islamic modernists worried about wholesale adoption of Western culture. Bahithat al-Badiya (Egypt, 1886–1918; chapter 5), while promoting education in modern subjects, suggested that "If we pursue everything Western we shall destroy our own civilization, and a nation that has lost its civilization grows weak and vanishes." Rida (chapter 6) assailed the faction of Egyptians that, "in imitation of the heretics of Europe and its liberals, is hostile to religion and despises the devout, who constitute the majority of the nation." Salim (chapter 49) criticized "*taqlid*" of Western manners, and Aghayev mocked the "Westernized Oriental" as "Western only on the surface." Aghayev warned, "Simply to transplant Western civilization to the Orient will only result in doubling the misery of the Oriental. One becomes neither Eastern nor Western, but something in-between, with all the weaknesses of the one without the qualities of the other."[95]

Modernists aimed these critiques at one another, just as religious conservatives aimed them at modernists as a whole. All modernists, presumably, considered themselves in happy equilibrium, rejecting existing customs where necessary while maintaining the most important Islamic values. Yet what to reject and what to maintain was frequently a subject of debate. One broad field of disagreement was the topic of popular religious practices associated with Sufism. Some modernists had Sufi backgrounds—the most influential modernist in Damascus, al-Jaza'iri (chapter 15), was a Sufi sage and justified his rationalism on thoroughly Sufi grounds.[96] Some modernists wished to maintain certain Sufi practices and beliefs, including Frashëri, who urged Albanian Sufi organizations to develop into a political party;[97] and 'Ubaydullah Sindhi (Sindh, India, 1872–1944), who defended Sufi mysticism as both "the basis of Islam" and "an international or purely human conception of a universal religion."[98] More commonly, modernists held Sufi practices to be abhorrent, especially the veneration of saints.[99] The profit to be had from such practices lured sham clerics eager to "gain fame and earn more worldly profit," according to Fakhreddin (chapter 33). "As a result, the Muslims were overwhelmed in economic and political affairs, and so were destined to be crushed under the feet of others." At the same time, reformist Sufi leaders condemned certain of their colleagues on similar grounds, accusing them of "spending their lives in the pursuit of the things of this world and lavish lifestyles,"[100] and trying to ban the commercialization of religious practices.[101] In relation to Sufism, as to other Islamic practices and beliefs, the scope

93. C. P. Skrine and Pamela Nightingale, *Macartney at Kashgar: New Light on British, Chinese, and Russian Activities in Sinkiang, 1890–1918* (London: Methuen, 1973), p. 157).

94. Audrey Altstadt, "The Azerbaijani Bourgeoisie and the Cultural-Enlightenment Movement in Baku," in Ronald Grigor Suny, ed., *Transcaucasia, Nationalism, and Social Change*, rev. ed. (Ann Arbor: University of Michigan Press, 1996), pp. 199–209.

95. Edward J. Lazzerini, "Beyond Renewal: The Jadid Response to the Pressure for Change in the Modern Age," in Jo-Ann Gross, ed., *Muslims in Central Asia: Expressions of Identity and Change* (Durham, N.C.: Duke University Press, 1992), p. 164.

96. Itzchak Weismann, *Taste of Modernity: Sufism, Salafiyya, and Arabism in Late Ottoman Damascus* (Leiden, Netherlands: Brill, 2000), part 2.

97. H. T. Norris, *Islam in the Balkans* (London: Hurst & Company, 1993), p. 188.

98. Mazheruddin Siddiqi, *Modern Reformist Thought in the Muslim World* (Islamabad, Pakistan: Islamic Research Institute, 1982), p. 19.

99. Frederick de Jong and Bernd Radtke, eds., *Islamic Mysticism Contested* (Leiden, Netherlands: Brill, 1999); Elizabeth Sirriyeh, *Sufis and Anti-Sufis: The Defense, Rethinking and Rejection of Sufism in the Modern World* (Richmond, England: Curzon, 1999).

100. Julia A. Clancy-Smith, *Rebel and Saint: Muslim Notables, Populist Protest, Colonial Encounters (Algeria and Tunisia, 1800–1904)* (Berkeley: University of California Press, 1994), p. 222.

101. F[rederick] de Jong, *Turuq and Turuq-Linked Institutions in Nineteenth Century Egypt* (Leiden, Netherlands: E. J. Brill, 1978), p. 170.

and meaning of cultural revival was contested both within and outside the modernist Islamic movement.

Political Reform

A second major goal of the modernists was the implementation of constitutionalism. Here too, Islamic dictates on human equality were marshaled in support. "[A]lthough God, most exalted, preferred some to others in endowments, He made them equal in accountability, with no distinction between the honorable and the base, the leader and the subordinate," wrote Tahtawi (chapter 1). "Equality means nothing but sharing the same laws, and being equal before them." Similarly, according to Abdullah Abdurahman (South Africa, 1870–1940; chapter 8): "If God made no distinction between man and man, we had no right to do so. And until we are regarded as equal in this country, there is no such thing as a democratic institution." Mustafa Fazıl Pasha (Turkey, 1829–1875) wrote in 1866, in one of the earliest manifestos of Islamic constitutionalism, that Islam dictates human fate in the afterlife, but does not limit "the rights of the people," and therefore cannot justify tyranny: "there are no Christian politics or Moslem politics," he argued, "for there is only one justice, and politics is justice incarnate."[102] Sayyid 'Abd al-'Azam 'Imad al-'Ulama' Khalkhali (Iran, mid-nineteenth–early twentieth century), writing soon after the promulgation of the first Iranian constitution, stressed that "God has not made any distinction among his obedient servants. Prophets and messengers, serfs and kings, the old and the young, men and women, servants and masters, religious authorities and the masses, descendants of the Prophet and non-Arab Muslims, the rich and the poor, are all equal and partners in their obligations, according to the laws of justice, fairness, and equality."[103]

Modernists referred to a variety of sacred sources to establish the legitimacy of constitutionalism. Namık Kemal (chapter 17) quoted the Qur'anic in-junction, "And seek their counsel in the matter" (Sura 3, Verse 159), concluding that "the salvation of the state today is dependent upon the adoption of the method of consultation." Chiragh 'Ali (North India, 1844–1895; chapter 39) argued that "the Qur'an does not interfere in political questions, nor does it lay down specific rules of conduct in the Civil Law," concluding that "the Qur'an or the teachings of Muhammad are neither barriers to spiritual development or free-thinking on the part of Muhammadans, nor an obstacle to innovation in any sphere of life, whether political, social, intellectual, or moral." Na'ini (chapter 13) quoted the Qur'anic verse, "He [God] cannot be questioned about what He does, but they will be questioned" (Sura 21, Verse 23), concluding that "Absolute power belongs only to God, yet [reactionaries] declared it un-Islamic to struggle against the absolute power of earthly tyrants." 'Ali 'Abd al-Raziq (Egypt, 1888–1966) quoted Qur'anic verses referring to the Prophet as a "warner" or a "reminder," not a "warden" or a "guardian," concluding that kingship was not required by sacred precedent.[104] Ibn Badis (chapter 9) quoting a speech of the first caliph, concluded that "It is the people that have the right to delegate authority to the leaders and depose them. No one can rule without the consent of the people."

These and other Islamic arguments accompanied constitutionalist movements around the Islamic world. Egypt promulgated a constitutionalist document in 1860, and a fuller constitution in 1882; Tunisia briefly in 1861 and then, after the colonial interlude, in 1959; the Ottoman Empire briefly in 1876, then again in 1908; Iran briefly in 1906, then again in 1909; and so on.[105]

Yet the modernists of this period did not necessarily intend constitutionalism to mean democracy, as it came to be understood over the course of the twentieth century: universal adult suffrage, reduction of monarchs to symbolic offices, and constitutional protection of a growing list of rights. Suavi (chapter 16) argued that "democracy is the highest form of egalitarian government and the most in accord with the holy law," but was "not possible when people lack morals, or unity, or in large countries" such as the Ottoman Empire, which needed a sultanate to

---

102. Şerif Mardin, *The Genesis of Young Ottoman Thought* (Princeton, N.J.: Princeton University Press, 1962), p. 281.

103. Sayyid 'Abd al-'Azam 'Imad al-'Ulama' Khalkhali, "A Treatise on the Meaning of Constitutional Government," trans. Hamid Dabashi, in Said Amir Arjomand, ed., *Authority and Political Culture in Shi'ism* (Albany: State University of New York Press, 1988), p. 337.

104. Kurzman, ed., *Liberal Islam*, pp. 32–34.

105. *Dustur: A Survey of the Constitutions of the Arab and Muslim States* (Leiden, Netherlands: E. J. Brill, 1966).

remain "in conformity with its geographical location, circumstances, and population." The best to be hoped for, he concluded, was to hold the sultan's ministers accountable to an elected parliament.

In addition, constitutionalists faced a tension between limiting state power to protect liberty and building sufficient state power to effect societal changes. Their solution to this dilemma lay in the idea that ruling by consent would increase the state's effectiveness, as in Khayr al-Din's formulation (chapter 2): "It is God's custom in His world that justice, good management, and an administrative system duly complied with be the causes of an increase in wealth, peoples, and property, but that the contrary should cause a diminution in all of these things." Some modernists adopted the recently developed European view that the role of the state lay in cultivating consent through training, as in a 1903 Egyptian educational text: "There is no way to educate and strengthen something, except by training and drilling it in the performance of its function, until it can accomplish it with smoothness, speed, and precision."[106]

Other modernists reversed the order and considered state power the prerequisite for all other reforms. The "first conditions of any progress and reform," wrote an Iranian educator, were "security and order"[107]—a view expressed in the Young Turk slogan of "Union and Progress."[108] Indeed, one strain of modernist Islam sacrificed political reform altogether for the sake of other reforms. In Afghanistan, for example, the monarch suppressed an Islamic constitutionalist movement in 1909, executing the movement's religious leader, Maulawi Muhammad Sarwar Wasif (Afghanistan, died 1909).[109] Thereafter, Afghan modernists such as Tarzi (chapter 14) abandoned hopes for constitutionalism and channeled their energies into lobbying the king to announce social and economic reforms. Tarzi praised the king in lavish phrases as "his great and enlightened majesty, the beacon of the nation and the religion," whose "ever-increasing innate talent and capability has caused continuous growth and advancement," making Afghanistan "the beam of the scale of justice and equality in Asia." Elsewhere, he wrote, a nation or fatherland "without Government, and Government without a King, would resemble inorganic substance or a car without an engine."[110]

Science and Education

Modern science held such power, in the world-view of modernist Islam, that it could only be described in terms generally reserved for divine entities, as in this statement by Afghani (chapter 11):

> How difficult it is to speak about science. There is no end or limit to science. The benefits of science are immeasurable; and these finite thoughts cannot encompass what is infinite. Besides, thousands of eloquent speakers and sages have already expressed their thoughts to explain science and its nobility. Despite this, nature does not permit me not to explain its virtues. Thus I say: If someone looks deeply into the question, he will see that science rules the world. There was, is, and will be no ruler in the world but science.

The power of science, Afghani continued, accounted for the reverses suffered by the Islamic world: "The English have reached Afghanistan; the French have seized Tunisia. In reality this usurpation, aggression, and conquest have not come from the French or the English. Rather it is science that everywhere manifests its greatness and power. Ignorance had no alternative to prostrating itself humbly before science and acknowledging its submission."

This oppositional pair, "science" versus "ignorance"—denigrating all forms of knowledge aside from modern science—paralleled the traditional opposition between the age of Islam and the pre-Islamic age of ignorance (*jahiliyya*). Indeed, numerous modernist Islamic authors made the parallel explicit, recounting the scientific advances of the early Islamic era and their influence on later European scientific developments. A cartoon in *Mulla Nasruddin*, for

106. Timothy Mitchell, *Colonising Egypt* (Cambridge, England: Cambridge University Press, 1988), p. 89.

107. Darius M. Rejali, *Torture and Modernity: Self, Society, and State in Modern Iran* (Boulder, Colo.: Westview Press, 1994), p. 48.

108. Şerif Arif Mardin, *Jön Türklerin Siyasî Fikirleri, 1895–1908 (Political Thought of the Young Turks, 1895–1908)* (Ankara, Turkey: Türkiye İş Bankası Kültür Yayınları, 1964).

109. Senzil Nawid, "State, Clergy, and British Imperial Policy in Afghanistan during the 19th and Early 20th Centuries," *International Journal of Middle East Studies*, volume 29, number 4, 1997, p. 598.

110. Asta Olesen, *Islam and Politics in Afghanistan* (Richmond, England: Curzon Press, 1995), p. 119.

example, showed a speaker castigating an audience: "Sirs! There are hundreds of [Qur'anic] verses and *hadith*s about science being obligatory upon all. The Europeans have taken our ancient science and reached civilization, but we have remained backward."[111] Ameer 'Ali (Bengal, 1849–1928; chapter 43) credited the Prophet Muhammad as well for his "devotion to knowledge and science . . . distinguishing him from all other Teachers, and bringing him into the closest affinity with the modern world of thought." The intellectual centers of the early Islamic centuries, Ameer 'Ali continued, developed "a true and strongly marked scientific spirit, which dominated over all its achievements. The deductive method, hitherto proudly regarded as the invention and sole monopoly of modern Europe, was perfectly understood by the Muslims."

Pride in the past greatness of Islamic science was coupled with dismay at later stagnation. Some attributed the shift to external forces, such as Ameer 'Ali's emphasis on destruction wrought by the Mongol conquest. Others attributed the shift to internal developments, as in Afghani's accusation that a religious elite "tried to stifle the sciences" and "was marvelously served in its designs by despotism." Frashëri (chapter 18) took this accusation a step further, suggesting that centuries of scientific stagnation undermined any pride in past accomplishments:

> The Europeans borrowed many things from us, that is to say from our ancestors or more precisely our coreligionists who lived eight or ten centuries ago; however, none of the things in their hands today is something that was borrowed from our ancestors. Europe borrowed a seed of civilization from the Islamic world, she planted that seed. It is natural that a seed should decompose in the earth in order to bear fruit. That seed decomposed; the cycle has been repeated many times, with the result that its very genus has changed. The knowledge that Europe derived from the scholars of Islam was very considerable by [the standards of] the time, but by present-day standards it is nothing.

Along similar lines, Azad ridiculed the attempt "to invoke the Qur'an to lend its support to the achievements of modern research in the different spheres of scientific thought, as if the Qur'an was delivered over 1,300 years ago just to endorse in advance, in the form of riddles, what for centuries, [European scientists] could find out for themselves without the aid of any revealed scripture."[112]

A countertheme in modernist Islam held that early Islamic science was a foreign import, not an expression of the original Islamic spirit. Yet this importation was a favorable sign of Islam's openness, in the view of Khayr al-Din (chapter 2): "If it was permissible for the virtuous ancestors to take such things as logic from outside their own religious community, and to translate it from Greek when they saw it as being among the beneficial instruments . . . then what objection can there be today to our adopting certain skills that we see we greatly need in order to resist intrigues and attract benefits?"

For others, importation was problematic. While expressing deep respect for science, many leading modernists also worried that excessive respect for science might result in Muslims' rejection of Islamic faith. Afghani accused Ahmad Khan of "naturism," and was in turn accused of atheism by conservative scholars.[113] The danger of atheism helped to motivate education reform, which was intended to compete with European-run schools by teaching modern science along with the belief that science was consistent with Islam. 'Abduh, would-be reformer of al-Azhar in Cairo, criticized Western-style schools for trying to turn Muslims into Europeans, which he likened to making chickens lay goose eggs.[114] Gasprinskii (chapter 29), pioneer of *jadid* schools in the Russian Empire, excoriated Russian-educated Muslims who knew European languages and sciences but were "unable to read and write in their own national language!" Ahmad Khan (chapter 40), founder of the Aligarh school in India, sought to pro-

---

111. *Mulla Nasruddin*, May 17, 1909, p. 12. Translation from Azeri by Hasan Javadi.

112. Abu'l-Kalam Azad, *The Tarjuman al-Qur'an* (*Interpretation of the Qur'an*), trans. Syed Abdul Latif (Bombay, India: Asia Publishing House, 1962), volume 1, p. xl. First published in 1930.

113. Sayyid Jamal ad-Din al-Afghani, "The Refutation of the Materialists," trans. Nikki R. Keddie and Hamid Algar, in *An Islamic Response to Imperialism: Political and Religious Writings of Sayyid Jamal ad-Din al-Afghani* (Berkeley: University of California Press, 1968), pp. 130–171; Nikki R. Keddie, *Sayyid Jamal ad-Din "al-Afghani": A Political Biography* (Berkeley: University of California Press, 1972), pp. 65–80.

114. John W. Livingston, "Muhammad 'Abduh on Science," *Muslim World*, volume 85, numbers 3–4, 1995, p. 224.

vide an Islamic response to English education, which left "the inner spirit dead."[115]

Women's Rights

"Except for the Pathan, the women have no enemy. He is clever but is ardent in suppressing women," a Pathan woman named Nagiria wrote in the journal *Pushtun* in 1919. "O Pathan, when you demand your freedom [from the British], why do you deny it to women?"[116] Similarly, women—and men—in many Islamic regions began to demand gender reforms of various sorts in the late nineteenth and early twentieth centuries, using an Islamic discourse. "Pay attention to every corner of the world, we are at the eve of a revolution," Fatma Nesibe Hanım (Turkey, mid-nineteenth–early twentieth century) told a women's conference in Istanbul in 1911.[117]

Among the most common themes in this segment of the modernist Islamic movement was the promotion of girls' schooling. Modernists justified girls' schools on various grounds. One focused on the rights of women. Rokeya Sakhawat Hossein (Bengal, 1880–1932), a pioneer in women's education in South Asia, emphasized this theme in her presidential address to the Bengal Women's Education Conference in 1926: "The opponents of female education say that women will become wanton and unruly. Fie! They call themselves Muslims and yet go against the basic tenets of Islam, which accords women an equal right to education."[118] As Mazrui (chapter 7), among many others, emphasized, "The Prophet himself says that women and men both should be educated."[119]

The rights of women extended to a variety of behaviors, including military service, that women of the early years of Islam engaged in, wrote Fakhreddin (chapter 33). According to Maghribi (chapter 27), "Many of the ways [the Prophet] used to treat his wives we see today as inappropriate and unsuitable," such as camel-racing with his wife and watching entertainment together in a mosque. Aside from education, though, modernists disagreed as to which rights women should enjoy. In 1917, Muslim women's organizations in Russia urged limits on polygamy, so that it would not infringe on the rights of first wives; the (male) All-Russia Muslim Congress, meeting the same year, took a more radical position, calling for a complete ban.[120] In 1918, a women's association in India called for an end to polygamy, emphasizing the Qur'anic guarantee of women's right to equal treatment by their husbands; other (male) modernists were scandalized, even one who had himself called for such a ban.[121] Similarly, modernists debated women's right to divorce and their right to participate in politics. The Azerbaijan People's Republic granted women's suffrage in 1918,[122] yet the republicans in Turkey refused, a refusal that Adıvar (chapter 28) called "perhaps a blessing," since women have thus "been protected from the danger of being identified with party politics, and their activities outside the political world could not be stopped for political reasons."

As these examples indicate, gender did not necessarily predict a modernist's position on any particular aspect of women's rights. Even *hijab*—modest "Islamic" dress—which Western observers took as a potent symbol of Muslim women's oppression, divided modernist Muslims along ideological rather than gender lines. In Iran, pioneering educator and editor Maryam Amid Muzayyan al-Saltana (Iran, died 1919), a woman, defended *hijab*, but published the work of other Iranian women who objected to it.[123] Qasim Amin (Egypt, 1863–1908; chapter 4), a man, and Nazira Zein-ed-Din (Lebanon, born circa

115. David Lelyveld, *Aligarh's First Generation* (Princeton, N.J.: Princeton University Press, 1978), p. 129.

116. Eknath Easwaran, *Nonviolent Soldier of Islam: Badshah Khan, A Man to Match His Mountains*, 2d ed. (Tomales, Calif.: Nilgiri Press, 1999), p. 105.

117. Aynur Demirdirek, "In Pursuit of the Ottoman Women's Movement," in Zehra F. Arat, ed., *Deconstructing Images of "The Turkish Woman"* (New York: St. Martin's Press, 1998), p. 78.

118. Sonia Nishat Amin, *The World of Muslim Women in Colonial Bengal, 1876–1939* (Leiden, Netherlands: E. J. Brill, 1996), p. 158.

119. Margaret Strobel, *Muslim Women in Mombasa, 1890–1975* (New Haven, Conn.: Yale University Press, 1979), p. 105.

120. Marianne R. Kamp, "Unveiling Uzbek Women: Liberation, Representation and Discourse, 1906–1929," Ph.D. dissertation, University of Chicago, 1998, p. 110.

121. Gail Minault, *Secluded Scholars: Women's Education and Muslim Social Reform in Colonial India* (Delhi, India: Oxford University Press, 1998), pp. 145–146, 289–290.

122. Swietochowski, *Russian Azerbaijan*, p. 129.

123. Afsaneh Najmabadi, "Crafting an Educated Housewife," in Lila Abu-Lughod, ed., *Remaking Women: Feminism and Modernity in the Middle East* (Princeton, N.J.: Princeton University Press, 1998), p. 101.

1905),[124] a woman, inveighed against *hijab*, preferring the middle-class garb of Western Europeans of the era; while Rida (chapter 6) and Kazım,[125] men, and Bahithat al-Badiya (chapter 5), a woman, defended it. Bahithat, by contrast, considered it appropriate for women to perform certain forms of work outside of the home, while the founder of the Society for the Progress of Women, Fatima Rashid (Egypt, died 1953), associated such work with a disturbing "third sex."[126]

A second strand justified girls' schools on the grounds of benefit to society. Qasim Amin (chapter 4) adopted the language of women's rights but also linked women's education to the aspirations of male modernists: "There is a way of raising yourselves up to the highest level of civilization—the kind of civilization you aspire to, and then some. It consists of liberating your women from the bondage of ignorance and *hijab* [here, isolation]." Tahar Haddad (Tunisia, 1899–1935) attacked those "condemning women to eternal ignorance, despite all the grave dangers for our present society and future generations that illiteracy presents. . . . It is critical that women have access to certain careers of social importance, such as medical treatment of infants and women's diseases, teaching in orphanages and kindergartens, and all the functions involved with health, education, and culture, without these activities preventing the accomplishment of her duties as mother of the family."[127] Training women for these roles—notice the gendered limits of Haddad's list, plus the recurrent association of women with family—would allow society to make use of human resources that were currently being wasted. Zaynab Fawwaz (Lebanon-Egypt, 1860–1914) objected to any limits on women's usefulness: "man and woman are equal in mental capacity and are two members of one social body, both of which are equally indispensable. . . .

God in His creation has set laws whose transformation cannot be decreed [by humans]. But this transformation would not occur through employing women in men's occupations or men in women's occupations."[128]

A variant of this argument, adopted so commonly that it may well constitute a third strand, held that schools would make women better mothers. Bahithat al-Badiya (chapter 5) made this case, responding to the view—common in global scientific discourse of the era—that education desexed women: "No matter how much a mother has been educated, or in whatever profession she works, this would not cause her to forget her children nor to lose her maternal instinct. On the contrary, the more enlightened she becomes, the more aware she is of her responsibilities. Haven't you seen ignorant women and peasant women ignore their crying child for hours? Were these women also occupied in preparing legal cases or in reading and writing?" The founder of the first girls' schools in the Sudan, Babikr Bedri (Sudan, 1860–1954), justified modern education on the grounds that it "would enable a girl to run her home in such a way as to attract educated young men of her own race, from among her relatives or fellow citizens. This would help to prevent our educated men from marrying foreigners, a thing which would bring to nought our efforts in educating them."[129] Even quite conservative religious scholars, such as *Maulana* Ashraf 'Ali Thanavi (North India, 1864–1943), could support women's education on the grounds that ignorance, "the ruination of the religion of the women of Hindustan, . . . went beyond the women to their children and in many respects even had its effects on their husbands."[130] This line of reasoning allowed some modernists to call for limits on girls' education; women needed only to learn child-rearing, home economics, and moral virtue. In Ahmad Khan's words: "The learning that will be beneficial today to women is the same that benefited

124. Nazira Zein-ed-Din, "Unveiling and Veiling," in Kurzman, ed., *Liberal Islam*, pp. 101–106. First published in 1928.

125. Nilüfer Göle, *The Forbidden Modern: Civilization and Veiling* (Ann Arbor: University of Michigan Press, 1996), p. 42.

126. Beth Baron, *The Women's Awakening in Egypt* (New Haven, Conn.: Yale University Press, 1994), p. 147.

127. Tahar Haddad, *Notre femme, la législation islamique, et la société* (*Our Woman, Islamic Legislation, and Society*) (Tunis, Tunisia: Maison Tunisienne de l'Édition, 1978), pp. 222–224. First published in 1930.

128. Margot Badran and Miriam Cooke, eds., *Opening the Gates: A Century of Arab Feminist Writing* (Bloomington: Indiana University Press, 1990), p. 223.

129. Babikr Bedri, *The Memoirs of Babikr Bedri*, trans. Yusuf Bedri and Peter Hogg (London: Ithaca Press, 1980), volume 2, p. 132.

130. Barbara Daly Metcalf, *Perfecting Women: Maulana Ashraf 'Ali Thanawi's Bihishti Zewar* (Berkeley: University of California Press, 1990), pp. 47–48.

them in the past, namely, religion and practical morality."[131]

Queen Surayya Tarzi (Afghanistan, 1897–1968), daughter of Mahmud Tarzi (chapter 14), combined all three sorts of arguments—benefit to family, benefit to society, and women's rights—in consecutive sentences in her announcement of the opening of the country's first girls' schools in 1921: "Women are in charge of bringing up the future generation, the most important responsibility in life. If we deprive women of education, we have, in effect, incapacitated half of our body and have destroyed our subsistence with our own hands. It was not in vain that *Hazrat* Muhammad (may peace be upon him) made the acquisition of knowledge obligatory for both men and women."[132]

The emphasis on women's role as mothers was mirrored in the modernist Islamic discourse on masculinity. The crisis and decline of the Islamic world was associated in male authors' writings with effeminate men—that is, men who did not embody the masculine roles associated with success in the modern world. Malkum Khan (chapter 12) goaded male readers by noting that certain women "have perceived the meaning and virtues of Humanity far better than the men, that is, better than our non-men." Fitrat (chapter 34) accused traditional religious scholars of pederasty—"indecent acts with a beardless youth"—identifying premodern maleness with homosexuality, as did a cartoon in *Mulla Nasruddin* showing traditionally garbed men groping and kissing dancing boys,[133] and a Turkish modernist accusing traditional religious scholars of "adultery, homosexuality, drinking": "How can we restore the vitality of this great religion with these *Shaykh al-Islam*s [religious officials], with these snuff-addicted preachers, with this army of vagabond *softa*s [seminary students] whose ideas of faith do not go beyond voluptuous desires to own beautiful girls and boys in Paradise?"[134] Iqbal (chapter 41) turned the image of emasculation onto modern-educated Muslim men, bemoaning "the brainy graduate of high culture"—

presumptively male—"whose low, timid voice betokens the dearth of soul in his body, who takes pride in his submissiveness, eats sparingly, complains of sleepless nights, and produces unhealthy children for his community, if he does produce any at all." Male modernists projected their conception of an idealized heterosexual family onto the nation as a whole, representing the nation as a female in need of male salvation and protection.[135] The male modernist, Bahithat protested, tends to be "as despotic about liberating us [women] as he has been about our enslavement. We are weary of his despotism."[136]

The Legacy of Modernist Islam

Many observers of the modernist Islamic movement, even many sympathetic observers, have said all along that it won't amount to much. One British supporter rescinded his optimism after being attacked in western Egypt in 1897, an experience that "has convinced me that there is *no* hope anywhere to be found in Islam. I had made myself a romance about these reformers, but I see that it has no substantial basis."[137] In 1916, a Christian missionary concluded from his study of Islamic modernism that "we need not expect much to result in the way of uplift to Islam from rationalizing and intellectual defence and pruning."[138]

Not all observers have been so critical. For example, the Orientalist Ignác Goldziher (Hungary, 1850–1921), noting the "efforts, in a large number of theological tractates, to find support in Qur'an and *hadith* for the requirements of modern political life, as also for the requirements of progress in civil life

---

131. Fazlur Rahman, *Islam and Modernity* (Chicago, Ill.: University of Chicago, 1982), p. 77.

132. Senzil Nawid, *Religious Response to Social Change in Afghanistan, 1919–29* (Costa Mesa, Calif.: Mazda Publishers, 1999), p. 221.

133. *Mulla Nasruddin*, May 19, 1906, p. 1.

134. Niyazi Berkes, *The Development of Secularism in Turkey*, 2d ed. (London: Hurst & Company, 1998), p. 378.

135. Lisa Pollard, "Nurturing the Nation: The Family Politics of the 1919 Egyptian Revolution," Ph.D. dissertation, University of California at Berkeley, 1997; Afsaneh Najmabadi, "The Erotic *Vatan* (Homeland) as Beloved and Mother: To Love, to Possess, and to Protect," *Comparative Studies in Society and History*, volume 39, number 3, 1997, pp. 442–467; Tavakoli-Targhi, *Refashioning Iran*, pp. 113–134.

136. Leila Ahmed, *Women and Gender in Islam: Historical Roots of a Modern Debate* (New Haven, Conn.: Yale University Press, 1992), p. 182.

137. Wilfrid Scawen Blunt, *My Diaries: Being a Personal Narrative of Events, 1888–1914* (New York: Alfred A. Knopf, 1922), p. 276.

138. Samuel Graham Wilson, *Modern Movements among Moslems* (New York: Fleming H. Revell Company, 1916), p. 171.

(the question of women, etc.)," concluded with cautious optimism, "These cultural tendencies, intimately related to religious life, that are making themselves felt in various parts of the Muslim world, carry the seeds of a new phase in the evolution of Islam."[139]

Many Muslims of the early twentieth century seem to have agreed with Goldziher's assessment. Thousands read modernist Islamic newspapers; hundreds of thousands of families sent children to reformed Islamic schools; millions of Muslims celebrated the constitutional revolutions in Iran (1906) and the Ottoman Empire (1908); millions more participated in the anticolonial movements led by Islamic modernists in North Africa and South and Southeast Asia. At the same time, millions opposed the modernist Islamic movement; but sympathy for the movement appears to have diffused beyond the elite intellectual circles that spawned it.

In midcentury, such sympathies largely dissipated, even among the educated. By the 1930s, the movement was in serious decline, its energies sapped by secular nationalism, socialism, and fascism, which emphasized the modernist aspects of modernist Islam; and by religious revivalist movements emphasizing the Islamic aspects. Among secularists, the Soviet Union witnessed the most spectacular denunciations of previous identities—Azerbaijani Islamic modernists signed an open letter admitting that "we were deceived and mistaken" in their earlier views, for example[140]—but similar transitions occurred even without the threat of Soviet purges. This split did not occur evenly throughout the Islamic world: modernist Islam was still arriving during this period in some regions, such as West Africa or China, where Ya'qub Wang Jingzhai (China, 1879–1949; chapter 52) and others only began to study in the Middle East in large numbers in the 1920s and 1930s; the Sudan, where Muhammad Ahmad Mahjub (Sudan, 1908–1976; chapter 10) and other college graduates developed a modernist-Islamic nationalism; and the Hadhramaut—where a "boomerang effect" brought modern-

ism via Southeast Asia.[141] In regions where Muslim scholars played an active role in nationalist movements—Algeria and Indonesia, for example—modernist Islam seems to have had greater staying power.

A recent critic has suggested that this bifurcation reflected a "disintegrative tendency" inherent in the juxtaposition of "modernist" and "Islamic."[142] Another approach might view the split-up of modernist Islam in terms of the weakening of liberalism throughout the world—not just among Muslims—during the Interwar period, with authenticity on the right and the "New Man" on the left crowding out the toleration of multiple identities, old and new. This approach might find support in the resurgence of interest in modernist Islamic figures among Muslim intellectuals of the late twentieth century, contributing to global intellectual trends shifting away from fascism and communism. Rachid Ghannouchi (Tunisia, born 1941) has dedicated his recent work on civil rights to Afghani, 'Abduh, and other modernists.[143] Chandra Muzaffar (Malaysia, born 1947) has republished excerpts from Ameer 'Ali and Azad.[144] The centennial of the death of Afghani recently led a high-level official in the Islamic Republic of Iran to praise modernism as "necessary for the survival of Islam at the theoretical, practical, political, and social levels."[145]

The modernist Islamic movement's primary legacy, the aspect that appears to attract contemporary Muslim thinkers, is its defining feature: the attempt to reconcile modern values and Islamic faith. Admitting

139. Ignaz Goldziher, *Introduction to Islamic Theology and Law*, trans. Andras and Ruth Hamori (Princeton, N.J.: Princeton University Press, 1981), pp. 236, 263. First published in 1910.

140. Audrey Altstadt, *The Azerbaijani Turks* (Stanford, Calif.: Hoover Institution Press, 1992), p. 131.

141. Peter G. Riddell, "Religious Links between Hadhramaut and the Malay-Indonesian World, c. 1850 to c. 1950," in Ulrike Freitag and William G. Clarence-Smith, eds., *Hadhrami Traders, Scholars, and Statesmen in the Indian Ocean, 1750s–1960s* (Leiden, Netherlands: Brill, 1997), pp. 224–229.

142. Seyyed Vali Reza Nasr, "Religious Modernism in the Arab World, India, and Iran," *The Muslim World*, volume 83, number 1, 1993, pp. 43–45.

143. Rachid al-Ghannouchi, *al-Hurriyyat al-'amma fi al-dawla al-islamiyya (Public Liberties in the Islamic State)* (Beirut, Lebanon: Markaz Dirasat al-Wihda al-'Arabiyya, 1993).

144. Chandra Muzaffar, ed., *The Universalism of Islam* (Penang, Malaysia: Aliran, 1979).

145. Mohammad Javad Hojjati Kermani, "Modernism, Islamic Movement, and the Islamic Revolution," *The Iranian Journal of International Affairs*, volume 9, number 1, 1997, p. 93.

that one has both modern values and Islamic faith is the first step in this reconciliation. Some of the admissions generated in the first century of modernist Islam may strike later readers as embarrassingly foolish and craven, such as references to European civilization as the world's sole civilization. But rejecting such formulations does not necessarily amputate the underlying values. Mass education, rapid international communication, and globalized commodities markets have generated huge populations in the Islamic world who are imbued with modern values such as cultural revival (defined in a particular manner), democracy (on Western lines), science and education (as practiced globally), and particular rights for women (as articulated by international organizations). Even Islamic revivalists share many of these concerns—though they might be scandalized by association with their modernist roots.[146]

Accepting modern values as modern is only the first step in reconciliation. The second step is to theorize the compatibility of such values with Islamic faith. This search for consistency may itself be a characteristically modern concern, as previous eras were less insistent on the discursive construction of a coherent individual self. Even some modernists have rejected such an attempt, such as Taha Husayn (Egypt, 1889–1973), who suggested that every human is composed of two separate parts, rational and emotional: "Both of these personalities are connected with our constitution and make-up, and we cannot escape from either of them. What, then, is to hinder the first personality from being scholarly, inquisitive, critical, and the second believing, assured, aspiring to the highest ideals?"[147] More commonly, the modernist Islamic movement has taken up the task through a process of double translation: modern values into Islamic terms, and Islamic values into modern terms. Translations are famously imperfect, and modernist Islam involves particularly difficult pairings: the Islamic concept of justice with the modern concept of law and judicial systems; the modern concepts of citizenship and rights with the Islamic concept of equality; the Islamic concept of consultation with the modern concept of constitutional democracy; and so on. Critics may argue that these concepts lose something in translation, but the modernist Islamic movement argued that they gain something through juxtaposition.

146. David D. Commins, "Modernism," in John L. Esposito, ed., *The Oxford Encyclopedia of the Modern Islamic World* (New York: Oxford University Press, 1995), volume 3, pp. 118–123.

147. Nissim Rejwan, *Arabs Face the Modern World* (Gainesville: University Press of Florida, 1998), p. 50.

SECTION I

Africa

The Extraction of Gold, or an Overview of Paris *and* The Honest Guide for Girls and Boys

Rifaʻa Rafiʻ al-Tahtawi (Egypt, 1801–1873) was a pioneering figure in the Arab intellectual awakening of the nineteenth century. Tahtawi was born in Tahta, Upper Egypt, to a rural family of modest means yet with a line of descent from the Prophet Muhammad. He studied for seven years at the famous al-Azhar mosque in Cairo, where his mentor nominated him to serve as religious leader for a student mission to Paris. Tahtawi stayed in France from 1826 to 1831, learned French, and became the mission's main translator. He also read the writings of major French thinkers. When he returned to Egypt, Tahtawi directed the Medical School, then worked as a translator for the Artillery School. In 1835, he ran the School of Foreign Languages, his own brainchild, which produced thousands of translated works in various fields. As a result of a falling out with Khedive ʻAbbas (reigned 1848–1854), Tahtawi was exiled to the Sudan, and was only able to return four years later, after ʻAbbas's death. He then assumed the directorship of the Military School and participated in several educational reform commissions. Tahtawi also served as editor of the official newspaper and an educational journal. Tahtawi translated two dozen French works and wrote several original books, including a didactic memoir of his experiences in France, excerpted here; a program for the reform of Egypt; and a book of guidance, also excerpted here, whose emphasis on the Egyptian *watan* (homeland) constituted one of the first statements of nationalism in the Arab world.[1]

The Extraction of Gold, or an Overview of Paris

Civil Rights Established for the French

[The French Constitutional Charter of June 4, 1814:]

Article 1: All Frenchmen are equal before the law.

Article 2: They pay, without distinction, a specified sum of money to the Treasury, each according to his wealth.

Article 3: Each one is qualified to attain any position or rank.

Article 4: Each one has an independent personality, whose freedom is guaranteed. Nobody may infringe upon it except in rights that are stipulated in the law and in the way the law is deemed applicable by the judge.

Rifaʻa Rafiʻ al-Tahtawi, *The Extraction of Gold, or an Overview of Paris* (*Takhlis al-ibriz ila talkhis Bariz*), translated from Arabic by Ihsan ʻAbbas, edited by Raʻif Khuri, revised by Charles Issawi, in *Modern Arab Thought* (Princeton, N.J.: Kingston Press, 1983), pp. 102–105; *al-Murshid al-amin li al-banat wa al-banin* (*The Honest Guide for Girls and Boys*), in Muhammad ʻImara, *al-Aʻmal al-kamila li Rifaʻa al-Tahtawi* (*The Complete Works of Rifaʻa al-Tahtawi*) (Beirut, Lebanon: al-Muʻasasa al-ʻArabiyya li al-Dirasat wa al-Nashr, 1973), volume 2, pp. 429–435, 469–477. First published in 1834 and 1875, respectively. Translation of second selection from Arabic and introduction by Emad Eldin Shahin. Thanks to Heba Mostafa Risk for her assistance with this translation.

1. Albert Hourani, *Arabic Thought in the Liberal Age: 1798–1939* (London: Oxford University Press, 1970), pp. 67–83; Khaldun S. al-Husry, *Origins of Modern Arab Political Thought* (New York: Caravan Books, 1980), pp. 11–31; Muhammad ʻImara, *Rifaʻa al-Tahtawi: Raʻid al-tanwir fi al-ʻasr al-hadith* (*Rifaʻa al-Tahtawi: Pioneer of Enlightenment in the Contemporary Era*) (Cairo, Egypt: Dar al-Mustaqbal al-ʻArabi, 1984).

Article 5: All who live in France may profess their religion as it requires, with no intervention by anybody; they shall be assisted to accomplish that, and anybody who molests them in this shall be stopped from doing so.

Article 6: The religion of the state is the Apostolic Roman Catholic faith.

Article 7: The maintenance of Catholic and other Christian churches shall be met by money of the Christians, and none of that money shall be allocated for the maintenance of places of worship that belong to other religions.

Article 8: No one in France shall be denied the right to print and publish their opinion, provided that it does not contravene the law. If it does, then it shall be suppressed.

Article 9: All property and possessions are inviolable and nobody shall encroach on the property of another.

Article 10: The state shall have the exclusive prerogative of compelling people to sell their property for the public welfare, provided that it pays an adequate price before acquisition.

Rights of the People Secured by the Parliament

The first article, that is, "All Frenchmen are equal before the law," means that all those who live in France, whether high or low, must, without distinction, be subject to the provisions of the law. Legal proceedings can be initiated even against the king himself, and judgment can be passed against him like anyone else. Consider this first article: it has great power in establishing justice, in helping the wronged and satisfying the poor by convincing them that they are great as far as legal proceedings are concerned. This criterion has become one of the most comprehensive principles among the French. It is clear proof of how highly justice is valued among them and how advanced their cultural program has become. What they hold dear and call liberty is what we call equity and justice, for to rule according to liberty means to establish equality through judgments and laws, so that the ruler cannot wrong anybody, the law being the reference and the guide. This is indeed a country to which the following verse applies:

And justice filled it from end to end,
And in it were happiness and sincerity.

In general, if justice exists in any country it must be considered as relative and not absolute, for absolute justice as well as perfect faith, complete purity, and similar things do not exist anywhere, nowadays. Thus there is no point in limiting impossible things to the ghoul, the griffin, and the faithful friend, of which the poet says:

When among the people of my time I found no faithful friend to choose,
I became certain that the impossible things are three:
The ghoul, the griffin, and the faithful friend.

This is not true about the griffin, because it is an existing species of birds mentioned by botanists. [Ahmad ibn Muhammad] al-Tha'labi [died 1035] in his *Qisas al-Anbiya* [*Stories of the Prophets*] mentions the story of the griffin and King Solomon and how it denied predestination. It is true that the griffin believed by the common people, Arabs and Franks [Europeans], to have the head of an eagle and the body of a lion, does not exist; yet it does exist as a bird.

The second article is purely political. It can be stated that had taxes been clearly set in Muslim countries, as they are in that country, this would have been a course of satisfaction, especially when *zakat* [alms tax], *fay'* [revenue from state lands], and booty cannot meet the need of the Treasury or are prevented from being levied totally. Taxes might have some roots in Islamic law according to some sayings of the Great *Imam* [Abu Hanifa, circa 699–767]. "*Kharaj* land-tax is the pillar of kingship" is an established maxim among ancient wise men. During my stay in Paris, I never heard any complaint against taxes, imposts, and other levies. People do not mind paying, because taxes are levied in a way that does no harm to the payer and at the same time benefits the Treasury, especially in that the wealthy are protected against injustice and bribery.

The third article does not cause any harm at all. One of its merits is that it encourages everyone to learn, so that all may be promoted to a higher position. Thus the French could acquire different kinds of knowledge and their civilization is not limited to one condition like that of the Chinese and the Indians, who believe in transmitting arts and crafts from father to son by inheritance. A historian states that the law of the ancient Copts assigned to everyone his own craft, which had to be inherited by his sons. The reason for such a procedure, according to [this historian], is that all arts and crafts were considered honorable. This procedure was necessitated by circumstances, for it helped them reach the degree of perfection in their arts, because the son usually improves on what he witnessed his father doing many times and does not direct his desire to another craft. This method usually cut the roots of covetousness and kept everybody content with his craft. Thus one does not aspire to what is higher but directs his attention to inventing new things that can carry his craft to a higher degree of perfection.

The answer to what this historian claims is that not everyone has the natural aptitude to learn his father's craft. To confine him to it might produce an unsuccessful craftsman, whereas if other crafts were open to him he would prove to be successful and achieve his aim.

The fourth, fifth, sixth, and seventh articles are very useful for both natives and foreigners. Thus the population of this country increased and its culture progressed with the many foreigners who migrated to it.

The eighth article encourages every man to express his opinions, to propagate his knowledge and to say whatever occurs to him if it does not harm others. In this way a man comes to know what his fellow men are thinking, especially on reading the daily sheets called "journals" and "gazettes," which publish up-to-date news, both domestic and foreign. Although these abound with innumerable lies, they still contain news which the people may wish to know. They may also contain newly established scientific matters, useful notices, or profitable advice, coming from the noble and the vulgar. Sometimes the latter discover what the former miss. It is said: "Do not look down upon a great opinion given to you by a lowborn man, for the pearl does not lose its value because of the mean status of the diver." A poet also said:

When I heard of him I heard of one, and when I
     saw him he was to me the whole universe
Every kind of game is in the belly of the onager
     and one man can represent all the good men.

One of the great merits of the newspaper is that if a man does an outstanding deed, whether good or bad, it is reported in the paper, and made known to all people, high and low. Thus the doer of good deeds is encouraged and the doer of evil ones restrained. If a man is wronged by another, he states his case in the newspaper to make it known to high and low, without any alteration in, or deviation from, facts; the case

gets to the courts and is dealt with according to established laws, making it thus a good lesson to others.

The ninth article is the heart of justice itself. It is essential to curb the oppression of the weak by the strong. For it to be followed by the tenth article is mere propriety.

A Discourse on the Homeland

The homeland [*watan*] is the nest of man, where he toddled and from which he emerged, the congregation of his family, and part of his inner self. It is the homeland whose soil, food, and air have raised him, whose breeze has reared him and in which he grew up. Abu 'Amr ibn al-'Ala' [linguist and poet, 689–770] said: what proves the freedom of humanity and the generosity of its nature is the longing for homeland, yearning for the return of compatriots, and weeping over the passage of time. Generous people long for their beloved ones like the lion longs for its jungle, and rational people yearn for their country like the high-born yearn for their resting-place. Free people do not prefer any country to their homeland, and are never patient being away from it. [. . .] Nothing keeps away sane people from their homeland except the search for eminence, if it could not be achieved within. [. . .]

It has been the custom that those who are away from the homeland where they spent part of their youth, yearn for it, whether they be Bedouin or city people. The Bedouins regret leaving Najd, and yearn for it the same way people might yearn for the gardens of Damascus. [. . .] So if we show some of the merits of the mother of the world and of the blessings [that is, Egypt], which is the quiver of God in His land, it appears to us that it is considered the first of all homelands in the world, which deserves its children's hearts to be inclined toward it. It is most worthy for the souls of its people who are separated from it to yearn for it.

The Egyptians' Attachment to Their Homeland

Nobody doubts that Egypt is an honorable homeland, even if we refrain from calling it the most honorable place. It is the land of honor and glory in the past and the present, and much came in its praise in clear [Qur'anic] verses and *hadith*s [traditions of the

Prophet], as if it was the image of everlasting paradise engraved across the earth by the divine hand of wisdom, which gathered life's merits in it, until it nearly confined them in its corners and regions. [. . .]

[Egypt is] described by all in terms of courage, enthusiasm, prudence, and leadership, in addition to intelligence, insight, pleasant attributes, and morals. [. . .] It has the right to be respected by all nations and faiths, and the states and kings of the world. In old times, they adopted much of its brilliance in science and knowledge, which engulfed the world and led it to towering heights.

It is still the pride of every time. Its exquisiteness adorns every place. Its share of civilization is immense. [. . .] It is said: Among Egypt's characteristics is the abundance of currency in it, and those who enter it and do not get rich, God will never enrich them. [. . .] Some said: Among Egypt's characteristics is that the Egyptian who seeks a homeland in another place lives in humiliation. Its kings and leaders were greeted as "mighty one," as stated in the Noble Qur'an. In general, countries are both praised and insulted. It was said: the world is Basra [a city in Iraq], and Baghdad has no equal. Al-Hajjaj [ibn Yusuf, governor, 660–714] used to say: Kufa [a city in Iraq] is a beautiful young girl that possesses no money; it is sought for its beauty. We say: Egypt is a young bride adorned with money and beauty, and is sought for its money and beauty. It now combines the old and the new; it is the source of splendor and pleasantries; it offers benefits to the seekers of the best; it is prominent in every art; and it is the urban [city] of Africa, and all else is a desert.

It is indeed across the nights and days a source of happiness, the heir of *Dar al-Salam* [the House of Peace, a description of heaven], and the adornment of the territories of Islam. Its king is mighty, its people are dignified and strong, loved by the children of [other] countries, adhering to the *hadith*: "Love of homeland is part of faith." By God's will, it is secure and safe against the accidents of time.

On the Children of the Country and Their Responsibility

The wisdom of the One Able King [God] has so destined that the children of the homeland are always united in language, in entering under the care of a single king, and in following a single law and a single

policy. This is what proves that God, most exalted, has prepared them for cooperation in the reform of their country, that they would be to one another like the members of one family, as if the homeland were the home of their parents and the place of their upbringing—so may it be a place for mutual happiness between them. The one nation should not be branched out into various parties with different opinions for what follows from this of quarreling, envy, hatred, and the insecurity of the homeland. One should not wish for his own happiness and the misery of others, especially that the *shari'a* and politics made them equal and required them to be on the heart of one man [united], and not to take as an enemy for them except that who inflicted failure on them with his deceit, so that the system of their rule is disturbed and the order of their path unravels. This is the evident enemy who does not like the people of the homeland to be secure of their country and to enjoy their freedom.

The Rights of the Citizen

Also, the children of the homeland—those who originated in it, or those who came and settled and adopted it as their homeland—are affiliated with it: first to its name, so they are called "Egyptian," for example; or to the people, so they are called "native"; or to the homeland, so they are called "patriot." This means that they enjoy the rights of their country. The greatest of those rights is complete freedom in social association. Patriots are not characterized by freedom except when they follow the law of the land and assist in its implementation. Their adherence to the rules of the country requires, implicitly, that the country guarantee them the enjoyment of civil rights and civil privileges. Only in this sense are they patriots and natives, meaning that they are considered members of the community. They relate to it as organs relate to the body. This is the greatest privilege in civilized nations. This privilege, one of the greatest virtues, has been denied to the people of most nations. When rulers reigned by whim, doing what they pleased, the people had no way to oppose their rulers or defend the rulings of the *shari'a*. They were not able to tell their kings what they saw as inconsistent, contribute to matters of policy and administration, or give their views on issues. They were like foreigners in government affairs, and they only held jobs or positions below their qualifications. Now ideas have changed, and those dangers have been removed from the children of the country. Now, true patriots can fill their hearts with the love of their homeland, because they have become members of it.

The Responsibilities of the Citizen

Patriots who are faithful in their love of homeland redeem their country with all their means, and serve it by offering all they possess. They redeem it with their soul, and repel anyone who seeks to harm it the same way a father would keep evil away from his child. The intentions of the children of the country must always be directed toward the country's virtue and honor, and not toward anything that violates the rights of their countries and fellow countrymen. Their inclination should be toward that which brings benefit and goodness. Likewise, the country protects its children from all that harms them, because of its possession of those characteristics. The love of homeland and the promotion of the public welfare are among the beautiful characteristics that get inculcated into each person, constantly, throughout one's life, and make every one of them loved by the others. No one could be happier than the human beings who are naturally inclined to keep evil away from their homeland, even if they must harm themselves to do so.

The quality of patriotism requires not just that humans demand the rights they are owed by their homeland. They must also carry out their obligations toward the country. If the children of the homeland fail to earn the rights of their country, then the civil rights to which they are entitled will be lost.

In olden times, the Romans used to force citizens who reached twenty years of age to give an oath that they would defend their country and their government. They required a pledge to this effect, the text of which is:

"May God be my witness that I shall carry the sword of honor to defend my country and its people whenever there is a chance I would be able to assist it. May God be my witness that I am willing to fight with the army or on my own for the protection of the country and religion. May God be my witness that I shall not disturb the serenity of my country, nor betray it or deceive it, and that I shall sail on the seas whenever necessary in all conquests that the government orders, and that I pledge to follow present and future laws and customs in my country. May God be my witness that I shall not tolerate anyone who dares violate them or undermine their order."

Based on this, it is understood that the Roman nation firmly adhered to the love of country, and that is the reason it reigned over all the countries of the world. When the quality of patriotism was removed, failure beset the members of this nation, its affairs were ruined, and the order of its system disintegrated by the numerous disagreements of its princes and the multiplicity of its rulers. After being ruled by one Caesar, it was divided between two Caesars in the east and the west, the Caesar of Rome and the Caesar of Constantinople. Power that had belonged to one mighty force was split into two minor forces. All its wars ended in defeat, and it retreated from a perfect existence to nonexistence. This is the fate of any nation whose government is in disarray, and whose state is disorganized.

On Civilizing the Homeland

Civilizing the country allows civilized people to improve their physical and moral condition. It improves morals and customs, perfects socialization, motivates people to be inclined toward commendable qualities, fulfils civic perfection, and promotes prosperity. This is what civilization is for the nation residing in the homeland. Individuals may differ with regard to [the level of] advancement and improvement. Civilization varies, both for nations and individuals. That is why you find one kingdom more advanced in civilization than another, and also one person more civilized than another with regard to the improvement of condition and status.

Contrary to civilization is crudity, which involves the lack of prosperity in the standard of living. There is no doubt that the laws delivered by the prophets are the essence of true civilization to be considered and adopted. The principles and rulings that arrived with Islam have certainly civilized all the countries of the earth, and the lights of right guidance reached beyond the horizons. God's Prophet [Muhammad], may peace and prayer be upon him, said: "I was sent to you with a clear Abrahamic *shariʻa*, that no prophet came with before. Had my brother Moses and all the prophets been in my time, they would have followed only my *shariʻa*." Anyone who practiced the science of the fundamentals of *fiqh* [Islamic jurisprudence], and learned its regulations and rules, would ascertain that all the rational deduction—which the minds of the people of civilized nations developed and used as the basis for the laws of their civilization and laws—hardly go beyond those fundamentals upon which the branches of *fiqh* were built, and around which transactions revolve. Similar to the science we call the fundamentals of *fiqh*, they have the science of "natural rights" or "natural law"—rational regulations, stipulating good and bad, upon which they base their civil laws. What we call the branches of *fiqh*, they call civil rights or laws. What we call justice and benevolence, they call freedom and equality. The love of religion and the desire to protect it, whose adherence distinguishes the people of Islam from other nations in power and defense, they call love of country. But for us, the people of Islam, love of country is but one of the branches of faith, and the protection of religion is the core of all pillars. Every Islamic kingdom is a homeland for all those in it who belong to Islam. It combines religion and patriotism. Therefore, its children are obliged to protect it, for both reasons. But the practice has run to confine [this love] to religion because of its importance, while still desiring the homeland. Zeal for one's country could be entirely for reasons of citizenship and status. This could be the case of the Qaysi, the Yemeni, the Egyptian, and the Syrian. However, in the homeland all humankind is equal. We find that parties, despite their differences, unite against the foreigner to protect their country, their religion, or their kind.

The benefits of civilization are numerous, and around them revolve all the sciences of life and destruction. That is why some have said: as civilization advances among the kingdoms of the earth, wars diminish, hostility decreases, conquests become less brutal, instability and revolutions become rarer and disappear completely, unlawful enslavement and bondage end, and poverty and humiliation vanish.

On the Reasons for Civilization

Also among the reasons for civilization on earth: adhering to *shari'a*; promoting science and knowledge; advancing agriculture, commerce, and industry; and discovering the countries that can help achieve all this, inventing machines and equipment that facilitate the path to civilization by providing the ways and means. Printing houses, for example, assisted education and learning, which are among the pillars of civilization. It is said that the first inventor of printed books in Europe was the German nation, and that it traveled from there to Chinese lands. The people of France at that time were in a deep sea because of blind ignorance, and in a bottomless pit because of coarseness. They believed that printers were sorcerers, and wanted to kill them. But they were saved by Louis XI, the king of France [reigned 1461–1483], who put the printing houses under his protection. Then printing reached the rest of the countries of Europe, and from there the countries of the East and Egypt.

Freedom of Opinion and Expression

Among the things that helped to broaden the scope of civilization in the countries of the earth is the kings' approval for scientists and possessors of knowledge to write legal, philosophical, literary, and political books. [There was an expansion] of freedom in this respect by disseminating [aspects of civilization] through print and pictures, especially in the daily newspapers of the countries of Europe, [thanks to] the law of freedom of expression. The only condition is that [this freedom] should not destabilize the government and should take a moderate path, without neglect or excessiveness.

Among the greatest supports to civilization is the freedom of navigation and travel, on land and sea. Travel brought all the kingdoms of the earth fortune, wealth, and familiarity with the wonders of the world. The Arabs of Islam used to travel to discover new countries and bring their people to the religion of the best of people [that is, the religion of the Prophet Muhammad]. They discovered countless lands and seas; they civilized countless people on the islands of the [Indian] Ocean and its shores. Then shrewd and attentive Europeans followed their example and discovered a new world, previously unknown to the ancients. The greatest aid in navigating the sea is the invention of the "compass," which is the "house of the needle." It was said to be invented by the Arabs of Islam, traveling to all sides of the [Indian] Ocean to spread Islam to the barbarian nations of these regions. It was [also] said that the house of the needle was invented by none but the Europeans. In sum, we may say: the Arabs invented this machine, and the Europeans worked to perfect and improve it, and to produce it in large quantities. It is a box, in which is fixed a magnetized iron needle, always heading toward the North Pole, and never deviating from it, except for a small deviation. Inside it are drawn the four directions: north, south, east and west. [The function of this compass] is to determine the blowing of the four original winds and the catastrophic wind. With this [compass] the captains at sea are guided toward their destinations. As a result, most kingdoms of Europe are masters of sea power. However, the greatest sea power is the kingdom of the British, then the kingdom of France and the Sublime State [the Ottoman Empire], which has a strong naval power, and whose ports which cannot be matched in impenetrability and security. The Egyptian government has important ports that could be [world] leaders, centers of trade in all sorts of exports and imports, aided by the advantage of the Mediterranean and Red Seas.

Policy experts have said that a kingdom's sea power should be relative to its land power, and in accordance with the greatness of its dominion. The most beneficial thing in demonstrating the sea power of a kingdom is that its banner be allowed to sail in the sea and to be respected throughout the seas of the world. Among the advantages of sea power is that it helps in promoting agriculture, trade, and industry, especially in colonies outside the kingdom. The nation that desires many ships and ports must increase the planting of forests and tree farms, to grow the proper wood so that the naval kingdom can build its fleet. If that is difficult, it must obtain the appropriate ships through purchase from foreign countries to the extent that satisfies its needs. Sea power is a plentiful source to broaden the scope of civilization, which is built upon justice and public freedom.

On Public Freedom and Social Equality

Freedom is the license for permissible action without an impermissible obstacle or a prohibited objection. The rights of all the people of the civilized kingdom are based on freedom. In a kingdom that has obtained its freedom, social association is permitted, and each individual may move from one house to another and from one place to another, without harassment or coercion. People may do as they please with themselves, their time, and their work. They are restrained only by the limits prescribed by law or politics, which are required by the principles of their just kingdom. Among the rights of civil freedom is the human being's right not to be forcibly exiled or punished, except by a legal or political ruling in accordance with the principles of the kingdom. People are not restrained from dealing with their money as

they please, and it will not be confiscated, except in accordance with the laws of the country. Their opinion on any subject may not be muffled, on condition that what they say or write does not violate the laws of the country.

The Types of Freedom

Freedom is divided into five types: natural freedom, behavioral freedom, religious freedom, civil freedom, and political freedom.

Natural freedom originated with humankind, and molded it. Humans cannot suppress natural freedom without being considered unjust. For example, eating, drinking, and walking—things common to all individuals, that they cannot do without, so long as they do no harm to the individual or to others. Overeating, for example, is not allowed, as is eating poison, or eating other people's food without their permission.

Behavioral freedom involves commendable conduct and noble morals. It is the attribute necessary for every member of the community—as deduced from the rules of reason, and as required by the integrity of the individual, since one's conscience rests upon the goodness of one's behavior in dealing with others.

Religious freedom is the freedom of faith, opinion, and doctrine, on condition that it adheres to the principles of religion, like the doctrinal views of the Ash'aris [followers of Abu'l-Hasan al-Ash'ari, 873–925] and the Maturidis [followers of Abu Mansur al-Maturidi, died circa 944], and the followers of *madhhab*s [legal schools] who exercise *ijtihad* [religious interpretation] on minor issues. The human being feels secure in following one of the *madhhab*s and in adhering to it in matters of worship. The same applies to the freedom of political *madhhab*s, that is, the opinions of the heads of official administrations in implementing their principles, laws, and decrees according to the codes of their countries. Monarchs and their ministers are unrestricted in the different ways [they formulate] political procedures, as long as they refer to consistent criteria, for that is good politics and justice.

Civil freedom involves the rights of a city's residents and communities toward each other. It is as if the social community formed out of the people of the kingdom, joining together to honor each other's rights, so that each individual has pledged to the others to help them in all their activities that do not violate the law of the country. [In return,] they do not oppose the individual, and they all repudiate anyone who would impinge on the individual's freedom, on condition that the individual does not trespass the limits of the law.

Political freedom refers to the state. It exists when the state assures all of its people their legitimate and recognized property, and the practice of their natural freedom without infringement of any kind. Thus, every individual may engage in all legitimate transactions regarding personal property, so long as one avoids harming one's compatriots. The government has thus guaranteed human happiness.

The Relation between Freedom and Happiness

Freedom, in all these meanings, is the greatest means for making the people of kingdoms happy. If freedom is built on just and sound laws, it will be a great means in comforting the people and making them happy in their countries. It provides a reason for their love of their countries. In short, the freedom of the people of every kingdom can be summed up in the right to do what is legal, and the right not to be coerced into doing what is unlawful in their kingdom. Every member of the community is allowed to enjoy all that is permitted in the kingdom. Restricting what people are allowed to do, without a legitimate reason, is considered to be a denial of their recognized right of happiness. Whoever restricts them arbitrarily has stripped them of a recognized right, and thereby would be infringing upon their rights, and opposing the laws of the country. If the freedom of the people is accompanied by the justice of monarchs, combining tolerance with firmness and reverence, the state need not fear freedom. The two rights [of the state and the individual] will counterbalance each other; and the ruler and the ruled will both be happy.

The Duty of the Free toward Their Country

As freedom is naturally imprinted on the hearts of humans, and as divine wisdom has decreed that humans be dignified above all others, and not denigrated or humiliated, so should they devote their freedom to honoring their country, their compatriots, and their ruler. If people feel obligated to serve their coun-

try, then they will not consider it an infringement upon their rights when the government collects taxes to fight enemies or contribute to government expenditures. This is part of their duty toward their country; and since the enemy transgresses by invasion, people will have to fight and repel him. This in reality is nothing but a protection of freedom. Among the splendors of the nation's freedom is that this nation also feels happy with the freedom of other nations, and is hurt by the enslavement of the nations of the world that have no freedom.

The greatest freedom in the civilized kingdom is the freedom of agriculture, trade, and industry. Permitting them is one of the principles of the art of governmental administration. Evidence has proven that this freedom is of the greatest public benefit, and that human beings have been inclined toward it for centuries, as civilization has advanced. The greatest difficulty for the person who appreciates the benefits of these arts is to see these spheres restricted. But the reason for the restriction might be that the monarchs of the kingdom perceive their subjects as unqualified for this freedom, because of their incomplete civil education. When education progresses and conditions improve, they will allow people the freedom of expanded spheres of agriculture, trade, and industry. Socializing people and improving their conditions will equip their minds with good judgment and [the ability] to handle huge operations.

Some wise people said: allow me to improve education, and I will devote myself to improving the conditions of the whole world. Human minds, once they reach a lofty level in understanding the knowledge of daily life, expand commerce and continuously invent equipment and machines contributing to the public welfare. People of that era strive to perfect the practice of their business and work. Clever people in agriculture, industry, and trade can record and document all their inventions in books, and abundant profits and gains, thriving day by day, will thus be multiplied by knowledge. It is not surprising for a kingdom, where the sciences of management and banking have progressed, where their strong principles and solid foundations have been mastered, to reap public benefits and financial fruits. It would not be surprising for the same benefits to be generated, and expanded in practice, among those who live nearby and compete with the people of that kingdom in these sciences. And freedom is associated with equality, and both are associated with justice and benevolence.

Equality

Equality among the members of a society is a natural human quality, which makes each one equal in civil rights to another. It encompasses civil and public freedoms, because all people share common attributes. Each has two eyes, two ears, two hands, and the senses of smell, taste, and touch. Each needs sustenance. Therefore, all are on equal footing in life, and have the same right to the necessities of life. They are all equal in this respect, and no one is preferred over others in terms of survival.

But if we examine the matter thoroughly, we find that this equality is illusory. Divine Providence has already privileged some over others. Some were granted magnificent qualities while others were not, and thus differed in moral makeup, and also in physical qualities, some bodies being strong and others weak. And although God, most exalted, preferred some to others in endowments, He made them equal in accountability, with no distinction between the honorable and the base, the leader and the subordinate. This is ordained and articulated in all the books revealed to His messengers, may peace and prayer be upon them. Equality means nothing but sharing the same laws, and being equal before them. This equality cannot be suspended by human legislation. If people can be proven to be equal in rights, it follows that they must cooperate to remove a public threat, as its removal would serve their public interest. If their country suffers a mishap, they must totally put aside their private privileges. They must adhere to equality and forget privilege. Thus, equality would be associated with freedom when the banner of war is brandished. To this a third character would be added: their concern for the continuation of their country's stability and public welfare, the prevention of internal disorder, and the resolution of the source of civil strife. Any nation that considers equality the basis of its laws and natural rights, and continues to observe this equality, will establish its freedom on firm grounds, and its kingdom will have a strong basis, without internal or external disturbances. It will be strong enough to defend its territories, protect its country, and fend off the aggression of its neighboring kingdoms. This nation is strong, inside and outside, and revered by all.

Equality in rights is nothing but the legal ability of the human being to do, attain, or prevent all that is possible for others to do, attain, or prevent legally. All people manage their property and rights in a similar manner, regardless of their status in the kingdom, noble or mean. All are equal in their conduct. It makes sense, therefore, that human equality in rights requires equality in the responsibilities that people owe one other. Equality in rights is associated with equality in obligations. As humans demand their rights, they must [in turn] fulfill their responsibility. Equality means trusting all the people of the kingdom, without distinction, to perform their obligations toward each other. Obligations are always associated inseparably with rights. In any case, the legal and political obligations around which the world revolves are based upon rational and sound principles devoid of inhibitions and doubts, because *shari'a* and politics are based on a wisdom that we can perceive, through worship, a wisdom that is known to God the Sustainer, most exalted and glorified. We cannot depend on what the mind likes or detests, unless *shari'a* law has stipulated its rightness or distastefulness.

Justice

Those who perform their duties and receive their proper due from others, and persevere in so doing, are characterized by justice. Justice is a quality that induces humans to be rightful in words and conduct, and to be just with themselves and others. Some philosophers perceived [justice] as the virtue of all virtues and the basis for human society, modernization, and civilization. It is the cornerstone of the establishment of kingdoms, whose affairs cannot be managed without it. All other virtues stem from justice. They form part of its attributes, but with specific names such as sympathy, chivalry, piety, love of country, sincerity of the heart, internal purity, generosity, moral decency, modesty, and the like. All these are the products of justice. The noble *hadith*, the saying of [the Prophet], may peace and prayer be upon him, [states]: "None of you is a believer until you love for your brother what you love for yourself." This is the highest level of justice, and it is consistent with the wisdom of the philosophers and the laws of the Messengers prior to Islam. It is supported by *shari'a* and nature, although the support of natural laws should not be taken into consideration unless it is stipulated by the Legislator.

2

Khayr al-Din

The Surest Path

Khayr al-Din al-Tunisi (Tunisia, 1822–1890) was a prominent reformer and effective states-man. Khayr al-Din was a Circassian who was enslaved and sold to a notable in Turkey, where he spent seventeen years before being brought to the court of the Tunisian ruler. Still a teenager, he studied in the ruler's palace and then joined the Bardo Military School, where he received Arabic and Islamic education and learned modern military sciences. Khayr al-Din's remarkable talents facilitated his ascendance to the premiership of Tunisia (1873–1877) and of the Ottoman Empire (1878–1879). He was the main inspiration behind the promulgation of a constitution and the establishment of a parliament in Tunisia in 1860, which he headed. As Tunisia's prime minister, he introduced influential financial, administrative, agricultural, and educational reforms. He founded the Sadiqiyya School in 1875, whose combination of Islamic and modern education produced much of the elite that later struggled for Tunisian independence from the French. His tenure as Grand Vizier of the Ottoman Empire was brief, lasting only eight months, and constrained by the autocratic tendencies of the sultan. After his dismissal, Khayr al-Din went into retirement in Istanbul. His major written work, the book excerpted here, contained Khayr al-Din's political visions and his program of reform. He advanced strong arguments for the acquisition of Western institutions, values, and practices that he considered compatible with the Islamic *shari'a*, prime among them the concept of liberty. Khayr al-Din argued that liberty, both personal and political, is crucial for peace and prosperity.[1]

In the name of God, the beneficent, the merciful.

Praise be to Him who made prosperity one of the results of justice and endowed mankind with intelligence, by which He made it possible for man to attain right conduct and the various gradations of knowledge. And commanded him to cooperate in good works and to fear God to the exclusion of idols or transgression.

I praise Him. He is to be praised at all times and in all tongues. And I pray for His servant and our master Muhammad, who was sent with the Book and the Balance. To whom it was revealed that God commands justice and charity. And I pray for his family and his companions, the guardians of his Holy Law,

which is suitable for all times. Whose rulings describe orbits around the two points of faith and God's protection.

After this invocation the compiler of these pages says, "May God guide him to the surest path."

After I had long contemplated the causes of the progress and backwardness of nations, generation after generation, relying on the Islamic and European histories I was able to examine, and on what the authors of both groups have written concerning the Islamic *umma* [community], its attributes, and its future, according to evidence which experience has decreed should be accepted, I decided to assert what I believe no intelligent Muslim will contradict and no one who

Khayr al-Din, *The Surest Path (Aqwam al-masalik)*, translated from Arabic by Leon Carl Brown (Cambridge, Mass.: Center for Middle Eastern Studies, Harvard University, 1967), pp. 71–96, 160–165. First published in 1867. Introduction by Emad Eldin Shahin.

1. Ahmed Amin, *Zu'ama' al-islah fi al-'asr al-hadith* (*Leaders of Reform in the Modern Era*) (Cairo, Egypt: Maktabat al-Nahda al-Misriyya, 1979), pp. 158–197; A. Alâaddin Çetin, *Tunuslu Hayreddin Paşa* (*Khayr al-Din*

Pasha of Tunis), 2d ed. (Ankara, Turkey: Kültür Bakanlığı, 1999); Albert Hourani, *Arabic Thought in the Liberal Age, 1798–1939* (London: Oxford University Press, 1970), pp. 84–95; Khaldun S. al-Husry, *Origins of Modern Arab Political Thought* (New York: Caravan Books, 1980), pp. 33–53; G. S. van Krieken, *Khayr al-Din et la Tunisie, 1850–1881* (*Khayr al-Din and Tunisia, 1850–1881*) (Leiden, Netherlands: E. J. Brill, 1976).

has been shown the evidence will oppose: if we consider the competition of nations in the fields of civilization and the keen rivalry of even the greatest among them to achieve what is most beneficial and helpful, it becomes clear that we can properly distinguish what is most suitable for us only by having knowledge of those outside our own group, and especially of those who surround us and live close to us.

Further, if we consider the many ways which have been created in these times to bring people and ideas closer together, we will not hesitate to visualize the world as a single, united country peopled by various nations who surely need each other. The general benefit to be derived from the experience of each nation, even when it is pursuing its own personal interests, suffices to make it sought after by the rest of mankind.

Whoever considers these two undoubtedly true principles, and who according to religion knows that the Islamic *shari'a* [religious law] is a guarantor for the two worlds, will necessarily recognize that secular organization is a firm foundation for supporting the religious system. Such a person will then be saddened to see that certain *'ulama'* [religious scholars] of Islam who are entrusted to take into consideration the changing circumstances of time in the application of the Law are opposed even to learning about domestic events, and their minds are empty of any knowledge of the outside world. This is undoubtedly one of the most imposing obstacles to a knowledge of the most appropriate course of action in this world.

Is it fitting that the physicians of the *umma* should be ignorant of its ailments? Or that they should direct their concern to acquiring the essence of knowledge to the exclusion of its contingent circumstances?

We are likewise saddened by such ignorance on the part of certain statesmen and a feigning of ignorance by others out of a predilection for despotism.

For this reason I was fired to believe that if I assembled what years of thought and reflection had produced, plus what I had seen during my travels to the various states of Europe where I had been sent by His Excellency the Bey [Muhammad al-Sadiq, ruler of Tunisia, 1859–1882], then my effort might not be without benefit, especially if it comes upon hearts working together in defense of Islam.

Thus, the object of this book is to remind the learned *'ulama'* of their responsibility to know the important events of these days and to awaken the heedless both among the politicians and all the classes of the people by demonstrating what would be a proper domestic and foreign conduct. It is also to call attention to these aspects of the Frankish [European] nations—especially those having close contacts or attachments with us—which ought to be known. This includes their own eagerness to learn about other nations. The folding-in of the globe, whose farthest distance is now connected with its nearest, makes this easier.

With God's help I have collected all possible information about European inventions related to economic and administrative policies, with reference to their situation in earlier times. I have shown their progress in the governance of mankind, which has led to the utmost point of prosperity for their countries. I have also noted the superiority formerly held by the Islamic *umma* (as attested by even the most important European historians) in the two fields of knowledge and prosperity at a time when the *shari'a* exerted its influence on the *umma*'s conditions, and all conduct was regulated accordingly.

The purpose in mentioning how the European kingdoms attained their present strength and worldly power is that we may choose what is suitable to our own circumstance which at the same time supports and is in accordance with our *shari'a*. Then, we may be able to restore what was taken from our hands and by use of it overcome the present predicament of negligence existing among us.

In addition, other material which the reader might properly expect on such a subject, including observations based either on precedent or reasoning, will be found throughout the several chapters.

I have called the book *The Surest Path to Knowledge Concerning the Conditions of Countries*. It is made up of an introduction and two books, each of which has several chapters.

With the guidance of God we seek the paths of integrity and correctness. Should this prove to be above my own powers, the indulgence of my distinguished readers is to be hoped for as a means of averting my own poverty. And good intentions are, if the All-High God so wills, a sufficient guarantee to the attainment of aspirations.

The motive for a work is its true beginning. Therefore it is appropriate that we set out our motive in writing. Nor will we be content to indicate what compelled us to compose this work. Rather we believe it important to build certain arguments upon it. Our incentive is a desire to accomplish two tasks leading to one ultimate goal.

The first task is to spur on those statesmen and savants having zeal and resolution to seek all possible ways of improving the condition of the Islamic *umma* and of promoting the means of its development by such things as expanding the scope of the sciences and knowledge, smoothing the paths to wealth in agriculture and commerce, promoting all the industries, and eliminating the causes of idleness. The basic requirement is good government, from which is born that security, hope, and proficiency in work to be seen in the European kingdoms. No further evidence is needed of this.

The second task is to warn the heedless among the Muslim masses against their persistent opposition to the behavior of others that is praiseworthy and in conformity with our Holy Law, simply because they are possessed with the idea that all behavior and organizations of non-Muslims must be renounced, their books must be cast out and not mentioned, and anyone praising such things should be disavowed. This attitude is a mistake under any circumstances.

There is no reason to reject or ignore something which is correct and demonstrable simply because it comes from others, especially if we had formerly possessed it and it had been taken from us. On the contrary, there is an obligation to restore it and put it to use. Anyone devoted to religion should not be deterred from initiating the commendable actions related to worldly interests of one religiously misguided. This is what the French have done. By ceaselessly emulating what they deem good in the work of others, they have attained the sound organization of their affairs in this world to be witnessed by all. Discriminating critics must sift out the truth by a probing examination of the thing concerned, whether it be word or deed. If they find it to be correct, they should accept and adopt it whether or not its originator be from among the faithful. It is not according to the person that truth is known. Rather, it is by truth that the person is known. Wisdom is the goal of the believer. One is to take it wherever one finds it.

When Salman the Persian [a companion of the Prophet], may God be pleased with him, indicated to the Prophet of God, may God bless him and grant him peace, that the Persians had a custom, when besieged

by the enemy, of surrounding their cities with a moat as a protection against attack, the Prophet of God, may God bless him and grant him peace, took his advice and dug a moat around Medina when it was attacked. He even worked in it himself in order to exhort the Muslims. 'Ali [ibn Abi Talib, son-in-law and fourth successor of the Prophet, reigned 656–661], may God honor him, has said, "Do not pay attention to who spoke, but pay attention to what was said." If it was permissible for the virtuous ancestors to take such things as logic from outside their own religious community, and to translate it from Greek when they saw it as being among the beneficial instruments—so much so that [Abu Hamid Muhammad] al-Ghazzali [1058–1111] said, "The learning of a man having no knowledge of logic is not to be trusted"—then what objection can there be today to our adopting certain skills that we see we greatly need in order to resist intrigues and attract benefits?

In the *Sunan al-Muhtadin* [*Traditions of the Rightly Guided*] by the Maliki scholar *Shaykh* al-Mawwaq [Abu 'Abdullah al-Gharnati, Andalusian judge, died 1492] is found the following, "The acts of non-Muslims which we have forbidden are those which violate the requirements of our canon law. There is no need to abandon acts practiced by non-Muslims that are in accordance with the *shari'a* categories of obligatory, recommended or permissible because the Holy Law does not forbid the imitation of anyone who does what God permits."

On the margin of *Durr al-mukhtar* [*The Selected Pearls*] by the learned *Shaykh* Muhammad Ibn 'Abidin al-Hanafi [jurist of Damascus, 1783–1836] is found the following, "There is no harm in imitation of that which is linked to the good of the believers."

Actually, if we reflect on the situation of those critical Muslims and the European actions they approve of, we find them refusing to accept *tanzimat* [administrative reforms of the nineteenth century] and its results, while not avoiding other things which harm them. We see them vying with each other in clothing, home furnishings, and such everyday needs just as in weapons and all military requirements. The truth is that all of these things are European products. There is no hiding the disgrace and the deficiencies in economic development and public policy which overtake the *umma* as a result. The disgrace is our needing outsiders for most necessities, indicating the backwardness of the *umma* in skills. The shortcoming in economic development is the failure to use our country's industries to process the goods we have produced, for this should be a major source of gain. Corroboration of this statement is in seeing, for example, our shepherd, or silk farmer or cotton farmer, defying fatigue for the entire year, sell the produce of his labor to the European for a cheap price, and then in a short time buy it back, after it has been processed, at a price several times higher. In sum, we now get only the value of our land's raw materials. We receive none of the increased value resulting from the manufacturing process, the basic means of creating abundance, both for us and for others. Under these circumstances, if we considered the total of what is exported from the kingdom and compared it with the imports and found that the two approximate each other, it would be the lesser of two evils, for if the value of imports exceeds the exports, ruin will unavoidably take place.

As for political imperfections, the kingdom's need for others stands as an obstacle to its independence and a weakener of its vigor, especially when linked to the need for military necessities, which if easy to purchase in peacetime are not easy in time of war, even at many times the value. There is no reason for all this except European technical progress resulting from *tanzimat* based on justice and liberty. How can a thinking man deprive himself of something which, in itself, he approves of? How can he lightly turn down what will benefit him, simply because of unfounded misgivings and misplaced caution? It is worth mentioning in this connection the statement of a European author on military policy, "Kingdoms which do not keep pace with the military inventions and tactics of their neighbors risk becoming, sooner or later, their prey." He singles out military matters because that is the subject of his book, but it is equally necessary to keep up with one's neighbors in all aspects of progress, military or non-military. Supporting what we have related is the statement of the Prophet, may God bless him and grant him peace, to 'Asim bin Thabit [companion of the Prophet, died 625] in the *hadith*, "Let him who fights, fight as his adversary fights." The meaning of this *hadith* is made clear in the advice of Abu Bakr [first caliph, reigned 632–634] to Khalid ibn al-Walid [Muslim general, died 642], may God be pleased with both of them, when he sent him to fight the apostates. He said, "O Khalid, may the strength and support of God be conveyed through you to those with you," and he went on to say, "May the people of al-Yamama be seized with fear. After entering their country, match caution with caution. When you meet a fighting party, fight them with the same weapons they use to fight you—arrow for arrow, spear for spear, sword for sword." If Abu Bakr had known this age, he would have said instead cannon, rifles, armored ships, and other such inventions needed for defense. Without these the state of preparation imposed by the Holy Law will not be attained. This requires knowledge of the capabilities of any potential aggressor and an effort to mobilize against him equal or superior strength, which also entails a knowledge of the means leading to this goal. For this reason it can be asked, can we today attain such a level of preparation without progress in the skills and bases of growth to be seen among others? Can this progress be successful without our implementing political *tanzimat* comparable to those we see among others? These institutions are based on two pillars—justice and liberty—both of which are sources in our own Holy Law. It is well known that these two are the prerequisites for strength and soundness in all kingdoms. Therefore we must press on to the purpose of this book which is to reveal the conditions of the European nations, including what might be suitable for the Islamic *umma*.

The present situation in the kingdoms of Europe has not long been firmly established. After the attacks of the northern barbarians and the fall of the Roman Empire in 476, Europe fell into a shocking state of savagery, lawlessness and oppression, beginning a movement of decline—which is naturally quicker than that of advance. Europe remained in the noose of slavery to its kings and oppressive grandees of the several nations, called *noblesse*, until the rule of Emperor Charlemagne [742–814], king of France, and most of the kingdoms of Europe in 768. He exerted every effort to improve the condition of the people by striving to promote knowledge, and in other ways. Then, after his death, Europe returned to its darkest period of ignorance and oppression by its rulers, as will be shown in detail. It is not to be imagined that Europe's peoples arrived at their present state because of a marked fertility or temperateness of its regions, for similar or even better conditions are found in other parts of the world. Nor is it due to the influence of their Christian religion. Although it does urge the enforcement of justice and equality before the law, Christianity does not interfere in political behavior, because it is founded on the concept of retirement from the world and asceticism. Even Jesus, upon him be peace, forbade his disciples from opposing the kings of this world in what relates to politics saying that he did not have dominion over this world, for the authority of his holy law was over the spirits and not the bodies.

Also, the imperfections existing in the provinces of the pope, leader of the Christian religion, because of his unwillingness to imitate the political ordering recognized in the rest of the European kingdoms, is a clear sign of what we have mentioned. Rather, Europe has attained these ends and progress in the sciences and industries through *tanzimat* based on political justice, by smoothing the roads to wealth, and by extracting treasures of the earth with their knowledge of agriculture and commerce. The essential prerequisite for all of this is security and justice, which have become the normal condition in their lands. It is God's custom in His world that justice, good management, and an administrative system duly complied with be the causes of an increase in wealth, peoples, and property, but that the contrary should cause a diminution in all of these things. This is well known from our Holy Law and from both Islamic and non-Islamic histories. The Prophet, may God bless him and grant him peace, has said, "Justice brings glory to the religion, probity to constituted authority and strength to all orders of the people, high and low. Justice guarantees the security and well-being of all subjects." A Persian maxim affirms, "The king is the foundation, and justice is the guardian. What has no foundation will be destroyed, and [what has] no guardian will be lost." The *Nasa'ih al-Muluk* [*Advice to Kings*, by al-Ghazzali] asserts that the possessor of authority needs a thousand qualities, all of which can be grouped into two. If he acts by these two he will be just. They are providing for the country's prosperity and the security of its subjects.

Anyone who leafs through the third section of Book One of *Muqaddima* [*The Prolegomenon*], by Ibn Khaldun [Tunisian historian, 1332–1406], will find conclusive proof that oppression foreshadows the ruin of civilization, whatever its previous condition. Man's natural propensities are such that unrestricted authority for kings brings about some kind of oppression. This has occurred today in certain Islamic kingdoms. It happened in European kingdoms during those centuries when royal despots had absolute power over God's creatures, without the restraint either of ordinances based on reason, since that was incompatible with their appetites, or of religious law, this being nonexistent in Christianity, which is built on retirement from the world and asceticism, as has been said. That some of the European kingdoms were on the verge of vanishing and losing their independence was due solely to their poor conduct resulting from the unlimited authority of kings, which is to be contrasted with the good behavior of their neighbors at that time from among the Islamic *umma*. This was the result of their rulers being restricted by *shari'a* laws applicable to both religious and secular matters. Among its carefully guarded principles are the release of the creature from the exigency of his own passions, the protection of the rights of mankind, whether Muslim or not, and consideration of the public interest appropriate to the time and the circumstances, giving priority to averting corruption over that of advancing the public interest, carrying out the lesser of two evils when one is necessary, and other matters of this nature.

Among the most important of the *shari'a* principles is the duty of *shura* [consultation] with which God charged His impeccable Prophet, may God bless him and grant him peace, although Muhammad could have dispensed with this since he received inspiration directly from God, and also because of the many perfections which God had placed in him. The underlying reason for this obligation upon the Prophet was that it should become a tradition incumbent upon later rulers.

Ibn al-'Arabi [Andalusian jurist, 1076–1148] has said, "Consultation is one of the foundations of the religion and God's rule for the two worlds. It is a duty imposed upon all men from the prophet to the least of creatures." Among the sayings of 'Ali, may God be pleased with him, is, "There can be no right behavior when consultation has been omitted." One of the principles upon which there is consensus is that every adult Muslim knowledgeable of what is forbidden is obliged to resist any forbidden act. Al-Ghazzali, the proof of Islam, has said, "The caliphs and kings of Islam want to be refuted, even if they should be in the pulpit."

'Umar ibn al-Khattab [second caliph, 634–644], may God be pleased with him, once said while preaching, "O people, let him among you who sees any deviation in me set it right." A man stood up and said, "By God, if we saw in you deviation we would rectify it with our swords." 'Umar replied, "Praise God who created in this *umma* him who would rectify with his sword my deviations." There can be no doubt that if a just *imam* [leader] such as 'Umar, vigorous in defending religion and the rights of the caliphate, had not believed such a harsh retort to be in accordance with the *shari'a*, he would not have praised God but would have been impelled to oppose it and to rebuke the man who spoke. Al-Ghazzali relates also in the section on "Commanding the Good and Forbidding the Evil" in the *Ihya'* [*Revival*] that Mu'awiyya [ibn Abi Sufyan, caliph, 661–680] withheld the people's allowances, and Abu Muslim al-Khawlani [famous ascetic, died 682] came before him saying, "This is not from your toil, nor from that of your father or mother." Mu'awiyya, after stilling his anger with water for ritual ablution, replied, "Abu Muslim is right. This is not the result of my toil nor my father's. Come forward for your allowances."

Without this type of resistance to authority, kingship would not be proper for mankind, because some form of restraint is essential for the maintenance of the human species, but if people exercising this restraint were left to do as they please and rule as they see fit, the fruits to be expected from this need to have a restrainer would not appear to the *umma*, and the original state of neglect would remain unheeded. It is essential that the restrainer should in turn have a restrainer to provide a check, either in the form of a heavenly *shari'a* or a policy based on reason, but neither of these can defend its rights if they be violated. For this reason it is incumbent upon the *'ulama'* and the notables of the *umma* to resist evil. The Europeans have established councils and have given freedom to the printing presses. In the Islamic *umma*, the kings fear those who resist evil, just as the kings of Europe fear the councils and the opinions of the masses that proceed from them and from the freedom of the press. The aim of the two [that is, European and Muslim] is the same: to demand an accounting from the state in order that its conduct may be upright, even if the roads leading to this end may differ. Ibn Khaldun has referred to what we have mentioned in the chapter on the imamate in his *Muqaddima* in saying, "Since kingship is an expression of the essential grouping together of humans, and its basic characteristic is domination and force, both of which stem from irradicable strength rooted in mankind, the judgments of the holder of authority usually turn aside from the right and are unjust to whoever is under him, for he usually demands of them that which is not within their power. This is because of his appetites. For this reason it is difficult to obey him. Group feeling is produced leading to turmoil and fighting. For this reason it is necessary to return to imposed political laws to which the masses will submit and let themselves be led to their authority as was the case with the Persians and other nations. If the dynasty violates such a policy its position will not be well established and its control will be incomplete. If these laws are imposed by the wisest, most important and most discriminating persons in the state then it is a policy based on human reason. If it is imposed from God All-High by means of a prophet who determines it, it is then a religious policy valid both for this world and the next."

The aforementioned benefit will be realized only if it remains respected through being preserved and protected by such precepts as commanding the good and forbidding the evil, as we have said.

Nor do we deny the possibility of finding among kings one who conducts himself properly in the kingdom without consulting "those qualified to loosen and bind" [political power brokers], and is moved by the love of justice to seek the aid of an informed loyal minister to advise him in complicated matters of public interest. However, this is rare and not to be taken into account, as it depends on qualities which are seldom combined in a single person—and even assuming these qualities were combined in a permanent manner in one person, they would disappear with his death. Thus we must assert that the participation of those qualified to loosen and bind with the kings in all policy matters (with responsibility for administration of the kingdom placed upon the ministers directly responsible, in accordance with precise, well-observed ordinances) is the situation most likely to bring about what is best for the kingdom. It is, at the same time, the best safeguard for the king.

Consideration of human nature thus makes it clear that there are only three types of kings. A king might possess complete knowledge, love what would benefit the country, and be capable of implementing the public interests through discriminating supervision. Or he might possess complete knowledge but have personal aims or appetites that would prevent him from carrying out the general public interests. Or he might be both lacking in knowledge and deficient in executive ability. These same three types can apply to the chief minister as well. It is clear that the obligation of consultation and ministerial responsibility in the case of the first type would not impede the complete knowledge from achieving its good purpose. Rather it would help him, since the opinions of all are an aid in attaining the public interest, just as this facilitates the maintenance of the monarchy in the king's family. If kings are more nearly like the last two types, then the imperative nature of consultation and responsibility would be clear, out of the need for opposition in the second case and for assistance in the third. In this way the condition of the kingdom is set right even if the governor is a prisoner of his appetites or is weak in judgment. As the translator of [John] Stuart Mill [English thinker, 1806–1873] has said, "The English nation reached its highest peak during the reign of George III [reigned 1760–1820], who was mad." This was only through the participation of those qualified to loosen and bind, to whom the ministers were responsible.

It might occur to some weak minds that to entrust with responsibility a minister endowed with good reputation would repair the disadvantages of the last two types, so there would be no need for those qualified to loosen and bind. This is manifestly a mistake, because the matter of advancing a minister to executive power or of removing him is in the hands of the king, and it is not to be imagined that the king would advance someone whom he knows would offer serious opposition to him. Assuming, however, that such a minister were appointed and his conduct commendable, then his situation would turn upon two possibilities. Either he would agree with the king and his retinue in their aims and appetites, showing in a manner hardly to be hidden that his own interests outweighed any concern about the harm done to the kingdom. Or he could oppose them and order those functionaries under him to carry out what the interests of the country require. In that case, where would he get this right and by means of what support would he be able to triumph over that opposition, especially if there is no Holy Law in operation to protect him from the factiousness of his enviers, whose fondest hopes would be to do him harm and in every way available to them to stop his beneficial activities which tend to diminish their personal profit? They might do this by carrying out his orders other than the way intended, or by delaying them beyond the

appropriate time in order to make manifest the defects and increase the errors, or by hiding his good qualities and making public his bad qualities in order to turn hearts against him. One of the supplications of 'Ali, may God be pleased with him, was, "God protect me from an enemy who carefully watches me. If he sees something good in me he conceals it, but if he sees bad he divulges it."

If God frustrates their hopes by granting such a minister success in his efforts to administer the kingdom, then they fall back on the tactic of defaming him before the king, saying, "He is acting independently of you. You are king only in name," and other such stories of the type spread by the unrighteous, which could find acceptance even among the thinking man who has not been forewarned, especially in eastern countries. How then in such a situation would it be possible for the minister to carry out the administration of the kingdom within the framework of the public interest, when this entails opposing the man who is both the judge and the plaintiff? Because of this second set of obstacles, the aforementioned minister is obliged either to choose the first situation of conformity and adopt the ways of dissimulation with the disastrous consequences resulting in harm to the homeland, the king, and even to himself, because the sweetness of agreement with the appetites in a situation out of which results destruction of the kingdom will later be followed by the bitterness of remorse, or the minister is obliged to resign from government service once and for all, for even if not for self-protection then in order to escape the consequences of concurring in what would lead to the destruction of the kingdom, which would necessitate punishment for the creator and censure of the creature. He may be permitted to endanger himself for the good of the country, but not his honor and reputation. The obedience to the king and the love of country required of him are realized only by his striving to advise on how to promote the public interest and ward off corruption, if he is able to do this. If not, then he must withhold his agreement to anything which would cause harm. Failing this, then his agreement, with the knowledge of the harm which would ensue, is treason.

It is clear from this that kingdoms administered without regular and well-observed laws under the supervision of those qualified to loosen and bind will be limited in their best and their worst to the person of the king. The extent of success will depend on his ability and probity. This is shown in the situation of the European kingdoms in past centuries, before the establishment of laws, for during that time they had ministers famous to this day for their complete knowledge and valor. Yet they were unable to cut the roots of imperfection growing out of the two types of royal tyranny referred to above. It should not be said that the participation of those qualified to loosen and bind with the princes in all aspects of policy would be a restriction of the *imam*'s jurisdiction or of his executive powers. This is an illusion which can be dispelled by reading *Qawanin al-wizara* [*Ordinances of Government*], by ['Ali ibn Muhammad] al-Mawardi [Iraq, circa 974–1058]. He has said in explaining the delegated vizierate: "This occurs when the *imam* chooses a vizier to whom he delegates authority to administer affairs as he sees fit and to implement them in accordance with his own independent judgment. The authority of this type of vizierate is not restricted, for God all High has related the speech of His prophet Moses, upon him be peace, 'Appoint for me a helper [*wazir*] from among my people, my brother Aaron. Increase my strength with him and cause him to share my task.' So, if this is permissible for the prophethood, it is even more permissible for the imamate."

Therefore, if the *imam*'s sharing his power with the delegated vizierate in the aforementioned manner is permissible and is not deemed a diminution of his general executive authority, then his sharing of power with a group—those qualified to loosen and bind—in all aspects of policy is even more permissible, because a group of opinions is more likely to attain the correct answer. For this reason when 'Umar ibn al-Khattab, may God be pleased with him, made succession to the caliphate a matter of consultation among six persons, he said, "If you divide two against four, then decide in favor of the four"—Sayyid al-Sanad [reference unclear] adds the commentary that his preference was for the majority, since their opinion was more likely to be correct—"and if you are equally divided then decide in favor of the party which includes 'Abd al-Rahman ibn 'Awf [a companion of the Prophet, died circa 652]."

On the other hand, *al-Maula* Sa'd al-Din [Taftazani, 1332–1389] in the *Sharh al-'Aqa'id* [*Explanation of "The Creed"*] does not even disallow the sharing of the executive authority of the imamate. He restricts his disallowing of multiplicity to whatever might create corruption. As he has stated in the course of an exposition, "The unauthorized imamate is the appointment of two independent *imams* with obedience owed to each of them separately, for this could create an obligation to obey conflicting ordinances, but all forms of consultation with a single *imam* are authorized." This is because the multiplicity of persons in no way contradicts the unity of the imamate, which is linked to the unity of commanding and forbidding. Commentators on Sa'd, such as 'Isam al-Din [probably al-Isfara'ini, died circa 1544] and 'Abd al-Hakim [possibly Siyalkuti, died 1657], have approved his statement, and [Ahmad ibn Musa] al-Khayali [died circa 1457] confirmed it in saying, "This also is to be agreed to." In sum, they all recognize the soundness of Sa'd's statement. It is thus clear how even more explicitly acceptable is consultation in general policy matters in the sense referred to here, for this is less extensive than consultation in all executive acts. In the former type of consultation there is no restriction upon either the general scope or the basic prerogatives of the imamate, for the view of those qualified to loosen and bind would be tantamount to that of the *imam*. It should also be noted that the *imam* is the one who would promulgate any decision, as he is the one having exclusive charge of implementation and direction, just as he has exclusive authority other executive activities not requiring the association of others, such as carrying out political and commercial relations with foreigners, appointing and dismissing administrators, execution of all judgments, and other such executive actions which are the very bases of the unity of command. Additional evidence is to be found in the words of the *imam* Ibn al-'Arabi, who said on the subject of special taxes taken from the people when the treasury is empty, "they should be taken publicly not secretly, the sums should be spent justly not appropriated exclusively, and in accordance with the views of the public, not arbitrarily."

As an additional element of clarification, let us try to understand this by means of a parable. The owner of a large garden, for example, in the management and care of his trees would not be able to do without the assistance of helpers knowledgeable about trees and what causes them to prosper or wither. Now it might happen that the owner of the garden wanted to cut some of the branches of his trees, believing that would strengthen the roots and increase the fruit, but his helpers disagreed, knowing from the basic principles of cultivation that pruning at that time would kill the tree at the roots. In such circumstances, to obstruct the owner's wish could not be considered a restriction on the scope of his supervision or his complete executive authority in his garden. Or the helpers might attempt to stop the owner in what he wanted to do because of the Holy Law. For example, if the owner should wish to sell the fruit before it was ripe, they would indicate to him that such action would displease the Creator of the trees, who is the true owner. This might oblige him to accept their advice in these two cases; but if not, the blame would fall upon him, and he would deserve to be deprived of the garden. Can it be argued that this was a restriction on the owner of the garden, when giving him his way would have been contrary to divine wisdom that the production of the world and the exploitation of the earth is for the sons of Adam? It is true that the yield from the garden belongs to its owner, but whether it belongs to him, to someone else, or even if his position was—as 'Umar, may God be pleased with him, said—like that of the orphan's guardian, one should not think that such action is a restriction upon the owner. It is well known that the *imam*'s freedom of action concerning the condition of his subjects does not extend beyond the limits of the public interest. Furthering the interests of the *umma* and managing its policies are matters which do not come easily to everyone. In such circumstances, to obstruct his will when he does something beyond the limits of permissible action is, as we have explained, a means of liberation from the unsoundness of that argument. Thus, there can be no prohibition on the type of consultation which has already been described. Whoever gives due attention to the matter of necessity, as *Shaykh* Ibn al-'Arabi has done (for he is our source in all that we have previously stated), would not hesitate to assert that this is necessary especially in these times characterized by a dearth of knowledge and an abundance of tyranny. In a conversation I had with a European notable, I was praising at length their king and mentioning his great knowledge of political fundamentals, when he replied that the king by his very nature and intelligence was incapable of acting in the wrong manner. "Then why," I asked, "are you so sparing in granting him freedom of action in government, and why do you wish to participate with him in the affairs of the kingdom, for you concede that given his qualities no such participation is needed?" He replied, "Who will guarantee to us that he and his descendants after him shall remain upright?"

Since what we have been presenting on this subject indicates that liberty is the basis of the great development of knowledge and civilization in the European kingdoms, we believe it imperative to demonstrate the meaning of liberty in actual practice, in order to avert any possible ambiguity.

The expression "liberty" is used by Europeans in two senses. One is called "personal liberty." This is the individual's complete freedom of action over one's self and property, and the protection of one's person, honor, and wealth. Each is equal before the law to others of the race, so that no individuals need fear encroachment upon their person nor any of their other rights. They would not be prosecuted for anything not provided for in the laws of the land, duly determined before the courts. In general, the laws bind both the rulers and the subjects. Liberty in this sense exists in all the European countries except the Papal State and the Muscovite state, for these two are despotisms. Although these two possess established laws, this is not enough to protect the rights of the *umma*, for the influence of those laws depends on the will of the king.

The second sense of liberty is political liberty, which is the demand of the subjects to participate in the politics of the kingdom and to discuss the best course of action. This is similar to what the second caliph, 'Umar ibn al-Khattab, may God be pleased with him, referred to in saying, "Whoever among you sees any crookedness, then let him set it straight," meaning any deviation in his conduct or governance of the *umma*.

Since the granting of liberty in this sense to all the people is most likely to cause a divergence of views and result in confusion, the people instead elect from among those possessing knowledge and virtue a group called by the Europeans the Chamber of General Deputies. We would call them those qualified to loosen and bind, even though this [latter] group is not elected by the people. This is because the avoidance of the reprehensible in our *shari'a* is in the category of those responsibilities which can be delegated. If some members of the community assume the responsibility, then the obligation is removed from the rest of the community. When such a group is so designated, this responsibility becomes a strictly prescribed obligation upon them.

The Chamber of Deputies is to be found in all European kingdoms except the Papal State and Russia. The chamber has the right to discuss in the presence of the ministers and other statesmen which lines of state policy seem to be beneficial or the contrary, and other such matters affecting the public interest, as will be seen.

In addition to this there remains to the public something else which is called freedom of the press, that is, people cannot be prevented from writing what seems to them to be in the public interest, in books or newspapers which can be read by the public. Or they can present their views to the state or the chambers, even if this includes opposition to the state's policy.

In this matter there are differences among the European states. There are those who have obtained this second liberty with the first, thus achieving absolute liberty. In others, the rulers have granted the people the second liberty subject to important conditions, for these governments have refused their subjects rights which it would be easy to bestow upon subjects of other states. This is because the conditions of kingdoms vary according to the aims of their subjects. Some subjects resist their kings only in order to have the right of opposing the state if it turns aside from the straight path, and to draw it toward a policy of benefit to the kingdom. In such circumstances it is easy for kings to grant complete liberty, because the ruler and the subjects share the same aim regarding the public interest.

There are those subjects who suppose that the reason for the struggle is to exacerbate factionalism and fanaticism, so that the subjects are divided into parties, with each seeking the policy which it believes most beneficial for the kingdom. Some believe the state should be a republic. Some would choose the monarch from a different family than the one favored by others. This causes the dynasty to believe that the opposition of the various parties, even if it appears to be confined to returning the state to the paths of public interest, actually hides an ulterior motive. As a result of this belief, some kings deem it permissible to abstain from granting complete liberty. This leads to the consequences already mentioned.

One of the duties in kingdoms that have granted liberty, even if only personal liberty, is that its subjects should repay having received this blessing by working to bring about its possible consequences and benefits. They can do this by concerning themselves with the various branches of knowledge and all kinds of industries, which can be reduced to four basic categories: agriculture, commerce, physical work, and intellectual activity. These four categories are the foundation of material well-being, which causes the growth of human ambition, and are a complement to liberty, which is based on justice and the sound organization of society.

Artisans, for example, must feel secure against being despoiled of any of the fruits of their labor or hampered in certain aspects of their work. What does it profit a people to have fertile lands with bountiful crops if the sowers cannot realize the harvest of what they have planted? Who then will venture to sow it? Because of the faint hope of the people in many lands of Asia and Africa, you find the most fertile fields uncultivated and neglected. There can be no doubt that the hostile action against property cuts off hopes, and with the severance of hope comes the severance of activities, until finally destitution becomes so pervasive that it leads to annihilation.

Among the most important things the Europeans have gathered from the lofty tree of liberty are the improvements in communications by means of railroads, support for commercial societies, and the attention given to technical training. By means of the railroads, products can be imported from distant lands quickly enough to be useful, whereas their importation was formerly impossible. They would have spoiled en route or the freight costs would have been several times the value of the goods.

With these societies the circulation of capital is expanded, profits increase accordingly, and wealth is put into the hands of the most proficient who can cause it to increase.

Through technical training wealth gains the necessary means of productive activity from among the ranks of those without capital. We have seen that the countries which have progressed to the highest ranks of prosperity are those having established the roots of liberty and the constitution, synonymous with political *tanzimat*. Their peoples have reaped its benefits by directing their efforts to the interests of the world in which they live. One of the benefits of liberty is complete control over the conduct of commerce. If people lose the assurance that their property will be protected, they are compelled to hide it. Then it becomes impossible for them to put it into circulation.

In general, if liberty is lost in the kingdom, then comfort and wealth will disappear, and poverty and high prices will overwhelm its peoples. Their perceptiveness and zeal will be weakened, as both logic and experience reveal.

Laws Should Change in Accordance with the Conditions of Nations *and* The Theology of Unity

Muhammad 'Abduh (Egypt, 1849–1905) was, along with his mentor Sayyid Jamal al-Din al-Afghani (see chapter 11), the most prominent figure of modernist Islam. Born to a peasant family of modest means in the Egyptian Delta, he received a traditional Islamic education in his hometown, then continued his education at the celebrated al-Azhar seminary. During Afghani's sojourn in Egypt (1871–1879), 'Abduh became closely associated with him and his reformist ideas. In 1882, 'Abduh was exiled to Beirut for his association with the 'Urabi revolt. In 1884, he joined Afghani in Paris, where they produced the famed journal *al-'Urwa al-wuthqa* (*The Strongest Link*), which agitated against imperialism and called for Islamic reform and unity. 'Abduh returned to Beirut, where he taught for several years before being pardoned by the Egyptian ruler. Returning to Egypt, he served as a judge and then as Egypt's leading religious official, al-Azhar administrative board member, and Egypt's Legislative Council member. 'Abduh devised programs for the reform of the educational system, the Arabic language, and the education of girls, and labored to introduce reforms in al-Azhar, the religious endowment administration, and the court system. 'Abduh's influence extended beyond Egypt, inspiring reformists throughout the Islamic world. The first piece presented here makes a case for legal reform; the second piece highlights the role of reason in understanding religion and the *shari'a*. Through a return to the fundamental sources of Islam, 'Abduh hoped to liberate the Muslim mind from traditional patterns of stagnation, enabling Muslims to address the requirements of modernity.[1]

Laws Should Change in Accordance with the Conditions of Nations

The First Creator, God the Sublime, entrusted to humanity two powers, one practical and one theoretical, so that through them we might attain the perfection intended for us. God also bound one of them to the other, making the perfection of the first dependent on the perfection of the second. Humanity is thus innately disposed to seek out a theoretical understanding and to discover the true state of matters before he begins any practical work, for he undertakes no task unless the results thereof induce him to do so. Now, not every activity produces the results desired; indeed, in order to do so, it must be accomplished in a particular fashion. Certainly, the ability to envision results and knowledge of the methods involved in activities are among those things that depend on the capacity for rational inquiry. If this

Muhammad 'Abduh, "Ikhtilaf al-qawanin bi-ikhtilaf ahwal al-umam" (Laws Should Change in Accordance with the Conditions of Nations), pp. 309-315 in *al-A'mal al-kamila* (*The Complete Works*), ed. Muhammad 'Imara (Beirut, Lebanon: Mu'assasat al-'Arabiyya li al-Dirasat wa al-Nashr, 1972); *The Theology of Unity* (*Risalat al-tawhid*), translated from Arabic by Ishaq Masa'ad and Kenneth Cragg (London: Allen & Unwin, 1966), pp. 29-40, 151-154, reprinted by permission of HarperCollins Publishers. Translation of first piece from Arabic by Devin Stewart. First published in 1881 and 1897, respectively. Introduction by Emad Eldin Shahin.

1. Charles C. Adams, *Islam and Modernism in Egypt: A Study of the Modern Reform Movement Inaugurated by Muhammad 'Abduh* (London: Oxford University Press, 1933); Osman Amin, *Muhammad 'Abduh* (Washington, D.C.: American Council for Learned Societies, 1953); Malcolm H. Kerr, *Islamic Reform: The Political and Legal Theories of Muhammad 'Abduh and Rashid Rida* (Berkeley: University of California Press, 1966); Ahmed Amin, *Zu'ama' al-islah fi al-'asr al-hadith* (*The Leaders of Reform in the Modern Era*) (Cairo, Egypt: Maktabat al-Nahda al-Masriyya, 1979), pp. 302-369.

capacity is fully developed, then work turns out in the best fashion, the benefit that results is greater, and the outcome is more complete.

For this reason, all humans are bent on rounding out their theoretical knowledge, first and in particular so that through it they might be guided to the proper methods for the work they perform in order to lead a full life. They also do so in order to distinguish results according to their relative benefits, so that they might put each result opposite a particular task, arranged in a known manner, beginning with that which produces benefits most quickly, is accomplished most easily, and is set forth most reliably.

Human knowledge is in effect a collection of rules about useful benefits, by which people organize the methods of work that lead to those benefits, so that they will not stumble along their path and confuse the beneficial with the harmful, thus encountering hardship and suffering at the hands of misfortune.

Since the conditions of nations depend on their collective stores of information, and the two are related in terms of cause and effect, each nation adopts rules for its activities and chooses laws for its circumstances in accordance with its power of theoretical investigation and its level of thought. At no time does it contradict the customs and traditional values that its natural disposition has established, unless fortune provides it the chance to ascend to a higher level of rational examination and a more elevated plane of thought.

Because laws are the basis of activities organized properly to produce manifest benefits, the results of theoretical inquiry, and the outcome of intellectual investigation, the laws of each nation correspond to its level in understanding. Laws vary in accordance with nations' varying levels of knowledge, or the lack thereof.

It is not permissible, therefore, to apply the law of one group of people to another group who differ from and surpass the first in level of understanding, because the law will not suit their state of thinking and will not match their customs and traditional habits. Otherwise, order among the second group will be disturbed, their path toward good sense will be obscured, and the road to understanding will be closed before them. They will consider the correct to be invalid and the right to be wrong. They will pervert the application of these laws, change them, and put others in their place, so that what is a cure for others will become a disease for them. This is because of short-sightedness on their part and ignorance of what these laws were intended to accom-

plish, what motivated them, and what made them necessary. Need is the guiding master, and the first teacher. When people properly recognize need, they strive to fulfill it. They are restricted by it, and do not go against its dictates and prescriptions. If the institution of laws within a nation is motivated by its need for them, it will not contravene them simply because of circumstances. However, people who were not induced by need to institute such laws do not consider them among life's fundamental necessities. They are not to be blamed for discarding such laws, and demanding that they abide by such laws would impose an impossibly difficult obligation. It is more appropriate for them to learn first what the need is, so that they might be equal with others in their level of knowledge and united with them in the consequences thereof.

It has been the custom of legislators in every age, in instituting laws, to take into account the level of intelligence of those for whom laws are to be instituted, so that the people will not find them unclear, incomprehensible, or devoid of discernible purpose. [Legislators have also customarily] paid full attention to customs and traditional habits. In establishing laws, they do not deviate from the harshness or leniency that customs and traditional habits require. A little reprimand suffices and the threat of a light punishment restrains many a group of people whose temperaments are readily compliant, whose spirits are noble, and whose senses are quick to be affected. Such people should have prescribed for them laws that suit their conditions. They should not be burdened with severe laws, for they will be harmed by these laws, like someone who takes more than the proper dose of medicine.

For example, suppose that one of these people we have described did something that required punishment. If imprisonment, for him, troubles his temperament and severely pains his spirit, because of his pride and delicate sensibility, and if the spirits of his clan and the inhabitants of his town cannot bear that someone should say "So-and-so was imprisoned for such-and-such a crime," the occurrence of such a thing to one of them would be a very great check against perpetrating the crime he committed. The sentencing of this criminal, then, to a more severe punishment, such as banishment, exile, or hard, humiliating labor, would be a clear injustice. It might cause his death soon thereafter, or produce long-lasting dejection and perennial rancor in the hearts of his folk and clan, due to their certainty that the ruling was wrong and the judge unjust. This would only lead, in the long run, to the fires of rebellion being lit and the heat of hatred flaming up among them. Either they would be destined to commit evil acts or else their spirits would be extinguished, their temperaments humiliated, and their pride utterly crushed, a miserable end indeed.

Many a nation has raised its members on coarseness and the shunning of delicacy. Their insides are filled with vileness and baseness, and their spirits are far from honorable. Such people are only deterred from perpetrating offenses or restrained from the pursuit of immoral aims by harsh laws based on severe punishments. It is a clear mistake to sentence a guilty party from among such a group to imprisonment, for example, since his spirit considers even harsher punishments to be trifling. The purpose of instituting laws is to prevent that which disturbs order, disrupts the structure of society, harms individual interests, and detracts from public welfare. If laws do not serve this purpose, then they are but empty burdens thrown on the shoulders of the people. Indeed, we should see them as merely widening the sphere of corruption and increasing instances of injustice.

As an example of what we have just stated, we may cite the former state of our own land. Some time ago, Egypt's inhabitants were barbarians who did not know what was good for themselves, for ignorance had a tight hold on them in that era. They did not pay attention to agriculture, despite the availability of the necessary means for it and the suitability of the soil. Landowners did not know the value of the land they owned. They continually wished that their properties would be transferred to someone else, so that they would not be burdened with paying the taxes that the government had imposed on them. They avoided tarrying in town long enough for the hands of the governors to grab them. Villagers left and settled in other villages, fearing that they could not survive through farming and seeking better ways to accumulate wealth and fortune. The government was thus compelled to force villagers to take possession of the land and farm it, instituting harsh laws for violators, including provisions for severe punishment. When the time came for the government to demand the royal taxes, the prisons filled up with those left behind by the others who had fled their villages, and the market for whips became brisk. It appeared that everyone had either fled, been imprisoned, or ached from beatings. The country regularly withered and

flourished at particular times of the year, without variation. It continued in this sorry state for a long time, until the populace's spirits became attached to work, and agriculture was made easy for them. Egypt entered a new stage of development as a result of measures which made the methods of farming easier and got the populace to remain in their villages. They adopted a unified plan for the farming of their lands and were no longer overly concerned with government taxes, because they had begun to learn the importance of agriculture, taking it seriously and competing in their crop yields. So the laws that the government had adopted to prevent farmers from fleeing, neglecting to work the land, and defaulting on the submission of taxes changed to a certain extent. Then various oppressive hands had successive control over them for quite a long period, but they remained settled in their properties. They grew tired of abuse, and their spirits longed for a just law by which the matter of their tax payments would be put in order. The hand of divine Providence brought to them, through the government of Tawfiq [Egyptian ruler, 1879–1892], someone who established for them a just law concerning this issue. With this new law, Egypt entered a new era, and the sound of the whip was removed from among its people. The punishment for falling behind in the payment of taxes was changed so as not to debase a person's honor, and public welfare was regulated according to laws that do not go against the inclinations of the populace, in a fashion different from that followed in earlier laws. This was a consequence of the difference between the two conditions and the change in the two inclinations, former and latter. If the punishment for falling in arrears in earlier times had been seizure of the owner's land, then falling in arrears would have been their dearest wish, so that they could be relieved of writing their names in the landowners' register. This recompense would have been a reward for them, in actuality, and not a punishment, but now it has become the most severe punishment.

The time has come for our government to turn its consideration to the laws of our courts, to make them appropriate for present conditions, choosing laws that are not difficult to understand, whose texts do not suggest multiple interpretations. The articles of the new law should not be the sort of general rules whose verdicts are meant to apply to various punishments for many diverse crimes. This will prevent the laws themselves from serving as a pretext for those who harbor immoral designs to play with people's rights as they wish. [We urge this] while recognizing the fact that those who exercise control over the law do not have the status of legislators able to derive the rulings which apply to the actual situations at hand from general rules or from texts which support interpretations contrary to their evident meaning.

Moreover, those of us who have legitimate claims are not beyond entertaining invalid suspicions and conjectures. We might suspect someone who is innocent of error or treachery, while the actual articles of the law do not provide a clear ruling and their texts are not transparent. This leads to repeated appeals for judicial inquiry: The matter takes a long time, the welfare of the people is obstructed, expenses increase, resentments grow strong, and the gates of corruption are flung wide open, given an abundance of legal cases and disputes, as is the case in our land at present. It is therefore necessary that the articles of the law be written explicitly, indicate rulings in a straightforward manner, apply to all possible cases, be set forth in logical categories, and use simple linguistic constructions.

The laws that have been in common use in our land up to now—in addition to being insufficient, too general, and written in an unclear style—are not precise and well organized, nor are they known by the people. Certain laws are known as "The Imperial Law," some laws are named "Regulations," some are called "Directives of the Ministry of Justice," some are called "Decisions of the Privy Council," others "Proclamations of Legal Rulings," some "The Royal Decree issued on such-and-such a date," and so on *ad infinitum*. How could this scattered mess reasonably serve as a law by which the people should abide? Even if they were informed of the law, it would remain inconceivable to them, because it is foreign to their conditions and beyond their capacity to understand.

It is necessary to reform this obvious flaw in our legal system, which has deprived people of their rights and jeopardized security. It behooves us to do this quickly and avoid wasting time in pointless discussions. The laws must fulfill all of the necessary restrictions and conditions, and should refer us back neither to the "Proclamations" nor to the "Regulations." This should facilitate the determination of legal rulings and make them conform with the exigencies of the present situation. The laws should suit the conditions of the populace and their level of comprehension, enabling them to understand the laws and abide by their require-

ments, each one according to his own situation. Otherwise, they will be nothing but ink on paper.

Scholars and political leaders of both ancient and modern times have long recognized that legislators and institutors of laws must always take into account customs and traditional habits in order to establish laws in a just and beneficial manner. Indeed, the conditions of nations are themselves the true legislator, the wise, regulating guide. The governing power is actually dependent on the capacities of its subjects; the former does not take a single step unless induced to do so by the latter. True, we do not deny that the preparation of means and measures depends on the governing power. The government imposes these things on its subjects willy-nilly, but these impositions must be in accordance with the capacity of those ruled. Changes in the form of government and the replacement of its laws depend on the citizenry's legitimate claims, and these are tantamount to the condition of the populace. The shift of the government of France, for example, from an absolute monarchy to a restricted monarchy, then to a free republic, did not occur by the will of those in authority alone. Rather, the strongest contributing factors were the conditions of the people, the increase in their level of thought, and their new awareness of the need to ascend to a state higher than their present one. By learning what their true obligations were, they were able to overcome all the outside forces that had stood between them and the attainment of their desires. Moreover, they only arrived at this noble goal after breaking through the obstacles that stood before them; otherwise, they could not have reached their goal or attained their desire.

Since the identification of the proper means and measures presents a difficult puzzle for human intelligence and discernment, it is extremely difficult to learn and acquire them in their essential forms. It often occurs that a certain group of people think themselves prepared to move to a higher level of civilization and legal organization, but the matter is not as they had imagined, so they end up regressing to a less desirable state. While they set out to make legislation and participation in the establishment of laws free and open to all, they are not safe from the machinations of special interests, nor do they possess the means necessary to prepare them for such an undertaking. The disease of discord spreads rapidly through their collective body, and the disorder of obstinacy pursues them relentlessly. They fail to arrive at correct decisions, settle on firm opinions, and give decisive verdicts. They spend ages in pointless argument, and so lose the benefits of decisive action and squander their own welfare. They are thus aptly described by the proverb, "He who hastens something on before its time, will be punished by being deprived of it." In sum, the form of civil rule for a nation is nothing but a reflection of the capacities that its members have acquired, including their familiar practices and the customs on which they have been raised. During the course of a nation's ascent or descent, its laws are inseparable from these capacities, no matter how much its classes change or its affairs vary. This is what makes intelligent people, when they desire to establish a sound system to regulate the nation's social life, strive first to change the people's capacities and traditional habits, placing genuine education before all else in order to be able to attain this goal. Indeed, they include in the governmental laws themselves chapters and sections that serve to regulate customary habits and preserve meritorious aptitudes, guide individuals in their activities and their conduct, so that their work may be transformed from a burden to a custom and natural disposition. In this way, morals may become virtuous and customs excellent, and the nation may follow the path of rectitude toward the best ultimate goal.

The Theology of Unity

The theology of unity (*tawhid*) is the science that studies the being and attributes of God, the essential and the possible affirmations about Him, as well as the negations that are necessary to make relating to Him. It deals also with the apostles and the authenticity of their message and treats of their essential and appropriate qualities and of what is incompatibly associated with them.

The original meaning of *tawhid* is the belief that God is one in inalienable divinity. Thus the whole science of theology is named from the most important of its parts, namely the demonstration of the unity of God in Himself and in the act of creation. From Him alone all being derives and in Him alone every purpose comes to its term. Unity was the great aim of the mission of the Prophet Muhammad, the blessing and peace of God be upon him. This is entirely evident from the verses of the mighty Qur'an, as will fully appear below.

The doctrine of unity could equally well be called scholastic theology. One reason for this lies in the fact that the chief point of debate at issue between the learned of the early centuries was whether the Qur'anic word was created or preexistent. Another may lie in the fact that theology is built on rational demonstration as alleged by each theologian in his spoken case. For in their rationality they only occasionally appealed to dogmatic tradition (*naql*) and then only after establishing the first principles from which they went on yet again to further deductions, like branches of the same stem. The name may perhaps also be credited to the fact that these scholastic methods of proof in theology were comparable to those of logic in its procedures of argument within the speculative sciences. So *kalam*, or scholastic theology, was used as a term in preference to logic, to denote the distinction between the two, with their identical procedures but differing subject matter.

This branch of science, dogmatic theology and prophetic interpretation, was known among the nations before Islam. There were in every people custodians of religion concerned with its protection and propagation, of which the first prerequisite is expression. They had, however, little recourse to rational judgment in their custody of belief. They rarely relied for their ideas and dogmas on the nature of existence or the laws of the universe. Indeed there is an almost total contrast between the intellectual cut and thrust of science and the forms of religious persuasion and assurance of heart. Oftentimes religion on the authority of its own leaders was the avowed enemy of reason, and all its works. Theology consisted for the most part of intricate subtleties and credulous admiration of miracles, with free play to the imagination—a situation familiar enough to those acquainted at all with the condition of the world before the coming of Islam.

The Qur'an came and took religion by a new road, untrodden by the previous Scriptures, a road appropriate and feasible alike to the contemporaries of the revelation and to their successors. The proof of the prophethood of Muhammad was quite a different matter from that of earlier prophecies. It rested its case on a quality of eloquence, belonging even to the shortest chapter of it, quite beyond the competence of the rhetoricians to reproduce, though in his recipience of the revelation he was simply a man. The Book gives us all that God permits us, or is essential for us, to know about His attributes. But it does not require our acceptance of its contents simply on the ground of its own statement of them. On the contrary, it offers arguments and evidence. It addressed itself to the opposing schools and carried its attacks with spirited substantiation. It spoke to the rational mind and alerted the intelligence. It set out the order in the universe, the principles and certitudes within it, and required a lively scrutiny of them that the mind might thus be sure of the validity of its claims and message. Even in relation of the narratives of the past, it proceeded on the conviction that the created order follows invariable laws, as the Qur'an says: "Such was the way of God in days gone by and you will find it does not change." [Sura 48, Verse 23] And again: "God does not change a people's case until they change their own disposition." [Sura 13, Verse 11] ". . . the shape of religious man as God has made him. There is no altering the creation of God." [Sura 30, Verse 30] Even in the realm of the moral it relies on evidence: "Requite evil with good and your worst enemy will become your dearest friend." [Sura 41, Verse 34] Thus for the first time in a revealed Scripture, reason finds its brotherly place. So plain is the point that no elucidation is required.

Saving those who give place to neither reason nor faith, all Muslims are of one mind in the conviction that there are many things in religion which can only be believed by the way of reason, such as the knowledge of God's existence, of His power to send messengers, of His knowledge of the content of their inspiration, of His will to give them particular messages, and, with these, many consequent points relating to the comprehension and evidence of prophetic mission. So Muslims are of one mind that though there may be in religion that which transcends the understanding, there is nothing which reason finds impossible.

The Qur'an describes the attributes of God, by and large, with a far surer accent of transcendence than the earlier religions. Nevertheless, there are several human attributes, which, in name or form, are made comparable, such as power, choice, hearing, and seeing. In what is ascribed to God we find points that have counterparts in man, like taking one's seat upon a throne, and like the face and the hands. The Qur'an deals at length with predestination and human free will, and takes controversial issue with those who exaggerate on both sides of this theme. It affirms the reward of good deeds and the retribution of evil deeds and leaves the recompense of approbation and punishment to the arbitrament of God. In this introduction there is no need to expatiate further on similar topics.

This Qur'anic esteem for the rational judgment, together with the use of parables in the allegorical or ambiguous passages in the revealed text, gave great scope to alert intelligences, therefore so inasmuch as the appeal of this religion to reason in the study of created things was in no way limited or hedged about with conditions. For it knew that every sound study would conduce to belief in God, as Qur'anically depicted. So it had no need of either excessive abstraction or over-rigorous definition.

The Prophet's day passed—he who was men's recourse in perplexity and their lamp in the darkness of doubt. His two immediate successors in the caliphate [Abu Bakr and 'Umar ibn al-Khattab, 632–634 and 634–644] devoted their span of life to repelling his foes and ensuring the unity of the Muslims. Men had little leisure at that time for critical discussion of the basis of their beliefs. What few differences there were they took to the two caliphs, and the caliph gave his decision, after consultation, if necessary, with the available men of insight. These issues, for the most part, had to do with branches of law, not with the principles of dogma. Under those two caliphs, men understood the Book in its meaning and allusions. They believed in the transcendence of God and refrained from debate about the implications of passages involving human comparisons. They did not go beyond what was indicated by the literal meaning of the words.

So the case remained until the events which resulted in the death of the third caliph ['Uthman in 656]—a tragedy which did irreparable damage to the structure of the caliphate and brutally diverted Islam and the Muslim people from their right and proper course. Only the Qur'an remained unimpaired in its continuity. As God said: "It is We who have sent down the Reminder and We truly preserve it." [Sura 15, Verse 9] And thus the way was open for man to transgress the proper bounds of religion. The caliph had been killed with no legal judgment and thus the popular mind was made to feel there could be free rein to passion in the thoughts of those who had not truly allowed the faith to rule in their hearts. "Lawless anger had possessed many of the very exponents of pious religion. Both worldlings and zealots together had overborne the steadfast people and set in motion a train of consequences they could only deplore.

Among the actors in that crisis of disloyalty was 'Abdullah Ibn Saba' [7th century, reputed founder of Shi'ism], a Jew who had embraced Islam and an excessive admirer of 'Ali [ibn Abi Talib, son-in-law and fourth successor of the Prophet, reigned 656–661] (whose face God honor) to the point of asserting that God indwelt him. Ibn Saba' claimed that 'Ali was the rightful caliph and rebelled against 'Uthman, who exiled him, He went to Basra where he propagated his seditious views. Evicted from there, he went to Kufa, taking his poison with him, and thence to Damascus, where he failed to find the support he wanted. He proceeded to Egypt where he did find collaborators with the dire consequences we know. In the time of 'Ali, when his school showed its head again, he was exiled to Mada'in. His ideas spawned a lot of later heresies.

Events took their subsequent course. Some of those who had pledged allegiance to the fourth caliph broke their fealty. Civil war ensued, issuing in the hegemony of the Umayyads [reigned 661–750]. But the community had been sundered and its bonds of unity broken. Rival schools of thought about the caliphate developed and were propagated in partisanship, each striving by word and act to gain the better over its adversary, This in turn gave rise to forgeries of traditions and interpretation, and the sectarian excess brought sharp divisions into Khawarij [extreme pietists], Shi'a [supporters of hereditary succession of the Prophet], and moderates. The Khawarij went so far as to declare their opponents infidels and to demand a republican form of government. For a long time they maintained their "excommunication" of those who resisted them, until after much fighting that cost many Muslim lives their cause grew weak. They fled into remoter parts but continued their seditious activities. A remnant of them survives to the present in certain areas of Africa and of the Arabian peninsula. The Shi'as carried their heresy to the point of exalting 'Ali or some of his descendants to divine or near-divine status, with widespread consequences in the field of dogma.

These developments, however, did not halt the propagation of Islam and did not deprive the areas remote from the center of controversy of the light of the Qur'an. People came into Islam in droves—Persians, Syrians and their neighbors, Egyptians and Africans, and others in their train. Freed from the necessity of defending the temporal power of Islam, great numbers were ready to busy themselves with the first principles of belief and law, in pursuance of the Qur'an's guidance. In this task, they gave due place to the delivered tradition without neglecting the proud role of reason or overlooking the intellect. Men of sincere integrity took to the vocation of knowledge and education, the most famous of them being Hasan al-Basri [642–728]. He had a school in Basra to which students came from every part, and various questions were examined. People of all religious persuasions had come into Islam without knowing it inwardly, but carrying with them into it their existing notions, seeking some kind of mediating compromise between the old and the Islamic. So after the tempests of sedition came the tensions of doubt. Every opinion-monger took his stand upon the liberty of thought the Qur'an enjoined. The newcomers asserted their right to an equal stake with the existing authorities, and schisms raised their heads among the Muslims.

The first theme of contention to arise was that of will—man's independence in willing and doing and choosing, and the question of the supreme sin unrepented of. Wasil ibn 'Ata' [founder of Mu'tazilism, died 748] and his [spiritual] master, Hasan al-Basri, differed on this issue and the former broke away, teaching according to his own independent lights. Many of the first Muslim masters, including Hasan al-Basri, or so it is alleged, were of the view that man truly has choice in the deeds which proceed from his knowledge and will. So they opposed the school of *jabr*, or determinism, which held that man in his volitional activity is like the branches of a tree swaying necessarily. Throughout the period of the rule of the sons of Marwan [Umayyad caliph, died 685], no effort was made to regulate the issue or to get people back to first principles and bring them to a common position. Individual idiosyncrasy had free play, though 'Umar ibn 'Abd al-'Aziz [caliph, 682–720] gave directions to [Muhammad ibn Muslim] al-Zuhri [died 741] to record the traditions he had come by, and he was the first tradition-collector.

These two problems, however, were not all. Controversy developed also over the question whether the real attributes of God should be posited of the divine essence or not. There was also the question of reason and its competence to know all religious principles, even the ramifications of law and matters pertaining to worship, which some espoused even to the point of excessive pleading of the Qur'anic text. Others limited the writ of reason to the first principles, as explained above. Others again—a minority—in a spirit of contention against the first group, totally repudiated reason and thus went counter to the

Qur'an itself. Opinions on the caliphs and the caliphate marched with those on matters of doctrine, as if
they were an integral part of Islamic dogma.

With the disciples of Wasil the paths diverged
further. For they had recourse to drawing congenial
ideas from the Greeks. They had the idea that it was
a work of piety to establish dogma by scientific corroboration, without discriminating, however, between what went back to rational first principles and
what was merely a figment of the imagination. So
they mingled with the tenets of religion what had no
valid rational applicability. They persisted on this
tack until their sects multiplied apace. The rule of the
'Abbasids [caliphs, 750–1258], then in the prime of
power, helped them and their views prevailed. Their
learned scholars began to write books. Whereupon
the adherents of the schools of the early masters took
up their challenge, sustained by the power of conviction, though lacking the support of the rulers.

The early 'Abbasids knew the extent of their debt
to the Persians for the successful establishment of
their power and the overthrow of the Umayyad state.
They relied strongly on Persian collaboration and
brought them into high positions among their ministers and retainers. Many of them thus came into
authority without any part or lot in Islam religiously,
including Manichee sectaries and Yazidis, and other
Persian persuasions, as well as utterly irreligious
people. They began to disseminate their opinions and
by attitude and utterance induced those to whom their
views were congenial to accept their direction. Atheism emerged, and views inimical to belief in God
became rife, to the point that [Abu Ja'far] al-Mansur
[caliph, reigned 754–775] ordered the issue of books
exposing their errors and negating their claims.

At this juncture the science of theology was still a
young plant, a still partly reared edifice. Technical
theology took its point of departure from its perpetual
principle, namely the study of the created order, within
the terms laid down by the Qur'an. There ensued here
the dispute over the createdness or uncreatedness
of the Qur'an. Several of the 'Abbasid caliphs adopted
the dogma of the Qur'an's being created, while a
considerable number of those who held to the plain
sense of the Qur'an and the *sunna* [the practice of the
Prophet] either abstained from declaring themselves
or took a stand for uncreatedness. The reticence arose
from a reluctance to give expression to what might
conduce to heresy. The dispute brought much humiliation to men of reason and piety, and much blood was

criminally shed. In the name of faith, the community
did violence to faith.

It was in this way that the lines were drawn between the thoroughgoing rationalists and the moderate or extreme upholders of the text of the law. All
were agreed that religious principles were a matter
of obligation for their followers, both in respect of
acts of worship and mutual dealings, and should be
stringently followed. It was recognized that the inner attitudes of heart and the spiritual life constituted
a binding obligation to which the soul must be set.

A further element in the picture was the sect of
the Dahriyyun [materialists], who believed in *hulul*
[the incarnation of God in humans] and sought to
foist upon the Qur'an the notions they brought with
them on assuming the externals of Islam. They
strayed far in their exegesis and pretended to find in
every plain deed some hidden mystery. In their handling of the Qur'an they were as far from the import
of the text as error is from truth. They were known
as the Batiniyya [esoterics] and the Isma'iliyya [a
gnostic Shi'i sect], as well as by other names current
among historians. Their schools of thought had a
disastrous influence on the faith and undermined
conviction. Their deviations and deeds are only too
familiar.

Despite the identity of purpose shared by the orthodox and those at issue with them, as to the com-
bating of these atheist sectarians, there were considerable areas of contention between them and the
vicissitudes were prolonged. This did not prevent
them, however, from mutual borrowing, each group
profiting from the other, until the emergence of
Shaykh Abu'l-Hasan al-Ash'ari [873–925] early in
the fourth century [A.H.]. He plotted a middle course,
as is well known, between the early "orthodox" and
the subsequent tendencies towards extremes. He
based dogma on the principles of rational enquiry.
The disciples of pristine loyalties doubted his views
and many maligned him. The followers of [Ahmad]
ibn Hanbal [780–855] called him an infidel and demanded his death. A number of eminent *'ulama'*,
however, came to his support, among them Abu Bakr
[Muhammad ibn al-Tayyib] al-Baqillani [circa 948–
1013], the *Imam al-Haramayn* [the *Imam* of Mecca
and Medina, that is, Abu'l-Ma'ali al-Juwayni, 1028–
1085], and [Abu Ishaq] al-Isfira'ini [died 1027]. His
school came to carry the name of "the people of the
sunna and consensus." Two powerful forces were
effectively overcome by these esteemed thinkers—

the temper that leans wholly on the literal and the instinct that runs off into the imaginary and the extravagant. Two centuries or so later these types survived only as insignificant pockets of opinion in the periphery of the Islamic world.

The disciples of al-Ash'ari's school, it should be remembered, having based their doctrine rationally on the laws of the universe, required the believer as a matter of obligation to hold the certainty of these rational premises and deductions in the same assurance with which he accepted the dogmas of faith, insisting that where proof was wanting, the to-be-proven was nonexistent also. That outlook continued until the rise of [Abu Hamid Muhammad] al-Ghazzali [1058–1111] and [Fakhr al-Din] al-Razi [1149–1209] and those who adopted their position, according to whom one or even several proofs could be shown to be false, and yet leave open the possibility of the object whose existence it was intended to demonstrate being substantiated from more adequate evidence. There was, they held, no justification for making the argument from the negative instance absolute. As for the schools of philosophy, they drew their ideas from pure reason, and the only concern of philosophic rationalists was to gain knowledge, to satisfy their intellectual curiosity in elucidating the unknown and fathoming the intelligible. They were well able to achieve their objectives, inasmuch as they were sheltered by the mass of religious believers who afforded them full liberty of action to enjoy and give rein to their intellectual interests, the pursuit of crafts and the strengthening of the social order through the disclosure of the secrets hidden in the universe—all in accordance with the divine mandate for such exploration by thought and mind: "He created for you all that is in the earth," [Sura 2, Verse 29] which exempts neither the seen nor the unseen. Not a single intelligent Muslim sought to debar them or to impede their findings, the Qur'an having espoused the high role of reason and confirmed its competence as the ultimate means to happiness and the criterion between truth and falsehood, worth and loss. Had not the Prophet observed: "You are most cognizant of the world and its ways," and given at the battle of Badr [in 624] an example of behavior based on intelligent discernment and the proof of experience.

Nevertheless, it is clear that most of the philosophers were subject to two influences that got the better of them. The first was an admiration for all that derived from the Greek philosophers, notably Plato [circa 427–347 B.C.] and Aristotle [384–322 B.C.],

and with it a too precipitate inclination to accept their authority. Second, there was the prevailing contemporary trend of will, and this had the more mischievous effects. For they got themselves into controversies obtaining among speculative thinkers in the field of religion. Though there were relatively few of them, they clashed with the beliefs predominantly held, and so came under attack. Then came al-Ghazzali and his school, who brought sharp criticism to bear upon the entire content of philosophical lore in the fields of theology and related themes, including the principles of substance and accident, theories of matter and physics, and, indeed, the whole gamut of rationality in relation to religion. Later exponents of this criticism became so extreme as to forfeit their following. Ordinary people turned from them and the specialists became indifferent to them. In due course, time precluded the results the Muslim world might have expected from their activities.

All this explains why matters of theology mingle with philosophy in the writings of later authors like ['Abdullah] al-Baydawi [Shafi'i scholar, died circa 1286], al-'Adud [al-Din al-Iji, Ash'ari scholar, died 1355], and others, and why various rational sciences became concentrated in a single pursuit, the assumptions and debates of which approximated more to a traditionalism than a rationalism, whereby the progress of knowledge was arrested.

Then there supervened the various successive insurrections aimed at the civil power, in which it was the obscurantists who got the upper hand, destroying the remaining traces of the rational temper which had its source in the Islamic faith. They betook themselves to devious by-paths, and students of the writings of the previous generations found themselves limited to mere wrangles about words and scrutiny of methods—and that in a very few books characterized by feebleness and mediocrity.

As a consequence, a complete intellectual confusion beset the Muslims under their ignorant rulers. Ideas which had never had any place in science found sponsors, who asserted things Islam had never before tolerated. Fostered by the general educational poverty, they gained ground, aided too by the remoteness of men from the pristine sources of the faith, They evicted intellect from its rightful place and dealt arbitrarily with the false and the valid in thinking. They went so far as to espouse the view of some in other nations who alleged an enmity between knowledge and faith. They took up highly misleading positions on questions of both morals and doctrine, things allowed and things forbidden, that is, and even the issues of Islam and the very denial of God. Their fantasies fell very far short of the real meaning of religion, while their ideas and language sadly misrepresented God. There can be no doubt that the consequences befalling the masses of men in their beliefs and principles from this prolonged disaster with its widespread confusion were grievous and heavy.

The foregoing is a summary of the history of theology, indicating how it was founded on the Qur'an and how at length partisanship sadly distorted its true goal and quality.

We must, however, believe that the Islamic religion is a religion of unity throughout. It is not a religion of conflicting principles but is built squarely on reason, while divine revelation is its surest pillar. Whatever is other than these must be understood as contentious and inspired by Satan or political passions. The Qur'an has cognizance of every man's deed and judges the true and the false.

The purpose of this discipline, theology, is the realization of an obligation about which there is no dispute, namely, to know God most high in His attributes that are necessarily to be predicated of Him and to know His exaltation above all improper and impossible attribution. It is, with Him, to acknowledge His messengers with full assurance and heart-confidence, relying therein upon proof and not taking things merely upon tradition. So the Qur'an directs us, enjoining rational procedure and intellectual enquiry into the manifestations of the universe, and, as far as may be, into its particulars, so as to come by certainty in respect of the things to which it guides. It forbids us to be slavishly credulous, and for our stimulus points the moral of peoples who simply followed their fathers with complacent satisfaction and were finally involved in an utter collapse of their beliefs and their own disappearance as a community. Well is it said that traditionalism can have evil consequences as well as good, and may occasion loss as well as conduce to gain. It is a deceptive thing, and though it may be pardoned in an animal, it is scarcely seemly in man. [. . .]

It is said by some that if Islam truly came to call diverse peoples into one common unity, and if the Qur'an says "You have nothing to do with those who divide over religion and make parties," [Sura 6, Verse 159] how does it come about that the Islamic community has been sundered into sectarian movements and broken up into groups and schools?

If Islam is a faith that unifies, why this numerous diversity among Muslims? If Islam turns the believer in trust toward Him who created the heavens and the earth, why do multitudes of Muslims turn their faces to powerless things that can neither avail nor harm, and apart from God are helpless either way, even to the point of thinking such practice part of *tawhid* itself?

If Islam was the first religion to address the rational mind, summoning it to look into the whole material universe, giving it free rein to range at will through all its secrets, saving only therein the maintenance of faith, how is it that Muslims are content with so little and many indeed have closed and barred the door of knowledge altogether, supposing thereby that God is pleased with ignorance and a neglect of study of His marvelous handiwork?

How does it happen that the very apostles of love have become in these days a people who nose around for it in vain? They who were once exemplary in energy and action are now the very picture of sloth and idleness?

What are all these accretions to their religion, when all the time Muslims have the very Book of God as a balance in which to weigh and discriminate all their conjectures, and yet its very injunctions they abandon and forsake?

If Islam really is so solicitous for the mind and hearts of men, why today in the opinion of so many is it somehow beyond the reach of those who would grasp it?

If Islam welcomes and invites enquiry into its contents, why is the Qur'an not read except by chanting, and even the majority of the educated men of religion only know it very approximately?

If Islam granted to reason and will the honor of independence, how is it that it has bound them with such chains? If it has established the principles of justice, why are the greater part of its rulers such models of tyranny? If religion eagerly anticipates the liberation of slaves, why have Muslims spent centuries enslaving the free?

If Islam regards loyalty to covenants, honesty, and fulfilment of pledges as being its very pillars, how does it come about that deception, falsehood, perfidy, and calumny are so current among Muslims?

If Islam forbids fraud and treachery and warns imposters that they have neither part not lot in it, how is it that Muslims practice deception against God, the sacred law, and the true and loyal believers? If it prohibits all abomination, whether evident or hidden, what is it we see among them, both secret and open, both physical and spiritual?

If Islam teaches that religion consists in sincerity before God, His Apostle, and fellow believers in both immediate and general relationships, if "man is the loser , save those who believe, do good works, and enjoin upon each other justice and patience" [Sura 103, Verses 1–3] and yet, not enjoining kindliness or forbidding evil, they go altogether to the bad, and their honest folk call and get no response, and if this which they quite fail to fulfill is in fact their most bounden duty, why is it that they thus so totally fail to counsel each other and lay upon each other squarely what the divine will requires? Why do they not hold to it with fortitude and speak truth about right and wrong? Who do they in fact take each their own way, letting things go as they will in rabid individualism, ignoring each other's affairs as if they were totally unrelated the one to the other, having nothing in common? Why do sons murder fathers, and daughters prove refractory toward their mothers? Where are the bowels of mercy, of compassion for a neighbor? Where is the just dealing the rich owe to the poor with their possessions? Rather the rich plunder even what remains in the hands of the wretched.

A glimmer of Islam, it is said, illuminated the west, but its full light is in the east. Yet precisely there its own people lie in the deepest glom and cannot see. Does this seem intelligible? Is there any parallel in the annals of men? Doesit not appear that the very Muslims who have known something of science are precisely those who, for the most part, instinctively regard Islam's doctrines as superstitious and its principles and precepts as a farce? They find pleasure in aping the free-thinking people who scoff and jeer and think themselves forward-looking. Do you not see Muslims whose only business with the scriptures is to finger their pages, while they preen themselves on being memorizers of their precepts and expert in their laws? How far they are from the rational study of the Qur'an which they despise and regard as worthless to religion and the world! Many of them simply pride themselves on ignorance, as if thereby they had evaded prohibited things and achieved some distinction. Those Muslims who stand on the threshold of

science see their faith as a kind of old garment in which it is embarrassing to appear among men, while those who deceive themselves that they have some pretension to be religious and orthodox believers in its doctrines regard reason as a devil and science as supposition. Can we not, in the light of all this, call God, His angels, and all men to witness that science and reason have no accord with this religion?

It may well be said that the foregoing has not exaggerated the plight of Muslims today, indeed, these several generations past. But is the objection the whole story? Parallels could be found in the descriptions of Islam in their day given by al-Ghazzali, [Abu 'Abdullah Muhammad] Ibn al-Hajj [died 1336], and other writers on religion, filling whole volumes, both about the general population and the intelligentsia. But the reading of the Qur'an suffices of itself to vindicate what I have said about the essential nature of Islamic religion, provided it is read with care to understand its real import, interpreted according to the understanding of those among whom it was sent down and to the way they put it into practice. To admit the validity of what I have said of its fine effects, it suffices to read the pages of history as indited by those who truly knew slam and the objective writers in other nations. Such Islam was—and is. We have earlier said that religion is guidance and reason. Whoever uses it well and takes its directives will gain the blessedness God has promised to those who follow it. As a medicine for human society its success when truly tried is so manifest that not even the blind and the deaf can deny or gainsay it. All that the objection just elaborated leads to is this: a physician treated a sick man with medicine and he recovered; then the doctor himself succumbed to the disease he had been treating. In dire straits from pain and with the medicine by him in the house, he has yet no will to use it. Many of those who come to visit him or seek his ministrations or even gloat over his illness could take up the medicine and be cured, while he himself despairs of life and waits either for death or some miraculous healing.

We have now set forth the religion of Islam and its true character. As for those Muslims who by their conduct have become an argument against it, these must be dealt with not here, but in another book, if God wills.

The Emancipation of Woman *and* The New Woman

Qasim Amin (Egypt, 1863–1908) was renowned for his support of women's liberation in the Islamic world. Amin was born in Alexandria to an Egyptian mother and a Turkish father, a former Ottoman governor of Kurdistan who had retired to Egypt following a major revolt in that province. After finishing his primary education at the aristocratic Ras al-Tin School and the Khedival School, Qasim Amin obtained a bachelor's degree in law in 1881 from the School of Law and Administration and was sent to France in an educational mission for five years to study law. There, he joined Sayyid Jamal al-Din al-Afghani (chapter 11) and Muhammad 'Abduh (chapter 3) and participated in their publication of the journal *al-'Urwa al-wuthqa* (*The Strongest Link*). After his return to Egypt, he joined the judicial system and worked as attorney general and judge. Amin's major works include *Les Egyptiens* (*The Egyptians*, 1894), in which he defended Islam's treatment of women, and *Tahrir al-mar'a* (*The Liberation of Woman*, 1899), to which 'Abduh secretly contributed sections. The latter book, whose introduction is presented here, called for an end to the seclusion of women, an improvement in their status, and widespread education of girls. The book generated heated controversy in Egyptian intellectual circles, to which Amin responded in *al-Mar'a al-jadida* (*The New Woman*, 1900)—whose conclusion is also presented here—adopting further liberal views, such as the need for women's participation alongside men in public life.[1]

The Emancipation of Woman

I call on every lover of truth to examine with me the status of women in Egyptian society. I am confident that such individuals will arrive independently at the same conclusion I have, namely the necessity of improving the status of Egyptian women. The truth I am presenting today has preoccupied me for a long time; I have considered it, examined it, and analyzed it. When it was eventually stripped of all confounding errors, it occupied an important place in my thinking, rivaled other ideas, overcame them, and finally reached the point where it became my dominant thought, alerting me to its advantages and reminding me of its necessity. I became aware of the absence of a platform from which this truth could be elevated from reflection to the unlimited space of appeal and attention.

A profound factor that influences human development and ensures its positive future is the strange power that compels a human being to communicate every scientific or literary idea once it crystallizes in the mind, and once it is accompanied by the belief that it will benefit the progress of future generations.

Qasim Amin, *The Liberation of Woman* and *The New Woman: Two Documents in the History of Egyptian Feminism*, translated from Arabic by Samiha Sidhom Peterson (Cairo, Egypt: © American University in Cairo Press, 2000), pp. 3–10; *al-Mar'a al-jadida* (*The New Woman*), in Muhammad 'Imara, ed., *Qasim Amin: al-'Amal al-kamila* (*Qasim Amin: The Complete Works*) (Cairo, Egypt: Dar al-Shuruq, 1989), pp. 511–518. Translation of second piece from Arabic by Lisa Pollard and Raghda El Essawi. First published in 1899 and 1900, respectively. Introduction by Emad Eldin Shahin.

1. Muhammad 'Imara, *Qasim Amin: Tahrir al-mar'a wa al-tamadun al-islami* (*Qasim Amin: The Liberation of Woman and Islamic Civilization*) (Cairo, Egypt: Dar al-Shuruq, 1988); Samir Abu Hamdan, *Qasim Amin: Jadaliyat al-'alaqa bayn al-mar'a wa al-nahda* (*Qasim Amin: The Dialectical Relationship Between Woman and Renaissance*) (Beirut, Lebanon: al-Sharika al-'Alamiyya li al-Kitab, 1993); Leila Ahmed, *Women and Gender in Islam: Historical Roots of a Modern Debate* (New Haven, Conn.: Yale University Press, 1992).

Communicating these findings supersedes concern over any negative consequences that may be incurred by the individual in presenting his knowledge. The impact of this power is recognized by anyone who has experienced a trace of it. Such an individual feels that if he fails to use this power toward the goal it is aiming to achieve, and if he does not use whatever strength he has to assist it in reaching that goal, it will eventually overcome him in the struggle, resisting him if he opposes it, coercing him if he tries to force it, and appearing in an unfamiliar form, like a gas that could not be contained through pressure. In fact, the pressure may cause an explosion that would destroy its container.

History offers numerous proofs of this phenomenon. The history of nations is saturated with disputes, arguments, sufferings, and wars that originated with the purpose of establishing the superiority of one idea or ideology over another. During these encounters victory was sometimes for truth and at other times for falsehood. This characterized Islamic countries during the early days and the middle ages, and continues to characterize Western countries. It is reasonable to state that the life of Western countries is a continuous struggle between truth and falsehood, between right and wrong: it is an internal struggle in all branches of education, the arts, and industry, and an external struggle among the various countries. This is especially obvious in this century when distance and isolation have been eliminated by modern inventions, and when the separating borders and forbidding walls have been torn down. These changes are reflected in the increasing number of individuals who have toured the whole world and who presently can be counted by the thousands. Likewise, the ideas of any Western scholar, when formulated in a book, are translated and published simultaneously in five or six languages.

Countries like ours have preferred a less ruffled existence. This is because we have neglected the nurturing of our minds to such an extent that they have become like barren soil, unfit for any growth. Our laziness has caused us to be hostile to every unfamiliar idea, whether a product of the sound principal traditions or of current events.

An intellectually lazy person whose arguments are weak is often satisfied, in refuting an apparent truth, to hurl a false remark and declare it a heresy in Islam. He only makes this false remark to avoid the effort of understanding the truth, or to disengage from the labor of research, or to avoid its application. It is as if God created the Muslims from clay especially set aside for them and freed them from obeying natural law, whose power dominates human beings and the rest of living creation.

Some people will say that today I am publishing heresy. To these people I will respond: Yes, I have come up with a heresy, but the heresy is not against Islam. It is against our traditions and social dealings, which ought to be brought to perfection. Why should a Muslim believe that traditions cannot be changed or replaced by new ones, and that it is his duty to preserve them forever? Why does he drag this belief along to his work, even though he and his traditions are a part of the universe, falling at all times under the laws of change? Can the Muslim contradict God's laws of creation—God who has made change a prerequisite for life and progress, rather than immobility and inflexibility, which are characteristic of death and backwardness? Is not tradition merely the set of conventions of a country defining the special customs appropriate to its life and behavior at a specific time and place? How can people believe that traditions never change, and at the same time maintain the understanding that traditions are one of the intellectual products of humans, and that human intellect differs according to historical era or geographical location? Does the presence of Muslims in various parts of the world imply a uniformity of traditions or ways of life? Who can pretend that Sudanese preferences are similar to those of the Turks, the Chinese, or the Indians; or believe that the Bedouin tradition is appropriate for an urbanite; or claim that the traditions of any country have remained the same since the creation of that country?

In truth, during a specific historical era every country has peculiar traditions and mores that match its intellectual state. These traditions and mores change continuously in an unobtrusive way, so that people living during that era are unaware of the changes. However, the changes are influenced by regional factors, heredity, intercultural exchanges, scientific inventions, ethical ideologies, religious beliefs, political structures, and other factors. Every intellectual movement toward progress is inevitably followed by an appropriate change in the traditions and mores of a society. Therefore, there should be examples of differences between the Sudanese and the Turks comparable to the differences in their intellectual status. This is a well-known, established fact. The differences between Egyptians and Europeans also need to be considered in this context.

We cannot consider traditions (which are merely a way of life for an individual, family, compatriots, and children of the race) to be the same in a civilized nation as in an ignorant, barbaric one, because the behavior of every individual in a society is appropriate to the intellectual abilities of that society and to the method by which its children are brought up.

This total interdependence between the traditions of a nation and its level of civilization and knowledge suggests that the power of tradition controls a country more than any other power, and that tradition is one of the most influential permanent components of a nation, and is least likely to change. Therefore, citizens of a nation cannot but comply with the existing traditions, unless they change, or unless their intellectual level increases or decreases. Thus I believe that traditions always overcome other factors in a society, and that they even influence the laws of that society. This belief is confirmed through daily observation of the laws and programs of our nation, which are usually intended to improve the state of affairs but are immediately turned around to become new instruments for corruption. It is not difficult to understand this phenomenon, because at times tradition may even supersede the existing religion, destroying or transforming it so that those who are most knowledgeable about religion eventually disown its existing form.

This is the basis of our observations. This evidence of history confirms and demonstrates that the status of women is inseparably tied to the status of a nation. When the status of a nation is low, reflecting an uncivilized condition for that nation, the status of women is also low, and when the status of a nation is elevated, reflecting the progress and civilization of that nation, the status of women in that country is also elevated. We have learned that women in the first human societies were treated as slaves. The ancient Greeks and Romans, for example, considered a woman to be under the power of her father, then her husband, and after him his eldest son. The head of the family had the absolute right of ownership over her life. He could dispose of her through trade, donation, or death, whenever and in whatever way he wished. His heirs eventually inherited her and with her all the rights that were given to the owner. Prior to Islam, it was acceptable for Arab fathers to kill their daughters, and for men to gratify themselves with women with no legal bonds or numerical limits. This authority still prevails among uncivilized African and American tribes. Some Asians even believe that a woman has no immortal soul, and that she should not live after her husband dies. Other Asians present her to their guests as a sign of hospitality, just as one would present a guest with the best of his possessions.

These traits are present among emerging societies, which are based on familial and tribal bonds rather than on formal structures. Force is the only law with which such societies are familiar. The use of force is also the medium of control for governments run by autocratic structures.

On the other hand, we find that women in nations with a more advanced civilization have gradually advanced from the low status to which they have been relegated, and have started to overcome the gap that has separated them from men. One woman is crawling while the other is taking steps; one is walking while the other is running. These discrepancies reflect the different societies to which these women belong and the level of civilization of these societies. The American woman is in the forefront, followed by the British, the German, the French, the Austrian, the Italian, and the Russian woman, and so on. Women in all these societies have felt that they deserve their independence, and are searching for the means to achieve it. These women believe that they are human beings and that they deserve freedom, and they are therefore striving for freedom and demanding every human right.

Westerners, who like to associate all good things with their religion, believe that the Western woman has advanced because her Christian religion helped her achieve freedom. This belief, however, is inaccurate. Christianity did not set up a system which guarantees the freedom of women; it does not guarantee her rights through either specific or general rules; and it does not prescribe any guiding principles on this topic. In every country where Christianity has been introduced and spread, it has left no tangible impact on the normative structure affecting women's status. On the contrary, Christianity has been molded by the traditions and manners of the specific nations in which it was introduced. If there were a religion which could have had power and influence over local traditions, then the Muslim women today should have been at the forefront of free women on earth.

The Islamic legal system, the *shari'a*, stipulated the equality of women and men before any other legal system. Islam declared women's freedom and emancipation, and granted women all human rights during a time when women occupied the lowest status in all societies. According to Islamic law, women are considered to possess the same legal capabilities in all civil cases pertaining to buying, donating, trusteeship, and disposal of goods, unhindered by requirements of permission from either their father or their husband. These advantages have not yet been attained by some contemporary Western women, yet they demonstrate that respect for women and for their equality with men were basic to the principles of the liberal *shari'a*. In fact, our legal system went so far in its kindness to women that it rid them of the burden of earning a living and freed them from the obligation of participating in household and child-rearing expenses. This is unlike some Western laws, which equate men and women only with regard to their duties, giving preference to men with regard to societal rights.

Within the *shari'a*, the tendency to equate men's and women's rights is obvious, even in the context of divorce. Islam has created for women mechanisms worthy of consideration and contrary to what Westerners and some Muslims imagine or believe. These will be discussed later,

Islamic law favors men in one area only—polygamy. The reason is obvious and is related to the issue of lineage, without which marriage is meaningless. This topic too will be addressed later. In summary, nothing in the laws of Islam or in its intentions can account for the low status of Muslim women. The existing situation is contrary to the law, because originally women in Islam were granted an equal place in human society.

What a pity! Unacceptable customs, traditions, and superstitions inherited from the countries in which Islam spread have been allowed to permeate this beautiful religion. Knowledge in these countries had not developed to the point of giving women the status already given them by the *shari'a*.

The most significant factor that accounts for the perpetuation of these traditions, however, is the succession over us of despotic governments. At various times and places, Islamic societies have been stripped of the political structures that delineated the rights of the ruler and the ruled, and that granted to the ruled the right to demand that the rulers stop at the limits established for them by the *shari'a*. In fact, their governments continually took on a despotic nature, with their sultan and his assistants having total authority. Thus they ruled however they wished, without restraint, counsel, or supervision, and they administered the affairs of their citizens without these having any say.

Yes, rulers, whether important or unimportant, are obliged to follow justice and avoid injustice. Experience demonstrates, however, that unlimited power is a temptation for abuse, especially when it is unaccountable, unchallenged by any other opinion, and unsupervised by any formal structure. This explains why for so many centuries absolute and autocratic rule was the norm for Islamic countries. Rulers administered these nations poorly and were excessive in their capricious tampering with the affairs of their subjects; quite often they even tampered with religion. There are a few exceptions to this pattern, but they are insignificant in contrast to the majority of cases.

When despotism prevails in a country, its impact is not limited to individual cases only, since it is central to the ideology of the supreme ruler. Despotism continues to flow from him to those around him, and they in turn influence their subordinates. A despot spits his spirit into every powerful person, who, whenever possible, dominates a weaker one. This attitude pervades the life of all individuals, regardless of the approval or disapproval of the supreme ruler. These despotic systems have also influenced the relationships between men and women—man in his superiority began to despise woman in her weakness. As a result, corrupt morals became the first sign of a country ruled by a despot.

Initially, one would assume that a person who experiences injustice would love justice, and that he would be inclined toward compassion, having experienced the suffering resulting from the catastrophes which have befallen him. Observation indicates, however, that an oppressed nation does not contain an appropriate and fit environment for the development of desirable virtues. The only plant that grows in an oppressed nation is that of depravity. Every Egyptian who has lived under despotic rule in the not-very-distant past knows that the village mayor, robbed of ten Egyptian pounds, reclaims a hundred pounds from his villagers, and that the village chief, struck with one hundred lashes, upon his return to the village takes his revenge upon a hundred peasants!

The natural implication of this situation is that human beings respect only force and are deterred only by fear. When women were weak, men crushed their rights, despised them, treated them with contempt, and stomped on their personality. A woman had a very low status, regardless of her position in the family as wife, mother, or daughter. She was of no importance, was ignored, and had no legitimate opinions. She was submissive to a man because he was a man and she a woman. She obliterated herself in the person of the man. She was allowed nothing in the universe except that which she concealed in the corners of her home. She specialized in ignorance and secluded herself with the curtains of darkness. A man used her as an object of delight and pleasure, amused himself with her whenever he wished, and threw her into the road whenever he wished. He had freedom and she had bondage; he had knowledge and she had ignorance; he had a mind and she had simple-mindedness; he had light and space and she had darkness and prison; he had absolute authority and she had only obedience and patience. Everything in existence belonged to him, and she was part of that totality of which he took possession.

Despising the woman, a man filled his home with slaves, white or black, or with numerous wives, satisfying himself with any of them whenever his passion and lust drove him. He ignored the prescribed religious obligations, which required good intentions for his actions and justice in his dealings.

Despising the woman, a man divorced her without reason.

Despising the woman, a man sat alone at the dining table, while his mother, sisters, and wife gathered after he was done to eat what was left over.

Despising the woman, a man appointed a guardian to protect her chastity. Thus a eunuch, a legal guardian, or a servant supervised, observed, and accompanied her wherever she went.

Despising the woman, a man imprisoned her in the house and boasted about her permanent restriction, which was lifted only when she was to be carried in her coffin to the grave.

Despising the woman, a man announced that she was unworthy of trust and honesty.

Despising the woman, a man secluded her from public life and kept her from involvement in anything except female or personal issues. A woman had no opinions on business, political movements, the arts, public affairs, or doctrinal issues, and she had no patriotic pride or religious feelings.

I do not exaggerate when I say that this has been the status of women in Egypt until the past few years, when we have witnessed a decrease in the power of men. This change is a consequence of the increased intellectual development of men, and the moderation of their rulers. We have observed that women at present have more freedom to look after their own affairs, that they quite often go to public parks in order to take the fresh air and to see the works of the Sublime Creator, displayed for the eyes of all humans, whether male or female. In fact, many women now accompany their husbands during their business trips to other countries. Likewise, many men have given women a special status within the family structure. This has occurred among men who are confident in their women and have no worries regarding their trustworthiness. This is a new kind of respect for women.

Yet we cannot claim that this change removes the need for criticism. In reality, the causes of criticism are not change but the conditions surrounding it. Among the most important of these are the firmly established tradition of veiling among the majority of the population, and the inadequate socialization of women. Were women's socialization effected in accordance with religious and moral principles, and were the use of the veil terminated at limits familiar in most Islamic schools of belief, then these criticisms would be dropped and our country would benefit from the active participation of all its citizens, men and women alike.

The Current State of Thinking about the Situation of Women in Egypt

Egyptians have, over the last few years, become aware of the poor state of their social order. They have begun to show signs of dissatisfaction with it, and felt the need to improve it. They have heard about the West, have intermingled with Westerners, spent time with many of them, and learned about the West's progress. When Egyptians saw the good life that Westerners enjoyed, their widespread influence and their indisputable word, as well as certain other advantages from which they themselves were forbidden—but without which life has no value—a desire spread among them to keep up with the West and its blessings. Leaders arose among them who competed with each other to disseminate new thoughts, thoughts which they believed would guide the community down the road to success. One would call for work and action, and another for harmony and unity, and for the rejection of any possible sources of discord. A third would call for love of the country and self-sacrifice in its service. A fourth, nothing less than increased adherence to the precepts of religion, and so on.

But one factor escaped the attention of these leaders: these ideas, and those similar to them, won't have any influence worth mentioning upon the community if they do not reach women, and if women do not understand their meanings. They will not have any influence if women are not favorably disposed to them, or are not filled with love for them, such that their children embody the perfect picture that represents human perfection.

This is because no social condition can be changed unless it is made the target of education. It is not enough for a reform program, no matter what its target, to consist merely of a government order issued to spur the masses to action, or of a speech designed to encourage its listeners to want to change. Nor can it consist merely of books and articles written about the benefits of change. These will merely inform a nation about the state of its deteriorating conditions; they are not the means by which people will change, nor are they the things that will transform a people from one state to another. Any and all change must be the result of a confluence of virtues, characteristics, morals, and customs which are not innate to the individual upon his birth. They cannot be had except through training, or, in other words, they cannot be had without women.

Hence, if Egyptians want to reform their current situation, they must begin with the roots of reform. They must believe that there is no hope that they will become a vibrant community, one that can play an important role alongside the developed countries, with a place in the world of human civilization, until their homes and their families become a proper environment for providing men with the characteristics upon which success in the world depends. And there is no hope that Egyptian homes and families will become that proper environment unless women are educated and unless they participate alongside men in their thoughts, hopes and pains, even if they do not participate in all of their activities.

This truth, despite its simplicity and its self-evident nature, was considered by certain people, upon its publication last year [in the author's book *The Liberation of Women*, 1899], to be a kind of lunacy. Legal scholars decided that it was an offense to Islam. And many graduates from the *madrasa*s [seminaries] saw it as an exaggerated imitation of the West. Some of them went so far as to say that it was a crime against the country and against religion. In their writings, they were even so deluded as to say that the liberation of Eastern women was something that the Christian nations were striving for in order to destroy Islam, and that any Muslim who supports women's liberation is not, in fact, a Muslim. These are delusions that the simple-minded are inclined toward and that the ignorant delight in believing, because they do not understand where their true interests lie. Such delusions prevent them from reaching the truth.

We have but one word with which to respond to such people: If the Europeans intended to destroy us, they would have only to leave us to our own devices! They have no more perfect method than to leave us in our present situation!

This is the indisputable truth, and no matter how much one group might try to hide it, or how much another group might try to neglect it, it will be made clear to everyone, sooner or later, just as the truth always is.

Anyone observing our present social situation will find proof of the fact that our women have broken away from their role as slave, and that there remains but a *hijab* [that is, a thin veil] between them and freedom. Such an observer sees:

1. A new awareness amongst the Egyptians of the necessity of educating their daughters, rather than teaching them nothing, as was their custom.
2. A decrease in the use of the *hijab* and its concomitant institutions, such as segregation, and a movement toward its obsolescence.
3. The displeasure that our youth takes in marriage along the lines that it is now practiced, as well as their desire to change that practice through [the institution] of engagement.
4. The government's interest, as well as that of certain Egyptians—at the head of them being His Excellency *Shaykh* Muhammad 'Abduh [Egypt, 1849–1905; see chapter 3], *mufti* [chief religious official] of Egypt—in reforming the *shari'a* [Islamic law] courts. Anyone who sees the report that His Excellency made regarding these courts will find a number of matters regarding the reform of the Egyptian family. The matter that is

most worthy of mention is the *mufti*'s statement about polygamy:

I am hereby raising my voice in complaint over the number of wives that poor men are marrying. Indeed, many of them take four wives; some have three, others two, without being able to support them. These men continuously fight with their wives over expenses and over their marital rights. Moreover, they will not divorce a single one of their wives and, thus, depravity continues to affect them and their children. [In this state] it becomes impossible for men and women to respect the limits that God has placed on mankind's freedom of action. [This condition] damages Islam and the Islamic community in ways too clear to explain.

This year, it happened that the wives of men who had been sentenced to life in prison, hard labor, or long prison terms, complained to the Ministry of Justice about their unhappy condition, with no means available for them to divorce their husbands and no family member who could support them or their children. The Ministry found itself in need of consulting the *mufti* about the legal recourses that could be adopted in response to such complaints. He studied the issue and others similar to it, and in response to them he produced eleven stipulations, in line with the Maliki *madhhab* [school of law], which we present below for the reader's benefit.

Stipulation One: If the husband refuses to provide for his wife despite the fact that he has a clear source of income, he is sentenced to pay alimony. If he has no clear source of income and continues to refuse to provide for his wife, the judge grants the wife a divorce from him on the spot. If the man claims financial incapability but cannot prove it, the judge takes the same action. But, if he can prove incapability, he is given a one-month grace period—no more—at the end of which he is considered divorced if he does not provide for his wife.

Stipulation Two: If the husband is ill or imprisoned and he refuses to provide for his wife, the judge grants him a period of time after which it is assumed that he will be cured or released from prison. If the period of illness or imprisonment is so long that harm or *fitna* [dissension] is feared, the judge grants the wife a divorce.

Stipulation Three: If the husband is absent for a short period of time, but before his departure he did not leave means of provision for his wife, the judge fixes a date by which he must send provisions. If he does not, the judge grants the wife a divorce after the fixed period elapses. In the case that he is absent for a long period or his destination is unknown, and it is proven that he has no means of providing for his wife, the judge grants the wife a divorce.

Stipulation Four: If someone owed the husband money, or if he left money in someone's trust, the wife has the right to ask to be provided for from that money. She also has the right to make a refutation of anyone who claims that she has no right to that trust, after swearing that she deserves to be provided for by the absentee, and after swearing that he, indeed, left nothing behind for her provision, and that he left no guardian to provide for her.

Stipulation Five: The judge's prerogative in divorcing a man from his wife for not providing for her is refutable. The husband has the right to remarry his wife if he proves his sources of provision and his willingness to support her through them. If he does not do both, any return to his wife is unacceptable.

Stipulation Six: If a man is lost in an Islamic land and there is no news of him, his wife has the right to raise the issue at the Ministry of Justice. She can, in front of the court, proclaim what she believes to be his fate, or his whereabouts. Then, the Minister of Justice should search for him in the areas where she believes him to be, either through the courts or by means of the police. If the Minister fails to find the lost husband, he sets for the wife a period of four years. If those four years pass, the woman must then wait out the time of her *'idda* [Qur'anic term of waiting before remarriage, apparently to clarify paternity]. Without then needing to return to the courts, she is allowed to remarry.

Stipulation Seven: If the absentee returns or proves to be alive, and if he does so before his wife's new husband consummates the marriage, not knowing that the absentee is alive, then the wife is returned to her original husband. If, in fact, the second husband knew all along that the original husband was alive, the wife is also returned to her original husband. If the death of the original husband is discovered during the wife's period of *'idda* or after it and before the new marriage contract is drawn or after it, the wife inherits her original husband's property if the second husband was ignorant of the first husband's death. However, if in fact the first husband died and the second husband knew of his death before consummating the marriage, then the wife inherits nothing.

Stipulation Eight: If a man dies in a conflict between Muslims, and it is proved that he indeed fought in said conflict, his wife is permitted to raise the issue before the Ministry of Justice. If after the Minister of Justice searches for the man, and after the period of *'idda* has passed, then the woman can remarry if she wishes, and his money goes to her heirs. If all that can be proven is that the man went along with the fighting armies, then the case is reverted to stipulations six and seven.

Stipulation Nine: The wife of a man missing as the result of a war between Muslims has the right to take her case before the Minister of Justice. After the minister has the man searched for, a period of one year is set. If that year passes and the man is not found, the woman then begins her period of *'idda*. She then has the right to remarry, and his money is inherited at the end of the year.

This process of setting a grace period is valid only in cases in which the absentee had, before disappearing, an income with which to provide for his wife, or in cases in which the wife does not fear seduction. Otherwise, the judge grants the wife a divorce once the woman's claim is proven to be true.

Stipulation Ten: If a dispute between a husband and wife becomes quite severe, and it cannot be solved through one of the means provided for in the Book of God, the case is brought to the provincial judge. He must then appoint two trustworthy arbitrators, one of them from the husband's family and the other from the wife's. It is best if they are neighbors. If it is difficult to find such arbitrators from among the members of their family, then they are chosen from among people outside of the family.

The arbitrators are then sent to the couple. If they are able to settle the dispute between the couple, so be it. Otherwise, they recommend divorce and bring the matter before the judge. He is required to rule according to what his appointed arbitrators have recommended. In this case, the divorce is revocable, and the arbitrators have no right to make it irrevocable.

Stipulation Eleven: The wife has the right to ask the judge to grant her a divorce if she is harmed by her husband. The *shari'a* does not permit a man to harm his wife, just as it does not permit desertion or beating or abuse without legitimate reason. It is in-

cumbent upon the wife to prove, by legal means, that her husband is harmful to her.

The *Shaykh* of al-Azhar lent his agreement to this project, and sent Muhammad 'Abduh the following letter:

To the *Mufti* of Egypt, may God keep you:

We have received your letter dated the fourth of Rabi'i al-thani 1318 [August 2, 1900], number 19, containing eleven stipulations, following the guidelines of the Maliki *madhhab*, about which you seek our opinion. We conclude as you do, and thus grant you our agreement. We thank you for high aspirations, as they are reflected in your interest in this venerable matter.

Signed,
Salim al-Bishri [Egypt, 1832–1917], the humble Maliki
Servant of knowledge and of the humble ones at al-Azhar

These two issues—that of polygamy and that of granting women the right to divorce her husband—are amongst the most important issues that I addressed in my book *The Liberation of Women*, and about which *Shaykh* Muhammad 'Abduh, a great religious scholar and a wise jurisprudent, has called worthy of his interest. He supports my suggestions about polygamy and divorce in a voice that is well heeded.

The sum of these facts—and then some—along with the things that one witnesses every day in Egyptian homes, foretells that the state of Egyptian women is in need of improvement.

This movement did not result from study. It grew, rather, through the influence of contact with Westerners, and according to the law known to natural scientists, which orders that every animal follow the nature of the environment in which he lives. The proof that our will does not interfere with this movement lies in the fact that when we pointed out the necessity of preserving and continuing the movement until our goals are met, we met with serious opposition even from those in whose selves and in whose homes the changes that we work for had already appeared.

There is nothing strange about this: It has always been our way to follow our whims.

If it makes no difference to us whether we spend our lives in excess or lack, richness or poverty, freedom or servitude, knowledge or ignorance, virtue or depravity, then it would be my opinion that there is no need for the freedom and the education that have been granted to Egyptian women up till now. If it makes no difference, then let men have a number of women, and marry a new woman every day, only to divorce her the next, and imprison their wives and daughters and sisters and grandmothers if they wish!! In Africa and Asia there are a number of countries in which women live entombed in their homes, from which they see no one and encounter no one. And amongst these nations there are those that have decayed to the extent that when a woman's husband dies she must kill herself, so that she may not enjoy life without him! What else can we do but direct our attention to these countries and ask them what the secret to the progress of their women is, in ignorance and isolation. Perhaps we will learn from them how to isolate our women and hold them back even further!!!!

But if what we hear and read about every day is true, that Egyptians want to create a living, advanced, civil nation, then we have the following to say to them:

There is a means of getting yourselves out of the poor condition that you complain about. There is a way of raising yourselves up to the highest level of civilization—the kind of civilization you aspire to, and then some. It consists of liberating your women from the bondage of ignorance and *hijab* [here, isolation]. This means was not our brainchild; we deserve no credit for its invention. Nations have used it before us, tested it, and put it to their advantage. Take a look at the Western nations; you will find amongst their women great differences. You'll find that the way American women are raised, and their morals and habits and manners, are not those of French women. And you'll find French women to be entirely different from Russian women. And you'll find that the Italian woman has nothing in common with the Swedish or the German woman. But all of these women, despite differences in their regions, nationalities, languages, and religions, share a common ground in one matter: they enjoy freedom and independence.

It is this freedom that has delivered Western women from their former state of decline. And once they were granted an education, women began to direct their energies, working alongside of men, to the establishment of and participation in charitable societies. This took place when women were given useful work—different, no doubt, from that of men. But just because this work is different does not mean that it lacks importance: women's work is like that of the merchant who spends his day bent over his goods in order to sell them, or the scribe who spends long hours in some governmental bureau writing an inter-departmental report. It is like that of the engineer who builds a bridge in order to make transportation easier, or the doctor who amputates a patient's limb in order to preserve life in other limbs. It is like that of the judge who mediates in the disputes that arise between people. But none of these has the right to call his work more useful to the social order than the woman who gives to society the gift of a well-raised man, useful to himself, his family, and his country.

We aren't saying the same things to you that others say, things like "Unite and be of help to one another," or "Cleanse yourselves of the faults that have crept into your morals." Nor are we saying, "Serve your family and your country," or any such slogans that get lost in the wind. We are teaching that the changing of the self requires more than a leader's advice, or a sultan's order, or a magician's magic, or a saint's miracles. Rather, it takes place, as we've said, through the preparation of young people ready to meet the requirements of a changing society.

This is the natural, long-term secret—one which is surrounded in difficulties. But the easiest of all difficulties is the one that ends in victory and success. And the shortest path is the one that delivers you to your goal.

A Lecture in the Club of the Umma Party

Malak Hifni Nasif (Egypt, 1886–1918), who used the pseudonym Bahithat al-Badiya (Seeker in the Desert), was born in Cairo into a literary family. Her father, who had studied at al-Azhar with Muhammad 'Abduh (see chapter 3), encouraged his daughter's education. She graduated from the first teacher training school for women in Egypt, the Saniyya School, where she later taught. On Fridays she gave women's lectures at the Egyptian University and elsewhere, which she published along with feminist essays in 1910. The present selection was one of these lectures, delivered to hundreds of upper-class women, and addressing some of the most sensitive social issues of the day: changing gender relations, the symbolic and practical implications of women's garb, and the need for legal change in women's status. The program listed at the end of the lecture formed the kernel of the more extensive set of demands that she sent in 1911 to the Egyptian Congress in Heliopolis, a meeting of (male) nationalists. Her life then took an abrupt turn when she married a Bedouin chief, gave up teaching, and went to live with him in the Fayyum oasis west of Cairo. She discovered he already had a wife—his cousin—and a daughter he expected her to tutor. Some of the sufferings she experienced and observed were expressed in her writings. In 1918, at the age of 32, she died of influenza. Her eulogy was the first feminist speech delivered by Huda Sha'rawi (1879–1947), founder of the Egyptian Feminist Union.[1]

Ladies, I greet you as a sister who feels what you feel, suffers what you suffer, and rejoices in what you rejoice. I applaud your kindness in accepting the invitation to this talk, where I seek reform. I hope to succeed, but if I fail, remember that I am one of you, and that as human beings we both succeed and fail. Anyone who differs with me or wishes to make a comment is welcome to express her views at the end of my talk.

Our meeting today is not simply for getting acquainted or for displaying our finery, but is a serious meeting. I wish to seek agreement on an approach we can take, and to examine our shortcomings in order to correct them. Complaints about both women and men are rife. Which side is right? Complaints and grumbling are not reform. I don't believe a sick person is cured by continual moaning. An Arab proverb says there is no smoke without fire. The English philosopher, Herbert Spencer [1820–1903], says that opinions that appear erroneous to us are not totally wrong, but there must be an element of truth in them. There is some truth in our claims and in those of men. At the moment there is a semi-feud between us and men because of the low level of agreement between us. Men blame the discord on our poor upbringing and haphazard education, while we claim it is due to men's arrogance and pride. This mutual blame which

Bahithat al-Badiya, "A Lecture in the Club of the Umma Party," translated from Arabic by Ali Badran and Margot Badran, in Margot Badran and Miriam Cooke, eds., *Opening the Gates: A Century of Arab Feminist Writing* (Bloomington: Indiana University Press, 1990), pp. 228–238. Speech delivered in 1909 and first published in 1910. Introduction adapted from the same volume, pp. 134, 227.

1. Soha Abdel Kader, *Egyptian Women in a Changing Society, 1899–1987* (Boulder, Colo.: Lynne Rienner, 1987), pp. 64–68; Leila Ahmed, *Women and Gender in Islam* (New Haven, Conn.: Yale University Press, 1992), pp. 179–185;

Margot Badran, *Feminists, Islam and Nation: Gender and the Making of Modern Egypt* (Princeton, N.J.: Princeton University Press, 1995); Beth Baron, *The Women's Awakening in Egypt* (New Haven, Conn.: Yale University Press, 1994); 'Abd al-Muta'al Muhammad Jabri, *al-Muslima al-'asriya 'inda Bahithat al-Badiya* (*The Contemporary Muslim Woman, in the View of Bahithat al-Badiya*) (Cairo, Egypt: Dar al-Ansar, 1976); May Ziyada, *Bahithat al-Badiya* (*Bahithat al-Badiya*) (Cairo, Egypt: Matba'at al-Muqtataf, 1920).

has deepened the antagonism between the sexes is something to be regretted and feared. God did not create man and woman to hate each other, but to love each other and to live together so the world would be populated. If men live alone in one part of the world and women are isolated in another, both will vanish in time.

Men say when we become educated we shall push them out of work and abandon the role for which God has created us. But isn't it rather men who have pushed women out of work? Before, women used to spin and to weave cloth for clothes for themselves and their children, but men invented machines for spinning and weaving and put women out of work. In the past, women sewed clothes for themselves and their households, but men invented the sewing machine. The iron for these machines is mined by men, and the machines themselves are made by men. Then men took up the profession of tailoring and began to make clothes for our men and children. Before, women winnowed the wheat and ground flour on grinding stones for the bread they used to make with their own hands, sifting flour and kneading dough. Then men established bakeries employing men. They gave us rest, but at the same time pushed us out of work. We or our female servants used to sweep our houses with straw brooms, and then men invented machines to clean that could be operated by a young male servant. Poor women and servants used to fetch water for their homes or the homes of employers, but men invented pipes and faucets to carry water into houses. Would reasonable women seeing water pumped into a neighbor's house be content to fetch water from the river, which might be far away? Is it reasonable for any civilized woman seeing bread from the bakery, clean and soft, costing her nothing more than a little money, to go and winnow wheat and knead dough? She might be weak and unable to trouble herself to prepare the wheat and dough, or she might be poor and unable to hire servants or to work alone without help. I think if men were in our place they would have done what we did. No woman can do all this work now, except women in the villages where civilization has not arrived. Even those women go to a mill instead of crushing wheat on the grinding stones. Instead of collecting water from the river, they have pumps in their houses.

By what I have just said, I do not mean to denigrate these useful inventions which do a lot of our work. Nor do I mean to imply that they do not satisfy our needs. But I simply wanted to show that men are the ones who started to push us out of work, and that if we were to edge them out today, we would only be doing what they have already done to us.

The question of monopolizing the workplace comes down to individual freedom. One man wishes to become a doctor, another a merchant. Is it right to tell a doctor he must quit his profession and become a merchant or vice versa? No. Each has the freedom to do as he wishes. Since male inventors and workers have taken away a lot of our work, should we waste our time in idleness or seek other work to occupy us? Of course, we should do the latter. Work at home now does not occupy more than half the day. We must pursue an education in order to occupy the other half of the day, but that is what men wish to prevent us from doing under the pretext of taking their jobs away. Obviously, I am not urging women to neglect their home and children to go out and become lawyers or judges or railway engineers. But if any of us wish to work in such professions, our personal freedom should not be infringed. It might be argued that pregnancy causes women to leave work, but there are unmarried women, others who are barren or have lost their husbands or are widowed or divorced, or those whose husbands need their help in supporting the family. It is not right that they should be forced into lowly jobs. These women might like to become teachers or doctors with the same academic qualifications. Is it just to prevent women from doing what they believe is good for themselves and their support? If pregnancy impedes work outside the house, it also impedes work inside the house. Furthermore, how many able-bodied men have not become sick from time to time and have had to stop work?

Men say to us categorically, "You women have been created for the house and we have been created to be breadwinners." Is this a God-given dictate? How are we to know this, since no holy book has spelled it out? Political economy calls for a division of labor, but if women enter the learned professions it does not upset the system. The division of labor is merely a human creation. We still witness people like the Nubians whose men sew clothes for themselves and the household, while the women work in the fields. Some women even climb palm trees to harvest the dates. Women in villages in both Upper and Lower Egypt help their men till the land and plant crops. Some women do the fertilizing, haul crops, lead animals, draw water for irrigation, and other chores. You may have observed that women in the villages work as hard as the strongest men, and we see that their children are strong and healthy.

Specialized work for each sex is a matter of convention. It is not mandatory. We women are now unable to do hard work because we have not been accustomed to it. If the city woman had not been prevented from doing hard work, she would have been as strong as the man. Isn't the country woman like her city sister? Why then is the former in better health and stronger than the latter? Do you have any doubt that a woman from Minufiya [a town in the Egyptian Delta] would be able to beat the strongest man from al-Ghuriya [a section of Cairo] in a wrestling match? If men say to us that we have been created weak, we say to them, "No, it is you who made us weak through the path you made us follow." After long centuries of enslavement by men, our minds rusted and our bodies weakened. Is it right that they accuse us of being created weaker than them in mind and body? Women may not have to their credit great inventions, but women have excelled in learning and the arts and politics. Some have exceeded men in courage and valor, such as Khawla bint al-Azwar al-Kindi [a companion of the Prophet, died circa 655], who impressed 'Umar ibn al-Khattab [second caliph, 634–644] with her bravery and skill in fighting when she went to Syria to free her brother held captive by the Byzantines. Joan of Arc [circa 1412–1431], who led the French army after its defeat by the English, encouraged the French to continue fighting and valiantly waged war against those who fought her nation. I am not giving examples of women who became queens and were adept in politics such as Catherine, Queen of Russia [reigned 1762–1796]; Isabel, Queen of Spain [reigned 1474–1504]; Elizabeth, Queen of England [reigned 1558–1603]; Cleopatra [queen of Egypt, reigned 51–30 B.C.]; Shajarat al-Durr, the mother of Turan Shah [reigned 1249], who governed Egypt [1250–1257]. Our opponents may say that their rule was carried out by their ministers, who are men, but while that might be true under constitutional rule, it is not true under absolute monarchies.

When someone says to us, "That's enough education," it discourages us and pushes us backward. We are still new at educating our daughters. While there is no fear now of our competing with men, because we are still in the first stage of education and our Oriental habits still do not allow us to pursue much study, men can rest assured in their jobs. As long as they see seats in the schools of law, engineering, medicine, and at university unoccupied by us, men can relax, because what they fear is distant. If one of us shows eagerness to complete her education in one of these schools, I am sure she will not be given a job. She is doing that to satisfy her desire for learning or for recognition. As long as we do not work in law or become employed by the government, would our only distraction from raising children be reading a book or writing a letter? I think that is impossible. No matter how much a mother has been educated, or in whatever profession she works, this would not cause her to forget her children nor to lose her maternal instinct. On the contrary, the more enlightened she becomes, the more aware she is of her responsibilities. Haven't you seen ignorant women and peasant women ignore their crying child for hours? Were these women also occupied in preparing legal cases or in reading and writing?

Nothing irritates me more than when men claim they do not wish us to work because they wish to spare us the burden. We do not want condescension, we want respect. They should replace the first with the second.

Men blame any shortcomings we may have on our education, but in fact our upbringing is to blame. Learning and upbringing are two separate things—only in religion are the two connected. This is demonstrated by the fact that many men and women who are well educated are lacking in morals. Some people think that good upbringing means kissing the hands of women and standing with arms properly crossed. Good upbringing means helping people respect themselves and others. Education has not spoiled the morals of our girls, but poor upbringing, which is the duty of the home, not the school, has done this. We have to redouble our efforts to reform ourselves and the young. This cannot happen in a minute as some might think. It is unfair to put the blame on the schools. The problem lies with the family. We must improve this situation.

One of our shortcomings is our reluctance to take advice from each other. When someone says something, jealousy and scorn usually come into play. We also are too quick to ridicule and criticize each other over nothing, and we are vain and arrogant.

Men criticize the way we dress in the street. They have a point, because we have exceeded the bounds of custom and propriety. We claim we are veiling, but we are neither properly covered nor unveiled. I do not advocate a return to the veils of our grandmothers, because it can rightly be called being buried alive, not *hijab*, correct covering. The woman used to spend her whole life within the walls of her house, not going out into the street except when she was carried to her grave. I do not, on the other hand, advocate unveiling, like Europeans, and mixing with men, because they are harmful to us.

Nowadays the lower half of our attire is a skirt that does not conform to our standards of modesty (*hijab*), while the upper half—like age, the more it advances, the more it is shortened. Our former garment was one piece. When the woman wrapped herself in it, her figure was totally hidden. The wrap shrunk little by little, but it was still wide enough to conceal the whole body. Then we artfully began to shrink the waist and lower the neck and finally two sleeves were added and the garment clung to the back and was worn only with a corset. We tied back our headgear so that more than half the head, including the ears, was visible and the flowers and ribbons ornamenting the hair could be seen. Finally, the face veil became more transparent than an infant's heart. The purpose of the *izar* [long outer garment] is to cover the body as well as our dress and jewelry underneath, which God has commanded us not to display. [Qur'an, Sura 24, Verse 31] Does our present *izar*, which has virtually become a "dress" showing the bosom, waist, and derriere, conform with this precept? Moreover, some women have started wearing it in colors—blue, brown, and red. In my opinion, we should call it a dress with a clown's cap, which in fact it is. I think going out without it is more modest, because at least eyes are not attracted to it.

*Imam*s [religious leaders] have differed on the question of *hijab*. If the get-ups of some women are meant to be a way to leave the home without the *izar*, it would be all right if they unveiled their faces but covered their hair and their bodies. I believe the best practice for outdoors is to cover the head with a scarf and the body with a dress of the kind Europeans call *cache poussière*, a dust coat, to cover the body right down to the heels, and with sleeves long enough to reach the wrist. This is being done now in Istanbul, as I am told, when Turkish women go out to neigh-borhood shops. But who will guarantee that we will not shorten it and tighten it until we transform it into another dress? In that instance, the road to reform would narrow in front of us.

If we had been raised from childhood to go unveiled, and if our men were ready for it, I would approve of unveiling for those who want it. But the nation is not ready for it now. Some of our prudent women do not fear to mix with men, but we have to place limits on those who are less prudent, because we are quick to imitate and seldom find our authenticity in the veil. Don't you see that diamond tiaras were originally meant for queens and princesses, and now they are worn by singers and dancers?

The way we wear the *izar* now imitates the dress of Europeans, but we have outdone them in display (*tabarruj*). The European woman wears the simplest dress she has when she is outside, and wears whatever she wishes at home or when invited to soirées. But our women are just the opposite. In front of her husband she wears a simple tunic, and when she goes out she wears her best clothes, loads herself down with jewelry, and pours bottles of perfume on herself . . . Not only this, but she makes a wall out of her face, a wall that she paints various colors. She walks swaying like bamboo in a way that entices passersby, or at least they pretend to be enticed. I am sure that most of these showy women do this without bad intentions, but how can the onlooker understand good intentions when appearances do not indicate it?

Veiling should not prevent us from breathing fresh air or going out to buy what we need if no one can buy it for us. It must not prevent us from gaining an education, nor cause our health to deteriorate. When we have finished our work and feel restless, and if our house does not have a spacious garden, why shouldn't we go to the outskirts of the city and take the fresh air that God has created for everyone, and not just put in boxes exclusively for men? But we should be prudent and not take promenades alone, and we should avoid gossip. We should not saunter moving our heads right and left. If my father or husband will not choose clothes I like and bring them to the house, why can't he take me with him to select what I need, or let me buy what I want?

If I cannot find anyone but a man to teach me, should I opt for ignorance or for unveiling in front of that man, along with my sisters who are being educated? Nothing would force me to unveil in the presence of the teacher. I can remain veiled and still benefit from the teacher. Are we better in Islam than Sayyida Nafisa [saintly scholar, 762–824] and Sayyida Sukayna [bint al-Husayn, great-granddaughter of the Prophet, died 736]—God's blessings be upon them—who used to gather with *'ulama'* [religious scholars] and poets. If illness causes me to consult a doctor, and there is no woman doctor, should I abandon myself to sickness, which might be light but could become complicated through neglect, or should I seek help from a doctor who could cure me?

The imprisonment in the home of the Egyptian woman of the past is detrimental, while the current freedom of the Europeans is excessive. I cannot find a better model than today's Turkish woman. She falls between the two extremes and does not violate what Islam prescribes. She is a good example of decorum and modesty.

I have heard that some of our high officials are teaching their girls European dancing and acting. I consider both despicable—a detestable crossing of boundaries and a blind imitation of Europeans. Customs should not be abandoned except when they are harmful. European customs should not be taken up by Egyptians except when they are appropriate and practical. What good is there for us in women and men holding each other's waists dancing, or daughters appearing on stage before audiences acting with bare bosoms in love scenes? This is contrary to Islam, and a moral threat we must fight as much as we can. We must show our disdain for the few Muslim women who do these things, who otherwise would be encouraged by our silence to contaminate others.

On the subject of customs and veiling, I would like to remind you of something that causes us great unhappiness—the question of engagement and marriage. Most sensible people in Egypt believe it is necessary for fiancés to meet and speak with each other before their marriage. It is wise, and the Prophet himself, peace be upon him and his followers, did not do otherwise. It is a practice in all nations, including Egypt, except among city people. Some people advocate the European practice of allowing the engaged pair to get together for a period of time so that they can come to know each other, but I am opposed to this and am convinced this is rooted in fallacy. The result of this getting together is that they would come to love each other, but when someone loves another, that person does not see the faults of that person and would not be able to evaluate that person's morals. The two get

married on the basis of false love and without direction, and soon they start to quarrel and the harmony evaporates. In my view, the two people should see each other and speak together after their engagement and before signing the marriage contract. The woman should be accompanied by her father, or an uncle or a brother, and she should wear simple clothing. Some might protest that one or two or more meetings is not enough for the two persons to get to know each other's character, but it is enough to tell if they are attracted to each other. However, anyone with good intuition can detect a person's moral character in the eyes and in movements and repose and sense if a person is false, reckless, and the like. As for a person's past and other things, one should investigate by talking with acquaintances, neighbors, servants, and others. If we are afraid that immoral young men would use this opportunity to see young women without intending marriage, her guardian should probe the behavior of the man to ascertain how serious he is before allowing him to see his daughter or the young woman for whom he is responsible. What is the good of education if one cannot abandon a custom that is not rooted in religion, and that is harmful. We have all seen family happiness destroyed because of this old betrothal practice.

By not allowing men to see their prospective wives following their engagement, we cause Egyptian men to seek European women in marriage. They marry European servants and working-class women, thinking they would be happy with them rather than daughters of *pasha*s and *bey*s [high officials and nobles] hidden away in "a box of chance." If we do not solve this problem, we shall become subject to occupation by women of the West. We shall suffer double occupation, one by men and the other by women. The second will be worse than the first, because the first occurred against our will, but we shall have invited the second by our own actions. It is not improbable, as well, that these wives will bring their fathers, brothers, cousins, and friends to live near them, and they would close the doors of work in front of our men. Most Egyptian men who have married European women suffer from the foreign habits and extravagance of their wives. The European woman thinks she is of a superior race to the Egyptian and bosses her husband around after marriage. When the European woman marries an Egyptian, she becomes a spendthrift, while she would be thrifty if she were married to a Westerner.

If the man thinks the upper-class Egyptian wife is deficient and lacking in what her Western sister has, why doesn't the husband gently guide his wife? Husband and wife should do their utmost to please each other. When our young men go to Europe to study modern sciences, it should be to the benefit, not the detriment, of Egypt. As these men get an education and profit themselves, they should also bring benefit to their compatriots. They should bring to their country that which will profit it and dispense with whatever is foreign, as much as possible. If a national manufacturer of silk visits the factories of Europe and admires their efficiency, he should buy machinery that would do work rapidly, rather than introduce the same European-made product, because if he does he will endanger his own good product.

If we pursue everything Western we shall destroy our own civilization, and a nation that has lost its civilization grows weak and vanishes. Our youth claim that they bring European women home because they find them more sophisticated than Egyptian women. By the same token, they should bring European students and workers to Egypt because they are superior to our own. The reasoning is the same. What would be the result if this happens? If an Egyptian wife travels to Europe and sees the children there with better complexions and more beautiful than children in Egypt, would it be right that she would leave her children and replace them with Western children, or would she do her best to make them beautiful and make them resemble as much as possible that which she admired in those other children? If the lowliest Western woman marrying an Egyptian is disowned by her family, shall we be content with her when she also takes the place of one of our best women, and the husband becomes an example for other young men? I am the first to admire the activities of the Western woman, and her courage, and I am the first to respect those among them who deserve respect, but respect for others should not make us overlook the good of the nation. Public interest is above admiration. In many of our ways we follow the views of our men. Let them show us what they want, We are ready to follow their views, on condition that their views do not do injustice to us nor trespass on our rights.

Our beliefs and actions have been a great cause of the lesser respect that men accord us. How can a sensible man respect a woman who believes in magic, superstition, and the blessing of the dead, and who allows women peddlers and washerwomen, or even devils, to have authority over her? Can he respect a woman who speaks only about the clothes of her neighbor and the jewelry of her friend and the furniture of a bride? This is added to the notion imprinted in a man's mind that woman is weaker and less intelligent than he is. If we fail to do something about this, it means we think our condition is satisfactory. Is our condition satisfactory? If it is not, how can we better it in the eyes of men? Good upbringing and sound education would elevate us in the eyes of men. We should get a sound education, not merely acquire the trappings of a foreign language and rudiments of music. Our education should also include home management, health care, and child care. If we eliminate immodest behavior on the street and prove to our husbands through good behavior and fulfilment of duties that we are human beings with feelings, no less human than they are, and we do not allow them under any condition to hurt our feelings or fail to respect us—if we do all this, how can a just man despise us? As for the unjust man, it would have been better for us not to accept marriage to him.

We shall advance when we give up idleness. The work of most of us at home is lounging on cushions all day or going out to visit other women. How does the woman who knows how to read occupy her leisure time? Only in reading novels. Has she read books about health, or books through which she can profit herself and others? Being given over to idleness or luxury has given us weak constitutions and pale complexions. We have to find work to do at home. At a first glance, one can see that the working classes have better health and more energy and more intelligent children. The children of the middle and lower classes are, almost all of them, in good health and have a strong constitution, while most of the children of the elite are sick or frail and prone to illness, despite the care lavished on them by their parents. On the other hand, lower-class children are greatly neglected by their parents. Work causes poisons to be eliminated from the blood and strengthens the muscles and gives energy.

Now I shall turn to the path we should follow. If I had the right to legislate, I would decree:

1. Teaching girls the Qur'an and the correct *sunna* [practice of the Prophet].
2. Providing primary and secondary school education for girls, and compulsory preparatory school education for all.

3. Instructing girls on the theory and practice of home economics, health, first aid, and childcare.
4. Setting a quota for females in medicine and education so they can serve the women of Egypt.
5. Allowing women to study any other advanced subjects they wish without restriction.
6. Bringing up girls from infancy stressing patience, honesty, work, and other virtues.
7. Adhering to the *shari'a* [Islamic law] concerning betrothal and marriage, and not permitting any woman and man to marry without first meeting each other in the presence of the father or male relative of the bride.
8. Adopting the veil and outdoor dress of the Turkish women of Istanbul.
9. Maintaining the best interests of the country and dispensing with foreign goods and people as much as possible.
10. Making it incumbent upon our brothers, the men of Egypt, to implement this program.

Renewal, Renewing, and Renewers

Muhammad Rashid Rida (Lebanon-Egypt, 1865–1935) was a prolific writer and one of the most important figures in Islamic modernism. Born in Tripoli, Rida attended a school established by *Shaykh* Husayn al-Jisr (Lebanon, 1845–1909), who believed in the need to combine religious and modern education. Rida therefore acquired a fair knowledge of modern sciences and European languages, while studying also the works of Abu Hamid al-Ghazzali (1058–1111) and Ibn Taymiyya (1263–1328), which reinforced his reformist and antimystical tendencies. Rida was greatly influenced by the reformist message of Sayyid Jamal al-Din al-Afghani (chapter 11) and Muhammad 'Abduh (chapter 3), and he moved to Egypt in 1897 to join 'Abduh, becoming one of 'Abduh's closest disciples and his biographer. Rida's monthly periodical, *al-Manar* (*The Beacon*), which he published from 1898 to 1935, was widely read and highly influential, disseminating the ideas of Islamic reform throughout the Islamic world. Like Afghani and 'Abduh, Rida believed in the compatibility of Islam and reason, science, and modernity. He advocated return to the original sources of Islam and the reinterpretation of the Qur'an to meet modern demands. Yet Rida was critical of some of 'Abduh's disciples who took modernist ideas to secular and liberal conclusions. He rejected the growing attempts to subordinate Islam to modernity and Westernization and in his later years tilted toward religious conservatism. The speech translated here, from late in his life, reflects Rida's vision of Islamic renewal and his concerns about the increased secularization of Muslim society.[1]

Part I

This is a lecture the publisher of this periodical [*al-Manar*, or *The Beacon*] delivered at the Royal Institute of Geography at the invitation of the Society of the Oriental League on a Ramadan night in the year 1348 [early 1930]. A large audience of scholars, writers, students of al-Azhar [University], outstanding students of the high schools, and virtuous women attended it, as well as some eminent European Orientalists. They were asked for their opinion after delivering it and attested to its moderation.

In the Name of God, the Beneficent, the Merciful

The Society of the Oriental League has entrusted me to deliver a lecture tonight on the issue of "Renewal, Renewing, and Renewers." My colleague in its board of directors, Doctor Mansur Fahmi [1886–1959], has kindly mentioned its title to you. I appeal to you to overlook and forgive any shortcoming. I begin with an introduction of the topic and what needs to be explained and examined.

Muhammad Rashid Rida, "al-Tajdid wa al-tajaddud wa al-mujaddidun" (Renewal, Renewing, and Renewers), *al-Manar* (*The Beacon*), Cairo, Egypt, volume 31, number 10, July 1931, pp. 770–777; volume 32, number 1, October 1931, pp. 49–60; volume 32, number 3, March 1932, pp. 226–231. Translation from Arabic and introduction by Emad Eldin Shahin.

1. Charles C. Adams, *Islam and Modernism in Egypt: A Study of the Modern Reform Movement Inaugurated by*

Muhammad 'Abduh (London: Oxford University Press, 1933); Shakib Arslan, *Al-Sayyid Rashid Rida wa ikha' arba'ina sana* (*Rashid Rida and Forty Years of Fraternity*) (Damascus, Syria: Matba'at Ibn Zaydun, 1937); Albert Hourani, *Arabic Thought in the Liberal Age: 1798–1939* (London: Oxford University Press, 1970), pp. 222–244; Emad Eldin Shahin, *Through Muslim Eyes: M. Rashid Rida and the West* (Herndon, Va.: International Institute of Islamic Thought, 1993).

Introductory Note on Our Need for Renewal in All Aspects

In a time that is afflicted by ideological, intellectual, political, Communist, and Bolshevik upheavals; in a time that is strained by religious, literary, and social chaos; in a time that is threatened by women's revolution, the violation of marital vows, the disintegration of the family, and the bonds of kinship; in a time in which heresy and unfettered promiscuity have erupted, as well as attacks on the nation's religion, language, and values, and its customs, dress, and origins, nothing remains stable to raise our youths and teach them respect.

In such a time, which I have described briefly, and which you know even better, the concepts of renewal, renewing, and renewers have become widely spread amongst us. Truly, we are in a dire need for renewal and renewers. Anything that could preserve our national character and religious heritage, and promote us in the paths of civic advancement has been revoked and corroded. All of our historical origins, the true religion, our blossoming civilization, and great empire, we have worn out and depreciated, even abandoned and forgotten. In our attempts to acquire the novel and borrow the modern we have only clung to the fringes and have never been able to reproduce it fully. What we have of the old and the modern is a shell of imitation, like the shell of an almond or a walnut that lies under the outer wooden layer; it is useless in itself and cannot preserve the core.

If our al-Azhar and religious institutions are in need of reform to renew the guidance of religion, our public and private schools are in even greater need of reform to renew our civilization, regain our independence, and fulfill all our interests. The corruption of education and socialization in them includes two dimensions: positive and negative. Our complaint against defects in the religious institutions is almost entirely negative, and we will explain the harm later. People of vision and understanding in this nation complain about both and propose one reform after the other.

We need an independent renewal like that of Japan to promote our economic, military, and political interests and develop our agricultural, industrial, and commercial wealth. With this renewal we shall become a dignified *umma* [Islamic community] and a strong state, while preserving our nation's religion, culture, laws, and language, and its national character of dress, good traditions, and values. [There is] no need for an imitative renewal like that of the Ottoman state, which ended in the disintegration of its vast sultanate, then in its termination and eradication from the world geographic atlas. Nor [do we need] a renewal like that of the Egyptian state, which started independently during the reign of Muhammad 'Ali the Great [ruler of Egypt, 1805–1849], then turned to imitation and ended with occupation and the loss of independence. If it had adhered to its initial plan, Egypt would have become a great sultanate consisting of the eastern part of Africa and the western part of Asia. It would have restored the glory of Arab civilization, and would have been charged with the leadership of the Muslim *umma*. It is still qualified to do so. All that it needs is to prepare, to exert the necessary efforts, to seek this goal when the time is ripe, and to achieve it with a worthy leader. On the throne today there is a king [Fu'ad, reigned 1922–1936] who demonstrates the willingness to do so, as everyone knows.

We need this glorious renewal, one that combines the modern and the old. We need renewers of civilization, like Muhammad 'Ali the Great, and renewers of knowledge and wisdom, such as Muhammad 'Abduh [Egyptian scholar, 1849–1905; see chapter 3] and Jamal al-Din [al-Afghani, Iranian pan-Islamic activist, 1838–1897; see chapter 11]—not the renewal of heresy and promiscuity, laxity and profligacy, espousing depravity in the name of the liberal arts [literally "naked arts"] and discouraging virtue under the pretext of freedom, liberation of the Oriental woman, and imitation of Western civilization. All these vices are old, not new, as known to those who are familiar with the history of Athens and Rome and other capitals of the ancient peoples. They weakened their states and eroded their independence. "And when We destroy a population, We send Our command to (warn) its people living a life of ease; and when they disobey, the sentence against them is justified, and We destroy them utterly." [Qur'an, Sura 17, Verse 16] [This means:] We order them with obedience and virtue, but they defied our order and pursued disobedience and depravity, preferring their own lust over the public interest. Therefore they deserved our statement, "Verily We shall annihilate these wicked people"; [Sura 14, Verse 13] our statement, "We would never have destroyed cities if their inhabitants were not given to wickedness"; [Sura 28, Verse 59] our statement, "Shall any perish but the ungodly?"; [Sura 46, Verse 35] our statement, "Your Lord would not surely destroy communities so long as the people are righteous." [Sura 11, Verse 117] This means that He [God] will not destroy them because of transgression on His part, when they are righteous in their deeds.

The modernizing reforms of Muhammad 'Ali the Great have become known, and the religious, political, and social reform of 'Abduh and Afghani are no longer unknown. His Majesty, seated on the throne of Muhammad 'Ali, as well as the princes and the nobility of Muhammad 'Ali's family, are the strongest basis for the military and civilizational renewal of the nation and the state, while preserving the nation's components and character, if the nation so requests. Muhammad 'Ali's folded turban, his wide garment, the garb of his officials and that of the students on his scientific missions [to Europe], did not preclude them from engaging in modernization, reviving the sciences, and achieving glorious accomplishments. But Amanullah Khan [ruler of Afghanistan, 1919–1929] lost his throne and shed the blood of his people in his attempts at imitative renewal by donning the [European] hat, adorning his wife, and shaving the beards of his statesmen!

Jamal al-Din [al-Afghani] and Muhammad 'Abduh have [formed] a scientific, rational, and reformist group, capable of following their footsteps and proceeding with their reforms insofar as the *umma* is willing to respond to them. The *umma* has seen the brilliance of one of them in political leadership,[2] which was inconceivable before [the *umma*] became ready to rise up with him and acknowledge his stature. Nonetheless, destructive individuals have assumed the leadership of renewal and monopolized the title of renewers. They urge the nation to abandon the guidance of religion, take off the apparel of virtue, take pride in the donning of the hat, allow the mixture of women and men in dancing [halls], swimming, seclusion, and travel, permit drinking and all types of sinfulness that follow. They criticize woman, who makes it her utmost concern in life to prepare herself to perform well what God has created her for, distinguishing her over man: that is, to be a good and virtuous spouse, an affectionate and educating mother, and an organized and frugal head of the household. They call the household her prison, even if it is like a garden palace, and the husband her jailer, even if he considers her as an angel in goodly pavilions. They entice her to disobey and disregard him, to allow whomever she pleases to enter his home, and to enter the home of whoever she likes without [her husband's] permission and approval. They also tempt her with positions in the government and attorneys' offices, and urge her not to consider such impediments as the burdens of pregnancy and labor, breast-feeding and nursing. Some even say that she is fit for wars and fighting, leading land and naval armies, marine and air fleets. [. . .]

They also entice youths with heresy and praise the pursuit of lust, trying to turn them and women into soldiers blindly obedient to their leaders. Advice and preaching are useless once they have deviated from religion. No advice can be heard during the pursuit of moral chaos and whims. It is quite sufficient [proof] of moral degradation and intellectual decay to concede [to their claim] that the old is repulsive and must be abandoned and despised just because it is old, and to deride those who would preserve [the past] by calling them reactionary.

A horde of heretics in this great country are at present attempting to assume this honorable title [of renewer]. None of them deserves this title, not for excellence in knowledge or wisdom, guidance or virtue, or in revealing unknown truths; not for initiating practices useful to the *umma* in preserving its true nature, developing its wealth, or restoring its glory. (I seek forgiveness from God because restoring the nation's glory, with its conquests and civilization, is considered by them as reactionary, and they despise those who call for that.)

All their wares in this marketplace are but chatter, sophistry, audacity in mixing right with wrong, and insolence in criticizing their opponents or critics. They engage in flagrant slander, not correct evidence, for truth has no sanctity for them, and they praise the extremist Turks who have tossed Islam behind them, destroying all the cornerstones of freedom: freedom of religion, opinion, speech, writing, dress, and work—[the very freedoms] that are glorified by the leaders of knowledge and modern civilization whom they claim to be following. Had it not been for the excessiveness of the Egyptian government, these pretenders would not have dared to voice these heretic calls to destroy [the government's] religion, values, and traditions. Their praise of the excessiveness of the Turkish heretics is not novel. It began with an earlier generation, and its product in

2. Sa'd Pasha Zaghlul [Egyptian nationalist leader, 1857–1927].

this generation has been the extinction of the Ottoman sultanate, which was the greatest sultanate in Europe, Asia, and Africa. Nothing remained of it except for a small, poor republic, less in number, affluence, knowledge, and civilization than the kingdom of Egypt, which was once a province of this sultanate. Now [Turks] want [Egypt] to follow [the Turkish state's] footsteps—its heresy and disavowal of the guidance of religion—so that [Egypt] will not be able to replace [Turkey] in what it is now qualified to do, that is, assume the leadership of 400 million Muslims [around the world].

When similarly false renewers deceived Amanullah Khan, and he tried to imitate the present Turkish state, they showered him with praise for unveiling women and forcing his people to wear hats. His heretical renewal ignited fires of revolution in his country against him and his government. He was forced to flee and abdicate his rule. There has been no real renewal in Afghanistan, no inclination for [building] schools, a military system, industry, and the like, though this process started in the last century during the reign of 'Abd al-Rahman [Khan, reigned 1880–1901].

Since the last century, the Turks have embarked on all the earthly renewal that the heretics called for. Further, Islam has neither prevented the evils of renewal, which it condemns, nor [opposed] the positive aspects, which it requires. [The Turks] have not pursued an independent path of renewal, like Japan, which preserved its religious and national character. They were imitators, and, therefore, they clashed with the imitators among the clerical scholars. They should have combined religious renewal and earthly renewal, the same way Europe has done with religious reformation and modernization.

Egypt preceded the Turks in this earthly renewal. The clerical scholars neither opposed nor helped [the process,] because renewal was carried out by one side. Had it been carried out by both sides, it would have been accomplished in a short time, as I will explain later.

The false renewers here do not consider existing conditions, because they imitate the heretics of Europe in their hostility to religious scholars. This blind imitation has made them disincline [people from religion], casting doubt on the doctrines of religion, criticizing its rules and regulations, undermining its scholars, claiming that science and philosophy have annulled it, accusing its *'ulama'* [religious scholars]

of being an insurmountable obstacle to the progress of the *umma*, an obstacle that must be removed just as dirt is removed from the road. Had they called for practical reform in the name of renewal, and then found resistance from religious scholars, they would have been justified.

The Alleged Renewal of the Heretics Constitutes a New Division of the Nation

This so-called renewal is almost becoming a real renewal of divisive strife. This could be worse than the divisions of ethnic and national extremisms and of political parties. The presence of a new party appears to complete the roster of divisions. [This party,] in imitation of the heretics of Europe and its liberals, is hostile to religion and despises the devout, who constitute the majority of the nation. *'Ulama'*, orators, and writers urge people to respond to this party, to declare their hostility and resistance to it. Leaders and elites are forced to call upon the government to prevent members of this party from pronouncing evil. This took place precisely as a result of the negative influence of someone who declared unheard-of rights for women at the University of Egypt.[3] Similarly, someone at the American University [in Cairo], in a lecture which he published and distributed, argued the necessity of equality between men and women, even in divorce and inheritance.[4] I heard the Friday prayer speaker, in the mosque where I pray, pity Islam and urge the fasting worshipers to defend the Qur'an, which its enemies scorned and accused of transgressions against women, and so on, after some of the notables[5] renounced that lecture and the newspapers unanimously criticized such nonsense.

This sort of strife occurred in Europe during the Middle Ages, which were the worst centuries for Europeans. There was a dark sedition, during which much blood was shed in the conflict between the freedom of knowledge and government on the one hand, and the authority of religion and church on the other. Recently, a similar situation took place in Afghani

---

3. Mr. Mahmud 'Azmi [1889–1954], whom we defeated in debate at the University, to judge by the support of the audience and his own admission.

4. Doctor Fakhri Faraj Mikhail al-Qibti.

5. His Highness 'Umar Pasha Tusun [1872–1944].

stan. However, I see the condition of Egypt as different from that of Europe during these centuries and that of present-day Afghans. We must repel this sedition before it spreads, to prevent this conflict before it escalates. This is exactly what I seek with this lecture. I see it as the greatest task that I can perform before the Society of the Oriental League, for the sake of dear Egypt and the entire Orient. [. . .]

Part 2

All of creation is new. The absolute original is the Creator, most glorified and exalted. Among the created, new and old are relative. Every old creature was once new, and every new one will become old. As a folk proverb says: "Whoever does not have a past will not have a future." This is a wise proverb that the knowledgeable may understand in senses that the common people cannot approach.

Renewal and renewing of the universe are among the divine general laws, generating order in our world and change and transformation in the phase of our existence. They operate [today] just as they operated for our parents and grandparents. "No change will thou find in God's way (of dealing): No turning off wilt thou find in God's way (of dealing)." [Qur'an, Sura 35, Verse 43]. [. . .]

What I stated in the introduction to a previous lecture, on coeducational schools, may be appropriate to state here as a summary:

> Renewing is a law of social association; renewal is part of nature and habit. It is counterweighed by the preservation of the old. Each has its place. There is no contradiction or opposition between them, provided that each is put in its place with no neglect or excess. [. . .]

> Part of renewal in human action is achieved by the instinct of independence, which is opposite of imitation, and the tendency for discovery and invention. Without them, humans would be similar to flocks of birds; their dwellings would not be more advanced than bee hives and ant hills.

Types of Renewal and Their Necessity

Social, political, civic, and religious renewal is necessary for human societies, in accordance with their nature and level of readiness. They enable societies to progress through the stages of civilization and ascend on the paths of science and knowledge. Even divine religion, which is based on the revelation of the wise God, with His grace, to selected creatures whose holy souls He prepared to receive it, has advanced along with the nature of human societies in their progress from one stage to another, until it was completed by Islam when they reached the stage of maturity and independence. Despite this completion, the narrators of *hadith* [accounts of the Prophet] tell us that [Muhammad,] the Seal of the Prophets, peace be upon them all, said, "God sends to this nation at the beginning of every century someone who renews its religion." Narrated by Abu Da'ud [al-Sijistani, died 889] in his *Sunan* [*Hadith Collection*]; [Muhammad ibn 'Abdullah] al-Hakim [al-Naysaburi, 933–1014] in his *Mustadrak* [*Supplement*]; [Ahmad ibn al-Husayn] al-Bayhaqi [994–1066] in *al-Ma'rifa* [*al-sunan, The Wisdom of the Collected Hadith*], and others from the *hadith* of Abu Hurayra [companion of the Prophet, died 678]. [Jalal al-Din] al-Suyuti [1445–1505] referred in his *al-Jami' al-saghir* [*The Lesser Collection*] to its correctness. The renewal of religion means renewing its guidance, clarifying its truth and certitude, refuting the innovations and extremism that its followers accrue, or their reluctance in upholding it and following its rules in managing the interests of humans and the laws of society and civilization. [. . .] This is the meaning of renewal and renewing, and it leads us [to conclude] that both the new and the old have their place, and it is a matter of ignorance to prefer one over the other in absolute terms. [. . .]

The True and Decisive Statement on New and Old

The true statement on this topic is that humans at all times need both the old and the new. In each there is good and ill, benefit and harm. Some people by nature tilt more to one or the other, in accordance with the nature of things and their type. Rarely is the new preferred, because of its newness, except by children and those women and men who are at their level. Rational and independent people do not shun the old and turn to the new unless there is a reason making it preferable, in accordance with the rule of logic. [. . .] A rational person may prefer the new for a reason related to its usefulness and utility, either in itself or for something outside it, such as the economy, appropriateness, patriotism, and nationalism.

Preferring the National to the Foreign

Preferring all that is national, either new or old, is a cornerstone of economic, political, and literary life in all vibrant nations, particularly the British, who became appalled by the spread of cheap German products in their country. They formed several associations to investigate means of prevention. I inquired in some pharmacies in Berlin and Munich about a French medication I usually carry during travel and keep back home. [. . .] The answer I received was, "It is French, it is French." They never denied its existence, but only gave as the reason [for its unavailability] that it was made by the French, not the Germans. I had to substitute that medication with a German one, a better one for that purpose. Had an Egyptian or Arab medication existed, I would have preferred it.

With this kind of nationalism and patriotism, the peoples of the West, faithful to their kind and devoted to their nation, have advanced. They prefer their own industries, commerce, laws, and other components and characteristics of the nation, over that which belongs to others. They preserve the regulations of the old British judges and their legal decisions more than we maintain the regulations that we believe to have been revealed by God, most exalted, let alone the regulations deduced through *ijtihad* [interpretation] by our leading scholars on the basis of our laws and principles. Our ancestors preceded the foreigners in taking pride in their legislature and other matters in the early years of Islam. An example is what happened between 'Umar [ibn al-Khattab, second caliph, 634–644], may God be pleased with him, and Mu'awiyya [a later caliph, 661–680]. When 'Umar arrived in Syria wearing his patched garment and riding his camel, Mu'awiyya observed: "O, Commander of the Faithful, the people of Syria are accustomed to seeing their rulers in splendid clothes. They do not fear anyone who is simple in attire and appearance." 'Umar responded, "We came to teach them how we rule, not to learn from them how they rule."

Similarly, ['Umar's] instructed his governors in foreign provinces to observe Arab garb. He wrote a letter to his governor in Persia, 'Utba ibn Farqad, forbidding [Muslims] to wear the dress of the Persians and ordering them to preserve their Arab customs. Part of what he said in the letter: "follow your grandfather Ma'add ibn 'Adnan [patriarch of the northern Arab tribes] in his toughness, perseverance, and harsh life style." The Arab descendants of Ma'add are like the Spartans. [. . .] The Arabs were able to preserve their national character in the provinces they conquered, so long as they obeyed these instructions and maintained their character, especially their language and religion. [Other] nations assimilated into them and were Arabized and Islamized. Those who abandoned these features were assimilated into other peoples. The foreigners imitated our ancestors in this respect, particularly the British. The heretical false renewers try to convince us to abandon all that, even rules of inheritance, in which the British differ from the laws of all other nations, allowing the eldest son to acquire the entire inherited estate of his parents, while the rest of his siblings receive nothing.

The Contempt of the Heretics and Copts for the Muslims in Urging Them to Abandon Their Religion

The contempt of the false renewers for us, the Muslims in this country, has reached such an extent that heretics and Copts have spoken at podiums and schools urging us to abandon our religion and our entire *shari'a*, not just the rules of inheritance. They argue that the government has abandoned the rules of the *shari'a* in such and such cases of the penal code and finances, and that we remained silent and accepted its judgment. Therefore, we must abandon all the rest of God's regulations regarding the personal status code, inheritance, marriage, and divorce. There is no difference for these renewing *muftis* [religious officials] between the two types of regulations. [. . .]

Part 3

In clarifying the need for religious and earthly renewal, and Islam's perspective and encouragement, I need to begin with a brief introduction on the stagnation of the religious scholars and its negative impact on rulers and seekers of political and social reform. [. . .] I include [. . .] statements by two Turks, [the first] by one of the most enlightened scholars of Islam and [the second] by an outspoken proponent of heresy. I then mention a statement of the wise man of the Orient [Afghani] about them.

[The first scholar] is the *Shaykh al-Islam* [chief Ottoman religious official] Musa Kazım [Turkey, 1858–1920; see chapter 23], God bless his soul. In his home in a suburb of Istanbul, he was explaining to me his plan for the reform of the government of Yemen. He formulated all its laws in accordance with the *shari'a*. [He also planned] to establish a unified commercial court to specialize in reviewing the cases related to foreigners and Jews. I suggested to him, "If you agree not to commit yourselves to Hanafi doctrine, I guarantee you that I can deduce from the vast Islamic *shari'a* all the rulings that the sultanate needs and that address the conditions of the present time, and so on." He responded, "I realize that this is possible, but what can we do with the official scholars of *fatwa*s [religious rulings]?"

He means that the Islamic clerical scholars charged with the issuance of official *fatwa*s for the state would oppose [such reforms]. Among the things I learned about them, and about the *Shaykh al-Islam*—who is restricted by them in the issuance of *fatwa*s—is that they do not issue *fatwa*s in accordance with the rules of the [Ottoman] *Mecelle-i Ahkam-ı 'Adliye* [*Compendium of Legal Statutes*, 1876], all of which conforms to *shari'a*, because it contains rules that contradict established statements of Hanafi doctrine. [. . .]

[The second scholar] is Doctor 'Abdullah Bey Cevdet [Turkey, 1869–1932; see chapter 21], editor of a magazine [*İctihad*, or *Rational Interpretation*] that he used to publish in Egypt before the [repromulgation of the Ottoman] Constitution [in 1908], because he was persecuted and not allowed to enter the Ottoman state. He is one of the founders of the Committee of Union and Progress [CUP, which came to power in the Ottoman Empire in 1908].

This man, who publicly declares heresy, helped me in Istanbul with the project of *al-Da'wa wa al-irshad* [Propagation and Guidance, an elite school that Rida established in Egypt in 1912]. He informed me that "if you succeed in this effort and establish an Islamic college, I will volunteer to teach there and deliver my health and science lessons in accordance with your approach in religious reform." I responded, "How is that possible, while you oppose religion?" He explained, "I oppose the religion of the *shaykh*s of Fatih and Sulaymaniyya [historic mosques in Istanbul], because it is impossible for us to progress while we follow the ideas of those people. But the understanding of Rashid [Rida] *Efendi* and *Shaykh* Muhammad 'Abduh of the religion of Islam helps progress and benefits the state. I would be the first to wish to serve Islam under your auspices." [. . .]

The *'ulama'* of Istanbul had a great influence on the nation and the government. The *'ulama'* of Egypt do not enjoy the slightest share of such an influence—how can they be accused of blocking civic progress, and where is this progress? When did they put up such a practical resistance that the government feared [to make reforms]? When I presented the project of *al-Da'wa wa al-irshad* to [Ottoman] Prime Minister Hüseyin Hilmi Pasha [1855–1922], God bless his soul, he told me: "This is a great project and necessary to the state. Its implementation depends on the acceptance of the *'ulama'* and the approval of the Committee of Union and Progress. I will speak to the *Shaykh al-Islam* to convince the scholars, and to [Colonel Mehmed] Sadık Bey [Şehreküştü, 1860–1940] to convince the Central Committee of the CUP. I will do my utmost to persuade them to use their influence on this matter." [General] Mahmud Şevket Pasha [Ottoman prime minister, 1858–1913], God bless his soul, also told me of the influence of the Turkish religious scholars, and then said: "The scholars in my country (Iraq) do not have such an influence. What is their status in Egypt?"

The Statement of Sayyid Jamal al-Din [al-Afghani] on the Turkish Scholars

The statement of al-Sayyid Jamal al-Din [al-Afghani], which I refer to here, and there are similar ones by him regarding the Muslim *'ulama'*, concerns the following incident:

During the time [Jamal al-Din] was at Istanbul, the emperor of Japan [Mutsuhito Meiji, reigned 1867–1912] sent a letter to Sultan Abdülhamid [II, reigned 1876–1909] seeking his friendship and saying that "each one of us is an Oriental king, and it is in our interest and the interests of our people to get acquainted, to establish friendly relations, and to promote cooperation vis-à-vis the Western states and peoples, who view us as one and the same. I see the Western people send missionaries to our country, evangelizing their religion because of the religious freedom we have. I see that you do not do the same. I would like you to send us preachers to evangelize for your religion (Islam), who can serve as an implicit moral link between you and us." The sultan was interested in this letter and ordered the formation of a committee of his advisors in Yıldız Palace for consultation. It included the *Shaykh al-Islam* and the minister of education, the two ministers officially concerned with this issue, Sayyid Jamal al-Din al-Afghani, most qualified in all respects, and others. They met with the sultan at Yıldız Palace and the discussion started. The *Shaykh al-Islam* and the minister of education suggested the formation of a delegation of scholars from the schools of Istanbul to be sent to Japan. Sayyid Jamal al-Din remained silent. The sultan directed his gaze at him and asked his opinion. He said what may be summarized as follows: "Your Majesty, these scholars turn even Muslims away from Islam. How could they be charged with convincing the Japanese to adopt Islam? [My] opinion is to develop a cadre of intelligent persons and provide them with a special education that qualifies them to fulfill this duty in the present age. It might suffice for the time being, for His Majesty to send a courteous letter to the emperor, along with an appropriate gift, mention to him that his suggestion has received the highest approval, and say that you will look into its implementation in a satisfactory manner." The sultan adopted this view, but without implementing the suggestion of special education for Islamic evangelists.

A Conclusion on the Objective behind the Two Renewals

I have mentioned the *hadith* on religious renewal: "God sends to this nation at the beginning of every century someone who renews its religion." The words of this text are [directly] related to our topic. We have explained its meaning at the outset of the lecture. The objective of this *hadith* focuses on the return to the simplicity and guidance of religion as it was in the beginning; to reunify the Muslims around their commonality, prior to disunity and discord; to justify individual *ijtihad*, except where [the revealed text's meaning is] self-evident; and to justify those who engage in *taqlid* [imitation], following the doctrine or the scholar whose knowledge they trust, without a divisive extremism that turns the nation into factions and mutually hostile groups. [. . .] Some of the means for this renewal include the revival of the Arabic language, in vocabulary, writing, and speech; the writing of books in easy modern styles; the spread of education and socialization, according to scientific methods; and the spread of Islamic teachings in the world.

If the nation needs renewal in maintaining its religion, which God has perfected, prohibiting innovation, it is in even more need of renewal in earthly affairs. Its interests differ in accordance to changes in time, place, and the condition of the people. The *shari'a* has taken all that into consideration, as stipulated in the books of *fiqh* [jurisprudence].

There are two kinds of this renewal in this regard. One relates to the public interest and our need for legislation. The Lawgiver [God] has recommended this type of renewal in the statement of the Prophet, may peace be upon him, "He who introduced some good practice in Islam and was followed (by people), he would be assured of reward like the one who followed it, without their rewards being diminished in any respect. And he who introduced some evil practice in Islam that was subsequently followed (by others), he would be required to bear the burden like that of the one who followed this (evil practice), without theirs being diminished in any respect." Narrated by Muslim [ibn al-Hajjaj, died 875] from the *hadith* of Jarir ibn 'Abdullah [companion of the Prophet, died 640]. Among these general practices are the foundation of the principles of useful sciences and arts and the establishment of schools, orphanages, and hospitals. Everyone is equally [responsible] for this renewal: individuals, groups, and governments. Some are particular to government, such as military affairs, on which depend the defense of the country and the protection of the *umma* from aggression.

The legislation connected with this renewal is entrusted in Islam to those in charge and to the group known as *ahl al-hal wa al-'aqd* [the people who loosen and bind]. They approve the legislation on the basis of consultation and the exercise of reason, in issues that are not stipulated as self-evident in God's revelation or the practice of the Prophet, according to recognized criteria. The *shari'a* prohibits *ijtihad* and all human legislation in the presence of a [self-evident] text.

The second type [of renewal in earthly affairs] relates to matters of livelihood, such as agriculture, industry, trade, and the issue of harmless practices. The *shari'a* has left this to the experience of the people. The Prophet, may peace be upon him, said in this regard, "You are more knowledgeable about your earthly affairs." Narrated by Muslim from the *hadith* of Anas [ibn Malik, servant of the Prophet, circa 612–709] and 'A'isha [bint Abi Bakr, wife of the Prophet, circa 614–678], may God be pleased with her. He commented on its meaning: "Whatever concerns the affairs of your religion is referred to me, and whatever relates to your earthly affairs, you are more knowledgeable about." Narrated by Ahmad [ibn Hanbal, 780–855].

In conclusion, legitimate renewal includes all that the *umma* and the state hold dear, such as the sciences, arts, and industries; financial, administrative, and military systems; land, naval, and air installations. All these are considered a collective duty in Islam, and the entire *umma* sins when it neglects them. The *shari'a* does not restrict the *umma* in pursuing them. The only restrictions are to avoid inflicting or generating harm and transgression (for example, exploiting the condition of the financially needy by collecting usurious interest from them), to observe the [jurisprudential] principle according to which "Necessity permits the impermissible," to assess the extent of this necessity, and to follow truth and justice.

Advice

Shaykh al-Amin bin 'Ali Mazrui (Kenya, 1890–1947) was the scion of a long line of religious scholars from the large Mazrui clan, which had immigrated to Mombasa, Kenya, from Oman during the 1700s. In the 1880s and 1890s, Arab colonial power in Kenya and Mombasa was replaced by British rule. Al-Amin sought to explain what appeared to him to be a topsy-turvy world, and to find direction for a future he felt was being lost. He was very aware of the nature of this debate as it was being discussed outside East Africa. He appears to have read the teachings and writings of contemporary authors such as Muhammad 'Abduh (chapter 3) and Rashid Rida (chapter 6). What is especially interesting about al-Amin, however, is the specific construction he gave to the singular historical character of Swahili Islamic society, as well as the localized dilemmas in which it found itself during Mazrui's lifetime. To address these issues, Mazrui wrote two short-lived newspapers in Arabic and Swahili in the early 1930s. Nothing has survived of those journals except for twenty-seven essays that he later collected into a little booklet, from which these excerpts are taken.[1]

How Do We Imitate the Europeans?

All people of the world have their customs and habits which are not like those of other people. This is because of dissimilarities people have in their cities, nations, and religions. And the foundation by which people know their way is their nationality, from which they derive their habits and customs. For this reason intelligent people in every tribe customarily hold fast to these roots and habits and customs because they fear becoming like the blackbird which lost its way and [took to] imitating that of the sparrow, whose identity was lost to him yet who could not become a sparrow, an existence which was neither this nor that.

We must take care that we do not change our customs to those of others who do not get along with us except in an emergency, and then [if we do so, we do so] only for the good, and [if we choose to change

to their ways, we should do so] only in ways that are good and which do not violate our religion.

I say this because every day we see ourselves mimicking whites, and not only in ways that are good and which do not contradict our religion.

We have imitated them in their habits; [it seems] we have only seized upon [things like] drinking wine and dressing as they do. I say [we should follow them only] in their good customs, like their pastimes, their ways of [conducting] meetings, their love of country, their solidarity, and other things like these; [however] in [other] things of ours, it does not benefit us to mimic them.

We also have wanted to follow them in their exertions. What we have observed of their exertions has been in their entertainment like football, golf, music, and dance, not in things like working or studying artisanry as they do. These are not the sorts of things we have taken to: to the contrary, we have left all

Shaykh al-Amin bin 'Ali al-Mazrui, *Uwongozi (Advice)* (Mombasa, Kenya: East African Muslim Welfare Society, 1955), pp. 6–8, 45–48. First published in 1931–1932. Translation from Swahili and introduction by Randall L. Pouwels. Thanks to Professor Thomas Hinnebusch for his valuable help with this translation.

1. Randall L. Pouwels, *Horn and Crescent: Cultural Change and Traditional Islam on the East African Coast, 800–1900* (Cambridge, England: Cambridge University

Press, 1987), pp. 97–124, 201–202; Shaykh Abdallah Salih Farsy, *The Shafi'i Ulama of East Africa, ca. 1830–1970* (Madison, Wisconsin: University of Wisconsin Press, 1989), pp. 120–122; Ahmed I. Salim, "Sheikh al Amin bin Ali al Mazrui: un réformiste moderne au Kenya" (Shaykh al-Amin bin 'Ali al-Mazrui: A Modern Reformist in Kenya), pp. 59–71 in François Constantin, ed., *Les voies de l'Islam en Afrique orientale (The Paths of Islam in East Africa)* (Paris: Éditions Karthala, 1987).

meaningful forms of employment to the Chaga, the Taita, the Kikuyu, and the Kamba.[2] They are the ones who do mechanical and railway work: they are the telephone workers; they are the ones who do radio and electrical work; they are the ones who make an effort to learn the work of lighting and craftsmanship and other modern forms of employment.

We have tried to follow the whites' ideas about knowledge, [the form of which] we have taken to be [merely] a twisting of the tongue when we say "yes,"[3] even learning salutations like "good morning" or "thank you," which are how you greet or thank someone in their language, as if the European language itself is all the knowledge we need. It has gotten so that people think there is no need for knowledge of [practical affairs like] business, agriculture, work, or other things!

Poor people of Mombasa! These days we cannot [even] see the difference between [genuine] knowledge and [mere] language. These casual employees of the Europeans who work as coolies and cooks and "boys," all [of them] speak the language of the whites even more than our own. Are these ones [now] to be taken to be scholars? No, rather as fools who belong to the lowest order [of society].

We have tried to imitate the Europeans in how we expect our women to act to the point that we expect them to be like theirs. We don't consider them to be proper women if they don't cut their hair [as white women do] or wear frocks. Or the knowledge European women have in fixing up their houses and making them comfortable and neat, and rearing their children in a healthy way, and with good customs and manners, and the ability they have in [doing] handy work and crafts and cooking, we have never regarded this twaddle as something that makes them civilized. It is a stinking mess, and [something] to make our women go around in circles.

2. [These ethnic groups were neighbors of the coastal Swahili. When the British made Mombasa the principal port city of their Kenyan colony, thousands of people from the up-country crowded into the city seeking work and the excitement of the new possibilities that the new order seemed to represent. They learned quickly about the new forms of employment and mastered English, the new skills and ideas needed to land jobs in light industry and transport. The Swahili and other Muslims found themselves to be minorities in their own city.—Trans.]

3. ["*Fot-fot* yes" in the original. I am unable to identify this reference.—Trans.]

Praise the Lord! Is it only in bad things that we see ways of following the whites' example? It seems we have become like flies, building only in sores, or like scavenger beetles becoming offended only by a good scent, and made happy by a stench, searching for filth.

I implore you, O Prophet! Show us the truth, and charge us with the vigor to follow it. Show us what is worthless, and arm us with the strength to prevent it.

Advice for Today's Muslims

These quarrels in which Muslims are involved these days reduce them to a contemptuous and humiliating condition that accomplishes nothing for them except to debase their religion, which requires [of them] their best and [demands that they] cleanse themselves of all that is base. Muslims these days are in [such] a state of division that they are their [own worst] enemies. One hardly sees a city anywhere where there are not Muslims, and Muslims among whom there are great differences.

For example, Mombasa has 75,000 people, and among these are many Muslims who are the most humiliated of all peoples. They are poor in learning, poor in wealth, poor even in fearing the people who lead them, poor in everything. One source of great dissension in Mombasa concerns the Banyan community—who number only a few people—and [yet] they have two daily newspapers, while Mombasa Muslims have none. And in the whole of Kenya there exists not one, single [Muslim] newspaper except this wretched little one of ours which is so little. It brings me great sorrow that Goans have their own school, while we have not one school in all our communities [Swahili towns of East Africa] except these Qur'an schools which a seven-year-old child enters and—God forbid!—leaves at a barely mature age, hardly knowing anything except how to read the Qur'an. And [even this] he is hardly able to read properly, nor know its meaning, even that of the *Fatiha* [opening verses of the Qur'an], which he recites all the time in his daily and nighttime prayers. So he finishes at the Qur'an school, and his father takes him and he goes and pushes him into the fire pit of the missionary school where there is great misfortune [for him].

Our advice to today's Muslims is to [encourage them to] build their *madrasa*s [seminaries] to teach their children what is in the *shari'a* [religious law] and what they need to know about life in this world as well. This *madrasa* itself [provides] a stratagem for protecting children from the temptations of the mission school, saves their religiosity, lifts them into the exalted ranks, and teaches them excellent manners and great strength of character. This will [ward off] disgrace and will encourage them to desire better things of themselves, since all Muslims want very much to be respected, as God Almighty showed in the Qur'an.[4] This respect cannot be realized except, first, by opening the way needed to accomplish this, nor is there any other means except through education that combines [matters of] Religion and the World.

This is the true way of advancing Muslims to a condition of pride and sublimation, the reason for lifting them up. But where is the money to build these *madrasa*s? I say the money is not lacking. Rather, all the people require is a plan, [and] then they should resolve to do this with their whole hearts; afterward they ought to make a great effort, so then there will be no problem that the money will be available.

The people of Mombasa number about 75,000, as I have already stated, and many among them are Muslims. We believe that Muslims number about half, and we, that is Arabs and Swahili, number around 12,000. So if we require every person among us to donate three shillings a year, we will collect 36,000 shillings in just one year. This will be sufficient to build the *madrasa*s that we need and to teach our children everything they need to know to benefit them in this world and in the Hereafter.

People suffering misfortune will say that this [plan] will cause them anxieties, but I say this must be and that we can do what is necessary to improve our resolve.

Every day we complain that our education is declining and that it is total nonsense to expect the government to improve it. God forbid, we are stingy with money! Do we think that great education will happen without a little application and with a lot of complaining?

We always want the government to treat us the same as the Indians. [Yet] have we thought even for a day of wanting to do as they do in giving as they do to educate their children? Indians each donate twenty shillings more than the Poll Tax they pay, and they do not see like you that [there is anything wrong in] teaching their children knowledge of the world. So why cannot we hospitable [that is, otherwise generous] people donate three shillings annually so our children can learn about religion and worldly matters too?

This is my plan and I place it before the eyes of our community for consideration. I ask God Almighty to help us to fulfill it.

The Community of Islam

"*Jama'a*" in the Arabic language means something which makes [many] people into one, [all] having a part in a certain matter. Countrymen, for example, are a family which encourages people who live in a particular city to participate in the reconciliation of their community, not in [creating] divisions between tribe and tribe, nor between religion and religion. And [it is the purpose of] the Muslim community to encourage all Muslims to be one family, eliciting harmony from their religion and avoiding harm. Thus it enjoins every Muslim to be a brother to another, not to [create] differences between Indian and Swahili, nor between Arab and Kikuyu, nor between European and Javanese, nor between the damned and the devout, nor between master and servant.

God Almighty has arranged all Muslims in a form of brotherhood by His word, which stated that "Muslims are brothers." And the essence of this brotherhood is in the fundamental objective of achieving unity, the abolition of different factions where every one defends only its own interests and causes harm to others. Confrontation saps people's strength. Even though their intention is to be united, they cling to their differences, each favoring only themselves.

Look at the armies of Islam which set out to conquer the cities of Iran in the time of our lord Abu Bakr [first caliph, reigned 632–634]. They were in four groups: 'Amr ibn al-'Asi [died 663] and his army, Abu 'Ubayda [ibn al-Jarra circa 581–639] and his army, Yazid ibn Abi Sufyan [died 683] and his army, and Shurahbil ibn Hasana [circa 570–639] and his army. No doubt all of these shared one goal, but their enmity was well known. Because of this

---

4. [The meaning is unclear: either that the Qur'an provides evidence of the great things Mazrui desires for Muslims, or that the Qur'an provides the wisdom by which Muslims can achieve great things.—Trans.]

estrangement they were unable to defeat the Iranians until Khalid ibn Walid [died 642] went and brought all four armies together, creating one army under his command, which is when they defeated the enemy.

Likewise, we have seen [how] the armies of the Allies in the Great War [World War I] were afraid of defeating their enemies so long as each country had its armies under its own commanders. But when they joined together under the command of General [Ferdinand] Foche [of France], not many days passed without victory. These [examples] show that tearing at each other does not strengthen people even though they intend to be harmonized.

A function of the Community of Islam is [to see] that all Muslims are like the connecting parts of a body, like the parts of our Lord, the whole thing: and if one [part] is sick, the whole is seized by Wild Cardamom Fever.[5] Furthermore, what is desirable is that it be like this between Muslims, each part [of the community] in respect to every other part. If the Community of Islam becomes this way, it will discourage some from organizing their own [exclusive] bonds, stopping them from bringing harm to others, and leaving [them] only [with] the duty a brother in religion owes another. It will permit them to help their brothers so they might bring about the desired harmony. And when, for example, does a rich person do harm when he tries to help his companion to be a rich man like him? Also, how bad does it appear to be when a person stops himself from rescuing a neighbor from a fearful danger in order that they might be like each other in vigor? Do we think we should distance ourselves from the bigotry of people when they were in the kind of ignorance [that existed] before the Prophet came, and follow what the Prophet told us? Should we not hold fast to our Islamic comradeship, thus saving each other? A Muslim is the brother of a fellow Muslim, just as the Prophet said.

5. [*Matungu* fever is a very painful sickness that is common in East Africa.—Trans.]

Democratic Institutions in South Africa

Abdullah Abdurahman (South Africa, 1870–1940) was the pre-eminent political leader of South Asians in South Africa in the first half of the twentieth century. Abdurahman's paternal grandfather was a former slave who founded a successful business in Cape Town; his father studied theology at al-Azhar in Cairo; Aburahman, by contrast, went to Scotland to study medicine, and established a medical practice on his return to Cape Town in 1895. Abdurahman soon entered politics, helping to found the African People's Organisation and serving as its president from 1905 until his death in 1940. Despite the imposition of suffrage restrictions on nonwhites, Abdurahman was elected to the Cape Town City Council and the Cape Provincial Council, running on a platform of unity among nonwhite peoples and a demand for equal civil and political rights with whites. Abdurahman's speeches rarely referred to Islam, perhaps because many of the South Asians and Africans whom he represented were not Muslim. However, in front of a Muslim audience—as in the speech described here, given to the Young Muslim Debating Society in Durban—he allowed himself passing references that linked his faith with his political beliefs. By the time of this speech, in the mid-1930s, Abdurahman's reformism was already losing favor with younger militants, who espoused communism and secular nationalism.[1]

Dr. A. Abdurahman, M[ember of] P[rovincial] C[ouncil], who arrived in Durban last week as a member of the Coloured Fact Finding Commission, was accorded a public welcome last Sunday morning at the Muslim Institute, Queen Street, under the auspices of the Young Muslim Debating Society. In introducing the speaker, the chairman, Mr. E. H. Ismail, said that the doctor needed no introduction and described him as the father of non-Europeans. Most of them were aware, said the chairman, that the doctor was a member of the Provincial Council and also occupied an important position on the Capetown City Council. He acted as leader to the South African Indian deputation that went to India in 1929. As a leader of the non-Europeans in South Africa he was second to none.

Dr. Abdurahman, who chose as his subject "Democratic Institutions in South Africa," said that it was a most interesting as well as a most difficult subject.

"Democracy," said the learned speaker, "is an ideal which arises from ideas and wishes of the people." As to what was meant by democracy, no two people would give the same answer. Democracy can be described as something in one's mind. The highest aim of any human being was to be happy. There were different conceptions of happiness. For instance, the drunkard regarded it as the height of happiness to get drunk, the religious man spent his time in prayers so that his soul may be saved and he found happiness there, then there was the individual that found happiness in pursuing his vocation.

The Aim of Democracy

It was the aim of democracy that every man in this world should have equal right to pursue happiness, and provided a man did not seek happiness in such a man-

"Dr. Abdurahman on Democracy," *Indian Views*, Durban, South Africa, July 19, 1935, p. 4. Introduction by Charles Kurzman.

1. Mogamed Tasleem Ajam, "Dr Abdullah Abdurahman," *Kronos: Journal of Cape History*, volume 17, 1990, pp. 48–58; Ian Golden, *Making Race: The Politics and Economics of Coloured Identity in South Africa* (Cape Town, South Africa:

Maskew Miller Longman, 1987), pp. 33–40; Gavin Lewis, *Between the Wire and the Wall: A History of South African 'Coloured' Politics* (New York: St. Martin's Press, 1987), pp. 198–204; R. E. Van der Ross, *The Rise and Decline of Apartheid: A Study of Political Movements among the Coloured People of South Africa, 1880–1985* (Cape Town, South Africa: Tafelberg, 1986).

ner as to disturb or injure others, no obstacles should be placed in his way. If a lover of music enjoyed himself by playing music in his own home, there should be nothing preventing him from doing so, but if he went out in the street disturbing others with his music, he should be prevented. The greatest gift that God had given to man was skill. It required skill to follow a trade or profession and it was the greatest sin in the world to prevent a man from exercising his skill by following his trade or vocation.

The Vote and the Franchise

"Democracy had nothing to do with the vote or the franchise," said the doctor. This was something that you can use to put your ideas into practice. The vote was merely an instrument to put your ideals into operation. A man, however, cannot follow all the ideas that pass through his mind. If he did so he would find himself in a lunatic asylum. Democracy meant that we were all equal, and this leads us to our religion, Islam, which also teaches us that we are all equal. God has given us the power of reasoning, which must be developed to its fullest extent. The Prophet of Islam had said that reasoning lighted the torch to heaven. If God made no distinction between man and man, we had no right to do so. And until we are regarded as equal in this country, there is no such thing as a democratic institution. If we study the history of the world, we find that there were no democratic institutions until a few hundred years ago. In a democratic institution a man is free, equal before God and man, and no restrictions are placed on him. It was stated in the American declaration of rights that every man was born free. If you admit this doctrine of everyone being equal, you cannot treat a class of people differentially. Though God had made us all equal, it was also true that he had made us different. There were different races and different colours, but this did not imply that we were not equal. There must be a purpose of God in creating the difference.

Custom and Tradition

While it is true that man is born free in this world, it is also true that there was such a thing as custom and tradition. From its birth, a child's character is molded by its parents, and custom and tradition mold his ideas for him. The tradition we have in South Africa is that the white man inherits certain rights immediately [as] he comes into this world. Not because he has any more intelligence than any one of us, but because of his birth. Immediately [as] you begin to treat a man in a privileged manner irrespective of his intelligence or character, you are departing from the ideals of democracy, and that is what we have here in South Africa. Man, here, is judged by something for which he is not responsible. Because he belongs to a different race, and is of a different colour, he is differentiated against.

The Two Groups

We can divide the population of South Africa into two groups. The privileged classes or the Europeans, who are in a minority, and the vast majority of unprivileged classes known as the non-Europeans. While the former inherit all the privileges of free citizenship, the latter inherit the restrictions and poverty of their parents. We must not expect the European in this country to be a democrat, because he comes out of a mold where the character is molded for him. It is impressed upon the white child to regard himself superior than those of a different colour. It will be years before the democratic ideals are impressed upon the Europeans of South Africa, and as long as we have different groups we shall have no democratic institutions.

Our Present System

The system of government in South Africa today can be compared with the system which prevailed 400 years B.C. They had then a democratic institution, but only for the privileged classes. There are already a number of Europeans who have realized that the system is wrong and unjust. We have the white labour or the civilized labour policy, which reserves skilled labour for the privileged classes. If there was a democratic institution in South Africa, this would not be the case. The privileged classes cannot continue to oppress the different classes forever. The Native is now aspiring for something higher, and the pressure of the privileged classes is becoming greater. As the oppressed classes consolidate themselves and show a united front, they will compel the Europeans to accede to at least some of their demands. We have seen that the group system leads to destruction. By consolidating the Native, the Coloured, and the Indian, we can gain much. The fear of physical force is driving the Boer and the Briton into one people. Why should we not consolidate our forces? We cannot achieve our ideal of democratic institution in a day or a week. We may not see it in our time, but come it must, concluded the doctor.

At the conclusion of the speech questions were invited and satisfactorily answered by the speaker. Mr. A[bdulla] I[smail] Kajee [1896–1947] thanked the doctor for the very interesting lecture and said that he agreed that there should be cooperation between the different groups. Mr. M. S. Badat proposed a vote of thanks, which was carried.

The Principles of Governing in Islam
From the Speech of [Abu Bakr] al-Siddiq

'Abd al-Hamid Ibn Badis (Algeria, 1889–1940) was an Islamic reformer, nationalist leader, and founder of the Association of Algerian Scholars. Ibn Badis was born in Constantine, Algeria, to a prominent Berber family and received religious education. In 1908, he joined the Zaytuna mosque in Tunis, where he was exposed to the reformist ideas of Sayyid Jamal al-Din Afghani (chapter 11) and Muhammad 'Abduh (chapter 3). After graduation, Ibn Badis returned to Algeria in 1913 to devote his career to Islamic reform, education, and nationalism. In response to the alienating policies of the French and the Francophile tendencies of the Algerian "évolués" (assimilationists), Ibn Badis formulated a program that asserted the Arab and Islamic identity of Algerians, stressed Arabic and Islamic education, and prepared Algerians for independence from the French. In addition, he proposed a modernist interpretation of the Qur'an that attributed the decline of Islamic society to mystical practices, intellectual stagnation, disunity, and political despotism. Ibn Badis articulated his views in several books and in his newspapers al-Muntaqid (The Critic) and al-Shihab (The Meteor). In 1931, he established the Association of Algerian Scholars to promote Algerian identity and Islamic reform and to combat the Sufi orders and the assimilationists. The Association opened hundreds of free Arabic and Qur'anic schools, advocated cultural and social reform, and combated practices that it viewed as corrupt. The article presented here reflects Ibn Badis's nonconventional response to the abolition of the Ottoman caliphate, which he held responsible for the repression and injustice of Muslim societies.[1]

When Abu Bakr al-Siddiq (may God be pleased with him) was sworn in as caliph [in the year 632], he ascended the pulpit and addressed the people with a speech that included the principles of governance. These principles have only recently been achieved by some nations, albeit with inconsistency.

This is the text of Abu Bakr's speech:

O People. I was entrusted as your ruler, although I am not better than any one of you.

Support me as long as you see me following the right path, and correct me when you see me going astray.

Obey me as long as I observe God in your affairs. If I disobey Him, you owe me no obedience.

The weak among you are powerful [in my eyes] until I get them their due. The powerful among you are weak [in my eyes] until I take away from them what is due to others.

'Abd al-Hamid Ibn Badis, "Usul al-wilayat fi al-islam, min khutba al-Siddiq (Allah ta'ali 'anhu)" (The Principles of Governing in Islam, From the Speech of [Abu Bakr] the Upright, May God Be Pleased with Him), al-Shihab (The Meteor), Constantine, Algeria, volume 13, number 11, January 1938, pp. 468–471. Translation from Arabic and introduction by Emad Eldin Shahin.

1. Salah al-Din al-Jurshi, Tajriba fi al-islah: Ibn Badis (A Case in Reform: Ibn Badis) (Tunis, Tunisia: Dar al-Raya li al-Nashr, 1978); Turki Rabih, al-Shaykh 'Abd al-Hamid Ibn Badis: Ra'id al-islah wa al-tarbiyah fi al-jaza'ir (Shaykh 'Abd al-Hamid Ibn Badis: Pioneer of Reform and Education in Algeria) (Algiers, Algeria: al-Sharika al-Wataniyya li al-Nashr wa al-Tawzi', 1969); Emad Eldin Shahin, "Abd al-Hamid Ibn Badis," in John L. Esposito, ed., Oxford Encyclopedia of the Modern Islamic World (New York: Oxford University Press, 1995), volume 2, pp. 161–162; Fathi 'Uthman, 'Abd al-Hamid Ibn Badis: Ra'id al-haraka al-islamiyya fi al-jaza'ir al-mu'asira (Ibn Badis: Pioneer of the Islamic Movement in Contemporary Algeria) (Kuwait City, Kuwait: Dar al-Qalam, 1987).

I say that and seek God's forgiveness for myself and for you.

The First Principle

No one has the right to assume any of the affairs of the *umma* [Muslim community] without their consent. It is the people that have the right to delegate authority to the leaders and depose them. No one can rule without the consent of the people. Rule cannot be bequeathed nor be based on personal considerations. This principle is derived from [Abu Bakr's] statement, "I was entrusted as your ruler." In other words, I was entrusted by others; and that is "you."

The Second Principle

He who manages an affair of the Muslim community should be the most qualified in this matter and not the best in behavior. If two persons share good behavior and qualifications, but one is better in good behavior and the other is more qualified for this matter, the one who is better qualified should be entrusted with this matter. Undoubtedly, qualification varies with the circumstance and the position. Someone might be qualified in a specific matter and position for possessing the characteristics suitable for that position. In this case, he should be entrusted with that post. On this basis, the Prophet appointed 'Amr ibn al-'Asi [died 663] to lead the army of Dhat al-Salasil and supported him with Abu Bakr, 'Umar [ibn al-Khattab, died 644], and Abu 'Ubayda ibn al-Jarra [circa 581–639], who were all under his command, though they were better than him. He also appointed Usama ibn Zayd [died circa 673] as a commander of an army that included Abu Bakr and 'Umar. This principle is based on the statement, "although I am not better than any one of you."

The Third Principle

Assuming the affairs of the people does not make the ruler better than anyone else. Preference is achieved through merit and deeds. If Abu Bakr was better, this was not due to his rule over them but because of his deeds and stances. This principle is also derived from the statement, "although I am not better than any one of you."

The Fourth Principle

The people have the right to monitor those in charge because they are the source of their authority and preserve the right to appoint or depose them.

The Fifth Principle

The responsibility of the people toward the ruler lies in offering assistance to him as long as they see him following the righteous path. They must support him, as they share with him the responsibility. This principle, as the previous one, is derived from the statement, "Support me as long as you see me following the right path."

The Sixth Principle

The responsibility of the people also lies in advising and guiding the ruler and pointing the righteous path to him when he deviates. The people must correct him if he misbehaves. This principle is based on the statement, "correct me when you see me going astray."

The Seventh Principle

The people have the right to question the rulers, hold them accountable for their actions, and make them follow the choice of the nation, not their own. The people have the final word, not the rulers. This is a result of the people's right to hold the rulers accountable and correct them when they are convinced that the rulers are not following the right path, and cannot convince the people otherwise. This is derived form the statement, "correct me when you see me going astray."

The Eighth Principle

Any one who assumes an affair of the people should declare the plan he is going to follow, so that the people become aware of and agree to it. He is not allowed to lead the people as he pleases, but as they please. This principle is based on the statement, "Obey me as long as I observe God in your affairs." His plan is the obedience of God. The people knew what the obedience of God in Islam entailed.

The Ninth Principle

The people will not be governed except by the law they voluntarily adopt, the law that realizes their interest. The rulers only implement the will of the people, who obey the law because it emanates from them, not because it is imposed on them by any other authority, be it of an individual or of a group. This makes the people feel free to manage their affairs on their own. Everyone in society will share this feeling. Freedom and sovereignty are a natural and legitimate right of every individual in society. This principle is derived from the statement, "Obey me as long as I observe God in your affairs. If I disobey Him, you owe me no obedience." Thus, they do not obey the ruler per se, but they obey God by following the law that He has revealed and that they have accepted for themselves. The ruler is delegated by them to apply this law to everyone, including himself. Therefore, if he deviates, he forsakes their obedience.

The Tenth Principle

All are equal before the law, regardless of their strength or weakness. The law should apply to the strong without any fear of their strength and to the weak without leniency for their weakness.

The Eleventh Principle

[The state] should protect the rights of the individuals and groups in society. The rights of the weak should not be forsaken because of their weakness, and the strong should not usurp the right of anyone because of their strength.

The Twelfth Principle

[The state] should maintain a balance in society when protecting the rights of its members. The dues should be fairly taken from the strong without transgression or weakening them. The rights of the weak should be granted to them without favor due to their weakness, so that they do not transgress against others. This principle and the two previous ones are derived from the statement, "The weak among you are powerful [in my eyes] until I get them their due. The powerful among you are weak [in my eyes] until I take away from them what is due to others."

The Thirteenth Principle

There should be a realization of a mutual responsibility of the ruler and the ruled in reforming society. They should always feel the need to continue working strenuously and seriously, and seek forgiveness from God, who oversees them. This is based on the statement, "I say that and seek God's forgiveness for myself and for you."

This is what the first caliph in Islam stated and implemented fourteen centuries ago. Are the civilized nations close to this today? Was Abu Bakr making these statements on his own? No, he was inspired by Islam. He addressed the Muslims at that time with what they already knew; had he done otherwise, they would not have accepted his speech. Were these principles known to or practiced by other nations then? No, nations were immersed in the darkness of ignorance and deterioration, suffering the chains of humiliation and enslavement under monarchical and clerical rule. These principles were not devised by men but were revealed by God, the All-Knowing and Wise. We pray to God to rescue us and all of humanity and grant us success in returning to these principles, without which there can be no salvation.

The Intellectual Movement in the Sudan: Which Direction Should It Take?

Muhammad Ahmad Mahjub (Sudan, 1908–1976) was a lawyer, judge, poet, anticolonial activist, and politician. Trained in colonial schools, he participated as a young man in the Sudanese intellectual reform movement that came to be known by the name of its journal, *al-Fajr* (*The Dawn*), founded in 1934. Mahjub and others in this movement sought to build a modern Sudanese identity by downplaying the sectarian and regional distinctions that divided the colony. This identity, as Mahjub argued in the essay translated here, was affiliated closely with the Arab Islamic world, notwithstanding the large number of non-Muslim non-Arabs in the south of the colony. In the 1940s and 1950s, Mahjub pushed to radicalize the Sudanese nationalist movement and helped write the Sudan's constitution and declaration of independence. Over the following two decades, he was by turns a top government official and a political prisoner, as democratic governments were succeeded by military ones. His final imprisonment and exile followed two terms as prime minister. Known as "the Boss," Mahjub left a political legacy that included repression of leftists and southerners, in addition to fervent defense of democracy.[1]

In all places and times, from the beginning of creation to this day and on to eternity, distinguished individuals and those with true culture have thought and will always think about realizing the ideal. Human effort is harnessed to achieve it, and lifestyle is improved to attain it. This ideal gives people a greater purpose for existence. Every aspect of life and each cultural ideology has its own sincere, dedicated advocates who do everything within their power to achieve outcomes that their followers among the masses perceive as difficult, if not impossible, to attain. If it were not for these sincere idealists, literature and the arts would never advance, because the nature of human beings is to fear dangers and to avoid them, to prefer the conventions of their parents, and to resist all change in ideas and action. Perhaps the universe would inevitably stagnate,

were it not for the appearance of a handful of talented, sincere, and dedicated idealists who blow the trumpet and encourage people toward a goal that has to be achieved by talented people like themselves. They insist that the goal they envision is necessary for themselves and others. They have the patience, the resilience, and the power of faith that makes them trust in ultimate victory.

The ideal life is important for humans, both as individuals and as part of a group with whom they have relationships based on nationality, blood, religion, common goals, public celebrations, and shared travails. Individuals and groups should recognize and attend to the ideal life, in all its branches and subdivisions: material life and intellectual life each have their place. In recent times, humans' goals have become deeply interconnected, making the prosperity

Muhammad Ahmad Mahjub, "al-Haraka al-fikriyya fi al-Sudan: 'Ila 'ayna yajib 'an tatajih" (The Intellectual Movement in the Sudan: Which Direction Should It Take?), in *Nahwa al-ghad* (*Toward Tomorrow*) (Khartoum, Sudan: Jami'at al-Khurtum, Qism al-Ta'lif wa al-Nashr, 1970), pp. 209–211, 215–217, 226–227, 233–234. First published in 1941. Translation from Arabic by Hager El Hadidi. Introduction by Charles Kurzman.

1. Muddathir Abdel-Rahim, *Imperialism and Nationalism in the Sudan: A Study in Constitutional and Political*

Development, 1899–1956 (Oxford, England: Clarendon Press, 1969), pp. 109–117; Afaf Abdel Majid Abu Hasabu, *Factional Conflict in the Sudanese Nationalist Movement, 1918–1948* (Khartoum, Sudan: University of Khartoum, 1985); Carolyn Fluehr-Lobban, Richard A. Lobban, Jr., and John Obert Voll, *Historical Dictionary of the Sudan*, 2d ed. (Metuchen, N.J.: Scarecrow Press, 1992), p. 133; Abdel Salam Sidahmed, *Politics and Islam in Contemporary Sudan* (New York: St. Martin's Press, 1996), pp. 35–41.

of an individual not only in contradiction with that of others but also with the prosperity and security of the group. A piece of candy in the hands of an oblivious child means the deprivation of his sad friend. A beautifully designed house, with cozy and luxurious furniture, is inhabited by an obtuse and insipid character, lacking in generosity; whereas the poet, the singing bird, the lyre player who nearly discovers the secrets of the universe, cannot find a lowly shack, let alone a luxurious abode.

This abominable contradiction is even more apparent in the relationship among nations than among individuals. However, in the world of culture and the universe of intellect, in mental activities that elevate humanity through novel findings and innovative opinions, this cutthroat competition does not and cannot exist. This is good news for human beings. They can find happiness in the world of culture and intellect, where they enjoy creating ideal visions and rising to achieve them. Generation follows generation, but the ideal is continuously rejuvenated, as are activities to achieve it.

It is easy to imagine a situation in which every race, nation, family, and individual has an equal share of culture, justice, comfort, and status. But this situation cannot be achieved unless the individuals, nations, and races whom God has granted the privilege of intellect and morality, and are thus able to shape the future, take it as their life mission to shower their culture, science, and wealth upon their neighbors, the seekers and the weak, with the intention of celebrating the highest ethical, intellectual, and material ideals of humanity.

But the teachings and generosity of a select elite are fruitless unless all people have reached a high degree of nobility. For some people do not benefit from education, and all effort to reform them is wasted—either because of the ignorance and stupidity bequeathed from past generations, or because of the evil that has overtaken them. How is it possible to rectify what time has spoiled? There is also a class of regressive and rigid people who do not accept innovative opinions even if they are right, who don't join a caravan unless they can maintain the idea that they are crossing the desert of life unaccompanied. There are also those self-interested individuals who have been blinded by their desire to preserve the status quo, in order to retain power, however illegitimate, and to hang on to the wealth derived from this power, however unethical. Reformists must do away with such

people in every time and place, and in every branch of material and intellectual life. Their self-interested recalcitrance must be confronted. Recalcitrance will evaporate when faced with loyal, selfless visionaries struggling for perfection. This struggle and ultimate victory in the battle between light and darkness, truth and falseness, progress and annihilation, depend on the zeal and integrity of the leaders of the renaissance, and on their innovativeness against the obstinacy of the propagators of rigidity and dissent.

An ideal does not know mediocrity; it requires perfection. And this is not imaginary, not a mirage. This is a conflict between people who care only about food, drink, clothing, and personal pleasures, and people who see that life is worthless when its short period is spent seeking common ordinary pleasures. Such [hedonism] is born out of ignorance, idiocy, and a stupidity that cannot imagine life as a continuous chain where the living depart, their vanishing bodies die, and their riches remain for future generations. That is why the propagators of reform and the worshipers of the ideal formulate plans that cannot be accomplished in their lifetime but must be pursued as long as life continues. They spread science and enlightenment without discriminating between classes, nations, and races. The progress of science and enlightenment weakens fanatic loyalties and competition between individuals and groups, erases differences and misunderstandings, and enables the exchange of trust and respect.

Such are the loyal reformists, the selfless propagators of the ideal, in every place and time. And we are not to be blamed for wanting to join them for a moment to formulate an ideal for the intellectual movement that we desire for this growing country. I don't pretend to be one of those talented people to whom the secrets of the era are revealed, who peek into the past of nations and understand the fate of their intellectual movements, who then look far into the future and reveal what it portends, the opinions and actions that it requires, and who lay out the truest ideals for the intellectual movement in their country. That is an honor I cannot claim. But I am going to attempt to study the past and present of this nation, and to study the past and present of the nations I have known. Following that, I will try to direct the intellectual movement in our nation toward what I see as the ideal. If I am successful, I will be satisfied. If I fail, let my solace be that this nation will never lack offspring to rectify my mistakes and reform my errors, to present us with the ideal that we will all work together to achieve. [. . .]

The history of Islam in this country [the Sudan] dates back to the year 22 A.H., or 642 A.D., when 'Abdullah [ibn Sa'd] ibn Abi Sarh [died 656] was appointed to invade Nubia at the head of 20,000 warriors. Since that era, Islam spread, with the *da'wa* [propagation] strengthening in this country until the Arab conquest of lower Nubia in 1318 A.D. and of upper Nubia in the year 1505 A.D. Thus Islam prevailed and became the religion of the majority of the population of this country.

The influence of Islam in this country is clear and tangible; you can see it in your [daily] comings and goings, and you can feel it in every action of the people of this country. Until recently, no movement could be successful in transforming or changing conditions unless it was a religious movement, or at least wearing the garb of religion. The story of the Mahdiyya is a recent example. The *da'wa* of al-Mahdi [Muhammad Ahmad, anticolonial leader, 1844–1885] was a religious *da'wa*, accepted by the people in the name of religion. As a result, they revolted against the corrupters [the colonial regime], expelled them from their country, and took over governance. If it had not been for religion, you would not have seen people dying for the sake of God and acting so bravely, seeking neither fortune nor prestige nor worldly position. The living envy the dead, who have won the honor of martyrdom. A nation with such religious fervor cannot tolerate opinions that have atheistic tendencies or break the norms of conventional morality. It accepts nothing from its intellectuals but honest words and sincere actions, virtue of the tongue and the hand, and honorable intentions.

In every place where Islam has spread, Arab literature and culture has [also] spread. The Scripture of God, the *sunna* [sacred precedent] of His Messenger, and the noble *hadith* [sayings of the Prophet] are not only in the Arabic language, but are also the purest sources of this language. It is necessary to learn, understand, and appreciate them in their original language. Muslims are very keen to come to understand and appreciate this legacy, and to become closer to the spirit of religion by studying its roots and following its precepts. That is why the Sudan was fortunate that the Arabic language spread in its lands, both because of the spread of Islam among its people, and because Arab blood has become the majority among its popu-

lation. The Sudan has remained, until the last conquest in 1898, far from the influence of European languages; there were no non-Arab languages heard in it except the Turkish language, and this was after the conquest of Muhammad 'Ali [Ottoman ruler of Egypt, 1805–1849] in the year 1820. And even then, the Turkish language was not the official state language, and was not taught in schools, but was only spoken by the Turkish rulers among themselves.

It is no wonder that the language of the people of the Sudan, especially in the desert, is the closest to classical Arabic. And it is no wonder that we find the people of the Sudan inclining toward [the classical genres of] *hamasa* [heroic] and *fakhr* [vainglorious] verse, whether in their songs or their poetry. They have great passion for all kinds of horsemanship. They are noted for their generosity and openhandedness, extending protection to their guests and taking care of their neighbors. They find meanness contemptible. They do not accept humiliation, and they are not happy with defeat. Any man among them, regardless of how poor he is, would not stain himself with the humiliation of begging, and would not stoop to relinquish public duty.

And the impact of Islamic religion and Arab culture in this country is most apparent in the legacy of the past generation—literary figures such as *Shaykh* Husayn al-Zahra' [died 1895], *Shaykh* al-Darir, *Shaykh* Abu'l-Qasim Ahmad Hashim [died 1934], and *Shaykh* [Muhammad 'Umar] al-Banna' the elder [circa 1847–1919]. Most of their poems were [in the genres] of *al-mada'ih al-nabawaiyya* [praise of the Prophet], *zikr shama'il al-rasul* [remembrance of the qualities of the Messenger], and the history of the Prophet's conquests and victories. Their verse also included some poetry [in the genres] of *fakhr*, *hamasa*, and *al-hath 'ala al-jihad* [inspiring sacred struggle]. Each one of these poems begins with a delicate *ghazal* [love poetry] in the manner of the ancient Arabs. This is not all the previous generation has given us; they also left a genre of literature that, despite its originality, has been ignored by the intellectuals among us. In fact, this literature is wonderful, and unique within its genre. I refer to the stories of the *mulid* [birth] of the noble Prophet which are read in *zikr* circles. If you had the good fortune to read the *mulid* by the leaders of the Tijaniyya [Sufi order] entitled "Insan al-kamal" (The Perfect Human), or to hear its narration, you would doubtless find it a wonderful literature, beautiful and harmonious narratives with fine examples of rhetoric and metaphor. The late *Shaykh* Muhammad Hashim wrote an introduction to the *mulid* that is a masterpiece of rhetoric in its expressions, structure, and meaning. All of these are examples of the influence of Islamic religion and Arab literature on our life. This influence is strong and ongoing; it still affects people's minds, readers and writers alike.

Such influence has also increased through contact with Egypt since the last invasion, because Egypt itself is under the sway of Islamic religion and Arab culture, despite its periodic tendencies to return to the pharaohs or to cling to the fringes of the West.

It is necessary for us to attend to this influence when we are attempting to direct the intellectual movement in this county. This influence warrants at least a brief discussion. And I state with increasing certainty that the impact of Islamic religion and Arab culture will remain part of our intellectual movement as long as this country exists, and as long as it has culture and intellectual movement. However, this impact will undoubtedly be subject to interaction with the modern opinions and Western ideas that we are acquiring. Both will be subject to the climate of this country and to ideas and imagination inspired by its geography and its nature. That is why we need to speak first about the effect of Western culture in our country, and second about the country's climate, geography, and nature, and the effect of all of these on the intellectual movement. We are attempting to draft the ideal of the intellectual movement, and to direct the movement toward the goal desired by its loyal, selfless, devoted offspring. [. . .]

Such has been the intellectual movement in our country up to now. And this is its future, as it appears to us through this exploration of the past and present of this country, the conditions required to achieve this desired intellectual movement, and the implications of its ideal.

So what is the ideal that this intellectual movement must follow? And how can it be reached? The ideal intellectual movement in this country will respect the religious practices of Islam, the true religion, and will work under its right guidance. It will be Arab in language and taste, inspired by the past and present of this country, making use of its nature and the customs, traditions, and dispositions of its people, elevated by all of these toward the goal of establishing a proper national literature. This liter-

ary movement will eventually be transformed into a political movement that leads to the independence of the country—political, social, and intellectual.

This ideal is the goal of the intellectual movement in this country. On the surface, it may seem remote, prohibitive, and hard to achieve; it calls for the effort of giants and the work of generations. But an ideal does not know mediocrity; it requires perfection. Let us make our ideal clear and draw the path to reach it. This country shall not lack dutiful, loyal, educated, and visionary offspring to take up the burden of its renaissance.

To complete our intellectual movement, we must grasp the Arab Islamic heritage. This effort awaiting us is unlike that of *Shaykh* Nasif al-Yaziji ([Lebanese Christian poet and philologist,] 1800–1871) and his companions, because the writings of the Arab Islamic heritage have already been published in Egypt and Syria. All that we need to do is devote ourselves to the study of this Arab Islamic heritage—a detailed study based on scrutiny, criticism, and interconnected comparisons so that we get the full benefit of this heritage.

Maybe someone will ask me: And what is the way to learn this Arab Islamic heritage and become inspired by it? So I will say that learning involves only dedication and study. And those among us who wish to revive this legacy, and to draw the best conclusions from it, so as to be armed with the strongest weapon possible, need to embark upon the study of the Arabic encyclopedias such as [*Kitab*] *al-aghani* [*Book of Songs*] by Abu Faraj al-Isfahani [897–967], *Mu'jam al-udaba'* [*Literary Biographies*] by Yaqut [al-Rumi] al-Hamawi [circa 1179–1229], *Wafayat al-a'yan* [*Late Greats*] by the judge Ibn Khallikan [1211–1282], and *Subh al-a'sha* [*Daybreak for the Sufferer of Night-Blindness*] by [Shihabuddin Ahmad] al-Qalqashandi [1355–1418]. And they need also to embark upon the study of the fundamentals of Arabic literature such as *Kamil* [*fi al-adab*] [*Literary Perfection*] by [Muhammad] al-Mubarrad [died 898], *Adab al-katib* [*The Art of the Scribe*] by [Abu Muhammad] Ibn Qutayba [828–889], *Bayan wa al-tabyin* [*Rhetoric and Clarification*] by al-Jahiz [circa 776–869], and others, too many to enumerate. In this way they will come to comprehend gradually the spirit of Arabic Islamic literature, to be dedicated to the service of the language of the ancestors, and to grasp the subject matter. Literature in its entirety is but subject matter and style. The subject matter comprises the different subjects treated by literary figures, which differ according to time and place. And the style is the way these subjects are treated. [. . .]

We have followed the intellectual movement in this country from ancient times until today, and we have seen the various states and the succession of civilizations that this nation has undergone and the creeds and beliefs adopted by its offspring. We have seen the cultures to which the nation was introduced, to which its people were exposed. And we have seen that this country and its people are the result of [different] blood groups, some Negroid and some Arab, along with the Turkish and the Abyssinian, and are born out of [an amalgam of] civilizations, among them the Pharaonic, the ancient and modern Arab, and the Western. And we have seen that they [the people of this country] worshiped the gods of the ancient Egyptians and adopted Christianity for a long period of time, and then adopted Islam, the true religion, as its creed, which it would not exchange for any other. It remains for us to see which ideal the intellectual movement needs to follow in this country.

The ideal vision that the intellectual movement has to follow is for this country to have an Arab Islamic culture backed by an acquired Western culture. They should be mutually supportive in creating a proper national literature that takes the subject of its artistic narrative from the dispositions of its people and their traditions, that composes its verse and appeals to the sensitivity of this nation's offspring by describing the scenery of its jungles, the shining of the silver moon in its deserts, its fertile valleys, and the gazelles of its dunes, and finds in these the sources for its artistic imagery. The feelings of the people, their sensitivities, their movements and silences, are the sources for music. The ideal vision gives attention to the writing of the history of this country in a way that instills patriotism in its youth and a sense of duty toward the land of the ancestors. The propagators of this literature should circulate useful political research, so that the movement may be transformed from a literary renaissance to a political one, resulting in the independence of this country—politically, socially, and intellectually.

This is our ideal: to protect our Islamic religion and hold fast to our Arab heritage with complete tolerance, a widened intellectual horizon, and an eagerness to study other cultures. All these will revive our national literature and arouse patriotic feelings, so to build a political movement that cannot be refused, because it is grows out of our essence. The goal we are striding toward is our independence—political, social, and intellectual.

This is our ideal. We must stride toward it and work together to achieve it, and all work that is not aimed at independence is worthless.

Come along! O youth of this generation, and its opinion leaders, let us work together to establish this ideal. Let us work to achieve it. Let us die, and the generation after us will work to realize it. Such is the eternal dream and the work of ages. Let the loyal, selfless, dutiful, and visionary offspring of this country work toward this ideal.

SECTION 2

Iran/Afghanistan

Lecture on Teaching and Learning *and* Answer to Renan

Sayyid Jamal al-Din al-Afghani (Iran, 1838–1897) was perhaps the most famous proponent of modernist Islam, and has enjoyed the stablest popularity of all modernists in the century since his death. Born in Asadabad in northwestern Iran, he adopted the name "Afghani" in order to distance himself from his Shi'i origins. He was educated at seminaries in Iran and Iraq, then studied modern sciences in India before coming to prominence as a royal adviser in Afghanistan in the late 1860s. Upon his expulsion, Jamal al-Din then spent a decade associated with academic reform—briefly in Istanbul, then for almost a decade in Cairo, before being expelled yet again. He spent much of the 1880s in Europe—in Paris, where he published the famous journal *al-'Urwa al-wuthqa* (*The Strongest Link*) with Muhammad 'Abduh (see chapter 3); and later in Russia. His final years were spent as a would-be adviser to the rulers of Iran and, after yet another expulsion, the Ottoman Empire, though both monarchs were suspicious of his loyalty and piety. As with his name, Jamal al-Din reinvented his political positions when necessary—supporting and opposing absolute monarchy, for example, and denouncing and offering to assist the British Empire. His consistent aim, however, was to revive the power and image of the Islamic world through modern-style reforms. The texts presented here—addressed to Hindus, in the first selection, and Christians in the second—offer Jamal al-Din's view that Muslims can and must adopt modern science as a means of civilizational survival.[1]

Lecture on Teaching and Learning

On Thursday, November 8 [1882], in Albert Hall, Calcutta, he said: [. . .]

Allow me to express my pleasure that so many Indian youths are here, all adorned with virtue and attainments, and all making great efforts to acquire knowledge. Certainly I must be happy to see such offspring of India, since they are the offshoots of that India that was the cradle of humanity. Human values spread out from India to the whole world. These youths are from the very land where the meridian circle was first determined. They are from the same realm that first understood the zodiac. Everyone knows that the determination of these two circles is impossible until perfection in geometry is achieved. Thus we can say that the Indians were the inventors of arithmetic and geometry. Note how Indian numerals were transferred from here to the Arabs, and from there to Europe.

These youths are also the sons of a land that was the source of all the laws and rules of the world. If one observes closely, he will see that the "Code Romain," the mother of all Western codes, was taken from the four *veda*s and the *shastra*s. The Greeks were the pupils of the Indians in literary ideas, limpid poetry, and lofty thoughts. One of these pupils, Pythagoras [Greek mathematician, circa 569–475 B.C.], spread sciences and wisdom in Greece and reached such a height that his word was accepted without proof as an inspiration from heaven.

Sayyid Jamal ad-Din al-Afghani, *An Islamic Response to Imperialism: Political and Religious Writings of Sayyid Jamal ad-Din al-Afghani*, translated from Persian and French by Nikki R. Keddie (Berkeley: University of California Press, 1968), pp. 101–108, 181–187. The first selection was a lecture delivered in 1882; the second piece was first published in 1883. Introduction by Charles Kurzman.

1. Nikki R. Keddie, *Sayyid Jamal ad-Din "al-Afghani": A Political Biography* (Berkeley: University of California Press, 1972); Elie Kedourie, *Afghani and 'Abduh: An Essay on Religious Unbelief and Political Activism in Modern Islam* (London: Cass, 1966).

[The Indians] reached the highest level in philosophic thought. The soil of India is the same soil; the air of India is the same air; and these youths who are present here are fruits of the same earth and climate. So I am very happy that they, having awakened after a long sleep, are reclaiming their inheritance and gathering the fruits of their own tree.

Now I would like to speak of science, teaching, and learning. How difficult it is to speak about science. There is no end or limit to science. The benefits of science are immeasurable; and these finite thoughts cannot encompass what is infinite. Besides, thousands of eloquent speakers and sages have already expressed their thoughts to explain science and its nobility. Despite this, nature does not permit me not to explain its virtues.

Thus I say: If someone looks deeply into the question, he will see that science rules the world. There was, is, and will be no ruler in the world but science. If we look at the Chaldean conquerors, like Semiramis [Sammu-ramat, Assyrian queen, ninth century B.C.], who reached the borders of Tatary and India, the true conquerors were not the Chaldeans but science and knowledge.

The Egyptians who increased their realm, and Ramses II [Egyptian king, ruled 1279–1213 B.C.], called Sosestris, who reached Mesopotamia according to some and India according to others—it was not the Egyptians but science that did it. The Phoenicians who, with their ships, gradually made colonies of the British Isles, Spain, Portugal, and Greece—in reality it was science, not the Phoenicians, which so expanded their power. Alexander [Macedonian king, 356–323 B.C.] never came to India or conquered the Indians; rather what conquered the Indians was science.

The Europeans have now put their hands on every part of the world. The English have reached Afghanistan; the French have seized Tunisia. In reality this usurpation, aggression, and conquest have not come from the French or the English. Rather it is science that everywhere manifests its greatness and power. Ignorance had no alternative to prostrating itself humbly before science and acknowledging its submission. In reality, sovereignty has never left the abode of science. However, this true ruler, which is science, is continually changing capitals. Sometimes it has moved from East to West, and other times from West to East. More than this, if we study the riches of the world, we learn that wealth is the result of commerce, industry, and agriculture. Agriculture is achieved only with agricultural science, botanical chemistry, and geometry. Industry is produced only with physics, chemistry, mechanics, geometry, and mathematics; and commerce is based on agriculture and industry.

Thus it is evident that all wealth and riches are the result of science. There are no riches in the world without science, and there is no wealth in the world other than science. In sum, the whole world of humanity is an industrial world, meaning that the world is a world of science. If science were removed from the human sphere, no man would continue to remain in the world.

Since it is thus, science makes one man have the strength of ten, one hundred, one thousand, and ten thousand persons. The acquisitions of men for themselves and their governments are proportional to their science. Thus, every government for its own benefit must strive to lay the foundation of the sciences and to disseminate knowledge. Just as an individual who has an orchard must, for his own profit, work to level the ground and improve its trees and plants according to the laws of agronomy, just so rulers, for their own benefit, must strive for the dissemination of the sciences. Just as, if the owner of an orchard neglects to tend it according to the laws of agronomy, the loss will revert to him, so, if a ruler neglects the dissemination of the sciences among his subjects, the harm will revert to that government. What advantage is there to a Zulu king from ruling a society poor and barefoot, and how can one call such a government a government?

As the nobility of science has been somewhat clarified, we now wish to say some words about the relations between science, teaching, and learning. You must know that each science has a special subject and deals with nothing but the necessities and accidents of that special subject. For example, physics treats the special features of bodies that exist in the external world, and with its own special qualities, and does not enter into other matters that are necessary to the human world. *Kimiya*, or "chemistry," speaks of the special features of bodies with regard to analysis and composition. Plant science, or "botany," fixes only plants as the subject of its discussion. Arithmetic deals with separate quantities and geometry with interconnected quantities, and similarly the other sciences. None of these sciences deals with matters outside its own subject.

If we observe well, we will learn that each one

of these sciences whose subject is a special matter is like a limb of the body of science. Not one of them can maintain its existence individually and separately, or be the cause of benefit for the human world. For the existence of each one of these sciences is related to another science, like the relation of arithmetic to geometry.

This need of one science for other sciences cannot be understood from the one science itself. Thus it is that if that science were isolated, progress would not be achieved in it, nor would it remain stable. Thus a science is needed to be the comprehensive soul for all the sciences, so that it can preserve their existence, apply each of them in its proper place, and become the cause of the progress of each one of those sciences.

The science that has the position of a comprehensive soul and the rank of a preserving force is the science of *falsafa*, or "philosophy," because its subject is universal. It is philosophy that shows man human prerequisites. It shows the sciences what is necessary. It employs each of the sciences in its proper place.

If a community did not have philosophy, and all the individuals of that community were learned in the sciences with particular subjects, those sciences could not last in that community for a century, that is, a hundred years. That community without the spirit of philosophy could not deduce conclusions from these sciences.

The Ottoman Government and the Khedivate of Egypt have been opening schools for the teaching of the new sciences for a period of sixty years, and until now they have not received any benefit from those sciences. The reason is that teaching the philosophical sciences was impossible in those schools, and because of the nonexistence of philosophy, no fruit was obtained from those sciences that are like limbs. Undoubtedly, if the spirit of philosophy had been in those schools during this period of sixty years, they themselves, independent of the European countries, would have striven to reform their kingdoms in accord with science. Also, they would not send their sons each year to European countries for education, and they would not invite teachers from there to their schools. I may say that if the spirit of philosophy were found in a community, even if that community did not have one of those sciences whose subject is particular, undoubtedly their philosophic spirit would call for the acquisition of all the sciences.

The first Muslims had no science, but, thanks to the Islamic religion, a philosophic spirit arose among them, and owing to that philosophic spirit they began to discuss the general affairs of the world and human necessities. This was why they acquired in a short time all the sciences with particular subjects that they translated from the Syriac, Persian, and Greek into the Arabic language at the time of [Abu Ja'far] Mansur Davanaqi [caliph, 754–775].[2]

It is philosophy that makes man understandable to man, explains human nobility, and shows man the proper road. The first defect appearing in any nation that is headed toward decline is in the philosophic spirit. After that, deficiencies spread into the other sciences, arts, and associations.

As the relationship between the preeminence of philosophy and the sciences has been explained, we now wish to say something about the quality of teaching and learning among the Muslims. Thus, I say that the Muslims these days do not see any benefit from their education. For example, they study grammar, and the purpose of grammar is that someone who has acquired the Arabic language be capable of speaking and writing. The Muslims now make grammar a goal in itself. For long years they expend philosophic thought on grammar to no avail, and after finishing they are unable to speak, write, or understand Arabic.

Rhetoric, which they call "literature," is the science that enables a man to become a writer, speaker, and poet. However, we see these days that after studying that science they are incapable of correcting their everyday speech.

Logic, which is the balance for ideas, should make everyone who acquires it capable of distinguishing every truth from falsehood and every right from wrong. However, we see that the minds of our Muslim logicians are full of every superstition and vanity, and no difference exists between their ideas and the ideas of the masses of the bazaar.

Philosophy is the science that deals with the state of external beings, and their causes, reasons, needs, and requisites. It is strange that our *'ulama'* [religious scholars] read *Sadra* [that is, *Sharh al- Hidaya*, or *Explanation of "Guidance,"* by Mulla Sadra, 1571–1640] and *Shams al-bari'a* [probably *Shams al-bazigha*, *The Rising Sun*, by Mahmud Jawnpuri

2. [In fact, the main translations were done later under al-Ma'mun (caliph, 813–833).—Trans.]

Faruqi, died 1652] and vaingloriously call themselves sages, and despite this they cannot distinguish their left hand from their right hand, and they do not ask: Who are we and what is right and proper for us? They never ask the causes of electricity, the steamboat, and railroads.

Even stranger, from early evening until morning they study the *Shams al-bari'a* with a lamp placed before them, and they do not once consider why if we remove its glass cover, much smoke comes out of it, and when we leave the glass, there is no smoke. Shame on such a philosopher, and shame on such philosophy! A philosopher is someone whose mind is stimulated by all the events and parts of the world, not one who travels along a road like a blind man who does not know where its beginning and end are.

Jurisprudence among the Muslims includes all domestic, municipal, and state laws. Thus a person who has studied jurisprudence profoundly is worthy of being prime minister of the realm or chief ambassador of the state, whereas we see our jurisconsults after studying this science unable to manage their own households, although they are proud of their own foolishness.

The science of principles consists of the philosophy of the *shari'a*, or "philosophy of law." In it are explained the truth regarding right and wrong, benefit and loss, and the causes for the promulgation of laws. Certainly, a person who studies this science should be capable of establishing laws and enforcing civilization. However, we see that those who study this science among the Muslims are deprived of understanding of the benefits of laws, the rules of civilization, and the reform of the world.

Since the state of these *'ulama'* has been demonstrated, we can say that our *'ulama'* at this time are like a very narrow wick, on top of which is a very small flame that neither lights its surroundings nor gives light to others. A scholar is a true light if he is a scholar. Thus, if a scholar is a scholar he must shed light on the whole world, and if his light does not reach the whole world, at least it should light up his region, his city, his village, or his home. What kind of scholar is it who does not enlighten even his own home?

The strangest thing of all is that our *'ulama'* these days have divided science into two parts. One they call Muslim science, and one European science. Because of this they forbid others to teach some of the useful sciences. They have not understood that

science is that noble thing that has no connection with any nation, and is not distinguished by anything but itself. Rather, everything that is known is known by science, and every nation that becomes renowned becomes renowned through science. Men must be related to science, not science to men.

How very strange it is that the Muslims study those sciences that are ascribed to Aristotle [Greek philosopher, circa 384–322 B.C.] with the greatest delight, as if Aristotle were one of the pillars of the Muslims. However, if the discussion relates to Galileo [Italian astronomer, 1564–1642], [Isaac] Newton [English physicist, 1642–1727], and [Johannes] Kepler [German astronomer, 1571–1630], they consider them infidels.

The father and mother of science is proof, and proof is neither Aristotle nor Galileo. The truth is where there is proof, and those who forbid science and knowledge in the belief that they are safeguarding the Islamic religion are really the enemies of that religion. The Islamic religion is the closest of religions to science and knowledge, and there is no incompatibility between science and knowledge and the foundation of the Islamic faith.

As for [Abu Hamid Muhammad] Ghazzali [1058–1111], who was called the Proof of Islam, he says in the book *Munqidh min al-dalal* (*The Deliverer from Error*) that someone who claims that the Islamic religion is incompatible with geometric proofs, philosophical demonstrations, and the laws of nature is an ignorant friend of Islam. The harm of this ignorant friend to Islam is greater than the harm of the heretics and enemies of Islam. For the laws of nature, geometric proofs, and philosophic demonstrations are self-evident truths. Thus, someone who says, "My religion is inconsistent with self-evident truths," has inevitably passed judgment on the falsity of his religion.

The first education obtained by man was religious education, since philosophical education can only be obtained by a society that has studied some science and is able to understand proofs and demonstrations. Hence we can say that reform will never be achieved by the Muslims except if the leaders of our religion first reform themselves and gather the fruits of their science and knowledge.

If one considers, one will understand this truth, that the ruin and corruption we have experienced first reached our *'ulama'* and religious leaders, and then penetrated the rest of the community.

I now wish to excuse myself, since, contrary to his promise, the principal caused this talk to be delivered only in an abbreviated form.

Answer of Jamal ad-Din to Renan

Sir,

I have read in your estimable journal of last March 29 [1883] a talk on Islam and Science, given in the Sorbonne before a distinguished audience by the great thinker of our time, the illustrious M[onsieur] [Ernest] Renan [French Orientalist, 1823–1892], whose renown has filled the West and penetrated into the farthest countries of the East. Since this speech suggested to me some observations, I took the liberty of formulating them in this letter, which I have the honor of addressing to you with a request that you accommodate it in your columns.

Monsieur Renan wanted to clarify a point of the history of the Arabs which had remained unclear until now and to throw a live light on their past, a light that may be somewhat troubling for those who venerate these people, though one cannot say that he has usurped the place and rank that they formerly occupied in the world. Monsieur Renan has not at all tried, we believe, to destroy the glory of the Arabs, which is indestructible; he has applied himself to discovering historical truth and making it known to those who do not know it, as well as to those who study the influence of religions in the history of nations, and in particular in that of civilization. I hasten to recognize that Monsieur Renan has acquitted himself marvelously of this very difficult task, in citing certain facts that have passed unnoticed until this time. I find in his talk remarkable observations, new perceptions, and an indescribable charm. However, I have under my eyes only a more or less faithful translation of this talk. If I had had the opportunity to read it in the French text, I could have penetrated better the ideas of this great thinker. He receives my humble salutation as an homage that is due him and as the sincere expression of my admiration. I would say to him, finally, in these circumstances, what al-Mutanabbi [915–965], a poet who loved philosophy wrote several centuries ago to a high personage whose actions he celebrated: "Receive," he said to him, "the praises that I can give you; do not force me to bestow on you the praises that you merit."

Monsieur Renan's talk covered two principal points. The eminent philosopher applied himself to proving that the Muslim religion was by its very essence opposed to the development of science, and that the Arab people, by their nature, do not like either metaphysical sciences or philosophy. This precious plant, Monsieur Renan seems to say, dried in their hands as if burnt up by the breath of the desert wind. But after reading this talk one cannot refrain from asking oneself if these obstacles come uniquely from the Muslim religion itself or from the manner in which it was propagated in the world; from the character, manners, and aptitudes of the peoples who adopted this religion, or of those on whose nations it was imposed by force. It is no doubt the lack of time that kept Monsieur Renan from elucidating these points; but the harm is no less for that, and if it is difficult to determine its causes in a precise manner and by irrefutable proofs, it is even more difficult to indicate the remedy.

As to the first point, I will say that no nation at its origin is capable of letting itself be guided by pure reason. Haunted by terrors that it cannot escape, it is incapable of distinguishing good from evil, of distinguishing that which could make it happy from that which might be the unfailing source of its unhappiness and misfortune. It does not know, in a word, either how to trace back causes or to discern effects.

This lacuna means that it cannot be led either by force or persuasion to practice the actions that would perhaps be the most profitable for it, or to avoid what is harmful. It was therefore necessary that humanity look outside itself for a place of refuge, a peaceful corner where its tormented conscience could find repose. It was then that there arose some educator or other who, not having, as I said above, the necessary power to force humanity to follow the inspirations of reason, hurled it into the unknown and opened to it vast horizons where the imagination was pleased, and where it found, if not the complete satisfaction of its desires, at least an unlimited field for its hopes. And, since humanity, at its origin, did not know the causes of the events that passed under its eyes and the secrets of things, it was perforce led to follow the advice of its teachers and the orders they gave. This obedience was imposed in the name of the supreme Being to whom the educators attributed all events, without permitting men to discuss its utility or its disadvantages. This is no doubt for man one of the heaviest and most humiliating yokes, as I recognize;

but one cannot deny that it is by this religious education, whether it be Muslim, Christian, or pagan, that all nations have emerged from barbarism and marched toward a more advanced civilization.

If it is true that the Muslim religion is an obstacle to the development of sciences, can one affirm that this obstacle will not disappear someday? How does the Muslim religion differ on this point from other religions? All religions are intolerant, each one in its way. The Christian religion (I mean the society that follows its inspirations and its teachings and is formed in its image) has emerged from the first period to which I have just alluded; thenceforth free and independent, it seems to advance rapidly on the road of progress and science, whereas Muslim society has not yet freed itself from the tutelage of religion. Realizing, however, that the Christian religion preceded the Muslim religion in the world by many centuries, I cannot keep from hoping that Muhammadan society will succeed someday in breaking its bonds and marching resolutely in the path of civilization after the manner of Western society, for which the Christian faith, despite its rigors and intolerance, was not at all an invincible obstacle. No, I cannot admit that this hope be denied to Islam. I plead here with Monsieur Renan not the cause of the Muslim religion, but that of several hundreds of millions of men, who would thus be condemned to live in barbarism and ignorance.

In truth, the Muslim religion has tried to stifle science and stop its progress. It has thus succeeded in halting the philosophical or intellectual movement and in turning minds from the search for scientific truth. A similar attempt, if I am not mistaken, was made by the Christian religion, and the venerated leaders of the Catholic church have not yet disarmed so far as I know. They continue to fight energetically against what they call the spirit of vertigo and error. I know all the difficulties that the Muslims will have to surmount to achieve the same degree of civilization, access to the truth with the help of philosophic and scientific methods being forbidden them. A true believer must, in fact, turn from the path of studies that have for their object scientific truth, studies on which all truth must depend, according to an opinion accepted at least by some people in Europe. Yoked, like an ox to the plow, to the dogma whose slave he is, he must walk eternally in the furrow that has been traced for him in advance by the interpreters of the law. Convinced, besides, that his religion contains in itself all morality and all sciences, he at-

taches himself resolutely to it and makes no effort to go beyond.

Why should he exhaust himself in vain attempts? What would be the benefit of seeking truth when he believes he possesses it all? Will he be happier on the day when he has lost his faith, the day when he has stopped believing that all perfections are in the religion he practices and not in another? Wherefore he despises science. I know all this, but I know equally that this Muslim and Arab child whose portrait Monsieur Renan traces in such vigorous terms and who, at a later age, becomes "a fanatic, full of foolish pride in possessing what he believes to be absolute truth,'" belongs to a race that has marked its passage in the world, not only by fire and blood, but by brilliant and fruitful achievements that prove its taste for science, for all the sciences, including philosophy (with which, I must recognize, it was unable to live happily for long).

I am led here to speak of the second point that Monsieur Renan treated in his lecture with an incontestable authority. No one denies that the Arab people, while still in the state of barbarism, rushed into the road of intellectual and scientific progress with a rapidity only equaled by the speed of its conquests, since in the space of a century, it acquired and assimilated almost all the Greek and Persian sciences that had developed slowly during several centuries on their native soil, just as it extended its domination from the Arabian peninsula up to the mountains of the Himalaya and the summit of the Pyrenees.

One might say that in all this period the sciences made astonishing progress among the Arabs and in all the countries under their domination. Rome and Byzantium were then the seats of theological and philosophical sciences, as well as the shining center and burning hearth of all human knowledge. Having followed for several centuries the path of civilization, the Greeks and Romans walked with assurance over the vast field of science and philosophy. There came, however, a time when their researches were abandoned and their studies interrupted.

The monuments they had built to science collapsed, and their most precious books were relegated to oblivion. The Arabs, ignorant and barbaric as they were in origin, took up what had been abandoned by the civilized nations, rekindled the extinguished sciences, developed them and gave them a brilliance they had never had. Is not this the index and proof of their natural love for sciences? It is true that the Arabs took from the Greeks their philosophy as they stripped the Persians of what made their fame in antiquity; but these sciences, which they usurped by right of conquest, they developed, extended, clarified, perfected, completed, and coordinated with a perfect taste and a rare precision and exactitude. Besides, the French, the Germans, and the English were not so far from Rome and Byzantium as were the Arabs, whose capital was Baghdad. It was therefore easier for the former to exploit the scientific treasures that were buried in these two great cities. They made no effort in this direction until Arab civilization lit up with its reflections the summits of the Pyrenees and poured its light and riches on the Occident. The Europeans welcomed Aristotle, who had emigrated and become Arab; but they did not think of him at all when he was Greek and their neighbor. Is there not in this another proof, no less evident, of the intellectual superiority of the Arabs and of their natural attachment to philosophy? It is true that after the fall of the Arab kingdom in the Orient as in the Occident, the countries that had become the great centers of science, like Iraq and Andalusia, fell again into ignorance and became the center of religious fanaticism; but one cannot conclude from this sad spectacle that the scientific and philosophic progress of the Middle Ages was not due to the Arab people who ruled at that time.

Monsieur Renan does do them this justice. He recognizes that the Arabs conserved and maintained for centuries the hearth of science. What nobler mission for a people! But while recognizing that from about A.D. 775 to near the middle of the thirteenth century, that is to say during about 500 years, there were in Muslim countries very distinguished scholars and thinkers, and that during this period the Muslim world was superior in intellectual culture to the Christian world, Monsieur Renan has said that the philosophers of the first centuries of Islam as well as the statesmen who became famous in this period were mostly from Harran [in Anatolia], from Andalusia, and from Iran.

There were also among them Transoxianan and Syrian priests. I do not wish to deny the great qualities of the Persian scholars nor the role that they played in the Arab world; but permit me to say that the Harranians were Arabs and that the Arabs in occupying Spain and Andalusia did not lose their nationality; they remained Arabs. Several centuries before Islam the Arabic language was that of the Harranians. The fact that they preserved their former religion, Sabaeanism, does not mean they should be considered

foreign to the Arab nationality. The Syrian priests were also for the most part Ghassanian Arabs converted to Christianity.

As for Ibn Bajja [Andalusia-Morocco, circa 1106–1138], Ibn Rushd (Averroes) [Andalusia-Morocco, 1126–1198], and [Abu Bakr Muhammad] Ibn Tufayl [Andalusia-Morocco, circa 1110–1185], one cannot say that they are not just as Arab as [Abu Yusuf Ya'qub] al-Kindi [Arabia, circa 801–866] because they were not born in Arabia, especially if one is willing to consider that human races are only distinguished by their language, and that if this distinction should disappear, nations would not take long to forget their diverse origins. The Arabs who put their arms in the service of the Muslim religion, and who were simultaneously warriors and apostles, did not impose their language on the defeated, and wherever they established themselves, they preserved it for them with a jealous care. No doubt Islam, in penetrating the conquered countries with the violence that is known, transplanted there its language, its manners, and its doctrine, and these countries could not thenceforth avoid influence. Iran is an example; but it is possible that in going back to the centuries preceding the appearance of Islam, one would find that the Arabic language was not then entirely unknown to Persian scholars. The expansion of Islam gave it, it is true, a new scope, and the Persian scholars converted to the Muhammadan faith thought it an honor to write their books in the language of the Qur'an. The Arabs cannot, no doubt, claim for themselves the glory that renders these writers illustrious, but we believe that they do not need this claim; they have among themselves enough celebrated scholars and writers. What would happen if, going back to the first period of Arab domination, we followed step by step the first group from which was formed this conquering people who spread their power over the world, and if, eliminating everything that is outside this group and its descendants, we did not take into account either the influence it exercised on minds or the impulse it gave to the sciences? Would we not be led, thus, no longer to recognize in conquering peoples other virtues or merits than those that flow from the material fact of conquest? All conquered peoples would then regain their moral autonomy and would attribute to themselves all glory, no part of which could be legitimately claimed by the power that fructified and developed these germs. Thus, Italy would come to say to France that neither [Cardinal

Jules] Mazarin [1602–1661] nor [Emperor Napoléon] Bonaparte [1769–1821] belonged to her; Germany or England would in turn claim the scholars who, having come to France, made its professorships illustrious and enhanced the brilliance of its scientific renown. The French, on their side, would claim for themselves the glory of the offspring of those illustrious families who, after [the revocation of] the edict of Nantes [in 1685], emigrated to all Europe. And if all Europeans belong to the same stock, one can with justice claim that the Harranians and the Syrians, who are Semites, belong equally to the great Arab family.

It is permissible, however, to ask oneself why Arab civilization, after having been thrown in such a live light on the world, suddenly became extinguished; why this torch has not been relit since, and why the Arab world still remains buried in profound darkness. Here the responsibility of the Muslim religion appears complete. It is clear that wherever it became established, this religion tried to stifle the sciences, and it was marvelously served in its designs by despotism.

[Jalal al-Din] al-Suyuti [Egyptian scholar, 1445–1505] tells that the Caliph [Musa] al-Hadi [reigned 785–786] put to death in Baghdad 5,000 philosophers in order to destroy sciences in the Muslim countries down to their roots. Admitting that this historian exaggerated the number of victims, it remains nonetheless established that this persecution took place, and it is a bloody stain for the history of a religion, as it is for the history of a people. I could find in the past of the Christian religion analogous facts. Religions, by whatever names they are called, all resemble each other. No agreement and no reconciliation are possible between these religions and philosophy. Religion imposes on man its faith and its belief, whereas philosophy frees him of it totally or in part. How could one therefore hope that they would agree with each other? When the Christian religion, under the most modest and seductive forms, entered Athens and Alexandria, which were, as everyone knows, the two principal centers of science and philosophy, after becoming solidly es-tablished in these two cities its first concern was to put aside real science and philosophy, trying to stifle both under the bushes of theological discussions, to explain the inexplicable mysteries of the Trinity, the Incarnation, and Transubstantiation. It will always be thus. Whenever religion will have the upper hand, it will eliminate philosophy; and the contrary happens when it is philosophy that reigns as sovereign mistress. So long as humanity exists, the struggle will not cease between dogma and free investigation, between religion and philosophy; a desperate struggle in which, I fear, the triumph will not be for free thought, because the masses dislike reason, and its teachings are only understood by some intelligences of the elite, and because, also, science, however beautiful it is, does not completely satisfy humanity, which thirsts for the ideal and which likes to exist in dark and distant regions that the philosophers and scholars can neither perceive nor explore.

The Law

Mirza Malkum Khan (Iran, 1833–1908) was an activist and pamphleteer who, in different periods of his life, alternately served and agitated against the Iranian monarchy. Born in the Armenian town of Julfa, next to Isfahan, Malkum and his father converted to Islam, but retained certain Christian practices. Malkum was educated in France on a government scholarship, and returned to Iran to teach at the country's first modern-style school, the Dar al-Funun (House of Sciences). A decade later, he was exiled for organizing secret societies devoted to freedom and equality—then hired the following year in the Iranian diplomatic service, rising to the post of ambassador in London. When he was fired in 1889 in a scandal over a proposed Iranian lottery, Malkum devoted himself to a journal called *Qanun* (*The Law*), which campaigned on behalf of constitutionalism. This journal, appearing periodically in forty-two issues over a decade, was smuggled into Iran, where its popularity threw the shah into "paroxysms of irritation and alarm," according to the British ambassador. The journal inspired the makers of the Iranian Constitutional Revolution of 1906, yet Malkum played no direct role in that movement, as he had ceased his oppositional activities upon reappointment to diplomatic service, as ambassador to Italy, in 1899. Issue number 10 of *Qanun*, translated here in its entirety—probably written entirely by Malkum, including the purported letters to the editor—demonstrates Malkum's vivid prose and some of his characteristic themes, including the necessity of conspiracy to promote the rule of Law.[1]

O intimate members of the royal household, O exalted courtiers of the shah! O ministers, O dignitaries of the state! Why don't you tell the shah, clearly and distinctly, how things really are? You who know what anger has gathered in the hearts of the people. You know how much the servants and subjects are subject to harassment. You know the level to which the provinces have been reduced. You see the ruthlessness with which the income of the state and the nation is being plundered. You know how ambassadors and all the Westerners trample on our rights. You know to what extent the existence of the state and the health of the monarchy are being shaken. A thousand times you have confided to one another that this cannot continue. So why haven't you told the shah of these matters? You say you are afraid that such words will displease the shah. Then what is the meaning of loyalty to the state? If you place personal safety over the interests of the state, then what difference is there between the aforementioned and cowardly traitors?

Look about you for a moment or two, and see how many regimes are being overthrown in this age of ours. How many monarchs are forced to flee. How many thrones have toppled, how many dear souls have been dragged through the dirt of degradation. All these calamities would not have occurred, but for the ruthlessness of the traitorous courtiers, who would not permit their meek rulers to be freed for one minute from the manacles of their sycophancy. If you have a speck of honesty and justice in service to your benefactor, these terrifying accounts would force you to speak out instantly. And if, unfortunately, you do not have enough manly candor to say openly how things really are, have enough sense at least not to

Malkum Khan, *Qanun* (*The Law*), London, England, No. 10, circa 1890. Translation from Persian and introduction by Charles Kurzman. Thanks to Mahmoud Sadri for translation assistance.

1. Hamid Algar, *Mirza Malkum Khan* (Berkeley: University of California Press, 1973); Edward G. Brown, *The Press and Poetry of Modern Persia* (Cambridge, England: Cambridge University Press, 1914); Isma'il Ra'in, *Mirza Malkum Khan* (*Prince Malkum Khan*) (Tehran, Iran: Bungah-i Matbu'ati-i Safi'alishah, 1971).

deny our words. Now that we have stumbled onto the path of nationalist martyrdom, out of insanity or loyalty, allow us to present the grievances of the speechless masses to the royal court without your taunting blows. Unless you want to maintain this good-natured shah, this wise shah, this oppressed shah, as leader of a group of enslaved beggars, allow—allow—us to make the bearer of these eminent qualities the emperor of the people of Iran.

Ever since the sound of *The Law* has rung out, from that moment the broken-hearted people of Iran have understood that they have invisible champions in this journal. On one hand, they have drowned us with petitions of grievance, and on the other hand they have gladdened us with support and useful information.

A noble and wise officer, who has served this munificent state for almost 40 years, writes from glorious Karbala [an Ottoman city, now in Iraq, site of an important Shi'i Muslim shrine]:

Nothing remains in this life for me. My property is gone. My reputation is gone. My servant's wages are gone. My family is gone. My brothers and kinfolk have all perished in the misfortune of service to this state. There is no scoundrel who has not afflicted me. There is no humiliation whose bitterness I have not tasted. Now that I have reached here, after a thousand troubles, I don't know which unbeliever to seek refuge with, so that I may be released from the grasp of these man-eating oppressors.

O dear brother, all of these calamities and bitternesses that you recognize as your personal portion are the lot of most of the people of Iran. What good is complaint and despair? Thousands were oppressed like you, whimpered, were destroyed, and left. If you truly think of yourself as having rights, as worthy of better than this standing, in the name of God the arena of Humanity[2] awaits you. With the talents and abilities that you have, not only can you save yourself, but you have the power to revive a whole country. For the thousand sacrifices that you foolishly made in devotion to the oppressors of the age, spend one

in the service of Humanity. Then you will see the poisons of misfortune change into tangible comforts and moral pleasures for your enjoyment!

We, the people of Iran, do not have the right to ask his imperial holiness why the state authorities have killed thus-and-such a minister. Why so-and-so plundered these houses. Why our kingdom is being ruined so. Why our nation has been bound to such abject servility.

His imperial highness would reply that you, the people of Iran, deserve this servility. If you were Men, if you had as much perception and zeal as other countries' women have, how would this handful of ignorant ministers of mine be able to rule over you so harshly and so confidently, you who number more than 10 million? If you had the sense to consider yourself Men, as others do, and to understand the meaning of unity, at least as well as some animals do, what foolish oppressor would dare to touch the rights of your Humanity?

A prince with good sense, who belongs to the rank of intimate courtiers of his royal majesty, writes:

You have lit an unusual fire. I see no head that is not full of enthusiasm for the Law. All the royal servants, who believed in Humanity less than anyone, have become great supporters of Humanity. Whenever they find a safe spot, their conversation is all praise and acclaim and yearning for the advancement of Humanity. Some weak-willed friends, who have become in spirit greater devotees of Humanity than we, have lately taken to slandering Humanity as much as they can in the presence of the shah, as a sort of *taqiya* [the Shi'i Muslim tradition of pious dissimulation]. But the depravity of their plan quickly came to light. Now, whenever someone speaks ill of Humanity and the founders of *The Law*, the shah, with that cleverness and slyness of his, immediately recognizes the purpose of such stupid hypocrisies.

But strangest of all is the rush of women toward the advent of Humanity. It happens that most of our noblewomen—in proportion with the intellect and prudence that they have developed far more than the men of our age—have perceived the meaning and virtues of Humanity far better than the men, that is, better than our non-men. My aunt—al-Saltana, in particular, who has really become crazy in her enthusiasm for this endeavor, has started a secret riot along with sev-

2. ["Humanity," in addition to denoting all people who have achieved enlightenment, refers specifically to members of the Society of Humanity, a secret organization that Malkum Khan founded around 1890 in conjunction with his journal *Qanun*.—Trans.]

eral of her friends in the royal quarters, especially among the highest ranks, that defies description.

Why should there be any surprise that the natural essence of the Iranians has appeared in this way, under the harsh blows of these times? Nobody said that the nation of this great race would remain buried forever in this graveyard of misery. On the contrary, the religious authorities and the masters of perspicacity have told us repeatedly that these times of misfortune will come to an end, and that the sun of enlightenment will breathe a new spirit into this blessed land.

Some ignorant old people and some shameless ignoramuses say that they despair of this people. The cause of this despair is their own idleness, not any defect in the zeal of the nation. Show [me] the people of any region of the earth who are more thirsty for progress and fit for work than Iranians. Although the various recent struggles of this kingdom have been fruitless, the cause of this is that none of the knowledgeable authorities divining the heavenly secrets have yet seen fit to show clearly where the destination is, and which path to take. Now that divine beneficence has opened the gates of Humanity in all directions, what further obstacles, what hesitations remain for the flowing currents of this nation's forces? Soon the rays of the sun of Humanity shall leave no stone in this kingdom numb and useless. Soon nobody will lack strength, as in the time of Ignorance [that is, the pre-Islamic period], and say, "Let us wait and see what the others do." Soon everyone of good sense will take on the duties of Humanity, alone, without waiting for others to act. You who read these words, you who call yourself a human being, you who wish to have the right to live in this world—for the defense of this right and the proof of your Humanity, what fresh disgrace are you awaiting, what miracles are you expecting from others?

A youth educated at the Academy of Sciences and Technology in Tehran [the leading modern-style school in Iran] requests that we publish these questions and answers here.

Why were this kingdom's concessions not given to the subjects of the kingdom?
Because we have decided that our subjects should remain as poor as possible.
Why are the people not allowed to send their children abroad for education?

Because we want our subjects to be as ignorant and blind as possible.
Why is the signature of other governments worth millions, and that of our government not worth a single coin?
Because our government, a thousand times a day, spits on its pacts and contracts.
Why has the king himself gone to Europe three times and not allowed his sons to go once in forty years?
Because it was decided that our princes should remain ignorant, inconsequential, and useless.
Why are uneducated and untalented individuals preferred to others?
Because we want the name and practice of science and art to fall into complete disuse in Iran.
Why have we become such deniers of science and enemies of wisdom?
Because science opens the people's eyes, and when the people find their voice and their courage, they say, "We are not animals, we want to be Men like others, we will defend our rights as Men." And this is certainly against the rules.

An individual from Isfahan writes,
"What is unlawful government?"
That which plunders its subjects at will, sells the rights of the nation to any foreigner who wants them, wastes the kingdom's treasures on any base whim, shamelessly exploits the salaries and claims of its employees, brazenly denies its obligations and pacts, and plucks out your eyes whenever it pleases, throws your family in the street, confiscates your property, and slits your stomach open.
What should we do to change this?
Become a human being and demand the Law.

We sincerely regret that we cannot respond personally to every one of the friends who have written on these subjects. Here, we can only allude to some of their statements in summary fashion. People of intelligence will easily identify their specific answer in these words that we set out.

M. D. The concession that you want to take from the government is useless, because the signature of our government is no longer worth anything.

A. J. The truth dawns where it is least expected.

A. N. It makes no sense for a man to be as fearful as you are.

S. M. I will send it, on condition that for the time being, you do not reveal how and where you received it.

A. S. Islam is the collection of divine laws, and Humanity is the observance of these laws.

Q. D. The remedy is just as you specified.

To all of the friends of *The Law*:

The office of *The Law* has relocated from its London address. The correspondence bureau has moved closer to Iran. From now on, please send all materials to one of the correspondents of *The Law* in Baghdad, Bombay, or Ashkabad.

O wise one of an exalted nature! What need is there for me to specify your noble name in these pages? A perceptive mind will have no trouble recognizing immediately that my words are meant for you.

You know the truth. The state and our entire existence have tumbled over a frightening precipice. We in the societies of Men are shouting to wake people up and prevent this terrible tragedy through the grace of the strength of Humanity. You, the noble child of the homeland, what right do you have in this widespread crisis to say, like those other non-men, "What's it to me?" Rest assured that up to this day, you have been unaware of the reality and dignity of your destiny. Your mission in the world is far loftier than the fanciful dreams that have rendered your true being useless. The numerous practical difficulties have nothing to do with this. Those individuals who hold high offices in the world, how are they better than you? If you would only look into your heart, your veins will testify that God created you for service to this nation. Why are you waiting to express your intrinsic nature, which was entrusted to your being for this great purpose? A thousand times you have wept bloody tears over the calamities of this dear homeland. For years you have wished for an opportunity for service. Now that divine will has appointed the rising sun of Humanity, in a manifest miracle, as the means of saving this kingdom, why do you hesitate to take up this timeless mission? What are you afraid of? After this, what heathen, what wretch could call into question the purity of Humanity? What need have I to tell you what sort of zealous disciples have undergone what type of sacrifices in this alliance of mutual support? You will soon be astonished and ecstatic to witness the divine intention of religious duty and the honor of erudition as the greatest of the *'ulama'* [religious scholars] of Islam take up the leadership

of this army of prosperity. To light this path of deliverance, what better torch than the science of the Islamic authorities? To fortify the hearts of the weak, what better reasoning than this word of enlightenment? We proclaim from first to last that we would never and in no way pretend to make a higher claim. We have not told and will not tell anyone to come and recognize us, to make offerings to us, or to obey us. On the contrary, we tell all people to make themselves a manifestation of Humanity, even among the tradesmen and soldiers and others whom no one counts among men of note. Everyone can advance into this arena of Humanity. We are prepared to give ourselves in service to them, life and limb. Why go this far? You who are reading these words, whatever meaning name and position may have for you, we accord you a higher meaning and position, and readily offer you the glad tidings that from this moment on, commanded by divine decree, you are appointed to the absolute trusteeship of these pages [that is, of the journal].

The performance of this great mission is to be devoted entirely to the knowledge and competence of your exalted soul. Among the largest services that the spirit of Humanity expects from that noble person, we draw your lofty attention specifically to the four following items.

First, bring the copies of *The Law* in an appropriate way to whatever places and people you see fit.

Second, appoint the trusteeship of Humanity to whatever person you deem deserving, with sufficient training, from among the *'ulama'*, the learned ones, and distinguished Men.

Third, because women in every kingdom and all eras have been the best proponents of the advancement of truth, particularly higher knowledge, it is incumbent upon you to appoint good and pure members of this respected half of the nation, by all legitimate means, as master of their sex and instigators of popular zeal.

Fourth, because some agents have lost all their possessions during their service to Humanity, and in fact have become spiritual martyrs for these truths, equity and manly duty demand that you strive to lend them assistance and relief to the extent of your powers of generosity. Furthermore, take great care that all members of Humanity give material aid, if only one dinar a month, to especially needy trustees.

What more can we say that your intellect and zeal have not already recognized? Beyond this, what need have we to impose on your noble time by reminding you of these things, by letter or in person? With all respect, and utmost pity, we urge you to take note if, at this point, at this very moment, the spirit of Humanity takes flight in the world of conscience, kisses your chosen forehead, and to complete this essay whispers in the ear of your intelligence the words:

God is great.

13   Muhammad Husayn Na'ini

Government in the Islamic Perspective

Muhammad Husayn Na'ini (Iran, 1860–1936) was an Iranian religious scholar who lived for decades at Shi'i seminary cities in Iraq, which was part of the Ottoman Empire until 1918. When the constitutional movement took power in Iran in 1906, Na'ini was the assistant to one of the leading scholars of Najaf, whom he helped in arranging an influential *fatwa* (religious ruling) issued in support of the constitutionalists. Three years later, Na'ini expanded on this theme in a treatise defending constitutional limits on power in Islamic terms—the introductory section of which is presented in this chapter. This treatise was widely distributed in Iran and provided theological support for the constitutionalists in the face of monarchist and clerical opposition. Na'ini later came to reject political involvement, famously—though possibly apocryphally—urging that all copies of his treatise be thrown into the Tigris River. Na'ini even supported the rise of the Pahlavi dictatorship in the 1920s. Yet his text survived long after its author's disavowal. Its biting criticism of both monarchical and clerical despotism has remained common knowledge among educated Iranians and a thorn in the side of successive dynasties in Iran, as well as the Islamic Republic.[1]

Thanks are due to God, Lord of the two worlds, and salutations are due to the noblest of the earliest and the latest and the seal of the prophets, Muhammad and his pure progeny, and damnation is deserved for all of their foes, until the Day of Judgment.

And then, those aware of the history of the world have come to realize that prior to the Crusades, the Christian nations and the Europeans were deprived not only of all the varieties of natural sciences but also of the sciences of civilization, practical reason, and political axioms. This was due either to the lack of such knowledge in their divine parchments or to adulteration of their heavenly books. After that fateful event [the Crusades], those nations attributed their defeat to their lack of access to civilizational sciences and their general ignorance. Thus they considered curing this mother of all ailments as the greatest of their goals and pursued knowledge as a lover who seeks after the beloved. So they appropriated the principles of civilization and politics

implicit in the Islamic holy books and traditions, and in the edicts of 'Ali [son-in-law and fourth successor of the Prophet] and other early leaders of Islam, as they have justly acknowledged in their earlier histories, as they have admitted that learning such principles and sciences conducive to such spectacular advances in such a short period of time would be impossible for unaided human reason. Therefore the progress and perseverance of the West in translation, interpretation, and application of these principles on the one hand, and the concomitant regression of the people of Islam and their subjugation at the hands of unbelievers [the Mongol conquerors] resulted in such a state that Muslims gradually forgot the principles of their own historical origins and even supposed that abject subordination is a necessity of Islamic life. Therefore they thought that the commandments of Islam are contrary to civilization, reason, and justice—the fountainhead of progress—and as such, they equated Islam with slavery and savagery.

Muhammad Husayn Na'ini, *Tanbih al-umma wa tanzih al-milla ya hukumat az nazar-i islam* (*Exhortation of the Faithful and Purification of the Nation, or Government from the Perspective of Islam*), 6th ed. (Tehran, Iran: Shirkat-i Sahami-i Intishar, 1960). First published in 1909. Translation from Persian and introduction by Mahmoud Sadri.

1. Abdul-Hadi Hairi, *Shi'ism and Constitutionalism in Iran* (Leiden, Netherlands: E. J. Brill, 1977); Baqir Parham, "Nigahi bih nazariyyat-i Na'ini" (A Look at Na'ini's Theories), *Chishm-andaz* (*Perspective*), number 5, 1988, pp. 48–77; Tawfiq Sayf, *Didda al-istibdad* (*Against Dictatorship*) (Beirut, Lebanon: al-Markaz al-thaqafi al-'arabi, 1999).

At this juncture in history, with God's benevolent support, the retrogressive trajectory of the Islamic world has been halted and slavery under the imperious passions of dictatorial rulers has been terminated [the reference is to the Iranian Constitutional Revolution of 1906, and possibly also to the Ottoman Young Turk Revolution of 1908]. The Muslim community has, thanks to the superb guidance and reasoning of its clerical leaders, become aware of the true requirements of its religion and its God-given freedoms. Thus they have endeavored to free themselves from the pharaohs of the time, and to restore their legitimate national rights of partnership and equality in all affairs. In their struggle to break the chains of slavery and in claiming their legitimate rights, Muslims have hazarded oceans of fire, from which they have emerged as a phoenix. They have faced martyrdom and spilled their pure blood in order to achieve the great privilege of national salvation and prosperity, and in this holy project they have followed the utterance of the prince of the oppressed, Husayn [grandson of the Prophet and third *Imam* of Shi'i Islam], who extolled "those who prefer noble death to the abject life of servitude."

The momentous edicts of the leaders of the Ja'fari religion [Shi'i Islam] in the city of Najaf,[2] and the subsequent edicts of the elders of Istanbul [Sunni Islam] who unanimously declared the struggle for these holy and legitimate goals [of constitutionalism] as a necessity of religion, exonerated Islam from acquiescing to such tyrannical and irrational rules. These were clear historical documents concerning the position of the Islamic leadership on the issue, thus silencing critical tongues. But the man-eating pack of wolves in Iran attempted to sustain the polluted tree of injustice, tyranny, and the plunder of the lives and property of the Muslims. Finding no better pretext for this than religion, they turned to the pharaonic declaration: "I fear for you, for they may change your religion." [Qur'an, Sura 40, Verse 26]

Thus they allied themselves with the pharaoh of Iran and revived the atrocities of Zahhak [a mythical Iranian tyrant] and Genghis [Khan, Mongol ruler, 1206–1227], and called it religion. Absolute power belongs only to God, yet they declared it un-Islamic to struggle against the absolute power of earthly tyrants. They dared to contaminate this sublime religion with such an insult; they dared to commit this grave affront to the prophet of Islam, even in God's sovereign domain. This is the extent of their injustice, that they at once affronted the Creator and His creation. Verily God spoke the truth in the holy Qur'an: "Therefore evil was the end of those who did evil, for they denied the signs of God and made fun of them." [Sura 30, Verse 10]

An authentic *hadith* [tradition of the Prophet] states: "When apostasy prevails on earth it is incumbent upon the knowledgeable to reveal their knowledge, and if they fail in doing so God's damnation will be upon them." Accordingly, silence in the face of such an outrage and derision of religion, and failure to support the holy religion in repelling such a mischief and injustice, is contrary to the duty, and even abets the injustice. So this lowliest of servants of the illustrious religion has taken it upon himself to discharge his responsibility, to render this service, and to reveal the incongruity of this apostasy with the essential necessities of Islam. It is my hope that with God's blessed succor this offering will achieve divine approbation, thus making it unnecessary for others to undertake such a task. "And I have no success except in God. I have put all my confidence in Him, I repent and take refuge in him. And he is the ultimate guide toward righteousness."[3]

Since the aim of this essay is to admonish the faithful concerning the necessities of the religion and to cleanse the nation of the apostasy [of tyranny], I have given it the title of "Exhortation of the Faithful and Purification of the Nation." I will organize it in an introduction, five chapters, and a conclusion.

Introduction: An Analysis of the Nature of Tyranny, Conditionality[4] of the Government, Achieving a Constitution and a Consultative Assembly of the People, and an Explanation of the Meaning of Liberty and Equality

2. [The author is referring to the joint edicts of three grand *ayatullah*s in Najaf, in today's Iraq, declaring the Iranian constitutional revolution to be in accordance with the spirit of Islam.—Trans.]

3. [This phrase is in Arabic but is not quoted from the Qur'an. Using such phrases in Persian texts is the equivalent of using Latin phrases in English texts.—Trans.]

4. [The term "conditionality" (*mashrutiyat*) also was used to mean "constitutionalism."—Trans.]

Be aware of the notion that all sages of Islam and of the nations of the world agree that some form of polity and government is necessary for the constitution of the society and the life of humankind, whether it be personal or group rule, legitimate or illegitimate government, freely elected, hereditary, or dictatorially imposed. Also, it is necessarily true that the maintenance of the honor, independence, and nationality of every nation, be it in religious or national affairs, is contingent upon their own endeavors. Otherwise, their privileges, the honor of their religion, the integrity of their country, and the independence of their nation will be utterly destroyed, regardless of how wealthy, progressive, and civilized they may be. That is why the pure *shari'a* [religious law] of Islam has designated the protection of the "essential constitution" of Islam as the highest of duties, specifying Islamic government as a holy duty invested in the institution of the imamate [Shi'i religious leadership]. (A detailed explication of this issue is outside of the scope of this essay.) It is evident that all worldly affairs are contingent upon government, and that the protection of every nation's honor and nationality is contingent upon self-rule, based upon two basic principles:

1. Protection of domestic order, education of the citizenry, ensuring that rights are allotted to the rightful, and deterring people from invading others' rights—these are among the internal duties of government.
2. Protection of the nation from foreign invasion, neutralizing the typical maneuvers in such cases, providing for a defensive force, and so on—these are what the experts in terminology call the "protection of the essential constitution" of Islam.

The *shari'a* canons concerning the upholding of these two holy duties are known as political and civilizational laws and are considered as the second subdivision of "practical reason."[5] This is why the greatest kings and emperors of Persia and Rome were adamant in choosing competent sages in theoretical and practical disciplines for the management of societal affairs. These sages realized the necessity and legitimacy of discharging such duties, and this real-

ization persuaded them to accept such responsibilities, despite their abhorrence of tyrannical rule. One can even surmise that the reason for any government, any system of taxation, any organization of forces in society, whether initiated by divine prophets or by sages, was to uphold these principles and discharge such duties. The pure *shari'a* too has endeavored to remedy the shortcomings [of government] and to stipulate its conditions and limitations.

The nature of the ruler's domination, in terms of the extent of the exclusiveness of its rule, can only be conceived of as one of two kinds: It is either "possessive" or "preservative."

The possessive form of government is the case in which a prince considers the nation his personal property to dispose of as his whims and desires dictate. He treats the nation like a stable full of animals meant to satisfy his passions and wishes. He rewards or punishes people insofar as they aid or impede him in realizing his ends. He does not hesitate to imprison, banish, torture, or execute his opponents, tear them to pieces, and feed them to his hounds. Or to encourage his pack of wolves to spill their blood and plunder their property. He can separate any proprietor from his property, and give it to his entourage. He upholds or tramples people's rights as he sees fit. He considers himself the sole possessor of the right to expropriate any holdings, to sell, rent, or give away any part of the nation or its rights, or to exact any taxes for his personal private use. His attempt to maintain order and to defend the nation is like that of a farmer toward his farm. If he wishes, he keeps it. If not, he gives it away to the obsequious bunch around him. On the slightest suggestion, he sells and mortgages national rights to finance his silly and hedonistic trips abroad.[6] He doesn't even hesitate to give himself leave for open sexual debauchery at the expense of his subjects, and still, he adorns himself with divine titles worthy of God. His courtiers help him identify his powers of tyranny, domination, passion, and anger with those of the nation. They help him to arrogate to himself God's attribute: "He cannot be questioned about what He does, but they will be questioned." [Qur'an, Sura 21, Verse 23]

---

5. [As distinct from "theoretical reason," in Islamic philosophy. The field of practical reason consists of three subdivisions: purification of the soul, management of society or politics, and home economics.—Trans.]

6. [This jab is meant particularly for the late nineteenth and early twentieth century shahs who sold exorbitant concessions to foreign corporations in order to finance lavish personal trips to Europe.—Trans.]

This form of government, because it is autocratic and arbitrary, is known as possessive, tyrannical, enslaving, imperious, and dictatorial. It is clear why each of these titles would be appropriate for such a form of government. The head of such a form of government is known as an absolute ruler, "owner of the yokes," dictator, and so on. The nation that is subject to such rule should be called servile, downtrodden, and oppressed. And insofar as they are alienated from their own resources and wealth, like little orphans, they may be called "children" as well. And insofar as their use for their rulers is like the use of crops for the farmer, they may be called "vegetative"! The degrees of dictatorship exerted by this form of government varies according to the personal attributes and rational faculties of the princes and their courtiers, as well as the degree of the awareness of nations of their rights and the rights of their rulers, and the degree of their devotion to monotheistic or polytheistic religions. (For this affects the leave they give to their rulers to lord over them as the sole arbiter and proprietor of their rights.) The most extreme form of tyranny is where the ruler declares himself God. Its power will be limited to the extent to which those subject to such a rule resist it. The rule is absolute if the citizens acquiesce to it, as happened under the rule of the pharaohs. And according to the old adage: "People follow the religion of their princes." They in turn treat their subordinates as petty tyrants. The root of this sprawling, degenerate tree is none but the nation's ignorance of its own rights and the rights of its rulers, and a general lack of responsibility, accountability, watchful deliberation, and checks and balances.

The second form of government is that in which rule does not belong to an absolute arbiter. Government is based on discharging the aforementioned legitimate responsibilities. It is a limited form of government, and the ruler's authority is rule-bound and conditional to the same extent.

These two forms of government are distinct both in their true nature and in their effects. Because the former is, in all its manifestations, based on domination and possession, the nation is hostage to the whims of the leaders. National resources are at the mercy of the ruling group. They are not responsible to anyone for what they do, so whatever they refrain from doing deserves profuse thanks. If they killed someone but didn't mutilate him and feed him to their hounds, they should be thanked. If they expropriated property but didn't rape the women, they should be thanked. Everyone's relationship with the ruler is that of a slave to his master—even lower than that! It is the relationship of the farm animal to the farmer. It is even lower than that: it is the relation of the crop to the crop owner. Their only value is to sate the needs of their owner. They have no independent right to their own life and existence. In short, this relationship is like the relationship of creation to the Creator. On the other hand, the nature and essence of the latter form of government are stewardship, service, upholding domestic order, and protecting the nation. This form of government is committed to using the nation's resources to meet the nation's needs, not to satiate the passions of the rulers. Therefore, the authority of the government is limited to the abovementioned matters, and its interference in its citizen's affairs is conditional upon the necessity of reaching those [national] goals. The citizens are partners with government in the ownership of the nation's powers and resources. Everyone has equal rights, and the administrators are all stewards, not owners. They are responsible to the nation, and the slightest infraction is punishable by law. And all citizens share the national right to question the authorities safely, and are safe in doing so. Nor does anyone protesting the government bear the yoke of servitude of the sovereign prince or his courtiers. This kind of government is called limited, just, conditional, responsible, and delegated. And it is evident why each of these designations would be appropriate for such a form of government. Those in charge of such a government are called protectors, guardians, just arbiters, and responsible and just rulers. The nation that is blessed by such a government is called pious, emancipated, gallant, and alive. (And again, it is evident why each of these designations apply to such a nation.) The nature of this government is analogous to loaning and delegating, and it can survive only in the absence of usurpation and violations of trust. That which protects this form of government and prevents it from degenerating into an absolute and arbitrary rule is none other than the principle of accountability, vigilance, and responsibility.

The most exalted means of ensuring that a government will not betray the trust of the nation in any way, is, of course, having infallible rulers. This is the same principle that we Shi'is consider as a principle of our religion. It is necessarily evident that anyone who partakes of the exalted status of an infallible leader will be innocent of base passions, blessed with wisdom, and endowed with many moral attributes (whose explanation falls beyond the scope of this essay). Due to divine protection, such a leader is immune even to the slightest oversight and neglect. In short, this is a status "whose true nature is incomprehensible for ordinary human beings."

However, given a lack of access to such divine leaders,[7] seldom does it happen that the king is just and virtuous and happens to choose a perfectly wise and chaste supervisor of the affairs of the state, as happened in the case of Nushirvan [Khosrow, king of Iran, reigned 531–579] and [his vizier] Buzarjumihr a long time ago. The level of vigilance, accountability, and responsibility and the partnership, equality, and honesty of the people and the government achieved under Nushirvan's rule was an exception, not a rule, in history. It is indeed rarer than the rarest of jewels. It is impossible to expect it to happen with frequency in history. Thus in the absence of divine leadership and the exceedingly rare incidents of just kingship, nations may attempt a pale likeness of such a rule only under two conditions:

First, by imposing the aforementioned limits so that the government will strictly refrain from interfering in affairs in which it has no right to interfere. Under these conditions, governmental powers are stipulated in degree and kind, and the freedoms and rights of all classes of the people are formally guaranteed, in accordance to the requirements of religion. Violating the trust of the nation on either side and in any form, whether by excess or penury, is punishable by permanent termination of the service and other penal measures applicable to betrayal of trust. Since the written document concerning political and civil affairs of the nation is analogous to "practical treatises" [compendia of ritual duties issued by a religious scholar], in that it sets limits and the penalty for exceeding them, such a document is called the constitutional law or the constitution. There should be no doubt about its universal application, with no conditions, except in areas of conflict with religious laws. Other considerations concerning this issue, and the points that must be observed in order to maintain the integrity of the constitution will be mentioned later, God willing.

Second, strengthening the principle of vigilance, accountability, and complete responsibility by appointing a supervisory assembly of the wise, the well-wishers of the nation, and the experts in internal and external affairs, so they can discharge their duties in preventing violation and wrongdoing. The people's representatives are comprised of such individuals and their formal seat is called "the Assembly of National Consultation." True accountability and responsibility will preserve the limits on power and prevent the return of possessive government only if the executive branch is under the supervision of the legislative branch, and the legislative branch is responsible to every individual in the nation. Slackening either of these two responsibilities will lead to the deterioration of the limits on power and reversion of constitutional government to absolutism in the first case, and to oligarchic autocracy of the legislature in the second. The legitimacy of the supervision of the elected legislative assembly rests conclusively on the will of the nation's selection, according to the principles of Sunni Islam, which relies on the contractual powers of the *umma* [the Muslim community]. But according to Shi'i Islam, this legitimacy rests in the principle of the supervision of the "the public representatives" of the Hidden Imam during his occultation.[8] Thus the legislature should either include some of the experts in religious law or be comprised of people who are given leave by such personages to adjudicate on their behalf. The correction and confirmation of the representative assembly's decisions by the grand experts in religious law will suffice, as we shall, God willing, explain later.

From what we have explained so far it is clear that the foundation of the first form of government [tyranny] is absolute power, possession of the nation, inequality of the citizens with the government, and irresponsibility of the leaders. And all of these stem from a disregard of the above two principles. All of the devastation and atrocities in Iran; all that has ruined religion, government, and the nation in that land, knowing no limits, is of this sort. "There is no need for explanation after exhibition!"

The foundation of the second [constitutional] form of government, as you have learned, is limited

---

7. [The last of the infallible Imams, according to Shi'i theology, went into occultation in 874.—Trans.]

8. [In Shi'i Islam, the Hidden Imam had "specific representatives" for the first seventy years of his occultation. Since that time, those knowledgeable in religion serve as his "public representatives."—Trans.]

to delegation in affairs beneficial to the nation. Contrary to the first form, this government is based on partnership, liberty, and rights, including the right to financial accountability and supervision of administrators. All these, as well, are the results of the application of the above two principles.[9] These two principles and their corollaries were constituted by the founder of the religion. So long as they were protected, and Islamic government did not degenerate from the second to the first form, the pace of the expansion of Islam was mind-boggling. After Mu'awiyya [reigned 661–680] and the children of al-'As came to power, and all the principles and corollaries of Islamic government were transformed into their diametrical opposites, the situation changed. Still, so long as other nations too were enslaved in tyrannies of their own, nothing much changed, and Islam continued to enjoy a measure of stability despite its tyrannical leaders. However, as soon as the other nations realized the natural foundations of progressive government, it was inevitable that they would prosper and that the Islamic nation would become their inferiors and, worse, be returned to the pre-Islamic savagery and ignorance, like animals, even plants, in the degree of their servitude. "Verily, God does not change the state of a people til they change themselves." [Qur'an, Sura 13, Verse 11]

At any rate, since the basis of the former is thralldom and of the latter liberty, the text of the holy Qur'an and traditions of the holy infallible ones have on several occasions likened the servitude of the tyrants to idolatry, the opposite of liberty. They have guided Muslims to free their necks from the yoke of wretchedness.

For example, the Qur'an tells that the Pharaoh ruled over the children of Israel, although they did not worship him as the Egyptians did, and were tormented and imprisoned in Egypt and prevented from leaving for the holy land. In one verse [Sura 26, Verse 22] Moses, may peace be upon him, tells the

Pharaoh, "You consider me indebted to your hospitality even though you have enslaved the Israelites?" In another blessed verse [Sura 23, Verse 47] the Pharaoh says, "whose people are our slaves." In still another verse [Sura 7, Verse 127] he says, "and we shall subjugate them." It is evident that the slavery of the Israelites is an expression of this subjugation. The noblest of all, the Prophet of Islam, greetings be to him and his pure progeny, has stated in the authentic and frequently quoted tradition: "When the children of al-'As reach 30 in number, they shall turn the religion of God upside down and take the servants of God as their own servants." [*Hadith* scholar Fakhr al-Din Turayhi, circa 1571–1674,] the author of *Majma' al-Bahrain* [*The Bahrain Collection*], interpreted the word "servant" as "slave." Similarly, [Muhammad ibn Ya'qub Firuzabadi, circa 1329–1414,] the author of *Qamus* [*The Concordance*], generalized the meaning of the word "servant" in this context to "serfs" and "subordinates." This generalization is further confirmed in the blessed verse [Sura 6, Verse 94]: "you have left behind your servants [upon death]." The prescient *hadith* of the Prophet of Islam concludes that once the number of the fruits of the evil tree of tyranny reach 30, they will alter God's religion and take people as slaves. The Prophet designated this number of wrongdoers as a critical threshold at which they would begin to transform the form of Islamic government from stewardship to tyrannical possession. 'Ali, the commander of the faithful, to whom is due the highest of prayers and salutations, elaborated on the sufferings of the children of Israel at the hands of the Pharaoh and his people in a sermon: "the pharaohs took them as slaves." He then expounded on the meaning of slavery: "then they subjected them to the worst tortures and made them drink the poisonous cup drop by drop. They continued to languish in this state of abject ruin and defeated subjugation. They couldn't find any way to refuse or defend themselves." In the same sermon 'Ali explained the reign of the leaders of Iran and Rome over the children of Israel and Isma'il [the Arabs]. Although in these cases the domination was not connected to deification of the kings, as was the case in Egypt, nonetheless 'Ali treated it similarly: "In those days, kings of Iran and Rome were their masters, banishing them from the lush arable lands around the Sea of Iraq toward arid areas of the inland." In another sermon, after a few complaints of

---

9. In the first days of Islam, these two principles were applied so completely that the second caliph ['Umar ibn al-Khattab, 634–644] was publically rebuked for wearing an extra garment, when everyone had received only one garment. He had to send for his son 'Abdullah to testify that his father's second garment was his, and that he had willingly given it to his father. On another occasion, when he asked to be corrected if he erred, he was reminded by his audience that he could be straightened by the sword if he diverged from the straight path.

his blessed heart concerning the hypocrisy and rebellion of the inhabitants of Iraq, in which he
warned them that as a result of this behavior they
will be deprived of his leadership and become slaves
of Umayyad rule [661–750], he said: "And they will
find the Umayyads evil masters after me." 'Ali used
the word "master" instead of "steward" here. This
is in agreement with scores of other traditions concerning the conversion of the form of government
in early Islam. The prince of the oppressed, ['Ali's
younger son] Husayn, equated obedience to the
Umayyad leaders with abject slavery. In reply to the
coarse and rude bunch of Kufans who had declared,
"We have descended upon you by order of your
cousin," he replied: "I shall not give you my hand
of allegiance as an inferior, nor shall I confess my
allegiance to you as a slave. You have limited my
options to two: death and servitude. And far be it
from us to accept servitude. God has forbidden it
to us, and to His Messenger, and to the faithful, and
to the pure of heart, and to the proud souls, and to
all those who prefer noble death to a life of servitude." He echoed his father's words: "How can a
head bent before God be made to bend to any
other?" Thus Husayn refused to acquiesce. In order
to preserve his freedom and monotheism, he offered
up his life, his property, and his family. He made
this generous sacrifice for the liberation of the community of the faithful, to cleanse its body of the
impurities of hedonistic passions. This is why all
others in the history of Islam who have followed
Husayn's blessed precedent, who have made similar sacrifices, are called "resisters of injustice" and
"heroes of freedom." Truly, they are all grain pick-
ers of this abundant harvest and dew drinkers of this
vast ocean of resistance and freedom-seeking.

Husayn, peace be upon him and all those who
were martyred with him, addressed Hurr ibn Yazid
Riyahi [a Kufan military officer], after Hurr had de-
fected from the enemy and stood [with Husayn],
ready to be martyred in his blessed stirrups: "You are
the free one, Hurr, as your mother named you [Hurr
means "free"]. You shall live as a free and heroic
soul, in this world as well as the next." Likewise, the
verse [Sura 24, Verse 55] declares: "God has promised to make those of you who believe and do right,
leaders in the land, as He had made those before
them, and will establish their faith which He has
chosen for them, and change their fear into security.
They will worship Me and not associate any one with

Me. But those who disbelieve after this will be rep-
robates." This verse as well as the closing clauses of
the "Promulgation" prayer [a prominent piece of the
Shi'i liturgy] refer to the return of his holiness the
twelfth Imam, the awaited Messiah—may our lives
be sacrificed for him. The acquiescence of the *umma*
to tyrants is likened here to polytheism. As Husayn
himself stated, "I hold no allegiance to any tyrant of
my time." Also, interpretations of the blessed verse,
"They consider their rabbis and monks as lords,"
[Sura 9, Verse 31] hold that the verse refers to [Jews'
and Christians'] unquestioning obedience toward
popes and their courtiers. *Taqlid* [imitation] of religious leaders who pretend to present true religion is
no different from obedience to political tyrants. Either one is a form of idolatry. The above verse that
rebukes imitation of the ill-intentioned clergy and
ambitious and hedonist hypocrites, also leads us to
the same conclusion. The difference between the two
forms of obedience is that political tyranny is based
on naked force, while religious tyranny is based on
deviousness and chicanery. The difference leads us
to believe that, in truth, the former is based on the
control of bodies while the latter stems from the control of hearts.

This argument confirms the astuteness and accuracy of the argument of some of the experts of this
science who divide tyranny into political and religious kinds. They consider them as interrelated and
mutually protective of each other! It is also evident
that uprooting this evil tree and liberation from this
abject slavery—possible only through the heedful-
ness and awakening of the nation—is relatively easy
in the case of political tyranny and extremely difficult in the case of religious tyranny, thus complicating resistance to the former form of tyranny as well.

The dismal condition of us Iranians is living testimony to the mutual support of these two forms of
tyranny and slavery. The two are allied and mutually
confederated. Thus the difficulty of getting rid of
political tyranny is rooted in religious tyranny's support of the political order. This will be, God willing,
further explicated in the discussion of the methods
of resisting the forces of absolutism.

We can conclude that obedience to the autocratic
orders of the rebellious tyrants of the *umma* and the
bandits of the nation is not only an injustice to one's
own life and liberty, which are among the greatest
endowments granted by God, holy be His names, to
human beings. In addition, according to the explicit

text of the worthy Qur'an and the traditions of the infallible ones, it is tantamount to idolatry, taking associates with God, for God only deserves the attributes of ultimate possession of the creation, and unquestionable authority in whatever He deems necessary. He alone can be free of responsibility in what He does. All of these are among His holy attributes. He who arrogates these attributes for himself and usurps this status is not only a tyrant and a usurper of the station of stewardship, but also, according to holy texts, a pretender to the divine mantle and a transgressor to His inviolate realm. Conversely, liberation from such an abject servitude not only releases the soul from its vegetative state and animal status into the realm of noble humanity; it also brings one closer to monotheism and the worship of God and His true and exclusive names and attributes. That is why liberating the imprisoned and usurped nations from the yoke of slavery and abject servitude and leading them to their God-given rights and liberties has been among the most significant goals of the prophets, peace be upon them.

Moses and his brother Aaron, peace be upon them and upon our Prophet, according to the text of the holy Qur'an, [Sura 20 , Verse 47] addressed the Pharaoh thus: "So let the Israelites come with us and do not oppress them." All they sought was to liberate the Israelites from slavery and torture, and take them to the holy land. They even guaranteed Pharaoh's continued reign and authority in his own land (as has been emphasized in ['Ali's] holy "sermon of disparagement" [of the devil]). Pharaoh's refusal and his persecution of the Israelites led to the drowning of the Pharaoh and his troops and the liberation of the Israelites. In his holy "sermon of disparagement," 'Ali, greetings to him, after the statements we have quoted above, argued that one of the advantages of the mission of the Prophet, peace be upon him, was liberation from the yokes [of the kings of Iran and Rome].

From the Prophet's biography, one recognizes the equality of a nation's people with their leaders in all laws and obligations and the great efforts of the Prophet, God's greetings be upon him, to establish this principle, thus guaranteeing the well-being of the *umma*.

Let us cite an example for each case. First, the principle of equality in property is evident in the incident in which [Muhammad's step-]daughter Zaynab [died 629] came to Medina and offered an heirloom in order to purchase the freedom of her husband, Abu'l-'Asi [ibn al-Rabi', a non-Muslim who had been captured by the Muslims in battle]. When she approached with the heirloom, an ornament that she had inherited from her mother Khadija [the Prophet's wife, died 619], may peace be upon her, the Prophet wept and announced that he would free her husband without payment. Yet he was careful to ask whether all the Muslims would forego their share of the payment before he returned the heirloom [to Zaynab]. Second, the principle of equality in decrees is evident in the case in which [the Prophet] did not discriminate between his uncle 'Abbas [ibn 'Abd al-Muttalib, died 652], his cousin 'Aqil [ibn Abi Talib, died circa 670], and other prisoners of war, when they were brought in front of him. They were given no special privileges, even in the binding of their hands and arms. Third, the principle of equality in punishment is evident in [the Prophet's] last sermon, when he asked all the faithful to exercise their right of just retribution if he has unfairly injured any of them. Someone claimed that [the Prophet's] riding crop had accidentally touched his shoulder during of the campaigns. The Prophet of Islam bared his shoulder and asked the man to retaliate if he wished. But the man was satisfied to kiss [the Prophet's] shoulder. Also, the Prophet once said in public that if my only daughter Fatima ever commits a crime, her punishment would not differ in the slightest from the punishment of any other wrong-doer.

It was for the revival of such a blessed tradition of leadership, and in order to abrogate the apostasy of discrimination in the distribution of favors, and to reverse the endowment of fiefs, and to uphold the principle of equality, that the commander of the faithful 'Ali encountered so many enmities and disturbances during his rule. Even senior disciples, such as 'Abdullah [Ibn] 'Abbas [an early Islamic scholar, 619–686] and Malik Ashtar [a great warrior, died 658] and the others, had been used to the practice of giving and accepting favors and discriminating based on the closeness of association [with the Prophet]. They preferred earlier Muslims such as the "Emigrants" [who accompanied Muhammad to Medina in 622] and the warriors of the battle of Badr [in 624] over later Muslims and newly converted Muslims like Iranians. So they would ask for favors [from 'Ali] and would, in every case, hear harsh rebukes. The story of 'Ali's refusal to provide for his needy brother from the treasury, his sharp rebuke of one of his daughters who wanted to borrow a necklace from the treasury for one night, and his refusal to allow his own son to borrow some honey from the public stock—which made even his enemy, Mu'awiyya [who would soon found the Umayyad dynasty] weep and extol his virtue as a leader—and countless other similar stories are examples of the justice and equality in Islam that put all other proponents of these virtues to shame.

All these endeavors served to preserve this central pillar of Islam and discharge the great responsibility of leadership in Islam. It was with a similar motivation, and in order to follow the glorious example of the praiseworthy prophets and their trusted stewards, that the godly jurisconsults and leaders of the Ja'fari [Shi'i] religion have resolved to free the faithful from the servitude of the tyrants in this auspicious age—which is, with God's help, the age in which the enslavement and decline of the Muslims are being terminated. They have resolved as well that in accordance with the maxim, "He who can't accomplish all should not abandon all," they ought to convert the form of government from possessive back to delegative. While the possessive form has caused the ruin of Islamic societies and the decline of Islamic states, the delegative form will protect against most forms of corruption and prevent the dominion of the infidels over the country. In this path [the religious leaders] have engaged in a struggle needed to protect the essence of Islam. Recognition of the need for change, and the brave, sober, and earnest attempt to bring about the end of absolutism and to replace it with limited government, has clearly sparked a backlash. The religious form of absolutism, in conformity with its ancient and ongoing duty to protect the evil tree of tyranny in the name of protecting religion, did its best to describe the life-sustaining principles of limited and responsible government in the most grotesque and reprehensible disguises—contrary to the Qur'an's warning: "Do not mix the false with the true, and hide the truth knowingly." [Sura 2, Verse 42] It portrayed the liberation of the nation from the clutches of unjust tyrants as illusory. (The reader of this essay knows such liberation to be the goal of all prophets and their just successors, and the origin of Islamic government, which was distorted by the evil tree of autocracy planted by the family of al-'As.) The proponents of religious despotism went farther and declared this struggle a denial of all moral limits and an attempt to spread apostasy. They even attributed

the outward appearance of women in the West (allowed by Christianity in places such as Russia, France, or Britain) to the political change from absolutism to constitutionalism, though this is as irrelevant to constitutional government as could be. Further, they mischaracterized the principle of equality of rights and powers, which the reader has learned from this essay to have been the practice of the Prophet of Islam and his just successors, for which 'Ali was martyred, as was his son Husayn. They said that this principle will erase all differences between Muslims and non-Muslims in affairs such as inheritance, marriage, even penal law; and that it denies any difference between children and adults, sane and insane, healthy and sick, the free and coerced, the able and the disabled, and so forth, in terms of their rights and duties. All of these issues, which are farther from the quest for constitutionalism than the sky is from the earth, they attached to the essence of this noble endeavor.

Because the salvation and prosperity of the nation, and the preservation of its essential rights, is contingent upon the limitation and responsibility of the government, they have mobilized to cloak this divine beneficence with ugliness. They do not realize that the sun cannot be covered over with mud, nor the Nile delta dammed with shovels. The Iranian nation—no matter how ignorant of the requirements of religion it is imagined to be, regardless of how unaware it may be of the evils of slavery and the advantages of liberty and equality—at least understands this much: Its sages and brave compatriots—be they clergymen, heroes, businessmen—would not have risen in order to achieve that which the proponents of religious despotism attribute to constitutionalism, but to attain freedom and equality. The leaders of the Ja'fari religion, too, had no motivation in authenticating this movement with such explicit edicts and orders, and in calling its enemies the enemies of the Imam of the age [the Hidden Imam], except to protect the essence of Islam and the integrity of the Islamic countries. This bunch of tyrants and oppressors of the *umma*, these depreciators of the *shari'a*, know full well that spreading corruption, anarchy, and debauchery can only strengthen the position of irresponsible, absolutist autocrats. They have no other objective in mind but to help their masters by committing these heinous acts. They know very well what we mean when we say that these so-called clerics "do more harm to the downtrodden Shi'is than the cursed troops of Yazid [circa 642–683] did to Husayn, peace be upon him"! They know how much we are hurt by their alliance with tyrants. They recognize that the blessed verse of the Qur'an [Sura 3, Verse 187] speaks of them: "And remember when God took a promise from the people of the Book, to make it known to humankind, and not keep back any part of it, they set aside [the pledge] and sold it away for a little gain; but how wretched the bargain that they made." They must realize that in this world and in the Hereafter, nothing but scandal and damnation will result from their support of tyranny. This is God's unchanging tradition, as stated in the Qur'an: "Such was God's tradition among those before you, and you will not find any change in God's tradition." [Sura 33, Verse 62]

It is time to rein in our pen, to describe this scandal no further, for it is sure to affect its own kind [that is, even proconstitutional clergy will suffer]. We shall postpone revealing their fallacies to appropriate sections in our five chapters. We shall bring the introduction to an end at this juncture with the following summary of the five ensuing chapters:

First: The foundation of government in the religion of Islam and in other religions, as well as in the cogitations of nonreligious philosophers, the sages of yore and thinkers of today, is none other than the second [constitutional] form. Devolution to the former [absolutist] form is among the apostasies of tyrannical rebels of all times and periods of history.

Second: During this period of the occultation [of the Hidden Imam], the *umma* is deprived of divine stewardship and [the Imam's] public representatives, whose rule has been usurped [by mortals]. Should one allow the former form of government to dominate—that is, compounded injustice, and usurpation upon usurpation—or is it incumbent upon Muslims to reduce the degree of injustice and usurpation?

Third: Based on the above-mentioned necessity to limit [the powers of] government, can one argue that the present form of constitutional government—based on the two principles of limitation of powers and responsibility of government—is the right answer and free of further limitations?

Fourth: Discussion and dispelling of some of the temptations and fallacies adduced against constitutional government.

Fifth: Explication of the conditions for the correctness and legitimacy of the process of electing the nation's representatives, and a summary of their responsibilities.

What Is to Be Done?

Mahmud Tarzi (Afghanistan, 1865–1933) was Afghanistan's foremost proponent of modernization and reform within an Islamic context, after Sayyid Jamal al-Din al-Afghani (chapter 11), whose birthplace is claimed by both Afghanistan and Iran. The son of a famed poet whose outspokenness led the family into exile, Tarzi spent more than 20 years in the Ottoman Empire, mostly in Damascus. Tarzi studied with Afghani for seven months in Istanbul, and also had intellectual contact with reformers in the Levant, Central Asia, and India. He returned to Afghanistan in 1905, opened a translation office, taught history and geography at a military school, and assumed editorship of *Siraj al-akhbar* (*The Lamp of the News*), the bimonthly periodical that became the cornerstone of modern Afghan journalism. He used this publication as a forum to spread his message of modernization, nationalism, and identity—Afghan, Eastern, and Islamic—among the elite of Afghanistan and neighboring Muslim states. Because of his break from ornate literary styles, Tarzi is sometimes referred to as the father of modern prose in Afghanistan. The specimen of Tarzi's work presented here is drawn from a book presented to subscribers of *Siraj al-akhbar* in September 1912. Tarzi's account of Afghan history is sketchy and not always factual, reflecting the version that enjoyed state sponsorship at the time. It is likely that Tarzi was one of the main architects of this version, just as Tarzi's model for education policy was later adopted by the state, forming the foundation of modern education in Afghanistan.[1]

The reign of the Great *Amir* [Dust Muhammad Khan, reigned 1826–1839, 1842–1863] passed in tranquility and total affluence. Great efforts were exerted for internal reform. All dependencies became attached to the central administration of Kabul, making Afghanistan a strong state with many dependencies. No thought, however, was given to foreign policy. Neither was anything done in the area of public education.

After the death of the Great *Amir*, once again the plague of disunity afflicted his sons and a destructive civil war inflamed the dynasty. Chaos and bloodshed ravaged the country. It was at this time that Baluchistan, Shalkut, the Diras, Peshawar, and other territories were lost.

We must say that there were two main reasons for such a civil war and fratricide. One was the practice of marrying a multitude of wives.[2] We do not call it polygamy, as the latter term signifies the number set by the *shariʻa* [Islamic law] of four wives that can only be allowed under specified conditions. By contrast, a multitude of wives means twenty, thirty, or forty wives, from each of whom would be born at least one child, good or wicked! The rival wives would instill discord in their children from their early days. Rivalries and antagonism among the nannies, the male attendants, and the nurses would also reinforce the discord. Second, there was a lack of proper

Mahmud Tarzi, *Chih Bayad Kard?* (*What Is to Be Done?*) (Kabul, Afghanistan: Siraj al-Akhbar, 1912), pp. 119–159. Translation from Dari and introduction by Helena Malikyar.

1. Vartan Gregorian, *The Emergence of Modern Afghanistan: Politics of Reform and Modernization, 1880–1946* (Stanford, Calif.: Stanford University Press, 1969); Sobir Mirzoev, *Literaturno-prosvetitel'skaia Deiatel'nost' Makhmuda Tarzi i Ego Gazeta Siradzh-ul'-Akhbar, 1911–1919* (*The Literary and Educational Activity of Mahmud Tarzi and his Newspaper, The Lamp of the News, 1911–1919*)

(Dushanbe, Tajikistan: Izd-vo "Irfon," 1973); Ashraf Ghani, "Literature as Politics: The Case of Mahmud Tarzi," *Afghanistan*, volume 29, number 3, 1976, pp. 63–72; May Schinasi, *Afghanistan at the Beginning of the Twentieth Century: Nationalism and Journalism in Afghanistan, A Study of Seraj ul-akhbar* (*1911–1918*) (Naples, Italy: Istituto Universitario Orientale, 1979); ʻAbd al-Bashir Shur, *Mahmud Tarzi-yi Afghani* (*Mahmud Tarzi the Afghan*) (Kabul, Afghanistan: Nasharat-i Ittihadiyya-i Zhurnalistan, 1988).

2. [Tarzi's sponsor, *Amir* Habibullah Khan, also had a multitude of wives and concubines in his harem.—Trans.]

education and discipline for the princes. From their birth, they would be addressed with royal titles and would spend their days playing games and seeking pleasure. Their scientific education would, generally speaking, remain limited to reading books in Persian and writing decrees and orders. They would be unaware of news from the outside world. Such innate ignorance and lack of education was so prevalent that no one could escape from its effects.

In the end, it was *Amir* Shir 'Ali Khan [reigned 1863–1865, 1869–1879] who captured the throne of Afghanistan, and once more the entire country was unified under one central command. He raised an army of about sixty to seventy thousand soldiers, who received modern military training. He also brought a number of reforms in the civil administration. In the end, however, *Amir* Shir 'Ali Khan made a political error in that he was deceived by the conspiracy of the Russian state and declared war on the English state. Consequently, he was defeated, fled to Turkistan, and died in Mazar-i Sharif. His son, *Amir* Muhammad Ya'qub Khan [reigned 1879–1880], who had been imprisoned by his father for many years, was released and, at such a sensitive time, ascended the throne. His unbalanced state of mind after a long imprisonment, added to the ill intentions of some royal advisors and an incompetent entourage, resulted in the new *amir* signing a most damaging and pernicious agreement with the English. This agreement resulted in the killing of [British official Louis] Cavagnari [in 1879] and the imprisonment and subsequent exile to India of the *amir* himself. The English occupied Afghanistan for the second time. The famous General [Frederick] Roberts [1832–1914], under the pretext of avenging Cavagnari, set up gallows in Kabul and began ordering the deaths of five, ten, or twenty innocent Afghans on a daily basis. A number of treacherous people, because of ignorance, lack of education, and ignorance of patriotism and religiosity, sold out their faith in religion for the vile carcass of worldly gains and committed all sorts of contemptible indecencies. Their names forever will be mentioned with damnation in the pages of Afghan history.

Most inhabitants, though, rose against the English. *Mullas* [religious scholars] everywhere declared *jihad* [holy struggle]. Women, men, old and young, anyone who could hold a weapon marched to the battlefield. The chaos of an uprising began to challenge the English. Their army was besieged at Shirpur, the garri-

son that the late *Amir* Shir 'Ali Khan had built as an excellent stronghold for the national army of Afghanistan. In Qandahar too, the English army was surrounded. The misery and destruction that had previously befallen the English was threatening them again, but this time in manifold. At this precise moment the news also struck like thunder that his late majesty *Amir* 'Abd al-Rahman Khan [reigned 1880–1901] had crossed the Amu River [from his exile in Central Asia]. If the Afghan nation could bring such calamity on the English without having a king or a military leader, imagine what kind of pandemonium and tumult could be handed to the enemy when such a valiant commander and chivalrous *amir* would lead such brave people. Like hungry lions, they were thirsty for the blood of the enemies of their homeland!

The esteemed English state employed a prudent policy and preemptively sent a delegation to the late *amir*, before the latter set out for Kabul. The delegation carried a confidential letter containing an offer for peace and negotiation. When his majesty arrived in the Charikar district of Kuhistan, approximately 300,000 armed civilians of the region and a number of soldiers from the regular army were ready to serve him. As a result of the agreement, which was signed at Zima, the English troops left Afghanistan in safety, and the control of the affairs of Afghanistan was passed on to the capable and strong hands of the wise, intelligent, and brave king. Here, it will not be an exaggeration if we say that because of this incident, the esteemed English state became greatly indebted to his majesty the late *amir*, for had he chosen, the *amir* could have brought much misery upon the English army. Therefore, if the good English state claims that it has approved the legitimacy of the Afghan government, the exalted government can also assert that it saved their troops from certain annihilation.

This ushered in an era of renewal for Afghanistan, as after a period of foreign domination, once again the independent state of Afghanistan was established. We will not discuss all the work and progress that was made during the tenure of his late majesty, as it has not yet been forgotten from our memories. In short, we will just mention that under his majesty's leadership Afghanistan became a mighty and powerful state, with all the aptitude and potential to establish and build a great Islamic state in Asia.

After the demise of that founder of the kingdom, came the turn of his eldest and wisest son, his great and enlightened majesty, the beacon of the nation and the religion, *Amir* Habibullah Khan [reigned 1901–1919]. This sovereign's ever-increasing innate talent and capability has caused continuous growth and advancement. So much so that at this moment Afghanistan has gained such an important place in the continent of Asia that it would be appropriate to call it the beam of the scale of justice and equality in Asia. It is precisely for this reason that one is compelled to pose the question:

"What is to be done at this time?"

Yes, Muslims must ask this question of one another. They must think and deliberate on their state of being. Time is very limited, and the opportunity for attack will soon be lost. One moment of negligence results in a day of damage. One day of damage entails a month of lagging behind. One month of lagging behind means a year of retardation. One year of retardation is an entire lifetime of regret. In this case, all the trees, stones, mountains, deserts, sky, and space would recite in unison:

"It is useless to have regrets later."

If we carefully study questions such as "What were we and what have we become?" and "What have they done?" we will arrive at the issue of "What is to be done?" Some say that even if we so desired, it would be impossible to return to the state of affairs as it appeared 1,300 years ago. The serenity, the justness, and the righteous morality of the four companions of the Prophet [the first four caliphs] ended with them, for in that golden time of happiness the rays of the light of that brightest of moons were still shining in the hearts of people, keeping them in clear conscience. The farther we have come from the brilliant sunshine of that era, the darker our hearts and minds have become.

We, however, consider this a lame excuse. We see the truth in a different light. We do not attribute our backwardness and the darkness of our age to the withdrawal of that light. That kind of light will not distance itself from us until the day of judgment. Were that light limited to a particular time period, all would have ended at the close of that golden age. But we believe that light shines over the entire world and for all time. The whole world will be enlightened by it until the end of days. The only reason for this darkness and this abject baseness of ours is that we have distanced ourselves from that light.

The Holy Qur'an is a sacred and steadfast book and a venerable right path that has been sent to guide and direct all of humankind. Alas, most of us Muslims have reserved that life-giving holy book for our dead, and read from it only for the souls of departed ones. We consider that great book, sent to heal and bless the inhabitants of the earth, as a book for the dead. More than in any other place, we hear recitations of the Holy Qur'an in cemeteries and before corpses! This is not to say that we must not recite the Qur'an for the souls of the dead—rather, the living should also read it to improve their own lives.

All of the miseries and adversities that have come upon us are from our ignorance of the Qur'an, and of our duties toward ourselves and toward humanity and the world. All our destitution and impoverishment is a result of ignorance and lack of education. The Holy Qur'an has shown us that knowledge is life and ignorance death, that knowledge is light and ignorance darkness. Regrettably, we read our Qur'an and memorize it too quickly without pondering its meaning. We do not apply this effective weapon to the needs of our time. Our Qur'an expresses and explains to us that all things in the universe are conquerable. Therefore, if we put into practice that which is taught to us, with the help of science and knowledge, we can achieve the conquest of all things, and put them to use for ourselves and our countries. If we dominate our mountains, mines, oceans, and rivers, we have done nothing more than obey the commands of our Qur'an.

Urgent Actions

O, our Muslim brothers! We have much urgent action to take and very little time. Whatever we do, we must do it fast. We must move fast and wake up at once, or else we will soon be hunted in our sleep, as happened to so many of us before.

First, we must read carefully our Holy Qur'an and make its glorious commands our guide for this world and the next. We must organize large gatherings of scholars, scientists, and specialists of Islam in each and every Muslim country. In those gatherings, we must carefully study the sacred book and translate its beneficial passages into all languages that Muslims speak. We must then publish the translations abundantly and distribute them to the entire Islamic world, so that Muslims learn that this is not just a book for the afterlife and for the dead, but one that covers the entire universe and all its creatures. In bestowing that book on us, He has bestowed the universe and its creatures on us.

It is because we are ignorant of the Qur'an that we commit such vile and immoral acts as bribery, falsehood, slander, hypocrisy, and bigotry. We cause resentment and envy by inventing lies and false accusations. We destroy any chance of brotherly sympathy and cooperation. We commit, with much certitude, these and many other unmentionable acts. Curiously, we feel that we have been absolved of all our sins when we bow in prayer a couple of times or recite a few passages of the Holy Qur'an. In fact, prayers benefit only one's self, while such acts [as bribery, lies, and the like] unsettle the foundations of Islam. Just as prayer is prescribed in the Qur'an, those vile acts are proscribed. Therefore, if we truly learned from our Qur'an, we would act differently.

Second, as the Holy Qur'an dictates, we must adopt unity as the very foundation of our principles. Let us begin with individuals, then spread this unity, this harmony and oneness, to all the tribes and clans of the various Islamic nations. This task, however, will require great sacrifice, effort, and perseverance. Societies, clubs, associations, and schools must be established all over the Islamic world, especially during the time of pilgrimage to the holy shrines of Medina and Mecca, where Muslims of different backgrounds gather. This unification must be based on the principles of survival, progress, and Islamic uplift. The land of the Franks [that is, Europe] has a great and uncontrollable fear of this Islamic unity. However, our aim and indeed the aim of all of Islam, is not to form a union and then confront the Christians, but rather to unite for the purpose of our own community's advancement, improvement, civilization, and cooperation. It would be a terrible crime to use the unification of Islam against Christianity. For example, to provoke the Muslims of India, China, or Turkistan against their respective ruling states would be to commit an atrocious crime. The purpose of their unity would be to replace malice and hypocrisy with benevolence, friendship, and harmony. Concurrently and jointly they should preoccupy themselves with the task of protecting the Qur'an, the faith, rights, and morality. Together with other Muslims they should try to reach the levels of education and sciences that their rulers possess. They should then spread their knowledge to their brothers, both free and needy, and

preserve their right to their own resources. Praise be to God, day by day we witness an increasing inclination toward such unity among Muslims. The Holy Qur'an commands unity. If Muslims are not yet there, it is because of their lack of understanding of the meaning of the Qur'anic ordinances. We find, for example, the Ottoman Empire struggling in an abyss of disunity. Iran is an even worse case, while Afghanistan also suffers due to the animosity, rivalry, and bloodshed that obviously prevails among its many tribes, clans, and races. It is therefore incumbent upon Muslims to draw strength from their absolute faith in the Qur'an and sow the seeds of unity in the field of the Islamic world, so that they may collect its fortuitous fruits.

Third, we must consider science and industry as a depreciated asset, and seek it aggressively. This is especially recommended for independent countries such as the Ottoman, Iranian, and Afghan states, which unfortunately make no use of their minerals, that is, their mines. European states, by contrast, not only exploit their own mines but also those of the entire world. In addition to natural resources, they are also capable of industrial production. This is simply because they have the knowledge and we do not. We remain deprived of thousands of things, for lack of knowledge, while others with the knowledge have acquired them. Minerals are but one example. To achieve this, there is only one remedy for Iran and Afghanistan, and that is to send and expose our children to schools, colleges, and workshops. There is no cure except to build an infrastructure in our countries for scientific education, especially at the elementary and secondary levels. If we start work today, we may see results in 10 years. The more we delay, the greater loss we will have to face.

Fourth, in the esteemed Ottoman Empire every citizen has become a soldier [in the Balkan Wars]. The same practice must be enforced in Iran and Afghanistan. The nation that does not take responsibility for protecting its nationhood and its statehood by participating in its country's armed forces has evaded its obligation toward its homeland and national honor. Such people will surely be punished in this world and the next. To suggest that all join the armed forces does not mean that the entire population of Afghanistan must simultaneously take up arms. It means that each and every citizen, without exception, upon reaching the age of twenty-one, should become a conscript. The duration of their training should be two years, at the end of which they will leave the military with the knowledge of military basics. In this manner, in a matter of a few years, the issue of all becoming soldiers will have been resolved.

Although there are many more things that we need to do, at this moment I will limit my humble suggestions to the above four items.

Epilogue and Apology

This humblest of creatures of the Creator of land and ocean has written this small and inadequate essay, and has presented it to readers along with the twenty-fourth issue of my newspaper, which is the last issue of the first year. Despite the fact that better-written essays on this topic have appeared many times in the Islamic press, I ignored my shortcomings and wrote this piece. My courage came from the conviction that speaking out and writing are always better than not saying or writing anything. No doubt the present work will not adequately and entirely answer the question, "What is to be done?" However, this humble essay will serve in opening the door for more writings of this sort, and in provoking thought and debate. It is therefore hoped that scholars and intellectuals who believe in the progress of Islam through such means will produce writings of their precious and beneficial thoughts and suggestions. Also, I hope that our generous readers will forgive any error or shortcoming that they may find in this humble work. In conclusion, I pray to the Almighty, in His sublime greatness, to bestow prosperity, progress, and enlightenment upon all Muslim brothers.

SECTION 3

Ottoman Empire

Reminding the Intelligent, Notifying the Unmindful

'Abd al-Qadir ibn Muhyi al-Din al-Jaza'iri (Algeria-Syria, circa 1807–1883) was an antico-lonial military leader and, later, a mystic scholar who strove to adapt Islam to the modern era through a reinterpretation of the teaching of the medieval mystic, Ibn 'Arabi (1165–1240). Born into a prominent Sufi family in western Algeria, 'Abd al-Qadir was chosen to lead the resistance to French occupation of the country in 1832. Following his surrender in 1847, during five years of captivity in France, he went through an acute spiritual crisis. At the same time, he was impressed by the material progress achieved in the West. His espousal of the scientific-rationalist approach and his criticism of blind imitation (taqlid) were consolidated in the form of mystical visions after his release, when he settled in Damascus. There, in addition to his efforts to prevent the anti-Christian riots of 1860, 'Abd al-Qadir dedicated himself to the mission of creating and guiding an elect circle of disciples toward the spiritual regeneration of the Muslim world. This circle adopted the modernist ideology of the Salafiyya, in contrast to the Islamic populist policies of Otto-man Sultan Abdülhamid II (reigned 1876–1909). The selections translated here come from a book—completed just before 'Abd al-Qadir's arrival in Damascus, and first pub-lished in French translation—stressing the compatibility of the scientific-rationalist approach with Muslim faith.[1]

On Knowledge and Ignorance

The intelligent person must consider the statement rather than the person who is stating it. If a statement proves to be true, one should accept it, whether this person is known to be a person of truth or of false-hood. For gold is derived from dust, the narcissus from bulbs, and antidotes from snakes. The rose is picked from among thorns. People should be mea-sured according to the truth, not the truth according to [the reputation of] people. The goal of the intelli-gent person is a word of wisdom, and he is prepared to receive it from whomever possesses it, be they commoner or notable. The lowest level of intelligent persons is to be distinguished from the common

people's level in certain things. Among them is not to feel disgust at honey even if it is found in a bleeder's glass. Intelligent persons recognize that blood is defiling in and of itself; it is not defiling because it is in this glass.[2] Since honey is not defil-ing, being within a vessel used for blood does not make it so, and there is no need to feel averse toward it. Most people yield to this false impression. When-ever a statement is ascribed to a person they believe to be good, they accept it, even if erroneous. But, if the statement is ascribed to someone they believe to be bad, they reject it, even if correct. They always measure the truth according to the person, rather than the person according to the truth. This is the utmost in ignorance and decadence. A person who needs an

'Abd al-Qadir ibn Muhyi al-Din al-Jaza'iri, *Dhikra al-'aqil wa tanbih al-ghafil* (*Reminding the Intelligent and Notifying the Unmindful*) (Beirut, Lebanon: Dar al-Yaqza al-'Arabiyya, 1966), pp. 33–38, 81–89. First published in 1855. Transla-tion from Arabic and introduction by Itzchak Weismann.

1. Muhammad ibn 'Abd al-Qadir al-Jaza'iri, *Tuhfa al-za'ir fi ta'rikh al-jaza'ir wa al-amir 'Abd al-Qadir* (*The Gift for the Visitor of the History of Algeria and Amir 'Abd al-Qadir*) (Beirut, Lebanon: Dar al-Yaqza al-'Arabiyya, 1964);

Raphael Danziger, *'Abd al-Qadir and the Algerians: Resis-tance to the French and Internal Consolidation* (New York: Holmes and Meier, 1977); Michel Chodkiewicz, *The Spiri-tual Writings of Amir 'Abd al-Kader* (Albany: State Univer-sity of New York Press, 1995); Itzchak Weismann, *Taste of Modernity: Sufism, Salafiyya, and Arabism in Late Ottoman Damascus* (Leiden, Netherlands: Brill, 2000).

2. [An old medical technique involved the removal of blood, often into glass cups.—Ed.]

antidote but shrinks from taking it upon learning that it is extracted from snakes is ignorant. This person should be made aware that such aversion is pure ignorance, and that it deprives him of the desired benefit. For knowledgeable people it is easy to distinguish between correct and false statements, between true and vain beliefs, and between worthy and repugnant deeds. Such things do not confuse them, and they do not follow others by imitating their beliefs and opinions. These are the marks of the ignorant.

People whom others follow are divided into two types. One is the knowledgeable, who help both themselves and others. Such a person measures the truth according to the evidence rather than accepting it blindly, and calls others to do the same. The other type is destructive of themselves and of others. They imitate the opinions and beliefs of their fathers and ancestors while neglecting their own judgment, and call upon others to engage in *taqlid* [imitation]. The blind cannot lead the blind. Even more reprehensible and unsatisfactory than imitating people, however, is the blind following of books. It is better to follow a beast than an imitator. The opinions of the *'ulama'* [religious scholars] and the devout are often contradictory and conflicting, since preferring [one opinion to others] without any grounds for doing so is unjustified, as it can be countered by equally valid arguments.

Every human being is capable, by nature, of perceiving truth. The relation of the mind [literally, the "heart"], the seat of knowledge, to the reality of things is like the relation of a mirror to colored forms that appear on its face one after the other. It is true, there are hindrances that may prevent the forms from being reflected in the mirror. These include a deficiency in the mirror's form deriving from the substance of the iron [from which mirrors used to be made], before it was given its round shape and polish; the poor condition and corrosion of the mirror, even if its shape is perfect; inaccurate direction of the mirror toward the objects, as when they are behind it; a barrier that is placed between the mirror and the form; and ignorance as to the location of the desired figure, which makes it difficult to turn the mirror toward it.

Similarly, the mind is a mirror capable of reflecting the forms of all phenomena. Minds may be devoid of knowledge because of these same five causes. One is deficiency in the mind itself, as in the case of a child's mind, which is still incomplete. A second cause concerns the impurity of worldly concerns and

the resulting wickedness that accumulates on the face of the mind. The endeavor to uncover the reality of things, and the avoidance of distracting occupations, would clear and purify the mind. Third comes its turning away from the direction of the desired truth. The fourth cause regards barriers (*hijab*). An intellect immersed in contemplating a certain truth may nonetheless miss it because of a [false] preconception that the man imbibed in his youth by way of uncritical acceptance and good faith. This is a formidable obstacle, which prevents most people from attaining the truth. Such people are veiled by traditional beliefs that have become deeply rooted in their souls and stiffen their minds.

Fifth is the ignorance of the direction in which the object is to be found. Seekers cannot attain a thing without referring to the relevant sciences. They must refer to them and arrange them in the specific way defined by the scholars. In this way they may find the necessary direction, and the reality of the object will be revealed to their minds.

Knowledge that is not self-evident can be caught only with the net of the acquired sciences. Moreover, every piece of knowledge can be deduced only from two antecedents, harmonized and combined in a definite manner. Their combination brings a third piece of knowledge, like the offspring produced from the copulation of male and female animals. Thus, to produce a horse, one cannot use an ass and a camel, but only a pair of horses. Similarly, every perception has two specific sources, combined in a specific way. Lack of knowledge of these sources, and of the nature of their combination, hinders that perception. As we mentioned, this is like ignorance of the figure's location. This is exemplified in the case of a person who wants to see the back of his head in the mirror. If he places the mirror in front of his face, he cannot direct it to reflect the back of his head, and if he places it behind his head, in the correct direction, he removes it from his eyes and can see neither the mirror nor the back of his head reflected in it. He needs another mirror to be put behind his head, while the first one remains in front of his eyes. Observing the appropriate position of the two mirrors, the back of his head will be reflected in the mirror directed toward it, and this will be reflected in the other mirror facing the eyes.

Similarly, in seeking knowledge and striving to understand things, there are odd paths that are even more oblique to the goal than the example of the mirror. These are the causes that prevent minds from recognizing realities. Normally, each mind is able, by divine providence, to perceive such realities. Like a person who cannot see what stands in front of him without moving the pupils of his eyes a great deal from side to side, so the mind will not perceive the reality of things if it does not move from concept to concept. These movements are called thinking and contemplation. And like the looking eye that cannot see without light, such as that of the sun, so the mind cannot perceive realities correctly without the lights of success and guidance from God, the most exalted.

Validating Revealed Knowledge

Know—may God give you success—that although the intellect attained eminence and an ability to explain the reality of things, there remains knowledge that it can neither achieve nor be guided to, but is obtained only by trusting and obeying the prophets and their successors. The sciences of the prophets are superior to intellectual knowledge, that which, as we have said, is inherent in the nature of the mind and which one finds when turning one's attention to acquire it. Nevertheless, although the intellect is separate from the information brought by the prophets that one is ordered to follow, it is capable of perceiving it, submitting to their commandments, and approving its content once they make it known to them.

The proof that there are suprarational sciences is that God, most exalted, created humankind devoid of any knowledge about His innumerable creatures, which only He can comprehend. He then gave humankind the sense of touch to discern tangible things of all types, but since humans could as yet grasp neither voices nor colors, they remained to humankind as if nonexistent. Thereafter, God created human sight, which enabled them to perceive part of the creation, insofar as they could go beyond the tangible. In the following stage He accorded them the faculty of discernment to recognize abstract realities beyond the tangible things. From there humankind proceeded to yet another stage, the stage of the intellect, which allowed them to perceive additional things. Then one progresses to another level, the level of the intellect in which one perceives matters imperceptible in any of the preceding levels. Beyond the intellect is a further level involving other matters from which the intellect is separated, which it cannot obtain by itself but rather requires [the aid of] someone else, just as the senses are separate from intellectual perception.

The sciences located in the mind are divided into two types: rational and revealed. By the term rational knowledge we mean that which is naturally commanded by the intellect, which is apart from indirect knowledge (*taqlid*) and revealed knowledge (*sama'*). This, in turn, is divided into self-evident and acquired knowledge. Self-evident, for example, is humankind's knowledge that a single item cannot be in two places at the same time, or that a thing cannot be both existent and nonexistent. People find such knowledge in themselves and recognize it without knowing where it comes from. I mean, they do not recognize the ultimate cause [of their knowledge]—that it is of course God who created it and guided them to that knowledge. Acquired knowledge is that obtained by learning, inference, and reflection. Another type of knowledge located in the mind is revealed knowledge, which is received from the prophets. It is obtained by studying the revealed books such as the Torah, the Gospels, the Psalms, and the Criterion [the Qur'an]. By understanding their concepts, they are revealed. By this [revelational knowledge] the intellect is perfected and delivered from illness.

Thus the rational sciences, although necessary, are insufficient to ensure our welfare, just as the intellect is insufficient to preserve bodily health. Humans need to know the particulars of medicine and remedies by learning them from doctors, since the intellect alone is incapable of arriving at them. Nevertheless, the intellect is the only means for comprehending such knowledge after it is learned. The intellect cannot do without the revealed sciences, and these cannot do without the intellect. Therefore, those who call on people to adopt pure imitative knowledge and avoid rationality are ignorant, while those who are satisfied with rationality at the expense of the revealed sciences are deluded. Beware not to belong to either of those groups but to combine them! The rational sciences are like nourishment and the revealed sciences are like medication. The sick may be harmed by food if they neglect their medicine. Similarly, the minds of all creatures are sick, and there is no treatment for them but the medications prepared by the prophets, namely the duties of worship. Those who are satisfied with rational knowledge will be harmed by it like the sick person who is harmed by food, as happens to some. It is said: a discerning person who grasps all of intelligible knowledge and affirms that the world has a creator has attained absolute perfection; humankind's felicity corresponds to its knowledge, and its distress corresponds to its ignorance. One's intellect brings one to this felicity.

Be careful not to assume that the revealed sciences are contradictory or incompatible with the rational sciences. On the contrary, everything the Prophet ordained is in full harmony with sound reason. It is true that there are certain details in the laws brought by the prophets that the intellect rejects, but this derives from the intellect's own shortcomings. Had it understood the method behind the stipulation, the intellect would have recognized that this is the truth, which one should not abandon.

An example from Islamic law (shar') involves the rulings concerning gold and silver. The law forbids their accumulation without giving part to the poor and needy; it prohibits the use of dishes and cups made out of them; it bans the sale of gold or silver for profit. Yet, if people were told to give part of them to the poor, or else they would be burnt in hell, they would surely reply, "This is unacceptable. I worked hard to gather them, so why should I now give them to people who were sleeping and resting? This is unreasonable!" If they were told not to eat and drink from golden or silver table utensils, or else they will be burnt in hell, they would similarly reply: "This is unacceptable. I will do with my property what I want and no one can dispute it. Why should I be punished for making use of my property? This is unreasonable!" And if these people were told not to sell gold and silver for profit or else they would burn in hell, they would again have said, "I buy and sell with the mutual consent of myself and my business partners. Without buying and selling, the world would be ruined and the public interest impeded. This is irrational!"

They are right [to say that it is irrational], since their intellect is incapable of understanding the punishment for such things and requires explanation.

It should be explained to them that the wisdom behind God's creation of gold and silver is their use for the sustenance of the world. In themselves these are merely two metals which have no utility. They ward off neither heat nor cold, nor do they nourish the body. Nonetheless everybody needs them. This is because every person has many needs, for nourishment and clothing. A person may lack necessities and possess unneeded things. For example, in the case of one who owns wheat but needs a horse, while a friend

owns a horse but needs wheat. An exchange will certainly take place between these two, and it would be necessary to assess the relative value [of these commodities], since the owner of the horse would not hand it over for just any amount of wheat. There is also no correlation between wheat and horses to allow exchanging them for a similar weight or shape. Thus one doesn't know how to assess the value of a horse in wheat, and transactions, in this example and its like, would become impossible. Consequently, people felt the need for an adequate medium to decide between them. For this reason God created gold and silver, to serve as a standard in all transactions. Accordingly, a horse may be worth a hundred dinars, and a certain amount of wheat has the same value.

Regulation by gold and silver is possible precisely because they have no purpose in themselves. God created them only to circulate among the people and serve as means of exchange. Their value is unified in relation to all commodities, and possessing them is like possessing everything. Thus, the owner of a horse, for example, owns only that particular horse. If he is in need of food, he may find that the one who has it prefers to buy a garment rather than a horse. It is therefore necessary to have something that seems to have no form, but actually has an overall significance, bearing an equal relation to the various commodities. It resembles a mirror, which has no color but reflects all the colors. Gold and silver have no purpose in themselves, but they are means for all purposes. Therefore, whoever uses them contrary to divine wisdom will be punished in the Hereafter, unless God permits. Those who hoard gold and silver without setting aside a certain amount for the poor thwart the underlying reason [of their creation], acting like one who imprisons a judge and prevents him from arbitrating and resolving disputes among the people. God did not create gold and silver especially for one person or another, but to circulate among all of them and serve as a standard. Undoubtedly, if the intellect understands that, it will confirm that hoarding gold and silver is an act of oppression and will justify punishment. God most high creates nothing in vain. He entrusted the living of the poor to the wealthy, but the wealthy have oppressed the poor and deprived them of the rights accorded them by God.

We therefore say: people who make dishes and cups out of gold and silver are oppressors. They are worse than those who hoard and amass [gold and silver], since their behavior is like that of a person who turns the judge of the city into a hatmaker, a tailor, a butcher—any job that could be performed by the meanest member of society. Copper, lead, and clay, rather than gold and silver, should be used for holding food and drink. These [chosen substances] can hold liquids, but clay, iron, copper, and lead, on the other hand, cannot fulfill the task of gold and silver. If the intellect knows this, it undoubtedly would not hesitate to approve of [this prohibition] and to punish those who transgress it.

We also claim that selling gold and silver for profit, turning them into objects of commerce in their own right, is contrary to divine wisdom. An owner of cloth, for instance, who wants to buy food might not be able to exchange food for cloth; he is therefore permitted to buy it with gold or silver, thereby obtaining his goal. [Gold and silver] are means to an end and not ends themselves. But owners of gold or silver who want to trade them for gold or silver are prevented from doing so, because by remaining restricted from circulation, the effect is as if they were hoarded. Moreover, thus obstructing God or the Prophet from conveying necessities to others is an act of oppression. The only purpose of buying gold and silver for their own sake is to hoard them, and when the intellect understands this [role] it approves both the prohibition and the punishment for transgressing it. Nevertheless, buying gold with silver, or vice versa, is permissible, since they differ in the ways they help satisfy the necessities of life, silver being more abundant and more easily divided among various needs. What is prohibited is interfering with its intended function, namely, to facilitate the attainment of other commodities.

Consequently, to those who sell silver or gold for a fixed period for profit [as a form of interest-making], such as selling at 10 to get back 20 after a year, we say that the foundation of society and the basis of all religions are to promote love and harmony, mutual assistance and cooperation. Those who are in need and find someone who will give them credit can assume the good-heartedness of their creditor and believe in his kindness. They will regard aid and support [of the creditor] as requirements. Prohibiting the sale of gold and silver at a profit over a fixed period thus preserves the utility of loans, which is among the noblest ends.

These few examples, from all that might be cited, make it clear that the revealed law is not incompatible with reason. All the commandments and interdictions of the prophets intend to be harmonious with reason. None of them contradicts it, though for some [rules] the human intellect alone is not a sufficient guide. However, when it is properly guided, it realizes and complies. Like the skilled physician who commands the secrets of various treatments that the ignorant think farfetched, so are the prophets, whose knowledge the intellect is unable to obtain save through instruction. The intelligent person is compelled to accept them, after inquiring into their truth.

Democracy: Government by the People, Equality

Ali Suavi (Turkey, 1839–1878) was a leading figure in the Young Ottoman political reform movement and in the search for Islamic justifications of constitutionalism. Trained both in religious and secular schools, Suavi held a variety of administrative positions before embarking on a career as a public intellectual in his mid-twenties. His pamphlets and sermons in the Şehzade Mosque in Istanbul—introducing modern political terminology, criticizing the government, and commenting on foreign relations—made him famous and led to his banishment to the provinces, whence he fled to Europe. In London and then Paris, Suavi published the journals *Muhbir* (*The Reporter*) and *Ulûm Gazetesi* (*Journal of the Sciences*), calling for constitutionalism in the Ottoman Empire. The article from *Ulûm Gazetesi* presented here, one of the first Ottoman works to use the term "democracy," maintains that Islamic precedent requires institutions of democratic consultation. In the 1870s, influenced by conservative European thinkers, he began to criticize constitutionalism, and in 1876 he appealed to Sultan Abdülhamid II (reigned 1876–1909) to be allowed to return to Istanbul. Upon his pardon and return, Suavi served as a court librarian, a teacher of young princes, and later the director of the Galatasaray Lycée, but his revolutionary sentiments had not disappeared. He was dismissed from Galatasaray in December 1877. In the following months, Suavi launched an unsuccessful uprising against the sultan, hoping to replace him with his elder brother, who was more sympathetic to constitutionalism. Suavi was killed during this attempt, known as the Çırağan incident.[1]

As is known, the forms of government are monarchy (sultanate), aristocracy (government of notables), and democracy (government by the people, equality).

During the early days of Islam, the form of government was democracy. That is to say, there was no sultanate, sultan, or king, but rather equality. Some words of Khalid ibn al-Walid [Muslim commander, died 642] (may God be pleased with him) will suffice to explain the [nature of] the Islamic government.

It so happened that a Byzantine commander named Bahan, [acting on behalf of] Heraclius [Byzantine emperor, reigned 610–641], engaged in a battle with the Companions [of the Prophet Muhammad] with troops numbering 600,000 [in one account] or 700,000 in another.[2] Bahan invited Khalid ibn al-Walid to his tent on the pretext of discussing the terms of an armi-

stice, but in reality to seize him by trickery. Upon Khalid's arrival at Bahan's tent with approximately a hundred courageous warriors, the latter rose and made a speech in Arabic: "Thanks be to God, who made our Lord Jesus the best of the prophets, our king the best of kings, and our [Christian] community the most excellent of communities."

When Bahan began his speech with these words, Khalid could not bear it and interrupted, launching into an oration to refute the words of Bahan:

Thanks be to God, who made us believers in Muhammad (peace be upon him), in your prophet Jesus, and in all the prophets, and who made our ruler,

[Ali Suavi], "Demokrasi: Hükûmet-i Halk, Müsavat" (Democracy: Government by the People, Equality), *Ulûm Gazetesi* (*Journal of the Sciences*), Paris, France, volume 2, number 18, May 17, 1870, pp. 1083–1107. Translation from Turkish and introduction by M. Şükrü Hanioğlu.

1. Hüseyin Çelik, *Ali Suavi ve Dönemi* (*Ali Suavi and His Time*) (Istanbul, Turkey: İletişim Yayınları, 1994); İsmail Doğan, *Tanzimatın İki Ucu: Münif Paşa ve Ali Suavi* (*The Tanzimat's Two Extremes: Münif Paşa and Ali Suavi*) (Istanbul, Turkey: İz Yayıncılık, 1991); Şerif Mardin, *The Genesis of Young Ottoman Thought* (Princeton, N.J.: Princeton University Press, 1962), pp. 360–384.

2. At that battle the number of Muslim troops was 41,000.

whom we ourselves chose to charge with our affairs, a man like us—so much so that if our ruler were to claim to be a king over us, we would immediately depose him. We would never think that our ruler was in any way superior to us, unless it be that he is more pious than us, and so on. That is to say, he possesses the virtue of piety required by the principle of Commanding Right and Forbidding Wrong.

Thus at a time when Byzantines, Armenians, and Europeans recognized kings, the men of God, that is to say Khalid and the Companions, thought this way about the Commander of the Faithful.[3] What this means is that at that time the Islamic government was a democracy. There was equality.

The following incident likewise throws light on the matter.

When cloth from the Yemen was divided among the Companions, 'Umar, the Commander of the Faithful, received the same share as everybody else.

One day 'Umar, wearing a robe made from this cloth, was addressing the Companions from the pulpit to encourage them to *jihad* [religious struggle], when one of the Companions arose and said, "'Umar, from now on we will not listen to you." 'Umar asked, "Why?" The Companion responded, "Because you have privileged yourself instead of remaining equal with us. Because during the division of the Yemeni cloth you too received your share. The robe that we now see on you cannot have been made from that piece. Thus you must have received a bigger piece than us to be able to make such a robe. In this way you have become privileged." Upon hearing these words, 'Umar turned to his son 'Abdullah [died 693] and said, "'Abdullah, answer this man." Thereupon 'Abdullah rose and answered the man: "'Umar, the Commander of the Faithful, wanted to make himself a robe from the cloth that he had received as his share, but it was not enough. So I gave my own share. Combining the two pieces produced such a robe." Then the objecting Companion said, "If so, we will continue to listen to 'Umar," and sat down.

May God be pleased with all of them.

Now that the meaning of democracy, government by the people, and equality is understood, we can go on to say that this form of government was established in a place and among a people [that were alike extraordinary], a single united, loyal, observant, and

pious community. They had no fear other than the fear of God, they had no work other than serving God, they had no institutions (*tanzimat*) other than good morals, in sum they were men of God. The system of equality that Plato [Greek philosopher, circa 427–347 B.C.] had merely imagined became a reality in their time.

Now a French party, which has been growing day-by-day in the name of freedom and equality, wants to annihilate the monarchy and create equality in a democratic system. But they do not have men of God among them—that is to say, they do not have an overpowering force in their hearts such as fear of God.

In their language, freedom is tantamount to saying whatever comes to one's mind and doing whatever one wants without any impediment. Thus an idea came to some Frenchmen, they did as they wanted, and published a newspaper to deny the existence of God in early May in Paris. Those who read this newspaper know well the improper and shameless language that they resort to against those who believe in God.

What will be the future of this nation that lacks a morality limiting liberties within the community if it does not possess an overpowering force to restrain freedom and license in such a shameless country? Undoubtedly this beautiful Paris, this prosperous France that the entire world strives to imitate, will be ruined in a year or two.

Democracy, [that is to say] equality, is a nightingale that can sing loudly only in the rose garden of good morality. Would such a beloved nightingale sing in such a dunghill of [corrupt] hearts?

Since French ideas on democracy have not remained confined to their country but are being disseminated through the press to the east, west, north, and south, they will one day cause trouble even in Istanbul, Cairo, Tehran, Bukhara, and Kabul. Therefore, let us take a glance at these lands of ours.

Morality in our big cities is worse than in those of the Europeans. We have reached such a position that a man who spends two hours in the company of a woman and controls his desire will be pointed out and reckoned to have miraculous powers. Do we not repeat in conversations and in our books as an extraordinary event that "[Mehmed] Ebussu'ud Efendi [Turkish religious leader, 1490–1574] found himself in the same room with a girl one night but controlled his desire and did not touch her."

In Europe, a man may stay with a woman for three days and nights, and it may not even occur to

3. At that time the ruler was 'Umar ibn al-Khattab [second caliph, 634–644].

him [to have sex with her]. This nevertheless is considered an indecent act. In our country, can this behavior, whether attributed to increased sexual desire due to the warmer climate, or to the passion aroused by veiling in the cities—no such impatience being observed among nomads and peasants—or to whatever cause, be brought under control with good morals or not? There lies the problem. All our situations and acts are similar to this matter of sexual desire. It is necessary for us to educate ourselves by refining our morals.

The present disposition of the peoples of our countries does not simply expect the government to regulate their material needs. Rather they look for a government that will also satisfy their moral needs—in short, one which will instill good morals in people through superior force. This superior force is the monarchy, that is to say the sultanate.

Today if even 'Umar came to us, what would he achieve?

For example, suppose someone got up and said: "Women too are human beings. They have the right to socialize with men. You yourself even dispatched women to war along with men." 'Umar would reply: "Those women, those men were not you. Those were decent people, but you are not."

Everybody knows that democracy is the highest form of egalitarian government and the most in accord with the holy law. Unfortunately, the people of Istanbul are not all like the *shaykh* of Gümüşhane [Ahmed Ziyaeddin Gümüşhanevi, Halidiyye Sufi leader, 1813–1893]. This is such a people that they did not even feel the loss of a vast territory like Algeria. It heard the rumblings in Samarqand, Tashkent, and Bukhara as if they were the buzzing of a mosquito. It bent down so low that 39 Âli Pashas could jump over it [a leading *Tanzimat* statesman and Ottoman grand vizier, 1815–1871].

We have become such a nation that when four of our school children gather, they start playing a game in which one of them becomes sultan and bestows high offices upon the others. When four of our elderly statesmen gather in the name of patriotism, each of them wants to announce his leadership and become commander.

What market can there be for the values of brotherhood and equality among a people with such morals?

Mustafa Fazıl Pasha [1829–1875, Egyptian prince and Ottoman statesmen who financed the Young Ottoman movement], who until yesterday led so many people in the name of freedom and patriotism, has been silenced with a membership in the Council of Ministers, despite the fact that he is as rich as Croesus and not in need of any high offices or imperial favors. He has not been affected in the slightest degree by the sighs of all those believers whom he encouraged in the name of patriotism and freedom and whom he made prisoners in the fortresses of Cyprus, Rhodes, and Acre.

A government is required that will not only satisfy the material needs but also see to the moral needs of such an immoral and leprous people. If a ruler like 'Umar is wanted, then one must have men of God like 'Uthman [third caliph, 644–656], 'Ali [ibn Abi Talib, fourth caliph, 656–661], and Khalid.

They once proposed the principle of democracy to Hajjaj [ibn Yusuf, one of the ablest governors under the 'Umayyad caliphate, 660–714]. He replied, "You be Abu Dharr [al-Ghifari, a devout companion of the Prophet, died 653], and I'll then be 'Umar for you."

"Verily an evil patron, and verily an evil friend." [Qur'an, Sura 22, Verse 13]

It is not just Hajjaj who says this. The political thinkers of modern Europe say the same. Jean-Jacques Rousseau [French philosopher, 1712–1778] says: "If there exist men of God, they should be governed by democracy."

In a book published this very year, entitled *Principes de la science politique* [*Principles of Political Science*], Monsieur [Félix Esquirou de] Parieu [1815–1893] states (p. 382): "In civilized societies the democratic way of government is excellent for the well-being of the majority. This way of government, however, must be ripened, sufficiently matured, and extremely well organized through the perfect education of times and obstacles."

Question: Since freedom and equality are among the rights of man, the proper form of government is the one that guarantees these rights. This form of government is democracy.

Answer: What a nice idea! What a sound conclusion! There is no doubt that this is so. Let us, however, move from theory to practice. Let us consider whether it is possible to establish democracy in this place or not? Here lies the problem. For when the term "sound" is used in Muslim jurisprudence and political science, the meaning of this phrase cannot be separated from feasibility, practicability, and utility. Monsieur Parieu says: "If the truth in question is not ripe and mature, it is not the truth, for in politics the truth cannot be separated from feasibility, practicability, and utility" (p. 386).

The same idea is expressed in the rule put forward by our own jurists: "One must not issue a legal opinion based on sound doctrine that is no longer practiced."

Is the only reason for the inapplicability of democracy in the Ottoman country bad morals? We have spoken about morals as an example. The fact that the country is divided between various continents, that it is inhabited by many peoples differing in language, custom, and religion, and its size are all obstacles in the way of democracy and equality.

However many republics may have come into being in the world up to now, they provide no examples to show that equality can be put into practice in a place like the Ottoman country; indeed they may rather indicate the contrary.

Where do we currently find democracy? In San Marino, do we not? That republic is composed of no more than 8,000 individuals, for all that they constitute a nation. Lübeck has a population of 30,000.

Is there anything remarkable about the fact that these and similar countries that resemble our small towns are suited by their situations to be governed by a republican regime? What is more, these countries have been living under the protection of [larger] powers.

The biggest republic in Europe is Switzerland, which is the size of our Danube Province. Its population is only two and a half million people.

It is, however, extremely suitable for its present system of government because of its circumstances. There the republic is nothing other than a federation of various states with each other. That is to say, in Switzerland each state joined the federation on condition that it would retain its autonomy and administration. What we have there is a federation where only two tongues exist (German, French). There are only 4,000 Jews in a population of two and a half million people; there is no other religion but Christianity. Moreover, each state is populated by one or another of the various Christian sects. For instance, Catholics and Protestants are not mixed. Nine cantons are exclusively Catholic, and seven exclusively Protestant. There are only six places in the twenty-two cantons where Catholics and Protestants are mixed. The Christians in Switzerland are extremely

pious and devout. This means that there is morality there, not like in France.

Finally, it was only recently that Switzerland become a federation divided into twenty-two cantons, and that a federal government was set up in Bern to have oversight [of federal affairs]. Previously, the term "republic" was just an empty title. This is because the form of government was not uniform: three cantons were aristocracies administered by aristocrats, six cantons were democracies; where then was equality?

Yes, one hears of a big republic in the New World, the United States of America. This country, however, cannot provide any model for our world. The American government was created by the federation and union of various independent provinces; it is a form of government suitable to that region and to the customs and circumstances of that region. It is divided administratively into states, counties, and townships, known respectively as Cities, Territories, and Districts. A region with a population of 600,000 people is called a state. Every state preserves its administrative independence and special privileges. There are 35 states, each of which joined on condition of preserving its administrative independence and privileges. This federation has a government in the city of Washington. This federal government is made up of a senate and a house of representatives. The president of the federal government is elected for four years. There is also a vice-president. The federal government does not intervene in the administration of the states, that is to say, the regions with populations of 600,000 each. It only administers the counties. Townships are governed from the nearest place.[4]

Something else that has to be said is that in truth democracy is an illusion. For is not its literal meaning government by the people? In Greek *demos* means people and *kratos* government. The basic idea of government by the people is that the people gather and decide in consultation on whatever regulations need to be made or decisions taken—just as in the days of the [early] caliphate people congregated in the mosque. While it may be possible to govern a little state with a small population through such gathering and consultation, how could this work in a larger state? How could the individuals composing such a population congregate? Doesn't everybody

---

4. [Ali Suavi must have garbled his source on the administrative system of the United States of America.—Trans.]

have work to do? How and when would they satisfy their needs?

We can therefore judge with certainty that it is not possible to establish a real democracy based on this conception. It is because of this impossibility that in the republics which exist today, the gathering of the people has given way to the gathering of deputies. The chamber of deputies that works best is that of Switzerland. There every 20,000 people participate in the chamber through electing a deputy. Does this not mean that the votes of 20,000 individuals are subsumed under this contract? As a matter of fact, since unanimity in chambers composed of many deputies is virtually impossible, experience has shown everywhere that one has to go by the majority opinion. Indeed the current rule is to go by the majority of the deputies actually present in the chamber.

Under these circumstances, is it not meaningless to call the opinion of the majority of the deputies present the opinion of the people? Unfortunately, such are the limits of feasibility and practicality. Having dwelt upon this matter, we have succeeded in differentiating the concepts of "soundness" and "political truth" at both the levels of theory and practice. Yet a conclusion has been reached from this discussion: "If a state accepts a chamber of deputies, it possesses the spirit of a republican form of government as far as is practicable."

If all these points about democracy have been understood, let us again consider how democracy and equality can be achieved in, for example, the Ottoman lands. How could these many different ethnicities, religions, sects, and tongues be gathered and united?

Could a federation be formed as in the case of America? To believe in the possibility of such an alliance is to believe in the possibility of Serbia in Europe forming a federation with Egypt in Africa, or Bulgaria in Eastern Europe forming one with Tunisia in Arab Africa—what a fantasy!

The point we have to grasp is that the Ottoman state, for example, must be a state in conformity with its geographical location, circumstances, and population, so that it has to be a sultanate.

However much republicanism puffs itself up, what can it actually accomplish in France, England, or anywhere else? We have to look at practice. When republican regimes were established in France and England, they became a source of corruption for the peoples of the world, and inimical to its good order. The French

republic assaulted the Orient as her initial act. She compelled the Ottoman state to enter into extremely harmful alliances with England and Russia. Yet how long-lasting these republics were to prove! Strangely enough, while the republicans in England and France speak about democracy, equality, and freedom, they have no wish to relinquish their hold over Canada, India, or Algeria. Just look how those Frenchmen talk pretentiously about freedom and equality, all the while seeking world domination like Caesar.

If there is going to be freedom and equality, let them ask the Algerian Arabs, who have absolutely no ethnic, religious, cultural, or geographical affinity with them [the French], whether or not they prefer their own rulers, however tyrannical they may be, to the French republic?

Question: Should the administration in Istanbul remain as it is now?

Answer: No, it should not. What should be done? The parliamentary [form of government should be adopted], that is to say government based upon the principle of consultation—the form which France has adopted this method in this very year 1870 A.D. What is the relevance of this method for us? In essence, our High Council [of Reforms] (*Meclis-i Âlî-i* [*Tanzimat*]) should be enlarged, a chamber of deputies elected by the people should be opened, and the ministers should be held accountable. The accountability of ministers means that their conduct of policy is discussed in the chamber of deputies. The members examine and question it, and the ministers respond. In the end, if the majority of the deputies give their approval with a majority of votes, the ministers keep their offices. And if the majority vote turns out to be against the conduct of policy by the ministers, then they leave office.

Question: Under the circumstances, would the treasury be able to raise money in a short period of time? Would the state be able to impose its authority over the provinces in this huge country?

Answer: These are entirely different questions. With the measures we have proposed, the Ottoman state would establish its state power on a strong foundation in the specific regions of Rumelia and Anatolia, where it currently is able to collect taxes and conscript soldiers directly. That's it. Only long-term policies will provide a remedy for fiscal problems. Bringing provinces under control requires overwhelming force. In our own opinion, the time has passed for the state in Istanbul to acquire such overwhelming force. There is no chance of this.

As far as Africa is concerned, if Tunisia, Tripoli in Barbary, and Egypt can come to their senses and unite, they will establish the best and the most enduring Muslim state in the world. If not, then the overwhelming power of Europe will conquer Africa.

In that event, Istanbul could only lodge a protest as strong as the one it made regarding Algeria. That's it.

For those who share our views, this is inevitable. That is to say, there is no remedy for it. But if Istanbul adopts a policy of attempting to create a unified African state, and henceforth favors the birth of such a state, then it will have found itself a great ally in the cause of its own survival. And until the Day of Judgment the Ottoman dynasty will be given honorable mention for this in the history books.

God knows best what is right.

And Seek Their Counsel in the Matter
[Qur'an, Sura 3, Verse 159]

Namık Kemal (Turkey, 1840–1888) was a leading advocate of constitutionalism and a famous poet and playwright. He received little formal education and spent much of his childhood accompanying his grandfather, a government official who served in various regions of the Ottoman Empire. In Kars, in eastern Anatolia, he studied Sufism. In Sofia, Bulgaria—then an Ottoman province—he learned Arabic and Persian, and produced his first poetry. In the 1860s, while working at the government Translation Bureau, he began writing newspaper articles on literature and social problems, especially women's education. He also joined a constitutionalist group later known as the Young Ottomans Society, and was banished from Istanbul through appointment as assistant governor of Erzurum. Kemal fled to Europe to publish an opposition journal, *Hürriyet* (*Liberty*). He penned most of the journal's articles—including the one translated here—explaining constitutionalism in an Islamic context and attempting to reconcile *shari'a* (Islamic law) with European theories of law. In 1870, Kemal returned to Istanbul and founded the newspaper *İbret* (*The Moral*), until performance of his patriotic play *Vatan yahud Silistre* (*Homeland or Silistria*) prompted public demonstrations, and he was exiled to Cyprus. Pardoned after three years, Kemal was appointed to the Council of the State, and worked on the commission preparing the Ottoman constitution. The following year, the sultan turned against constitutionalism and had its proponents arrested. Kemal was banished to the islands of Rhodes and Chios—now in Greece—where he continued to write, defending Islam against Europeans' accusations of backwardness.[1]

Being created free by God, man is naturally obliged to benefit from this divine gift. General freedom is protected within society because society can produce a preponderant force to safeguard the individual from the fear of the aggression on the part of another individual.

Accordingly, the service rendered by society in this world is the creation of a preponderant force, absolutely indispensable for the protection of freedom, upon which the continued existence of humanity is dependent. Thus the constitutive element of sovereignty, which is charged with the establishment of right and the suppression of wrong, is that force that comes into being from the conjunction of individual forces. Therefore, just as all individuals have the natural right to exercise their own power, so too conjoined powers naturally belong to all individuals as a whole, and consequently in every society the right to sovereignty belongs to the public.

A *shar'* [religious law] proof of this claim is the following legal rule:

Namık Kemal, "Wa shawirhum fi'l-amr" (And Seek Their Counsel in the Matter), *Hürriyet* (*Liberty*), London, England, number 4, July 20, 1868, pp. 1–4. Translation from Turkish and introduction by M. Şükrü Hanioğlu.

1. Ömer Faruk Akün, "Namık Kemal," *İslam Ansiklopedisi* (*Encyclopedia of Islam*), volume 9 (Istanbul, Turkey: Maarif Matbaası, 1971), pp. 54–72; Mehmed Kaplan, *Namık Kemal* (*Namık Kemal*) (Istanbul, Turkey: İstanbul Üniversitesi Edebiyat Fakültesi, 1948); Mithat Cemal Kuntay, *Namık Kemal Devrinin İnsanları ve Olayları Arasında* (*Personalities and Events from the Time of Namık Kemal*), 2 volumes (Istanbul, Turkey: Maarif Matbaası and Millî Eğitim Basımevi, 1944–1957); Şerif Mardin, *The Genesis of Young Ottoman Thought* (Princeton, N.J.: Princeton University Press, 1962), pp. 283–336; Mustafa Kemal Özön, *Namık Kemal ve İbret Gazetesi* (*Namık Kemal and the Newspaper "The Moral"*) (Istanbul, Turkey: Remzi Kitabevi, 1938).

If the people of a town gathered and appointed someone as *qadi* [judge] over themselves to judge cases arising among them, the judicial activity of this person could not be valid; judicial authority would still belong to the *qadi* appointed by the state because jurisdiction is a right of the government. But if the people of a town gathered and pledged allegiance to someone for the sultanate or caliphate, this person would [indeed] become sultan or caliph, while the previous sultan or caliph would retain no authority whatever, because the imamate is a right of the *umma* [the Islamic community].

The public cannot perform the duties attached to this right for themselves, so the appointment of an *imam* [leader] and the establishment of a government are indispensable. This is obviously nothing other than society's delegating the performance of the aforementioned duties to some of its members. Accordingly, monarchs have no right to govern other than the authorization granted to them by the *umma* in the form of allegiance [*bay'a*], and the authorization granted to ministers through appointment by monarchs. The apt saying in the *hadith* [tradition of the Prophet] "the leader of the tribe is its servant" hints at this.[2]

Each *umma* can delegate command to a greater or lesser degree, according to its exigencies and ethics. It is nevertheless one of the basic principles of governance that, "regardless of time, place, and circumstance, state authority should be realized in the way which will least limit the freedom of the individual." For example, no *umma* would wish to infringe this principle by such actions as appointing one of its members permanently as an absolute ruler, or bestowing legislative authority upon a [single] individual. Even if it wishes to do so, it could not rightfully proceed, because an individual has no right to wrong himself, neither does the public have the right to violate the rights of individuals. Furthermore, since it is a consequence of natural law that the circumstances of one generation affect the succeeding generations, no society can have the authority to choose a way of acting that would harm those who come after it.

---

2. [Traditionally this saying of the Prophet was understood to commend a willingness on the part of someone in high office to perform small private services for his inferiors (as opposed to "pulling rank"). Here Namık Kemal uses it rather to present rulership as a public service.—Trans.]

There are two major means to keep the state within the limits of justice. The first is to emancipate the fundamental principles of the administration from the domain of implicit interpretations and to make them public. The excuses, cavils, and denials that may emanate from the state would thus be checked.

The second is the method of consultation, which takes the legislative power out of the hands of the members of the government.

The state is a moral personality. The making of laws is tantamount to its will, and the execution [of laws] is its actions. As long as both of these are held in the same hands, the actions of the government can never be saved from the unfettered exercise of will. Thus the necessity for a council of the *umma* arises from this.

Let us glance at the fundamental regulations of our administration. Today we are in possession of the Rescript of Gülhane [Ottoman reform program of 1839], the Rescript of Reform [Ottoman decree of 1856 guaranteeing equal rights for members of all religious communities], and the recently delivered imperial speech [of 1868, including a liberal critique of the Ottoman legal system]. Some rules that may be described as fundamental principles can be deduced from the general character of these documents by taking the real and essential meaning of certain phrases into consideration. Yet none of these documents has the clarity and methodical structure to constitute a base for the administration of a civilized state.

Furthermore, some of these documents contain limitations denying the freedom of the people, embodied in such phrases as "without reaching the degree of freedom," and in some others many superfluities regarding the details of administration are found.

Since the rights of man are determined by reason and tradition, and the present state of affairs of our civilization is evident, the aforementioned imperial rescripts and decrees must be corrected by bringing these two principles into conformity. That is, their superfluities should be pruned, their obscurities should be clarified, and the necessary principles should be formulated—for example, the requisite freedom for everyone to scrutinize the state and criticize the actions of the government, either verbally or through publication, given that sovereignty belongs to the people. After this, a rescript of fundamental principles should be issued to ensure that the administration of the Ottoman state is indeed based upon freedom and justice. The inevitable consequence of this is the method of consultation, which is the very object of our discussion.

Let us first consider the truth of this Eastern Question which is so much talked about: As is known, Russia wants to annihilate the Sublime State [Ottoman Empire], while the Western states prevent her from carrying this out. And yet, while Russia has been attempting to accomplish her goal by provoking the Christian subjects of the Sublime State, Europe has been helping the complainants whom Russia has encouraged to come forward. At first glance, these actions may appear as a major contradiction. However, in fact, it is our state that compels the Europeans to follow this course.

When the Russians sent [Knyaz Aleksandr Sergeyevich] Menshikov [Russian general, 1787–1867] to Istanbul [in 1853] to protect their coreligionists [and the Crimean War broke out], the Western Powers sacrificed their resources and the lives of their men along with us in order to resist Russian intervention. At the end of the conflict, however, they proposed to us the reformation of our tyrannical administration. At that juncture the Sublime Porte should have succeeded in preventing all foreign interventions and securing our future existence by correcting the fundamentals of the state and obtaining a collective European guarantee as a constitutional state. Instead, the Sublime Porte mollified Europe by granting certain privileges to the Christians alone. Furthermore, by including these reforms in the Treaty of Paris, they [Ottoman statesmen] both promised to reform the conditions of the Christian subjects in the name of the sultan and granted the [European] guarantor states a right of supervision in this matter.

Now whenever Christians make allegations against the state, whether true or false, these result in their acquisition of rights. This is because the fundamentals of the administration are corrupt, the officials are not accountable, there is no consultation, and there is no oversight on the part of the *umma*. For these reasons the Europeans do not believe us, regardless of the magnitude of the privileges granted to the Christians to whom we have promised reform, and despite all the talk about their prosperity. And since the Europeans are accustomed to freedom, they say, "Could a country that lacks deputies to scrutinize the rules and make the ministers accountable enjoy order?" and "Can a man be free without being able to criticize members of the government verbally or through publication?" Another misfortune is that when members of the government speak about the contentedness of the people, Europeans conclude that the Muslims are ignorant of the pleasure of freedom and readily submit to the noose of oppression.

What will be the result of all this? The state will undoubtedly sink if it does not modify its present absolutism.

It is true that the Western Powers have defended us up to now, for the sake of protecting their commercial interests and safeguarding the European balance [of power] against the aggression of the northern savages [Russia]; and in the future they will continue to do so as much as they can.

Yet given these [Christian] complaints of victimization, the Western Powers cannot refrain from putting pressure on us, or at least standing as the protector of rebels, because they do not want to leave Russia alone in its intervention. This is an era in which nobody can resist public opinion. The claim that "rule belongs to the victor"[3] cannot be applied unless concealed behind a thousand curtains of deceit, even if a clear preponderance exists. In any case, the idea of granting autonomy to each and every ethnic group in the Ottoman lands and thereby creating a confederation like Germany has been debated in Europe for a long time. However, this idea does not enjoy much currency for now, because those famously shrewd European states know that this policy would be vulnerable to separatism, and there can be no barrier against Russia as strong as a united Ottoman state. In spite of this, every intelligent person realizes that as long as this tyrannical administration prevails in the state, foreign interventions cannot be stopped.

The continuation of foreign intervention (as is well known, the treasury lost three or four million purses [1.5 or 2 billion Ottoman piasters] because of the Crete insurrection alone) will soon reduce the state to a condition in which it lacks the power to resist Russian invasion as well as the [Ottoman] allies could do. Then the Europeans will be compelled to choose the lesser of two evils [that is, a costly intervention to defend the Ottomans or a costly acceptance of Russian domination of the region].

No means other than the method of consultation can be found to dispel these troubles. Then it will be

---

3. [This saying is generally taken to mean "one judges by the mainstream, ignoring exceptional cases."—Trans.]

known that everyone is free. Then Europe will treat us as a civilized nation, instead of regarding us as a scarecrow planted against Russia, as is now the case. Then if the people of a province resort to arms under the pretext of being oppressed, when they have deputies in the council of the nation, they will be unable to justify their claim to Europe. Therefore, almost all external threats toward the state will be eliminated.

Let us now glance at the internal dimensions of the matter:

To begin with, even the ministers cannot deny that today the nation is faced with the threat of extinction. One of the major reasons for this is that the country's wealth is in sharp decline. Would buildings and other expenses have plunged the treasury to its present level if we had already adopted the method of consultation and established an assembly of the people? Could the internal debt of 22 million liras have been raised to 40 million through consolidation? Would [the government] have had the audacity to declare that the value of the consolidated long-term debt was 29 million liras, when it was calculated as less than 26.5 million [liras]? Would the [tax] regulations for salt, tobacco, and road construction, whose thousand harms caused the destruction of so many regions, have been put into effect? On what basis can we assume that the future actions of the government will not conform to its past habits, so long as our administration maintains its present character? Is it not a matter of experience that trying what has already been tried can only lead to regret?

Second, we should not forget the fact that our people harbor a deep hatred and mistrust toward the present administration. Everybody views official declarations as attempts at disinformation. In fact, even when the government distributed cotton seed to the provinces free of charge because of the American Civil War, some farmers refused to accept it. When asked the reason for their rejection of this munificence, they responded: "Nothing good can come from the state. Who knows what hidden agenda there may be? We would not dare to accept it."

And how could people not be mistrustful? A hundred thousand policies have been put into effect. All caused harm because the foundations are corrupt. Many persons who had the confidence of the public came to occupy high office, but they could not accomplish anything, for the same reason: the rottenness of the foundations. Is there any possibility that in the future people will have a warm affection for

the government unless they themselves supervise the administration? Furthermore, when a while ago the French emperor used the occasion of the Cretan crisis to advise the Sublime Porte that it should seek the public opinion of the people of Turkistan [Turkey] regarding the necessary reforms, the Sublime Porte responded by saying: "We cannot commit suicide by drinking so lethal a poison as public opinion."

In fact, the opinion of the public is not a poison but an elixir of health. Just as a physician can only help individuals regain health with the support of their organs, so also the administration's measures to reform the character of the state, which is a moral personality, depend upon the assistance of the people who are the constituent elements of the state. The only measure that will eliminate the present oppression and profligacy, and put an end to the mistrust of the people, is the adoption of the method of consultation. In fact, what has been said above proves this claim.

As for the imagined detrimental effects that would stem from the adoption of the method of consultation, in reality these have no basis. First, it is said that the establishment of a council of the people would violate the rights of the sultan. As was made clear in our introduction, the right of the sultan in our country is to govern on the basis of the will of the people and the principles of freedom. His title is "one charged with kingship" [*sahib al-mulk*], not "owner of kingship" [*malik al-mulk*, a title reserved for God in the Qur'an, Sura 3, Verse 26]. His Imperial Majesty the sultan is heir to the esteemed Ottoman dynasty, which established its state by protecting religion. It was thanks to this fact that the [Ottoman sultan] became the cynosure of the people and the caliph of Islam. The religion of Muhammad rejects the absolutist claim to outright ownership [of the state] in the incontrovertible verse: "Whose is the kingdom today? God's, the One, the Omnipotent." [Qur'an, Sura 40, Verse 16][4]

Second, it is argued that the religious and cultural heterogeneity of the Ottoman lands and the ignorance of the people are reasons against this [the adoption of consultation]. In the gatherings of highly important personages, it is asked how a people speaking seventy-two different tongues could be convened in one assem-

---

4. [Namık Kemal appears to have deliberately omitted a word—*al-yawma*—that shows that the verse refers to the Day of Judgment.—Trans.]

bly, and what kind of response would be given if [some of] the deputies to be convened opposed dispatching troops to Crete because they wished to protect the Greeks, or raised an objection to appropriations for holy sites and pious foundations.

O my God! In all provinces there are provincial councils. Members from all denominations serve in these councils, and all of them debate issues in the official language [Turkish]. How can anybody speak of linguistic heterogeneity in light of this obvious fact? Is it supposed that a council of the people is a seditious assembly whose members are absolutely independent, and whose administration is not based on any rules? Once the fundamental principles and the internal regulations of the assembly are issued, who would dare to protect those, like the rebels of Crete, who desire to separate themselves from the integral nation? Who would dare to say a word about [Islamic] religious expenditures [purchasing non-Muslim land], in return for which [non-Muslim communities] have acquired real estate valued several times more?

Let us come to the matter of ignorance. Montenegro, Serbia, and Egypt each have councils of the people. Why should [our people's] ignorance prevent us [from having a council], if it did not prevent these lands? Are we at a lower level of culture than even the savages of Montenegro? Can it be that we could not find people to become deputies, whose only necessary qualification will be attaining the age of majority, when we can find people in the provinces to become members of the State Council, membership in which is dependent upon possessing perfected political skills?

O Ottoman liberals! Do not give any credit to such deceptive superstitions. Give serious thought to the dangerous situation in which the nation finds itself today. While doing so, take into consideration the accomplishments that the opposition has already achieved. It will be obvious that the salvation of the state today is dependent upon the adoption of the method of consultation, and upon continuing the opposition aimed at achieving this method of administration. If we have any love for the nation, let us be fervent in advancing this meritorious policy. Let us be fervent so that we can move forward without delay.

Transferring the New Civilization
to the Islamic Peoples

Şemseddin Sami Frashëri (Albania-Turkey, 1850–1904) was a leading Ottoman intellectual, journalist, and linguist. One of seven children in a prominent Albanian family, he learned European languages at a Greek high school and Middle Eastern languages from special lessons at Islamic schools. Following graduation, he worked for the governor of Ioannina, and then the press bureau of the Sublime Porte in Istanbul. At the same time, he published his own articles and plays, which resulted in his banishment through appointment as editor of the official gazette of Tripoli, in North Africa. The following year, he was granted an imperial pardon and returned to newspaper work in Istanbul. Şemseddin Sami was the author of the first modern geographical and historical dictionary of the Ottoman Empire, and many other lexicons. He also established a series called the "Pocket Library" to publish short essays for the general public. It seems that he suppressed his more radical opinions in these pamphlets—on the Islamic roots of European civilization, for example, and the veiling of women. Furthermore, his attempt to translate the Qur'an into Turkish was frustrated by the authorities, and he was compelled to destroy the parts he had completed. Meanwhile, his newspaper articles—including the one translated here—were outspoken in promoting positivism and modernization. These publications, along with his participation in Albanian cultural activities, caused the government to treat Şemseddin Sami as suspect. Although he was appointed to official positions, he was asked to conduct his studies at home and lived his last years under virtual house arrest.[1]

As may be understood from our previous articles on [Europe's] history and state, although civilization passed through many hands before reaching those of the Europeans, in comparison to modern-day European civilization those ancient civilizations—for all that the later ones were always more perfect than the earlier—are like mere drawings made on a wall with coal by a child in comparison to a painting by the famous artist Raphael [Italy, 1483–1520]. In addition, those old civilizations have already been destroyed; dealing with them is a duty reserved to history and to the science of archaeology. Many works of Islamic civilization—the latest of the ancient civilizations—and of its predecessor Greek civilization are extant, but given the existence of [modern] works and beacons, whose number is increasing daily, having recourse to these ancient works, or contenting oneself with them, is tantamount to trying to benefit from the wick of an oil lamp in the presence of sunlight. Thus the scholars and philosophers of present-day civilization consider Aristotle [Greece, 384–322 B.C.] and Ibn Rushd [Andalusia-Morocco, 1126–1198] as two great mentors of civilization and hold them in high esteem; yet in today's schools they do not teach Aristotle's *History of Animals* or *The*

Şemseddin Sami Frashëri, "Medeniyet-i cedidenin ümem-i islamiyeye nakli" (Transferring the New Civilization to the Islamic Peoples), *Güneş* (*The Sun*), Istanbul, Ottoman Empire, volume 1, number 4, 1883–1884, pp. 179–184. Translation from Turkish and introduction by M. Şükrü Hanioğlu.

1. Hikmet Turhan Dağlıoğlu, *Şemsettin Sami Bey: Hayatı ve Eserleri* (*Şemseddin Sami Bey: His Life and Works*)

(Istanbul, Turkey: Resimli Ay Matbaası, 1934); İsmail Hakkı, *On Dördüncü Asrın Türk Muharrirleri: Şemseddin Sami Bey* (*Turkish Authors of the Fourteenth Century* [A.H.]: *Şemseddin Sami Bey*) (Istanbul, Ottoman Empire: Kasbar Matbaası, 1895); Agah Sırrı Levend, *Şemsettin Sami* (*Şemseddin Sami*) (Ankara, Turkey: Türk Dil Kurumu Tanıtma Yayınları, 1969).

Canon of Medicine by Ibn Sina [Iran, 980–1037]. They rendered great services to humanity; they each lit a lamp in gloomy centuries enveloped in the darkness of ignorance. Gradually people left this environment of darkness, finding the way with the help of their lamps. At last the sun rose, the light of education flooded the world. The duty we owe to those lamps today is simply to cherish and respect them for their role in getting us out the darkness. To go beyond this and to draw a curtain of ignorance and fanaticism in front of the light of the sun, and to content ourselves with the weak light of those lamps, is sheer folly.

Therefore, saving the Muslim peoples from ignorance and once again bringing them to civilization are among the most important priorities of any zealous person who loves his religious community and fatherland, since the survival and glory of Islam are contingent upon this alone.

It is true that religious zeal would impel a man to be content with the lamp which he knows to have been lit by his ancestors; yet it is essential that reason and wisdom should overcome any such feeling. Today, however much effort and expense is required to revive the medicine of Ibn Sina, the wisdom of Ibn Rushd, and the chemistry of Jahiz [Iraq, circa 776–869], to extract their books from underneath the dust of libraries and translate them into the various Muslim languages, to publish them, and to found schools and colleges devoted to teaching them, we must make the same effort and go to the same expense to put into circulation among us the best scientific works of our own century. For just as we cannot cure even malaria with the medicine of Ibn Sina, so we can neither operate a railroad engine or steamship, nor use the telegraph, with the chemistry of Jahiz and the wisdom of Ibn Sina. For this reason, if we wish to become civilized, we must do so by borrowing science and technology from the contemporary civilization of Europe, and leave the study of the works of Islamic scholars to the students of history and antiquity.

It is a regrettable circumstance that, because today civilization seems to belong exclusively to the Christian nations, ignorant masses of our own nation take it to be a symbol or requisite of Christianity, and thus deem distancing themselves from it and guarding themselves against it to be a religious duty.

We can affirm that it is not the religion of Islam which prevents Muslim nations from becoming civilized; rather the cause is the religious difference and conflict which exists between the Muslim and the civilized nations—in other words, the fact that present-day civilization is in the hands of the Christian nations.

To avoid such fanatical reactions on the part of the people, some of our literary figures who are unhappy with this situation have attempted to make European civilization seem less loathsome in the eyes of the people, and so to make them warm to the new sciences and pave the way to transfer contemporary civilization to the Islamic nations. In order to achieve this goal, they used newspapers, books, pamphlets, sermons, and all available means to spread the view that European civilization was borrowed from the Muslims, that Islam is no obstacle to true civilization, and that most of science and technology which we see in the hands of the Europeans today is made up of Muslim discoveries. This effort of these people is a most worthy one. But because there is as much exaggeration as truth in what they assert, one senses that alongside the good they have done, they have also done some harm. This effort has gone to extremes by exceeding the limits of necessity. Just as a large dose of medicine intended to cure an illness creates a new one, so a new idea has arisen from this exaggeration, and although it is less detrimental than the first, its harmfulness cannot be denied. The number of people among the Muslims who view European civilization as a product of unbelief contrary to and incompatible with Islam has decreased, thanks to the efforts of these preachers of civilization. Yet as a result of their exaggerations, the number of those people who have acquired a new fanaticism—viewing European civilization as something stolen from us, imperfect, and an imitation, and insulting that civilization while maintaining that the true civilization is ours—has correspondingly increased.

This new fanaticism is like an illness arising from an overzealous physician's treatment. Shattering this fanaticism is a most weighty duty for those who want to be of service in civilizing the Muslim nations. This duty compels us to say the following to those who have acquired this new fanaticism: The Europeans borrowed many things from us, that is to say from our ancestors or more precisely our coreligionists who lived eight or ten centuries ago; however, none of the things in their hands today is something that was borrowed from our ancestors. Europe borrowed a seed of civilization from the Islamic world, and planted that seed. It is natural that a seed should decompose in the earth in order to bear fruit. That seed decomposed; the cycle has been repeated many times, with the result that its very genus has changed. The knowledge that Europe derived from the scholars of Islam was very considerable by [the standards of] the time, but by present-day standards it is nothing. At that time she borrowed a lamp from us in order to escape from the darkness of ignorance which surrounded her; but once she had reached a bright place with the help of the light of that lamp, she no longer needed it, and threw it away. Can we wax proud of this? There is nothing here to be proud of; rather we should be ashamed of it, because, after dropping this lamp and allowing it to go out, we do not even desire to benefit from a sun of civilization which rises and shines before our very eyes. Some among us say "this is not a sun but a time just before dawn," while some of us say "this is an imitation of our old lamp," thereby preferring to remain in darkness by closing our eyes!

Had the pioneers of Islamic civilization such as [caliph Abu] Ja'far [al-]Mansur [reigned 754–775], [caliph] Harun al-Rashid [reigned 786–809], and the caliph Ma'mun [reigned 813–833], who established the caliphate on the ruins of Babylon, viewed Greek civilization with similar contempt, maintained that that civilization was derived from, and a mere imitation of, the civilization of their ancestors the Chaldeans, or that depending on works of Greek pagans contradicted Islam, would the Islamic civilization of which we are so proud today have materialized? Although Greek civilization was no longer an ongoing enterprise at that time, and had ceased to exist, children of the Companions of the Messenger of God (may God bless him and grant him salvation) borrowed it in its entirety, revived it, and held Greek sages, in whose footsteps they proudly followed, in high esteem and paid tribute to them. Why then do we not want to benefit from European civilization, accusing it sometimes of blasphemy and polytheism

and sometimes of being an imitation? Are the European people of the book [Christians and Jews] more profligate in their religion than the ancient Greek pagans, or are we more pious than the children of the Companions of the Prophet who had the honor of conversing with the Messenger of God?

In Europe, too, fanaticism was often an obstacle on the road to civilization, Islamic scholars were viewed as sorcerers, and those cultivating the sciences were accused of heresy and severely punished. There too at first appeared some scholars who tried to reconcile religious texts with science, and to eliminate fanaticism by appeasing it. But because fanaticism is not the sort of monster that can be won over with kindness, it has brutally destroyed those who have attempted to appease it. Finally, the intellectuals gathered together, hand in hand, and waged a war against fanaticism with axes, crowbars, and gunpowder; they demolished it, and only then did civilization begin to move forward. In our society, too, in order to achieve progress in civilization and save the Muslim nations from the ignorance and Bedouinism that are precipitating their annihilation, for all intents and purposes a war must be declared against fanaticism to crush it by force and thus open the road to civilization.

Far from damaging religion, this would in fact greatly benefit it; for fanaticism is the rust of religion, and just as within a short time rust eats up and destroys even the best steel, so also fanaticism stains even the most truthful religion and rots it. The rust of fanaticism must be removed from religion so it shines with its true and essential luster, and its future is secured. There is as great a difference between religion and fanaticism as there is between light and darkness. The darkness of ignorance and fanaticism must be removed so that the light of knowledge and true religion may together illuminate and reinvigorate people's minds and hearts. There is no alternative.

Summary of the Causes of Stagnation

'Abd al-Rahman al-Kawakibi (Syria, 1854–1902) was one of the most influential Islamic reformist thinkers in the eastern Mediterranean at the end of the nineteenth century. Born into a well-established family of notables in Aleppo, al-Kawakibi received a thorough education in the Islamic sciences and in the major Islamic languages of the region: Arabic, Ottoman Turkish, and Persian. In the 1870s, he edited the official paper in Aleppo, *al-Furat* (*The Euphrates*), and established two independent newspapers, both of which were short-lived. Despite holding a number of administrative and public posts in Ottoman Syria, al-Kawakibi experienced chronic persecution by the authorities, leading him ultimately to settle in Egypt in 1898. He died suddenly in Cairo in 1902, possibly poisoned by agents of the Ottoman sultan. Al-Kawakibi's thought was influenced by his contemporaries Sayyid Jamal al-Din al-Afghani (chapter 11) and Muhammad 'Abduh (chapter 3), among others. His historical significance in the Islamic modernist trend of thought lay in his elaboration of an Arab pan-Islamism intended to reform the decaying Muslim world, privileging Arabs over non-Arabs and advocating the establishment of an Arab caliphate. In this process, al-Kawakibi decentered the primacy of the Ottoman Turks and transformed them into an internal, problematic other. The following selection is drawn from al-Kawakibi's famous account of a fictional series of meetings in Mecca, at which twenty-three representatives from around the Muslim world—including thirteen Arabs—assemble to discuss pan-Islamic resurgence and criticize Ottoman tyranny.[1]

The Seventh Gathering, Wednesday, 24 Zi'l-Qa'da 1316 [April 5, 1899]

On the morning of this day, the association assembled, and the minutes of the preceding [meeting] were read, in keeping with the rules.

"Mr. President," [the fictional delegate from Mecca] said, addressing al-Sayyid al-Furati.[2] "In addition to your attention to organizing meetings and fulfilling editorial duties, the association expects also to benefit from your personal views concerning the cause of stagnation, which is the topic under discussion, after summarizing all of the opinions that the honorable brethren have mentioned, whenever they have been expressed knowledgably and consistently in hearing, writing, reading, and reviewing—you are the most wide-ranging of us, intellectually.

"In addition, the association requests the eminent Damascene and the eloquent Alexandrian [fictional representatives from Damascus and Alexandria] to cooperate in writing down your speech, that is, to take turns listening to the spoken statements and writing them down, because, like the rest of the brethren, neither of them knows short-hand, which is used in such situations."

The eminent Damascene looked at his colleague [from Alexandria], who indicated his approval, then said: "We are willing to render this service."

'Abd al-Rahman al-Kawakibi, "Umm al-Qura" (The Mother of Towns [Mecca]), in *al-A'mal al-kamila lil-Kawakibi* (*The Complete Works of Kawakibi*) (Beirut, Lebanon: Markaz Dirasat al-Wahda al-'Arabiyya, 1995), pp. 358–367. First published in 1902. Translation from Arabic and introduction by Joseph G. Rahme.

1. Joseph G. Rahme, "'Abd al-Rahman al-Kawakibi's Reformist Ideology, Arab Pan-Islamism, and the Internal Other," *Journal of Islamic Studies*, volume 10, number 2, 1999, pp. 159–177; Eliezer Tauber, *The Emergence of the Arab Movements* (London: Frank Cass, 1993), ch. 5; Khaldun S. al-Husry, *Three Reformers: A Study in Modern Arabic Political Thought* (Beirut, Lebanon: Khayats, 1966); 'Abbas M. al-'Aqqad, *al-Rahhala Kaf* (*The Traveler K*) (Cairo, Egypt: Matbu'at al-Majlis al-'A'la, 1958).

2. [Al-Sayyid al-Furati—probably the alter ego of the author—was the fictional representative of northern Syria, primarily Aleppo, and parts of northern Iraq.—Trans.]

Al-Sayyid al-Furati said: "[I shall comply] out of affection and obedience though I am really incapable, my speech is feeble, and I have little to offer." Then he turned away from the desk, and the eminent Damascene and eloquent Alexandrian took his place. [Al-Furati] did not linger and plunged into his speech. He said:

"It can be concluded from our blessed association's deliberations that this stagnation, as already discussed, stems from the totality of numerous causes, not from one or a few causes that can easily be resisted. Some of these causes are fundamental, and some are derived from fundamental [causes]. Yet all of them can be reduced to three categories: religious causes, political causes, and moral causes. I will read to you summaries from the index list that I extracted from the association's studies, distinguishing the fundamental [causes] with the letter F and the derivative [causes] with the letter D, as follows."

The First Kind: Religious Causes

1. Effect of the doctrine of predestination on the ideas of the *umma* [Muslim community]. (F)
2. Effect of asceticism on effort, work, and beauty of life. (D)
3. Effect of dissension [arising] from debates about religious beliefs. (F)
4. Giving oneself over to specious ideas and artificial distinctions in religion. (F)
5. The abandonment of religious tolerance and leniency in religious practice. (F)
6. Religious severity by later legists in contrast to the pious early Muslims. (F)
7. Confusion of the *umma*'s beliefs due to the plethora of conflicting opinions in the derivative details of religious laws. (D)
8. Inability to relate statements to practices in religion due to adulteration and severity. (D)
9. Introduction of scriptural borrowings, fables, and harmful innovations into the religion by deceitful *'ulama* [religious scholars]. (F)
10. Belittling of religion by the exploiters of Sufism, treating it as entertainment and a game. (D)
11. Corruption of the religion by the obscurantism of the flatterers, through additions, omissions, and fanciful interpretations. (D)
12. Introduction of innumerable superstitions into the public sphere by deceivers and worshipers of the dead and their shrines. (F)
13. Alienation of Muslim minds [literally, "hearts"] through the threats of astrologers, geomancers, of magic and humbug. (D)
14. Deceit of liars and flatterers [who state] that in religion there are secret matters and that knowledge is a veil. (F)
15. Belief that the philosophical and rational sciences are incompatible with religion. (F)
16. Penetration of manifest or hidden polytheism into the beliefs of the laity. (D)
17. Failure of practicing *'ulama'* to affirm divine unity. (D)
18. The surrender to *taqlid* [imitation of previous scholars] and the abandonment of reflection and the quest for guidance. (D)
19. Undue allegiance to *madhhab*s [schools of law] and the opinions of recent writers, forsaking scriptures and the path of the pious early Muslims. (D)
20. Neglecting the wisdom of the community, of the Friday [prayer], and of the *hajj* [pilgrimage] assembly. (F)
21. Obstinacy in denouncing religious freedom in ignorance of its merits. (D)
22. Requiring what would not be required if one sought guidance from the Book [the Qur'an] and the *sunna* [practice of the Prophet]. (D)
23. Burdening Muslims with that which God has not demanded, and belittling of that which is commanded. (D)

The Second Kind: Political Causes

24. Policymaking is divorced from power and responsibility. (F)
25. Fragmentation of the *umma* into factions and political parties. (D)
26. Denial of the *umma*'s freedom of speech and action, and loss of its security and aspirations. (D)
27. Loss of justice and equality of rights among the *umma*'s [social] strata. (D)
28. The leaders' natural inclination toward deceitful *'ulama'* and ignorant Sufis. (D)
29. Denial of a livelihood and honor to practicing *'ulama'* and seekers of knowledge. (F)
30. Honoring knowledge by stipends through which rulers give preferment to the elite, while delegating service in religion to the ignorant. (F)
31. Reversal of the practice of taking property from the rich and giving it to the poor. (F)
32. Requiring leaders, judges, and religious officials [to implement] matters that destroy their religion. (D)
33. Banishing noble and liberal leaders, and associating with flatterers and the wicked. (F)
34. Coercion and mistreatment of high-minded, rightly-guided leaders. (D)

35. Loss of the power of public opinion through suppression and division. (D)
36. Foolishness of most leaders and their persistence in unwise policies. (D)
37. Stubborn and arrogant insistence of most leaders on despotism. (D)
38. Submersion of leaders in luxury and carnal appetites, and their avoidance of any kind of glory other than ostentation and wealth. (D)
39. Restriction of political concern to taxation and the military. (F)

The Third Kind: Moral Causes

40. Immersion in ignorance and acquiescence to it. (F)
41. Descent into alienation by those who are successful in religious and worldly affairs. (D)
42. Lingering in apathy as a way of comforting the self. (D)
43. Loss of mutual counseling and giving free rein to hatred of God. (F)
44. Dissolution of the bonds of religious responsibility. (F)
45. Corruption of teaching, sermonizing, orating, and giving spiritual guidance. (D)
46. Loss of religious and moral education. (F)
47. Loss of the strength of associations and the by-product of their continued existence. (F)
48. Loss of collective financial strength because of the neglect of *zakat* [alms tax]. (F)
49. Abandoning action because of low expectations. (D)
50. Neglecting the demand for general rights, due to cowardice and fear of disappointment. (D)
51. The dominance of flattery's fabrications, servility, and lowliness. (D)
52. Preference for earning a living in the military and in government service, rather than industry. (D)
53. Delusion that religious knowledge is found among turbans [that is, traditional religious scholars] and in everything that is recorded in the Book. (D)
54. Enmity toward the higher sciences because of the comfort of ignorance and abasement. (F)
55. Estrangement from engagement with and discussion of public affairs. (F)
56. Inattention to the avoidance of polytheism and its evil portents. (F)

Then al-Sayyid al-Furati said: "These summarize the causes of stagnation that the brethren of the as-sociation have set forth, disregarding repetitions, as one would suppose. Inasmuch as the disorder that exists in the fundamental administration of Islamic governments has an important role in producing the general stagnation, I therefore add the following causes to the ones already discussed by my distinguished brethren, enumerating them by means of the headings of the problem only. Were I to give details and explain them, it would take too long and we would digress from the aim of our gathering.

"Moreover, the causes that I will mention are the fundamental origins of the disorder in the current policies and administration of the Ottoman empire, this most powerful state whose affairs concern all Muslims. It has experienced most of these disorders in the last 60 years, that is, after it rushed to reorganize its affairs [in the Tanzimat reforms of the mid-19th century]. In doing so, it damaged its ancient foundations and did not improve either *taqlid* nor its blameworthy *bida'* [innovations], so that its condition deteriorated, especially in the last 20 years, during which time two thirds of the kingdom was lost and the remaining third was destroyed. Among the factors determining the ruin of the state was the loss of men and the squandering of the sultan's power for the sake of preserving his noble self and persisting in his autocratic policies.

"As for the rest of the Islamic kingdoms and emirates, they too share some of these fundamental problems. Furthermore, they suffer from other, more harmful and bitter conditions whose exposition and thorough examination would take too long. The causes I wish to discuss in summary form are the following."

The Policy and Administration of the Ottomans

57. Standardization of administrative and penal laws despite differences in the characteristics of the empire's parts and differences in the inhabitants in terms of [their] races and customs. (F)
58. Heterogeneity of juridical laws, and the confusion of the judiciary in [dealing with] analogous cases. (F)
59. Adherence to the principle of centralized administration despite the distance of certain parts from the capital; administrative leadership should reside in those distant parts [so as to know] the situations and the particular features of their inhabitants. (D)

60. Adhering to the principle that administrative leadership and governors are never held accountable for their actions. (D)

61. Administrative confusion resulting from inattention to the integration of morals with procedures among ministers, governors, and commanders. The state must select them from among all the races and nationalities found in the kingdom in order to satisfy them. (D)

62. Adhering to [the practice of] racial inconsistencies in the hiring of [government] employees, with the aim of complicating understanding between the employees and the [local] inhabitants and rendering it impractical for them to intermix and secure the administration; this makes agreement upon administrative policy impossible. (D)

63. Adhering to a policy of customarily giving special authority to certain families—like the rulership of Mecca and the rulership of the large tribes of the Hijaz, Iraq, and the Euphrates—who are incapable of administering them; as a result, the governor enrages those whom he rules, and is detested by them; [all this] so that they will not ally with him against the state. (F)

64. Adhering to the practice of appointing to particular positions in certain professions, like the *Shaykh al-Islam* [chief religious official] or the Minister of Defense, people despised by their colleagues in the *'ulama'* or the army, so that the leader and the led will not agree on any important matter. (D)

65. Gross discrimination among various subject races regarding subsidies and penalties.

66. Carelessness in the selection of [government] employees and [civil] officials, needlessly employing too many of them with the purpose of sustaining cliques, favorites, and habitual flatterers.

67. Permissiveness in reward and reproof due to inattention to whether administrative matters are done well or badly, as if the empire had no master.

68. Inattention to fostering religious requirements, such as erecting rules that conflict with religious law, in the absence of some compelling policy concern, or when there is need, but with no attention to explaining to the *umma* and seeking their indulgence for it, through seeking to convince them and satisfy their concerns.

69. Loss of the sanctity of religious law and the force of [secular] laws, by not abiding by and executing [religious law], and insisting on administration being methodical in name but arbitrary in practice.

70. Failure to attend to the customs of the inhabitants, their morals, and their welfare, so as to gain their affection, not just outward obedience.

71. Obtuseness toward or willful neglect of the needs of the times, the challenge of events, and the progress of the inhabitants, due to a of lack of concern for the future.

72. Suppression of awakened thought in an effort to forbid its growth, development, and [to suppress] inquiry into administrative activities, their merits and defects; though the suppression of natural growth is utterly futile, temptation and [corrupting] inducements are the result, as well as hatred toward the administration.

73. Preferential treatment of those base in descent, in morals, and in education, who hold sway over free persons and have authority over those who are their superiors; this neglect of matters by those who are responsible for them leads necessarily to the debasing of the administration.

74. Administration of the treasury in a loose manner, without any supervision; purchasing without budgeting; extravagance without reprimand; and damage without any accounting, until the empire became mortgaged to foreigners with heavy debts that are being paid with [the loss of] territory, sovereignty, blood, and rights.

75. Administration of important political and civilian interests without consultation of the subjects, and the [government's] refusal to discuss them—even though its damage in every act of omission and commission was well known.

76. Administration of property in a centralized manner, silencing experts who know of its defects, so as to prevent their divulging what they really know, lest the public learn the truth of the matter. If the public were to learn it would speak, and if it spoke, it would act, and then there would be a great uprising.

77. Administration of external affairs through bootlicking, appeasement, the compromise of rights, bribery, capitulations, and money; the administration expends all of that on its neighbors so that they will turn a blind eye to the [country's] destructive, painful sights, and they will put up with the rotten stink of their rule. Were it not for those sights and smells, the neighboring countries would have no means to exert pressure, despite the enmity and hatred that God planted among them till the Day of Resurrection.

Then al-Sayyid al-Furati said: "Some of these causes I have mentioned are old maladies inseparable from the administration of the Ottoman government since its establishment, or for centuries, and some of them are temporary manifestations that will disappear with the disappearance of their producers. Perhaps one could be patient with them, were it not that the danger has come close—may God forbid it—to the heart, as was indicated by the president in his first remarks."

Then he said: "Connected to these causes are a few miscellaneous causes that I shall examine after enumerating them in summary fashion, as follows."

Miscellaneous Causes

78. Differences in the natures of the subjects and the shepherds.
79. Heedlessness or negligence in organizing the matters of daily life.
80. Heedlessness of the need to apportion labor and time.
81. Heedlessness of [the need to] yield to expertise.
82. Heedlessness of balancing [military] power and preparedness.
83. Abandoning attention to educating women.
84. Inattention to the fitness of wives [that is, the development of qualities that make them of suitable status to their husbands].
85. Weakness of character, that is, general apathy.
86. Withdrawal from life and apathy.

"As to the incongruence of morals between the shepherds and the subjects, it has a great significance. As is apparent to those who contemplate and scrutinize the histories of nations, the greatest and most successful kings and conquerors—such as Alexander [Macedonian king, 336–323 B.C.]; 'Umar [ibn al-Khattab, second caliph, 634–644] and Salah al-Din [Ayyubid sultan, 1169–1193], may God be pleased with them; Genghis [Khan, Mongol ruler, 1206–1227], [Mehmed] the Conqueror [Ottoman sultan, 1451–1481], Charles V of Germany [Holy Roman Emperor, 1519–1558], Peter the Great [Russian tsar, 1696–1725], and [Napoléon] Bonaparte [French consul and emperor, 1799–1815]—did not accomplish their great feats except through sincere determination. They had a genuine and complete congruence with their subjects and armies in morals and instincts, so that they were truly heads to those bodies, not like a camel's head on the body of a bull, or the reverse. It is only this congruence that makes the umma consider its leader to be its head, so that it gives itself

wholeheartedly, without resentment or [the need for] coercion. Success can not be had in any other way, as the wise al-Mutanabbi [classical Arab poet, 915–965] said: 'The people exist only through kings; will Arabs succeed with 'ajam [non-Arab] kings?'

"There is no disagreement about the fact that one of the most important maxims of governments is to adopt the characters of the subjects, and to unite with them in habits and tastes, even if the habits are not good in themselves. The least a foreign government should do is conform to the subjects' characters, even if the commitment be temporary, at least until it succeeds in attracting them to its language, then to its morals, then to its nationality, as did the Umayyads [reigned 661–750], the 'Abbasids [750–1258], and the Muwahhidun [Almohads, North African dynasty, 1130–1269], and as the European colonial states would like to do in the present era. Similarly, all of the non-Arabs who established states in the Islamic world, such as the Buyids [Turkish dynasty, 932–1062], Saljuqs [Turkish dynasty, 1038–1194], Ayyubids [Kurdish dynasty, 1169–1260], Ghurids [Afghan dynasty, circa 1149–1215], Circassians [probably the Mamluk dynasty in Egypt, 1250–1517], and the descendants of Muhammad 'Ali [ruler of Egypt, 1805–1849, of Albanian-Turkish origin] acculturated, so that it was not long until they become Arabized and molded by the characteristics of the Arabs. They intermingled with them and became part of them, just as the Tatar Moghuls [that is, the Mongols] became Persians and Indians. The only exception in this regard was the Turkish Moghuls—that is, the Ottomans, who, on the contrary, take pride in preserving the otherness of their subjects, so that they do not seek their Turkification, nor do they agree to become Arabized; the contemporary ones are becoming Frenchified or Germanified. There is no rational cause for such [behavior] except their intense hatred toward the Arabs, as can be proved by the proverbs about Arabs that flow from their tongues:

—their use of the phrase 'dilenci Arab,' that is, 'Arab beggar,' for Arabs of the Hijaz.

—their use of the phrase 'kör fellah,' meaning 'rude peasant,' for Egyptians.

—'Arab Çingenesi,' that is, 'Arab Gypsy'; 'Kıbti Arab,' that is, 'Egyptian Gypsy.'

—their saying about the Arabs of Syria: 'Ne Şam'ın şekeri ve ne Arab'ın yüzü,' that is, 'It is worth putting up with the Arabs for the sweets of Damascus.'

[Literally: 'Neither the sweets of Damascus, nor the face of the Arab.']

—their use of the term '*Arab*' for slaves and black animals.

—their saying, '*pis Arab*,' that is, 'filthy Arab.'

—'*Arab aklı*,' that is, 'Arab mind,' or small; '*Arab tabiatı*,' that is, 'Arab taste,' or corrupt; '*Arab çenesi*,' that is, 'Arab jawbone,' or excessive babble.

—their saying, '*Bunu yaparsam Arab olayım*,' that is, 'If I do that, may I become an Arab.'

—their saying, '*Nerde Arab, nerde tambura*,' that is, 'Where there is an Arab, there is a lute.'

"To all that, the Arabs do not reciprocate, except with two expressions. The first is the Arab saying about them: 'Three were created for oppression and decay: lice, Turks, and the plague.' And the second expression: calling [Turks] 'Byzantines,' an indication of suspicion about their Islamic faith. The cause of this suspicion is that the Turks did not serve Islam, except for the establishment of a few mosques—and if it were not for their rulers wanting to have their names mentioned from the pulpits, even these would not have been established.

"Moreover, they joined Islam in blind obedience to their grandees, in fear of astrological misfortune, and in respect for fire-pits, which added greatly to existing superstitions."

Then al-Sayyid al-Furati said:

"I beg pardon from al-Maula al-Rumi [the fictional Turkish delegate], because he knows that I do not exaggerate, and if it were not for the religious necessity, of which he is aware, I would not have spoken so clearly and openly. For [it is said that] the sincere counselor is the one who makes you weep, not the one who makes you laugh."

Mr. President said: "Our brother al-Sayyid al-Furati is a well-spoken orator and a worldly knight, and the research to which he pointed deserves much discussion. But today our time has drawn to a close, and therefore we adjourn till our appointment tomorrow, if the Exalted Master permits."

Ijtihad and the Refutation of Nabhani

Mahmud Shukri al-Alusi (Iraq, 1857–1924) was the foremost proponent of religious reform in late Ottoman Iraq. A prolific writer, he addressed such controversial religious
issues as independent reasoning (*ijtihad*) in Islamic law and innovations in worship. He
also contributed to the reform movement by searching for and publishing the works of
earlier scholars like Ibn Taymiyya (1263–1328). His modernist inclination appears in arguments for the harmony of modern scientific views, like heliocentrism, with the Qur'an.
Alusi came from a long line of prominent religious scholars, the most famous of whom
was his grandfather, the author of a major exegesis of the Qur'an. After a traditional
religious education, he taught in several Baghdad mosques and seminaries. Around 1890,
he began to criticize popular veneration of saints' tombs and the inclusion of music and
dance in Sufi rituals. In 1902, conservative scholars plotted to remove him from Baghdad
for allegedly spreading Wahhabi ideas, but their effort failed. Alusi gathered a small number of religious students who continued to pursue Islamic reform in Iraq. He is also notable for attracting the attention of European scholars. He befriended the great French
Orientalist Louis Massignon (1883–1962), and he won a prize from the Stockholm Oriental Languages Academy for his three-volume history of the pre-Islamic Arabs. This selection is excerpted from a polemical attack, published anonymously, on a scholar who
objected to *ijtihad*. After the Ottoman Young Turk Revolution of 1908, his publishers
wrote Alusi's name by hand on each copy of the book.[1]

The time has come for the pen to gallop along the
racecourse of debate, stirring up the dust of controversy in the face of the most intractable opponent,
who has mounted the steed of obstinacy. I ask God,
the Exalted, not to allow the tip of my pen to descend
into false accusation, but to safeguard me against
wrongdoing and lapses in word and deed, for God is
the Protection and Refuge from all ills. I will achieve
success only through Him; on Him I depend, and to
Him I turn in repentance.

[Yusuf] al-Nabhani [Palestine-Lebanon, 1850–
1932] wrote, "The first section of the introduction,
on the termination of *al-ijtihad al-mutlaq* [unre-
stricted or absolute freedom of Islamic legal inter-
pretation]—a capability claimed, falsely, by the
Wahhabi [scripturalist] group and other ignorant
heretics from various Islamic *madhhab*s [legal

schools] who admire them." I made this discussion
into a separate treatise, entitled *al-Siham al-sa'ibah
li-ashab al-da'awi al-kadhiba* [*Arrows that Strike
Those Who Make False Claims*]. After presenting the
prologue of that treatise, [al-Nabhani] continued, "I
hold that the claim of *ijtihad* in this age—by
[Wahhabis] and others, no matter how learned—is
false. It should be ignored, and should not be relied
upon." He also stated, "I responded to those who
claim *ijtihad* in this age in my book *Hujjat Allah 'ala
al-'alamin* [*God's Proof to Mankind*]. I cited on this
issue statements of religious scholars such as the
Imam [leading scholar] ['Abd al-Wahhab] al-
Sha'rani [1492–1565], the *Imam* [Abu'l-'Abbas] Ibn
Hajar al-Haytami [1504–1567], *Imam* ['Abd al-
Ra'uf] al-Munawi [1545–1621], and others, which

Mahmud Shukri al-Alusi, *Ghayat al-amani fi'l-radd 'ala
al-Nabhani* (*The Utmost Desire, a Refutation of Nabhani*)
(Cairo, Egypt: 'Abd al-Qadir al-Tilimsani, 1907), volume 1,
pp. 44–60. First published in 1903. Translation from Arabic
by Hager El Hadidi, edited by Devin Stewart. Introduction
by David D. Commins.

1. Muhammad Bahjat al-Athari, *Mahmud Shukri al-Alusi
wa-ara'uhu al-lughawiyya* (*Mahmud Shukri al-Alusi and his
Views on Language*) (Cairo, Egypt: Jami'at al-Duwal al-
'Arabiyya, 1958); Ibrahim Samarra'i, *al-Sayyid Mahmud
Shukri al-Alusi wa-bulugh al-'arab* (*Mahmud Shukri al-Alusi
and the Rise of the Arabs*) (Beirut, Lebanon: al-Mu'assasa al-
Jami'iyya li'l-Dirasat wa'l-Nashr wa'l-Tawzi', 1992).

should serve to persuade every person endowed with common sense and sound understanding." Then he said, "As for *ijtihad*, it is not claimed today except by those of defective mind and religion, unless it is through *wilaya* [here, an outstanding mystic's special status or closeness to God], as was stated by the great *Shaykh* Muhyi al-Din Ibn al-'Arabi [1165–1240]." Then he quoted *al-Jami' al-saghir* [*The Small Compendium*], by Ibn Hajar, which al-Munawi also quoted in the beginning of his large commentary on this book: "[Ibn Hajar] said, 'When Jalal [al-Din] al-Suyuti [1445–1505] claimed *ijtihad*, his contemporaries attacked him and criticized him en masse. They wrote him a petition presenting a number of legal questions on which Shafi'i jurists had proposed two different rulings considered equally valid. They demanded that if he had even the lowest level of *ijtihad*—that is, *ijtihad al-fatwa* [the ability to select among the legal opinions proposed within a particular legal school]—then he should explain the opinion he considered most acceptable in this regard, and provide the appropriate evidence according to the rules of *ijtihad*. Al-Suyuti, however, sent back the petition without writing any answer, and excused himself, saying that he was busy with other concerns that prevented him from looking into the matter.' Ibn Hajar said, 'Contemplate the difficulty of this level, I mean *ijtihad al-fatwa*, which is the lowest of all the levels of *ijtihad*, and it will become apparent to you that anyone who claims it—let alone claims unrestricted *ijtihad*—is addlepated and his thinking disturbed, like someone who rides blindly and strikes randomly.' [Ibn Hajar] said, 'Even if someone could conceive mentally of the level of unrestricted *ijtihad*, he would be too ashamed before God to claim it for any person of these times.' Moreover, [Ibn Hajar] said, '[Taqi al-Din] Ibn al-Salah [al-Shahrazuri, 1181–1245] and his followers stated that [*ijtihad*] had terminated about 300 years before their time, and Ibn al-Salah was about 300 years ago, since he lived in the sixth century [A.H., or 12th century A.D.], so as of today it has been discontinued for 600 years'—that is, with respect to the era of Ibn Hajar, who lived in the tenth century. So [*ijtihad*] has now been discontinued for about a thousand years, for we are in the seventeenth year of the fourteenth century [A.H., or 1899–1900 A.D.], the year I [al-Nabhani] wrote the book *Hujjat Allah 'ala al-'alamin*."

[Al-Nabhani] said, "Ibn al-Salah cited a scholar of the Islamic jurisprudence to the effect that, after the era of [Abu 'Abd Allah Muhammad] al-Shafi'i [767–820], there has not been a *mujtahid mustaqil* [independent interpreter of the law]." [Al-Nabhani] said, "Then Shihab al-Din Ibn Hajar said, 'If there has been a longstanding debate among leading scholars of the legal tradition concerning whether or not *Imam al-Haramayn* [the *Imam* of Mecca and Medina, that is, Abu'l-Ma'ali al-Juwayni, 1028–1085] and *Hujjat al-Islam* [the Proof of Islam] [Abu Hamid Muhammad] al-Ghazzali [1058–1111] are among those who have produced authoritative variant opinions [*wujuh*, singular *wajh*] within the Shafi'i legal school, what then might you think about others? Indeed, the leading scholars said about [Abu'l-Mahasin] al-Ruyani [13th century], the author of *al-Bahr* [*The Sea*], that he was not among those who produced *wujuh*—this despite [al-Ruyani's] statement, "If all of al-Shafi'i's texts were lost, I could dictate them from memory." If such great scholars are not qualified for *ijtihad al-madhhab* [the ability to interpret within a particular legal school], how then could those who cannot even understand the greater part of their expressions correctly allow themselves to claim a higher level, that of unrestricted *ijtihad*? Glory be to You, O God! This is great slander!'" Then [al-Nabhani] quoted a number of statements by scholars corroborating his view that *ijtihad* had been discontinued. This senseless jabber continues until the end of his discussion of this topic, indicating his ignorance, his bankruptcy of all knowledge, and the falseness of his claim. To mention all the fallacies included in his discussion would take a long time, so instead we will criticize his argument in general, and not in its details, as follows.

Al-Nabhani's thesis will be addressed according to the following points:

The First Point

To attribute the call for *ijtihad* to the Wahhabiyya—the term [al-Nabhani] uses for those who share the beliefs of *Shaykh* Muhammad Ibn 'Abd al-Wahhab [1703–1787]—is a false accusation, a lie, and a slander against them. All the people of Najd follow the school of the *Imam* Ahmad ibn Hanbal [780–855], may God be pleased with him, adopting his opinions on the individual points of law and agreeing with him on theology and articles of faith. *Shaykh* Muhammad stated this explicitly in many of his treatises. He did not claim *ijtihad*, nor did he call on anybody to adopt him as an authority. He did, however, enjoin doing good and forbid doing evil. To associate the people of Najd and those who follow the *sunna* [the practice of the Prophet] with the *Shaykh* and to consider them a sect of Muslims apart from the *ahl al-sunna* [people of the *sunna*, that is, Sunni Muslims], is an injustice and an aggression; it is a false and slanderous accusation. Even more odd is that the adjective designating the *Shaykh* should be al-Muhammadiyya [and not al-Wahhabiyya], since 'Abd al-Wahhab is *Shaykh* Muhammad's father, and it was the *Shaykh*, not his father, who supported the articles of faith, commanding good and forbidding evil, so to call students and supporters of the *Shaykh* Wahhabiyya is either plain ignorance or an insult, both of which are clearly wrong.

The Second Point

The topic of *ijtihad* has been exhausted, for the scholars of Islamic jurisprudence have discussed it extensively, particularly in the book *al-Muwafaqat* [*The Reconciliations*] by Ibrahim ibn Musa al-Shatibi, died 1388]. Despite that, some relevant issues should be mentioned here in brief. The scholars have declared that *ijtihad* is the utmost exertion of effort on the part of a jurist in order to arrive at a probable ruling. [Such cases] involve a *mujtahid al-mutlaq* [unrestricted interpreter]. Conditions [permitting such interpretation] are legal capacity—and not probity [that is, the full requirements for someone to act as an official witness in court cases], which is only necessary for adoption by others of a *mujtahid*'s verdict in a court case—and aptitude. This aptitude involves the rational capacity for acquiring necessary knowledge of the law as a whole, or knowledge of the particular case at hand alone, *ijtihad* being divisible, and mental acuity, an innate, keen understanding of the intended meanings of speech, so that he might be able to deduce legal rules from evidence, recognize similar and dissimilar cases, properly analyze cause and effect, and recognize validity and invalidity. This ability is the foundation of the legal craft. Stupid or incompetent people are incapable of *ijtihad*. [A *mujtahid*] must also attain a mid-level [or higher] expertise in the Arabic language and theology; be learned in the Qur'anic

verses and *hadiths* [narratives of the Prophet] with legal content; be familiar with legal issues on which consensus exists, abrogating and abrogated scriptural prooftexts, single and multiple chains of transmission, the occasions of Revelation, and the condition of *hadith* transmitters and texts. [For technical matters of *hadith* science and theology,] it is sufficient for the *mujtahid* to rely on the assessments of *hadith* experts and leading theologians. It is preferred that he be able to search for contradictory evidence. The rank lower than that of absolute or unrestricted *mujtahid* is *mujtahid* restricted to a *madhhab*, who is able to derive legal rulings from the texts of his *Imam* [the eponymous founder of the school of law to which he belongs]. Below this is *mujtahid al-futya* [interpreter restricted to the legal opinions already proposed within a single school], who becomes thoroughly versed in the law and able to perform *tarjih* [demonstrating the preponderance of one alternative ruling over another]. In addition, the scholars of jurisprudence mentioned numerous issues under this rubric that we need not relate, then disagreed on whether it is permissible for an age to be devoid of a *mujtahid*. Some held that it is permissible, and even that it actually occurs. Others held that it is not permissible, citing as evidence the *hadith* [of the Prophet], "A group of my nation will continue supporting the truth until God's command arrives"— that is, the Hour of Judgment. This issue will be discussed below, God willing.

This is a summary of the jurisprudents' discussions of the topic, and you have learned that the conditions they laid down for *ijtihad* are not impossible but may exist in any era. You have also learned from our summary of their statements that they did not claim that the gate of *ijtihad* is closed, nor was this implied by their argument, nor was it indicated by a scriptural prooftext from the Qur'an or the *sunna*, the references to which we must turn in cases of disagreement. God, the Exalted, said: "O you who believe, obey God and the Messenger and those in authority among you; and if you are at variance over something, refer it to God and the Messenger, if you believe in God and the Last Day. This is good for you and the best of settlements." [Qur'an, Sura 4, Verse 59] The opinion that *ijtihad* has terminated is not supported by any evidence; therefore, it should be dismissed, thrown back in the face of the person who espouses it, and returned to the one who upholds it.

The Third Point

The *hadith* expert [Muhammad] Ibn al-Qayyim [al-Jawziyya, 1292–1350] said, in response to this opinion [that *ijtihad* has been terminated]: "*Muqallids* [those who engage in *taqlid*, or the adoption of an authority's opinion without independent proof of its correctness] have flouted God's decree and His law with a false judgment that openly contradicts the statements of His Messenger, peace be upon him, thereby emptying the earth of people who uphold God's proofs for Him and stating that no scholar has existed since the early eras of Islam. One group of [*muqallids*] said, 'No jurist has the right to choose between alternative legal rulings after Abu Hanifa [circa 699–767] and [his students] Abu Yusuf [Ya'qub al-Kufi, died 798], Zufar ibn al-Hudhayl [died 775], Muhammad ibn al-Hasan [al-Shaybani, circa 750–805], and al-Hasan Ibn Ziyad al-Lu'lu'i [734–819].' This is the opinion of many Hanafi jurists. Bakr [Abu al-Fadl ibn Muhammad] ibn 'Ala' al-Din al-Qushayri, the Maliki jurist [died 955], stated that nobody has been able to choose between legal rulings since the year A.H. 200 [816 A.D.]. Others have said that nobody has been able to select rulings after ['Abd al-Rahman] al-Awza'i [707–774], Sufyan al-Thawri [716–778], Waki' ibn al-Jarrah [died circa 812], and 'Abdullah ibn al-Mubarak [736–797]. [Another] group said that nobody could choose rulings after al-Shafi'i. The followers of al-Shafi'i disagreed about whose opinions should be relied upon among those associated with him, who could produce a *wajh* that others of lesser status could adopt in their judgements and rulings, and who could not. They divided [legal scholars] into three levels: a first group who produced *wujuh*, such as Ibn Shurayh [possibly Shurayh ibn al-Harith al-Kindi, 7th century], al-Qaffal [Abu Bakr Muhammad ibn 'Ali al-Shashi, died 976], and Abu Hamid [al-Ghazzali, died 1111]; a second group who produced *ihtimalat* [preferable variant rulings] but not *wujuh*, such as Abu'l-Ma'ali [al-Juwayni]; and a third group who produced neither *wujuh* nor *ihtimalat*, such as Ibn Hamid [reference unclear] and others. They also disagreed about when the gate of *ijtihad* was closed, upholding many diverse opinions, none of which has God granted any authority [a reference to the Qur'an, Sura 12, Verse 40, and Sura 53, Verse 23].

"According to these scholars, the world is devoid of those who uphold God's proofs for Him; those who speak with knowledge have vanished from the earth. No one is allowed any longer to examine God's Scripture [the Qur'an] or the *sunna* of His Messenger, peace be upon him, to extract the rulings of the Sacred Law. No one should rule or give a legal opinion without considering the statement of the one he imitates and follows. If the authority agrees with what is contained in the Qur'an and the *sunna*, the jurist gives a verdict or legal opinion accordingly; otherwise, he rejects the scriptural evidence and does not accept it. These opinions [about the closing of the door of *ijtihad*], as you see, have reached the utmost level of invalidity, falsehood, and contradiction. They represent the espousal of religious positions without any basis in knowledge, the rejection of God's proofs, and the abandonment of the Qur'an and the *sunna* of His Messenger as sources for the rulings of the Sacred Law. God, however, will ensure the completion of His Light and make manifest the truth of the saying of His Messenger that the earth shall never be devoid of those who uphold God's proof for Him, that a group among His *umma* [the Muslim community] shall remain faithful to the genuine Truth that He revealed through [the Prophet], and that every hundred years, He will continue to send to this *umma* someone to renew its faith.

"Concerning these invalid opinions, it is sufficient to object to those who uphold them: If no one is allowed to choose between rulings after those you have mentioned, by what right can you choose to adopt certain scholars as authorities and not others? How do you forbid a man from choosing positions that *ijtihad* leads him to adopt, in agreement with the Scripture of God and the *sunna* of His Messenger? How do you allow yourselves to choose *taqlid* of a particular [*mujtahid*], and how do you force the entire Muslim community to follow him, forbid *taqlid* of others, and consider him more acceptable for *taqlid* than others? What gives you the right to perform this selection, which is not supported by any evidence, whether a scriptural prooftext from the Qur'an or the *sunna*, an instance of consensus or legal analogy, or a statement of a companion of the Prophet, while you forbid selection of what has been demonstrated in the Scripture, the *sunna*, and the statements of the Companions?

"One should also object to this opponent: If, according to you or others, it is not permissible to choose between rulings after [A.H.] 200, how do you permit yourself—you who were not born until sixty years after the year 200 [apparently a reference to al-Qushayri]—to select the opinion of Malik [ibn Anas, 710–796, founder of the Maliki *madhhab*], rather than those of Companions [of the Prophet] who were more knowledgeable than he, or jurists from the major cities who are equal to him, or later jurists? According to this position, [the Maliki jurists] Ashhab [died 819], Ibn al-Majishun [died 829], al-Mutarrif ibn 'Abdullah [died 835], Asbagh ibn al-Faraj [died 838], Sahnun ibn Sa'id [777–855], Ahmad Ibn al-Mu'adhdhal [ninth century], and other jurists of the same rank would have been able to choose between rulings to until the end of the last month of the year 200, but when the new moon of the month of Muharram in the year 201 appeared and the sun disappeared, on that night [July 30, 816] they would have been prohibited—all of a sudden—from choosing what they had been free to choose before.

"One should object to the others: Is it not one of the great catastrophes and wonders of the world that you grant only the *imam*s you mentioned the capability to select rulings, to engage in *ijtihad*, to express an opinion about the religion of God on the basis of personal judgment and analogy, while you deny the capability of selection and *ijtihad* to the protectors of Islam—the most learned of the Muslim community concerning the Scripture of God, the *sunna* of His Prophet, and the sayings and legal opinions of the Companions—such as Ahmad ibn Hanbal, al-Shafi'i, Ishaq Ibn Rahwayh [circa 778–853], Muhammad ibn Isma'il al-Bukhari [810–870], Dawud ibn 'Ali [founder of the Zahiri *madhhab*, died 884], and their likes, despite their wide knowledge of the *sunna*, their ability to distinguish authentic from inauthentic *hadith* reports, their efforts to record the sayings of the Companions and the Successors [the following generation of Muslims], their precise examination [of texts], and their ingenious use of evidence? When those among them who upheld the validity of legal analogy used this method, their analogies were the most accurate, the least questionable, and the closest to the texts of scripture. [Yet you refuse to grant them this status,] despite their extreme piety, the God-given affection of the faithful towards them, and the tremendous respect accorded to them by the Muslims, both scholars and the masses.

"Though each group of them argues for the preference of the particular [*mujtahid*] whom they accept as an authority on the basis of some type of superi-ority—precedence in time, asceticism, piety, acquaintance with teachers and authorities whom later scholars did not meet, or the vast number and illustrious status of their followers, unmatched by those of other scholars—the other groups can argue as much or even more for their own chosen authority's superiority on these points or others. It is also possible to object to all of these contending groups as follows: This opinion of yours, in order to hold water—if you insist on adhering to a contradiction—forces you to leave aside the opinion of your chosen authority in favor of the opinions of Companions and Successors who were earlier, more knowledgeable, more pious, more ascetic, and blessed with more numerous and more illustrious followers. How can one compare the followers of ['Abdullah] Ibn 'Abbas [619–686], ['Abdullah] Ibn Mas'ud [died circa 652], Zayd ibn Thabit [died 665] and Mu'adh ibn Jabal [died 627], or the followers of 'Umar [ibn al-Khattab, second caliph, 634–644] and 'Ali [ibn Abi Talib, fourth caliph, 656–661], with followers of later *imam*s in numbers and revered status? What of Abu Hurayra [companion of the Prophet, died 678], for example, about whom al-Bukhari wrote, 'Eight hundred men, both Companions and Successors, transmitted knowledge from him.' What of Zayd ibn Thabit, one of the companions of 'Abdullah Ibn 'Abbas? Where among the followers of [later] *imam*s can one find the likes of [the 7th and 8th century scholars] 'Ata' [ibn Abi Rabah], Tawus [ibn Kaysan], Mujahid [ibn Jabr al-Makki], 'Ikrima, 'Ubayd Allah ibn 'Abd Allah ibn 'Utba, and Jabir ibn Zayd? And where among the followers [of later *imam*s] can one find the likes of the two Sa'ids, ['Amir ibn Sharahil] al-Sha'bi, Masruq, 'Alqama [al-Kufi], al-Aswad [ibn Yazid], and Shurayh? Where among the followers [of later *imam*s] are the likes of Nafi', Salim, al-Qasim [ibn Muhammad], 'Urwa [ibn al-Zubayr], Kharija ibn Zayd, Sulayman ibn Yasar [al-Hilali], and Abu Bakr ibn 'Abd al-Rahman [al-Makhzumi]? What made [later] *imam*s more fortunate with their followers than these [earlier figures] with *their* followers? It is true that the latter enjoyed the status of their era, so perhaps their greatness, fame, and elevated status prevented later scholars from following their example, as if [the later scholars] had said: 'These [early Muslims] were too lofty for us, and we are in no way their equals.' They stated this explicitly and testified to it against themselves, for their status did not allow them to derive religious learning directly from the Qur'an and the *sunna*. They would say: 'We are not capable of this, not because of defects in the Qur'an or the *sunna*, but because of our own incapacity and defects. We have therefore made do with [the opinions of] someone who is more knowledgeable of [the Qur'an and *sunna*] than we are.'

"One should object to them: Why do you blame those who follow the teachings of [the Qur'an and *sunna*], make [these scriptural texts] the arbiters of their disputes, bring their suits to them for a verdict, and hold up scholars' statements to them for comparison, accepting statements that agree with [these sources] and rejecting those that contradict them? Just because you have not yet reached this bunch of grapes, why do you deny it to those who have reached it and tasted its sweetness? Why do you limit that which God's bounty, that human reason or imagination cannot fathom, has made broad? Even if jurists live in your era, grow up with you, and have a close kinship with you, God bestows gifts upon whom He wishes among his worshipers. God, glory be to Him, censured those who opposed the prophecy [of Muhammad] by arguing that He had denied it to prominent men and town leaders, giving it to someone else of lesser stature, saying: 'Are they the ones who dispense the favor of your Lord? It is He who apportions the means of livelihood among them in this world, and raises some in position over others, to make some submissive. The favors of your Lord are better than what they amass.' (Sura 43, Verse 32)

"The Prophet, peace be upon him, said, 'My nation is like rain; one does not know which is better, its beginning or its end.' God, glory be to Him, informed us that the foremost believers (who will reside in Heaven) are 'a multitude of those of old, and a few of those of later time.' (Sura 56, Verses 13–14) God, glory be to Him, also informed us that [He] 'raised among the Meccans a messenger from amongst them, who recites His revelations to them, reforms them, and teaches them the Scripture and the Law, for before him they were clearly in error.' (Sura 62, Verse 2) He also said, 'And for others among them who have not joined them yet. He is mighty and wise.' (Sura 62, Verse 3) Then He related, 'That is the bounty of God, He gives whosoever He please. God is master of great bounty.' (Sura 62, Verse 4)" This ends the statement of the *hadith* expert Ibn Qayyim al-Jawziyya in his book *I'lam al-muwaqqi'in* [*The Notification of Court Clerks*].

Ibn Qayyim's passage makes it perfectly clear that the statements made by al-Nabhani—following his deviant predecessors—are evidence of his ignorance and bankruptcy in the fields of knowledge, in both their subsidiary topics and their fundamental theories, since only one who is more ignorant than the son of an owl,[2] such as himself, would uphold his thesis.

The Fourth Point Indicating the Invalidity of the Ignoramus al-Nabhani's Thesis

Any knowledge which has no evidence to indicate it is unacceptable. *Ijtihad* is not like a prophecy so that it could be said to have been sealed by so-and-so. As for prophecy, texts from the Qur'an and the *sunna* provide evidence that it has been sealed. God, the Exalted, said, "Muhammad is not the father of any man among you, but a messenger of God and the seal of the prophets." (Sura 33, Verse 40)

In the *Sahih* [*Collection of Sound Hadiths*], al-Bukhari cites Abu Hurayra, who quotes the Prophet, peace be upon him, as saying, "I and the prophets before me are like the following example: A man builds a fine and beautiful house, except for a single corner brick. The people walk around it and wonder at its beauty, but they say, 'Would that this brick be put in its place!' I am that brick, and I am the last of the Prophets." The fact that prophecy has been sealed is also supported by rational proofs such as the perfection of the *shari'a* [sacred law], its inclusion of legal rulings for all ages and times, and its miraculous preservation from change and modification, while being the most moderate of faiths, without any exaggeration or shortcoming.

All of this indicates that prophecy ended with the Seal [Muhammad], peace be upon him. For *ijtihad*, however, we have seen no evidence of its termination, either in the Book of God or the *sunna* of His Messenger, peace be upon him, or even in the sayings of the Companions. Rather, we have seen evidence indicating that the science of *shari'a* and its scholars shall continue until the Hour of Reckoning. Kumayl ibn Ziyad al-Nakha'i [died circa 778] said, "'Ali ibn Abi Talib, may God be pleased with him, took my hand and brought me out with him near the cemetery. When we reached the desert he began to sigh, then said, 'O Kumayl ibn Ziyad, people's hearts

---

2. [In Iraq, the owl is held to be the epitome of ignorance.—Ed.]

are vessels; the best among them are those that are most capacious. Remember what I am telling you. There are three types of people: the divine scholar, the student who learns as a means to salvation, and the riffraff rabble, who follow anyone who shouts, bend with every wind, remain impervious to the light of knowledge, and fail to resort to a solid support. Knowledge is better than wealth. Knowledge guards you, but you guard wealth. Knowledge grows the more you give away'"—or according to another version, "the more you put it into practice"—"'but wealth decreases as you spend it. Knowledge is the ruler and wealth is the one ruled. The love of knowledge is a creed to adhere to. Knowledge gains for a scholar obedience during his lifetime and fine praise after his death, but the effect of wealth disappears once it is exhausted. The hoarders of money die, while scholars live on. Here is knowledge! Scholars shall live on until eternity. Though they themselves might be lost, their likes shall live on in the hearts [of humankind]. Look, here! Here is knowledge!' and ['Ali] pointed to his chest. 'If unworthy bearers become attracted to it, it may end up in the hands of people who cannot be trusted. They might use the tool of religion for worldly gain, trying to gain power over the Qur'an with His proofs and ascendance over His worshipers with His blessings, or merely follow the people of truth, without any insight in their bosom, so that doubt penetrates their heart at the first sign of specious challenge, or be bent on the pursuit of delights, easily driven by lust, or obsessed with gathering and piling up wealth. Such people are not ones who call to the faith. They are most like sa'iba camels.[3] Their knowledge dies with the death of its bearers. O God! Yes, indeed, the earth will never be devoid of those who uphold God's proofs, lest His proofs and pronouncements come to nought. These [persons] are few in number, yet their statements are great in the eyes of God. Through them, God defends His proofs so that they might convey them to their peers and plant them in the hearts of people like themselves. Knowledge brings them near the truth of re-

ality, so that they find easy what the affluent find difficult, and they welcome that which frightens the ignorant. Their bodies live in this world, while their souls ascend to divine heights. These are the representatives of God on earth and the propagators of His religion. Oh, how I long to meet them! I ask God's forgiveness for myself and for you. If you wish, you may leave.'" This was recounted by Abu Nu'aym [al-Isfahani, 948–1038] in Hilyat al-awliya' [The Adornment of the Saints] and by other authors. Abu Bakr al-Khatib [al-Baghdadi, 1002–1071] said, "This is a fine hadith, one of the best in letter and in spirit."

Imam Ibn Qayyim al-Jawziyya has interpreted this hadith in detail in his book, Miftah dar al-sa'ada [The Key to the Abode of Happiness], where he wrote about 'Ali's statement, "O God. Yes, indeed the earth shall not be devoid of those who uphold God's proofs for Him": "This is confirmed by the following authentic hadith of the Prophet, peace be upon him: 'A group of my community shall remain steadfast in the Truth, not affected by their tormentors or detractors. Until God's command arrives, they shall remain so.'" [This hadith] is also confirmed by the report related by [Abu 'Isa Muhammad] al-Tirmidhi [died 892], citing Qutayba, Hammad ibn Yahya al-Abahh, from Thabit, from Anas [ibn Malik, companion of the Prophet], who reported, "The Messenger of God, peace be upon him said: 'My nation is like rain: one does not know which is better, its beginning or its end.'" [Al-Tirmidhi] said: "This is a reliable but uncommon hadith." It is related that 'Abd al-Rahman ibn Mahdi [died 813] considered Hammad ibn Yahya al-Abahh a trustworthy transmitter. He used to say, "[Hammad] is one of our shaykhs [respected teachers]." In the same chapter, on the authority of 'Ammar [ibn Yasir, died 657] and 'Abdullah ibn 'Amr [died circa 680] [appears the report]: "If there were no mujtahid to uphold God's proofs in the last [days] of the umma, they would not be described as having such good qualities."

Also [the report]: "This nation is the most perfect of nations, the best nation ever brought to the people. Its Prophet is the seal of the prophets, and there will be no prophet after him. God made its scholars to succeed one another, so that the outstanding features of the faith might not be erased and its signposts not vanish. Among the Israelites, prophets continually succeeded one another, so that they were [always] led by prophets; the scholars of this nation are like the prophets of the Israelites." In another hadith, as well:

---

3. [In pre-Islamic Arabia, the term sa'iba (unhindered) applied to camels accorded an honored status because they had born a large number of offspring or as the result of a vow on the part of the owner. They were allowed to roam, pasture, and drink freely, and were exempted from most labor. This and related customs are rejected in the Qur'an. (Sura 5, Verse 103) Alusi's point here is that scholars who do not pass on their knowledge cease to benefit society.—Ed.]

"This knowledge will be passed on by the virtuous and reliable members of each successive generation." This *hadith* shows that Islamic religious knowledge is immune to the distortions of extremists, the pretenses of liars, and the misinterpretations of the ignorant. It indicates that knowledge will continue to be carried through the ages, century after century. In the collection of sound *hadith*s of ['Abd al-Rahman Ibn] Abi Hatim [circa 854–938], there is a report of al-Khawlani [Abu Idris or Abu Muslim, died 699 or 682] who said that the Messenger of God, peace be upon him, said: "God will continue to plant in this faith seedlings that serve to maintain obedience." These seedlings of God are the people of knowledge and pious works. If the earth were to become devoid of scholars, it would be devoid of seedlings of God. We have quoted sufficient material for the purpose at hand.

We have learned from this [fourth] point the invalidity of the senseless drivel the ignoramus al- Nabhani included in the introduction to his book. He is far from knowledge and enlightenment, without intellect or discernment. We leave this matter up to God.

The Fifth Point

[Al-Nabhani's] statement—"As for *ijtihad*, it is not claimed today except by those of defective minds and defective faith, unless it be through *wilaya*, as was stated by the great *Shaykh* . . ."—has neither meaning nor effect. We have already noted that it is not possible for an era to be devoid of a *mujtahid*, as Hanbali and traditionalist scholars of Islamic jurisprudence have stated. Why do those who fulfil the conditions for *ijtihad*, who are prepared to derive their religion [directly] from the Scripture and *sunna*, have defective minds and defective faith? Is this not but the statement of an ignorant person who has been struck by the touch of Satan? Then, what is the meaning of his statement: "unless it be through *wilaya*"? Have any religious scholars, experts in jurisprudence or the points of law, ever considered this term part of the topic of *ijtihad*? But it is no wonder that such ranting come from an ignorant heretic like al-Nabhani. Indeed, the ignorant injure themselves more than their enemies do. In addition, the *Shaykh* Muhyi al-Din [Ibn al-'Arabi] is among those who claimed *ijtihad al-mutlaq*, as the texts of his books indicate. He said in one of his poems:

They claim that I follow Ibn Hazm [994–1064], but I am not among those who say, "Thus spoke Ibn Hazm,"
Or anybody else. Rather, my words are, "The text of the Scripture avers." That is my judgment.
Or, "The Prophet says," or "The scholars have agreed unanimously on the opinion I profess." That is my knowledge.

Muhyi al-Din, God's mercy be upon him, indicated in these verses that he deduces legal rulings from the Scripture, *sunna*, and consensus; according to him, these three alone are the sources of the law, and not legal analogy. This point will be treated exhaustively in the appropriate place below.

The Sixth Point

[Al-Nabhani] quoted Ibn Hajar al-Makki as saying, "When Jalal [al-Din] al-Suyuti [1445–1505] claimed *ijtihad*, his contemporaries attacked him and criticized him en masse. They wrote him a petition presenting a number of legal questions on which Shafi'i jurists have considered two disparate rulings equally valid. They demanded that if he had even the lowest level of *ijtihad*—that is, *ijtihad al-fatwa* [the right to choose from among alternative legal opinions]—then he should explain the opinion he considered most acceptable in this regard, and provide the appropriate evidence according to the rules of *ijtihad*. Al-Suyuti, however, sent back the petition without writing any answer, and excused himself, saying that he was busy with work that prevented him from looking into this matter."

I respond that even if Ibn Hajar related the text of the quotation accurately, he is not trustworthy, for he fabricated even greater lies than this against the *Shaykh al-Islam* [Ibn Taymiyya, 1263–1328], and his lies are apparent, as will be seen in what follows. The response in defense of *Imam* al-Suyuti, mercy be upon him, is that the *mujtahid* need not have all the knowledge contained in the Preserved Tablet.

It is said that *Imam* Malik was asked 40 questions and said in response to 36 of them, "I don't know." This has been transmitted by the *Imam* Abu Hanifa and others. ". . . and not even a little of His knowledge can they grasp, except what He will." (Sura 2, Verse 255)

The Seventh Point

As for Ibn Hajar's statement—"'Ibn al-Salah and his followers stated that [*ijtihad*] had terminated about 300 years earlier, and Ibn al-Salah was about 300 years ago, since he lived in the sixth century [A.H., or 12th century A.D.], so, as of today, it has been discontinued for 600 years'—that is, in relation to the time of Ibn Hajar . . ."—my response is: This statement is beneath consideration on account of the arguments of the *hadith* expert Ibn al-Qayyim we have presented in the third section above and the texts and evidence of the falseness of this statement that we included there. Ibn Hajar's argument shifts, however, and his statements are inconsistent. He states here that *ijtihad* had been discontinued 600 years before his era, whereas he wrote in his book *al-Jawhar al-munazzam* (*Strung Jewels*) in the course of insulting *Shaykh al-Islam* Ibn Taymiyya:

> The *Shaykh al-Islam* Taqi [al-Din] al-Subki [1284–1355, a critic of Ibn Taymiyya], the great scholar of mankind, whose brilliance and *ijtihad* as well as righteousness and scholarly excellence are generally acknowledged, may God bless his soul and brighten his tomb, undertook to refute [Ibn Taymiyya] in an independent work in which he presented valuable and excellent arguments, precisely and clearly setting forth the correct approach through brilliant proofs. May God thank him for his effort, and continue to shower him with divine mercy and favor.

See how Ibn Hajar claims a consensus here on the *ijtihad* of al-Subki, because he follows the same heretical and whimsical approach and method, but then cannot bring himself to admit the *ijtihad* of one whose lofty status neither al-Subki himself nor his teachers could even approach. I am referring to Abu'l-'Abbas Taqi al-Din Ibn Taymiyya, may God the Exalted have mercy upon him. In *al-Jawhar al-munazzam*, in addition to the preceding statements, [Ibn Hajar] said: "The outrageous statements Ibn Taymiyya made—even though they were a horrendous offense whose sinful effect will never be undone, and a calamity whose misfortune will reflect on him until the end of time—are not surprising coming from him, for he let himself be so seduced by his whims, desires, and demons that he saw fit to attack the great *mujtahids*. The poor man did not realize that he was committing the foulest of sins." [Ibn Hajar's text] continues in this manner, making it apparent to any impartial judge that Ibn Hajar followed his

whims and chose the path of error. May God treat him with His justice.

The point here is that the words of fanatics such as these, because they speak according to their whims, cannot be used in valid arguments. They do not adhere to the evidence, but follow the worst of paths. The argument of the heedless al-Nabhani has crumbled and cannot be granted any serious consideration.

The Eighth Point Indicating the Invalidity of the Ignoramus al-Nabhani's Thesis

Each of the *imams* has stated that if a *hadith* is sound, it must be followed and its purport must be accepted. That is why many of the *imams* have stated that one must accept the sound *hadith* and forsake all statements by *mujtahids* that contradict it. In the book *I'lam al-muwaqqi'in*, [Ibn Qayyim al-Jawziyya states], "The four *imams* [the founders of the four primary Sunni *madhhabs*] forbade the blind adoption of their own opinions and sharply censured adherence to their statements without proof. Al-Shafi'i said that he who seeks knowledge without proof is like someone who gathers firewood at night: he might, without realizing it, pick up a bundle of fire wood with a snake in it and so get bitten. [This statement] is cited by [Ahmad ibn al-Husayn] al-Bayhaqi [994–1066]." Isma'il ibn Yahya al-Muzani [791–878] said at the beginning of his *Mukhtasar* [*The Abridgement*], "I have summarized this from the teachings of al-Shafi'i and the gist of his statements in order to make them more accessible to the interested student, but at the same time I would have him know that al-Shafi'i prohibited the blind adoption of his own opinions or those of others. Therefore, may [the student] examine [al-Shafi'i's teachings] for the sake of his faith and exercise caution for the sake of his soul." Abu Da'ud [al-Sijistani, circa 817–889] said, "I asked Ahmad [ibn Hanbal], 'Is al-Awza'i more deserving of being followed, or Malik?' He said, 'Don't imitate either of them for your faith. Adhere to what has come down from the Prophet, peace be upon him, and the Companions. After these, one is free to accept or reject the opinions of the Successors [the generation after the Companions].'" Ahmad differentiated between *taqlid* and *ittiba'* [critical acceptance]. Abu Da'ud said, "I heard [Ahmad ibn Hanbal] say that *ittiba'* means following what has come down from the Prophet, peace be upon him, and from his Companions. After that, one is free to accept or reject the opinions of the Successors." [Ibn Hanbal] also said, "Don't imitate me, and don't imitate Malik, al-Thawri, or al-Awza'i. Rather, draw from the sources that they draw from." [Ahmad ibn Hanbal] said, "It is a sign of limited understanding that a man base his exercise of religion on *taqlid*." Bishr ibn al-Walid [8th century] reported that Abu Yusuf said, "Nobody is allowed to adopt our opinion until he knows the evidence on which it is based." Malik stated explicitly that anyone who abandoned the words of 'Umar ibn al-Khattab for the words of Ibrahim al-Nakha'i [666–715, a generation later] needs to repent, so what about those who abandon the words of God and His Messenger for the words of one like Ibrahim, or one lesser than he?! Ja'far al-Firyabi said: "Ahmad ibn Ibrahim al-Dawraqi told me that al-Haytham ibn Jamil told him: 'I said to Malik ibn Anas, "O Abu 'Abdullah! People among us have written books, and one of them, having written that someone related such-and-such, citing 'Umar ibn al-Khattab, and someone else related such-and-such, citing Ibrahim [al-Nakha'i], then adopted the words of Ibrahim." Malik inquired, "Did they consider the words of 'Umar to be authentic?" I replied, "It was a transmission as reliable as that from Ibrahim." Then Malik stated, "These [people] should be asked to repent."'"

The Ninth Point

The dim-witted al-Nabhani's opinion implies that the statements of one who is accepted as an authority today are to be given more weight than authentic prophetic *hadith*s that contradict the opinions of the *mujtahid*, and this is the essence of error. I have heard a Turkish judge say: "If I were to see a text in *Munyat al-musalli* [*The Wish of the Worshipper*, a Hanafi legal text by Sadid al-Din Kashghari, 13th century], and a *hadith* in *Imam* al-Bukhari's *al-Sahih* that contradicts this text, I would accept what is in the *Munyat* and leave aside the *hadith* from *al-Sahih* and not rule by it." Just look at this stupidity and tremendous ignorance.

Shaykh al-Islam Abu'l-'Abbas Taqi al-Din Ibn Taymiyya, may God bless his pure soul, was asked about a man who studied law according to one of the *madhhab*s and became accomplished in it, but then studied *hadith* at a later time and found authentic *hadith*s, not abrogated, restricted, or contradicted by any known scriptural text, which went against elements of his *madhhab*. Should he practice according to the *madhhab* or practice according to the *hadith*s that contradict his *madhhab*?

[Ibn Taymiyya] answered: "Praise be to God, Lord of the worlds. It has been established in the Qur'an, *sunna*, and consensus that God, the Exalted, made obedience to Him and His Messenger, peace be upon him, a religious duty for His worshipers. He did not require this nation's obedience to any particular person, in everything he commanded and forbade, except His Messenger, peace be upon him. Thus *Siddiq al-Umma* [The Truthful One of the Nation, Abu Bakr, first caliph, 632–634], the best [of the Muslim community] after its Prophet, peace be upon him, said: 'Obey me as long as I obey God, the Exalted, for if I disobey God, the Mighty and Sublime, you owe me no obedience.' All [of the four *imam*s] agreed that no one is infallible, in all of what he commands and forbids, except God's Messenger, peace be upon him. That is why several of the [four] *imam*s instructed [people] to pick and choose from the speech of anyone except for the Messenger of God, peace be upon him [who must be obeyed]. These four *imam*s, mercy be upon them all, warned people not to adopt all of their own statements blindly, as was their duty. *Imam* Abu Hanifa said, 'This is my opinion. It is the best I can do, and if someone comes up with a better opinion, we will accept it.' That is why, when Abu Yusuf, the most learned of Abu Hanifa's disciples, met with the *imam* of Dar al-Hijra [Medina], Malik ibn Anas, and asked him about the *sa'* measure, alms to be paid for vegetables, and various species [a debate raged over which sorts of produce were subject to alms-giving requirements], Malik, God's mercy be upon him, informed him what was indicated in the *sunna* concerning these [matters], and [Abu Yusuf] responded, 'I cede to your judgment, O Abu 'Abdullah, and had my master [Abu Hanifa] seen what I have, he would have ceded likewise.' Malik, God's mercy be upon him, used to say, 'I am only human. I am sometimes correct and sometimes wrong. You must compare my statements with the Qur'an and *sunna*,' or words to this effect. Al-Shafi'i, God's mercy be upon him, used to say, 'It is limiting to a man's knowledge to adopt the opinions of other men regarding matters of his faith.' He also said, 'Don't adopt your faith from men, for they are bound to make mistakes.' Established reports relate that the Prophet, peace be upon him, said, 'When God wishes somebody well, He makes him knowledgeable in matters of religion.' Implicit in this statement is that those whom God, the Mighty and Sublime, does not make knowledgeable in matters of religion are not wished well by Him, so that the acquisition knowledge of religion is a religious duty. To acquire knowledge of religion means to know the rulings of the *shari'a* through the appropriate scriptural evidence. Those who do not know this do not have knowledge of religion.

"Some people, however, might be incapable of acquiring knowledge of religion; they are only required to do what they can. Some say that anybody capable of using evidence to establish proof is absolutely prohibited from *taqlid*. Others say that *taqlid* is allowed without restriction. Still others say that *taqlid* is allowed only when necessary, such as when the time allowed for producing such a proof is limited—this is the most correct of these opinions, God willing. *Ijtihad* is not a monolithic capability, but may be parceled and divided. A man might be a *mujtahid* in one particular field, topic, or issue, but not in another field, topic, or issue. Each person's *ijtihad* varies according to his ability. If someone examines an issue that has been disputed by scholars and finds scriptural prooftexts that appear to corroborate one of the disputed opinions and are not contradicted by any other known texts, he is faced with two options. First, he might follow the opinion of the later jurist, just because he is the *imam* of the *madhhab* in which he studied law—but this is not a legitimate legal proof, only a mere convention contradicted by the conventions of others who have studied in the *madhhab*s of other *imam*s. Second, he may follow the opinion that seems more likely to him, in view of the texts that indicate it. In this case, his agreement with one *imam* implies taking issue with another, but the prophetic texts remain protected from violation in practice—and this is the more correct option.

"We have made this partial concession only because someone might object that the speculative ability of this particular person might be limited and his *ijtihad* regarding this issue might be incomplete. If, however, he were capable of complete *ijtihad*, such that there would not exist any evidence on the side of the opposing opinion sufficient to reject the scriptural text, then such a person would be required to follow that text. If he did otherwise, he would be following speculation and the dictates of whim, and

would be most disobedient toward God, the Exalted, and His Messenger.

"His situation would be completely different from that of someone who claims that the opposing opinion is supported by proof which carries more weight than the scriptural text, but says that he does not know what that proof is. To this person, one should respond that God, the Exalted, said, 'So fear God as much as you can.' (Sura 64, Verse 16) Your best attempt, in terms of knowledge and understanding of the law, indicates that the first opinion is more likely, so you must follow it. If you later find that the text is contradicted by more convincing evidence, your situation would then be like that of the independent *mujtahid* when his *ijtihad* changes. To change from one opinion to another because of some truth which becomes apparent is praiseworthy. This is to be distinguished from insisting on an opinion unsupported by any proof, shying away from an opinion that has been proved clearly, or shifting from one opinion to another simply out of custom or whim—such acts are reprehensible. When a *muqallid* [person engaging in *taqlid*] has heard a *hadith* and then abandoned it—especially if it was narrated by a person with a record of probity—such a case, if it indeed occurs, is not an excuse to abandon the scriptural text. Our writings in defense of the distinguished *imam*s have demonstrated that they had some twenty reasons for abandoning practice according to certain *hadith*s. We have shown that they were justified in their rejection of certain *hadith*s for these reasons. We, too, are justified in rejecting these *hadith*s for these same reasons. However, if one person rejects a *hadith* in the belief that it is not authentic, that its transmission is anonymous, or some such reason, but another person knows at the same time that this *hadith* is authentic and that its transmitter is trustworthy, then the reasons of the first person are invalid with respect to the second person. Whoever abandons a *hadith* on the grounds that the clear meaning of the Qur'an, or legal analogy, or the practice of some of the Ansar [early Muslims of Medina] contradicts it—and at the same time, it becomes apparent to another person that the clear meaning of the Qur'an does not contradict it, and that the text of a sound *hadith* has priority over the unambiguous texts of the Qur'an, legal analogy, and the deeds [of the Ansar]—then the first person's reason [for rejecting the *hadith*] no longer holds with respect to the second person. Legal understandings occur to people's minds or remain hidden to them in a process we cannot entirely fathom. This is especially the case if someone abandons a *hadith* because he believes that its use was abandoned by the Muhajirun [early Muslims who fled from Mecca to Medina] and the Ansar—the people of Medina and others—who are said not to have abandoned a *hadith* unless they believed it to have been abrogated or contradicted by a preferable [*hadith*], but later hears that the Muhajirun and Ansar did not in fact abandon this *hadith*, that some of them, or some Muslims who heard it from them, practiced in accordance with it, or other such reasons which render invalid the evidence that contradicts the scriptural text.

"Suppose someone were to challenge this petitioner who is seeking guidance [to whose question Ibn Taymiyya is responding], asking, 'Are you more knowledgeable or is the *Imam* so-and-so?' This would be a corrupt comparison, because *Imam* so-and-so has been contradicted on this issue by his equals among the other *imam*s. You are not more knowledgeable than this or that *imam*. In relation to each other, the various *imam*s are like [the Companions of the Prophet] Abu Bakr, 'Umar, 'Uthman [died 656], 'Ali, Ibn Mas'ud, Ubayy [ibn Ka'b, died circa 652], Mu'adh, similar prominent figures, and others. These Companions were equal to one another in debate. If they were at odds about something, they deferred the question to God and His Messenger, even though some of them were perhaps more knowledgeable than others in certain areas. Debate among [later] *imam*s is similar.

"People abandoned the statements of 'Umar and Ibn Mas'ud, may God be pleased with them, regarding the performance of *tayammum* [performing ritual ablutions with sand or dry ground when water is not available] on the part of someone with a major ritual impurity, and adopted the statements of Abu Musa al-Ash'ari [died 662] and others because of the evidence from the Qur'an and *sunna* they cited. They abandoned the statements of 'Umar regarding the blood money due for the loss of fingers or toes, adopting instead the statement of Mu'awiyya ibn Abi Sufyan [caliph, 661–680], because of the statements he transmitted from the Prophet, peace be upon him, saying, 'This and that are equivalent.' A certain person, arguing with Ibn 'Abbas about temporary marriage, said to him, 'Abu Bakr said [such-and-such] and 'Umar said [such-and-such]!' So Ibn 'Abbas said, 'Stones are about to rain down on you from the sky! I tell you that the Messenger, peace be upon him,

said [one thing], and you tell me that Abu Bakr and 'Umar said [something else]!' When [Ibn 'Abbas] was asked about [temporary marriage], he declared it permissible. His interlocutors objected, presenting as contradictory evidence the statement of 'Umar, so he showed that 'Umar had not intended what they claimed. But they pressed him, so he remonstrated: 'Who has more right to be followed, the Messenger of God, peace be upon him, or 'Umar?' The people [tend to forget this,] despite their awareness that Abu Bakr and 'Umar are more knowledgeable than Ibn 'Umar ['Umar's son] and Ibn 'Abbas, may God, the Exalted, be pleased with them. If this gate is opened [to adopting later *imam*s as ultimate authorities], it would be necessary to turn away from the commandments of God, the Exalted, and His Messenger, peace be upon him. Each *imam* would have the same status among his followers as a prophet among his people, and this would alter the religion. This is similar to what God, the Exalted, faults the Christians with in His words, 'They consider their rabbis and monks and Christ, son of Mary, to be gods apart from God, even though they had been enjoined to worship only one God, for there is no god but He. Too holy is He for what they ascribe to Him!' (Sura 9, Verse 31) God, glory be to Him, knows best."

The Tenth Point

One understands from the words of the dim-witted al-Nabhani that for the last thousand years Muslims, east and west, have had to adopt the opinions of one of the four *mujtahid*s, and that anyone deriving his faith from the Qur'an and *sunna*, or adopting the opinions of others—such as a Companion or some other figure—has departed from the path of correctness and followed a way other than that of believers. This is one of the implications of his false words and worthless statements. It is to be rejected, and no scholar of recognized learning has ever professed it.

From the book *I'lam al-muwaqqi'in*, by the *hadith* expert Ibn al-Qayyim, mercy be upon him: "Must the person seeking a *fatwa* engage in [a type of] *ijtihad* in order to choose the right *mufti* for consultation, appealing only to the one he estimates is most knowledgeable and most pious—or not? Concerning this issue, there are two schools of thought, as we have already discussed: the correct opinion is that he ought to, because everyone is commanded to fear God as much as one can." [Ibn al-Qayyim] states: "When two *mufti*s differ over an issue, and one is more pious while the other is more knowledgeable, which one should be followed? There are three approaches to this issue, which have been presented above. Is the layperson obliged to follow one of the well-known *madhhab*s or not? There are two opinions on this issue. One is that [the layperson] is not obliged—and this is the correct and undeniable opinion. This is because there are no religious duties except what God and His Messenger have imposed, and God and His Messenger have not obliged anybody to follow the *madhhab* of an ordinary man, adopting as his faith this man's opinion and no one else's. The noble [early] centuries of Islam and the early generations of Muslims came and went entirely free of such practices. Moreover, a *madhhab* is not appropriate for laypeople. Even if they follow one, they ought not to, because only those who possess the means of rational inquiry and deductive reasoning and are versed in the various *madhhab*s on account of this ability, or those who have read a book on the points of law according to this *madhhab* and have learned the legal opinions and statements of its *imam*, are entitled to claim a *madhhab*. Someone who is not qualified for this at all, but nevertheless says, 'I am a Shafi'i' or 'I am a Hanbali,' and so on, does not become so by his mere utterance of such a statement. It is as if he had claimed to be a jurist, a grammarian, or a professional secretary: one does not become such things just by saying so. This is clarified by noting that one who says he is a Shafi'i, a Maliki, or a Hanafi claims that he follows this *imam* and adopts his path, which can only be true if he takes after [the *imam*] in knowledge, learning, and deductive reasoning. With his ignorance and the extreme disparity between him and the *imam* in behavior, knowledge, and scholarly method, how can he properly claim to be related to him except through an empty claim, a statement devoid of all meaning? It is not imaginable that a layman can properly have a *madhhab*. Even if it were possible, neither he nor anyone else would be under the obligation to follow the *madhhab* of an ordinary man, such that he would have to accept all of his opinions and reject the opinions of all others. This disgraceful heresy has recently befallen the Muslim community; none of the leading scholars of Islam has ever professed this opinion, for they are higher in degree, more distinguished in status, and more knowledgeable of God and His Messenger than to

impose such an obligation on the people. More outlandish than this is the opinion of those who state that one is obliged to follow the *madhhab* of a particular scholar, and even more outlandish is the opinion of those who state that one is obliged to adopt one of the four *madhhab*s.

"O God, how astonishing! The *madhhab*s of the Companions of the Messenger of God, peace be upon him, and the *madhhab*s of the Successors and their successors, and all the *imam*s of Islam, have died and altogether ceased to exist, except for the *madhhab*s of four souls from among all the leading scholars and jurists. Has any of the leading scholars ever held this opinion, or called for it? Does a single word of their statements indicate it?!

"The obligations imposed by God, the Exalted, and His Messenger upon the Companions, the Successors, and their successors are the same obligations imposed on all who succeed them until the Day of Resurrection. Religious duty does not differ or change, though it might differ in terms of execution or amount according to variations in ability, time, place, and circumstance—but this is also inherent in the obligations imposed by God, the Exalted, and His Messenger. Those who consider that a layperson can have a *madhhab* say: 'He believes that this *madhhab* he has adopted is the truth, so he must fulfill the obligations of his belief.' If what they say is correct, then it would be prohibited for him to petition legal scholars outside his adopted *madhhab*, to follow the *madhhab* of an *imam* comparable, or even preferable, to his own, or other untenable implications of evident invalidity that indicate the invalidity of the premise on which they are based. Indeed, these ideas would require that, when faced with a text by the Messenger of God, peace be upon him, or a statement by the [first] four caliphs that contradicts his *imam*, such a person be required to reject the text or the statements of the Companions, and give precedence over them to the opinion of the *imam* he follows. On the contrary, the true position is that he may petition a legal opinion from any of the followers of the *imam*s or others that he wishes and that he is not obliged by the consensus of the Muslim community, nor is the *mufti*, to limit himself to the positions of one of the four *imam*s. Moreover, the scholar should not be limited to the *hadith* transmitted by the people of his region or any other region. If a *hadith* is sound, he should follow it, whether it be Hijazi, Iraqi, Syrian, Egyptian, or Yemeni. In addition, by consensus of the Muslims, one is not obliged to limit oneself to the seven well-known variant readings of the Qur'an, but if the reading one adopts matches the unpointed text of the Uthmanic codex, is correct in terms of Arabic grammar and usage, and has a sound chain of authority, one may read and pray according to it, by consensus. Even if one reads a version which departs from that of the Uthmanic codex, but which the Messenger of God, peace be upon him, and the Companions after him read, then it is permissible to read according to it, and prayer performed using it remains valid, according to the most correct opinion. The second opinion is that prayer performed using it is invalid. These opinions are both reliably reported from the *Imam* Ahmad [ibn Hanbal]. The third opinion is that if he prays the standard prayers using it, he has not fulfilled his obligation, but if he uses it in other prayers, they are not invalid. This is the opinion espoused by Abu al-Barakat Ibn Taymiyya, on the grounds that, in the first case, the requirements for the standard prayer were not completely met, and that, in the second, no invalidating element occurred. However, [the petitioner for legal opinions] may not seek out the easiest obligations among the various *madhhab*s or seek out what he wishes from whatever *madhhab* he finds to contain it. Rather, he must endeavor to seek the truth as far as this is possible."

Conclusion

It should be apparent to you, from the arguments presented in the ten points above, that the miserable al-Nabhani's thesis concerning the closing of the gate of *ijtihad* is false and heretical. We know necessarily that no single man during the time of the Companions engaged in the blind adoption of all of the opinions of another Companion, not dismissing any of his opinions while dismissing all the opinions of others. Nor did such a person exist among the Successors, or the successors of the Successors. Let the *muqallidun* try to prove us wrong by identifying a single man who followed their disastrous ways in the virtuous centuries, as they were termed by the Messenger of God, peace be upon him [that is, the first three centuries of Islam]. This heretical innovation, for which the Messenger, peace be upon him, expressed blame, occurred in the fourth century [A.H., or 10th century A.D.]. *Muqallid*s, who follow their supposed authorities in everything they say, permitting or prohibiting the taking of women, lives, and property, without knowing whether this is right or wrong, are in grave danger. They shall be in a difficult position before God [on the Day of Resurrection], when those who made religious arguments without knowledge will realize their error, for they did so without any justification.

The *hadith* expert Ibn al-Qayyim criticized *muqallid*s extensively in his book *I'lam al-muwaqqi'in*, refuting the arguments of the ignorant concerning the termination of *ijtihad*, and other respected scholars have also written useful books on this issue. Had this ignoramus [al-Nabhani] not raised the issue—even though it has nothing to do with the topic of his book—we would not have needed to open our mouth or move our pen concerning it.

Preface by the Translator

Abdullah Cevdet (Turkey, 1869–1932) was a leading publicist and freethinker who used Islam to promote modernization and materialism. Cevdet was a devout Muslim and had even written a eulogy of the Prophet, until his education at the Royal Military Academy in Istanbul turned him toward European materialism. According to Cevdet, "science is the religion of the elite, whereas religion is the science of the masses." He therefore argued that materialism should be promoted in Islamic terms—"stitched onto an Islamic jacket," as he put it. In 1889, he helped to found the Ottoman Union Committee, later called the Committee of Union and Progress, whose opposition to Ottoman absolutism led to their exile. In 1904, he founded the journal *İctihad* (*Rational Interpretation*) in Geneva, Switzerland, later moving it to Cairo, Egypt. While Europeans considered the journal Islamist, it faced considerable opposition from Ottoman Muslims, culminating in the unprecedentedly negative reaction to Cevdet's Turkish translation of Reinhart Dozy's controversial work on the history of Islam. This translation—whose introduction is presented here—was banned, and all existing copies were confiscated. Despite having founded the organization that came to power in the Constitutional Revolution of 1908, Cevdet could not return from exile until 1911. In subsequent years, Cevdet became increasingly open in his campaign against religiosity, including a notorious article ridiculing prayer. In the Turkish Republic, Cevdet's closest associates entered parliament, while he was stigmatized as a collaborator of the European Allies' occupation of Istanbul after World War I, and as a Kurdish nationalist.[1]

History, in effect, is like a motion picture that transmits the conditions and transformations of the world to vision, through reading; to the sense of hearing, through listening; and to the center of perception and consideration, which we call consciousness, through one or both of these.

To put it in another way, history is similar to a photographic plate that has not been touched up, the lines and details of which are neither toned up or down, a photograph exactly reflecting the original. Real history is like that, and must be like that. Other books that are not like this and yet are still called history are either negligently written works or take advantage of negligence. It was necessary to bring into existence a "History of Islam" that truly possesses the requisites and specifics of a real work of

history, and to submit it to the attention and consideration of our brothers in religion. I deliberately use the words "bring into existence" because I have verified that there is no such history [of Islam] in the three major Islamic languages, Arabic, Persian, and Turkish. The reason for this deficiency should be sought mainly in the absolutism of Muslim rulers. History is the most eye-opening branch of the sciences. It is obvious that open eyes cannot coexist with absolutism and disinformation. People with open eyes can discern oppression and freedom and will develop a desire for justice and truth. The folly of Muslim tyrants who claim to be the shadow of God and whose tyranny and treachery overshadow the most cruel and treacherous of creatures is best

---

Abdullah Cevdet, "İfade-i Mütercim" (Preface by the Translator), in Reinhart Dozy, *Tarih-i İslamiyet* (*The History of Islam*) (Cairo, Egypt: Matbaa-i İctihad, 1908), volume 1, pp. 3–8. Translation from Turkish and introduction by M. Şükrü Hanioğlu.

1. M. Şükrü Hanioğlu, *Bir Siyasal Düşünür Olarak Doktor Abdullah Cevdet ve Dönemi* (*Doctor Abdullah Cevdet: A Political Thinker and His Time*) (Istanbul, Turkey: Üçdal Neşriyat, 1981); Karl Süssheim, "'Abd Allah Djevdet," *Encyclopedia of Islam*, Supplement, edited by M. Th. Houtsma *et alia* (Leiden, Netherlands: E. J. Brill, 1938), pp. 55–60.

summarized in the awful truth embodied in the following couplet of *Shaykh* Sa'di [Iranian poet, 1184–1292]:

The distress of mind of one who seeks justice
Can overthrow the king from his realm.

We strongly sensed the Muslims' need for a "History of Islam." We have found a "History of Islam" that possesses the required qualities among the superb works of the famous Dutch Orientalist, Professor Doctor [Reinhart] Dozy [1820–1883]. We have restricted ourselves to the judgment of "wisdom is the believer's stray camel: wherever one finds it, one appropriates it." We have translated this work [first published in 1863], which is a product of an absolutely impartial good sense, and which possesses the qualities of enormous erudition and thorough research, into Turkish from its French version entitled *Essai sur l'histoire de l'islamisme* [*Essay on the History of Islam*].

"The author is from the Netherlands, a non-Muslim, thus a stranger to the religion [of Islam]. So is it possible to trust what he says?" To this inevitable question we respond in the following manner: Being a Muslim does not consist in [having a Muslim] name, fasting, and performing the prayers. "Religion is social relations (*mu'amala*)" [a *hadith*, or tradition of the Prophet]; religion is nothing other than social relations. Learned, virtuous Doctor Dozy, who spent his entire life in teaching and study, and who strove to enlighten the minds of God's people and to be beneficial to them, is a thousand times more Muslim than vagabond Hamids [a reference to the Ottoman sultan, Abdülhamid II, reigned 1876–1909], whose deeds and desires are nefarious. It is our own Prophet who says, "The Muslim is one from whose hand and tongue people are safe," "The best of men is he who is the most useful to people," and "One hour's search for knowledge is better than a thousand years' acts of worship." Every learned and virtuous person is a Muslim. An ignorant, immoral person is not a Muslim even if he stems from the lineage of the Prophet. Culture and virtue will reduce all religions to one religion, that of justice and truth, and are already doing so:

The warring of 72 sects ignore.
Failing to find the truth, mere fables they
   explore. [Hafiz, Iranian poet, circa 1325–
   1390]

Doctor Dozy has covered the history of Islam down to about forty years ago. The history of Islam during these last forty years is reproduced from our erudite friend A. Guy's article entitled "Islam in the Last Forty Years." Mr. A. Guy is a young Orientalist. He has such a high degree of knowledge of Islamic affairs and of the obscurities of the Islamic religion that it would be appropriate to say that he has no match among the *'ulama'* [religious scholars] of Islam.

His massive volume "Sources of Islam," soon to be published in French, will make it clear how tireless a researcher this young Orientalist is, and what an outstanding zeal for understanding he possesses.

The method that we have followed in translating this essay is the same method that we have always used with a religious scrupulousness; it is nothing other than preserving the textual integrity of the original. There are only four letters which we have added to the text, placing them in parentheses: they are "S.A." for *salla'llahu alayh wa sallam* [May God bless him and grant him salvation], and "R.A." for *radiallahu anh* [May God be well pleased with him].

Some of our observations and additions are given at the bottom of the pages as footnotes; they have been differentiated from the footnotes of the author by appending to them the initials "A.C."

We are of the opinion that today there is no book more beneficial to the Muslims, none the attentive reading of which would be a more absolute necessity, than the *History of Islam*. The times for naive or misleading works full of silly tales and deceptions is long passed thanks to the enlightenment of evolution.

We should possess the courage to face the truth regardless of how harsh it is and how strongly it contradicts our former beliefs and feelings. Bravery is not only just exposing ourselves to the bullets of the enemy. We must possess the power to abandon the undignified dignity of our ignorant selves in the face of the divine magnificence of reality and truth, and of adorning ourselves with the decoration of the sublime grief of truth. We should demonstrate our bravery by displaying a moral courage of this kind. If we seriously consider the *hadith* of the Prophet, "Religion is social relations"—which, as we have said, states that religion is nothing other than social relations—then it is plain how far most of us Muslims are inadequate in our religion, or even lack it altogether. The best acts of worship are those aiming to benefit and save all God's people, beginning with one's own self, or even sacrificing oneself.

Those ignorant pietists who are not aware of this subtle social aspect of the exalted religion of Islam can only confirm the truth of the famous couplet by *Maulana* Jalal al-Din al-Rumi [Iranian poet, 1207–1273]:

With head on the ground and backside in the air,
He considers to be God the place of his prayer![2]

True Islam cannot coexist with ignorance and oppression. If we take into consideration the fact that the word "Muslim" is derived from the word "salvation," it may be easily understood that Islam cannot live in places where ignorance and oppression prevail, and that ignorance and oppression cannot take root in places where Islam rules supreme.

Here then is the aim of the study of history: by examining the affairs and changes of the past and drawing on the adventure of our fathers and grandfathers, to reach a life-giving conclusion, and to derive a salutary lesson of awakening.

We repeat and confirm that the aim of translating and publishing this work is to present for the understanding of the Muslims a book the study of which could provide such a lesson.

"Peace be upon those who follow right guidance!" [Qur'an, Sura 20, Verse 47][3]

---

2. [Cevdet used this couplet in other writings as well to criticize Islamic fanaticism, for example *Dilmesti-i Mevlana* (*Rumi's Language of Spiritual Intoxication*) (Istanbul, Ottoman Empire: Orhaniye Matbaası, 1921), pp. 17–18.—Trans.]

3. [In the Qur'an, Moses and Aaron are instructed to speak these words to the Egyptian pharoah, and they have become a conventional nongreeting to unbelievers at the end of letters. Here Cevdet's intention must be to exclude Muslim fanatics but include Dozy and Guy.—Trans.]

The Principles of Consultation and Liberty in Islam *and* Reform and Review of Religious Writings

Musa Kazım (Turkey, 1858–1920) was a leading member of the 'ulama' (religious scholar) branch of the Committee of Union and Progress, an Ottoman senator, and *Shaykh al-Islam* (chief religious official) of the Ottoman Empire. Educated in a traditional manner, Musa Kazım taught religious studies at seminaries and modern schools in Istanbul until the Constitutional Revolution of 1908, defending Islam against its Christian critics and defending constitutionalism against its Muslim critics. On the day of the revolution's triumph, he authored a thirteen-page manifesto on Islam and constitutionalism, translated in the first part of this chapter. Under the new regime, he became a member of the Ottoman Senate and an organizer of clerical support for the regime. In 1910, he was appointed *Shaykh al-Islam*; after a series of resignations and removals, he was reappointed in 1911, 1916, and 1917. His opponents frequently accused him of being a freemason; he denied the charges in a pamphlet in 1911, maintaining that he was a devotee of the Naqshibandiyya Sufi order. During World War I, Musa Kazım published a pamphlet defending the Ottoman government's declaration of *jihad* (holy struggle), extending the duty of *jihad* to all Muslims, not just Ottomans. Following the Ottoman defeat, he was tried in a military court along with other leaders of the Committee of Union and Progress. Due to illness, the British exempted him from imprisonment on Malta and banished him instead, first to Bursa and then to Edirne, where he died in 1920.[1]

The Principles of Consultation and Liberty in Islam

The divine ordinances that our lord Muhammad, Prophet of the end of times and apostle sent to men and genies, whose exalted mission happily coincided with the period of the human mind's highest development, was enjoined to communicate from God to all mankind can be divided into two groups: those concerned with the other world, and those concerned with this world. Each of these can then be subdivided into two groups: matters of fundamental principles, and matters of detail.

The fundamental ordinances pertaining to the next world are concerned with matters of doctrine, while

Musa Kazım, "İslamda Usul-i Meşveret ve Hürriyet" (The Principles of Consultation and Liberty in Islam) and "Kütüb-i Kelamiyye'nin İhtiyacat-ı Asra Göre Islah ve Te'lifi" (Reform and Review of Religious Writings According to the Requirements of the Age), in Musa Kazım, *Külliyat-ı Şeyh'ül-İslam Musa Kazım: Dini, İçtima'i Makaleler (Collected Works of Shaykh al-Islam Musa Kazım: Religious and Social Essays)* (Istanbul, Ottoman Empire: Evkaf-ı İslamiye Matbaası, 1919), pp. 243–247, 289–293. The first selection was published as a manifesto on July 24, 1908; the second piece was a speech delivered at the Şehzade Club in Istanbul on August 20, 1909. Translations from Turkish by M. Şükrü Hanioğlu and Yektan Türkyılmaz, respectively. Introduction by M. Şükrü Hanioğlu.

1. Sadık Albayrak, *Son Devrin Osmanlı Uleması İlmiye Ricalinin Teracim-i Ahvali (Biographies of Notable Religious Scholars of the Late Ottoman Era)* (Istanbul, Turkey: Millî Gazete Yayınları, 1981), volumes 4–5, pp. 157–158; Abdülkadir Altınsu, *Osmanlı Şeyhülislamları (Ottoman Chief Religious Officials)* (Ankara, Turkey: Ayyıldız Matbaası, 1972), pp. 233–237; *Osmanlı İlmiye Salnâmesi (Yearbook of Ottoman Religious Scholars)* (Istanbul, Ottoman Empire: Matbaa-i Âmire, 1916), pp. 626–628; David Kushner, "Şeyh-ül-Islam Musa Kazım Efendi's Ideas on State and Society," pp. 603–610 in *V. Milletlerarası Türkiye Sosyal ve İktisat Tarihi Kongresi, Tebliğler* (Fifth International Congress on the Social and Economic History of Turkey: Communications) (Ankara, Turkey: Türk Tarihi Kurumu Basımevi, 1990).

ordinances on details pertaining to the next world are concerned with acts of worship. In addition, the fundamental ordinances pertaining to this world relate to the administration of the affairs of the country, while ordinances on details pertaining to this world are about transactions and punishments.

Without having fundamental ordinances pertaining to the next world, executing ordinances on details pertaining to the next world would be absolutely useless. For example, it is self-evident that worship and acts of piety would not be of the slightest benefit to someone who does not believe in the existence of God and His uniqueness. Similarly, it cannot be imagined that anything will be gained from implementing ordinances on details pertaining to this world unless the corresponding fundamental ordinances are executed. For example, unless justice and equity are respected, no benefit can be expected from the punishment of criminals.

The basic principles of the fundamental ordinances pertaining to this world are:

Consulting the *umma* [Islamic community] in every matter.
Respecting justice and equity in every matter.
Entrusting the affairs of the country and the interests of the *umma*, which are a divine charge, to qualified persons.

Our proofs of these are noble Qur'anic verses (and some *hadith*s [narratives] of the Prophet), like the following:

And seek their counsel in the matter. [Sura 3, Verse 159]
And their affairs [are decided in] consultation among them. [Sura 42, Verse 38]
When you judge between men, you should judge justly. [Sura 4, Verse 58]
Be just; it is closer to piety. [Sura 5, Verse 8]
If you speak, be just even if the matter concerns a relative. [Sura 6, Verse 152]
God commands you to deliver to the owners that which is held in trust with you. [Sura 4, Verse 58]

In the first of these verses, God orders His Messenger to consult with the *umma* in every matter. Since, as explained in the science of jurisprudence, an order to do something entails that its contrary is forbidden, it is established that according to the exalted tenor of this noble verse, failure to consult with the *umma* was absolutely forbidden, even to that

great Messenger to men and genies who was the recipient of God's revelation. If such a holy person, who had received God's revelation, was commanded to consult with his *umma* in every matter, then all Muslims, especially the exalted caliphs, are all the more obligated to consult with the *umma*.

In the second verse, God shows that the affairs of Muslims consist in consultation among themselves. With this, He confirms in a categorical fashion that the order for consultation is the greatest pillar of Islam. Thus all those who bear the exalted title of "Muslim" are under the obligation to obey this heavenly order and divine command.

In the third verse, God orders us to make judgments between people with justice and equity, and this reveals that rendering justice in all cases is a religious duty.

In the fourth verse, it is enjoined: "Be just, for this is the closest thing to piety."

Likewise, in the fifth verse, it is enjoined: "You should not deviate from justice whenever you speak, even if the matter concerns your closest relative."

The sixth verse tells us that "God commands you to deliver to the owners that which is held in trust with you." Since the content of an order stems from something that is incumbent, it is absolutely clear, according to the tenor of this verse, that entrusting the affairs of the nation and matters of the state—the greatest and most important of all trusts—to those who are qualified is one of the duties incumbent on their authority.

God specifies those who are qualified for this sacred trust in the noble verse: "The noblest among you in the eyes of God is the most pious." [Sura 49, Verse 13] It is clear from this exalted verse that the foremost quality that persons undertaking the duties of the religious community must possess is piety. Aristocratic birth and nobility play no part whatsoever in this matter. Piety means avoiding the violation of the rights of God and humans, and it is thus dependent without any doubt upon knowing those rights. Therefore, a person who would undertake one of the duties of the religious community must be well-informed about that duty, and be one of those powerful and capable people who are distinguished by their integrity and ability.

Accordingly our Prophet, the teacher of all beings, the most perfect of salutations be upon Him, personally always favored consulting his *umma* in every matter of public import. During his lifetime, he entrusted the administration to those who were qualified for it. In this regard, he paid no attention to such considerations as kinship or friendship. All the appointments made by the Prophet were based upon competence. He never deviated from justice and equity in the slightest degree in any matter.

Integrity, competence, justice—these were the qualities that the Messenger of God wanted! These are the virtues that the Prophet sought! While he was alive, while he was leaving this world, his hopes were always, always directed to these: Integrity, competence, and justice!

It is well known that three days prior to his departure to the next world, he ascended to the blessed pulpit and demonstrated to his *umma* and all his Companions with his last breath that he was justice incarnate in these lofty words:

O my *umma* and companions! If I have taken anybody's property, here is my property, let him come forward and take it. If I struck anybody in the back, here is my back, let him come forward and strike me in the back.

Thanks to such superior virtues of his, he left forever in the hearts of the *umma* an inextinguishable affection for himself, an affection that is genuine, sincere, and free from hypocrisy of all kinds. The rightly guided caliphs [that is, the first four successors of the Prophet], who were honored with that sacred post after him, literally followed in the sublime footsteps of the august Messenger. In this way they showed to all peoples who were lost in the darkness of ignorance, and groaning under the yoke of slavery, the meaning of humanity, civilization, freedom, equality, justice, prosperity, and happiness.

Thus on these firm foundations laid down by our Prophet, a virtuous government, the like of which has never been seen on the face of the earth, was established and this bright sun of truth spread the glitter of justice to all regions of the world, thanks to the assiduous and unremitting efforts of the rightly guided caliphs. Within a short time, [this government] shone the light of happiness on more than a hundred million wretched people who were longing for freedom, yearning for justice, and craving for equality. It was such a virtuous government that all peoples who took refuge in its protection, be they Muslims, non-Muslims, Christians, or Jews, one and all enjoyed equal rights. In the eyes of the law, the right of a Christian or a Jew was owed the same respect as the rights of the caliph.

What justice this was, what freedom, what equality! A Jew comes and is tried along with a caliph. If one of them sits, the other cannot be left to stand. If one of them is called by his name, the other cannot be called by his honorific or title.

All these are uncontested facts. Here is history, the history of humanity! Here are deeds, the deeds of Islam. Study them, examine them! Is it possible to see a sign of the smallest degree of inequality, the smallest degree of injustice, the smallest degree of arbitrariness? Do you need proofs for the fact that Islam treated everyone equally, without distinction of race, creed, religion, and nationality, and that it granted everyone his personal liberty and all his legitimate rights?

Here is a famous trial for you! This is a trial in which 'Ali [ibn Abi Talib, fourth successor of the Prophet, 656–661] is defendant and a Jew is plaintiff. The two are at law in the court of *Qadi* [Shurayh ibn al-Harith al-Kindi, judge in Kufa, 7th century]. Hasan ['Ali's son, 624–669] comes to give evidence in favor of his father. The judge refuses this. 'Ali accepts this, and shows no sign of resentment. The judge calls the Jew by his name but mentions 'Ali by his honorific as "O Father of Hasan!" This angers 'Ali. He senses a hint of inequality in this. That is what that virtuous government was like, that is what the leaders of that state were like, that is what the justice, equality, and freedom dispensed to the subjects of that government were like.

This is such a firmly established truth that today all civilized peoples around the world are obliged to admit and acknowledge it.

Thus it is clear that the fundamental principles that form the bases for humanity and civilization—principles such as consultation, equality, freedom, and justice—are a legal right granted by God 1300 years ago to Muslims and all human beings. This right was quite simply given to us by God. Nobody else is entitled to claim to have conferred it. But, alas, after the time of the rightly guided caliphs, the political ordinances of religion were cast in a different mold, persons acceding to the caliphate thought of their own personal interests. They yielded to their hedonistic desires, and in order to realize their aims, they usurped these rights, this freedom, this equality, this justice granted to the Muslim *umma* and to all human beings by God as a favor for which gratitude is due. Affirming that "obeying those in authority is a binding duty" [paraphrase of Qur'an, Sura

4, Verse 59], they failed entirely to take into consideration the conditions that limit this obedience. They wholly uprooted the firm pillar of Islam from its foundations. They set a bad example for those who came after them. They spoiled the faith of ignorant people, who were ignorant of the conditions that prevailed at the beginning of Islam and of the ordinances of the holy law, telling them that "Islam prevents progress." The result was that this false idea prevailed in all regions of the world until the fortunate day of the accession to the throne His Royal Highness [Abdülhamid II, Ottoman sultan, reigned 1876–1909].

Since God is the true protector of this religion of Islam and has promised to preserve and forever protect the freedom-granting ordinances of the illustrious *shari'a* [religious law] of Muhammad, our sultan immediately upon his accession to the caliphate put the principle of consultation into effect and promulgated the constitution [in 1876], with the exalted intention of carrying out the duties of the caliphate with which he had been charged by God.

However, he was unable to put the ordinances comprehended in this exalted law [the constitution] into effect, owing to the incitations and instigations of certain traitors to the religion and nation. Thank God, today such false obstacles have been entirely removed, and thus His Royal Majesty feels that the time to put this exalted law into effect has come, and he has set about carrying out this sacred duty made incumbent upon him by God. And because of this, he has placed all the Islamic world and humanity at large in his debt. May God bless His Royal Majesty and make him successful with His divine guidance, and make the Islamic community and Ottoman nation always happy and cheerful with the gift of such freedom. Amen.

Reform and Review of Religious Writings According to the Requirements of the Age

During the first years of Islam, the obvious meanings of the verses [of the Qur'an] and *hadith* [narratives of the Prophet] were deemed sufficient. Especially during the time of our Prophet, everyone would settle issues they were confused about by asking the Prophet directly. There was no need to write or read books—any issue related to either the religious or temporal realms was settled in this way. It was not deemed necessary to write books.

Then in the time of Successors [to the Companions of the Prophet], differences emerged. As a result, to maintain the unity of Islam, books began to be written. Because, if there are differences of opinion, this could lead to conflict, and divisions might arise among the Muslims. God forbid that the emergence of divisions would, by weakening the power of the *umma*, lead to its destruction. For that reason, they began at that time to prepare books in an attempt to eliminate conflicts and distinguish truth from error.

In particular, books on the science of theology were written. It was said that the possessors of understanding would recognize the truth. And this worked. However, in these books there was no mention of philosophy, as the philosophical sciences had not yet been introduced to Islam. Each issue was interpreted by reference to a verse or a *hadith*. This was the mode of thinking of the ancient *'ulama'* [religious scholars], because that was the need at the time.

Later, the philosophical sciences were introduced to Arabic through translation. As a result, many other disciplines and *madhhab*s [schools of thought] emerged. For instance, up to that time nobody knew about the "Aristotelian" school, because there was no mention of it. This was the first [new philosophy] to appear. Similarly, nobody knew what "naturalism" meant; there was no such notion. These ideas, appearing along with all those [new] disciplines, also had their adherents, but they were few. Later, the Aristotelians turned out to be the most popular, and the number of its followers increased significantly. Consequently there emerged a need to defend religion against these people. As the need to defend religion against both polytheists and Aristotelians was perceived, books began to be written for this purpose: that is, philosophy was added into the science of theology, because this was necessary. This is the science of theology practiced by contemporary *'ulama'*.

But how did this happen? First, the *'ulama'* studied these sciences, then they defended the beliefs of Islam against philosophy, writing books for this purpose. This went on for a very long time. Later, the polytheist school failed to attract much support, [so] the major struggle was against the Aristotelians. Eventually, the Aristotelians also disappeared. That is, science changed, and the Aristotelians' principles were overturned. Hence there was no longer a need to defend against them. Since there were no adherents of these sciences and no one to support and advocate these disciplines, why should we protect religious rulings by articulating defenses against them?

After the disappearance of these philosophies, the "materialists" took their place. Inevitably, naturalists also gained in popularity. Now a need arose to defense against these [philosophies]. Just as the prominent *'ulama'*, especially the recent generation, struggled against the naturalists, Aristotelians, and polytheists, and succeeded [in this struggle], now a need arises for us, too, to struggle against our contemporary opponents.

"Is it appropriate for us to alter [the earlier struggles]? Let us continue with the model of their [earlier] struggles. . . ."

If someone makes this argument, we would reply:

"Very well, but against whom?" Since there is no faction of scholars—or as they are recently called, philosophers—pursuing this mode of thinking, why should we put forth these defenses?

[Aristotelians used to say:] "This universe is composed of 13 spheres. The first is earth, the second is water, the third is air, the fourth is light, and there are nine celestial spheres, all of which are concentric. These celestial spheres are eternal, and the type and kind of the remaining spheres are also eternal. Thus, the universe is eternal."

Now nobody says such things. Therefore even if we say we are defending Islam by shouting, "No, you are wrong to call [the world] eternal, it may be created," what would be the use? Today's philosophy agrees with us: "Yes, the earth is finite." And the creatures on it are also finite.[2] Then [they say]: "What we call the heavens are not nine concentric spheres, as Ptolemy [ancient astronomer, 2nd century] argued. Such a heaven does not exist." Even if we say it does, who would listen [to us]? Since the adversary does not even accept the existence of the heavens, how can we convince them by saying that it is created? Philosophy currently believes that space is infinite, and that the bodies in it are similarly infinite. With regard to form, these bodies are finite; only the fundamental atomic particles are eternal. There is no form in this universe that is eternal—all are finite, only atomic particles are eternal.

2. [Musa Kazım is playing with two meanings of the term *hadith*, translated here as "created": in the Islamic argument, it means "created by God"; in the modern scientific argument, it means cosmologically "finite."—Ed.]

This is the argument of today's philosophy. So if we argue against them that the heavens are not eternal, but created—they will laugh at us. "What are you talking about?" they will say.

[We might respond:] "Then humans are not eternal, but created."

"Of course they are created. The earth is divided into many layers, and humans only recently appeared on the upper layer. Do you know nothing about geology? This is obvious. Who says that humans are eternal?"

"I do not know, someone said it once upon a time. I am arguing against that."

Then they will say, "Find those people and argue against them." So it is obvious that our current teaching must be reformed accordingly. There is an urgent need for the writing of books that will refute the philosophy of our era.

But if it is said, "We will repeat the old arguments anyway"—then that is a different matter. But religion cannot be defended in this way. The Aristotelians also accept the existence of God, saying: "God exists. There must be a cause of the existence of this universe, and this is the prime mover (*wajib al-wujud*). But this prime mover is necessary [that is, the philosophical system must assume God's existence], not autonomous [as in Islam]. For this reason, the universe is eternal, since that which emanates from a necessary agent is eternal. Since God is necessary, the universe is eternal, because the universe emanated from Him, and emanated without any cause." We used to argue against this: "No, God is not necessary, but rather autonomous."

If you say this now to contemporary philosophers, they will laugh at us. "What are you talking about?" they will say. There is no God, according to their theory, much less "necessary" and "autonomous." Thus, there is no use in mentioning the issues of necessity and autonomy.

The ancient authorities concluded that "God has no attributes. He is the True One. Therefore it is absurd to represent Him with certain attributes. Since God is the prime mover, He is free of necessity. If He had attributes, how could He be the True One? Then there would be a need for attributes, but such a need is incompatible with his being the prime mover. He is self-existent, omniscient, almighty, all-desirous, and so on. Knowledge is identical with Him, power is identical with Him, anything that we call an attribute is identical with Him."

The Mu'tazilites [early Muslim rationalists] also adhered to this [line of thinking], as they acknowledged. Perhaps one could now make a similar defense: "No, God has attributes, God is omniscient in knowledge, almighty in power, immortal in life. He is all-desirous in His will, and all-speaking in His word." If you said this against our opponents, they would tell us, "We do not accept the basis [of your argument], much less the matter of the attributes." In brief, our opponents today, that is, the philosophers, do not accept the divine and the prophetic. Actually, some naturalists have accepted the existence of God. However, if you investigate the matter further, what they call God is Nature.

Therefore, our most pressing task is to review the theological books in accordance with present needs. And how are we to do this? First of all, we have to know the sciences of our opponents. Otherwise, it is impossible to argue against them. Indeed, earlier 'ulama' did just this. First they were educated in the sciences of contemporaneous philosophers, then they convinced them with their words. Now if we try to defend ourselves with our present level of knowledge, we will be ridiculous. Because we do not know. First of all, let us be educated in those sciences. Then let us defend Islam on the basis of these sciences. Now it is time to recognize this need. There is no use in displaying fanaticism in this respect. In fact, it would be harmful. The literature shows that all of the 'ulama' in every era wrote books in accordance with the needs of the day. As a result, later 'ulama', in translating philosophy into Arabic, deemed it necessary to reform the science of theology, and added many new topics from naturalists and theologians. We have the same need. We must also reform the theological books in accordance with the needs of our era.

Guiding Mankind to Act on the Basis of Telegraphic Messages

Jamal al-Din al-Qasimi (Syria, 1866–1914) was the leading proponent of Islamic modernism in early twentieth-century Damascus. His publications numbered more than two dozen and covered religious disciplines such as Islamic law, theology, and exegesis; Muslim religious customs; and Arab history. He came from a family of minor religious functionaries and obtained his religious education from the city's leading religious scholars. Qasimi emerged as a proponent of reformist ideas in the 1890s, but he was not able to openly publish his work until the Ottoman Constitutional Revolution created a freer political climate in 1908. He was one of a handful of liberal religious scholars in Damascus who favored constitutional government. Moreover, a younger generation of Syrians with inclinations toward Arab nationalism drew inspiration from his call for an Arab cultural and literary revival. His religious and political views made him the object of Ottoman suspicions and conservative scholars' hostility. Consequently, he endured several episodes of persecution. His religious writings focused on two themes. One exhorted Muslims to overcome historical divisions into rival legal schools and sects by returning to the Qur'an and the practice of the Prophet as the only bases of authority. The other emphasized the rational character of Islamic beliefs and practices. In this passage, Qasimi seeks to demonstrate that Islamic law possesses methods and principles, in particular the principle of *ijtihad* (independent reasoning), that allow for the adoption of new technology. To support this view, Qasimi cites an extensive series of classical Islamic authorities and texts.[1]

In the name of God, the beneficent, the merciful

Praise God, lord of the worlds. Prayer and peace on our master Muhammad, seal of the prophets, and on his exemplary family and Companions, and on their sincerely believing Successors until the Day of Judgment.

A judge asked me if he may act according to well-established information in a telegraphic message from an authority, such as a governor, another judge, or another trusted source, announcing on the basis of legally acceptable evidence the start or the end of Ramadan [the month of dawn-to-dusk fasting], given that celestial bodies rise at the two places at the same time.[2] I replied to him on the basis of the legal opinions of famous *'ulama'* [religious scholars] on this issue, and I shared with him both general and detailed texts about it. I told him that *'ulama'* of the last century and current leaders of knowledge have devoted much attention to the issue of the telegraph. They have lent it meticulous scrutiny and have taken the utmost care in understanding it. Some favor acting according to it in both social transactions and religious rituals; while others would act according to it only in certain categories of transactions; yet others favor using it in beginning and breaking the fast, depending on the conclusions they reach in undertaking *ijtihad* [independent reasoning]. I said that I have not heard of a single major scholar who has

Jamal al-Din al-Qasimi, *Kitab al-irshad al-khalq* (*Book of the People's Guidance*) (Damascus, Syria: Matba'at al-Muqtabas, 1911), pp. 2–11. Translation from Arabic and introduction by David D. Commins.

1. Nizar Abazah, *Jamal al-Din al-Qasimi* (*Jamal al-Din al-Qasimi*) (Damascus, Syria: Dar al-Qalam, 1997); David D. Commins, *Islamic Reform: Politics and Social Change in Late Ottoman Syria* (New York: Oxford University Press, 1990); Zafir Qasimi, *Jamal al-Din al-Qasimi wa-'asruh* (*Jamal al-Din al-Qasimi and His Era*) (Damascus, Syria: Maktabat Atlas, 1965).

2. [The timing is essential because Ramadan is deemed to begin and end with the appearance of a new moon.—Trans.]

issued a legal opinion against acting according to telegraphic messages in all circumstances. There is no such report from any renowned scholars whose legal opinions are followed. What kind of scholar could fall into such confusion on this matter when he knows that the telegraph is the prop of kingdoms' vital affairs? Is it possible for the most perfect of all laws to neglect a matter of general public benefit, especially one of the greatest technical advances, when the principles of the *shari'a* [Islamic law] provide for every time and place? The lofty *shari'a*'s basic legal principles cannot invalidate the telegraph; rather, they connect it to similar matters that are well known. They remove the mask of obscurity from the face of controversy with the extensive study and reasoning of its profound thinkers. Because the legal opinions of the *'ulama'* on this issue tend to be fairly brief, I have sought to explain in detail their sources. For in generality resides confusion, while in detail there is neither doubt nor conjecture. This is what has prompted me to compose this book. I seek the assistance of the Exalted One who gives success in arriving at the correct conclusion.

Preface on Method

Part One: The excellence of Islam includes the applicability of its principles to the laws of civilization. Islam's magnanimity includes the way specific regulations can be derived from its basic legal principles. Ancient and modern generations have adapted to new situations on the basis of well-known principles. Every age has men who uphold God's will with proofs. The basis for knowing the proper statute for any given case is its evidence.

The excellence of Islam includes the applicability of its basic legal principles to the laws of civilizations; the suitability of its principles to the needs of every time and place; basing its rulings on bringing benefit and preventing harm; its distinction in removing encumbrances and fetters; its opening the doors of ease and facility; and its blocking the ways of anguish and difficulty.

Its magnanimity includes the rise of the *madhahib* [schools of Islamic law] from its wise sources; the acquisition of its principles from the luminous niche of its lamp [the Qur'an]; and the breadth of its specific regulations to allow for the adoption of necessities and luxuries, however much inventions and discoveries multiply.

Islam's qualities include its guidance to methods of discovering laws through extensive study and reasoning, so that experts may easily relate all beneficial inventions to Islam's stipulations, certainties, generalities, and apparent meanings. Furthermore, Islam provides for the adoption of beneficial inventions because of its magnanimity and its agreement with ease and mercy.

Both ancient and recent jurisprudents, mercy and contentment be upon them, have adopted new conveniences and ways of life according to the basic legal principles and specific regulations of the *shari'a*. If that were not the case, then why are there so many huge volumes of rulings and abundant legal opinions on various cases? Are they not for novel situations that have arisen in both recent and ancient times? Of course they are. Thus it is necessary to adapt to novel situations in human society on the basis of the well-known principles of the true religion. Doing so helps people in both religious and worldly matters, and allows them to live according to firmly established customs.

The founders of the legal schools, God be pleased with them, acquired their stature and are considered exemplars of knowledge because they attained such proficiency in deriving specific regulations and such judiciousness in religious understanding that their knowledge became the standard of the religious sciences. They reached this distinction only by plunging into the details of affairs after studying the underlying rationales of existence, tracing every specific regulation to a basic legal principle, and adopting a statute on the basis of that principle. A sage once said, "The Muslims' *mujtahids* [religious scholars qualified to perform *ijtihad*] have taken into consideration many principles of their law and adapted to the customs of various places and times, according to the Book [the Qur'an] and the *sunna* [the precedents and advice of the Prophet]. Therefore, the Islamic legal schools, taken altogether, suffice for the discovery of all religious laws to regulate social transactions in all parts of the world, while complying with the basic principles of religious rulings." He supports this opinion by referring to such principles of legal extension as custom and the consideration of benefits.

The introduction of the telegraph resembles earlier innovations that did not exist in the time of the Companions or the Successors or the founders of the legal schools, but on which contemporary legal experts have issued legal opinions—innovations such as cannons and clocks used for fasting and prayer, and countless other matters in worship and social transactions. The telegraph is but a drop in the ocean of discoveries and inventions in coming ages, including conveniences and benefits for people of all classes—as the Qur'an states, "There will be created what you do not know." [Sura 16, Verse 8] If we do not adopt the telegraph according to fixed principles of discovery through reasoning and analogy, then do we not congeal religion and block the way of ancient and recent generations, and forever constrict what God made wide through understanding and discovery?

One of the Muslims' greatest blessings is that every age has men who uphold God's will with proofs and clarify obscure issues with proper methods. This is evident from the numerous religious judges in every place who rule on issues that were not stipulated in the two noble sources [the Qur'an and the *sunna*]. They extract rulings from the two sources by resorting to extensive study and reasoning. The abundance of legal opinions and judges is an emblem of the survival of *ijtihad* until the Day of Judgment. Every age has men who uphold the *shari'a* with proofs. Anyone who wishes may refer to the book, "The Virtue of the Notables," by *Imam* [Jalal al-Din] al-Suyuti [Egyptian scholar, 1445–1505], which contains long lists of *mujtahid*s—and that was in just one particular place. How many other men would be counted in all places? Indeed, it would be a boundless ocean.

Some worthless fellow might suspect—and it is said that suspicion is a sin—that current advocates of scholarly reform intend to use *ijtihad* to establish a special legal school and to call on believers to adhere exclusively to it, to deviate from the views of the founders of the *madhahib*, and to detract from the nobility of earlier generations. God save us from such ignorance and misunderstanding! Whoever thinks this way is more lost than a herd of cattle. What reasonable person would call for an increase in sectarianism and divisiveness? Instead, the intention is to arouse the concern of leading scholars to become familiar with issues through evidence, to research their sources, to explore the books of the ancestors and the founders of the *madhahib* on basic legal principles and specific regulations, to become familiar with the ways of extracting and discovering rulings and with the proofs of agreement and disagreement, then to aspire for the strongest evidence and to seek the firmest opinion, as was the custom of the upright

ancestors and numerous later generations. Later generations depend on earlier ones for all their scholarship and for the treasures they stored. But mental faculties vary from one person to the next. Grasping the purposes of the *shari'a* and the underlying rationales for deriving specific regulations, discerning the kernel from the husk in various matters that are the subject of *ijtihad* because they are not textually stipulated—these are paths that the ancestors pursued and methods followed by prominent men to the present day. Ahmad Ibn Faris [possibly al-Qazwini, religious scholar, 10th century], God have mercy on him, said, "Who forbade later generations from contradicting earlier ones? Do not accept the view of whoever says, 'The former left nothing for the latter.' Leave aside the view of another who says, 'How much did the former leave for the latter?' Is this world nothing but changing times? Does not every time have its men? Are not the sciences after the fundamental principles anything but the fruits of understanding and reason? Who ever restricted excellence to a particular age and stopped it at a certain time? Do not later men study, compose, and see things like earlier men? What would you say to contemporary jurisprudents if they needed to know the statute for a situation that had never before occurred? Do you not know that every heart has a mind, and every mind reaches its own conclusion? Why do you constrict what is wide, forbid what is permitted, and block the clear way? If people were limited to the books of the ancients, then a great deal of knowledge would be lost, penetrating minds would go astray, articulate tongues would be blunted, and we would hear nothing but repetition. Do you urge the revival of what the ages have covered over, the renewal of what the passage of time has worn out, the relegation to files of what contemporary minds have created, and the denial of this era? Even so, if one sought that, he would miss the mark and you would still read of new discoveries that will thrill and delight you."

The jurisprudents stipulated that the *mujtahid* must know those situations that are the subject of consensus [one of four bases of Islamic law, along with the Qur'an, the *sunna*, and analogy], so that he would not give a legal opinion in opposition to consensus. [Abu Hamid Muhammad] al-Ghazzali [major Iranian religious scholar, 1059–1111] wrote, "The desired end is that one know that his legal opinion is not opposed to consensus, either by virtue of knowing that it agrees with one of the legal schools or by knowing that this is an unprecedented occurrence with which the authors of consensus had no familiarity; that is sufficient."

Part Two: On the opinions of the founders of the madhahib *about the essence of jurisprudence and jurisprudents.*

The *Imam* Badr al-Din [Muhammad ibn Bahadur] al-Zarkashi [Egyptian religious scholar, circa 1344–1392] wrote, "Jurisprudence includes several meanings. First is knowledge of the rulings for cases according to a text or through discovery of rulings through reasoning. On this the masters have written extensive commentaries. Second is knowledge of combining likenesses and distinguishing between differences. On this meaning there are so many discussions among the ancestors that some say that jurisprudence consists only of difference and likeness. Third is the discussion of knotty issues for the purpose of sharpening the mind. Fourth are sophisms, quizzes, riddles, and legal fictions. Fifth is knowledge of the principles and exact rules by which specific regulations are derived. This last kind is the most valuable, the most general, the most complete, and the most perfect. By it the jurisprudent becomes prepared to undertake *ijtihad*. It is truly the root of jurisprudence."

The second meaning is called "the science of similarities and likenesses." *Imam* al-Suyuti wrote, "It is a great science by which one becomes thoroughly acquainted with the real meanings of jurisprudence, as well as its sources and its underlying rationales. One becomes proficient at understanding it and develops a command of it. One is able to make connections and extract meanings, to know the rulings for unprecedented events that do not cease with the passage of time. Therefore, some of our masters have said, 'Jurisprudence is the knowledge of likenesses.'"

Imam al-Ghazzali wrote, "The scholar is the heir of the Prophet, God's prayer and peace be upon him, only if he is thoroughly acquainted with all of the *shari'a*'s meanings. Its meanings and underlying rationales are attained at first only by the prophets, and they are discovered through reasoning, after the prophets' instruction about them, only by the *'ulama'*, who are the heirs of the prophets, upon them be peace."

He also wrote, "The specific regulations are known through the basic legal principles, not on the basis of those principles' literal meanings, but on the basis of implied meanings. For example, the saying

of the Prophet, upon him be peace, 'The judge should not issue a decision when he is angry,' is also understood to imply that he does not judge when he is in discomfort because of hunger, pain from an illness, or a need to urinate."

Shaykh Muhammad 'Abduh [modernist Egyptian religious scholar, 1849–1905; see chapter 3], God have mercy upon him, wrote, "How much stubborn ignorance is removed solely by maintaining clear distinctions between categories? Who could get confused about the meaning of jurisprudence in the Prophet's saying, prayers and peace be upon him, 'To whomever God wishes well, He gives understanding of religion?' One may hold the view that jurisprudence consists of cramming in one's mind *shari'a* rulings issued by specialists in deriving regulations, without distinguishing between perceptive ones and those who blindly imitate precedent. You can eliminate the confusion for such an arrogant one and remove his ignorance by saying, 'Knowledge of *shari'a* ordinances falls into two categories. One type consists of perceiving the intentions of the law in every ruling and understanding the underlying rationale of its ruling in every ordinance. God provided laws for his servants so that they may enjoy happiness in both worlds; that purpose does not change from one age of history to another, and it is unconditional. The perceptive individual finds application for the basic legal principles in all eventualities, however much people's conditions change, as long as people endure. The only one who has this quality is the judicious believer who hears and hearkens to God's call with his heart and mind, not with arrogance and pride.

"'The second type takes the forms of rulings from numerous disputations and crams them with the ideas of one partisan side in a kind of battle of minds, knowing only that something came from somebody without looking at the time and place of the speaker or the opinion. This type gets the same result for both the believer and the unbeliever. A good person, a wicked person, one who suspends the law with legal fiction, one who acts according to the law, one who stands at its limit: All reach the same conclusion.'

"If the categories are kept distinct, then confusion disappears, and the meaning is made clear, even to simpletons."

Imam Wali Allah al-Dihlawi [Indian religious scholar, 1703–1762] wrote, "Knowing the purposes on which rulings are based is an exact science. Only an individual with a refined mind and upright understanding delves into it. The Companions [of the Prophet] who were jurisprudents learned the rules of deriving specific regulations, of making things easy, and of religion by witnessing the circumstances in which commands and prohibitions were issued, just as the doctor's students know the purposes of the medicines that he prescribes by long practice and experience. The Companions attained the highest rank in knowing the law's purposes."

Part Three: On how the Companions, the Successors, and the founders of the madhahib used analogy and reasoning to derive specific regulations for events that are not stipulated in the Qur'an or the sunna.

Imam [Muhammad] Ibn al-Qayyim [al-Jawziyya, religious scholar, Damascus, 1292–1350] wrote, "When one seeks to know the ruling for something, one should first consult the Qur'an. If it contains no ruling, then one consults the *sunna*. If that contains no ruling, then one consults the rulings of the rightly guided caliphs [the first four successors to the Prophet], and then the sayings of the Companions, God be pleased with them. If none of these sources contains a ruling, then one performs *ijtihad* and seeks the closest ruling in the Qur'an, in the *sunna* of God's Messenger, God's prayer and blessing upon him, and in the rulings of his Companions.

"The Companions allowed this practice, they acted on it, and they affirmed each other's practice. It is related from Abu 'Ubayda [companion of the Prophet, circa 581–639], Abu Nu'aym [religious scholar, Isfahan, 948–1038], and Sufyan ibn 'Uyayna [religious scholar, Hijaz, died circa 813] that 'Umar ibn al-Khattab [companion of the Prophet and second caliph, 634–644], God be pleased with him, wrote to Abu Musa al-Ash'ari [companion of the Prophet, died 662], 'The office of judge is a well-established duty and an established custom. So understand that when litigants seek a decision on a matter that is not in the Qur'an or the *sunna*, you should use analogy and know like examples that are the basis for analogy. Then resolve on what you think is most beloved to God and what is most likely to be right.'"

Ibn al-Qayyim further wrote, "'Umar's instruction to use analogy for cases not covered in the Qur'an or the *sunna* is an authority for proponents of using

analogy in *shari'a*. They have said, 'This letter from 'Umar to Abu Musa was not rejected by any Companion. They agreed that rulings could be issued on the basis of analogy. It is one of the basic principles of the *shari'a* and it is indispensable for the jurisprudent. God guided His servants to use it for situations not covered by His book [the Qur'an]. He compared the second generation to the first generation in various places. He made the first generation the root and the second its branch. He compared the life of the dead after death to the life of the earth after the death of vegetation. He compared all new creation, which his opponents denied, to the creation of the heavens and earth—just as the second generation followed the first. He compared life after death to awakening after sleep. He coined comparisons and used them in various instances. They are all rational comparisons by which He instructs His servants to realize that the ruling of something is the ruling of its like. All likenesses are the bases of comparisons from which are known the rulings of similar things. The Qur'an contains around forty examples that include the comparison of a thing to its like and show that they have the same ruling. God, be He exalted, said, 'These are likenesses we offer the people, but only those who are knowledgeable understand.' [Qur'an, Sura 29, Verse 43] Using analogy in coining likenesses is a property of the mind. God gave people the instinct and the mental ability to detect similarity in two similar objects, to reject the notion that they are dissimilar, to distinguish between two different objects, and to reject the notion they are similar. It is said that the axis of inferential reasoning in its entirety involves equating similar objects and keeping separate different objects.'"

It is well known that 'Ali ibn Abi Talib [the Prophet's son-in-law and fourth caliph] and Zayd ibn Thabit [a companion of the Prophet] used analogy for determining inheritance in the case of a grandfather and brothers. 'Ali likened their relationship to a torrent from which there branch out tributaries, then tributaries of tributaries. Zayd compared their relationship to a tree from which a limb branches off, and then limbs of limbs. Their view was that the grandfather does not preclude the brothers from inheriting. ['Abdullah] Ibn 'Abbas [619–686] compared molars to fingers and said, "Take them as an example of a comparison." Muhammad ibn al-Hasan [al-Shaybani, Hanafi scholar, circa 750–805] said, "Whoever knows the Book and the *sunna*, the sayings of the

Companions of the Messenger (God's peace and blessing upon him and his family), and the findings of the Muslim jurisprudents—they are able to perform *ijtihad* on whatever new situation may arise, and they may judge accordingly, and practice accordingly in their prayer, fasting, pilgrimage, and indeed any religious duty or prohibition. If they perform *ijtihad* and study the case, comparing the case at hand to its most similar analogue, and they are unable to act on this, or if they err, they must say so."

The *Imam al-Haramayn* [the *Imam* of Mecca and Medina, that is, Abu'l-Ma'ali al-Juwayni, 1028–1085] said, "The basic issue in this matter is the *hadith* [saying of the Prophet] related by Mu'adh [ibn Jabal, companion of the Prophet died 627], God be pleased with him, and reported by [*hadith* collectors] Abu Da'ud [al-Sijistani, died 889], [Abu 'Isa Muhammad] al-Tirmidhi [died 892], and [Ahmad ibn al-Husayn] al-Bayhaqi [994–1066]. The *hadith* concerns the time when the Prophet, God's blessings and peace be upon him, wanted to send Mu'adh to Yemen. The Prophet said to him, 'How would you act as judge?' He said, 'I would judge by God's book.' The Prophet then said, 'And if you do not find a ruling in God's book?' He said, 'By the *sunna* of God's Messenger.' The Prophet then said, 'And if you do not find it there?' He said, 'I would perform *ijtihad* and spare no effort,' and he struck his chest. Muhammad said, 'Praise God to give success to the messenger of the Messenger of God, as he has pleased the Messenger of God.' This *hadith* may not come from either of the two major canonical *hadith* collections [those of al-Bukhari, died 870, and Muslim ibn al-Hajjaj, died 875], but it is rated as sound in another collection. It is sound indeed. *Al-Hafiz* Ibn Hajar [al-'Asqalani, Egyptian religious scholar, 1372–1449] wrote, 'Abu al-'Abbas [al-Tabari] Ibn al-Qass [jurist, died circa 946] relied in establishing the soundness of a *hadith* on studying with the leaders of jurisprudence and *ijtihad*, and he said that this is sufficient to dispense with rote learning of *hadith*s from specialists.'"

From this *hadith* it may be gleaned that the Lawgiver determined the *mujtahid*'s [method of] ruling. It is one of God's laws by His decree. [Muhyi al-Din] Ibn 'Arabi [Iberian religious scholar, 1165–1240] refers to this: "All of the *mujtahid*s have a firm foothold in the prophetic heritage and are the heirs of the prophets in deriving specific regulations. But they do not possess the law, because if it were not for the

material which the Lawgiver gave them from His law, they would not be able to derive laws."

Part Four: On the necessity of ijtihad *about new occurrences; that the way to know them is by* ijtihad, *not* taqlid *[imitation of a leading religious scholar].*

In every age novel occurrences must inevitably come under some ruling. Whoever is asked about them must issue a legal opinion after striving to the utmost to reach the proper decision. It is well known that a religious judge either belongs to a particular legal school or is independent (as I explained at length in my book, *The Legal Opinion in Islam*). Al-Ghazzali wrote, "It is agreed that if one exhausts *ijtihad*, and a particular ruling appears to be correct, then one is not allowed to follow its contrary, act on any other opinion, and abandon one's own opinion. But if one has not yet undertaken *ijtihad* and has not studied the matter, and if one is incapable of *ijtihad*—as commoners are—then he may resort to *taqlid*. There is disagreement, however, as to whether a scholar capable of *ijtihad* must perform it, or if he is permitted to imitate somebody else, even if the scholar has researched an issue, studied the evidence in order to reach an independent opinion, and is not deficient in learning." The Judge [al-Ghazzali] chose to forbid a scholar from imitating anyone else. He felt this was appropriate, and he cited as evidence the Qur'anic passages:

> So take heed, O people of vision! [Sura 59, Verse 2]
>
> Those who ponder would have known it. [Sura 4, Verse 83]
>
> Do they not contemplate what the Qur'an says, or have their hearts been sealed with locks? [Sura 47, Verse 24]
>
> In whatever matter you disagree, the ultimate judgment rests with God. [Sura 42, Verse 10]
>
> If you are at variance over something, refer it to God and the Messenger. [Sura 4, Verse 59]

"All this amounts to a command to ponder and investigate; it is not addressed to commoners; it is addressed only to religious scholars. The imitator abandons contemplation, reflection, and investigation."

Al-Ghazzali goes on to say, "*Taqlid* is accepting another's opinion with no proof; it is not a path to knowledge in either basic legal principles or specific regulations. Sophists claim that the path to knowing the truth is *taqlid*, and that *taqlid* is obligatory. The falseness of their view is demonstrated in a number of ways. We oppose their opinion with the following passages from the Qur'an:

> Do not follow that of which you have no knowledge. [Sura 17, Verse 36]
> Speak lies of God you cannot even conceive.' [Sura 2, Verse 169]
> We bear witness to only what we know. [Sura 12, Verse 81]
> Say, 'Bring your proof.' [Sura 1, Verse 111]

"All of this is about imitation and the command to seek knowledge. Therefore, the *'ulama'* have high standing. The Qur'an says, 'God will raise those of you who believe and those who have knowledge to high ranks.' [Sura 58, Verse 11] Muhammad (peace be upon him) said, 'The men of rectitude in every generation bear this knowledge, they banish from it the distortions of the excessively zealous, the interpretations of the ignorant, and the presumptions of liars. This is not attained by imitation but by knowledge.'" Thus wrote al-Ghazzali. From these words it is known that in order to discover rulings for novel occurrences, one must have recourse to the possessors of knowledge, namely, the *mujtahids*. There is no way to know the rulings or to assure the heart on such matters except by *ijtihad*, as al-Ghazzali (God be pleased with him) stated.

The Muslim Woman: Polygamy Can Be Prohibited in Islam

Mansurizade Mehmed Sa'id (Turkey, 1864–1923) was a religious scholar and politician whose radical ideas on polygamy and other issues caused heated debates during the second Ottoman constitutional period (1908–1918). Born into a family in Izmir that had produced many *'ulama'* (religious scholars), Mansurizade Sa'id followed the same path, gaining fame for his knowledge of Arabic literature and jurisprudence and serving on the regional appeals court. He also wrote for modernist journals and newspapers, arguing that Islam was not an obstacle to progress, and that it could be reconciled with modernization. In 1907, Mansurizade Sa'id worked with the secret Committee of Progress and Union, and after its rise to power in the revolution of 1908, he served in various official capacities, including negotiations with the Austro-Hungarian government over its annexation of Bosnia and Herzegovina. He also taught Muslim jurisprudence at the Law School in Istanbul. Mansurizade Sa'id was elected to parliament twice from Saruhan and once from Menteşe, serving from 1908 until 1918. In 1914, he was seriously considered for the office of *Shaykh al-Islam*, the chief religious authority of the Ottoman Empire, but was not appointed because of his radical religious views, which had caused an outcry in Islamist circles. Among these views was his position that polygamy could legitimately be banned in an Islamic country, as expressed in a series of articles excerpted here.[1]

"Since polygamy is permitted in the Islamic *shari'a* [religious law], Islam cannot refuse to accept polygamy." "In Islam polygamy has to be accepted." "Polygamy is forbidden in other religions and nations, but in Islam its prohibition is not possible." "The religion of Islam is different from other religions in regard to the issue of polygamy." Because of such wrong opinions and beliefs, the Islamic *shari'a* has been subjected to a great deal of criticism on the part of Europeans and civilized peoples in general. They imagine that medieval savagery still prevails in the Islamic world as a result of the *shari'a*. Islamic attempts to counter this veritable flood of negative comment serve only to strengthen the slander, calumny, and baseless accusations directed

against the *shari'a*. These antagonists have been carrying on their hostile propaganda on the basis of their belief that the *shari'a* contains a legal doctrine regarding polygamy. Meanwhile those who defend Islam, seeking to preserve this doctrine, never cease to speak of the advantages of polygamy, and to maintain that it is in accordance with reason.

The disputes continue to no purpose, because not one of the defenders of Islam has set out the true position: that there is no preferred doctrine in the *shari'a* regarding polygamy, that it is an issue left to the discretion of the rulers, that Islam in no way hinders the prohibition of polygamy, and that polygamy is not an issue which raises difficulties from the viewpoint of the *shari'a*, or needs extensive discussion.

[Mansurizade Sa'id], "İslam Kadını: Ta'addüd-i Zevcat İslamiyetde Men' Olunabilir" (The Muslim Woman: Polygamy Can Be Prohibited in Islam), and "İslam Kadını: Ta'addüd-i Zevcat Münasebetiyle" (The Muslim Woman: On Polygamy), *İslam Mecmuası* (*Islam Journal*), Istanbul, Ottoman Empire, numbers 8 and 11, 1914, pages 233–238 and 325–330. Translation from Turkish and introduction by M. Şükrü Hanioğlu.

1. "Mansurizade M. Said Bey," *İş ve Düşünce* (*Labor and Thought*), number 25, November-December 1959, pp. 2–3; Mecdut Mansuroğlu, "Mansurizade Sait Bey," in Ahmet Halil, editor, "Mansuroğlu Ailesi ve Kültür Tarihimizdeki Hizmetleri" (The Mansuroğlu Family and Their Contribution to our Cultural History), *İş ve Düşünce* (*Labor and Thought*), number 27, January-March 1961, pp. 6–8.

Let us then set out a truth which is accepted by the founders of all the [four Sunni] schools of law and by the jurists at large, one which cannot conceivably be doubted, since it stems, as I will explain, from a revealed text.

It is this: the verse "obey God and the Messenger and those in authority among you" [Qur'an, Sura 4, Verse 59] commands absolute obedience to the authorities.

This verse states that the authorities should be obeyed regardless of what they order or prohibit. Since the verse does not mention any restriction concerning the matters in which the authorities should be obeyed, it follows that, as explained in the relevant science, this is an ordinance of unrestricted application, and it is thus to be understood that it is obligatory to obey the authorities in whatever they order or prohibit. Thus the ordinance we learn from this verse is unrestricted and unconditional.

There is, however, a point to be made here. It would indeed seem logical to say that the fact that the ordinance is unconditional means that even if the authorities go against shari'a, prohibiting things it commands and ordering things it prohibits, it is still necessary to obey the authorities. And yet it is impossible to imagine any law at all—not just the shari'a—which would disregard its own commands and prohibitions in this way, and enjoin obedience to commands and prohibitions which contradict them. Is it to abandon its own demands and impose conformity to demands that are incompatible with them? Suppose that the authorities give the order, "Do not obey the Lawgiver [God]." In such a case, how could it be a duty imposed by the shari'a to obey the authorities? Would not the shari'a have been voided altogether?

Thus it is obviously necessary to supplement the unconditional command to obey the authorities, which the verse contains, by adding as a condition that the commands and prohibitions of the Lawgiver must not be violated. But limiting the scope of the text in this way means establishing an exception to the unconditional character of the ordinance, an exception which specifies that one should not obey when the command of the authorities contradict commands and prohibitions of the shari'a. Thus it could be objected that such an exception, which seems to contradict texts but in reality is laid down by texts, is not established by scholarly opinion based upon personal judgment and analogical reasoning. One

cannot resort to opinion in the face of a text; on issues pertaining to texts, there is no place for ijtihad [interpretation].

An exception of this kind is established by self-evident reason and necessity; it is in the nature of a narrowing of the scope on the basis of reason. While it is impermissible to limit the scope of texts by recourse to scholarly opinion, it can be done on the basis of reason. When the legal theorists enumerate ways in which the scope of texts can be limited, they mention reason as the first of them. In sum, reason is one thing, and scholarly opinion is another. The scope of texts can be limited through reason, but not through scholarly opinion, because on issues where there is a text, there is no place for such opinion.

Thus, in the view of the jurists, limiting the scope of the verse and explaining the exception to it mean that if the authorities order the contrary of something that is obligatory according to shari'a, or order the performance of something that is forbidden by shari'a, in short if they go against the orders and prohibitions of shari'a, then there is no duty to obey them.

The reason is that if the authorities are obeyed in such a matter, then the Lawgiver is being disobeyed, and this is sin. The Prophet has stated that "no obedience is due to a creature in a matter involving disobedience to the Creator."

Thus on this question of obedience to the authorities, the views of the jurists and opinions of the schools are unanimous. We encounter neither disagreement among the schools nor clashes of opinion.

This is because, as I have explained, this is an issue that is fully resolved on the basis of reason and revelation.

Because ijtihad is not permissible on issues where there is a text, there is no place for it in the face of such a clear-cut text; in the same way, there is no possibility of opposing self-evident reason. In sum, it is established by clear evidence of reason and revelation that it is a duty to obey all the orders of the authorities regardless of what they are, subject to the condition that these must not contravene the shari'a. If, however, they contravene the orders and prohibitions of the shari'a, then according to the shari'a it is not permissible to obey them. Of these two judgments, the first rests on revelation, and the second on reason. Both of them, as I have explained, are incontrovertible ordinances free of any dispute or disagreement.

From this it follows that it is a duty to obey all orders or prohibitions of the authorities in matters regarding which the *shari'a* neither commands nor forbids—things that are neither obligatory nor forbidden, but simply licit. This is because in such cases the authorities are not ordering the omission of an obligatory act or the performance of a prohibited act. Thus this ordinance is free of any doubt or uncertainty; and it is the unambiguous sense of the text.

No disagreement among the schools or conflict of scholarly opinion can take place regarding the meaning of such texts.

Accordingly the authorities have broad power to issue orders and prohibitions on all matters regarding which the *shari'a* takes no stand, a power that is not subject to limitation.

Since, as I have explained, the authorities have no authority to prohibit something obligatory or command something prohibited, if their authority in such permissible issues were denied, they would be left with no authority according to the *shari'a* to order or prohibit anything, and the verse would have no force or meaning.

The *shari'a* grants to the authorities a power so great that it considers their commands and prohibitions tantamount to its own. If the authorities order something, then their orders have the force of a legal obligation just like commands of the *shari'a*. Similarly, if they prohibit something, this will become something prohibited under the *shari'a*. It decrees that anything that the authorities prohibit becomes prohibited by the *shari'a*, because the *shari'a* decrees that obeying the authorities is a duty.

Thus the *shari'a* reinforces the commands and prohibitions of the authorities. Can any greater authority be imagined?

Had the authorities not been empowered by the *shari'a* to order and prohibit, the *shari'a* would have voided rather than confirmed their [right to] command and prohibit—just as it decrees, as I have explained, that if the authorities ban something commanded by the *shari'a* or order an act which is prohibited by it, this will not be valid; it voids such orders and prohibitions of the authorities.

In sum, it is an established, indubitable, and inconvertible fact that the authorities have a wide authority in ordering or prohibiting within the general category of licit things; this rule has no exceptions, and cannot be restricted in any way. This authority is based upon an unambiguous legal text.

Now polygamy is precisely something which is neither commanded nor prohibited in the *shari'a*, and which is simply declared to be licit by the [Qur'anic] verse that states, "Marry the women who please you, two, three, or four." [Sura 4, Verse 3]

The authorities, that is to say the government, thus have full power to prohibit polygamy outright or to subject it to certain conditions. As I have explained, there is no obstacle to this in the *shari'a*, since in the view of *shari'a* the authorities have a wide power to issue orders or prohibitions and to legislate, in matters that are licit. If such a law were to be issued, the *shari'a* would confirm rather than invalidate it, since it would be an order issued by the authorities. The ordinances of the *shari'a* on polygamy would then be neither more nor less than the contents of this law.

It is the same with marriage and divorce. As with polygamy, there exists no command or prohibition of the *shari'a* regarding them, and only their permissibility is specified. Thus it is beyond any doubt that, in the eyes of the *shari'a*, the authorities have full power to make laws which accord with the community's general moral values regarding these issues. It is also worth mentioning that some of those who discuss the subject of polygamy want to resolve the question by arguing that according to the *shari'a* polygamy is conditional on fairness [in the treatment of co-wives], which is impossible to achieve; therefore, they say, it is necessary to ban polygamy by making a law against it.

It is indeed true that fairness is unattainable in polygamy, and that it is therefore necessary to prohibit it by law. It appears, however, that the *shari'a* does not countenance such a solution, since it explicitly declares polygamy to be licit. Thus no resolution is to be found in this line of argument. The discussion goes on and on, and the *shari'a* continues to be criticized.

Thus there is nothing to be gained in the face of such an imaginary prohibition by saying that fairness cannot be attained in polygamy, and that it is therefore necessary to prevent it by making a law against it. The reason is that if the prohibition conflicts with what is allowed, the prohibition prevails. This is not only one of the basic principles of jurisprudence but is also in accord with the demands of reason and the fundamental law of nature. Thus as long as the prohibition actually exists, that which is allowed cannot be implemented or have any effect. Therefore, as I stated at the outset, it is necessary to explain that there is no such prohibition in the *shari'a*, and it is simply imaginary. The issue of fairness is of secondary importance, and it would merely be one reason for the law, among others.

[. . .] The issue of the prohibition of polygamy in Islam is essentially a straightforward matter; it is not something invented by me on the basis of my own scholarly opinion, as [Babanzade] Ahmed Na'im Bey [1872–1934] maintains. It is something that necessarily follows the principles of jurisprudence and a very explicit verse. So much so that the time has long come to show the real face of the *shari'a* in relation to an issue which has been covered with the dark veil of ignorance and fanaticism for many years, and which at the same time has generated endless and fruitless debates. [. . .]

If it is objected that a law prohibiting polygamy would not serve the public interest, this would raise a different issue. Our aim here is simply to point out that it is within the powers granted to the authorities by the *shari'a* to make laws regarding matters which are licit, when there is a public interest in doing so. It is also worth mentioning that, while the fundamental rational principle that "the discretionary power of the ruler may only be used beneficially" does restrict the broad power of the authorities in ordering and prohibiting to a certain degree, there is nevertheless no doubt that this restriction is of the type discussed in my original article. That is to say, it is a restriction arising from reason, and not from scholarly opinion.

Thus there is no conflict of opinion or scholarly disagreement concerning the scope of the verse. There is only the arrogant and stubborn clamor of ignorance and fanaticism arising from the panic at the prospect that this could make it possible to prohibit polygamy. The verse is quite explicit and unequivocal. No jurists resorting to their own opinion, no commentators on the Qur'an, can restrict or limit the verse in question. [. . .]

25

Islam and Modern Civilization

Ziya Gökalp (Turkey, 1876–1924) was a founder of Turkish nationalism. Encouraged by his father, an admirer of Namık Kemal (see chapter 17) and other modernists, he sought both Western and Islamic educations. The tension he experienced between the two led to a suicide attempt in 1894, and Gökalp lived with a bullet in his brain until his death. In 1898, he was arrested for his contacts with the Young Turk opposition, spent a year in prison, and was restricted to his home town of Diyar-ı Bekir, where he served in minor government positions and, according to his own account, read hundreds of books in French on sociology, psychology, and philosophy. Following the Constitutional Revolution of 1908, he quickly became an important figure in the Committee of Union and Progress. In 1912, he was elected to parliament from Ergani Madeni and turned down the post of minister of education; in 1913, he became a professor of sociology at the University of Istanbul and taught sociology at a modern-style religious school, the Darü'l-Hilafeti'l-Âliye. In addition, he published widely, applying theories of idealism to Ottoman society. In his most famous articles, such as one presented here, Gökalp promoted the "Turkification, Islamification, and modernization" of the Ottoman Empire. In 1919, following the Ottoman defeat in World War I, he was court-martialed as one of the leaders of the Committee of Union and Progress, and exiled to Malta for two years. On his return, he resumed his writing and was elected to parliament from Diyar-ı Bekir.[1]

In one of our previous essays we have put forth the thesis that Islam and modern civilization are compatible. There are two possible procedures to verify this thesis: the first is to compare the foundations of Islam with those of modern civilization directly; the second is to enquire whether the points of incompatibility or agreement between Christianity and modern civilization present favorable or unfavorable implications for Islam. Here we shall first follow the second course, because it will show us that to the extent to which Christianity remained remote from the principles of Islam, it failed to reconcile itself with modern civilization, and that it was able to reconcile

itself with modern civilization only to the extent to which it approached [the principles of] Islam.

There is strong evidence for the argument that Islam is the most modern religion and in no way conflicting with modern science.

The first reason for the existence of a fundamental opposition between Christianity and Islam should be sought in the social conditions existing at the time of their rise. Christianity originated within a community that was under the domination of a powerful state and that had no hopes for political independence. Islam, on the other hand, flourished among a people free from external domination who had the capacity to establish an independent

Ziya Gökalp, "Islam and Modern Civilization," in *Turkish Nationalism and Western Civilization: Selected Essays of Ziya Gökalp*, translated from Turkish by Niyazi Berkes (London: George Allen and Unwin, 1959), pp. 214–223. First published in 1917. Introduction by M. Şükrü Hanioğlu.

1. Uriel Heyd, *Foundations of Turkish Nationalism: The Life and Teachings of Ziya Gökalp* (London: Luzac & Company, 1950); Ali Nüzhet, *Ziya Gökalp'in Hayatı ve Malta Mektupları* (*Ziya Gökalp's Life and Malta Letters*) (Istanbul, Turkey: İkbal Kütüphanesi, 1931); Şevket Beysanoğlu, *Doğumu'nun 80. Yıldönümü Münasebetiyle Ziya Gökalp'in İlk Yazı Hayatı, 1894–1909* (*Ziya Gökalp's Early Life as a Writer, 1894–1909, on the Occasion of the 80th Anniversary of His Birth* (Istanbul, Turkey: Diyarbakırı Tanıtma Derneği Yayını, 1956); Rıza Kardaş, "Ziya Gökalp," in *İslam Ansiklopedisi* (*Encyclopedia of Islam*) (Istanbul, Turkey: Maarif Matbaası, 1988), volume 13, pp. 579–617; Cavit Orhan Tütengil, *Ziya Gökalp Sosyolojisinin Temel İlkeleri* (*The Foundations of Ziya Gökalp's Sociology*) (Ankara, Turkey: Kültür ve Turizm Bakanlığı Yayınları, 1987); Hilmi Ziya Ülken, *Ziya Gökalp* (*Ziya Gökalp*) (Istanbul, Turkey: Kanaat Kitabevi, 1939).

state, although they lacked such an organization at the time. "State" means a public authority which has the power to enforce its judicial rules over the individuals whose safety it undertakes. At the time of the rise of Christianity, the Roman state and its laws were in force. Christianity found a political organization already in existence, and thus it took the matters of organizing a government and maintaining laws as matters outside the concern of religion. It accepted the separation of state and religion as a principle, and formulated it in the slogan "render unto Caesar that which is Caesar's and unto God that which is God's." Thus, Christianity seems at first sight like a religion that has left judicial powers entirely to the government and has concerned itself exclusively with pronouncements on matters of righteousness and ethical teachings.

The real nature of things, however, was not that way at all. Christianity, by accepting the state outside of religion, was relegating the state to a non-sacred realm. It did not appropriate the state to itself because it looked down on it. This attitude, originally due to the fact that the Romans were foreign to the early Christians both from the point of view of nationality and of religion, did not disappear altogether even when the conditions changed. Although Christianity took on political government outside of the realm of religion, it nevertheless brought to the world a new government under the name of Heavenly Kingdom. Thus, two kinds of government came into existence in Christendom, one as the non-sacred, temporal government, and the other as the sacred, spiritual government. If Christianity had not found an already existing order of state at the time of its birth, it would have attempted undoubtedly to create one, and then it would have regarded it as a sacred being of its own creation. As this government would have been within the religion and, as such, a sacred institution, no need would have been felt to establish a spiritual government. If this had happened, there would be no duality of temporal and spiritual governments but, rather, something similar to the case existing in Islam.

Europeans who have compared Christianity and Islam usually believe that Islam's acceptance of judicial matters as part of religion, and of the state organization as part of religious organization, is a defect in Islam. Even some Muslims who have received their ideas from the same sources think the same way. However, when the problem is investigated more

carefully, it appears that this is not a defect but, on the contrary, a merit.

In Islam, religious provisions are divided into three categories—those relating to piety, to morality, and to judicial affairs. All of them are religious because they are sacred. Religion is the sum total of all beliefs that are taken as sacred by an *umma* [religious community]. Aesthetic and rational rules are non-sacred, and therefore they are outside of religion. Islam takes ethical and legal rules as religious rules and thus makes them sacred. This conception is contrary to the interpretations of ethics and law from the point of view of utilitarianism, historical materialism, and the doctrine of social contract. Over against these points of view, it attributes to them a supra-individual, sacred, and transcendental character. Modern sociology entirely justifies and confirms this point of view of Islam.

Although Islam brings everything sacred under religion, at the same time it divides them into three categories, ascribing to each a different sanction. The sanctions of the rules of piety are otherworldly sanctions; those of the judicial rules, legal sanctions; and of the ethical rules, the sanctions of *'urf* [community mores]. In Islam, which commands in accordance with *ma'ruf* [the good] and prohibits in accordance with *munkar* [evil], criteria of ethical rules are *'urf*. All the investigations of modern sociology have but confirmed the same thing.

When Christianity accepted the need for a spiritual government, it did not take it as a mere metaphysical expression. This government, although spiritual, would not content itself with a mere spiritual sanction; it would also demand a material sanction. Islam believed in the existence of a supreme court in the Hereafter, where the accounts of piety of our actions would be settled. Christianity, in its attempts to support its spiritual government by a material sanction, went much farther by bringing that court into this world and institutionalizing it, in the Middle Ages, in the so-called courts of inquisition. In Islam, the maxim "*shari'a* [religious law] decides for *zahir* [outward appearance]" is well known. The spiritual courts of Christianity extended their penetrating inquisitiveness to the realm of the inner private conscience of man and attempted to measure the faith of persons. But the spiritual government was composed not only of these courts. It also had its councils, which were a sort of parliament legislating laws on matters of piety and making ecclesiastical laws.

As politics is based on national sentiments perceived by men of action through experience, the rule of the majority in political matters may be an adequate basis. On these matters the opinions of the experienced ignorant may, in many cases, be better than those given by inexperienced learned persons. Thus, in politics, the fact that the learned are few and the ignorant many may not be an obstacle to the rule of the majority. Matters of piety, on the other hand, are entirely matters of learning and specialization. Thus, it is not permissible to decide matters of piety on the basis of the rule of the majority in such Councils, and to make such decisions obligatory. The opinion of the majority cannot be binding on matters of piety, just as it cannot be on questions of science. The majority commits few mistakes on political matters, and no great harm proceeds from them. On matters of piety, on the other hand, the error is greater and its consequences for otherworldly salvation are more dangerous. For this reason, Islam never constituted any Council and never made enactments on any matter of faith or worship on the basis of majority opinion, as if this were issued as law. The Councils did not content themselves with promulgating beliefs and prayers in the form of laws, but they issued laws providing earthly punishments for matters of conscience, forgetting that only the sublime court of the Hereafter can do this. As spiritual public authority was vested in the Councils and in the Papacy, the decrees of the latter were regarded as binding when the Councils were not in session. The interpretations of the popes were infallible, like those of the decrees of the Councils. The meaning of the Islamic saying "*Ijtihad* [rational interpretation] does not abrogate *ijtihad*" will be understood better when we compare it with the idea of infallibility of the popes and Councils, which may abrogate all opinions of the learned. In Islam, the *fatwa* [religious ruling] issued by a certain office does not prevent the *mufti*s [religious officials] from issuing *fatwa*s in accordance with their own opinions. The *hadith* [tradition of the Prophet] saying, "Consult yourself, et cetera," shows how wide are the limits of the freedom of *ijtihad* in Islam. The acceptance of the maxim, "*Ijtihad* does not abrogate *ijtihad*," does not mean that a judicial decision does not abrogate others. A judicial decision abrogates another act of a court, but one *ifta'* [ruling] does not abrogate another *ifta'*. The *Shari'a* Examination Board [an Ottoman institution] abrogates the decisions of the *shar'* [religious law] courts by cassation, and the *qadi*s [judges] as delegates of the caliph, are under the obligation of following what the caliph has decreed on those matters which are subject to *ijtihad*. The *mufti*s, on the other hand, do not have to make their *ifta'*s within such limitations. In Christianity the "*mufti*s" have to follow the "*fatwa*s" of the pope or of the Councils. In the Greek Orthodox Church, too, the decrees of the Holy Synod have the authority of a kind of *ifta'* in a similar manner. In Islam, any person who has the qualifications to *ifta'* has the right to exercise it, but no one may ever have the same authority on the basis of position. Only Revelation is the authority behind the *ifta'*.

Islam's inclusion of judicial provisions into the provisions of religion, and its acceptance of the sacredness of the state, is not a shortcoming but a merit, for if it had seen government and law as profane and secular institutions, it would have invented a spiritual government such as we find in Christianity. It was because Islam did otherwise that organizations having a spiritual authority or the authority to issue decrees on matters of faith, such as Councils, Holy Synods, Inquisition courts, and ecclesiastical courts, were not established in it. Islam did not establish institutions contrary to the laws of nature and life, such as a priesthood. It was because Islam had brought state, law, and court into the realm of the sacred that those traits such as loyalty to the secular ruler, a genuine fraternity and solidarity among the believers, sacrifice of interests and life for the sake of *jihad* [holy struggle], tolerance and respect towards the opinions of others, which are the very basis of a permanent order in society, were cultivated among all Muslims as common virtues.

Let us now look at the modes of relation between spiritual and temporal governments, and the differences existing between these and the regime accepted in Islam.

These modes of relations may be reduced to four basic regimes: The first form is what we may call Papalism, which is based on the universal authority of the popes. In this form, all authority on matters of both piety and politics are combined in the office of papacy. According to this system, Christian ecclesiastical sovereigns in general, such as bishops, are subject to the authority of the pope. Gregory VII [pope, 1073–1085] had said: "Why should not the papacy, having acquired the right of leadership in spiritual matters, also acquire the right to conduct temporal affairs? Temporal powers may see the glories of sovereignty higher than those of the bishops. The differences between the two will be understood by looking at their origins. Rulership is the product of the vanity of man, while the bishopric is the institution of God." Long before these words were uttered, Saint Ambrose [bishop, 339–397] had declared that the superiority of the bishop over the ruler is like the superiority of gold over silver. These declarations from the authorities suffice to expound the Catholic view on the matter.

The second form is Caesaro-Papism. This form, which existed in Russia, means that the ruler has the functions of papacy. Since the end of the sixteenth century, the Muscovy patriarchs, supported by the Russian episcopates, severed themselves from the Patriarchate of Constantinople, and since then they began to get supreme power into their hands, which caused the tsars some concern. Consequently, at a Council which convened at Moscow in 1666, Nikon [1605–1681] was dismissed from his office. However, this defeat did not stop the successors of Nikon from following the older policy. Finally, in 1720, Peter the Great [tsar, 1682–1725] declared himself the head of the Russian Church and put an end to the ambitious aims of the patriarchs. The next year Peter assembled a Holy Synod composed of archbishops, bishops, and archimandrites. The Holy Synod was headed by the tsar, the members were appointed, and decisions were ratified by him to be enforced. Thus, the tsar became an absolute ruler in religion over matters of faith, worship, and discipline.

This regime disrupted the safe conduct of both political and religious affairs. In accordance with political considerations, tsars could intervene in the foundations of religion by forcing the Holy Synod to issue decrees contrary to the provisions of religion. They thus arrested social progress and prevented political and social innovations, by utilizing men of religion, who became their most loyal instruments, in their attempts to keep people under their absolute rule. However, that was the result of the efforts to find a remedy against the principles of Christianity which were unfavorable to the establishment of an independent government. The Russians could establish an independent state only by accepting the papacy of the tsars.

The third system is the concordate system. The relation between temporal and spiritual governments found a solution in the Orthodox Church in the form of a harmful but durable system, while in Catholicism it remained in constant anarchy. Popes used to claim authority over political matters, and the rulers declined to accept such claims because just as religion cannot recognize a power above itself neither can the state. In the Orthodox Church, religion was sacrificed for the sake of the state. In Roman Catholicism, on the other hand, popes wanted to sacrifice the state for the sake of religion, and sought as vicars of God to become the rulers of the rulers over the earth, following the ancient Roman Caesars. When the temporal rulers were powerful, they rejected such a condition of dependence, which is contrary to the nature of state, and issued decrees about the limits of this authority of the bishops within their territories. When the popes realized that they were unable to curb the powers of the kings, they began to negotiate with them, trying to conclude concordats that would be in their own favor as far as possible. But these concordats were never made sincerely. The popes accepted them only temporarily in order to regain once again complete jurisdiction under a favorable situation. They even did not conceal their belief that these concordats were unilateral only, and that they were not binding on the Church. The history of Europe is full of such concordats, continuously changing and always dragging both sides into conflicts.

The fourth system is the separation of the state from the Church. The impossibility of maintaining the relationship between the state and the Church under the concordat regime was realized at last in France, and the French Parliament [after the revolution of 1789] decided to separate these two powers from each other completely. From that time on, France did not have an official religion, and the churches ceased to have any official character. They would be just private associations under the Statute of Associations. Thus, the state became completely laicized and religion unofficial. Although this has been a grave source of sickness for the French nation, it was nevertheless a necessary consequence of Catholicism.

The only natural consequence of the conflict of Christianity with the political government could be either Caesaro-Papism or laicism. The ideal [of the universal authority] of the "popes" has been realized only in Tibet. But this was due to a tricky measure of the Chinese government. In the first century of the *hijra* [the exodus of Muslims from Mecca in 622 that marks the beginning of the Islamic calendar], the kingdom of Tibet had conquered a great portion of China and Turkistan and had established a great empire. The Chinese succeeded in expelling the Tibetan king by encouraging the Dalai Lamas [Tibetan Buddhist religious leaders] and supporting them with military forces. From that time on, Dalai Lamas remained in Tibet as absolute sovereigns; but the Tibetan people came to their present state of backwardness under such a government.

The above explanations show that Christianity is irreconcilable with a modern state. Let us now look at Islam from that point of view. In Islam, both state and law are within religion. The provisions of religion comprise judicial rules and prescriptions of piety. The execution of judicial functions are given to the caliph. The *faqih*s [Islamic legal scholars] proven to be qualified as *mufti*s are charged with the task of purveying the provisions of piety. They are under the judicial authority of the caliphs but are not bound in their *ifta*'s by the latter's opinions. *Qadi*s are delegates of the caliph and exercise their judicial functions as his deputies and, thus, on the matters which are subject to *ijtihad* they are bound to follow the judgment preferred by the caliphs, even if this judgment is not in accord with the *ifta*', or even if it is beyond the opinions of any of the four schools of *fiqh* [Islamic jurisprudence], because the caliph's opinion and decree is "to be carried out judicially" and, as such, it is of the nature of law, whereas any opinion which is to be carried out as *ifta*' is not of a legal nature.

There are, for example, several judgments given as *ifta*'s in the *fiqh*s of the Shafi'i, Maliki, and Hanbali schools [three of the four main Sunni legal schools], which the *mufti*s of these schools follow in their *ifta*'s. In the Ottoman lands, on the other hand, the *qadi*s judged only according to the Hanafi *fiqh* [the fourth legal school]. Thus, only the pronouncements of the Hanafi *fiqh* were judicially followed and had assumed the nature of law; those of the other three schools remained subject to *ifta*'. Furthermore, the Ottoman caliphate had accepted only five of the books of *fatwa* of the Hanafi school as subject to judicial application, and the *qadi*s judged only on the basis of these. But even the Hanafi *mufti*s were not under any obligation to restrict themselves to these five books of *fatwa*. The codification of the *Mecelle-i Ahkam-ı 'Adliye* [*Compendium of Legal Statutes*, 1876] was meant only to show the provisions to be judicially followed by the *qadi*s, and not to be provisions followed in *ifta*'s of *mufti*s.

It follows from these considerations that *mufti*s are absolutely free and independent in declaring the provisions of piety, although they are dependent upon the ruler or the caliph, because the caliph, although having judicial authority, lacks any authority over matters of piety such as the Catholic pope or the Russian tsar enjoyed. However, the *mufti* does not have any authority over matters of piety either. The *mufti* only has the authority of *ifta*', simply because of his competence in learning. There is a great difference between "authority" and "competence." Thus, the judicial right belongs exclusively to the caliph, since he has judicial authority. But the *ifta*' authority of the *mufti* does not give the right of *ifta*' to him exclusively. There is no question of a right of *ifta*'; there is only the question of competence in *ifta*'. The fact that the *mufti* has no authority over matters of piety shows that there is no *ifta*' government of the *mufti*s in addition to the judicial government of the caliphs. There is only one government in Islam, which is the caliph's government. Thus, the caliph is entirely independent in his judicial government; and the *mufti* is equally independent in teaching and declaring the provisions of piety. Neither do judicial provisions obstruct the safe application of the provisions of piety, nor do the latter intrude into the safe course of the judiciary.

In one of our previous essays, we have shown that *qada*' [judgeship] and *ifta*' cannot be united in one office. But there are exceptions to this rule. There was no harm in their unification in the Prophet Muhammad's person. He was in a position which would not confuse the two, because, in addition to these two functions, he had the function of *risala* [prophetic mission] also. Whenever he failed in either of the first two, revelation corrected him.

In a secondary form, *ifta*' and *qada* may unite in the caliph, because the *qadi*s who are the caliph's delegates have to follow his opinion. If the *qadi* is dependent in his judicial action and independent in his capacity as *mufti*, he will be in a difficult position. What will happen if his opinion does not agree with the caliph's opinion? Therefore, it would be strange for him to exercise his *ifta*' according to his own opinion after judging the contrary opinion of the caliph. Furthermore, judicial provisions have been compromised with certain exigencies under legal casuistry. When the *qadi* follows them, and when he acts as a sort of judiciary, how can he issue a *fatwa* in contradiction to it? How can he have two consciences at the same time to pronounce the same thing both permissible and nonpermissible? The *qadi* may exercise *ifta'* only if he can face these difficulties in his position.

Let us now turn to our main topic. It has been seen above that Islam is not contrary to a modern state, but, on the contrary, the Islamic state means a modern state. But how did it happen that the modern states came into existence only in Christendom?

When we study the history of Christianity, we see that, following the Crusades [11th–13th centuries], a new movement started in Europe, which was then acquainted with Islamic culture. This movement aimed at imitating Islamic civilization and religion. It penetrated Europe with time, and finally culminated in Protestantism as a new religion entirely in contra-distinction to the traditional principles of Christianity. This new religion rejected the priesthood, and the existence of two kinds of government, spiritual and temporal. It also rejected the papacy, the Councils, the Inquisition—in short, all institutions which had existed in Christianity—as contrary to the principles of Islam. Are we not justified if we look at this religion as a more or less Islamicized form of Christianity? The modern state came into existence in Europe first in the Protestant countries. The constitutional regime appeared in England, the first nation-state was established in the United States, and the first culture-state came into existence in Germany. The racialist sociologists would believe that the superiority in civilization of these nations and of the Scandinavian nations was due to the fact that these nations belonged to the Germanic and Anglo-Saxon races. The sociologists of religion, on the other hand, believe that the decline of the Latin nations was due to their Catholicism, the backwardness of the Russians was a consequence of their Orthodoxy, and the progress of the Anglo-Saxon nations was the result of the fact that they had freed themselves from the Catholic traditions and approached the principles of Islam. If these principles taken by Protestantism from Islam were factors in this progress, do they not also constitute an experimental proof that Islam is the most modern and most reasonable religion? This being so, how is the attempt of the statesmen of *Tanzimat* [Ottoman administrative reforms of the 19th century] to organize the Islamic community in imitation of the [minority] "communities" existing in our country justifiable? Christian organizations appeared in a dependent people and they might suit only dependent "communities." Free nations and free states can reconcile themselves only with the institutions of Islam, because Islam originated in a free people who wanted to create an independent state.

Letter and Response

Džemaluddin Čaušević (Bosnia, 1870–1938) was a controversial religious reformer and educationalist. Son of a local religious leader in northwestern Bosnia, Čaušević received his early education from his father and thereafter at a Bosnian seminary school in Bihać. At the age of seventeen, he continued his studies in Istanbul, receiving both a traditional education and enrolling at the School of Law. Around 1900, Čaušević visited Cairo, where he met Muhammad 'Abduh (chapter 3) and attended his lectures for several months. 'Abduh left a lasting impression on Čaušević, who always referred to the Egyptian scholar as "Respected Teacher." Upon his return to Bosnia in 1903, Čaušević began his career as an Arabic language teacher and a member of the supreme council of the Bosnian Islamic community. Between 1914 and 1930, he served as *Reis al-Ulema*, the highest-ranking Islamic dignitary in the Kingdom of Yugoslavia. For Čaušević, the key reason for the malaise of Muslim society was poor education, rooted in the pitiful state of its educational institutions. He dedicated himself to the cause of educational reform with a missionary zeal typical of modernist Islam. He sought to promote literacy by introducing a simpler type of Arabic script for the Bosnian language. In 1937, he co-authored a Bosnian translation of the Qur'an, along with a commentary. Čaušević ran into opposition from conservative Muslims. As the following piece shows, the conflict spilled into a newspaper polemic with a respected community leader from Sarajevo, who accused him of contravening Islamic ordinances regarding veiling.[1]

[Letter from Hadži Mujaga Merhemić (Bosnia, 1877–1959) to Čaušević:]

Most enlightened sir!

The Majlis al-Jama'at [Community Council] has received your response of December 22 [1927] to our letter of the 20th of the same month, via the regional District Waqf-Ma'arif [Endowments-Education] Board, and has studied it with care.

First, the Majlis al-Jama'at notes with regret that you have failed to answer the main point of our letter, that is, concerning your statements to our press associates, which you also confirmed by your later statements.

The Majlis al-Jama'at expressed its concern that the manner in which the debate about these purely religious issues is being relayed to the press and the public could have very harmful consequences. Unfortunately, this concern has proven to be well-founded, and we can now see that this issue is discussed more by the unqualified than by the qualified, and in a way that hardly serves the interests of the Islamic community, and is detrimental to the issue itself. It is with regret that the Majlis al-Jama'at must state that you are responsible for this issue's having taken a direction it should never have followed.

Furthermore, the Majlis al-Jama'at has concluded from your response that your statements to the press,

Mehmed Džemaluddin Čaušević, "Pismo i Odgovor" (Letter and Response), *Novi Behar* (*New Bloom*), Sarajevo, Yugoslavia, number 19, 1928, pp. 290–295. Translation from Bosnian and introduction by Asim Zubčević.

1. Enes Karić, *Twentieth Century Islamic Thought in Bosnia-Herzegovina* (Sarajevo, Bosnia and Herzegovina: El-Kalem, 2001), pp. 107–224; Hfz. Mahmud Traljić, *Istaknuti*

Bošnjaci (*Prominent Bosniaks*), 2d ed. (Sarajevo, Bosnia and Herzegovina: Rijaset, 1998), pp. 51–58; Muharem Dautović, *Bibliografija Radova Džemaludina Čauševića* (*Bibliography of Works by Džemaluddin Čaušević*) (Sarajevo, Bosnia and Herzegovina: Takvim, 1998); Smail Balić, *Das unbekannte Bosnien* (*The Unknown Bosnia*) (Köln, Germany: Böhlau, 1992), pp. 339–344.

and the remarks you now quote in your response, are inconsistent for the following reasons:

1) The statements you made to the press, without explanation or qualification, show that you favor unveiling women, and are in favor of a step that cannot be harmonized with the *shari'a* [Islamic law] injunctions that Muslims of all *madhhabs* [schools of Islamic law] have upheld to this day, and to which we also strictly adhere, and which we by no means abandon.

2) It is stated in your response that you were instructed by your "Respected Teacher" [Muhammad 'Abduh, Egypt, 1849–1905; chapter 3] how to deduce legal rulings from the Qur'an, and to express your opinion accordingly, and so you say that a woman may go outside her home with her face unveiled, even though this judgment of yours contradicts other *shari'a* proofs, which Sunnis can in no way renounce, and without which they cannot survive. This is known from the whole literature bequeathed to us by the early Muslims, and upon which all of us Muslims have acted, with the exception of some heretics.

Enlightened sir! We surmise from your explanation, as you say yourself, that you wish to interpret Islam and its rules according to your own ability only, and to impose this upon others, whereas this contravenes the understanding of all *mujtahids* [religious scholars], who do not accept the isolated *ijtihad* [interpretation] of even much greater authorities [preferring to rely on *ijma'*, the consensus of authorities].

'Ulama' [religious scholars] throughout the Islamic world agree that all those who engage in *ijtihad*—which is restricted solely to those questions for which there is no manifest meaning from the reigning *madhhabs*—must be endowed with all the conditions for *ijtihad*, which your Respected Teacher surely did not possess, and only then may they become involved in the interpretation of such questions as call for great responsibility. The *'ulama'* of Islam count these people among the third category of jurisprudents, and call them *mujtahid fi'l-mas'ala* [scholars permitted to engage in *ijtihad* only on specific issues].

Let us take a glance at the history of legislation and see who these people are, and what kind of *'ulama'* belong to this category. The *'ulama'* of Islam do not find the preconditions for belonging to this category even in the case of the famous [Ahmad ibn 'Ali al-]Jassas [917–982], in whose shadow all the *'ulama'* of our century, including Respected Teacher, pale into insignificance.

Acting upon the clear meaning of the Qur'an involves great responsibility, since it requires a degree of education that the *'ulama'* do not find even in much greater authorities than those of the *'ulama'* of our century.

Enlightened sir! You say you deduce that it is permissible to unveil the face of women from Sura 24, Verses 30 and 31 [of the Qur'an]. In this you cite Jassas, taking only what suits you, and do not mention all that is in Jassas's *Ahkam al-Qur'an* [*Judgments of the Qur'an*]. Jassas deduces from the entirety [of sources] a ruling that a woman must be veiled, except in most exceptional cases, from which it by no means follows that—as you interpret it—she can go out in the street with her face unveiled.

You say in your statements that a woman may even go outside her home with her face unveiled without violating the injunctions of the Qur'an. We do not know how you have come to this conclusion.

You are aware of the fact that the five daily prayers were obligatory in Mecca, and that the way a woman should cover during prayer was determined at that time. It is said here [in the Qur'anic verse just cited] that a woman must cover everything except for her face, hands and feet. Later on a verse to which you refer was revealed, and which clearly states "and put their veils" [over their bosoms] and so on. [Sura 24, Verse 31]

If a woman is to cover everything except her face, hands and feet according to the very first injunction, what could be the legal force of the second verse?

Later on, yet another verse was revealed in which it says: "draw their outer garment over them" and so on, [Sura 33, Verse 59] from which it also follows that something else is to be covered apart from what has already been prescribed, so in what way do you derive a ruling that one should remain with what was prescribed for daily prayer?

The Noble Qur'an further says: "and do not display your adornments, as in the days of paganism," [Sura 33, Verse 33] which the *'ulama'* interpret to mean that a woman must not show her adornments, and if a woman's face is not her adornment, what else could it be? It also says in the noble verse, "and as for elderly women" and so on to the end [of the verse], [Sura 24, Verse 60] from which it indubitably follows that even in the case of old women who have no prospect of marriage and cannnot awaken a man's desire, it is better for them to be veiled.

In view of all the above-quoted verses, Jassas also finally states in his *Ahkam al-Qur'an* that a woman ought to be veiled, except during daily prayer.

Since the revelation of the verse concerning veiling, during the time of the Prophet, peace be upon him, the Companions [of the Prophet], the Successors [to the Companions], and to this day, women have been veiled, which is the best proof of your interpretation being wrong, since they surely knew the Noble Qur'an better than you do.

Enlightened sir! On this occasion we shall mention the interpretation and understanding of this matter by a great contemporary Islamic scholar, the late [Mehmet] Zihni Efendi [Turkey, 1845–1913], respected by all the *'ulama'* of our time, as testified by his good word and reports mentioned in it by a great pure one, the famous [Hoca Eminefendizade] 'Ali Haydar [Turkey, 1852–1918], and others.

This renowned Arabist, whose abilities even you cannot deny, has a different understanding and interpretation of the Qur'an from yours. On page 113 of his work of jurisprudence, *Mufarakat ve Münakehat* [*Separations and Marriages*], he says: "To say that the face is non-intimate (*na-mahrem*), outside the daily prayer, amounts to unpardonable error."

This work of his was approved by the religious officials [of the Ottoman Empire] and served as a handbook for all higher schools until the government of [Mustafa] Kemal Pasha [Atatürk, leader of Turkey, 1922–1938]; no one ever raised a voice against this ruling of his, nor did anyone call him a conservative or obscurantist on account of this; rather, he was respected and acknowledged by all, with litterateurs calling him the Noble One of the Age, while jurists call him the *imam* [religious leader] of our time.

3) It seems from your response that you take no account of these depraved times, but in an age when the whole civilized world is seeking ways to restrict female immorality, and when all the elders of other faiths are shouting, "Cover yourself," with your statements you unfortunately give our women, who are at present veiled, a justification for unveiling.

Concerned about Islamic morals, the Majlis al-Jama'at was the first to raise its voice a few years ago and take the initative in the establishment of a committee for the protection of morals. Although this was your duty [as Reis al-Ulema], the Majlis al-Jama'at took it upon itself to found this committee with the aim of uplifting those females who have faltered

morally. In an attempt to check the spread of immorality, the Majlis al-Jama'at asked the Mufti [leading religious official] of Sarajevo whether it would be permissible to unveil women who cannot be dissuaded from the immoral life in any other way, and thus stigmatize their actions, while protecting others who are veiled and chaste from temptation. The *fatwa* [ruling] from the Mufti was that even such women must not unveil.

4) It is said in your response that you would rather see one unveiled Muslim woman who makes an honest living, than one who is called veiled, and who parades herself flirtatiously in public places. We understand from this that you attach greater importance to the poor material conditions of Muslims than to religious injunctions. To this day we have not had the good fortune to see you taking any action that would enable our poverty-stricken women to earn an honest living without being exposed to all the temptations that threaten them in these depraved times, even when they are veiled, let alone if we were to throw her into the streets unveiled and lacking a proper upbringing.

If, by good fortune and by virtue of your duty, you had initiated this kind of action, we are convinced that all the Muslims of Bosnia and Herzegovina would have followed you on this path by now and be grateful to you, and we are firmly convinced that you would have achieved greater success in this than by allowing these purely religious issues to be discussed and dealt with in the newspapers, and by permitting unqualified people to meddle in these matters.

For no reason whatsoever, you made a statement in the premises of the Gajret [Effort Association], beginning with the words: "One cannot blaze a trail without being provocative" (*Gajret* newspaper, December 16, 1927, number 24), but we do not know whom you wish to provoke, and with whom you wish to engage in dispute, and against whom you wish to draw battlelines.

Taking into account the stir which your statements have caused among the citizens, on account of which there were calls for your action to be condemned in open meeting, the Majlis al-Jama'at, with the intention of protecting your standing and forestalling public debate about these purely religious matters, made representations to you through official channels, which you have treated with irony; instead of treating the matter as an official secret, you have given both our letter and your response to the daily press, from which it clearly follows that you wish and intend these purely religious issues be debated publicly, thus substantiating your statement given to the *Gajret*: "One cannot blaze a trail without being provocative."

Unfortunately, this challenge of yours has met with a response, since we have recently read in the Belgrade [newspaper] *Politika* [*Politics*] some observations by a so-called defender of your ideas, who does not shy away from calling a *hadith* [tradition of the Prophet] from the *Kutub al-sitta* [*The Six Books*, that is, the six most highly respected *hadith* collections] false and untrue.

When we read this, we rightly expected you to raise your voice against this unseemly scandal, but unfortunately that too failed to take place, since you did not react to this outrage.

As for the issue of religious endowments, the Majlis al-Jama'at has to state with regret that you have also raised these issues in a place where they do not belong at all. Endowment issues fall within the jurisdiction of a forum of ours, which is the only authority qualified and competent to discuss these issues. Making statements outside this forum could only have as its purpose to open the way for pressure on the Waqf-Ma'arif Board to stray from the path regulated by the endowments law.

The Majlis al-Jama'at is of the view that respect for endowment letters and the principles of the institution of the endowments have preserved the autonomous endowments, because we all witness how the central endowments foundation ended up, by buying bank shares, and that destiny could befall them too, through unification of the endowment property.

As for the question of wearing hats, on this issue the *'ulama'* have already taken a stand, and with reference to your *fatwa*, have expressed their view, which went contrary to your *fatwa*, and which was made public through special pronouncements. It is also known to the Majlis al-Jama'at that the *'ulama'* of Egypt have issued *fatwa*s concerning the wearing of hats, in accordance with all four *madhhab*s. These *fatwa*s were officially confirmed by the Shaykh al-Islam, the Shaykh al-Azhar and the Mufti of Egypt [leading religious officials], and are totally opposed to your decision on the matter and your recent statements.

Copies of the representations sent you by the Majlis al-Jama'at on the 20th of last month were also sent to the members of the Majlis al-'Ulama'; in the response it received to these representations, the members do not share your view either, just as they do not approve of individual declarations in these important matters, which justifies the Majlis al-Jama'at's reasons for warning you of the conclusions of the clergy with regard to your views.

The best proof that the view of Majlis al-Jama'at is wholly valid on all the issues mentioned in our representations is the statement from the Supreme Mufti of Belgrade, the enlightened Zeki Efendi, published in the Belgrade *Politika* of December 31, 1927, in which he gave a statement quite appropriate to his post, as befits the office he occupies, and referring to *shari'a* regulations, as well as the statement given through Mufti [Ibrahim] Maglajlić [Bosnia, 1861–1936].

In accordance with all of the above-mentioned, the Majlis al-Jama'at considers it its duty to state that your letter contains no real response to the questions asked that could satisfy this Majlis al-Jama'at.

Finally, the Majlis al-Jama'at must especially note also that its representations are an official document, and according to our education and the mores of the profession, greetings are not included in official communications, while you have treated this with irony in a manner unbecoming to a person who takes himself seriously, such as yourself.

Sarajevo, January 12, 1928
President H. M. Merhemić

To the Sarajevo Waqf-Ma'arif [Board of the] Majlis al-Jama'at, via the regional District Waqf-Ma'arif Board in Sarajevo

I have received your letter of January 12, and here is my response:

My responses are in accordance with what God prescribes in the Qur'an, and although I am familiar with what *shari'a* jurists and commentators have said, I prefer to abide by the prescriptions of the Qur'an, because it is eternal and for all times. This is what the Qur'an itself prescribes for me, since it prescribes reflection, study and research. In this regard I do not need your authorization, and therefore it is needless to gainsay me what God Almighty has called upon me to do. It was particularly excessive to criticize my former and present professors. The hierarchy of *shari'a* jurists is well known to me. This hierarchy is man-made, and was not prescribed in the Qur'an.

If you refer to that hierarchy so that you can say, "This person is better than that," this is wrong, because only He who sees all, hears all, and knows all can know who is better than whom. No religious scholar has ever spoken to me in such terms as you have. It is well-known that all four great *imams* [the founders of the four main Sunni *madhhabs*] always used to say, "We do not compel anyone to accept what we consider to be right; everyone is free to use a source, if he can; we ask no one to follow us blindly." Apart from this, you know that the faith of Islam recognizes no forum that could prohibit what the Qur'an has made permissible. In Islam, you cannot call someone *kufr* [unbelief] unless he himself so wishes.

You say that all Muslims to this day have adhered to the *shari'a* ordinances concerning the veiling of women, which does not accord with the truth. First of all, there are places in our homeland where Muslim women go out with their faces unveiled, yet conduct themselves very properly and decently. Furthermore, our courtship customs show that we have never followed that jurisprudential ruling. Moreover, our girls of twenty or more have not even covered those parts that Sura 24, Verse 31 requires be covered. The *'ulama'* have observed all this for centuries, but have not claimed that it did not exist. And now, the Majlis al-Jama'at wishes to turn a blind eye to this, so it claims that everything is covered. Quite apart from this, I know of areas in Turkey where Muslim women went out with faces unveiled even during the time of the caliphate and the religious officials [that is, during the Ottoman Empire]. During my studies at the time of the late Sultan Abdülhamid [II, reigned 1876–1909], and at the very time when the late Zihni Efendi was publishing his works, institutes of higher education for women were being opened in Istanbul, attended by thousands of students, all of them mature girls, taught by female Muslim teachers and professors with faces uncovered. All this was known both to the caliph himself and the Shaykh al-Islam as well as to *muftis*, judges, and military judges, and yet, by God, not one so much as paid a glance to Zihni Efendi's mistake. I am familiar with a good part of Arabia and all three parts of Egypt. There too things are not the way you imagine them. In Egypt, Muslim women who work in fields and factories go about with faces and hands uncovered. It is the same in Upper Egypt, while in the Nubian desert, near Lake Chad, live the Tuareg Muslims whose men veil their

faces and whose women go unveiled. In Egypt, Muslim girls who study wear special garments, and their faces are unveiled. All the women teachers in girls' schools are Muslims, and they go about with their faces unveiled. The situation is similar in Yemen, from Kawkaban to Taghz and Lahj. Moreover, there they carry on their heads a large basket like an umbrella, which they call "*muzilla*." And I have been informed by a reliable source that even in Persia, where the veiling of women has been most strictly enforced, there are places where Muslim women go unveiled. The same goes for Afghanistan, while in Russia, Muslim women too have been unveiled for a long time now, and play a prominent role in the field of science, while some are doctors, and many are teachers and book-keepers.

I did not use citations from Jassas to interpret my responses to you. I mentioned them to someone else and quoted his interpretation as an example. Kindly, therefore, take a closer look at my first letter. What I quoted from Jassas also corresponds to the Qur'an, because I do not invoke *al-Hidaya* [*Guidance*, by Burhanuddin Marghinani, died circa 1197], nor many other *shari'a* jurists who share similar views, but only the Qur'an. I affirm, and both my former and present professors also affirm, that the Qur'an demands purity of heart and soul, and decent conduct, from both men and women.

You refer to Sura 24, Verse 31, emphasizing certain words. . . . God alone knows what you meant, because you did not even wish to explain them. In this passage it is said that Muslim women should place a "*khimar*" over their bosoms. It was the custom in Arabia for women to wear a type of dress through which one could see the bosom, and this was not appropriate for modesty, so there came the order to cover those parts. All of this verse, from "And put" to the end, refers to those secret adornments that cannot be displayed to anyone without necessity, other than to one's husband and close relatives. There is not a word in it about covering the face. "*Khimar*" is similar to our shawl, which the women in Yemen, who wear a basket on their heads, put over their shoulders and fasten at the neck and bosom. In San'a' they draw the *khimar* over their heads and tie it at the neck so that the two ends cover the bosom, as understood from the words "over their bosoms."

You refer to some first command concerning veiling, and you have concluded from this verse that everything must be veiled, even the face. This interpretation is entirely false, since the verse is very clear. The verse says that Muslim women should cast down their eyes, guard their private parts for this is purer for them, and not reveal their adornments, save such as are outward; these are the hands and the face, because these are a woman's outward adornment. In Sura 24, Verse 30, Muslim men, too, are required to cast down their eyes and guard their private parts, from which it clearly follows that the main thing—both for men and women—is a good upbringing and moral conduct, without which even veiling serves no purpose.

You also refer to Sura 33, Verse 59, and emphasize certain words, saying that something should be covered in addition to what was prescribed earlier. This is not at all what is to be understood here. It says that [women] should put on a *jilbab* [outer garment] and draw it close to themselves, and that women should not go about bare-chested. What is demanded here is modest dress, and there is not a word about veiling the face, except that some commentators interpret it to mean that the *jilbab* should be held in the hands in such a way so that only one eye can see, and this interpretation is taken as a difficult way [of performing a religious duty].

You refer to Sura 33, Verse 33, again considering certain words only, and so you conclude what absolutely cannot be understood from the verse. This verse is a special injunction concerning the noble wives of our Prophet. The verse calls upon the wives of the Prophet not to leave their houses without necessity, and not to behave in the street in the manner of women in the age of ignorance . . . and to remember what is recited in their homes, so as to learn the great signs of God and the Wisdom. . . . There is not a word in that verse about veiling women's faces. I said in my first letter (bearing in mind these injunctions): whoever is able to do so, let him conform to the injunctions concerning the most noble wives of our Prophet, and let him spread learning at home and teach his womenfolk skills, but I assure you that there are very few able to do so these days.

You also refer to Sura 24, Verse 60, and again deduce something that is not in the verse. The verse says that women who are past child-bearing and have no hope of marriage may—without committing a sin—put off their clothes, that is, the *jilbab* and *khimar*, but that it is better for them to guard their chastity and not to flaunt their adornments. Again, there is nothing here about veiling the face.

You hold it against me that I take no account of these depraved times, from which it follows that you did not understand me. For twenty-four years you have not understood me, so it seems that you will never understand me. I have always stood for what I affirm and answer for. During the war [World War I], when a workshop for sewing and mending military uniforms was set up, I recommended to many Muslim women that they work there to earn a living. Every time I went to the camp where the workshop was housed, I would always say to the Muslim women: "Behave nicely and decently, do not tarnish the name of Islam, and it is better for you to earn a living honorably than to be a burden on someone else." On that occasion, when they asked me, I said that they could have their faces and hands uncovered. When a delegation came to me asking to take these Muslim ladies away from the workshop, I explained everything to them, saying, "Each one who joins the workshop earns six crowns a day, and there are some who make as much as 12 crowns, or even 18. If you can secure a hundred crowns a month for every one of them (and there are now 140 of them) until the end of the war, I shall take them away immediately, but their places will be filled by others who can barely wait to be taken on." At this remark of mine the gentlemen asked for the workshop to be moved to the Kolobara and for a Muslim to supervise it, to which I replied that this was impossible for technical reasons. They left, and the women continued to work until the end of war.

Six years ago, when speaking in the Begova Mosque of the verse "a mother should not be made to suffer on account of her child," [Sura 2, Verse 233] I gave it a rather broad interpretation. I well remember what I said on that occasion: A mother must not harm her child in bringing it up, nor must a father in supporting it, but the ignorance of parents is the greatest harm to children. Then, adhering to the interpretation of my former and present teachers, I elaborated how, according to *shari'a* rules, it is the major duty of every girl to learn the prescriptions on bringing up children and to know the basic rules for protecting a child's health, and how this is something every girl must learn before marriage. I said that it is a duty of all Muslims to disseminate knowledge, both men and women. I explained the difficulties associated with [male doctors performing] the medical examinations needed by Muslim women, and so I emphasized the need to train Muslim women as doctors, and said that this was an individual duty [incumbent upon each Muslim]. I said at that time that Muslim women can pursue their studies with their faces unveiled.

I have criticized some members of the Gajret [Association], even in the Gajret premises. I said that they were a Muslim association, and that as such they were duty-bound to take care of the religious upbringing of the Muslim children entrusted to them, since they [through their association] have taken upon themselves a parental duty. I reproached them for not maintaining religious teachers in their boarding schools, so that the children could become more knowledgeable about religious prescriptions and the proper recitation of certain Qur'anic verses. I criticized them because they took Muslim girls who were unfamiliar with religious prescriptions to an exhibition in Novi Sad and beyond, and during Ramadan at that, and I said that this was inappropriate. Furthermore, I also criticized those who wore hats, both within the Gajret and outside it, and I said to them that it was not proper of them to fail in performing their religious duty, not to come to the mosque for prayer and listen to my lecture, not to come into contact with Muslims and help them with their knowledge. I called upon them to hold lectures, each on his profession, and gave the example of the intelligentsia of our fellow citizens of other religions; I stressed that they too should contribute wholeheartedly to the welfare of the Islamic community.

Therefore, your reproach that I have not done my duty is out of place. I have performed my duty as has no other Reis before me. For almost eight years I have been interpreting religious truths in the Begova Mosque, and I elaborate and recommend what is beneficial for the Islamic community. Having pointed a finger at the shortcomings of our religious upbringing, I have also recommended some remedies. I well remember saying on many occasions, while interpreting God's commands on mutual help, that all Majlis al-Jama'ats and regional boards should have a list of all the Muslims in their area. They should have a list from which it could be seen who has a guardian and tutor and who has not, how many children go to school and how many do not, who has a job and what kind, as the basis for determining what is best for every sector of the Islamic community. I said then that it is not right to expect of the Reis that he take care of every matter himself. I emphasized

that we should all be together, and I would be there too. Despite legal regulations which tie my hands, I have also done more in the field of education than any other Reis. I do not want to lay too much emphasis on all that I have done for the Islamic community, but I must tell you that I am very sorry that the very Majlis al-Jama'at which should best appreciate my work should reproach me for not performing my duty. If all the Majlis al-Jama'ats were to say the same, then I would have to affirm that the Muslim community in Bosnia and Herzegovina is ungrateful and does not know how to appreciate its people.

The words "one cannot move ahead without being provocative" were not used in the sense you attribute to them. While I was speaking on the Gajret premises about ways of making use of endowment buildings and property, particularly graveyards, someone shouted, "That would provoke the people," to which I replied, "One cannot move forward without being provocative," and I mentioned the example of building shops in front of the Ferhadija Mosque. I said that there had been complaints while the shops were being built outside the Ferhadija, and that a friend of mine had come to me angry that the mortal remains of his aunt had been exhumed and buried outside the Ferhadija *mihrab* [prayer niche facing Mecca]. There is no irony in my letter whatsoever. I am completely sincere and I sincerely express my thoughts, and therefore it was needless to ascribe to me any kind of irony. I am very far from that.

I hardly read our newspapers here, and even the Belgrade press; moreover, I had no time to read this letter of yours until three days ago. I do not know, therefore, who said what. Furthermore, until recently I did not even know that my responses had been characterized as a kind of statement, and you have probably also accepted that. Anyway, many things have been said about the Qur'an too, yet a gem remains a gem, and the hot sun keeps on shining. When you read that attack, you could have responded, since every Muslim is bound to speak and defend the truth.

There is not a word in my letters and responses about coercion, and in this regard you are completely wrong. I respect everyone's opinion, even if it does not agree with mine. Anyone who knows me well can confirm that. At the same time, I have quite a different understanding of the endowments and endowment letters from yours. In any case, those who come after us will be able to see who was right.

I do not know what makes you bring up the issue of wearing hats now. I gave a response regarding hats as long ago as early 1914. And what I said is true. I know what the *'ulama'* have said, but I also know that this does not correspond to the true source of Islam. As a matter of fact, the *'ulama'* of Egypt have said nothing new. They have said [quotation in Arabic], "In wearing a hat for the sake of *kufr*, *kufr* there will be. . . ." If someone intends *kufr* in putting on a hat, it will constitute *kufr*. And I say too, if someone means to become a *kafir* [unbeliever] by wearing a particular type of dress, he will become a *kafir*. Thus intention and will are crucial. If someone does not desire *kufr*, nothing can drive him into *kufr*.

I know that you have addressed a letter to my friends, because they told me so. I respect everyone's opinion, just as I respect the opinion of my friends and of *Hajji* Mufti Maglajlić, and even that of the supreme mufti, although I may not know what they said, but I value my own opinion the most, because that is how I was brought up. I impose nothing upon anybody, not even among my own circle. The Majlis al-Jama'at may take my response any way it wishes. A time will come after us when what Džemaluddin said and intended will be better understood.

The main Islamic centers of Afghanistan, Iran, and Egypt and their decision-making factors have already taken account of the serious upbringing of their womenfolk. The Muslims of these countries have been saying for a long time now that we must shake off our lethargy and disseminate knowledge in all sectors of the Islamic community, as the Qur'an demands, and they demonstrate this by their actions in Afghanistan and Iran, where special professional schools for womenfolk have been opened in which women study various sciences and are introduced to various skills and crafts. In addition, workshops have been opened for the employment of needy and able women. Egypt takes pride in these establishments, and in the hundreds of its educated ladies, who make a great contribution to their homeland in various fields. These Muslims feel the need for Muslim women to be educated in all the professions required by the Islamic community. They say that we must have Muslim women doctors, women teachers, women able to work in the sanitation departments, and women versed in various arts and crafts, as did our forefathers in previous centuries. We cannot, they say, get the better of Europe if we do not make the other half of our strength equal to the struggle and *jihad* [religious struggle]. . . . These decision makers, who represent millions of Muslims, know the Qur'anic injunctions and the life of the pious early Muslims better than all of us.

Necessity is a very powerful motive force. Necessity compels one to relinquish difficult ways of performing religious duties and to move to easier ways. It was on this basis that the *shari'a* jurists set out their arguments. Time achieves wonders. Time changed the *feredža* [full black mantle, worn with face-covering] into the *peča* [a gauzy veil over the face] with *vala* and *zar* [light outer wraps]. Time is changing both the *zar* and the *vala* into the *jilbab* known as *mantija* [mantle] and the semi-*vala*. There is a firm desire to draw a line of upbringing and pure education, so as not to go too far, so as to preserve what is most important—purity of heart and soul, while also meeting one's needs.

At the beginning of your letter, you pronounce me guilty of giving responses, from which I can see that you have not read my letter carefully, or perhaps you doubt my exposition. Am I guilty if someone is desirous of confusing terminology? Three days ago a meeting on municipal elections was held in the reading room; after discussions on the subject, a friend of mine, for whom I had done all I could and even what I should not have, stood up and said, no more no less, "Forget the elections and all that. Do you know that our religion is in danger? The Reis wants to put hats on our heads and to unveil our women." And he went on to say, agitatedly, "Let him wear a hat and unveil his own wife." Nobody among the Muslims present wanted to put him right or tell him that the religion is in danger from another quarter, which the Reis fears too—from ignorance. Not even the person who later read the letter from the Majlis al-Jama'at without my answer did so. If this was not incitement to rebellion, I don't know what is. I do not know of any reason for discussing this at meetings devoted to municipal elections. I have two unsigned letters sent from here to some districts, in which Muslims are called to rise up against Reis Čaušević's heresy. These letters were brought to my attention and for my use by Muslims, and time is already revealing both their authors and those who sent them. I am not the one, therefore, who is opening up a line of attack, but my best friends who are doing so against me.

I have not told anyone to wear a hat, I have not told anyone to unveil his wife. I merely interpret the truth and the easy paths of religious duty, and the needs that time has brought and continues to bring upon us. The Majlis al-Jama'at may take my answer however it wishes. There is nothing to prevent it, and I am only glad that the Majlis al-Jama'at will uphold the rules of the *shari'a* and has no intention of giving them up. You would have received this response more quickly and clearly had you come to me, and you would have received an answer concerning the Mufti of Sarajevo's *fatwa*, but—well—you do not accept even my greeting, proving thereby that your letters are official, and so I withdraw my previous "*Salaam aleykum*" [Peace be upon you]!

Sarajevo, January 27, 1928
Džemaluddin

Muhammad and Woman

'Abd al-Qadir al-Maghribi (Lebanon, 1867–1956) contributed to the development of modernist journalism in Egypt, Lebanon, and Syria during the late Ottoman and early French Mandate periods. The son of a religious law court official, he studied at a school established in Tripoli, Syria, by *Shaykh* Husayn al-Jisr (Lebanon, 1845–1909), a cautious advocate of reconciling natural sciences with Islamic theology. Inspired by the work of Sayyid Jamal al-Din al-Afghani (chapter 11), Maghribi left Ottoman Syria for Egypt in 1905, where he began his journalistic career. He returned to Lebanon after the Ottoman Young Turk of 1908 and published a modernist periodical, *al-Burhan* (*The Proof*). In 1914, he went to Medina to participate in the establishment of an Islamic college, but the outbreak of World War I abruptly ended that effort. While many other Arab modernists supported Arab separation from the Ottoman Empire, Maghribi remained loyal to Istanbul. He spent the war years teaching at an Islamic college in Jerusalem and writing for a pro-Ottoman newspaper in Damascus. Later, Maghribi worked on behalf of Arabic language reform at academies in Syria, Egypt, and Iraq. He is best known for emphasizing moral reform as the key to resolving social and economic problems. In this selection, Maghribi cites evidence from the Prophet's relationship with his wet nurse and two of his wives to argue that Islam allows women to maintain active roles in society. In addition, he elaborates a common modernist position on the standing of women in Islamic law regarding divorce, polygamy, inheritance, and legal testimony.[1]

There are many possible topics for speeches, and many speech parties. These parties are made successful by their hosts, but they should also be made so by the proper choice of topic and by their pleasant atmosphere. Where, my sirs, can I find a topic [for my speech] as superior as this party? Truly, to take into consideration the suitability of the topic to the party is the most difficult task.

One day, I explained the word "women" in the presence of an educated girl. I said that it means "shunning," "expulsion," and "delay," and from the word comes "*al-minsa'h*," which is a stick—because the shepherd expels his sheep with it. The girl got angry and said: "Then the Arabs called women 'women' because they are excluded, shunned and expelled?!!" I wondered about her conclusion, and I prayed to God to guard me against her stubbornness, and I answered her objection with what I believed would please her on the whole.

And then, after I was invited to speak at this party, one day I saw the same girl reading a book with great interest. So I asked her: "What is this book?" She said: "al-Zubaydi."

[Ahmad ibn Ahmad] al-Zubaydi [circa 1409–1488], sirs, is [author of] a religious book summarizing all the *hadith*s [narratives of the Prophet] collected by [Muhammad ibn Isma'il] al-Bukhari [the foremost compiler of *hadith*, 810–870].

So I encouraged her to read it, and I praised her choice of that book to read, instead of those books that girls are usually fond of. The girl finished read-

'Abd al-Qadir al-Maghribi, *Muhammad wa al- mar'a* (*Muhammad and Woman*) (Damascus, Syria: no publisher indicated, 1928). The essay was first presented as a speech to the Syrian Association for the Education of Youth in Beirut, on January 11, 1928. Translation from Arabic by Hager El Hadidi. Introduction by David D. Commins.

1. Muhammad Farid 'Abd Allah, *'Abd al-Qadir al-Maghribi wa-ara'uhu fi al-lugha wa-al-nahw* (*'Abd al-Qadir al-Maghribi and His Views on Language and Grammar*) (Beirut, Lebanon: Dar al-Mawasim, 1997); Sami al-Dahhan, *al-Qudama' wa-mu'asirun* (*People of the Past and Present*) (Egypt: Dar al-Ma'arif, 1961); Muhammad As'ad Talas, *Muhadarat 'an 'Abd al-Qadir al-Maghribi* (*Lectures on 'Abd al-Qadir al-Maghribi*) (Cairo, Egypt: League of Arab States, 1958).

ing al-Zubaydi. As she was about to lay it down, she turned to those around her and said: "I did not find in all the *hadith*s that I read in this book anything that would make you feel that the Prophet, peace be upon him, had any disdain towards woman. On the contrary, I saw him honor her and put her on equal footing with men in [religious] commandments and duties. So where did the accusation that our *shari'a* [Islamic law] degrades woman or teaches any lowering of her standing come from?!!"

I do not hide from you, sirs, that my happiness about her deduction this time made me forget my disappointment with her conclusion the first time. I became even happier when I realized that I had found the topic for my speech for this party. And I called out: "I found it. I found it!" Just like Archimedes: "I found it. I found it."

Yes, I found the topic, sirs, but I didn't find the time needed to give it its due, because the Education Association—I thank it anyway—did not give me time for a speech at a party. It gave me time only for a phone call. So forgive me if I hasten or if I gloss over certain aspects.

The Arabs, due to the nature of their countries and the constitution of their temperaments, saw in woman their delight and their comfort, so they loved her and almost worshiped her. And due to the nature of their social relations and their customary system of raid and capture, they saw woman as both a cause of their pleasure and their affliction with shame. So they perceived her as an evil omen; so much so that female babies were sometimes buried alive. So the Arabs were caught between two forces: pulled by the nature of their region and their temperament, which attracted them to woman, and pulled the other way by their social system and their wars, which distanced them from her.

Muhammad, peace be upon him, was born in the Arabian peninsula, the people of which, as we have described, were given to these two tendencies. He confirmed the first instance, affection toward woman, and blessed it by announcing: "Another of His signs is that He created mates of your own kin of yourselves, so that you may get peace of mind from them, and has put love and compassion between you." [Qur'an, Sura 30, Verse 21]

And he denounced the second case, the case of disfavor toward woman. He elevated her standing, returned her to the throne of her domain, and called out, saying: "The woman is the mistress of her abode." "The woman is the guardian of her husband's abode and she is responsible for her flock." The purpose of Muhammad's prophecy is not only to proclaim the oneness of God, but also to preach on behalf of woman and to celebrate her return to the throne of her domain.

'Umar ibn al-Khattab [the second caliph, 634–644] said: "By God, in pre-Islamic ignorance we did not consider women, until God revealed about them what He revealed and foreordained what He foreordained for them."

And for those who follow the stages of the life of the Prophet, peace be upon him, they realize the causes that made his noble spirit receptive to this female revelation.

His father died, and then his mother, when he was only a few years of age. So his nursing was taken over by an Abyssinian girl named Baraka, nicknamed "Umm Ayman." And this girl worked to raise him and serve him until he turned twenty-five. So he was happy with what he saw from his nurse in terms of affection and care. And he felt the first of women's functions in this existence: woman as woman, even if she was an Abyssinian and a slave, and did not belong to the blood line of the Arabs, nor was of noble descent.

And then the Divine Providence willed to move Muhammad to live close by the most eminent woman among the Quraysh [the dominant tribe of Mecca]. So he married the lady Khadija bint Khuwaylid [554–619]. Something new in the life of Muhammad: he moved on to another phase of knowing woman, and of examining her roles. And he was no longer the youth who was served by his humble nurse. So he honored her; but the youth who is loved by a noble woman also loves her in return. He was a youth of twenty-five, and she was a middle-aged woman in her forties. As if the Divine Providence saw that in his youth he still needed the affection of a woman who had age, experience, and wealth, so was his marriage to Khadija facilitated.

Her first husband had died, so many eminent Quraysh men asked for her hand in marriage. But she had refused them all, preferring to keep her independence and to tend to the business of her trade. She was looking for a trustworthy man, to make him her business agent. So she found Muhammad. She not only found him honest with her money, but also with her heart, so she entrusted him with all.

All those who saw Muhammad, peace be upon him, and heard his speech felt that he would play a role in the renaissance of the Arabs, and their salvation from ignorance. And this was not hidden from Khadija; she believed that her fiancé was going to be a great man, and an educator of nations and generations, so her fondness for him increased, and so too her desire for his affection.

Anas [ibn Malik, servant of the Prophet, circa 612–709] said: "The Prophet, peace be upon him, was with his uncle, Abu Talib, so he took his permission to go to his fiancée Khadija, so he gave him permission. And he [Abu Talib] sent a slave-girl called Naba'a to follow him [the Prophet], telling her, 'See what Khadija says to my nephew Muhammad.'

"Naba'a said, 'I saw something strange. The moment Khadija heard him, she went out the door and took his hand and held it to her chest and neck. Then she said to him, "I swear by my father and mother, I cannot do this thing (that you have barred me from doing). But I hope that you are the Prophet that will be revealed. If it is you, then recognize my rights and my standing and pray to the God that reveals you that he would reveal you to me." Muhammad answered her: "By God, if I am he, I will never forget what you have done for me. And if it is somebody else, the God you have served will never neglect you."'"

Muhammad didn't have money or property, and he lacked the means for comfortable living, but this became available when he married Khadija. So what does he do? Does he use the money and the prosperity of his wife for play, repose, and delight?

No. The youthful Muhammad used his wife's money to free his heart from worries about the family, as he used her affection and her obedience to dedicate his time to worshiping his Creator, and to performing the great work that preoccupied him.

Here is Muhammad secluding himself from people and taking refuge in a cave in Mount Hira,' talking to his God and asking Him to guide His people. Here is Khadija his wife, encouraging him and giving him confidence, patience, and certainty in himself. Here she is preparing food for him to eat during his long seclusion. Here is Muhammad's Magdalene in vigil at the foot of the mountain where her husband has isolated himself, and her heart is filled up with anticipation, faith, and confidence in the future.

In this way we see how the prophecy was born in the hand of a woman, Khadija, whereas its birth was not witnessed by any of the men. Neither Abu Bakr nor 'Umar [two of the Prophet's closest male followers] heard it, nor did 'Ali [the Prophet's son-in-law] or Mu'awiyya [caliph, 661–680].

Then Khadija died. Abu Bakr, the oldest of the companions of Muhammad, peace be upon him, wished to have the honor of his kinship, so he married his daughter 'A'isha [circa 614–678] to him. 'A'isha was not only [the Prophet's] wife, but also his student. And that is the third of Muhammad's stages with woman: Baraka the Abyssinian cares for him in his childhood, and the elder Khadija embraces him and encourages him in his youth, and 'A'isha the faithful makes him happy and becomes his disciple in his old age.

Muhammad experienced woman in all of his life's stages, and he exchanged affection with her as a child, as a youth, and as an elder. And she had enough influence in his life to make him elevate her standing, and declare her freedom, and put her on an equal footing with men.

And one of the strangest coincidences is that the Makun council convened during the time of Muhammad, in the year 586, and discussed Is woman a human being? [The council] stated that she is a human being but was created to serve man.[2] As soon as this verdict was reached in Europe, Muhammad contradicted it in the Hijaz and raised his voice saying: "Women are sisters to men."

But he said to men: Are you not eager to enter paradise? This paradise that you are so desirous of is "under the feet of mothers," and every woman is a mother, if not in fact then in her female power.

Nobody has said so much to honor woman as this saying given by Muhammad. If people thought of woman as the devil, Muhammad saw her as a protective charm against the devil.

He asked one youth among his companions, who was called Mu'adh ibn Jabal [died 627]:

"O Mu'adh, do you have a wife?"

"No."

"You are then a brother to the devils."

In other words, you should have protected yourself from the devils by marrying a woman. And

2. [This reference is unclear. No major Christian council was held in 586, though the Council in Trullo of 692, a century later, did decree that women should be silent in church, as they are "to be in subjection, as the law also saith" (Canon 70, quoting the Bible, 1 Corinthians, chapter 14, verse 34).—Ed.]

Muhammad, peace be upon him, wanted, by honoring woman and elevating her standing in the eyes of men in this way, to make them understand that their new renaissance is built on the shoulders of both sexes together—men and women—just like the great universal renaissances. And when the Arab women saw this renaissance that Muhammad raised them into, they were extremely happy with it, and were active to enrich themselves with it, to such an extent that when they saw themselves cheated in some of their rights they gathered in a meeting and decided to tell the Prophet about their demands through a representative among them, one of the companions of the Prophet, Asma' bint Yazid [died 693].

Asma' came to the Prophet and said to him: "I am a messenger; behind me is a group of women, and all of them say what I say and are of the same opinion."

So she presented to the Prophet the demands of the women who sent her. The Prophet satisfied their demands, and declared his happiness with her discourse and her courage, and turned to the companions around him and said: "Have you heard a woman's speech better than this woman asking about her religion?"

This statement is enough [to show] that he encouraged woman and emphasized the importance of her standing. The Prophet, peace be upon him, did not like to be autocratic in matters related to woman's marriage; he gave her the right to marry whomever she chooses and prefers to live with, on condition that this marriage does not degrade the honor of her clan.

One woman, Barira, was a slave of noble 'A'isha, so she freed her. Barira was married to a man called Mughith. So when she had her freedom she had the right to choose to remain married to Mughith or not. And it appears that Barira was not comfortable living with Mughith. So she declared that she did not want him as her husband. This was difficult for Mughith to handle, as he loved her a great deal. So he tried to win her favor, but she refused. Here is Barira walking in the roads of Medina, and poor Mughith walks behind her. Tears fall on his cheeks, and people look at him, and have pity on him. Yet Barira does not have compassion and does not have mercy.

"O Barira, have mercy on him. Have sympathy for his situation. Have pity for him."

"No! I don't want him."

They told the Prophet about Barira and Mughith. So he called her to him, and talked to her about him,

so she said to him: "Are you giving me an order, O Messenger of God?"

[The Prophet said:] "No, but I am mediating for him."

"No, I do not want him."

So the Prophet did not contradict her and did not blame her for using her freedom thusly, despite the fact that she was the freed slave of his wife; rather he turned to his uncle 'Abbas [ibn 'Abd al-Muttalib, died 652] and said to him: "O 'Abbas, don't you wonder about Mughith's love for Barira, and about Barira's hatred towards Mughith?"

And just as the Prophet, peace be upon him, acknowledged a woman's right to independence in her private affairs, he considered it her right also to participate along with men in public service. The most important of these public services in this era was giving support to the expansion of Islam, and resisting those who opposed it. Women made great contributions in this domain. And a group of the Prophet's companions' women used to accompany the army and serve the warriors.

Umm 'Atiyya said: "I used to make food for the warriors, and keep their tents, and tend their wounds, and take care of their sick."

And Umm Sinan said that when the Prophet wanted to go to Khaybar, she came to him and told him: "Shall I accompany you in this voyage? I can supply the water bag, and heal the sick and the wounded and take care of the men."

[The Prophet responded:] "Come along with God's blessing. You have friends who asked to accompany me, and I gave them permission. Be with my wife Umm Salama [died 679]." As for Umm Kabsha, when she asked his permission to accompany him, he told her no. So she told him: "I medicate the sick and take care of the wounded."

"Sit down, I don't want people to say that Muhammad's invasion is accompanied by a woman."

So you see, sirs, how the Prophet explained not taking her with him by his concern that it would spread among the tribes that Muhammad had no men nor heroes, for he fights with those who have anklets. He did not tell her, "Sit down, accompanying warriors is not your business."

And Anas said: "In the battle of U'hud [in 625], I saw 'A'isha, the wife of the Prophet, and with her my mother Umm Salim, [their garments] rolled up. I could see their anklets as they jumped with water bags on their backs, emptying them in the mouths of the thirsty and then coming back to fill up and returning to empty them in their mouths again."

Here is another woman, Rafida the Muslim. She did not accompany the army but had pitched her tent in the mosque of the Prophet and would heal the wounded and medicate the sick. And when the leader of the companions of the Prophet, Sa'd ibn Mu'adh, was wounded in the Battle of the Ditch [in 627], the Prophet, peace be upon him, told them: "Take him to Rafida's tent." This was Rafida's role in time of war. As for the time of peace, she used to bring the handicapped and the unfortunate to her tent to take care of them and alleviate their suffering. The tent, Rafida's tent, was a blessing: It was a military hospital during war and a shelter for the handicapped during peace.

A heathen warrior came to Umm Hani' [bint Abi Talib] and asked her for protection, so she gave it to him. When some of the Prophet's companions objected and wanted to nullify it, she got angry and complained to the Prophet, who told her: "We give protection to whomever you have given protection, O Umm Hani'." This act was an interference in military and political affairs, and the Prophet acknowledged that she had the right to do what she did. He did not tell her: "This is not your business, [restrict yourself rather to] taking care of cooking, adorning your self, and raising children."

But in spite of that, my ladies, Muhammad saw that adornment and household management were the most elevated of women's functions. As he was proud of the Quraysh woman who protects her husband's money and takes care of raising her children—at the same time, he liked the woman who did not forget her femininity and did not ignore her adornment, and did not hinder her maternity in one way or another, to the extent that he hated to see no trace of dye in a woman's palms (dye was the most beautiful adornment in past eras).

Umm Sinan said: "I pledged Islam to the Prophet, so he looked at my hands with no traces of dye, and said, 'None of you should change her nails; but tie her hand even with a belt.'" So he encouraged them to use dye and to wear a bracelet, even one made of leather, on her wrist.

Muhammad, peace be upon him, knew that woman's psychology[3] and instincts related to her sex, so he

treated her according to what he learned about her: he was always accommodating and kind and talked to her tenderly.

Many of the ways he used to treat his wives we see today as inappropriate and unsuitable: among these are taking them on his travels. And if one of them wanted to ride, he gave her his knee to step on and mount her saddle. Whenever he was in the desert with her, he would race her great distances for sport and to entertain her. On a feast day in Abyssinia, he let her enter the mosque to watch their games with spears, similar to today's games with sword and shield.

The Prophet, peace be upon him, used to have a neighbor from Persia. This Persian invited him for food, but did not invite his wife, the noble 'A'isha. The Prophet did not accept the invitation without 'A'isha, so he invited her. It is as if the Prophet saw that failing to invite her was a humiliation to her, and that is why he refused the invitation if she was not invited also.

He prohibited a man from beating his wife and noted that beating her was not appropriate for the marital relationship between them: he beat her at midday and then praised her at night, and insisted on winning her favor. A man cannot do both!

English laws still, today, allow the husband to beat his wife, albeit with a stick that is not thicker than a finger.

And the Prophet, peace be upon him, used to honor his nurse, Baraka the Abyssinian, and used to say to the companions: This is my mother, after my mother. He used to joke with her sometimes. She asked him for a camel to ride. So he promised to give her the offspring of his she-camel. She shouted, "And what should I do with the offspring of a she-camel, will it be able to carry me? I want a camel." The companion laughed and said to her, "O Baraka, woe unto you, and aren't all camels just the offspring of a she-camel?" And one morning the Prophet saw [some] women coming back from a wedding accompanied by their sons. So he stood up and called out, saying: "O God, you are among the most beloved people to me. O God, you are among the most beloved people to me."

Yes, sirs, he loved women because they raise men just as Baraka raised him in his orphanhood. They help men in their great renaissances, as Khadija helped him in his renaissance. And they spread culture and science as 'A'isha did by spreading his cul-

---

3. [Maghribi uses the word *nafisa*, derived from *nafs* (psyche), as a neologism for "psychology."—Trans.]

ture and delivering to his *umma* the rules of his *shari'a*.

Muhammad's preaching on woman and his liberation of her from her old slavery is not hidden from European scholars, even those who are unfair. The Orientalist André Servier [France, flourished 1890s–1920s] said the following in a book he called *L'Islam et la psychologie du musulman* [*Islam and the Psychology of the Muslim*, 1923]:

> Muhammad creates the conditions that make the woman join his camp and does not speak about her except with all kindness, and strives to improve her situation. The women and children before him did not inherit. Previously, the closest [male] kin to the deceased inherited the dead man's women, along with what he inherited as a whole in money and slaves. With Muhammad's renaissance, he gave woman the right to inherit. And made it a duty to be positive towards her.

Then Servier said:

> Those who want to confirm Muhammad's extreme care for woman should read his speech in Mecca, in which he admonished his audience to take care of women. Muhammad is not ignorant of the fact that if the woman is a captive during the day, she is mistress in the night, and her power is ever great.

This is what André Servier said, and despite his attack on Muhammad he could not help but state that Muhammad liberated woman.

The German scholar Driesman [possibly Heinrich Driesmans, German racial ideologist, 1863–1927] declared that Muhammad's giving the woman her freedom is the sole reason for the renaissance of the Arabs and the rise of their civilization. And for that reason, when his followers took away this freedom, they degenerated and their civilizations declined.

The statement of André Servier that "Muhammad is not ignorant of the fact that the woman is a captive during the day" mocks and casts aspersion on Islam, and we have the right to criticize him for it: We do not know the reasons that made André Servier and his colleagues claim that the Muslim woman is a captive or like a captive.

What are the issues they refer to, I wonder: the veil, divorce, polygamy, classification of inheritance, and qualification for [legal] testimony? We cannot speak of these five issues at length because of the limited amount of time on one hand, and because these issues have received lengthy arguments among Muslims and others, so that talking about them has become boring. In spite of this, I will say a few telephonic words about them:

The first of these issues is the veil. My word about it is that human beings, since the day they reached this social stage, have aristocratic classes that consider it in their interest to distinguish themselves, to veil themselves or reduce interaction with other classes, and it is the same with kings and queens and also high people and their women even today.

The prophecy of Muhammad, peace be upon him, has nothing to do with what is aristocratic. He did not institute a veil between himself and the mass of people. They used to enter his house to receive knowledge as students enter their teachers' schools. But some of these students overstayed their welcome. 'Umar advised him to prevent people from coming to his house, but the Prophet did not agree with him, preferring to exercise what we call today "democracy," and to avoid royal behavior. Then the situation got worse, so a revelation was revealed that [the Prophet's wives] should be veiled, and people should be prevented from coming to [the Prophet's] house except under special circumstances. This is the only aristocratic element that Muhammad was forced by extreme necessity to adopt.

Then the Muslims began to imitate their Prophet, following the precept: "The people follow the religion of their kings." So they veiled their women until every Muslim woman became a veiled queen and every Muslim house a royal court. But how bad is the future of a nation with no working women, and only veiled queens! The Islamic veil, ladies and gentlemen, is a remnant of the traces of aristocracy of woman and her royalty in Islam, and not a remnant of her humiliation and her slavery.

My word on the veil is complete. I now move on to my second word, about the inheritance of a daughter being half that of her brother.

This is the Islamic *shari'a* rule that everybody in England seems to know about, by which inheritance does not pass to daughters, and their father's wealth is given only to the eldest of the sons. That is because the eldest son is the head of the family, bearer of its title, and keeper of the tradition of its glory. This is very similar to the common Islamic view of male offspring in the family. Since the sons are following their fathers in his family, they need more money than their sisters, who get incorporated into other families, where they are not financially responsible. So then the issue is not one of preferring men to women, but rather a social and economic issue.

Lately it has become apparent to factory managers that the average capacity of a woman is less than half the average of a man's capacity, and that is why they doubled his wage.

The third among the five issues is that the [legal] testimony of a woman is viewed as half a man's testimony. And my word in answering is that the reason behind the rule is not that Muhammad believed that the woman is lowly or that she lies in her testimony. But he sees that the woman is far away from the battleground of the work that men do, in which there are many tricks and treacheries. That is in addition to the woman's weak self-confidence, gullibility, and lack of discipline. They might trick her by calling her beautiful. Imagine if they use other words of flattery and praise?!!

This is the psychology of the woman that Muhammad, peace be upon him, recognized, so he saw to it that she be backed up by one of her sex when she testifies in court. Each would remind the other, and they would cooperate to confirm the issue they are testifying about. The classification of testimony then is a reflection of the belief that women are angelically naïve, and not a belief in their baseness or dishonesty. However, Muhammad, peace be upon him, preferred woman to man in some aspects of testimony: in matters concerning women, the testimony of a man is not accepted by itself, whereas her testimony alone is accepted.

This is indication enough about popular trust in women and its belief in her propriety.

Among the issues on which the civilized world casts aspersions about Muhammad, peace be upon him, is religious law of divorce. But this atrocity they now share with us, on a much wider scale.

Muhammad knew that no matter how much we try to investigate to make the couple compatible in their ethics and temperament, there will always be the possibility of mistakes in this investigation. The disparity between the couple's character many times leads to a souring of marital affection and reducing the happiness of the family. So they resort then to separation. In many cases this separation is in the interest of the woman, as she gets rid of her evil husband.

Despite that, Muhammad hated divorce and decreed patience. In the Qur'an: "Live with them with tolerance and justice, even if you do not care for them. For it may well be that you may not like a thing, yet God may have endowed it with much goodness." [Sura 4, Verse 19]

The Muhammadan revelation encouraged the man to act contrary to his feelings in consideration for the woman, so he said to man: If you feel hatred towards your wife, who says that this hatred does not have a lot of goodness in it? Be patient with her then.

To that extent Muhammad encouraged people to avoid divorce. But his followers did not follow his *shari'a*, so calamity befell them. And this cannot be blamed on him. Don't you see that with natural laws themselves, such as the laws of health and sickness, for example, people don't follow them, so misery befalls them? This is not the fault of physicians, nor the Divine Providence that created those laws. The fault is with those who contradicted them. Cicero [Roman orator, 106–43 B.C.] said: "Whoever is unhappy, it is his fault."

The Muslims used divorce to excess. They divorced with no limit or condition. The Christians were also excessive [in the opposite direction]: they did not divorce at all, even when it was necessary. Both groups ended up miserable, so the Muslims in Turkey went back to limiting the parameters of divorce, and the Christians in America and England expanded the parameters. The result should be a balanced, reasonable medium in divorce, and that is what Muhammad wanted in codifying divorce.

Now to the last of the five issues that Muslims are faulted with: polygamy. My word on this subject requires a bit of courage in stating. And despite that, I will do my best to avoid insinuations and imputations. I would say first that Muhammad, peace be upon him, did not address only one class of people with his laws, as other lawmakers did. He addressed all classes and all nations, among them the barbaric nation, the half-civilized nation, and the civilized nation.

Muhammad, peace be upon him, says to each nation with regard to polygamy: Take from my flexible laws what is appropriate to your milieu and your social situation.

So if one class of people said, "We don't acknowledge multiple wives," Muhammad would tell them: "Good work, because in my *shari'a*, polygamy is permissible and not a duty." But there would be another group, in Africa or China for example, constrained by their social situation or the disposition of their temperament to adopt polygamy. So when Muhammad invites these people to his religion, he does not force their temperament to his preference, and doesn't ask them to renounce polygamy, so as not to make it difficult for them as long as they are in this stage in their social evolution. Therefore he allowed them to practice polygamy, particularly if one of the couple is barren, or that the number of women has increased due to the demand for men in war, as happened in Europe [during World War I], or for any other reason.

But we come back and say, Why should we concern ourselves with the nations that Muhammad has allowed to have polygamy due to their milieu and temperaments? These civilized nations themselves have multiple wives in actual practice and deny it in words, and insult those who allow polygamy.

Muhammad knew the temperament of human beings and studied the nature of their masculinity deeply, for he struggled with this nature face to face and told them, "Are you in fact not impatient with one type of food? Are you not driven by your nature and temperament, or by other causes, to know a second woman other than your legal wife? Wipe this nature from your souls, and I will wipe polygamy from my laws."

And how is denial useful in this issue? If we do not see, don't we have ears to hear?

These men that want to know women other than their legal wives are not told by Muhammad: "Know them against the law [*haram*]. And put your offspring in the homes for abandoned and orphaned children." On the contrary, he tells them: "If you have to do it, know the second woman through religious tolerance. Know her through a religious official, and don't know her at the hands of Satan."

In the law of Muhammad, allowing a second wife thus fulfills a need in rebellious human nature, which cannot be resisted in some persons.

All who expect polygamy to pose a danger to the family should also expect the same from taking mistresses. The family is exposed to dangers in non-Islamic milieus, just as it is in Islamic milieus.

We have learned that some lawmakers in Europe are currently thinking of promulgating a law concerning secret multiple cohabitation, in order to limit the scope of its evil, and to save the family from the misery that it causes.

This is, ladies and gentlemen, what I wanted to say on the subject of Muhammad and woman.

And you have seen that Muhammad came to preach in favor of woman and to give her freedom. And that divorce and the other of the five issues [just discussed] do not taint this freedom in any way. Rather, if Muhammad, peace be upon him, wanted woman to be free in a judicial sense, he also wanted her to be free in an ethical sense.

The free woman who is not free makes life bitter. As for the truly free woman, she becomes the source of comfort, a pearl in the heart of gatherings, and a star on the forehead of her nation.[4]

---

4. [A white blaze on the forehead of a horse has long been a prized mark of beauty in Arab culture.—Trans.]

Turkey Faces West

Halide Edib Adıvar (Turkey, 1882–1964) gained worldwide renown as one of the first female writers and activists of the contemporary Islamic world. She received a traditional primary education, then enrolled as one of the first Muslim pupils at the American College for Girls, a missionary school in Istanbul. During high school and afterward, she translated numerous European novels and was deeply impressed by literary naturalism. Following the Constitutional Revolution of 1908, she began writing newspaper articles promoting Social Darwinism, positivism, and Turkism. Following World War I, Halide Edib participated in the founding of the Wilson Principles Society in Istanbul, but she turned to nationalism after the Greek occupation of Izmir in 1919. In fiery public speeches, she maintained that European bias against Islam had played an important role in the heavy-handed punishment and occupation of the Ottoman Empire. She joined the nationalist campaign in Anatolia and served at the front as a journalist with the rank of corporal (later sergeant). Yet her subsequent opposition to nationalist leader Mustafa Kemal (Atatürk, 1881–1938) caused her to leave Turkey in 1924, returning only in 1939. During this period she lectured and wrote prolifically in English. In her most important religious statement, a series of lectures delivered in India—excerpted in this selection—Halide Edib argued that separation of religion and state would rejuvenate Turkey and Islam. In 1940, she became professor and chair of the English Literature Department at Istanbul University; she also represented Izmir in the Turkish parliament between 1950 and 1954.[1]

The Turk perhaps was never a nationalist in politics. Empire builders rarely are. Their ultimate and highest ideal in politics is inevitably some form of democracy. When the Turk became a Muslim, the democratic side of his nature was strengthened, for democracy is the dominating aspect of Islam. That part of Western idealism which preached equality among men took hold of the Ottoman mind at once. The Ottomans could not grasp the nationalist side of it, the separation of small groups into independent states. For their lack of understanding in this field they suffered more than any other race by the advent of Western ideals in the Near East.

Down to *Tanzimat* [Ottoman administrative reforms of the 19th century], the Ottoman Turks had believed that only Muslims could be politically equal. With *Tanzimat* they believed that all men could and ought to be politically equal, and once the principle applied in a mixed society of men, they could not conceive of the reason for political disintegration. This was their external lack of understanding.

In the advent of Western Ideals there was a greater and more important question. Islamic society was something different from Western society. Could it be possible to effect an all-round Westernization without altering the very nature of Islamic society? The Muslim state might reform its army upon modern lines, it might adopt the mechanical side of civilization with regard to transport, it might open special schools for training in certain professions and arts; it might even proclaim the equality of Muslims and non-Muslims—Islam had already proclaimed the rights of man in other lines a thousand years ago. But was it possible to alter the nature of Islamic society

Halidé Edib, *Turkey Faces West: A Turkish View of Recent Changes and their Origin* (New Haven, Conn.: Yale University Press, 1930), pp. 76–82, 226–232. Introduction by M. Şükrü Hanioğlu.

1. Uğurol Barlas, *Halide Edib Adıvar: Biyografya, Bibliyografya* (*Halide Edib Adıvar: Biography, Bibliogra-*phy) (Istanbul, Turkey: Yurttaş Yayınları, 1963); Ayşe Durakbaşa, *Halide Edib: Türk Modernleşmesi ve Feminizm* (*Halide Edib: Turkish Modernization and Feminism*) (Istanbul, Turkey: İletişim, 2000); İnci Enginün, *Halide Edib Adıvar* (*Halide Edib Adıvar*) (Ankara, Turkey: Kültür Bakanlığı, 1989).

without altering Islam in itself'? And what was the dominating difference between Islamic society and that of the West which did not allow Westernization internally? It was the Islamic law. No change could be made in that aspect. Divine law administered by the *'ulama'* [religious scholars] of the realm in Islamic society did not permit change. Hence superficially, the creative and critical faculties of the Turk seemed far behind those of Western peoples. But was Muslim Turkish society as immobile and stagnant as the other Islamic societies? Was there not an objective psychology at work all the time beneath the surface, trying to change or throw off all obstacles to its growth? We can find the right key to the changes in Turkey in recent times, in a study of the Turkish soul, struggling between religious orthodoxy and a freer, more vital racial instinct, in a long effort to express itself. As soon as we penetrate beneath the surface immobility, and observe how he freed himself from the rigid Arab rationalism of the Islamic Middle Ages, and how he threw off the tyranny of the Persian spirit which had tied him down to the repetition of ancient and uncongenial forms of thought, we see clearly the difference between the Muslim Turk and the other Muslims in the world.

The most static aspect of life in Islam is law, and religious law had given its character and shape to Turkish Islamic society. But from the very moment when the Turks had accepted Islam, and originated the class—*'ulama'*—which was to preserve them from stepping outside the Divine Law, they began unconsciously to take those steps for change. In the eyes of the world, modern Turkey has only recently become a secular state, and to the casual observer it looks as though the change had been carried out by a single act overnight, and forced upon the Turks by the power of a terrorist government. But Turkey was not changed by one single step from a theocratic state into a secular one. The change is a logical culmination and result of a series of lesser changes in development. Nor is it yet complete. The final and latest secularization is only understandable [in the context of change] in the Ottoman Empire which has been going on for centuries.

The Arab mind has a metaphysical conception of the universe. It looks upon legislative power as belonging to God, and executive power to the caliph; and it regards the doctors of law as intermediaries between God and the caliph, who are to control the executive and see that he carries out the laws of God.

If he fails, they are to cancel his contract and elect another caliph by the consent of the Islamic people. Semites, as well as Arabs, had formulated this conception of Divine Law before Muhammad did so. It was the Scriptures which ruled the Semitic peoples, and it is the Scriptures which rule them still.

It was different with the Turk. In his pre-Islamic state he had been accustomed to be ruled by man-made laws, and he is by nature more inclined than the other Islamic peoples to separate religion from the ordinary business of life. It is true that his laws were made for him by his chiefs, but all the same they were man-made. This streak in his psychology made itself felt immediately during the earliest centuries after his adoption of Islam.

When the Ottoman Turks founded the vast and complicated Ottoman state, sultans and governments began to make laws outside the Divine Law. It is true that these began as royal enactments and dealt with military and feudal organizations, which were virgin soil and unforeseen by the *shari'a* (Islamic law). Nevertheless, the precedent was contrary to the teachings of the orthodox doctors, and no Arab, no other Muslim state, would have dared to do such a thing. This was the first stage. Sulayman [reigned 1520–1566], called the Magnificent in the West, is known in Turkish history as the Lawgiver (*Qanuni*), the maker of laws. The very name is a direct contradiction of orthodox principles [that call God the sole Lawgiver]. Sulayman created the embryo of a criminal code which gradually replaced some of the texts of the *shari'a* in penal matters. Such primitive measures as the cutting off of a thief's hand, the stoning of adulterers, and the flogging of wine drinkers, were replaced by imprisonment or fines. They are still applied in the kingdom of Ibn Sa'ud [circa 1880–1953, founder of Saudi Arabia], who prides himself on having restored the Hijaz to Islam.

In Sulayman's time the word *qanun* (man-made law) entered Turkish jurisprudence side by side with *shari'a* (God-made law). The *qanun* was at first in an inferior position, but it gradually gained ground and expanded until it overshadowed the *shari'a*. The very name *qanun* is a direct contradiction of orthodox principles, and in those days out of all the Islamic states it existed only in the Ottoman Empire.

The proclamation of *Tanzimat*, 1839, which declared the political equality of all the church nations [that is, religious communities], also introduced an entirely new series of man-made laws. A criminal code, taken from the French code of 1810, a commercial code, and a judicial organization copied from France, with a Tribunal of the First Instance, Courts of Appeal, and a Court of Cassation, all came into existence. After *Tanzimat*, therefore, two kinds of courts existed side by side in the Ottoman Empire: (1) The *shari'a* courts, with only Muslim judges, which were only concerned with family matters, marriage, divorce, and inheritance of the Muslims in the Empire; (2) the *nizamiye* [state] courts, where Christian, Muslim, and Jewish judges sat side by side and judged all the Ottoman subjects according to the laws of the realm. The penal section was derived entirely from the French legal system; the civil section was the codified *shari'a*, or *Mecelle*[-*i Ahkam-ı 'Adliye, Compendium of Legal Statutes*, 1876]; and the procedure throughout was French. Hence, by the middle of the nineteenth century, the Ottoman Empire had passed from God-made to man-made laws in a very large section of her jurisprudence.

To all these changes the *'ulama'*, the doctors and judges of Islamic law, made no opposition. With the Turkish outlook on life, which is readier to separate this and the next world from each other, they accepted changes in the laws which would have made the *'ulama'* of other countries denounce the Turks as heretics. No other believers in the Islamic law but Turks in those days could have permitted a separate criminal code and a separate commercial code without deeming the foundations of Islam shaken. Yet the opposition to these changes had not come from the *'ulama'* but from the rank and file of the army, which was reactionary up to the time of Mahmud [II, Ottoman sultan, reigned 1808–1839]. The Muslim Turks of the *'ulama'* class considered only one feature of the Islamic law as unchangeable, that part which concerned the family, and this they intended to keep within the boundary of God-made law. [. . .]

The adoption of the Swiss code in place of the Islamic family law in 1926 was a reform of a much more serious nature. It could have been put through without much coercion, although there would have been some bitter criticism.

A year after the sultan's government had been abolished [in 1922] in Constantinople [Istanbul], there was serious discussion whether the revised family law of 1916, abrogated by the sultan's government in 1919, should be restored with or without alterations. In 1924 the National Assembly took up the question, and it aroused great interest, especially among the women of the cities and of Constantinople in particular. At a large meeting of women in the Nationalist Club there was elected a committee of women to study the situation and send a petition to the National Assembly. The committee made a selection of the family laws of Sweden, France, England, and Russia, and having found the Swedish law most desirable, it sent a translated copy with a petition attached to it to the National Assembly. Their petition had at the time no definite result. But there was a group of very keenly interested young deputies working for the adoption of a Western code rather than the restoration of the revised family law of 1916. Mahmut Esat Bey [Bozkurt, 1892–1943], the young deputy of Smyrna [Izmir] who became Minister of Justice in 1925, was one of the leading spirits in the movement. In 1926, the law following the Swiss code was passed. It can be termed perhaps one of the two most significant and important changes that have taken place during the dictatorship. This particular law will mean the final unification of the Turk with the family of European nations, by giving the Turkish family that kind of stability which constitutes the Western Ideal of the family.

The adoption of the Swiss law, which is entirely Western, instead of revision and alteration of the Islamic family law, which could have made marriage a freer if a less stable institution and brought it nearer to the present Russian family law, was one more triumph in Turkey of the Western Ideal over the Eastern Ideal, and one of more permanent import than is realized at present.

The educational rights that Turkish women have gained are no longer questioned even by the smallest minority, and the sphere of women's work has been constantly widening. It is perhaps a blessing that they have not obtained the vote. Thus they have been protected from the danger of being identified with party politics, and their activities outside the political world could not be stopped for political reasons.

In the Turkish home, women continue to be the ruling spirit, more so, perhaps, because the majority contribute to the upkeep by their labor. At the present time, offices, factories, and shops are filled with women workers in the cities; and in addition to their breadwinning jobs, and sometimes in connection with them, women have interested themselves in child welfare and hygiene, and in organizing small associations to teach poor women embroidery, sewing, weaving, and so on. The favorite profession of Turkish women today, after teaching, is medicine. All this is the city aspect of the situation. In the rural districts, women still continue to live their old life with its drudgery, and will continue to live under these conditions until a more up-to-date agricultural system is adopted and the rudiments of education can be given in those districts. It would not be an underestimate to say that something like 90 percent of the Turkish women are very hard workers; the question is not how to provide more work for them but how to train them better for their work and to give them more leisure. The small percentage of the idle rich (much smaller in Turkey than elsewhere) do on a miniature scale what the idle rich of other countries do. Unfortunately, Turkey is judged by the life and attitude of these idlers, who are conspicuous to the eyes of the traveler, rather than by the hard-working majority.

On the whole, within the last twenty years women in Turkey as elsewhere have profited by changes more than men. It has been fortunate for Turkey that the emancipation of women there was the result of an all-party program rather than a sex struggle. The contribution of the Republic [of Turkey, founded 1923] to women's social emancipation in the introduction of the new civil code has brought the movement to its highest and historically its most important stage. But a generation at least must pass before its full effects can be seen. The general criticism that with Westernization a great deal of evil and Western immorality has penetrated into Turkish customs is not very important. The evil affects a small number of the idle, while the good penetrates into the majority, although more slowly.

In 1928, the clause in the Constitution which declared Islam the state religion was abolished. In the foreign press this step was criticized very severely, on the ground that it amounted to the abolition of religion in Turkey. This criticism was not only superficial but inaccurate. If religion, in the best sense, is in any danger of losing its hold on the Turkish people, it is not due to absence of governmental interference but to governmental interference itself. The men who sponsored this measure may or may not have been atheists, but the measure itself does not do away with religion. No secular state can logically have a basic law which establishes a state religion. The abolition of the clause from the Constitution was therefore in true and necessary accord with the nature of the new Turkish state at its last stage of secularization. "Render therefore unto Caesar the things which are Caesar's, and unto God the things that are God's." [Bible, Books of Matthew, chapter 22, verse 21; Mark, chapter 12, verse 17; Luke, chapter 20, verse 25] The Turks have at last rendered up the things that were Caesar's or the state's; but Caesar or the state still keeps things which belong to God. Unless the Presidency of Religious Affairs is made free, unless it ceases to be controlled by the office of the Prime Minister, it will always be a governmental instrument. In this respect the Muslim community is less privileged and less free than the Christian Patriarchates. These are free institutions which decide upon all questions of dogma and religion according to the convictions of their particular group. The Islamic community is chained to the policy of the government. This situation is a serious impediment to the spiritual growth of Islam in Turkey, and there is always a danger in it of the use of religion, for political ends.

Now that the state has freed itself entirely from religious control, it should in turn leave Islam alone. Not only should it declare, "Every major Turkish citizen is free to adopt the religion he (or she) wishes to adopt," but it should also allow the Muslim community to teach its religion to its youth. Now that the schools give no religious instruction, and the religious institutions are abolished, the Islamic community, if it is going to last as a religious community, must create its own means of religious teaching, its own moral and spiritual sanctions. Further, in the ritual and in the fundamentals of worship, there are likely to be changes among the Muslims in Turkey. Those changes should be allowed to take place without governmental interference. The occasional proposals by the university professors of new forms of worship in Islam—such as substituting organ music for vocal music, entering the mosques without taking off the shoes, placing benches so that the faithful may pray seated, and doing away with a number of complicated body movements in prayer—have met with profound displeasure. All these changes might take place by the wishes of the people, but governmental interference in this most sacred part of men's rights would constitute a dangerous precedent. It would fetter the religious life of the Turks and bring politics into religion. The fundamental meaning of the long and very interesting phases of secularization is that Turkish psychology separates this world from the next. To take religion out of the political state, but at the same time to keep the state in religious affairs, is one of the contradictory aspects of the last phase which must be corrected.

Not only in Turkey, but wherever religion is interfered with by governments, it becomes a barrier, and an unremovable one, to peace and understanding. Yet the fundamental doctrine of every religion is peace and the brotherhood of men. If only religions could be freed from political influences all over the world, the barriers between peoples of different creeds would break down sooner than one supposes.

SECTION 4

Russian Empire

First Steps toward Civilizing
the Russian Muslims

Ismail Bey Gasprinskii (Crimea, 1851–1914), Tatar reformer, educator, and publicist, was the most influential architect of Islamic modernism among the Turkic subjects of the Russian Empire. Gasprinskii—also known by his Tatar name, Gaspırali—was educated in both traditional Islamic and Russian schools, and was being trained for a career in the Russian military until he abandoned his studies to spend three years in France and the Ottoman Empire. Returning to Crimea in 1875, he became a school instructor and served four years as mayor of Bakhchisarai. From the early 1880s until his death, Gasprinskii devoted his efforts to challenging intellectual assumptions and sociocultural practices that he believed condemned Muslims to cultural inferiority in the face of modern Western technological, military, political, economic, and intellectual hegemony. His primary tool was print, notably the Russian- and Tatar-language newspaper *Perevodchik/Tercüman* (*The Interpreter*), which Gasprinskii founded and edited for the last thirty years of his life. Education stood at the center of his modernist project, and Gasprinskii also called for the development of a common Turkic literary language, the establishment of mutual-aid societies, and cooperation with the Russian government and people. Gasprinskii's influence, intellectually moderate and consummately practical, came to be felt throughout Turkic Russia as well as in Turkey, Egypt, and South Asia. The essay translated here assesses the first two decades of Islamic modernism in Russia, highlighting key directions and accomplishments and (although not included here) listing a bibliography of the "new" writing, fiction and nonfiction, that he felt defined the cutting edge of the new society.[1]

At the present time, despite the fact that the Muslim subjects of Russia lag far behind [other peoples], and that they share in so little of modern life, this great [Muslim] society is not all that incognizant [of what is happening around it]; and one cannot deny that within it a revival is taking place. Granted that this revival is not imposing; and so long as you do not pay close attention you will not even notice it. Yet it is enough for us that with some attention it can be observed, because it undoubtedly represents the beginning of progress and civilization.

Twenty or twenty-five years ago, God be praised, although a considerable number of [Muslim] religious works were published in Russia, only three items dealing with science and literature were written in our language [that is, all of the Turkic dialects of the Russian Empire]. Of these, one was the [*Qutadghu*] *Bilik* [*The Wisdom of Royal Glory*, by

Ismail Bey Gasprinskii, *Mebadi-yi Temeddün-i Islamiyan-i Rus* (*First Steps Toward Civilizing the Russian Muslims*), translated from Tatar by Edward J. Lazzerini in "Gadidism at the Turn of the Twentieth Century: A View from Within," *Cahiers du monde russe et soviétique* (*Annals of the Russian and Soviet World*), volume 16, number 2, April–June 1975, pp. 245–277. First published in 1901. Introduction by Edward J. Lazzerini.

1. Alan W. Fisher, "A Model Leader for Asia, Ismail Gaspirali," and Edward J. Lazzerini, "Ismail Bey Gasprinskii (Gaspirali): The Discourse of Modernism and the Russians," pp. 29–47 and 48–70, in Edward A. Allworth, ed., *Tatars of*

the Crimea, 2d ed. (Durham, N.C.: Duke University Press, 1998); Edward J. Lazzerini, "Ismail Bey Gasprinskii's *Perevodchik/Tercüman*: A Clarion of Modernism," pp. 143–156 in H. B. Paksoy, editor, *Central Asian Monuments*, (Istanbul, Turkey: Isis Press, 1992); Thomas Kuttner, "Russian *Jadidism* and the Islamic World: Ismail Gasprinskii in Cairo, 1908," *Cahiers du monde russe et soviétique* (*Annals of the Russian and Soviet World*), volume 16, 1975, pp. 383–424; Hakan Kırımlı, *National Movements and National Identity among the Crimean Tatars* (*1905–1916*) (Leiden, Netherlands: E. J. Brill, 1996).

Yusuf Khass Hajib, 11th century] published by the Orientalist [Vasilii Vasil'evich] Radlov [Russia, 1837–1918], the second was the almanac of Qayyum Efendi Nasiri [Tatarstan, 1825–1902], and the third comprised the comedies of Mirza Fatih 'Ali Akhundov [Azerbaijan, 1812–1878]. Two of these works appeared in Kazan, while the third was published in Tiflis. At that same time, a Turkic-language newspaper entitled *Ekingi* [*The Sower*] was founded in Baku by Hasan Bey Melikov [Zerdabi, Azerbaijan, 1842–1907]. Although it had only a brief existence [1875–1877], the newspaper cast a ray of light, like a lightning bolt, upon [long] dormant ideas.

Even though a few works such as the tale of *Tahir ve Zühre* [*Tahir and Zühre*] were available [at that time], these cannot be included [in our discussion] because of their lack of literary significance. [Among Muslims] the state of general knowledge was regrettably pitiful. Unaware of the discoveries of Johannes Kepler [German astronomer, 1571–1630] and [Isaac] Newton [English physicist, 1642–1727], Muslim society viewed the world and universe through the eyes of Ptolemy [ancient astronomer, 2nd century], and was heedless of both contemporary affairs and the lifestyles of other nations. In short, whatever may have been the circumstance of the civilized world 400 years ago, we Muslims find ourselves today in exactly the same circumstances; that is, we are 400 years behind!

But now, in this same Islamic world characterized by a dearth of knowledge, a lack of information, and torpor, one can discern a slight revival, a degree of awakening and understanding. This revival is not the result of some external influence, but is a marvelous, natural phenomenon born from within.

In 1881 we published an essay in Russian entitled *Russkoe musul'mantsvo* [*Russian Islam*]. Therein we called upon Muslims to write and translate works concerning science, literature, and contemporary progress. Praise God, for we were fortunate that our appeal coincided with the intentions and thoughts of many others. As a result, today, some twenty years later, as many as 300 scientific and literary works have been published in our own language. I realize that for a people numbering in the millions, the publication of 300 items in twenty years is not a great deal. Nevertheless, compared with the three works that I mentioned above, 100 times those three is not insignificant.

Generally speaking, the contents of these 300 national works are such as to encourage people to read and learn. Among the books themselves are those that discuss geography, introductory philosophy, astronomy, the preservation of health, and other useful knowledge. "New method" primers and reading books, plays, and one or two national novels make up the literary contributions.

The authors of the above are young *mulla*s who have been trained in our national *madrasa*s [seminaries] and who, through self-education, have acquired scientific knowledge. But those youth who have entered the [Russian] gymnasia and universities have not yet shown a service to our national literature. Although the *mulla*s have taken many steps forward, these others have just made a beginning.

There is a very simple explanation for this regrettable state of affairs. While our enlightened, educated Muslims know Russian and European languages, and while they enter various professions such as medicine, engineering, mining, and law, they are unable to read and write in their own national language! There is no educated Russian who does not read and write his own native tongue, no educated Austrian, Pole, Georgian, or Armenian who is not literate in his own national language. Unfortunately, this is not the case with our people.

Above all else, Islam makes two demands [on its adherents]: one is education, the other is prayer. As a consequence, in every place where Muslims are found, a *maktab* [primary school] is built for the former and a mosque for the latter. Depending upon the locality, they are constructed either of stone, wood, or felt cloth. Those of sedentary Muslims are found in fixed places; those of the nomads are portable and travel along with them. Everyone knows that the Islamic world's largest and most important buildings and building complexes consist of *maktab*s and mosques. In every village, in every quarter, somehow or other one will find a place of instruction. In Russia, at a time when education was hardly considered, and there were only two Russian schools to be found in the whole country, every Muslim village had one *maktab* apiece. But if in former days these schools sufficed and were competent, we must all acknowledge that to meet the demands of today they are in need of reform.

For several years I was in the teaching profession, and [during that time] I became intimately acquainted with conditions in the Russian schools and Muslim *maktab*s. [In the latter] the poor students would rock at their reading desks for six or seven hours every day for five or six years. There were many nights when I was unable to sleep because of my bitterness and regret at seeing them deprived of the ability to write and of a knowledge of the catechism and other matters, and their inability to acquire, in the end, anything other than the talent for repeating an Arabic sentence.

School time was being wasted. The teaching of skills, techniques, the Russian language, and other matters was [so inadequate] that a fifth-year *maktab* student could neither perform his daily prayers properly nor write a simple letter. A remedy had to be found for this state of affairs. It was necessary to complete the teaching of religion well and in a short time, and then to find a way to provide [the students] with the skills, languages, and information needed for today's world.

It was because of this that we opened a discussion of the "new method" in 1884 in *Terjuman* [*The Interpreter*], the newspaper that we had founded in 1883. A graded and phonetic primer was published, and a *maktab* in Bakhchisarai was changed over to this method and system. The visible progress made by the students of this *maktab* compelled other schools to adopt the method. In six months, after mastering reading and writing in the Turkic language and the four basic arithmetical processes, the novice students had begun lessons to learn Arabic, and were reading a book that taught the elements of religion. [Their successes] reverberated in far-off provinces, and today the "phonetic method" has spread all the way to Chinese Turkistan. [In the intervening period] over 500 old [method] *maktab*s have been reformed. Because the opportunity presented itself, Russian language teachers have been invited to a number of *maktab*s, and one hears that perfect Russian has been acquired with ease (for example, in *maktab*s in Bakhchisarai, Sheki, Kuldzha, Shirvan, Nakchivan, and other places).

Great success has been achieved in awakening public opinion concerning the *maktab*, because Muslims are an alert people who, once they are exposed to something, come to know and understand it. Consequently, I am hopeful that there will be other reforms and that the idea of change will not be reserved only for primary schools. Reform of Arab *madrasa*s as well has been engraved on the heart of the nation. After spending eight or ten years studying grammar, which is the primary section of the Arabic and Islamic sciences, and after "imprisoned

in the *madrasa*" for 15 years, the student does not know Arabic. He will have come across the names of [religious scholars such as Abu Hamid Muhammad al-]Ghazzali [1058–1111], [Muhammad ibn Isma'il al-]Bukhari [810–870], and [Sa'd al-Din] Taftazani [1322–1389], but will have had no acquaintance with the likes of 'Ali Husayn Ibn Sina [scientist and philosopher, 980–1037], [Abu Ibrahim al-]Farabi [lexicographer, died 961], or Ibn Khaldun [historian, 1332–1406]. Consequently, it dawns on many men that this is not a very sound or reasonable way to terminate their education. Thanks to this [realization], and with the intention of renovating the educational method, they have been rather successful in reforming and reorganizing the following *madrasa*s: the Zinjirli in Bakhchisarai, the Barudi in Kazan, the Osmanov in Ufa, and the Husaynov in Orenburg. In order to facilitate the reaching of Arabic, newly organized grammar books have been published. For example, there are the works of Ahmed Hadi Efendi Maksudi [1867–1941] [published] in Kazan.

The search for knowledge does not take this path alone. Profiting from the state-run primary schools, Muslim students are entering [Russian] gymnasia and universities in order to become acquainted with contemporary progress and learning, and the number who complete [these schools] is increasing. Twenty years ago one of our people had received a university education; now such people number more than 100. Fifty Muslim young men who have received a [Russian] higher education and who have entered the professions of engineering, medicine, law, et cetera, can be found in Baku alone. There are also those who have been educated in, and returned home from, French and German universities.

It is noteworthy that there is a greater number of Muslims in the southern provinces who study Russian than there is in the inner provinces. We hope that our coreligionists up and down the Volga will recognize that they are being delinquent in this matter, and that they will endeavor to become acquainted with contemporary progress through a knowledge of the Russian language. There are thousands of scientific and technical works written in Russian; it is necessary to profit from them.

In a similar way, the national theater is the product of recent years. Besides the comedies of Mirza Fatih 'Ali [Akhundov], which have been around for some time, several new comedies have been written and published. Theatrical plays in the national language have appeared in Baku, Karabagh, Gendzhe, and Bakhchisarai. In Baku, a permanent theatrical company has been formed, and one or two plays have been translated from Russian. Armenian, Georgian, and Jewish girls serve the roles of women. We are thankful [for all of this], but it cannot be denied that our theater rests on one leg.

One notices traces of awakening and progress among Muslim women, who have remained even further behind in comparison with Muslim men. If you want proof [of progress in this area], I can only give you a little. In the last days of winter there is a white flower that grows in the snow; surely you know it. If this blooming flower is not proof that summer has arrived, it is a certain sign that the beginning of summer is near. There are some signs just like this one [with regard to the advancement of our women]. Twenty-five years ago [Khanifa Khanim,] the respected wife of Hasan Bey [Melikov Zerdabi] (who was one of our journalists), was the only Muslim woman who had received an education; now there exist perhaps twenty such women. In St. Petersburg, in a women's medical [nursing?] school, three Muslim women are studying medical science, and one is practicing medicine. It is well known that two Muslim women are writing, and their results are being published. Let them be examples and models for emerging authors. This world is one of hope; why should we despair?

Charity, giving alms, and helping others are fundamental to the Islamic faith. Because of this, God be praised, we can say that there is no one who does not tithe, give alms and [other assistance]. All contribute within their means, and thus every year a great deal of money is dispensed in this way. Nevertheless, while there are those who help themselves to these charities, there are others too ashamed to do so and, as a result, go hungry. Aware that there is a lot for some and nothing for others, the public has begun to rectify the situation. In recent years, to provide order to charitable activities and to increase the opportunities for such projects, the idea of the "charitable society" has emerged. Twenty-five years ago in all of Russia there was only one Muslim charitable society, in Vladikavkaz. Today such societies have been established and are performing their tasks in each of the following places: Khankerman, Kazan, Troitsk, Semipalatinsk, Ufa, and Hadzhi Terhan.

[The extent of] publishing activity and the book trade is the most concrete testimony to the degree of advancement and progress of a nation; it is the most direct proof. Twenty years ago there were two printing presses in Muslim hands: that of the 'Abdullin Tag publishing house in Kazan, and of the Insizade press in Tiflis. Now there exist the "Terjuman" press in Bakhchisarai, the press of Ilias Mirza Boragani [1852–1942] in St. Petersburg, of the Karimov brothers in Kazan, of Mulla [Ghilman ibn] Ibrahim Karimov [1841–1902] in Orenburg, and of Doctor Akhundov and 'Ali Merdan Bey [Topchibashev, 1862–1934] in Baku. In all, we have progressed from two such establishments to eight.

I am leaving it up to each reader to make his own evaluation as to the degree of progress and advancement that has been made in each of the areas [of Muslim life] about which I have been writing.

What Is Reform?

Munawwar Qari Abdurrashidkhan oghli (Turkistan-Uzbekistan, 1878–1931) was the leading reformist figure in Tashkent, the capital of Russian Turkistan. Born in a family of Islamic scholars, Munawwar Qari received a seminary education in Tashkent and Bukhara. He opened Tashkent's first new-method school in 1901, which soon became the largest and best organized in the city. Munawwar Qari also wrote many textbooks for such schools, and ran a publishing house specializing in modernist works. He was also editor and publisher of *The Sun*, one of the region's first nongovernmental newspapers. He continued to work in the field of education in the early Soviet period, but fell afoul of the regime by the late 1920s and was arrested and sent off to prison camp in 1931. The editorial translated here provides a succinct account of the Central Asian modernists' critique of their society and their desiderata of reform, as articulated during the optimistic days in the wake of the Russian Revolution of 1905.[1]

For several years, newspapers have been writing about the need for the reform of schools, colleges, the [Muslim] Spiritual Administration, morals, the government, et cetera, et cetera. No rational person can deny that reason and tradition, the *shari'a* [Islamic law] and the present age, all require these reforms. All recognize this. But reform doesn't come about merely by our recognizing the need for it. It needs action and effort. Therefore men devoted to the nation have appeared from every direction, endeavoring to do what is necessary for reform. Under their leadership, in many provinces [of Russia] we see, if nothing else, the reform of schools and colleges, where subjects suitable to the present age are being taught according to the principles of the science of education.

Let's come to Turkistan: Are we Turkistanis heeding the example of our coreligionists and doing something to reform ourselves? And have we recognized that all aspects of our existence are in need of reform? No, gentlemen, I dare not answer this question, for while there are many among us who, aware of the contemporary world, recognize the fact that all aspects of our society, but especially our schools and education, are in need of reform, there are also many who, having spent all their lives as if in a dark house,

isolated from everybody, consider all reform to be corruption, and portray all reformers as mischief-mongers. Under their influence, Muslims [are content to] sell their happiness in the afterlife in return for banquets and parties, and laying out feasts for religious leaders and officials. As a result, they go not just into debt but cannot even pay their rents. Fie, fie—such is [our] happiness in this world and the next. Is this situation not in need for reform? Indeed, the things most in need of reform are [precisely] our banquets and parties. Our honor, indeed our humanity, depends on this.

Our whole aim in working day and night and accumulating wealth seems to be to populate these banquets and parties and thus to gain fame and honor in society. Therefore the pomp and expenses involved in these grows every year, and these innovations have become habit among us. If the poor do not host these banquets and parties, they are reviled by people; if they do so, they are forced to postpone them for many years to accumulate [the necessary money], and therefore their sons remain uncircumcised until the ages of fourteen or fifteen. If we look at these banquets and parties honestly, it will be obvious that they produce no good and are nothing but extravagance.

[Munawwar Qari Abdurrashidkhan oghli], "Islah ne demakdadur" (What Is Reform?), *Khurshid* (*The Sun*), Tashkent, Turkistan, September 28, 1906, p. 1. Translation from Uzbek and introduction by Adeeb Khalid.

1. Sirojiddin Ahmad, "Munavvar Qori," *Sharq yulduzi* (*Star of the East*), number 5, 1992, pp. 105–119; Adeeb Khalid, *The Politics of Muslim Cultural Reform: Jadidism in Central Asia* (Berkeley: University of California Press, 1998).

Although some faults may not be apparent to us because they have become habit, they are quite obvious to foreigners. But there are other faults that appear detestable even to our own eyes, yet we continue in them, claiming that they are the traditions of our forefathers. The fact is that we have added many commentaries and glosses to the traditions of our forefathers. In a couple of years, these commentaries and glosses become integral parts of the "text" itself and are associated with our forefathers. Therefore, all our acts and actions, our ways, our words, our schools and seminaries, our methods of teaching, and our morals are corrupt. If we continue in this way for another five or ten years, we are in danger of being dispersed and effaced under the oppression of developed nations. But the curtain of ignorance has so shut our eyes that we don't [even] know to what extent we have fallen behind. As for those who do know, we pay them no heed; indeed, we answer those who talk of reform with nothing but anger. We are content to judge ourselves only with reference to one another, saying, "I'm richer, or wiser, or more learned than so and so," and feel proud of it. That's why daily we go down the path of extinction.

O coreligionists, O compatriots! Let's be just and compare our situation with that of other, advanced nations. Let's secure the future of our coming genera-tions and save them from becoming slaves and servants of others. The Europeans, taking advantage of our negligence and ignorance, took our government from our hands, and are gradually taking over our crafts and trades. If we do not quickly make an effort to reform our affairs in order to safeguard ourselves, our nation, and our children, our future will be extremely difficult. Reform begins with a rapid start in cultivating sciences conforming to our times. Becoming acquainted with the sciences of the present age depends upon the reform of our schools and our methods of teaching. Our present schools take four or five years to teach only reading and writing, and our colleges take fifteen to twenty years to study introductions [to canonical texts] and the four readings. To hope for them to impart a knowledge of the sciences of the present age is as futile as to expect one to reach out to a bird flying in the sky while standing in a well. The most necessary and beneficial path for the reform of schools and colleges for all Muslims is the one laid out by the resolutions passed at the Muslim congress in Nizhnii Novgorod [in August 1905]. To endeavor to implement these plans and regulations in all Muslim provinces [of the Russian empire], and to establish organizations and to counsel on this behalf is the most sacred responsibility of all learned and wealthy notables. If we ignore this [now], it will be too late.

Islam and Democracy

Ahmed Aghayev (Azerbaijan, 1869–1939) was born into a Shi'i family and, during his youth, identified his homeland with predominantly Shi'i Iran. During his studies in Paris, where he was acquainted with reformist Turks from the Ottoman Empire, he came to see Azerbaijanis in ethnic rather than religious terms. This emphasis on Turkic identity did not make him a chauvinist; he decried the communal violence that wracked Baku in 1905 and joined a Peace Committee of twelve pledging their personal wealth against damage wrought by members of their community. His many contributions to the lively Baku press, one of whose newspapers he edited in 1906–1907, made him a leading figure in the Turkist movement. In 1909, after the Ottoman constitutional revolution, he traveled in Anatolia and wrote a series of newspaper articles outlining his vision of peaceful ethno-religious diversity in Ottoman and Russian lands, and arguing for the compatibility of Islam and democracy—as in the excerpt translated here. After the collapse of the Russian Empire, he returned to the Caucasus and worked with the newly founded Democratic Republic of Azerbaijan (1918–1920). En route to the Paris Peace Conference, he was detained by the Allied Powers for his work in the Young Turk government and interned on Malta until 1921. By then, Azerbaijan had been incorporated into the Soviet Union, and Aghayev—now known by his Turkish name Ahmet Ağaoğlu—lived out his life in Turkey, where he contributed to the 1924 constitution and campaigned for free-market economic policies.[1]

Throughout the world a spirit of awakening has encompassed the Muslims; unusual state revolutions have occurred in two Muslim states—Persia [1906] and Turkey [1908]—that are considered the bulwarks of Islam. [This process] naturally draws the attention of Europe once again to the study of Muhammad. In addition, [Muslim] state representatives, publicists, and scholars are taking an interest—only insofar as this scholarship is compatible, in its basic origins, with the state, societal, and ethical ideals—with contemporary life, [and] with the foundations of European civilization.

Does Islam tolerate free, liberal institutions? Is it able to adapt itself to the demands of such institutions? How does it look upon power? Does it permit Muslims to mingle with other non-Muslim peoples, does it permit [non-Muslims] to enjoy the same rights as Muslim peoples?

These questions, awakening interest in Europe, were picked up from the western press and transferred to the Constantinople [press], where they raised heated debate.

As an answer to these questions, but without saying a word [directly] about them, the Turkish *Shaykh al-Islam* [chief Ottoman religious authority, Mehmed Cemaleddin Efendi, 1848–1917] issued within days a brochure in three languages—Turkish, Persian and Arabic—and these brochures have been sent out by the thousands to every corner of the Muslim world.

If we consider the high position of the present *Shaykh al-Islam*, his authority throughout the Muslim world, and the fact that the best *'ulama'* [religious scholars] of Turkey took part in writing this brochure

Ahmed-bek Aghayev, "Islam i Demokratiya" (Islam and Democracy), *Kaspii* (*The Caspian*), Baku, Azerbaijan, Russian Empire, September 5, 1909, p. 3. Translation from Russian and introduction by Audrey L. Altstadt.

1. Audrey L. Altstadt, *The Azerbaijani Turks: Power and Identity under Russian Rule* (Stanford, Calif.: Hoover Institution Press, 1992); Fahri Sakal, *Ağaoğlu Ahmed Bey* (Ankara, Turkey: Türk Tarih Kurumu Basımevi, 1999); A. Holly Shissler, *Turkish Identity between Two Empires: Ahmet Ağaoğlu and the Development of Turkism* (London: I. B. Tauris, 2002); Tadeusz Swietochowski, *Russian Azerbaijan, 1905–1920: The Shaping of National Identity in a Muslim Community* (New York: Cambridge University Press, 1985).

and consulted with the *Shaykh al-Islam*, then this brochure must be regarded as nothing less than [the equivalent of] a papal encyclical, the political and social credo of the Muslim clergy.

The content of this brochure is of interest also for Russia, with its 25 million Muslim citizens. In Russia, as in all Europe, opinion about Islam is sharply divided. Some, like the late philosopher [Vladimir S.] Soloviev [1853–1900] and Professor [E. K.] Petrov [1863–1908] in Russia; [George] Rawlinson [1812–1902], [Joseph D.] Carlyle [1759–1804], and [Friedrich] Max Mueller [1823–1900] in England; Barteleli and Saint-Iner[2] in France consider Islam a doctrine that is compatible with the foundations of present-day contemporary civilization and ethics. Others, such as Ernest Renan [France, 1823–1892] and [Alfred Le] Châtelier [France, 1855–1929], consider it an enemy of all culture and all progress. Renan, for example, sees in past Muslim culture a movement created in opposition to [the spirit of] Islam by peoples who converted to Islam and despised it. This movement perished, in the end, from obligations [imposed] by Islam itself. He expresses it literally as follows: "Islam inevitably surrounds the head of all of its adherents with threefold armor of fanaticism, prejudice, and ignorance; not one ray of light can penetrate this armor and enter the mind of the Muslim."

This harsh opinion of a prominent thinker and writer about Islam has divided and still divides many, and this in turn creates a social opinion and mood divorced from reality which leads to incorrigible errors in relation to Muslims.

This is why, to follow the trends of social thought among Muslims, to be precisely informed about the character of the evolution achieved by their religion [and] their worldview, is not only of intellectual interest but also has sociopolitical meaning.

I am deeply convinced that, notwithstanding all the accelerated interaction with Muslims and the huge development of Oriental studies in Europe in general and in Russia in particular, [Europeans] still do not understand Islam or Muslims. In the judgments of Europeans about Muslims, certain elements still predominate—bias, prejudice, and even intoler-

ance, which they [got] from their own ancestors and which future generations, for centuries, will carry as an instinct, always ready to be awakened.

A centuries-old battle is not easily forgotten, and the battle of Christianity with Islam, which began virtually from the day the latter was born, is an indelible fact of history! Properly speaking, the battle is not yet over. Beaten unconscious, having seemed powerless, defenseless, Islam again awakens, again wants to take its place, to do its part for the fate of humanity. This sparks interest, but together with interest, also some fear. What lies ahead? What remains? In the face of this question, involuntarily and unconsciously, old instincts awaken in every European, as formulated most forcefully in the eighteenth century by [François Marie] Voltaire [French philosopher, 1694–1778], who put in the mouth of Muhammad the follow verse:

> I must rule the prejudiced universe in the name of God,
> My empire will be destroyed if the man is recognized.

The famous expert of the East, Mr. [Le] Châtelier, warned Europe some twenty-five years ago about the revival of Islam, invited her [Europe] to establish a coalition against [Islam], and not to permit it to rise.[3] The best independent people, including for example [Pavel N.] Miliukov [Russian historian and politician, 1859–1943], are not able to free themselves from these old prejudices and their judgments about Muslims and Islam are always spoiled and distorted by them.

We are deeply convinced that it is incorrect to raise even in principle the question of the relationship of the three monotheistic religions—Christianity, Judaism and Islam—to contemporary civilization. These religions themselves contain today elements of contemporary civilization. They proceed one from the other, they confess one and the same origin. All of them preach faith in One God, in an afterlife, in repayment for good and evil. Judaism created Christianity and both together [created] Islam; this was the last, emerging in a special historical medium and conditions. [It] created medieval Arab culture which through two channels, Byzantium and Spain, influenced Europe, [and] having acquainted

---

2. [These may be references to Barthélemy d'Herbelot (1625–1695) and Georges Saint-Yves (born 1867), author of *À l'assaut de l'Asie: la conquête européenne en Asie* (*To the Assault of Asia: The European Conquest in Asia* (1901).—Ed.]

3. [Le] Châtelier, *L'Islam au XIXe siècle* [*Islam in the 19th Century*, 1888].

the Christian and Jewish world with ancient Greek culture, prepared the ground for the epoch of the renaissance of science and art.

In this way, the whole question boils down to this: How can one understand a given religion in a given time, the relation between them, and the uses to which [the religion] is put?

Religion, like science and art, is a force; this force can be used for good or evil. In the Middle Ages, Catholic Christianity surely was an obstacle to initiatives; [it] opposed science, art, and the development of free thought! Jan Huss [Czech religious reformer, circa 1370–1415], Galileo [Italian astronomer, 1564–1642], Giordano Bruno [Italian scientist, 1548–1600], and others underwent torture in the name of Christianity! But it is not the Gospel that is guilty in all this; it is its interpreters, the moral torpor, the mental ignorance of [their medieval] contemporaries. It is not so anymore; having at one time handed over Joan of Arc [French leader, circa 1412–1431] to be burned, having damned her as a fiend of an evil spirit, the papacy now elevates her to sainthood. The holy fathers at one time sold indulgences and religious offices, and propounded the theory of the Divine Right [of monarchs] as an unshakable foundation. Now they consecrate republics, work out the bases of Christian socialism, and reconcile religion to the sciences!

It is the same with Islam. Immediately after its emergence, Islam created one of the most dazzling civilizations; but then, under the force of known historical circumstances, the analysis of which is not part of the present letter, it fell into the hands of people who were ignorant and savage, who turned it into an instrument of evil. In the name of Islam wild blasphemies and horrible crimes were committed; fires were kindled and people were tortured for their ideas, feelings, and convictions. But even so, the Qur'an was no more guilty than was the Gospel for the horrors of medieval Europe.

Now the Qur'an is undergoing such an evolution as the Gospels never did, and in this respect, the brochure of the *Shaykh al-Islam* is the brightest contribution.

Is the Period of *Ijtihad* Over or Not?

Abdullah Bubi (Tatarstan, 1871–1922) was a famous teacher and reformist theologian who long opposed the czarist regime. After studying in Arabia, Cairo, and Beirut, he and his brother returned to their home village of Izh-Bobino and established a reform-style school. Despite the small size of the village, this school was renowned among Muslims throughout the Russian Empire as a leader in reformist education, offering a variety of subjects—even French—in addition to traditional Islamic studies. At the same time, Bubi participated along with other reformist scholars in congresses of Russian-empire Muslims, at which he supported demands for democratic rights and called for women's suffrage. In 1911, Russian police charged the Bubi brothers with subversive activities against the Russian government and closed their school. Their allegedly subversive, anti-Russian, and antigovernmental activities included close contact with the Ottoman pan-Turkist party and the propagation of pan-Islamist ideas, including a vision for ending the historical conflict between the Sunni and Shi'i sects. Anti-modernist Islamic scholars cooperated with Russian prosecutors at the trial, painting Bubi as a dangerous dissident. In addition to his educational activities, Bubi wrote several works of religious scholarship. In the book excerpted here, Bubi argues that the period of *ijtihad* (rational religious interpretation) did not end in the early Islamic era, and that Muslims are not bound by the positions of the great scholars of the distant past. Rather, he writes, Muslims must reclaim this right and duty, which medieval obscurantists and despots have for centuries denied them.[1]

Human thought has been advancing day by day, and even the most ignorant and foolish are dazzled to see the results of this progress. In such an era, it is foolish to say that "understanding the Qur'an is limited to those who lived in the past; now they are extinct, and no more of them will be born until the end of time." It is also foolish to waste precious time responding to such claims. However, when do things ever go the way you want them? I wish that the truth had not been lost among illusions of all sorts. That way such delusions would not be written in the name of science, and therefore we would not feel it necessary to respond to such questions.

Who would have imagined that Islam—which based itself on reason and thinking, and in every sentence addresses reason and thinking—would be deprived of the freedom of *ijtihad* [rational religious interpretation] and would be left under the yoke of *taqlid* [imitation of great scholars]? I wish this were just imagination. That way such troubles would not beset Muslims. Children think highly of the mistakes their elders make, such us drinking alcohol. Likewise, because of their misunderstanding of the aims and conditions of Muslims in the past, [some of] our recent Muslims adopt and imitate whatever actions—even those that are destructive—that past Muslims performed. Unfortunately, the problem was not limited to this. The troublesome practice of *taqlid* spread so widely that it shook the very structure of Islam and caused Islam to deviate from its original path. Under the lash of oppression, the light of Islam was nearly extinguished. It is this *taqlid* that caused recent Islamic legal scholars to devote hundreds of pages to menstruation, a topic not even mentioned in the Qur'an, while failing to pay any attention to morality, which makes up a very large part of the Holy Book of the Muslims. I wish they had spent just

Abdullah Bubi, *Zaman-i Ijtihad Munqariz mi, Dägil mi?* (*Is the Period of Ijtihad Over or Not?*) (Kazan, Tatarstan, Russia: Millät Kütübkhanäsi, 1909), pp. 2–13. Translation from Tatar and introduction by Ahmet Kanlıdere.

1. Ahmet Kanlıdere, *Reform within Islam: The Tajdid and Jadid Movement among the Kazan Tatars (1809–1917)* (Istanbul, Turkey: Eren Yayıncılık, 1997), pp. 142–143; Azade-Ayşe Rorlich, *The Volga Tatars* (Stanford, Calif.: Hoover Institution Press, 1986), pp. 75–76, 97–99.

one tenth of their time considering the moral values that the Qur'an orders, rather than indulging themselves in matters of religious law. If they had done that, perhaps Muslims would not be in their present state of ignorance and misery. If recent Muslims allowed reason to reach the truth, as early Muslims did, there would be no accusations of perdition and disbelief, and no words of hate. Only Satan rebelled against the compassion of God. Why do you accuse your brother of blasphemy and heresy just because he has a different opinion or has criticized the thought of a Muslim from the past. Why do you tell him, "You will not be able enter God's paradise?" Companions of the Prophet [Muhammad, 570–632] and the founders of the four Muslim orthodox schools also differed in opinion on many matters. However, they never accused each other of heresy and they did not regard each other as foes. Thus, it is said that there was less disagreement of opinion between [Abu 'Abdullah Muhammad] Shafi'i [767–820] and Abu Hanifa [circa 699–767] than between [the two leading followers of Abu Hanifa,] Abu Yusuf [Ya'qub al-Kufi, died 798] and Muhammad [al-Shaybani, circa 750–805].

Since their disagreement represented freedom of thought and speech, it was beneficial for the *umma* [Muslim community]. However, the time came when Muslims set aside their original sources and began thoughtlessly to imitate the sayings of certain individuals from the past. Each party bound itself to a particular leader and stuck fanatically to this path, although God criticized Jews and Christians [for similar acts], saying, "They worship their rabbis and their monks as gods, apart from God." [Qur'an, Sura 9, Verse 31] Each party became the foe of any other that differed in opinion. None of the parties desired to know the reasoning of the others. All of the parties insulted one another, and spoke ill of one another, and thought only about increasing the number of their followers. Selfishness increased along with quarrels and disputes. None of the parties sought to find the truth, but instead sought only to best each other and show that they alone were right. These disputes, rather than benefitting Muslim society, substantially weakened it. It was as though this saying of God was addressed to them: "The people of the Book did not differ until knowledge had been given to them." [Sura 3, Verse 19]

Everywhere [in the Qur'an], God invited people to reason. Consequently, Islam bases itself upon independent thinking. *Taqlid* and Islam are mutually contradictory. If this principle of independent thinking had continued and gained strength, right would have been separated from wrong, and people would have avoided *taqlid*. However, things did not happen that way. The Qur'an criticized the people of the book [Jews and Christians] for altering their [holy] book and imitating the words of their religious elders unreservedly, mixing what is right and what is wrong. Likewise, our religious elders of later days blindly imitated the sayings of their elders. They say: "The statements of the founders of the *madhhab*s [the principle schools within Sunni Islam] must be obeyed. Their words must be given precedence over the decisive words of the Qur'an and *hadith*s [sayings of the Prophet]." On the other hand, when the words of their religious elders contradict the words of founders of the four *madhhab*s, they follow the elders, saying: "In comparison with the words of the Qur'an and *hadith*, as well as with the words of the founders of the four *madhab*s, the words of these religious elders provide more illuminating information for us. Therefore, the seeming contradiction in their words results from a deficiency in our understanding." Thus, the followers of each party obeyed the founders of the four *madhhab*s only in such matters that their own religious elders declared appropriate, and they chose the path of *taqlid*, though this has been declared wrong unanimously. In doing so, they made Islam narrow, even though the Qur'an said: "God does not wish to impose any hardship on you"; [Sura 5, Verse 6] "God wishes ease and not hardship for you." [Sura 2, Verse 185] With the curtain of *taqlid*, they closed the wide paths of *ijtihad* and the solutions to many difficult matters which can be found in God's Book and His Prophet's practice. Since they do not use their minds, and they resist every reasoned argument out of ignorance, it is impossible to talk with them, too. Perhaps they should just be sent to a lunatic asylum. The troubles that Muslims have suffered because of them are much greater than the benefits they brought. They were useful only to oppressive rulers and sultans.

Oppressors always benefit from ignorance and try to fish in muddy waters. Above all, they fear knowledge and learning. Nothing causes knowledge to disappear so well as *taqlid*. In order to pacify people and oppress them, the first step is to abolish the idea of freedom and *ijtihad*. For this reason, oppressors welcome the *fatwa* [religious ruling] that says, "The time for *ijtihad* is over," by either coopting or threatening the scholars of their time.

Today the illness of *taqlid* has became so widespread and firmly rooted that a person who calls for a return to the Qur'an and *sunna* [the practice of the Prophet] will be hated, ostracized, and attacked with curses. God—may He be exalted!—said, "Do you claim that Ibrahim [Abraham], Isma'il [Ishmael], Ishaq [Isaac], Ya'qub [Jacob], and their offspring were Jews or Christians?'" [Sura 2, Verse 140] None of the great prophets accepted the yoke of *taqlid*, they only obeyed the truth which comes from proof. *Taqlid*, following, and the repetition of everything heard or read as though one were copying from a book—all are *bid'a* [later innovations]. The Prophet was sent precisely to end these distortions and to return to the original scriptures. Followers who follow without reason were criticized with these words: "When they face their punishment, those who were followed will disown their followers." [Sura 2, Verse 166] God criticized those who talk without evidence or knowledge, calling them the followers of Satan: "Do not walk in the footsteps of Satan, your acknowledged enemy. He will ask you to indulge in evil, indecency, and to speak lies of God you cannot even conceive." [Sura 2, Verses 168–169] It is a very strange thing that recent scholars turn away from the Qur'an and *hadith* and cling to a *madhhab*, even though a mountain of proof has been brought before them. Because of their ignorance, they think that they will protect the faith with *taqlid*. The protection of religion will not be achieved by *taqlid*, by turning away from the Qur'an and *hadith*, by intervening between God and humankind, or by causing people's hearts to lose the love of God. Therefore, God said: "When it is said to them, 'Follow what God has revealed,' they reply: 'No, we will follow only what our fathers practiced.'" [Sura 2, Verse 170] In order to demonstrate the wickedness and wrongness of *taqlid*, God also said in the same verse: "Even though their fathers were senseless men lacking in guidance." In saying this, God recognizes as beasts those who do not understand what is said to them and who do not ask for proof. If those who favor *taqlid* possessed understanding hearts, just this verse would be sufficient to demonstrate the wickedness of considering old customs as holy, and the wrongness of turning away from the Qur'an and *hadith*.

This verse tells us that all who favor the path of *taqlid* are in the wrong, because in seeking the truth they do not look for any proof from those they follow. Those who seek the truth would probably find it in the end. If they fail once, on their second attempt they would think it over and so have a better chance of finding the truth. For this reason, mindful people would not employ fake excuses and leave God's words and blindly follow a person, however brilliant. They would see clearly that people may make a mistake, no matter how good and mindful they are. Therefore, it is necessary to check the proof before following somebody, rather than just obeying. Do not look at who said a thing, but look at what is said. Thus, God said in the Qur'an: "Give glad tidings to My creatures. Those who listen to then follow the best it contains are the ones who have been guided by God, and are men of wisdom." [Sura 39, Verses 17–18] For this reason, in his book *Munqidh min al-dalal* (*The Deliverer from Error*), Imam [Abu Hamid Muhammad] al-Ghazzali [1058–1111] thanked God for releasing him from *taqlid*, so that he would draw beneficial ideas from each of the four *madhhab*s, while making sure that their sources are authentic (although those who favor *taqlid* called this "compilation"). That is, he was pleased that he rose from the level of *taqlid* to the level of scrutiny. As is well known, those who favor *taqlid* saw compilation as inappropriate or *haram* [religiously prohibited]. But is there any evidence that it is *haram*? If anyone claims that there is, he is welcome to prove it! They have no evidence. These people resemble those whom God described: "Among them are heathens who know nothing of the Book, but only what they wish to believe, and only lost in fantasies." [Sura 2, Verse 78]

The scholars of the people of the book changed the scriptures, and with their various interpretations they moved away from divine rules. They gave importance to their fancies and held these fancies above the Scriptures. They grew proud of their predecessors from the Golden Age and thought that this was sufficient for their happiness. Thus, their religion moved away from its bases and became corrupted and died. We read about these events now and smile at them in astonishment. However, we are not aware that we are following the same path they did. Also, we are not aware that we deserve the saying of the Prophet: "[Unfortunately,] you will obey your predecessors." We never remember that these verses show the wrongfulness of *taqlid*, and that the Muslims of the early period of Islam agreed upon this matter. Again, we do not remember that at that time, the ignorant learned faith from the learned only after checking their reasoning, and if there was no proof they did not follow them blindly. *Shari'a* [religious law] does not forbid those who have found their way through reasoning to obey; however, if the reasoning is unknown, how can we know who has used their mind? For that reason, after criticizing those who followed their ancestors without reasoning, God delivered the following example: "The unbelievers are like a person who shouts to one that cannot hear more than a call and a cry. They are deaf, dumb, and blind, they fail to understand." [Qur'an, Sura 2, Verse 171] That is, those who follow blindly resemble sheep. Just as the sheep are led by the voice of the shepherd, and do not understand this voice, nor their fortune and misfortune, so those who accept a belief or religious law without deduction cannot understand their fortune or misfortune. This verse clearly shows that imitating without reasoning is the business of unbelievers; according to this verse, those who do not know their religion with proof but understand simply through passive submission, cannot be considered believers. The meaning of belief is not to tie people to a certain *madhhab* as an animal is tied to its halter, but to raise up their minds in science and learning. Only then can people understand what is good or bad and abstain from the wicked by knowing its undesirable consequences. Only then will it be possible to invite civilized nations to Islam. At the present time, if we say to civilized nations: "Here is our *shari'a*. It is codified by the religious scholars of early Islam and nothing can be added to their interpretations. You will not understand such matters, because a long time has passed from the time of understanding the Qur'an! For that reason, you have to accept the words of the legal scholars, even though their words contradict the Qur'an and *hadith*. You should practice these [teachings] without considering whether they suit the conditions of the era! You must do exactly this. If you do otherwise, you will deviate from Islam." If we assert all of this, will they have any love for Islam? Will they abandon their intellect and follow what some old legal scholars have said, therefore putting themselves in the position of an ignorant person? How can you convince these people with [religious scholars such as Shamsuddin] Quhistani [Hanafi scholar, died circa 1543] and Levleciyye [reference unclear]? They will not follow the words of the old legal scholars, except

by using their minds. If we proceed while practicing our religion in such a manner of submission, how can we bring the civilized nations closer to us and to our religion? On the contrary, God forbid, we would cause our own learned people to sicken of Islam, and thereby we would cut the ground out from under our own feet.

In order to gather Muslims around Islam and to raise our national glory, we need to inquire into Islam and return it to its original condition, while permitting all to understand it with their own mind. When this is done, Muslims will not be stagnant and stuck to *taqlid*, nor will they be satisfied with vague fancies and sanctify the old ideas. Rather, they will understand the mysteries of the Qur'an and the benefits of the duties God presented, and the wisdom behind the ordering of such duties. God praised those thusly: "Those to whom We have sent down the Book, and who read it as it should be read, believe in it truly." [Sura 2, Verse 121] Their belief will be stronger, and they will be happy in this world as well as in the next world. They will not slip into *taqlid* and mix their belief with pernicious innovations and customs for lack of understanding of their religion. God criticized those as follows: "Those who deny it will be losers." [Sura 2, Verse 121] They will think with their own minds but will not contradict the freedom of thought by imposing their own ideas. They intend to return to the Qur'an and the *sunna*. However, they will base a forced interpretation of the Qur'an and *hadith* on the words of the founders of the four orthodox schools. Rather, they will accept the words of the founders if they are in accordance with these sources; otherwise they will reject them. They will also follow the principle of the companions of the Prophet, the generation that followed, and the founders of the four orthodox schools, saying, "Everyone is free in matters of *ijtihad*." It is true that in our time *madhhab*s and controversies have increased. However, among the *mujtahid*s [religious scholars] of the early period of Islam, there was no fanaticism and such controversies did not cause the Muslims to fight one another or to cut off friendly relations with one another. People who had a great enough ability to understand acted according to their own interpretation in controversial issues. They did not hate those who asked them to refer to the Qur'an and *sunna*, nor did they accuse others of heresy. They tried to understand each matter by expending as great intellectual effort as they could. They also tried to infer religious rules from the four basic sources of Islam: the Qur'an, *sunna*, consensus, and the method of analogy. They did not glorify old scholars while demeaning later ones. And they did not claim that later scholars could not reach the level of the older ones, no matter what effort they expend. Contrary to the claims that one has to have a deep knowledge of Qur'anic exegesis and *hadith* and related sciences in order to become a *mujtahid*, they knew that it would be sufficient to know the Arabic sciences of text and style as well as the aims of the *shari'a* as [Ibrahim ibn Musa] Shatibi [Andalusian scholar, died 1388] wrote in his *Muwafaqat* [*The Agreements*]. For that reason, Shatibi claimed that it is all right for a *mujtahid* to follow a non-*mujtahid* in determining the authenticity of a *hadith* which is fundamental for making *ijtihad*. Abu Hanifa, who was unanimously accepted as a *mujtahid*, was only able to know a quite small number of *hadith*, because the place where he lived had a limited degree of *hadith* narration.

Since God's creation is progressing day by day, therefore the latest religion, Islam, is the most perfect religion of all the religions. Similarly, it is quite possible and in accordance with God's *sunna* that in our time there might be scholars of the same degree as, or better than, the scholars of the past. For this reason, the Prophet forbade people to substitute others for God and His Prophet, saying: "Any innovations other than our way belong to those who invented them and are rejected," while the founders of the four orthodox schools forbade others to imitate them.

Abu Hanifa [founder of the Hanafi *madhhab*] and his companions said, "It is inappropriate to obey a *fatwa* without knowing its underlying basis." Again, Abu Hanifa said, "If my word contradicts the Qur'an and *sunna*, you should abandon it!" Thus he made his meaning clear beyond any doubt or hesitance. Malik ibn Anas [710–796, founder of the Maliki *madhhab*] said, "Since I am a human being, I am fallible. For this reason, you should think about my opinion! If it is in accordance with the Qur'an and *sunna*, you may follow it. If not, you should set it aside!" Again, Malik ibn Anas once said, while pointing out the grave of the Prophet: "Only the owner of this tomb is not to be rejected. All others might be rejected. In addition, *Imam* Shafi'i [founder of the Shafi'i *madhhab*] said, "It is not appropriate to obey any person but the Messenger," while *Imam* Ahmad [ibn Hanbal, 780–855, founder of the Hanbali *madhhab*] said: "Follow nobody in your religion!

Follow only our Prophet and things narrated by his companions!" Elsewhere, *Imam* Ahmad clearly explained: "Do not follow me, or Shafi'i, Malik, [Abu 'Amr 'Abd al-Rahman] Awza'i [died 774], or [Sufyan al-]Thawri [716–778], but make use of the sources from which they derive their teaching!"

As is evident, all of the founders of the four orthodox schools of Islam agreed upon the wrongness of imitation. They engaged in *ijtihad* and expressed their opinions, but they did not impose upon anybody else by asserting that their opinions had to be accepted. Everyone was free to accept or not accept. Abu Hanifa said, "This is my opinion. If anyone brings a better explanation, I will accept that one." In the same way, when *Imam* Malik was asked to compel the agents of Harun al-Rashid [caliph, circa 763–809] to act according to the principles put forth in his work *al-Muwatta'* [*The Well-Trodden Path*], he declined, saying: "The Prophet's companions spread all over different countries, and there are *hadith*s in every nation that other nations have not heard of." *Imam* Shafi'i used to forbid his students to follow his words in the presence of *hadith*, saying, "If the Prophet's words become evident to a person, it is not correct to leave aside the *sunna* in favor of anybody's word." In the same way, *Imam* Ahmad rejected the writing down and codifying of the religious rulings he gave. They knew that they might have fallen into error in some of their judgments and stated this clearly. They never introduced their rulings by saying, "Here, this judgment is the judgment of God and His prophet." If Abu Hanifa's judgment had been accepted without question, nobody—not Shafi'i, *Imam* Muhammad, *Imam* Abu Yusuf, or anybody else—would have gone against him. If, as later scholars supposed, respect for a teacher meant to follow all of his words or to act without thinking, even though this word might contradict the sacred sources, *Imam* Muhammad and *Imam* Abu Yusuf would have been the first to follow their teachers.

You imitators! You go too far in respecting your teachers, saying, "He is good and could not be mistaken." Thus you follow even the most ignorant and foolish person and fail to remember that nobody except the prophets is free from making mistakes. Your case resembles that of people who try to find their way by looking at the stars in the sky, even though Mecca is directly in front of them. Although religious proofs are clearly visible to you, you turn away and follow the words of a legal scholar! You have seen with your own eyes the words of the legal scholars, whose scholarly books you believe in count reason fundamental for science. You deny that reason is fundamental in the matter of understanding religious proofs! Therefore, you yourself fail to follow these books and these [supposedly] infallible men. You yourself say that it is necessary to follow these leaders, but you go against their consensus, that it is not proper to follow anybody! You yourself claim that it is not proper to step outside of the four orthodox schools, but again you keep saying that up to the the end of the fifth century [A.H., or twelfth century A.D., that is, several centuries after the founding of the orthdox schools], *ijtihad* continued! It is quite obvious that even at the end of the fifth century there were many scholars practicing *ijtihad*.

[. . .] A *mufti* [religious leader] has to be a legal scholar. Without a doubt, he must also be a *mujtahid*. Even the Shafi'i school contended that even judges should be *mujtahids*. The Hanafi school contended that it is appropriate to appoint a person other than a *mujtahid* as a judge only on condition that he be under a *mufti* capable of *ijtihad*. *Hidaya* [*Guidance*, by Burhanuddin Marghinani, died circa 1197] laid down the condition that a judge should be capable of making *ijtihad*. [*Binaya fi*] *sharh al-Hidaya* [*Structure of Explanation of "Guidance"*, by Badr al-Din 'Ayni 1361–1451], *Mukhtasar al-Wiqaya* [*Abridged "Defenses"*, by 'Ubaydallah Mahbubi, died circa 1346], and *Multaqa al-abhur* [*Confluence of the Seas*, by Ibrahim Halabi, died circa 1549] accepted *ijtihad* only as a preferred condition, while *Fath al-qadir* [*The Powerful Victory*, by Muhammad Ibn al-Humam, circa 1388–1459] stated clearly that "it is not proper to follow a person incapable of *ijtihad*, according to the schools of Shafi'i, Malik, Ahmad, as well as our scholar, Muhammad [al-Shaybani, a founder of the Hanafi school, circa 750–805]." And finally, *Majma' al-anhur* [*Confluence of Streams*, by 'Abd al-Rahman Shaykhzada, died circa 1667] quoted *Fath* [*al-qadir*]: "According to the methodology of legal scholarship, a *mufti* should be capable of engaging in *ijtihad*." That means that, although there is controversy about appointing a person incapable of *ijtihad* as judge, it is unacceptable to appoint a person who is incapable of *ijtihad* as *mufti*. This shows that appointing *mufti*s and judges never became extinct. Therefore, the time for *ijtihad* must never have become extinct.

Ibn Taymiyya

Rizaeddin bin Fakhreddin (Tatarstan, 1858–1936) was a leading figure of the Tatar renaissance. Born in a village in Samara, Fakhreddin did not study in Bukhara, as other leading religious scholars of the era did. Instead, he pursued his studies within Tatarstan, becoming a member of the Muslim Religious Board, the *Sobranie*, in his early 30s. He turned to journalism in 1906, publishing the longest-lived Tatar journal of the era, *Shura* (Council). Fakhreddin then returned to clerical activities in 1921, serving as *mufti* (religious leader) of the European region of Russia until his death in 1936—though never praising the Soviet regime that allowed him to hold this position. Fakhreddin was a prolific author. Using the archives of the Muslim Religious Board, he wrote a two-volume history of Tatar scholars that remains the best source on the subject. He also wrote tracts on the condition of the Muslims of Russia; pedagogical works on students, women, men, and family; and biographies of numerous famous figures, including the modernist Sayyid Jamal al-Din al-Afghani (chapter 11) and various medieval scholars. The present selection, the conclusion to Fakhreddin's biography of Ibn Taymiyya (1263–1328), links medieval religious reform with contemporary modernist goals. According to Fakhreddin, the rise and decline of nations are closely connected with the strength of their belief systems. The renaissance of the Muslim world, he argues, requires the removal of superstitions that have corrupted Muslim belief, and a return to the beliefs of the early Muslims.[1]

Progress and regress, the strengthening and the decline of religious communities [*umma*s], are based on the beliefs on which they establish themselves. Belief is the axis of all revolutions and the political, economic, scientific, and literary struggles that take place in the world. Likewise, belief is the source of every kind of discovery and invention, religious as well as scientific renewal and reform. The problems, disputes, alliances and disagreements among mankind, and all their accompanying difficulties and troubles, come from belief.

When their belief serves as a guide, the most miserable nations climb upward; however, when their beliefs are coerced, the most powerful religious communities fall to the bottom in a confused and scattered state. They leave behind only their names—on documents and manuscripts, on buildings and in books, written in small or great numbers.

For this reason, if a nation makes progress, one should look at its belief. However, if a nation displays signs of regression, it is urgent to study its belief, and the necessary precautions should be taken accordingly. The same thing can be said for human beings. A person who says, "God created me unlucky, I am unfortunate," falls into desperation and becomes unsuccessful in life. However, a person who has a strong belief and says, "If this thing is within the power of human beings, why can't I do it?"—this person will be successful. For this reason, if we wish the advancement of a nation, first we have to correct its belief system.

Under the motivation of Islamic belief, Arabs, who had previously fought unending battles among

Rizaeddin bin Fakhreddin, *Ibn Taymiyya* (*Ibn Taymiyya*) (Orenburg, Russia: Vaqt Matbaʻasï, 1911), pp. 128–139. Translation from Tatar and introduction by Ahmet Kanlıdere.

1. Ahmet Kanlıdere, *Reform within Islam: The Tajdid and Jadid Movement among the Kazan Tatars (1809–1917)* (Istanbul, Turkey: Eren Yayıncılık, 1997), pp. 50–52; Azade-Ayşe Rorlich, *The Volga Tatars* (Stanford, Calif.: Hoover Institution Press, 1986), pp. 53–58; Mahmud Tahir,

"Rizaeddin Fahreddin," *Central Asian Survey*, 1989, volume 8, number 1, pp. 111–115; İsmail Türkoğlu, *Rusya Türkleri Arasındaki Yenileşme Hareketinin Öncülerinden Rızaeddin Fahreddin (1858–1936)* (*Rizaeddin Fakhreddin (1858–1936), A Pioneer of the Renewal Movement of the Turks of Russia*) (Istanbul, Turkey: Ötüken, 2000); Ömer Hakan Özalp, *Rizaeddin bin Fahreddin* (Istanbul, Turkey: Dergah Yayınları, 2001).

themselves, gained a new life. They established a brotherhood among themselves and attained a unifying consensus. Holding a sword in one hand and the Qur'an in the other, they went out from the wilderness and expanded into a vast range of lands. While some were conquering countries and cities, still others occupied themselves with trade. They became the successors of [Julius] Caesar [Roman emperor, died 44 B.C.] and left their footprints throughout the world. Places dominated by the family of Mundhir [the Lakhmids], the Himyarids, and the Ghassanids [dynasties based in present-day Iraq, Yemen, and Syria] became the cradle of Islam. The science of the Muslims became known everywhere, and the earth's surface grew prosperous with the works of Islam. At a time when transportation was difficult, Muslim caravans traveled from south to north and from west to east. Great bazaars filled up with the goods of Muslim merchants, and the Muslim trade network reached to the shores of Andalusia. It was considered most unacceptable for a Muslim to remain idle, to envy and covet another person's property. As if in a busy factory, the entire Muslim world was involved in similarly intense activities.

What was the reason for this extraordinary pattern of innovation and wondrous activity? There is no need to ask; the reason was the change in their belief. Numerous verses of the Qur'an and *hadith* [sayings of the Prophet] changed the belief of these immoral Arabs and led them to a true path. According to the noble Qur'an: "He made for you all that the earth contains"; [Sura 2, Verse 29] "And we taught him [David] the art of making coats of mail"; [Sura 21, Verse 80] "Do not forget your part in this world"; [Sura 28, Verse 77] "And that each man shall receive only what he strives for"; [Sura 53, Verse 39] "And when the prayers are over, spread out in the land, and look for the bounty of God"; [Sura 62, Verse 10] "It is God who has subdued the ocean for you, so that ships may sail upon it by His command, and you may seek His bounty, and may render thanks happily. He subjugated for you whatever the heavens and earth contain, each and every thing. Verily there are signs in this for those who reflect"; [Sura 45, Verses 12–13] "It is He who made the earth subservient to you, that you may travel all around it, and eat of the things He has provided; and to Him will be your Resurrection." [Sura 67, Verse 15] According to *hadith*: "There is no better food for a man than food he has earned by his own labor. Even the

prophet David ate food which he had grown with his own hands"; "It is better for a man to make a living at hard work than to beg from another, whether that one gives or not"; "If a Muslim plants a tree or grows grain, and someone, or a bird or wild animal, eats from it, this is counted as charity for the Muslim."[2]

If this righteous belief had remained in existence among Muslims, civilization in its real meaning would have appeared in the Muslim world. Schools, teachers and students in these schools, scholars and artisans, inventors, factories, architects, engineers, doctors and professors—all those people the Europeans have today, would have come from the Muslim world. Unfortunately, the later Muslims did not follow the path of the earlier Muslims. They lent their ears to those merchants of religion who forbade, in the name of religion, the trades and businesses that were necessary for the happiness and prosperity of humankind. In addition, whether it was adopted from Christianity or invented by coincidence, some people were given titles of sainthood, though the Prophet had said nothing about this. The common people surrendered themselves to such persons, contrary to the clear prohibition: "Do not follow that of which you have no knowledge." [Qur'an, Sura 17, Verse 36] These persons were believed to be "master of two worlds" [heaven and earth], "the best of all creation," and "the pole of the universe," and people began to submit their wishes to these saints, requesting help from their spirits in humble supplication.

As a result of such belief, like a factory standing idle, the Muslim world remained completely idle and vacant. Attention was not paid to the factory of the world that God described in the verse: "And you will find no change in the law of God." [Qur'an, Sura 48, Verse 23]

It is futile to resist machines and to struggle against nature, and it will not bring any benefit, only damage, since it is not easy to hold rivers by obstructing and damming them.

While the Muslim world remained idle and superstitions replaced divine belief, enemies seized the opportunity and attacked Islam from all sides. The beautiful countries and riches that the Muslims had inherited fell into the hands of their enemies. They lost their spirit, too. They should have learned from these misfortunes and drawn moral lessons from such

---

2. [Muhammad ibn Isma'il] Bukhari [810–870], [*Collection of Authentic Hadiths*,] volume 3, pp. 9, and 66.

conditions. However, their spirit could not awake, as its illnesses had become ingrained. Rather, in keeping with the saying, "Heal me with that which is itself a sickness," their condition worsened. They drank, one after another, the wine of somnolence, and even asked for more. They were surprised when they heard the sound of the Europeans' cannons and weapons, but this did not awaken them. On the contrary, after staying inactive for some time, this led them to the tombs of their ancestors, spirits, and religious leaders, who are (to use the term of a contemporary writer) "living idols." Rather than seeking help from God alone, and acting in accordance with the teachings of the Qur'an, they sought help from dead people. The fate of those who do not walk the proper path is deprivation and misery. That was the result in this case.

Our statements apply to the general tendency of people. However, ever since the Age of Prosperity [the era of the Prophet], a small group of people adopted the principle of speaking only the truth, fearing nobody. They did not approve of popular practices. But power was in the hand of others, and for this reason their voice was not heard. They could not express themselves adequately. Since the death of the caliph 'Ali [ibn Abi Talib, 656–661], public opinion was on the common people's side and the people of Piçen Pazari prevailed everywhere.[3] Those who study the historical facts will know that the opinion of the people overwhelms the truth. As a result, the most famous personalities of Islam were accused of being infidels and heretics.

If some undeserving people are given the title of saint, the limits of the ensuing misfortune are difficult to estimate. To see this, one should study [the history of] the Christian world. From the same causes came the same consequences. This is a known fact; there is no doubt in that. For this reason, the Muslim world fell into the condition that the Christian world experienced in the medieval age. The names of saints became sources of sustenance. The names of Muslim saints became means of earning a living. Their tombs and the surrounding areas filled with miracle sellers and peddlers of saintly intercession. Although it went by a different name, a class of clerics formed with a similar function. The names of great saints became the tools of trade.

It was necessary to show the greatness of saints in order to earn more money. For this purpose, strange powers and marvelous occurrences were shown as proof. In the end, tens or hundreds of lies were added to a true fact, along with the invention of numerous miracles and marvelous events. Even though it was not stated openly, by implication saints were given the function of "the One who created all beings and gave food to all creation" [that is, God]. When the Muslim forces gained a small victory over their enemies, these men attributed this to the help of saints, and imposed this upon people in place of faith. When a defeat occurred, they attributed this to a failure to obtain the approval of saints (that is, too little money had been donated), and they threatened the ignorant people.

In order to gain fame and earn more worldly profit, as much exaggeration as possible is needed. Therefore, some make their own *shaykh*s [holy men] the friend of Khizr Ilyas [a mythical prophet].[4] Some go even further and make him an intimate friend of the Prophet, exploiting this alleged friendship for their own benefit. Others have their spiritual guides conquer cities and defeat their enemies, who they make flee in disorder (just as in the siege of Vienna [in 1683], the Christian clergy attributed the Turks' failure to the help of saints). Still some others make those (who deny their *shaykh*s) live in misery, while some lengthen their life through the power of a saint.[5] The books of miracles are full of such adventures and stories.

Those men to whom the title of "helper of creatures" was given, whose names were exploited for profit, will not be blamed. They would not have approved of such lies and the extravagant praise and miracles attributed to them. The real blame should go to those who prey upon the people and consume their property by such means.

Some people accepted Jesus, peace be upon him, as God, and others attributed supernatural peculiarities to 'Ali and his sons. There is no doubt that these honorable figures would not consent to such claims. And they would not excuse those who do this out of excessive feelings of love. Likewise, those leading figures of the Muslim community, such as ['Abd al-

---

3. [Piçen Pazari was a Muslim market in Kazan known as the bastion of Tatar conservatism.—Trans.]

4. [The author writes Khizr and Ilyas separately, as if referring to two separate personalities.—Trans.]

5. ['Abd al-Rahman Jabarti, Egyptian historian, circa 1753–1825], *'Aja'ib al-athar* [*Marvelous Works*], volume 1, p. 147.

Qadir] Jilani [1077–1166, founder of the Qadiriyya Sufi order], Ibrahim ibn Adham [730–777, Central Asian ascetic], Habib [al-]'Ajami [died circa 747, a famous Sufi from Basra], [Muhyi al-Din] Ibn 'Arabi [1165–1240, Andalusian mystic] and [Baha'uddin] Naqshband [1317–1389, founder of the Naqshbandi Sufi order], [Ibrahim ibn 'Abd al-'Aziz al-]Dasuqi [circa 1235–1277, founder of Dasuqiyya Sufi order] and [Ahmad al-]Badawi [1200–1276, founder of the Ahmadiyya Sufi order], [Ahmad al-]Rifa'i [circa 1106–1182, founder of the Rifa'iyya Sufi order] and [Ahmad] Yasawi [died 1166, Central Asian mystic], and others would not be pleased with those who seek help from them by bowing and prostrating before their tombs. Just as those who claim Jesus to be God should not be considered his followers, those who attribute superhuman peculiarities to 'Ali and his sons, and those writers who write exaggerated things about them, should not be counted as [true] followers of 'Ali. Acts of respect that contradict the spirit of the Qur'an and *sunna* [the practice of the Prophet] cannot be considered proper. People's pleasures and conscience cannot be taken as proof [in religion], and their traditions and customs cannot be considered guiding principles. On the matter of respect, our proof is the proof of the Qur'an and *sunna*. True reason does not contradict this.

As a result of all these [mistaken] beliefs, Muslims who had been advancing rapidly on the path of progress stagnated. Schools fell into ruins, men of learning lost the respect and worth they used to possess. Any lazy creature could be called a religious leader, and any insane person could be appointed as religious scholar. The Muslim world was ruined and became filled with wretched mendicants. India, with its treasuries of gold, and Turkistan, the spring of learning, became victims of such beliefs. Likewise, Marrakech, Andalusia, Egypt, and the Turkmen were ruined by such thought. No trace remained of the learning and scholars of the first generation of Muslims. Hypocrisy, mischief, eulogy, and superficial observance replaced serious piety and sincerity. Very bright, trusting young men, holding a rod and rosary in their hands, belonging to a religious order, became minor clergymen, traveling from house to house, loitering and wasting Muslims' property. Unqualified individuals attained the post of scholar and became tools of oppression, interpreting religion according to the wishes of oppressors and tyrants. No

trace of self-respect or love of nation was left. A time came when the names of the companions of the Prophet, great scholars, and the early Muslims were exploited for worldly gain and human desires. As a result, the Muslims were overwhelmed in economic and political affairs, and so were destined to be crushed under the feet of others. They sank into the depths of hopelessness, disappointment, degradation, and insult. "We belong to God, and to Him we shall return." [Qur'an, Sura 2, Verse 156] "The oppressors will now come to know through what reversals they will be overthrown." [Qur'an, Sura 26, Verse 227]

So, when did these [mistaken] beliefs spread among the Muslims, such as the power of the spirits and the dead, and the *shaykh*s' being "masters of the two worlds," and resurrection from death, and so on? And through whom were such beliefs introduced? We have no evidence that such beliefs existed in the Age of Prosperity, and among the early Muslims. The Honor of the Universe, our Prophet himself, worked to dig trenches, wore armor, did housework, and sewed his own clothes. His successors lived in the same way. They toiled and took up the burden of conquering the Arab tribes, as well as the lands of Khosrow [king of Iran, reigned 531–579] and Caesar. During this time many events occurred that turn a youth's hair gray. However, none of them laid their responsibilities on the backs of the people or took themselves to the tombs [of holy men] to ask for help from the dead. Some cruel men threw stones over the Ka'ba at Mecca, and others stole the sacred black stone [of the Ka'ba]. Still other unfortunates entered the city of the Prophet [Medina], insulted the Muslims there, and behaved disrespectfully at the Holy Garden [the tomb of the Prophet]. At such a time, no spirit gave any help, and the dead did not use their spiritual power. Nor did the [dead] *shaykh*s of Turkistan or the teachers of Bukhara or the descendants of the Prophet in the Maghrib wield any power—we do not even know whether they themselves were saved when they passed away from this world. According to God's *shari'a* [religious law], is it possible to believe in the power of the dead?

Not only men but also women performed great duties in the Age of Prosperity. Since they were knowledgeable, knowledgeable of a cause, they did not remain helpless and weak like those who are sickly and lowly. They endured every difficulty by saying, "It is better to die with honor than to live debased." During time of war they assisted and treated the wounded. Indeed, they performed the job of those in the army who [today] give medical treatment. These things happened before the eyes of the Prophet. In the battles of Qadisiyya and Yarmuk [years 636 and 637], they fought in the same ranks with men, and even went ahead of them. They did not stay behind passively believing in the spirit of the Prophet and his companions. It is recorded in the history of Islam that in the Maysan war [633–636], Muslim women brought about the victory over the enemy. These were the Muslim women that European writers described: "These women are no less than their men in fighting. If they fall into captivity they are capable of protecting themselves from any harassment." It was the sons of these women who made the Europeans tremble.

As if there were not enough charity cases occupying the streets, sitting and filling the best places, placing a heavy burden on the *umma*, new things called "the fountain of holy men" and "the mountain of the saints"[6] are constantly being invented in many places just to waste people's property for the sake of a religious order. Their purpose in this is well known. Now, just look at the forbears, and then look at the successors! The difference between them is so great that it is difficult to see any connection between the two. Now, instead of lions sit monkeys, while the seats of real scholars are occupied only by robes. Those whose foresight is not blinded would see and know this, and their conscience would not deny it.

If Muslims desire a happy life and a secure future, if passing their lives by serving others like slaves, carrying brooms and axes along the streets looking for jobs, are not their ultimate aspirations—then they should try to understand Islam in the same way the early Muslims understood it, and they should revive themselves. Rather than constructing mausoleums, they should build schools; rather than handing out money to those who beg around sacred sites, they should spend their money on education; rather than

wasting their money on fountains for the holy and the tombs of saints, they should help educate students, establish poorhouses, and build hospitals to provide services for Muslims in need. It is undoubtedly a crime against religion and an [irresponsible] exaggeration to call mere worldly affairs "religion," and to vulgarize the name of religion for those things that the Prophet did not deliver. "Tell them: 'O people of the Book, do not overstep the bounds of truth in your beliefs.'" [Qur'an, Sura 5, Verse 77] [Muhammad said:] "Do not go beyond the limits of your religion; those who transgressed fell into ruin by exceeding the bounds of their religion."

It became a custom to repeat everything written in hagiographies of praiseworthy figures. *Isnad*s [chains of authority, that is, the books' sources] are not really examined. No attention is paid to reason or the rules of logic.[7] However, in a biography every piece of information and fact is examined meticulously, and partisanship is avoided as much as possible. Since the work we have written [a biography of Ibn Taymiyya] is not a hagiography, but a biography, we examined major works in our library for positive and negative accounts of Ibn Taymiyya, and then produced this work. Then we gave it as a gift to honorable personages, who must endure the torments of those who pass their time insulting the likes of Ibn Taymiyya, a man who spent his life in the service of religion and community. The best consolation for those who suffer is to see others suffer like them. If we had the power we would sacrifice our world for them, but we have only our books and pens.

Since we do not consider anybody infallible but prophets, it is inappropriate to claim anybody's word or thinking to be completely true. Despite depth in learning and skill in reasoning, anybody can make mistakes. But those mistakes which are the result of free reasoning would be more valuable than those actions that habit deems correct; for that reason, it is not a wise man's business to fight against every mistake he sees. Right words should be accepted no matter who utters them, and wrong words should be

---

6. [The mountain of the saints, Khojalar Tavi, was a sacred location in the Volga-Ural region of Russia. See the polemic against pilgrimages to the site by 'A. 'A. Rashidi, *Khojalar Tavi ya ki Yalgan Hajj* [*The Mountain of the Saints, or a Fake Pilgrimage*] (Kazan, Tatarstan, Russia: Ornak Matbaasi, 1909).—Trans.]

7. When Muhammad 'Abduh [reformist Egyptian scholar, 1849–1905; see chapter 3] was imprisoned, this was attributed to the miracles of *Shaykh* [Muhammad] 'Illaysh [conservative Egyptian scholar and Sufi leader, 1802–1882]. However, when *Shaykh* 'Illaysh was imprisoned, this was not attributed to Muhammad 'Abduh.

rejected regardless of who said them. "Take that which is pure and leave that which is impure." [Arabic saying]

Our service in writing this work consisted of gathering and evaluating knowledge and insight that had been written in various places. If necessary, readers should judge every matter according to their own reasoning, and in problematic matters they should act in accordance with the advice: "Should you disagree about something, refer it to God and the Messenger." [Qur'an, Sura 4, Verse 59] By doing this they will obtain the consent of the Prophet, peace be upon him. The most peculiar aspirations of the men of learning and respect must be to seek the truth and to kneel in the presence of the truth. "Let us not go astray, O Lord, having guided us already. Bestow on us your blessings, for You are the benevolent." [Qur'an, Sura 3, Verse 8]

Debate between a Teacher from Bukhara and a European

Abdurrauf Fitrat (Bukhara, 1886–1938) was the most prominent modernist figure in Russian Central Asia. The son of a prosperous merchant, Fitrat received a traditional Islamic education in Bukhara before being sent to Istanbul by a Bukharan benevolent society in 1909. The four hectic years Fitrat spent in Istanbul were formative of his worldview. He returned to Bukhara in 1914 and became involved in cultural and educational activities. In 1917, when the Russian revolution opened up possibilities for political action, Fitrat emerged as one of the main leaders of the Young Bukharans, as the reformist intellectuals began to style themselves. When the Bukharan People's Soviet Republic was proclaimed in 1920, Fitrat served as the chief economic advisor and minister of education. Fitrat's political stance of Bukharan nationalism proved unpalatable to the Soviet regime in Moscow, and he was ousted from public office in 1923. He spent the rest of his life as a scholar of the Turkic cultural heritage of Central Asia, publishing numerous works on the language, literature, and music of Central Asia. Fitrat was arrested in 1937 during the Great Purge and executed the following year. *The Debate between a Teacher from Bukhara and a European* (published in Istanbul in Persian, 1911), excerpted here, was the most popular work of Muslim reformism in Central Asia before 1917, for the new-method schools defended by Fitrat here lay at the center of the reformist agenda in Central Asia.[1]

EUROPEAN: Mr. Teacher! Some years ago Bukhara had an independent, powerful government and a population of ten million people. After the defeat [in 1868] of Amir Muzaffar [ruler of Bukhara, 1860–1885], the pomp of kingship was replaced by an emirate; the magnificence of independence turned into the state of a protectorate; the population was reduced to one third, and the land reduced to one tenth. From those days until these, foreign intervention, with the help of your own negligence [literally, the negligence of you sleepers on the deserts of ignorance], has brought the emirate to such a state of exhaustion that it resembles a formless statue. If you continue much longer in your old neglect; if you do not have pity on your religion and people; if you do not begin to think about saving your nobility and honor; if you forget the rights of your motherland, and if you betray the dignity and greatness of your world-conquering ancestor [Amir] Timur [reigned 1370–1405], you will cast this statue from the compass of memory, and you will sleep forever in the land of dishonor, lowliness, and anonymity.

TEACHER: My brother, you frighten me. My soul is about to leave my body. For God's sake tell me what the cure is! What is the remedy for this incurable disease? Where shall we turn? What shall we do?

[Abdurrauf] Fitrat Bukharayi, *Munazara[-yi] Mudarris-i Bukharayi ba yak Nafar Farangi dar Hindustan dar barah-yi Makatib-i Jadida* (*Debate between a Teacher from Bukhara and a European in India about New Schools*) (Istanbul, Ottoman Empire: Matba'a-i Islamiyya-i Hikmat, 1911–1912), pp. 30–53. Translation from Persian by William L. Hanaway. Introduction by Adeeb Khalid.

1. Hisao Komatsu, *Kakumei no Chūō Ajia: aru Jadiido no shōzō* (*Revolutionary Central Asia: Portrait of a Jadid*) (Tokyo, Japan: Tokyo University Press, 1996); Stéphane A. Dudoignon, "La question scolaire à Boukhara et au Turkestan russe" (The Education Question in Bukhara and Russian Turkistan), *Cahiers du monde russe* (*Annals of the Russian World*), volume 37, 1996, pp. 133–210; Adeeb Khalid, *The Politics of Muslim Cultural Reform: Jadidism in Central Asia* (Berkeley: University of California Press, 1998); Edward A. Allworth, *The Preoccupations of 'Abdalrauf Fitrat, Bukharan Nonconformist: An Analysis and List of His Writings* (Berlin, Germany: Das Arabische Buch, 2000).

What distress must we suffer to smell the scent of liberation from this misery?

EUROPEAN: Be patient and I will tell you.

TEACHER: I have no patience left. Tell me!

EUROPEAN: Even if you did not want to know, I would have told you. Now that you are impatient, I shall certainly tell you.

TEACHER: Tell me at once!

EUROPEAN: I'll tell you, but . . .

TEACHER: For God's sake don't abandon us. Explain to us.

EUROPEAN: Mr. Teacher, I shall certainly tell you, but I am afraid that you won't accept it.

TEACHER: I say, if you tell us the remedy for our incurable disease, why should we not accept it?

EUROPEAN: The remedy is this: you should open new schools. Instead of the nonsense of studying obscure points of Arabic grammar, you should study the new sciences, which produce rapid results and great benefits. Bring teachers from Istanbul, which is the capital of your Prophet's caliph [that is, the Ottoman sultan] and is famous for the abundance of its learning and the prevalence of its new industries. Try to have what the Christians possessed to make them victorious over you.

TEACHER: Fine, fine. Now I understand what you are driving at. Now I see that all of your worries over Islam were false. I am certain now that all of your professions of friendship for Bukhara had no basis. You only wanted to deceive us. You poor fool, don't you know that your opportunity for misleading us has passed? Long ago we unmasked your friends who wanted to lead us astray.

EUROPEAN: What are you saying? What have I said to be worthy of such reproaches? Why do you react so coldly merely on hearing the expression "new schools"? Tell me, what have you seen of new schools? What have you heard about these useful sciences, so that if what I have said is bad, I can repent and apologize?

TEACHER: Poor fellow, you are afraid of me. One of these new schools that you are talking about was opened in Bukhara. It continued for a year, but our great 'ulama' [religious scholars] understood the truth of the matter, had no time for it, and closed it.

EUROPEAN: (Greatly amazed) Teacher, explain this more clearly. Do you mean that a new school was opened in Bukhara and the 'ulama' would not allow it [to continue]?

TEACHER: Yes, yes. Our 'ulama', our pious, law-supporting 'ulama', after they learned the truth of it, closed the school.

EUROPEAN: I beg of you, tell me what the truth of this school is, that your 'ulama' should forbid such a useful thing once they understood it.

TEACHER: You ignoramus, you still keep on saying "useful school." Do you think that I am still fooled by you? Listen: in only a few years that school would have made infidels out of our children.

EUROPEAN: You have made a claim with no proof.

TEACHER: What do you mean with no proof? I have a thousand proofs.

EUROPEAN: Excellent. First tell me how you knew that this school would have made infidels out of your children.

TEACHER: You have not seen and do not know the 'ulama' of Bukhara. They are great men. Each one of them teaches a thousand persons. Their horses have five sirs [about a third of a kilogram] of gold around their necks. Why shouldn't our pure, honorable 'ulama' have discovered the truth of this?

EUROPEAN: You poor teacher! If you think that I do not know the state of the 'ulama' of Bukhara, you are mistaken. I am well aware that the 'ulama' run after boys in the streets during the period of study, and spend their nights in some corner drinking. After they have finished [their studies], they debase their manhood for a pittance at the door of a qadi [judge]. As soon as they have become a qadi or a government official, they seize the lives and property of the poor unfortunate people as if they were an inheritance from their fathers. If they become a great teacher or religious leader, they drink the blood of their students who are far from home, in the name of the "opening" [of the school year] and gifts. How can we have any hope of miracles from this group? What you said about each one teaching a thousand students is true, but tell me what they teach. What science do they teach those thousand poor souls that will serve them any use in this world or the next? In exchange for selling their property for twenty years to give gifts to their honorable teachers, what do they learn other than the nature of the lam of hamd and the augmentation of the third radical [elegant Arabic grammatical details] and other such trivia? What benefit is there for their religion or their world from learning this nonsense? And what does this practice of the Magi [the Zoroastrians, or polytheists in general] of putting five sirs of gold around their horses' necks have to do with miracles?

TEACHER: (With great fear) You stupid prattler, are you calling our *'ulama'* Magi?

EUROPEAN: Never. Never would I think such a rude thought about your *'ulama'*, but I do say that this conduct of theirs has nothing to do with miracles. Furthermore, your *shari'a* does not permit such activity.

TEACHER: What do you mean it does not permit it? These things are the glory of learning, and the *shari'a* orders that learning be glorified.

EUROPEAN: It is strange that you have brought up a religious question again. You Bukharans are deceived, and are neglectful of the truth of the commands of your religion. During his whole lifetime your Prophet never needlessly mounted his horse, to say nothing of putting five *sir*s of gold around its neck and deploying several retainers out ahead. If you look carefully at the history of the great men and *'ulama'* of your faith, you will see what their life was like, what their state was, what their habits were. Then you will understand clearly that your conduct is nothing but an offshoot of the conduct of the Magi. In the light of all these illegalities, with what conscience do you make claims to miracles?

TEACHER: Alright, let's put miracles aside. One of the reputable members of the *'ulama'* who became a teacher and who has studied these new principles carefully, informed the rest of the *'ulama'*.

EUROPEAN: Although I am very sorry that your *'ulama'* accepted this pure lie without any proof, and although it is my duty to seek the reasons from you, still my aim is to awaken you from the sleep of neglect. Therefore I must explain to you about that teacher who calls reformers infidels and who calls useful new principles illegal. Please tell me, was that man a native of Bukhara or a foreigner?

TEACHER: He was a foreigner.

EUROPEAN: Was he an Ottoman or an Iranian subject?

TEACHER: He was a Russian subject.

EUROPEAN: From which group was he?

TEACHER: He was a Tatar.

EUROPEAN: Do you know anything about him? In other words, do you know how great a traitor this man was to his own people and country?

TEACHER: No.

EUROPEAN: This man so betrayed his fellow countrymen in religious and worldly affairs that today he is cursed by every feeling Tatar.

TEACHER: Again you have begun speaking ill of our *'ulama'*.

EUROPEAN: I am not speaking ill of them. I am speaking the truth, for they say that one should not hide the truth. That person is a traitor. He never spares any Muslim evil. Now, by arousing you to forbid the new schools and by bringing harm to Islam, he seeks a reward from the enemies of Islam. If you wish, I will enumerate right now the injuries that he has caused to his people and country.

TEACHER: No, there is no need to do so. Since I do not know anything about that, I cannot confirm what you have said. In any case, no intelligent person could accept that a teacher from Bukhara could be a traitor.

EUROPEAN: Be still; do not reason falsely. In a city where sometimes they make illiterates preachers, if they make a traitor a teacher what is so strange about that? How is that impossible?

TEACHER: I do not say that it is impossible. What I am asking is that with what conscience can an intelligent and pious teacher betray his people and country and bring harm to Islam in Bukhara in order to be accepted by the enemies of the religion?

EUROPEAN: It is nonsense to characterize a teacher as intelligent and pious, because in a country where the position of preacher is not dependent on intelligence, to say nothing of piety, neither is the position of teacher. Secondly, you ask with what conscience can one question acceptance. Listen: with the same conscience with which such and such a learned man extorted money from his students,[2] or with which such and such a religious official took a usurious profit, or with which such and such a religious official committed indecent acts with a beardless youth, betraying the entire world of Islam.

TEACHER: You cannot establish the legality of the new schools with all this. The *'ulama'* of Bukhara, nay all the people of Bukhara agree that the new schools are unlawful.

EUROPEAN: The agreement of a group of people on a matter without proof or reason is madness. It brings about nothing and has no importance. Didn't

2. [Fitrat has a character explain this form of extortion (*joz' keshi*) elsewhere in the essay: "Each group of pupils has a leader who is called the 'reader to the group.' At the time of the distribution of the [school's endowment stipend] funds, the leader must write the names of those in his group and take them to the teacher, so that the teacher can give him the money to divide for them. Then the teacher orders the leader to write down several more names on his list. Whatever is left over after the division, the leader gives to the teacher."—Trans.]

the infidels of Mecca agree on calling the Prophet a liar? Don't the Christians agree that the person of God is a trinity? Just as their agreement has no credibility, neither has yours. Unanimity must be based on logical and traditional proofs, not on surmise and coercion.

TEACHER: My dear fellow, what business have you saying such words; you who have not attended a *madrasa* [seminary] and have not studied our sciences? The prophet said, "My people do not come together in error." When there is general agreement there is no longer room for question.

EUROPEAN: Yes, yes, this *hadith* [saying of the Prophet] is sufficient for the legality, even the necessity of the new school. You yourself know that you are not the only people in the Muslim community. Wherever there is Islam, there are Muhammad's people. Indian, Afghan, Ottoman, Arab, Tatar, and Iranian Muslims generally affirm the necessity of these schools, and you deny it. Although there is not complete agreement, still look and see which side the majority is on.

TEACHER: Since it was established among us that this school was not legal, words like this have no value.

EUROPEAN: With what proof was it so established?

TEACHER: This school would have made infidels of our children.

EUROPEAN: The point is that I say and the whole Islamic world says that it won't make your children infidels, but rather it will make them perfectly civil, patriotic Muslims.

TEACHER: No, no. It is agreed that this school will make our children infidels.

EUROPEAN: By God, if I asked you for proofs til doomsday you would say nothing but "so and so said it." Nevertheless, let me ask you this: do you know what they taught in this school that lasted for a year in your city?

TEACHER: Yes, I know. At the end of the year they sat for an examination on the subjects studied. Some of the '*ulama*', including myself, were present. They performed in a praiseworthy manner on the examination, which covered reading and writing Persian, introductory religious questions, history, ethics, arithmetic, and geography.

EUROPEAN: At that time did any of the children utter a blasphemous word or commit a disgusting act?

TEACHER: No, no. In that session the children were all very polite and looked just like Muslims.

EUROPEAN: Did you see any blasphemous words in the books that were in that school?

TEACHER: No. On the contrary, all the books were useful and worth being taught.

EUROPEAN: Have you heard that any of those children uttered anything repugnant to Muslims outside of school?

TEACHER: Never. On the contrary, unlike the children of the old schools, they did not enjoy childish games and were disgusted by them.

EUROPEAN: Were the children of this school indolent in their ablutions and prayers, or were their ablutions and prayers otherwise?

TEACHER: It was never this way. On the contrary, these children tried to outdo their elders in ablutions and prayers.

EUROPEAN: Please stop joking. How can it be that a seven-year-old child performs his ablutions and prayers more properly than a seventy-year-old man?

TEACHER: What I said is correct; it is not a joke. Most of our adults are not literate, and those who are do not know anything more than two or three lyrics of Hafiz [Persian poet, circa 1325–1390] and ['Alishir] Nava'i [Central Asian poet, 1441–1501], while these children are well informed on religious matters. It is for this reason that the children's ablutions and prayers are more proper than those of the adults.

EUROPEAN: Was the teacher of this school an infidel or an unknown person?

TEACHER: Heaven forbid! Their teacher was a pious Muslim and one of the learned men of Bukhara.

EUROPEAN: Then notwithstanding all these excellent qualities which you yourself have admitted, how do you know that this school would have turned your children into infidels?

TEACHER: Now you have started to argue again. I did not say that this school was good. My point was this: these good-for-nothing modernists, who can outdo the devil in craft and trickery, have employed good tools and excellent methods to make infidels of our children. First, they make themselves look benevolent by teaching religion to the children; then as soon as they have deceived us, like that religious official, they set to their basic task, which is making our children unbelievers.

EUROPEAN: Is it true that a religious official became a supporter of the new principles?

TEACHER: Yes, and one of his sons was in that school.

EUROPEAN: Is that religious official an educated man, or is he like the ordinary religious officials of Bukhara?

TEACHER: Ah! He is very much a scholar. Like the rest of the great scholars, all of his learning is not just in logic or grammar or theology. On the contrary, he is an expert in all matters, be they religious, logical, doctrinal, or philosophical. Moreover, he is pious and would lay down his life for Islam.

EUROPEAN: Now, my dear sir, with regard to the Noghay[3] teacher, you asked with what conscience could he accept treachery. Why did you not wonder with what conscience a person who in your words is learned and pious, could be satisfied with having a group of Muslims turned into unbelievers, one of whom was his own son?

TEACHER: That religious official did not know the truth about this school.

EUROPEAN: How could it be that an ignorant teacher who did not even know the grammatical form of zaraba Zayd [a typical example in elementary Arabic textbooks] could knowingly condemn the school, and a famous, learned, and pious religious official unwittingly declare it legal? Well, did you know in how many years this school would have made infidels of your children?

TEACHER: Yes, in four years.

EUROPEAN: Do you know the "program" of this school?

TEACHER: What is a "program"? Talk to me in the language of Muslims [literally: speak "Muslim" to me].

EUROPEAN: Well then, do you know the list of courses in the new school?

TEACHER: When should I have examined these unlawful books to know this?

EUROPEAN: Do the others of your 'ulama' who have condemned the new principles know, or not?

TEACHER: What an unintelligent man you are. One man opened a new school, another declared it illegal, the 'ulama' accepted this and closed the school. Before this, who knew that such a school existed in the world, to say nothing of its books.

EUROPEAN: Are your 'ulama' not aware of the passage in the Qur'an that says, "Do not utter the lies your tongues make up: 'This is lawful, and this is

forbidden'"; [Sura 16, Verse 116] that they should condemn something without investigation, merely on the word of a stranger? If you were truly educated people and did not have corrupt personal interests, certainly you would accept something that the whole Islamic world has accepted and deemed necessary. You would turn away from this vain fanaticism and meaningless opposition, or at least investigate it so that you would not be ashamed before the True Judge on the day after the Resurrection. Now, I have a proof of the harmlessness of this school even stronger than the first one.

TEACHER: Tell me.

EUROPEAN: For some time these schools have been open in Istanbul, Baghdad, Egypt, India, Noghayistan [Tatarstan], and the Caucasus, and not one person in any of these places has become an unbeliever. On the contrary, they have attained perfection in their faith and learning. Notice how in these times the Christians have concentrated all their efforts on refuting Islam, and every day write and publish a number of books to this end. The 'ulama' of Istanbul, India, and Egypt are producing books hourly to refute them, and they engage their great priests in daily debates. I have not heard that the 'ulama' of Bukhara, on the other hand, have written one line to refute the Christians. In this very year 1328 [1910] they have opened such schools in Afghanistan and Medina, the Prophet's city. In Medina in particular, a great celebration was held on the opening day of this school, and nobody condemned it or said that it would make infidels of their children. What makes you say such a thing?

TEACHER: Aside from producing unbelievers, this new school is illegal in several other respects.

EUROPEAN: Fine. Now at least you have admitted that this new school has not made infidels out of your children.

TEACHER: Do you think that I have gone mad that I should admit such a thing? After four years this new school would certainly have made our children infidels.

EUROPEAN: What proof do you have?

TEACHER: What proof is needed? The Noghay teacher said so.

EUROPEAN: Do you have any evidence other than the word of this Noghay?

TEACHER: No.

EUROPEAN: How strange! Why do you believe a foreigner whose disloyalty and trouble-making are known to all, who lied in order to secure his liveli-

---

3. [The Noghay were a Turkic people originally centered around Kazan. The term was often used interchangeably with Tatar.—Trans.]

hood, and disbelieve me when I produce tangible evidence? For example, I say that these schools have been operating for some time in Istanbul, Egypt, Baghdad, India, Noghayistan, and the Caucasus, and still have not made an infidel out of anyone. On the contrary, they have made all of the students more learned, more civilized, and more patriotic than before. Thus it is clear that the statement of that Noghay fellow who said that in four years it would make the children infidels was a lie. In addition, this year such schools were opened in Afghanistan and Medina and nobody said anything [against them]. From this it is clear that that Noghay's statement was a fraud. Now, since you have seen India, tell me whether the people there keep the *shari'a* more firmly than the Bukharans or not.

TEACHER: The Indians were better Muslims than the Bukharans.

EUROPEAN: Have you seen or heard that any of the Muslims there [that is, in India] have denied the unity of God or the prophethood of Muhammad or the truth of the Qur'an or any of the commands of the *shari'a*?

TEACHER: Absolutely not! They are excellent Muslims.

EUROPEAN: A new school has been open there for twenty years, and according to your own words it has not made any of them unbelievers. Is there any further doubt as to the untruth of that Noghay's words?

TEACHER: Suppose that the new schools do not make infidels of our children. They are still illegal for several other reasons.

EUROPEAN: Illegality is another problem. Now, after my statement, can you still affirm what that corrupt Nogay said?

TEACHER: All right. From what you have said, I know that these schools would not make unbelievers of our children. I still have a little doubt, though.

EUROPEAN: About what?

TEACHER: Why did that Noghay teacher tell such a useless lie for nothing?

EUROPEAN: I answered this objection before. Since it was established that that person is a traitor to the people, then he did not just tell that lie for nothing but found some profit in it.

TEACHER: That is clear, but with what conscience can a Muslim scholar act to harm Islam?

EUROPEAN: O dear! I have told you several times that most of your scholars have no conscience. With what conscience can such and such a learned man engage in treachery, or a certain religious official take

usury, or this or that religious official behave improperly with a beardless youth? This teacher, too, worked on behalf of the unbelievers against Islam. Now what do you say? Are you certain that the new school would not make unbelievers of your children?

TEACHER: Yes!

EUROPEAN: Do you understand that this Noghay fellow uttered this lie on behalf of the enemies of Islam?

TEACHER: Yes!

EUROPEAN: Then what do you say about the new school?

TEACHER: The school is illegal.

EUROPEAN: For what reason?

TEACHER: We have a thousand reasons.

EUROPEAN: Fine. Now if you state all of your reasons at once and then I answer them, the matter will not become clear. It would be better if you gave your reasons one by one so that we can examine them.

TEACHER: My first reason is that in this school the children sit on chairs.

EUROPEAN: Very well, what happened because of this?

TEACHER: You do not know the *shari'a*. The Prophet said: "He who likens himself to a people, then he is one of them." Sitting on a chair is a Russian practice. If the children sit on chairs, through this imitation of the Russians they will become Russians themselves.

EUROPEAN: Bravo, honorable traditionist [that is, one who studies the *hadith*s, or traditions, of the Prophet]. First of all, the man who uttered the *hadith* that you quoted also said: "He who says 'There is no God but God' shall not enter the fire." That is to say that whoever proclaims the unity of God will not go to hell. If the meaning of the first *hadith* is what you mean, then these two *hadith*s are contrary to each other. You hear one *hadith* from your fathers and grandfathers, but you do not examine the books of *hadith* carefully. The great *hadith* scholars explain the above *hadith* in this manner: "He who likens himself unto a people out of love for them and inclines toward their religion, then he is one of them." Second, if this much imitation is sufficient for becoming an infidel, then your *'ulama'* are Magi because their custom of adorning their horses' heads and necks with gold and silver is a custom of the Magi. Third, God created your eyes and ears like the eyes and ears of the Russians. What harm has come to your religion from this?

Fourth, the Russians did not invent chair-sitting. The first person to sit on a chair was one of the great Companions, Mu'awiyya ibn Abi Sufyan [first Umayyad caliph, reigned 661–680]. Fifth, examine your conscience for a moment. How can it be that someone who reads the Qur'an (which was sent down by the Creator of the world and its creatures through a mighty angel to the Best of Creatures, that is, the Messenger of God) while he is sitting on the ground or on thorns and rubbish is called a Muslim, while someone who reads it with the greatest reverence while sitting on a chair is called an infidel? Sixth, if you close an Islamic school because the students there sit on chairs, then why do you allow the Russian school to continue even though they both sit on chairs and learn the Russian language there?

Seventh, in a country where the leaders drink the blood of the people and commit adultery, where the 'ulama' make a usurious profit, betray the rights of the pupils and create discord among the Muslims, where the students drink alcohol, and where the rich have ceased paying alms and commit a great many sins and nobody has prevented them from doing this, nor will they, why do you forbid a useful school just because of chair-sitting? If your 'ulama' are really 'ulama', they should be "the heirs of the prophets" and "like the prophets of Israel." In spite of the fact that God had prohibited oppression in the verses "God does not wish injustice to the creatures of the world" [Sura 3, Verse 108] and "God does not show the unrighteous the way," [Sura 3, Verse 86] why don't they strive to root out the basis of oppression, which is so widespread in Bukhara? For example, in spite of the fact that a single spark of the oppression and despotism of a certain governor burned a vast area of—[the region is left unnamed], so that 20,000 of Muhammad's people emigrated from there to neighboring countries, nobody has asked what is becoming of them, or why they left their homeland, or what the reason is for the ruin of their homes. On the contrary, they made the oppressor the supporter of the—government, and a flood of oppression by such and such a judge ruined the prosperous state of—, uprooted the foundation of a decent life for God's creatures, and claiming that he was wise and pious, the government was given over to him.

Praise God, I still remember that in Marv I met one of those fleeing from the despotism of—. I asked the reason for his flight, and he said, "I had a beautiful wife. Apparently the eldest son of our governor

had heard of her. To satisfy his lust and desire, he sent for me and asked me to send her to him. I refused, and however many sweet promises and fearful threats he made, I refused more firmly. They had no choice but to let me go. Four days later the sergeant-at-arms of the governor came to see me looking like one of the chief guardians of Hell and, accusing me of burglary, bound me hand and foot and carried me away. As soon as the governor's eyes fell on me, it was as if I had escaped several times from him, and without any investigation he put me in jail. After I had spent some time in prison I was forced to present 2,000 tangas[4] to the governor and a thousand to his men, and I was set free. Hoping for some peace, I hurried home. As soon as I reached my house, alas, I saw that the door was open, and there was no sign of my wife and property. I ran here and there like a madman. One of the neighbors said that after I had been jailed, the godless son of the governor sent someone to my wife. The poor thing was afraid and escaped without telling anybody, and the oppressor was so angry that he ordered my property seized. When I heard this I could not bear to stay there any longer. I found my wife in another village, sold my house cheaply, and came here."

Amazing! Aren't these unfortunate people human beings? Aren't they Muhammad's people? Did God not lay down the foundations of justice for the well-being of the people? Doesn't the shari'a forbid oppression so that they may rest easy? I can say with complete confidence that today in every corner of Bukhara a thousand kinds of oppression and cruelty exist, of which the above story is a mild example. However hardhearted, beastly, and pitiless a person may be, it is impossible not to weep at the ruined state of this fallen people. Yes, it is just this that provided the means for the Russian conquest. It is this same oppression that has turned prosperous Bukhara into a land more ruined than the worst wasteland elsewhere. If I ask people, from water-carriers and porters to the greatest nobles of Bukhara, they will all be in accord in preferring the Russian government, which is hostile to Islam, to this irreligious Islam.

The result of this is obvious. If your 'ulama' are really 'ulama', then let them think about putting into effect the divine commands. Let them clear the field

---

4. [A coin used in Central Asia and northern India, worth approximately 15 Russian kopeks in late nineteenth and early twentieth century Bukhara.—Trans.]

in the name of God and bring some progress to Islam. Let them free a group of Muhammad's people from the weight of oppression and rescue Islam from the domination of infidels. Let them prevent a governor who is neither God nor prophet nor saint nor angel, who has neither four eyes nor eight feet, who is neither learned in religion nor artful in politics, who is also, in short, illiterate, from imprisoning one of the best of his subjects, causing his wife to flee, and plundering his property.

TEACHER: These things are not the responsibility of the *'ulama'*, but of the *amir* [the ruler]. How can the *'ulama'* speak against the *amir*?

EUROPEAN: You are lying! His Majesty the *amir* would never, under any circumstances, countenance such oppression of his subjects. The fact is that His Excellency is alone, and it is humanly impossible for him personally to watch the condition of each of his subjects individually. Therefore he sends a person as governor over a group of people. This person collects what they owe to the treasury and maintains order among them. He sends two trustworthy members of the *'ulama'*, designated as *qadi* and *ra'is* [religious leader], along with him to observe his behavior. As soon as he commits an unlawful action, they report it so that he can be dismissed. As soon as these two members of the *'ulama'* reach there, they begin every kind of illegal behavior, to say nothing of leading the governor down a bloodthirsty path. While the unfortunate subjects have no sleep as a result of the wounds of the spears of oppression from these three enemies of mankind, they report to the king that the people are sleeping in the cradle of ease. If the cries of the miserable oppressed should deafen the ears of those in heaven, they write that the people do nothing but pray that the government be everlasting and daily-improving. If it should happen one day that these oppressed people think that they have a king, and that their king is just and kind, and that they should go and present a petition to the king in the hope that he would free them from the tortures of these grandsons of the Lord of Hell, it would do them no good to arrive at the royal court. Despotic wolves have so surrounded the king that even if the peoples' petition became a mosquito and escaped their notice, it would be impossible for it to reach the king. No. Halfway along they [the courtiers] would tear up the petition, lie to the *amir*, cause the people to be severely flogged, send them back, and they would return to their homes in a worse state than before. Now,

tell me what the fault of the *amir* was in this. In 1327 [1909–1910], when Tura Khwaja Sudur was appointed governor of Qarshi, he reported the oppression of the judges to the late *amir*. A royal edict was issued ordering the judges and chiefs to limit and fix the gratuities of their attendants. Unfortunately, the good Sudur was the only person who carried out the order. If you *'ulama'* would report the oppression of the governors to the king and say that cruel governors are giving the king a bad name, and if you say that a despotic government—in keeping with the verse "the wicked will have none to help them" [Qur'an, Sura 2, Verse 270; Sura 3, Verse 192; Sura 5, Verse 72]—will not endure, certainly he will accept what you say. But what is the use; you *'ulama'* of Bukhara are always busy with your sensual desires and have not thought of the progress of Islam or carrying out the divine commands. Truly we have strayed from our subject. What other proofs do you have of the illegality of this school?

TEACHER: If this school should remain in Bukhara for 10 years, all of the schools would be ruined and studying would collapse.

EUROPEAN: If your point here is that learning would be removed from Bukhara, or, in other words, that those associated with the schools would consider the acquisition of knowledge as blasphemy or a sin, then this is false. Just as I have said before, these schools have been operating for years in India, Baghdad, Egypt, the Caucasus, and Kazan, and the inhabitants of these places are many times more learned than the Bukharans. You have admitted that the Indians are more learned and pious than the Bukharans. If you say that "the special method of study that the Bukharans have will be ruined and another substituted for it," what harm for the world of Islam would this have? Let us look at this matter in some detail.

The old method of study, according to you, was like this: the children at age seven go to school and study for ten years and learn to read and write Persian. After this they toil in the seminary, pay all that they own to the schoolmaster, study for twenty years, and finish not knowing any more than the nature of the *lam* of *hamd* and the augmentation of the third radical. Even after studying Arabic for twenty years they are unable to speak it. After they finish, instead of going out to serve Islam and guide the people to the right path, they trample their human dignity underfoot before their fellow men for a meager livelihood. For a minor teaching job they make an illiterate judge's house into the exalted Ka'ba [the sacred site in Mecca] and his doormen into angels of mercy.

The new method of study is this: A child is sent to school at the age of six. At nineteen, the child has become a learned, pious, patriotic, religious, nationalistic, honest, and just person, obedient to all the commands of Islam and possessed of all the characteristics of humanity. The period of study in the old school and seminary was thirty years, and in the new one, thirteen years.

The quality of the old studies was thus: first of all the student enters upon ten years in a miserable, wretched, dark, stuffy room, strongly resembling a corner of a prison or a stable. Every day they have two lessons, accompanied by blows and humiliation from a teacher of the character of the Angel of Death. This is how it goes: "read and pass on!" Nobody cares whether yesterday's lesson is well learned or today's understood.

The nature of the new studies is this: The pupils enter a large building which is pleasant and exhilarating, and which has been built according to hygienic principles. It is situated among spacious gardens and seems like a castle in heaven. Every day they have three lessons (on which they will be examined) from noble, well-favored teachers who do not frown. Between each lesson they have a recess of 15 minutes in the gardens.

The results of the old studies are this: During their period of study the students do no gainful work and spend most of their time in the direst poverty and indebtedness. Because they are so poor they do not marry. After they finish at the age of thirty-seven they must spend at least three years wandering about in search of a livelihood, and by that time they are forty. It is clear that the life span of many of today's men is forty years. Then most of the graduates die without marrying, to say nothing of repaying their debts. Thus the population of Muslims will decrease and some Muslims carry off the property of the people, which is against the *shari'a*.

The results of the new studies are these: The children of the rich will study in private schools, and poor children will attend public schools. They will study in all comfort, and after they have finished, whatever work they turn their hands to—be it teaching, the military, trade, craftsmanship, shopkeeping, or farming—they will find their job easily and without humiliation, and perform it well. Under the old system, because of the length of the course, they withheld

from women the dignity of acquiring knowledge, not conforming to the *hadith* that says, "Seeking knowledge is obligatory for all Muslim men and women." Under the new system, they send a girl to school at the age of six. If they so desire, they may give an educated girl, capable of reading the [Qur'anic] commentaries and *hadith*, to be married at the age of eighteen or fourteen. It is clear now that wherever the new system is in effect for ten years, the old system will naturally break down. This will not harm Islam; on the contrary, it will benefit it.

TEACHER: How can it not be of harm to Islam? The system which the religious scholars, the sages, and our fathers and grandfathers endured will pass away and a new system, invented by unbelievers, will take its place.

EUROPEAN: First of all, the new school is not the invention of unbelievers. Even if it had been invented by the infidels, since it is beneficial to the Muslims in their present condition, what part of the world would be ruined if they adopted it?

TEACHER: No part of the world would be ruined, but if we prefer the new principles to our old system, of necessity we will be preferring infidelity to Islam.

EUROPEAN: Just as the new principles were not invented by the unbelievers, neither is the old system the method of the great men and religious scholars of Islam, such that it would become necessary to prefer infidelity to Islam. Imagine that your method was the method of the great men and religious scholars of Islam; today you have found an easier and more useful method. If you should adopt this, what harm would it have for Islam?

For example, after your fathers and the great men and religious scholars set out on the pilgrimage, they would mount a horse or an ass and spend six months getting from Bukhara to Baghdad or Bombay. From there they would board a sailing ship and in a year's time reach Mecca. After performing the pilgrimage it would be three years and some months before they returned to Bukhara. Now that the infidels have invented trains and steamships, everybody has completely abandoned the way that the great men of your religion traveled, and in the space of twenty-five days they reach Mecca by a means which the infidels invented. The religion has not been lost, and the world has not been ruined. On the contrary, in Bukhara in the old days only twenty people a year were able to make the trip to the Ka'ba, while now a thousand people go. The question of studying is just the same.

Under the old system, women are deprived of learning and most of the men live in illiteracy, and in every generation one or two great scholars appear. Under the new system, because it is easier, both women and men will become learned.

Similarly, during the time of the Prophet and his companions the Qur'an was written in Kufic script on the shoulder-blades of sheep. For a long time now they have been writing it on paper in the *naskh* script because it is easier, and still the sky has not fallen down. The question of studies is the same. The will of God that matters be facilitated is the basis of the *shari'a*, as He says, "God wishes ease and not hardship for you," [Sura 2, Verse 185] and "God would like to lighten your burden, for man was created weak." [Sura 4, Verse 28]

Why Did the Muslim World Decline While the Civilized World Advanced?

Religious scholar, journalist, politician, and author, Musa Jarullah Bigi (Russian Tatarstan, 1875–1949) was one of the most important figures of the Modernist Islamic movement in Russia. Born in Rostov-on-Don, Bigi was raised by his mother, who sent him to a Russian elementary school. He was later trained at religious schools in Kazan, Bukhara, Istanbul, and Cairo, where he studied with an associate of Muhammad 'Abduh (chapter 3). On his return to Russia, he turned to political activism, attending and recording the discussions of the major meetings of the Muslims of Russia. In addition, he taught at a reformist seminary in Orenburg, wrote articles for the reformist press, translated Sufi classics into Tatar, and wrote several books on Islamic jurisprudence. Bigi's work was widely read by religious scholars in Russia and the Ottoman Empire, but not always well received. Bigi was so outspoken in his espousal of Western science and his criticism of traditional Islamic scholarship that even some of his fellow modernists disapproved. Traditionalists called him a heretic. His books were banned by Ottoman authorities, and he was forced to leave Orenburg because of conservatives' hostility. In this typically strongly worded selection, Bigi ascribes the progress of the "civilized world"—which he equates with Europe—to the freedom of thought generated by the Protestant Reformation. He stops short of calling for an equivalent Reformation in Islam, but the selection makes clear why Bigi's critics accused him of aspiring to serve as the "Martin Luther of Islam."[1]

Today there is a large gap between Europe and the Muslim world. The former, determined never to step down, has established itself on the thrones of leadership, politics, and governance; occupied the treasures of the whole world; and concentrated all power in its own hand. The latter, like a captive, was deprived of all political life, and cannot even manage its own affairs. Like a convict, the Muslim world remains everywhere under someone else's control.

There must be a reason for this disparity. While there may be secondary reasons, the real reason is one. However, it is difficult to demonstrate it clearly. It is often difficult to determine properly the real reasons in historical facts and social situations. The civilized world has striven, through the power of the sciences and education, to subjugate both nature and nations. At the same time, the Muslim world has remained inert and remiss. For this reason, the Muslim world declined while the civilized world advanced.

Was that the main reason?

If this was the main reason, what accounts for the former's striving and the latter's inertia?

The light of the sciences and education started in the civilized world in the eighth century. Why then did it remain weak for so many centuries? Why did it die out each time it arose? Why didn't it come to life until the sixteenth century? Why couldn't the effects of progress became widespread [until then]?

Beginning in early sixteenth century Germany, the mind of the civilized world freed itself through

Musa Jarullah Bigi [Bigiyef], *Khalq Nazarïna Bir Nichä Mäs'älä* (*Several Problems for Public Consideration*) (Kazan, Tatarstan, Russia: Äliktro-Tipografiyä Ümid, 1912), pp. 33–39. Translation from Tatar and introduction by Ahmet Kanlıdere.

1. Ahmet Kanlıdere, *Reform within Islam: The Tajdid and Jadid Movement among the Kazan Tatars (1809–1917)* (Istan-
bul, Turkey: Eren Yayıncılık, 1997), pp. 52–56; Azade-Ayşe Rorlich, *The Volga Tatars* (Stanford, Calif.: Hoover Institution Press, 1986), pp. 59–61; Abdullah Battal-Taymas, *Musa Carullah Bigi* (Istanbul, Turkey: Sıralar Matbaası, 1958); Ahmet Kanlıdere, "Rusya Türklerinden Musa Carullah Bigi (1875–1949)" (Musa Jarullah Bigi (1875–1949) of the Russian Turks), M.A. thesis, Marmara Üniversitesi, Istanbul, Turkey, 1988.

the [Protestant] Reformation from religious restrictions and the captivity of the clergy, allowing science and knowledge to breathe freely.

The Reformation, beginning with small issues, rapidly gained great power and provided crucially important ingredients for the civilized world: humans attained their humanity, reason achieved its autonomy, its independence, its freedom, its power. From that time on, human reason moved quickly, unchecked, and began to conquer all the treasures of nature. Mankind recovered its powers of understanding, its powers of action, from the hands of the Catholic clergy and began to move eagerly on the path of science and action. Progress was impossible when reason was imprisoned by popes within the walls of the church. In recent centuries, the works of progress developed rapidly.

The civilized world progressed by saving reason from church authority. At the same time, Muslim *madrasas* [schools] were busy studying the commentaries of medieval theology [*kalam*]. Muslim writers were addicted to, and were proud of, writing commentaries on such texts. At that time, the mind of the Muslims was captive in the hands of unoriginal jurisprudents and philosophers. It must have been this widespread stoppage of brains that caused the mind of the Muslim world to remain lifeless and motionless, and therefore to decline.

The days of the great reformer Martin Luther [German founder of Protestantism, 1483–1546] coincided with the days of the greatest of the Ottoman sultans, Sulayman the Magnificent [1494–1566]. At that time Christian states were weaker than the [Ottoman] Islamic state. However, through reformers like Martin Luther, the Christian world entered on the path of progress; meanwhile, through religious scholars and leaders such as Ibn Kemal [Kemalpaşazâde, Turkish scholar, circa 1468–1534] and [Mehmed] Ebussu'ud [Efendi, Turkish religious leader, circa 1491–1574], the Muslim world went into decline. That is, while the civilized world progressed through the freedom of reason, through the captivity of reason the Muslim world declined.

As if prophesying these great historical facts, the blind Muslim philosopher Abu al-'Ala' [al-Ma'arri, Arab poet, 973–1057] said in his *Luzumiyyat* [*Necessities*]:

They progressed but we went to sleep.
They rose up thanks to our decline.

The ways of progress naturally differ from the beds of ignorance.

If a person's mind becomes captive and is deprived of reason and judgment, it weakens the will for activity, and that person suffers the sickness of inertia. Then even a weak thing can have a great influence on that person.

It must be for this reason that monastical ideas, spread by dervishes—sermons ceaselessly cursing this-worldly life, thoughts seeking comfort and happiness in poverty, Sufi philosophy seeing Satan's work in everything—become influential on the minds and hearts of Muslims suffering from captivity.

For this reason, the Muslim world languished in inertia, intellectually and physically. For this reason, the Muslim world went into decline, while the civilized world progressed. For this reason, a big gap opened between the Muslim world and the civilized world. For this reason, one descended into captivity, while the other was promoted to the honor of rulership.

This is my approach in this matter. This opinion became clear in my mind after studying the political and cultural history of Islam. My conviction became even clearer when I read the works of authors writing about the reasons for the [Muslims'] contemporary situation and remedies for recovery.

Because of the belief that strengthened in my heart, I began to act, consciously or unconsciously. Whatever I wrote, whatever I said, it was all with the guidance of this belief. In every word of mine, in every line I wrote, I had only one thought: to free reason from its captivity; to demolish the confines built by the *madhhabs* [schools of Islamic law]; to break the restrictions of the *madhhabs* completely; to liberate our free will and willpower from their weakness. That is, to free our reason and to strengthen our willpower.

This was my sole purpose, for the main reason for the current situation of the whole Muslim world was the captivity of reason and weakness of willpower.

I certainly believe in the righteousness, greatness, holiness, and heavenliness of Islam. For this reason, the teachings of such a holy religion as Islam should not be confined to the narrow circles of the *madhhabs*. It is a great error to confine Islam to such narrow circles. This is the reason that I deny the limitations of the *madhhabs*.

According to Islam, reason did not used to be confined. It was unrestrained and respected as the proof of the divine. Islamic governments viewed the freedom of reason and thought as fundamental rights, as natural rights. In the age of the *salaf* [the pious ancestors; the first Muslims], there was no narrowness favoring any single *madhhab*. Abandoning reason, confining its power, seeing sciences and education as enemies and cursing its members, labeling freedom as unbelief—all of this insanity must have spread to Islamic philosophers from the Inquisition courts, which continued in the Catholic world for seven centuries. Otherwise, such insanity could never have been reconciled with the spirit of Islam.

The brutality of the Inquisition spread easily into the blood of Islamic philosophers, poisoned by disputes, into the hearts of philosophers swollen with the desire to maintain appearances and break minds. In the name of religion, the Islamic philosophers imposed this brutality on the Muslim world. This calamity, introduced in the name of religion, took root in the minds and hearts [of Muslims]. For this reason, the mind of the Islamic world, its willpower, virtually all its strength became captive. This captivity was the main cause of all disorders and calamities.

Escaping this captivity is the only way to enter onto the path of healthiness. Without freeing mind and willpower, all other remedies are useless and fruitless.

For this reason, I pursued a career of freedom in reasoning, thought, and understanding. I denied the restrictions favored by the followers of the *madhhab*s and stood courageously against the experts of the *madhhab*s in many matters. This was not intended to suggest that the great ones of the past were in error, but to demonstrate my belief in the freedom of thought and reason, my belief in Islam's sublime expansiveness.

I devoted myself to this career, which was like a prologue to our salvation from captivity. It was not harmful for the future, but certainly useful.

I limited myself to writing novels and such, because I doubted my poetic abilities would produce great literature, my mind would produce great thoughts, and my heart would produce great emotions. I saw no use in introducing small thoughts and low feelings into readers' hearts.

I presented many issues to the Muslims of Russia to destroy and demolish the restrictions imposed upon the human mind, willpower, and thought by the experts of the *madhhab*s. Surely my intentions were good. If this goal is achieved, its benefits would be great. None of these were minor issues. In view of the situation of our society, in view of the continuous development of the teachings of Islam, all of these issues were definitely important. Certainly, these issues were more beautiful than love stories and other erotic works, and without their ill effects.

I would like, God willing, to discuss some of the most important of these matters in the next chapter. To conclude this chapter, allow me to present my opinion of our contemporary literature.

In my opinion, the language of our literature is not very correct. Our literature is full of errors of grammar, syntax, and rhetoric. If today's writers corrupt our language through negligence, the language developed by our ancestors will deteriorate. The branches of Turki, originally derived from a single source, will bear no fruit for [Pan-Turkic] unity, and will grow further and further apart.

In my opinion, our contemporary literary production is not suitable to our needs. Love stories, translations from other nations' novels, frivolous and foolish works, and eroticism—none of this is suitable to our needs.

The civilized world has everything. Our future will not please us if we—who are weak in all respects, with all our needs unmet—imitate only the play and games of the civilized world, if we close our ears to the lessons of the civilized world's "bitter experience," if we close our eyes to the causes of ever-increasing murder, dissipation, poverty, and illness.

What we need today is to restrict our literature to serious works; to adopt with all our strength what we need from the civilized world, such as science, education, and industry; to put aside plays and novels; to educate our children with the spirit of trade, agriculture, and activity.

In my opinion, this alone is the path to salvation and the road to progress.

The Patricide

Mahmud Khoja Behbudiy (Samarqand, 1874–1919) was the leading figure among the reformist intellectuals of Russian Central Asia. Born on the outskirts of Samarqand in a family of Islamic scholars, Behbudiy received a traditional Islamic education and worked for most of his life as *qazi* (judge) and *mufti* (jurisconsult). An eight-month trip to Arabia, Transcaucasia, Istanbul, and Cairo brought Behbudiy in contact with currents of cultural reform in the wider Muslim world. Upon his return to Samarqand, Behbudiy began his public career, writing in support for the reform of Muslim education, social customs, and public mores. Behbudi contributed copiously to every newspaper published in Central Asia. In 1913, he launched his own newspaper, *Samarqand*. When financial problems led to its closure, Behbudiy started *Ayina* (*The Mirror*), a weekly magazine which he published almost singlehandedly for the next twenty months. Behbudiy also wrote and published a number of textbooks for new-method schools and established a reading room in Samarqand. Behbudiy was also an advocate of the theater, primarily because he saw it as an effective way of spreading the message of reform. In 1913, he published *Padarkush* (*The Patricide*), the first modern play written in Central Asia, and presented here in translation. The earnest didacticism of the text is typical of modernist writing in Central Asia, as is the faith in the power of knowledge and education to cure all social ills.[1]

Dedicated to the present jubilee commemoration of the Battle of Borodino [1812], and of delivering Russia from the invasion of the French.

Cast of Characters

Mr. Rich [*Bay*],[2] 50 years old

Tashmurad (Young Mr. Rich), Mr. Rich's son, 15 to 17 years old

Mentor, a *mulla* [religious teacher] with modern ideas, 30–40 years old

Intellectual (in European clothes), a Muslim nationalist who has learned Russian

Khayrullah, Mr. Rich's private secretary, 18–20 years old

Tangriqul, murderer of Mr. Rich

Dawlat and Nar (green youths)

Liza, Russian woman of ill repute

Artun, Armenian tavernkeeper

Police Chief, 2 Policemen, 2 Officers

3 Men (Mr. Rich's neighbors)

Mrs. Rich, a woman of 35–40 years

First Act

(Mr. Rich sits in the front room with Khayrullah.)

MENTOR: (Enters.) Peace be upon you.

MR. RICH: Upon you, too, if you please. (Stands up, exchanges greetings, shows Mentor a place, sits down.)

MENTOR: May God the Most High increase Bay's wealth even more than it is now (gives benediction).

Mahmud Khoja Behbudiy, *Padarkush* (*The Patricide*), translated from Uzbek by Edward A. Allworth in "Murder as Metaphor in the First Central Asian Drama," *Ural-Altaischer Jahrbücher/Ural-Altaic Yearbook*, volume 58, 1986, pp. 84–93. First published in 1913. Introduction by Adeeb Khalid.

1. Ahmad Aliyev, *Mahmudkho'ja Behbudiy* (Tashkent, Uzbekistan: Yozuvchi, 1994); D. Alimova and D. Rashidova, *Makhmudkhodzha Bekhbudii i ego Istoricheskie Vozzreniia* (*Mahmud Khoja Behbudiy and his Historical Vision*) (Tashkent, Uzbekistan: Ma'naviyat, 1998); Stéphane A. Dudoignon,

"La question scolaire à Boukhara et au Turkestan russe" (The Education Question in Bukhara and Russian Turkistan), *Cahiers du monde russe* (*Annals of the Russian World*), volume 37, 1996, pp. 133–210; Adeeb Khalid, *The Politics of Muslim Cultural Reform: Jadidism in Central Asia* (Berkeley: University of California Press, 1998).

2. [A *bay* is a rich man. The author does not give this character a personal name.—Ed.]

MR. RICH: O blessed soul, God grant that his prayers are accepted.

MENTOR: Right, Friday evening is the time a prayer is accepted.

MR. RICH: Welcome, sir!

MENTOR: Good health, good health (places hands on his breast).

MR. RICH: Khayrullah! Bring some tea and a tray.

KHAYRULLAH: Very well. (Brings tea and tray. Serves tea; they partake. Tashmurad comes in rudely, without a greeting.)

TASHMURAD: Father! I'm going out for a good time. Gi'me some money!

MR. RICH: My son, who will you go with?

TASHMURAD: With big brother Tursun.

MR. RICH: (Giving money from his purse.) Come in on time, now, and don't go to disreputable places!

TASHMURAD: So long, so long, oh you talk so much. (Goes off.)

(Mentor looking at Mr. Rich and Tashmurad disapprovingly, shakes his head.)

MR. RICH: Let's talk awhile together, sir!

MENTOR: Very well, very well. Young Bay has grown up, I see. God grant him long life. Does he study in a new method school or an old school?

MR. RICH: Why, he studies in neither.

MENTOR: Do you expect to educate him in your own home?

MR. RICH: No, no. I certainly haven't planned to educate my son.

MENTOR: Really! Why don't you educate him? Learning is a religious duty, and besides, knowledge is the reason for worldly honor and eternal nobility.

MR. RICH: To my way of thinking, the reason for worldly honor is wealth. As for the afterlife, God's will be done. So, we see that men honor the wealthy man more than the learned man. Look, in particular, the banks multiply, magnates become members, everyone honors the members. Even the ones who have business pay dearly for the members' goods. More than that, banks won't give money to men who haven't obtained the courtesy of a member. Then, businessmen go bankrupt and there are fewer and fewer. Did you know that?

MENTOR: What you say suits the present day, but the honors of members and wealthy men are ephemeral, only until people's eyes are opened. Meanwhile, just those who have their own business respect them. As for the learned man, the entire country honors him; in other words, a learned man's knowledge is honored.

MR. RICH: Our wealth is honored, too—never mind by Muslims alone—it's honored among Russians and Armenians, as well.

MENTOR: Let's put honor aside. If you educate your son, he will keep your accounts, he will know his devotions and his Muslim way of life very well, and he'll become a reward for your good deeds.

MR. RICH: Paperwork is easy. I give Khayrullah, here, seven rubles a month. He does paperwork daytimes and housework nights, and before I go to sleep he even gives a massage and reads a book to me.

MENTOR: You must without fail educate young Bay, so that he will know the field of Islamic law and the religious requirements.

MR. RICH: I don't consider that teaching the field of Islamic law is needed, for I have no intention of making him a legal advisor or a prayer leader and mosque clerk, inasmuch as my wealth will suffice for him.

MENTOR: What do you say about the requirements for religion?

MR. RICH: I'm acquainted with the obligatory prayers myself for the five worship times. I'll give instruction myself.

MENTOR: What do you say about reading and writing? In fact, an illiterate man serves absolutely no purpose.

MR. RICH: There you're mistaken, because I'm illiterate; nevertheless, I'm one of the magnates of this city, and I know about everything.

MENTOR: Perhaps you became a wealthy man somehow in an earlier day but now don't dream of becoming wealthy. Knowledge is required for someone to live. We observe that over the past 20 to 30 years all business matters passed into the hands of Armenians, Jews, and other foreigners. Our lack of education is the reason for this. We see that uneducated, affluent young men waste their fathers' property and finally become destitute; therefore, I suggest that you educate your son.

MR. RICH: O Mentor! Are you my inquisitor? The son is mine, the wealth is mine; what is it to you? You're one of the educated people, but you've got no bread to eat. Considering your plight, how can you admonish me! Khayrullah! Lock up the living room, I'm sleepy.

(Khayrullah gathers up the tray and dishes and stands waiting.)

MENTOR: (Toward the audience:) Money must be had for studying and becoming a learned man, but here you have the attitude of our wealthy men. So, if things go on like this, God preserve us. We shall be disgraced on earth and in the Hereafter. Learning was always a religious duty for every Muslim, male or female. Where did it stop! Oh, my! In our predicament, (toward Mr. Rich:) Mr. Rich! I placed upon you the obligation of doing a pious deed, and that way, according to Islamic law, I relieved myself of responsibility for the affair, as I had to. God willing, we shall observe the situation of your son, who sprouts a mustache but does not say his ABC's, even with a switch to help him. And you will also be a sinner for not educating him. (Mentor takes snuff.)

MR. RICH: Say, Mentor! I don't need an advisor. You've annoyed me. (Toward the audience:) This man made me miss my work and my sleep. Khayrullah! Lock the living room. (Mentor, offended, quickly goes out; Mr. Rich's chagrin persists.)

(An educated Muslim enters, hangs up his overcoat and staff on a peg. Bay glances reluctantly again and again).

INTELLECTUAL: Peace be upon you.

MR. RICH: (With aversion) Upon you, too. Khayrullah! Bring a chair! This man won't be able to sit on the floor. (Brings chair.) (Bay sits, smokes a cigarette.)

INTELLECTUAL: Good Bay, I see you're out of spirits. Can you tell me why?

MR. RICH: A certain *mulla* visited me just a short while ago and said, "you don't educate your son," and exasperated me terribly. It was so hard for me to get rid of him that it was like throwing him out. We went so far we almost had a brawl.

INTELLECTUAL: Well, it must have been a diverting and interesting incident. (Toward the audience:) God be praised! There seems to be a *mulla* in this town who assigns pious deeds to the wealthy. One must locate this good, upright *mulla* and visit him. Dear Mr. Rich! Don't let this upset you, but I have also intended for some time to say a few words to you about this exact thing. And, because the hour for saying it seems to have been deferred until this very moment, I'll now ask that for a few minutes you lend me your ear and let me speak about the benefits of knowledge.

MR. RICH: (Staring, again and again) Now I understand. You, too, want to press me, saying "educate your son." (Toward the audience:) Today I got up on the wrong side of the bed. Things I had not even thought of happened to me. Evidently, we fall out

of the frying pan into the fire. Khayrullah! Bring me a water pipe! (Both silent.) (Water pipe comes, Mr. Rich smokes, coughs.)

MR. RICH: Khayrullah!

KHAYRULLAH: At your service, sir!

MR. RICH: Make up my bedding. I'm sleepy (yawns). Tomorrow there is a lot of work to do. One must get to bed on time (again a yawn).

KHAYRULLAH: Right, at once.

INTELLECTUAL: (Seriously) Dear Mr. Rich! I told you I intend to speak about fields of knowledge necessary for the nation, but you don't seem to want to hear my opinions! Once again I say: lend me your ears. These words are valuable for you and the nation!

MR. RICH: Do you make people listen to your opinions by pressure and force? Or did you come to torment me?

INTELLECTUAL: No, in reality I came just now for another matter, but I kept my vow about discussing learning, and for this very reason have changed my intention and decided to explain about knowledge to you: If only wealthy men like Your Honor would make an effort to educate the nation's boys.

MR. RICH: (Toward the people:) Oh, if only I had not told the story about Mentor. All right, since you will not drop it, say what you have to say as quickly as possible. I'm getting sleepy (yawn, y- y- y-). "Educate people's boys," he said, eh?

INTELLECTUAL: This is a new and different age. In this age, as the wealth, land, and property of people without knowledge and skill slip from their fingers with every passing day, morals and authority also get out of hand. And even religion weakens. Therefore, we must make an effort to educate Muslims. Meantime, our holy religion has certainly made it a duty for us to study every sort of beneficial science from the cradle to the grave. This commandment is a commandment of Islamic law. For us Muslims, especially in this age, two classes of learned men are required—one of them the scholar of the spiritual, the other the scholar of the temporal. The scholar of the spiritual will become the prayer leader, preacher, seminary instructor, school teacher, civil and criminal court judge, and Muslim legal advisor, and will conduct the religious, moral, and spiritual affairs of the populace. Pupils who enter this class will most likely, first of all in Turkistan and Bukhara, study the field of religion, and of Arabic, and also a little Russian; then, go to Mecca, Medina, Cairo, or Istanbul to complete religious studies. Let them become thoroughly learned men! (Mr. Rich dozes.) Did you understand me, Mr. Rich?

MR. RICH: (Raising his head) Yes, yes, go on talking. You have my attention.

INTELLECTUAL: In order to become scholars of the temporal, it is imperative first of all—after having instructed the boys in the Muslims' writing and reading, and after having made known the requirements of religion and the language of our own nation—for them to attend the regular primary schools of our government. That is, after their having studied and completed high school and the primary schools of the city, it is a must to send the boys to the universities of Petersburg, of Moscow, to teach them medicine, law, engineering, the field of jurisprudence, of commerce, of agriculture, of manufacturing, of economics, of physics, of pedagogy, and others. It is imperative to become a real companion to the homeland and state of Russia. And it is necessary to enter civil service, so that the homeland and the nation of Islam may be served according to our way of life and the needs of our age. And, one must enter the service of the crown, so that a benefit will be conveyed to the Muslims, and also in order that they may become companions to the Russian state. And the Muslim boys as well who have studied in this manner must be sent to the universities of Western Europe, America, and Istanbul for practical experience. Didn't our blessed Prophet say: "Seek knowledge, even though it be in China!"? (Mr. Rich asleep.) These things will not come about unless through money and the generosity of magnates like you. For example, the wealthy men and philanthropists of the Caucasus, Orenburg and Kazan Muslims spend a great deal of money for knowledge, and have their penniless boys educated. (Toward Mr. Rich:) Of course, you have understood what I said, esteemed Mr. Rich! Mr. Rich! Ri-i-ich!

MR. RICH: (Dozes, raises head, yawns.) Yes, yes.

INTELLECTUAL: At present, a bad habit we Turkistan people have is that when a person studies Russian and enters crown service, if he puts on an official uniform, people censure him. Or, if a Muslim boy wears the uniform of the regular government primary school, they jeer. If he is a carriage driver and a manual laborer, he puts on the old clothes of the Europeans, or, being a young fellow, if he puts on a dancer's costume, no one will say a thing. This is the height of stupidity and lack of knowledge about the world. Isn't that so, honorable Mr. Rich?!

MR. RICH: (From his sitting position, leans over to one side and slumps down.) Sn-sn-sno-snore. . . .

INTELLECTUAL: O Lord God! Have mercy on the community of Islam and especially on us Turkistanians. (Wipes away tears with a handkerchief, exits.)

(Curtain falls.)

Second Act

(Tavern scene; three people sit with young Mr. Rich.)

TANGRIQUL: Tonight, I don't know why, the drinks don't affect me. Since sundown prayer I've emptied a dozen bottles. The pimp's beer didn't touch me! Fill 'em up, let's drink!

(Nar fills up the glasses.)

ALL: To Tashmurad's health, to young Mr. Rich, hurrah! Hurrah! Hurrah! (They drink.)

DAWLAT: Pals! I drank the wine, and now sweet Liza came to my mind. O, Liza dear!

ALL: O Liza dear, well Liza dear, are you near?

NAR: Tyrannical fate inflicted her absence on me. In the name of God, she's got t' come.

DAWLAT: Nothing'll come of this grumbling. We'll call the owner. My father died; we'll have a celebration.

NAR: Gi'me your hand! Hey, you son of a bitch (squeezes his hand). Fair enough!

DAWLAT: Hey, come on, Tangriqul! You don't make a sound. You go along taking in everybody's words. There's a right time for a man and a right time for a lion to act. Speak up, don't you respect these people? We're also worth something. Pal! When you're this way, drunkenness is seriousness. Be as happy as you can.

TANGRIQUL: Pals! We have no secrets from you. To tell the truth, I drank the wine. It hit me, and you said "Liza"; now, if I'm really in this myself, I'm hot for Liza. So 'til you bring Liza, you can't make me talk. But, can you really bring her, eh, Dawlat old man!

DAWLAT: Don't worry about your desire. As for Liza, this time you'll see her by your side. If she won't come, I'll kill 'er.

NAR: Young Bay! Have you an itch for the young lady?

TASHMURAD: Fine, go on, send somebody. Get the party warmed up.

TANGRIQUL: You waste a lot of time talking. If you're the one who gives orders, give them. Have her come right away. Let's have some fun. (Dawlat rings.) (Artun, the Armenian tavernkeeper, enters.)

ARTUN: What d'y' say?

DAWLAT: Have someone go to Liza's, so she'll come!

ARTUN: In here!

DAWLAT: Yeh, would y' rather bring her in this place, or to a tomb?

ARTUN: Beg pardon, I only asked.

DAWLAT: All right, all right! Send somebody!

ARTUN: Look, you know what! Liza said to me: "Don't send me anyone without 15 silver rubles!" So, gi'me fifteen silver rubles and carriage fare, too. Let's send Nicholas. If not Liza, let him bring someone else. Have a good time!

DAWLAT: Can't you bring her first and then get the money?

ARTUN: Dawlat, old man, I told y' Liza won't come to me 'til she gets advance payment, right! You know your ownself, this infidel gal isn't mine.

(The drinkers stare at one another in dismay, reach into their change purses.)

TANGRIQUL: Artun! Wait a second, we'll give you some money.

ARTUN: At your service (goes out). (The pals' ex-hilaration subsides; they quiet down.)

DAWLAT: Pour, let's drink. (Nar fills them up.)

TANGRIQUL: It spoiled everything when she had to get the money ahead of time.

DAWLAT: If she's stubborn, that's the way she'll be. Have you any money? All of you get it out. (They all get money out; Dawlat counts; it doesn't add up to five rubles.) Nothing can be done with this. A way out has t'be found.

NAR: (Mockingly) O young Mr. Rich! But what are we beggars to you! The money doesn't come out of your purse. That's young Mr. Rich's character. (Points with his hand.)

DAWLAT: Don't worry, Nar! I thought of something, if young Mr. Rich agrees.

TANGRIQUL: What d'y' mean?

DAWLAT: Just a minute! Before you find out what it may be, let's drink to young Mr. Rich's health. (Tangriqul pours, they drink to health of young Mr. Rich.)

DAWLAT: Young Mr. Rich! Wednesday's celebra-tion, like tonight's, will either be once in a lifetime, or it won't; a particular night won't be repeated a thousand times. If it's all right, I'll pair you off with Tangriqul. You'll go together, and you'll point out

your father's strongbox. Tangriqul will take care of the rest.

TASHMURAD (Young Mr. Rich): Tangriqul, brother, will you go?

TANGRIQUL: If buddies give the orders, I'll go to the other world, even if that's your townhouse.

DAWLAT: What d' y' say, Nar!

NAR: I'm one of the group, too. If you say so, I'll go.

DAWLAT: No, the two are enough. People mustn't get suspicious when they see them—tomorrow is another day.

NAR: Young Mr. Rich! Do you know where your father's strongbox is located?

TASHMURAD: In my father's bedroom.

DAWLAT: How many doors does his bedroom have?

TASHMURAD: Three.

DAWLAT: Which door will you enter by?

TASHMURAD: One of the doors opens from my mother's room. I'll go in and open the door located on the court side. Then brother Tangriqul will come in.

DAWLAT: Good boy! You must have done some thieving before. Nar! Fill 'em up, let's drink! (Nar fills them, they drink.) (Dawlat to Tangriqul and Tashmurad:) Do you plan to go now?

TANGRIQUL: Of course, why not go? (Dawlat gives his pistol to young Mr. Rich. Nar takes a knife from the leg of his boot, gives it to Tangriqul. They con-ceal them and stand up.)

DAWLAT: (Looking at the pair) Good luck, heroes!

TANGRIQUL: So he'll get it . . . (Dawlat takes Tangriqul to one side, gives sign and secret informa-tion and instructions.)

NAR: Amen, God.

ALL: God is great. (Dawlat gives benediction.) (Tangriqul and Tashmurad go out.) (Dawlat and Nar drink and sing.)

(Curtain falls.)

Third Act

(As is customary, Mr. Rich asleep on bedstead, strongbox in one corner of the room.) (Tashmurad enters stealthily through one door, looking this way and that, opens another door and stands aside.)

TANGRIQUL: (Enters, a key and an iron tool in his hands, knife at his belt; goes to the strongbox, uses key. Strongbox won't open; he looks at Tashmurad. With a gesture, asks what to do. Tashmurad signals him to break open the strongbox with the iron tool. Tangriqul breaks open strongbox with iron tool. Mr. Rich rouses at the noise of the strongbox.)

MR. RICH: (Starts up, seizes club.) Help, help (runs toward Tangriqul).

TASHMURAD: (Comes and grabs the club.)

TANGRIQUL: (Stabs Mr. Rich in armpit with knife.)

MR. RICH: (Collapses and falls.) Aaah, my soul! (Wheezes, tumbles, dies.)

TANGRIQUL: (Lifts moneybag from strongbox; hides knife and iron tool on himself; voices of some people heard from outside.)

People: What's wrong, someone cried for help. (Mr. Rich's wife enters with several men. They see Tangriqul and Tashmurad.)

TANGRIQUL: Tashmurad, shoot! (Tashmurad fires pistol in the air, they run away, now pointing the weapon at people who entered.)

MRS. RICH: Oh, thanks to a monster, what a day this is, help, police! (Slaps hands together, throws self on Mr. Rich, tears her face and hair.) Ey, Tashmurad, dead before your time! Vomit blood! If only you had perished of smallpox. Akh, Tashmurad, the patricide. Help, pol-i-i-ce!

MENTOR: (Enters.) Mother dear! For you, there is no alternative but patience. The causes of this unhappiness and calamity are backwardness and stupidity, ignorance and lack of training. Stupidity wrecked your home. Ignorance deprived you of home and family. Ignorance will send your son to Siberia. The misfortune of having no training will remove your beloved child from your heart and make his life separate from you. Your boy's father didn't train him or educate him. In the end, he ran into misfortune. Evil associates led him astray, so you became a victim of backwardness.

MRS. RICH: (Writhing) Ay, oh oh my boy. O, my master. Ah, o o o oh.

MENTOR: But your master turned a deaf ear to my admonition, and in the end, a terrible thing like this happened . Now, there is no recourse for you beyond bitter restraint, mother dear! May God grant you patience.

MRS. RICH: (Sobs hysterically.) O, my boy. Ah, my master. I've been cut off from both of them. They'll send my husband to the grave, my boy to Siberia. Oh oh oh h h.

(Curtain falls.)

Fourth Scene

(The same tavern as in the second act.)

NAR, DAWLAT: (Sit drinking and singing.)

TANGRIQUL and TASHMURAD: (Enter sweating and exhausted; hide pistol and bloody knife to one side; taking out moneybag; throw it on the table; sit down.)

TANGRIQUL: Bring a water pipe, hey!

ARTUN: (Brings a water pipe; they smoke. Artun exits.)

TANGRIQUL: (Taking Dawlat to one side, speaks confidentially, makes gestures.)

DAWLAT: ("Calmly.") (Speaks in undertone, with gestures; makes them quiet down.) (Opens moneybag, peers in, is delighted. Claps Tangriqul and Tashmurad on the shoulder.) Good work! Good work! (Rings bell; Artun enters.)

ARTUN: What'll y' have?

DAWLAT: Here, take the money, get Liza right away.

ARTUN: At your service. she'll come at once. (Takes money; they drink.)

LIZA: (Enters.) Good evenun'. (Exchanges greetings with everyone.)

DAWLAT: Glad y're here, tanks, y'come.

LIZA: Merci. (Sits down.)

DAWLAT: Fill 'em up! T' Liza's health!

NAR: (Pours, makes bow.) To Liza's health, hurrah, hurrah. (They drink.)

DAWLAT, NAR: (Sing a song; the sound of a whistle comes from outside. The tramp of feet is heard. The gathering becomes agitated, startled. Armed policemen, a police chief, and officers burst in.)

LIZA: (Runs away.)

POLICE: (Seize the four individuals; some look for culprits and search all around. They find the bloody knife and pistol, and turn the pistol over to the Police Chief. He sniffs it, examines it, empties cartridges.)

TANGRIQUL and TASHMURAD: (Run off; officers seize them.)

TASHMURAD: (Weeps, cries and cries, becomes extremely agitated.)

POLICE CHIEF: (Makes a signal. Bringing arm fetters, they shackle Tangriqul and Tashmurad. Hands of the other two are tied.) (Forms criminals and officers in a line.)

MENTOR: (Enters; looks at criminals, shows regret. Toward the audience:) That is the fate of backward and untrained boys; and if their fathers had educated them this robbery and patricide committed by them wouldn't have taken place; and they wouldn't have drunk liquor this way, and would not have incurred blood guilt unjustly. They would not remain in Siberia and in chains all of their lives, and on the Judgment Day stay in Hades. And if these people didn't drink liquor, they wouldn't remain in torment and suffering in the world, and in the Hereafter, to all eternity. O, truly, it is ignorance which murdered Mr. Rich and plunged these young men into an eternity of torment. It is untutoredness and backwardness which destroyed our life and made Mr. Rich's son weep, without a country, exiled, expatriated; rootlessness, the slavery of poverty and want, and humiliation, all are the fruit and consequence of ignorance and untutoredness. The people who have made progress in the world progressed by means of knowledge. When people became prisoners and wretched, it was from ignorance. So long as we are untrained and do not educate our children, evil events and ill luck must continue to reign among us. There is no way, other than studying and educating, to put an end to these affairs. May God the most high grant others the benefit of example and give you patience.

POLICE CHIEF: (Imperiously) Move along, prison, march! (They start off.)

(Curtain falls.)

Doctor Muhammad-Yar

Abdulhamid Sulayman, writing under the pseudonym Cholpan (Uzbekistan, 1893–1938) was one of the founders of modern Uzbek literature. As poet, playwright, novelist, and translator, Cholpan left an indelible imprint on his cultural milieu. The son of one of the wealthiest merchants in Andijan in the Ferghana Valley, Cholpan attended a so-called Russian-native school. His precocious talents led him to public life when still in his teens. He was also an active participant in the modernist reform movement in Central Asia. After the Russian revolution of 1917, Cholpan produced his greatest work, although his emphasis shifted much more to nationalism. He was arrested and executed in 1938, one of the innumerable victims of Stalinist terror. The story translated here is arguably the first piece of modern prose fiction in the Uzbek language. Serialized in a newspaper in 1914, it played an influential role in Central Asian modernism. The story is very much a juvenile work—Cholpan was a teenager when he wrote it. Still, for all its artlessness and its implausible plot, the story incorporates many of the central themes of modernist rhetoric in Central Asia: the power of knowledge, the value of collective action, patriotism, and a fascination with cosmopolitan modernity, and an intense didacticism.[1]

In a dark corner of Turkistan, in the town of—, lived a poor, sixty-year-old barber called Haji Ahmad. His wife had died of consumption after struggling bravely with it for nine months. She left behind a son called Muhammad-Yar. Haji Ahmad was known in his town as Haji Barber, because at the age of fifteen he had gone on *hajj* [pilgrimage to Mecca] with his father. His father died on the *hajj*, and Haji Ahmad traveled alone in Egypt, Istanbul, Fars, Morocco, Baluchistan, Baghdad, Iran, and Afghanistan, as well as in inner Russia, for 10 years before returning home. As a result of his travels, he could speak Persian, Arabic, Russian, and English. But because he had suffered many hardships in his travels due to his ignorance, he energetically set about educating his son Muhammad-Yar as soon as he was old enough.

When Muhammad-Yar was ten, a teacher from Russia, a graduate of the Great Seminary in Ufa, arrived in town. He had been in town only for a week

or two when he heard of the barber "who read newspapers and knew seventy-two languages," and went to his barbershop to meet him. Muhammad-Yar was also there. At a sign from his father, he got up and welcomed the teacher with the utmost respect. Haji Ahmad and the teacher sat and talked for a long time. During the conversation, Haji Ahmad said, "I have only this one son. I want to educate him according to the needs of the times. If you are willing, give him a good national education, so that afterwards I may have him taught in a government school." After some thought, the teacher accepted. Haji Ahmad closed his shop and took the teacher to his house. The young Muhammad-Yar studied enthusiastically with the teacher. And he spent his spare time not at tea houses, parties, and brothels, as uneducated boys do, but in physical training under the guidance of a Russian officer, and in reading useful books. In this time, he mastered all the commands of Islam, as well as history and geography. After a year, Haji Ahmad wanted to send his beloved son to a government school. But alas! He had no money. This poverty was very op-

Abdulhamid Sulayman Cholpan, "Do'khtur Muhammadyor" (Doctor Muhammad-Yar), edited by Sirojiddin Ahmad and Ulughbek Dolimov, *Sharq yulduzi* (*Star of the East*), 1992, number 1, pp. 132–138. First published in *Sada-yi Turkistan* (*The Voice of Turkistan*), Tashkent, Russian Turkistan, July 4, July 25, August 10, October 26, November 5, and November 12, 1914. Translation from Uzbek by Adeeb Khalid and Ken Petersen. Introduction by Adeeb Khalid.

1. Adeeb Khalid, *The Politics of Muslim Cultural Reform: Jadidism in Central Asia* (Berkeley: University of California Press, 1998), pp. 104–105; Naim Karimov, *Abdulhamid Sulaymon o'ghli Cho'lpon* (*Abdulhamid Sulayman Cholpan*) (Tashkent, Uzbekistan: Fan, 1991).

pressive and threatened to deprive the poor child of all excellence and learning.

Having no other choice, Haji Ahmad and the teacher went to all the notables of the city in search of help. Some of the merchants refused them entry as soon as they saw the teacher's [modern] dress, while others received them; some, seeing Muhammad-Yar's beauty, offered him a salary as secretary and personal servant. However, our Haji Ahmad knew what these men were up to and therefore refused to give his beloved son to them. Poor Haji Ahmad gave up hope of receiving any help from the rich merchants and began to explore other avenues. At this time, numerous wedding feasts were being celebrated in the town,[2] while gamblers and drunks knifed each other, and human blood cried, "Ignorance! Ignorance!" as it flowed. One after the other, all the student aid societies had closed.

In the meantime, the teacher prepared to leave town. At nine o'clock, Haji Ahmad went to the railway station along with his son to see the teacher off. On the way back, they came upon gamblers fighting over money. Haji Ahmad went up to separate them and give them advice. One of them came up and strangled Haji Ahmad to death, and injured Muhammad-Yar. As he gave up his life, Haji Ahmad looked at his son and said, "My son! Instead of a legacy . . . I . . . leave . . . you . . . as security . . . study . . . study . . . study . . ."

Muhammad-Yar decided to seek out the murderers of his father and exact revenge. But the real murderer of his father was not these men but rather ignorance; so he peacefully buried his father and resolved to struggle against ignorance. As for the weapons in the struggle against ignorance, his father had already told him that they were not cannons, guns, pistols, daggers, or bows and arrows, but only "Study! Study! Study!"

The barbaric murder of his father, and the sorrows at seeing his homeland, Turkistan—which had once created a name for itself through knowledge and learning—swimming in a river of ignorance, made Muhammad-Yar fall ill with tuberculosis. The effects of the disease began to show on his face, though it did not afflict him fully. At this time, a big fire broke out in the town and destroyed six or

seven neighborhoods, leaving the Muslims hungry on the streets. In their midst was an Armenian shop as well, but its loss was smaller because the shop was insured. And what of our Muslims? Our Muslims didn't even know what insurance was. Those who knew what it was thought it was illicit, and therefore would have none of it. Seeing this state of affairs, how was it possible to remain unmoved? As he saw this state of affairs, poor Muhammad-Yar's illness began to worsen.

In the new city, an admonitory film called "Drunkenness and Its Terrible Consequences" was showing at the Admonition theater. No matter how bad he felt, he could not stay away. He waited impatiently for the evening in order to see the consequences of this accursed drunkenness.

At last, after the evening prayer, he set off on foot for the Admonition theater. [As the film played,] a shot rang out from the yard of the theater. The film was stopped and everybody ran outside. Poor, weak Muhammad-Yar, too, was among them. What a sight! In the yard of the city theater, drunks playing cards had argued over a small amount of money; one of them had taken out a handgun and shot the other. The culprit was apprehended and the injured taken to the hospital, but he died along the way. The culprit, thoroughly confused, shot himself in the theater's yard.

Two young Muslims said goodbye to this world due to ignorance. The horrible consequences of drunkenness were truly on display.

Seeing this, Muhammad-Yar fainted. The police took him to the city hospital. Muhammad-Yar had no father, no mother, no relatives . . . There was no one to ask after him. Ah, loneliness! Ah, orphanhood! Ah, the cause of it all: Ignorance! Go! Disappear!! Die!!!

Muhammad-Yar got better after a month's treatment in the hospital. As he left the hospital, the doctors recommended that he go to the Caucasus for treatment, and that he study while there.

Muhammad-Yar told the doctors of his pennilessness. The doctors consulted for a while and then gave him a letter that entitled him to be treated in any hospital in the Caucasus without having to pay a kopek. Muhammad-Yar left the hospital and went home. There was no one there: no father, no mother . . . What a sad sight! He rented the house to a Russian for six months for 225 rubles, and set off, at seven o'clock, for the railway station to see if there was a train. But there was no train until nine the next

2. [Lavish celebrations were a major focus of modernist Islamic criticism in Central Asia.—Trans.]

morning. Sadly, he went back home and became an overnight guest in his own house.

The next morning, he was at the railway station, waiting for the train. At last, twentieth-century civilization arrived, snorting like a dragon, spewing water in every direction . . . Muhammad-Yar was about to leave his homeland. It was a strange sight at the station, as Muhammad-Yar's heart began to break.

A Muslim had lost his bags! Another didn't know the name of the station he was going to and therefore had bought a ticket for the wrong station. Confronted with such scenes, Muhammad-Yar was left immobile. At last, after the second whistle, he got up and began to look for a place in the third class. The sad scenes mentioned above were in evidence in even greater force here. One Muslim had a bloody nose from fighting with another; another Muslim was taken away by train officials and beaten. Muhammad-Yar was left immobile. He left the car and, standing on one side, began to look around. An Armenian from some dark corner of the Caucasus had opened a shop at the station and had become rich. Two of his sons studied in government schools. Local Muslims, on the other hand, spent all their incomes on circumcisions and funerals, and were all in conditions of poverty and humiliation. His heart sank again; again, the nervousness . . . He was absorbed in thought. The third whistle came. The horseless carriage of the twentieth century announced its departure and began to move noisily forward. With that, Muhammad-Yar had left his sacred homeland and was on his way to other lands, to see other societies. He entered the third car and began walking around aimlessly. His head was full of worries about Turkistan. Suddenly somebody called out, "Muhammad-Yar!"

Muhammad-Yar looked up. It was Petr, the Russian officer who had given him physical training.

"Where are you going?" Muhammad-Yar asked the officer.

"I've been transferred to a different station on military business. Where are you going?" he asked.

Muhammad-Yar thought for a while and then said, "Into exile."

"Why?"

"To study—study—study."

"Is your father all right?"

Tears came to Muhammad-Yar's eyes at this question. "He's dead," he replied.

Hearing these words, the officer's eyes too filled with kind tears.

Muhammad-Yar borrowed a pair of binoculars from the officer and went out into the corridor. The train was marching on, spewing water onto the soil of his homeland and attracting the attention of the local Muslims living in the vicinity. Muhammad-Yar stood looking at the distant mountains through the binoculars. His eyes filled with tears and he addressed the homeland he was leaving behind:

"O black mountains who have seen the troops of Genghis [Khan] and [Amir] Timur [Central Asian rulers, died 1227 and 1405]. O old mountains who have seen the older epochs of my land Turkistan! Tell honestly: Now you see the civilization of the 20th century too! Seeing that this stallion of 20th-century civilization can cover a three-day journey in 10 hours, why do my compatriots stand around with their mouths agape? Why don't they do anything to enter this civilization? How long will they keep these two-wheeled carts that don't belong on the streets?

"O compatriots! How long this ignorance? Why this heedlessness? After all, you too are human beings! Act like human beings! Why don't you make use of the fruits of knowledge and education that you see before you? Why don't you participate in these things? Awake from your sleep. Struggle! Seek out knowledge, education, skills! The time has come—indeed, it is past!"

At seven in the evening, the officer and Muhammad-Yar parted, and Muhammad-Yar went to his place and fell asleep.

A few days later, Muhammad-Yar found himself at the great railway station of Baku. With his bundle and other things in his hand, he quickly descended from the train and took a carriage to the city center. The city of Baku, famous for its Muslim millionaires, wealthy Muslim merchants, many Turkic societies, and charitable funds worth millions, seemed wonderful to Muhammad-Yar. He went to the offices of the city's premier newspaper, *The Caucasus*, a 10-page daily which circulated in every Muslim city. He explained his circumstances in detail to the editor, who replied, "I'll seek a solution."

Muhammad-Yar left the offices to see the city. That night he spent in a hotel called "The Caspian Sea," which had been built according to Eastern architectural traditions by one of the city's [Muslim] millionaires. In the morning, he bought a copy of *The Caucasus* from a famous bookstore. At the top, he saw the following announcement:

ANNOUNCEMENT: From the Muslim Benevolent Society: We wish to send Muhammad-Yar, a 14-year-old coreligionist who has come here in search of knowledge from our neighbor Turkistan, to a government school at our expense. There will be a meeting of the Benevolent Society on this matter at 7:30 this evening. All the esteemed members must gather punctually at this time. Mr. Muhammad-Yar should also be present. Respectfully, The Director.

At half past seven that evening, after some discussion among members, the Society decided to give Muhammad-Yar a scholarship on condition that he lecture in Baku and its environs for two years after completing his studies. Muhammad-Yar had struck good fortune indeed. From here on, he would be able to reap the fruits of all the struggles he had endured. He was ready to serve his homeland and his nation with his body and soul.

Muhammad-Yar, who had received no aid in his own land from his compatriots, had achieved his hopes through the efforts of the youths of Baku. That is, he entered the city school, achieving his most sacred goal. Now he would serve his homeland and the compatriots who had humiliated him. Muhammad-Yar thought about his land and his place, and it made him cry.

One evening, he was reading a newspaper on a bench in the city park when he saw the headline, "The First Theater Performance in Turkistan." When he finished reading the story, he could hardly sit still, and began to jump for joy. Meanwhile, one of his friends among the young journalists of Baku had appeared and was startled at his jumping. He caught him by the shirt-tail, sat him down on the bench, and asked, "Muhammad-Yar! Why are you so happy?"

Muhammad-Yar could only say, "The first theater p . . . p . . . performance in T . . . Tur . . . kis . . . stan." The Baku journalist sat for a while, then got up and left. When Muhammad-Yar looked at the time, it was midnight. Nobody was left in the park, so Muhammad-Yar also stood up and left.

As exams approached, Muhammad-Yar worked day and night. At last, the exam came. Muhammad-Yar stood first among his classmates. Because of his unstinting labors, Muhammad-Yar began to show signs of illness again. On his doctors' recommendation, he went to the waters of Borzhum for a month of treatment.

Now, again with the help of the same benevolent society, Muhammad-Yar entered the Baku *gimnazia* [Russian school]. He loved his lessons so much that he didn't leave school, even on holidays. Hours passed, then days, then years. The time eventually came for Muhammad-Yar to leave the *gimnaziia* as well. At last, it was time for his final exams. Muhammad-Yar stood first again and won a gold medal for his efforts. Muhammad-Yar entered the medical faculty of Petrograd University—again with the help of the Benevolent Society and the efforts of the Baku merchants. In his second year there, he wrote *Students for Life*, a novel based on the lives of *madrasa* [traditional-school] students in his native Turkistan. It had twelve chapters—no novel of this size had ever appeared about national life in Turkistan. The novel was even translated into Russian and published by a Russian journal in Petrograd. This novel was so well written that nobody—even if they spent forty to fifty years in a *madrasa*—could have better described the *madrasa* students and how they spent all their time hanging around samovars instead of studying. A year before he finished his studies at the university, he wrote *Guests of the Capital*, a play about Turkistani merchants in Moscow and Petrograd. This play showed with consummate expertise the insults suffered by uneducated merchants in the hotels of the capitals, simply because of their ignorance of language and science. This book Muhammad-Yar translated into Russian himself and published. Along with some friends, Muhammad-Yar staged the story as a play in Petrograd to support themselves. Muhammad-Yar played the lead role himself and received much applause. After expenses, the players were left with 3,000 rubles for themselves.

Finally, exam time came. Muhammad-Yar stood first yet again, and received his doctor's diploma. But still he did not return home. With the help of the philanthropic merchants of Baku and his own money earned from the theater, this Turkistani student went to Switzerland to gain practical experience in Swiss universities.

All his school friends were present at the railway station to see him off on the evening train. A poor Turkistani boy, having finished Russian schools through his hard work and energy, was on his way to study in one of the most advanced countries of Europe.

Here then was the fruit of his labor, the fruit of his hard work, the harvest yielded by his efforts. May this be an example . . . an example . . . an example . . . Such are the benefits of benevolent societies, the product of solidarity, the fruits of unity . . .

Our Turkistani child reached the capital of Switzerland on the "stallion of civilization," and enrolled as an auditor in the medical faculty of the university. The poor student spent seven years in Switzerland, enduring good times and bad with patience and steadfastness. At last, he left Switzerland. Traveling through the lands of Italy, Turkey, Rumania, and Bulgaria, he reached Odessa, and then Baku.

All the young intellectuals of Baku were present at the railway station to receive Muhammad-Yar, their "spiritual father," and gave him a banquet with fifty or sixty people in attendance. He taught in the Muslim medical courses that had begun in Baku three years before and then got ready to return to his homeland, Turkistan. Having taken leave of his mentor in Baku, he asked his advice of helping his homeland, which seemed to be swimming in a sea of ignorance. When his mentor gave his permission, all the young intellectuals of Baku came to see him off at the steamer docks in the evening. His mentor gave him a gold watch with the inscription, "Souvenir of Baku." Those present asked for a brief speech. Muhammad-Yar gave a short speech from the deck. The audience applauded him loudly and began tossing flowers at him. Finally, the steamer gave a whistle and, ruffling the waters of the sea, set off toward Turkistan.

Muhammad-Yar's speech given from the deck of the steamer was as follows:

"O spiritual brothers! And O spiritual fathers! I was a poor student who came to your city in search of knowledge and education from the darkest corner of Turkistan. With the national effort of your zealous inhabitants, I followed education through Russian universities all the way to European ones. In reality, this is all the fruit of benevolent societies and publishing companies. I too will roll up my sleeves to help my land and work to awaken my brothers who are left behind in ignorance. I sincerely thank my spiritual home Baku, and you, my spiritual parents, and acknowledge your help in awakening us Turkistanis, who are like dragon fish in the river of ignorance, and helping us find the path." At this point, the steamer began to move slowly. "Be well, my fathers and brothers!" he finished.

The mechanical fish, splitting the water, was bringing a servant to his homeland. At last he alighted in a savage place and mounted the "stallion

of civilization." Where were the seas and waters with their delicate breezes? Where were the beauties of the Alps that he had seen a few years earlier in Switzerland, France, and Italy? Where were the Swiss villages built atop the Alps, where they spend their earnings in educating their beloved children, and not on feasts, *uloq*,[3] dancing boys, or providing embroidered clothes for noblemen, *mulla*s [religious teachers], and other fat-bellied types? Now they were all gone! In their place were low buildings made of thatch and mud, and the Muslims living in them in an orphaned state! The Uzbeks, Kazaks, Turkmens, and other Muslims, having spent their incomes on dancing boys, *uloq*, and drink, or on providing expensive garments and brocades for teachers, noblemen, and the wealthy, had become slaves to their landlords.

Ah! Ah! Ah! Muhammad-Yar, who had seen progress and civilization and who knew all, was deeply affected at seeing this baseness in his own nation, among his own people. Sometimes tears flowed from his eyes. On top of it all, inside the train, disorderly Muslims slept noisily and were beaten by the conductors for having lost their tickets. Muhammad-Yar couldn't stand it any longer. He went to the corridor and stared with tear-filled eyes at the majestic mountains visible in the distance—historic mountains which in the times of his ancestors had borne huge forts—and the peaks, rivers, forests, and sands. The beautiful scenes, the distant, tall, green mountains, were no less than in Switzerland. The water flowing in the rivers and the fertile land that gave to whomever sowed it—they were in no way inferior to America. Because of uneducated merchants, ignorant "scholars," false noblemen, and wastefulness, it resembled nothing. Even the Chinese were not so lazy!

How wonderful would it be if the people understood what was good for them—if they opened national schools and colleges, sent their children to European universities, and produced doctors, lawyers, journalists, skilled merchants and engineers—and if each one of them stuck to his duties and looked out for the good of our people. Such were his thoughts. But he couldn't believe this could happen. The farther we go, the farther behind we seem to fall.

---

3. [*Uloq* is a traditional game akin to polo, in which competitors struggle for the possession of the carcass of a sheep. It was accompanied by carnivalesque celebration and betting.—Trans.]

No, no! If intellectuals like Muhammad-Yar began to appear in every town in ones or twos, that would almost be enough. Muhammad-Yar's head was filled with many thoughts all the way to his town.

His town approached. Since he had left, five or ten intellectuals had emerged in his town too. They welcomed him. They got into a carriage and set off for the old city. There were all sorts of changes in the Russian part of town: new hotels, houses, parks, shops, theaters, schools; the streets were paved, the alleys wide, the electric lamps resembled Switzerland! The part of town where Muslims lived, however, was exactly the same. More grief. . . . Muhammad-Yar got down in front of his own house. It had been redone in the European manner by the Russian who had rented it from Muhammad-Yar for 225 rubles for six months. Muhammad-Yar saw him and introduced himself in Russian.

The Russian said, "I rented it from you for six months. No one appeared after six months, or a year. In the third year, I built this. It cost 5 or 10 thousand rubles. But three years ago, I finished recovering all the money. In the last three years, I made 9,000 rubles from 3,000. I'll vacate your place quickly and also give you 5,000 rubles. Please forgive the rest."

[Muhammad-Yar said:] "If you don't have a place, stay here. I only need two rooms here."

"I have another nice place. I'll move there. I would have given you 9,000 rubles, but 4,000 went for improvements."

Muhammad-Yar happily accepted. The next morning, the Russian vacated the house and gave Muhammad-Yar 5,000 rubles. Muhammad-Yar began to live happily in the spacious place. He rented out the shops below the house and, with the permission of the government, opened a private clinic upstairs and began treating patients—the wealthy for a fee, the poor for free. He made fifty to sixty rubles every day from his practice alone.

He bought a small plot in a village. Because of Muhammad-Yar's effort and God-given luck, he struck oil. Now millionaires came to Muhammad-Yar to work with him. On one hand, he started his own business; on the other, he gathered the few intellectuals in town and opened a benevolent society to which he gave a lot of money. A reading room opened in the city. This year, Muhammad-Yar began publishing an illustrated weekly called *Homeland* and a daily newspaper called *News*. When he raised the issue of vocational schools, many opponents emerged, so in its place he started summer courses for teachers where they were given lectures on the principles of education. Thus houses of learning began to proliferate in a small town, which became a model for others. The Turco-Tatar press began calling Muhammad-Yar "Doctor Muhammad-Yar, Servant of the Nation."

SECTION 5

South Asia

The Flow and Ebb of Islam

Khwaja Altaf Hussein Hali (North India, 1837–1914) was a pioneer in modern Urdu poetry. He came from a learned family in Panipat, United Provinces, and ran away to Delhi to pursue his studies. He was forced to return home and get married, then ran away again to pursue higher education. While working at the Punjab government book depot in Lahore, revising translations from English into Urdu, he developed an interest in English poetry and Western literary criticism. This interest led him to show his own verses to well-known poets of the era, Ghalib (1797–1869) and Shaifta (died 1869), who encouraged and sponsored him as he explored modern, humanistic themes, rather than romantic stock images that were popular at the time. Symptomatic of his altered mentality was the change of his pen name, from *Khasta* (distressed, exhausted) to *Hali* (modern, up-to-date). As both a poet and literary critic of great influence—his discussion of poetry prefacing his own collected poems is a classic—Hali evolved new styles of Urdu expression. Like many other Indian modernists of the era, Hali came into the sphere of Sir Sayyid Ahmad Khan (see chapter 40), for whose journal Hali wrote the long poem *Musaddas*, which is excerpted here. (The term "*Musaddas*" refers to the format of six lines per stanza.) The poem nostalgically laments Muslim decline, but also offers a message of hope and reform. It is the pioneering work in a genre emerging in Urdu that combined ethical and political themes with a strong Islamic orientation.[1]

The State of the Religion of Islam

But as for that dilapidated hall of the true religion,
    whose pillars have been tottering for ages,
Which will remain in the world only a few days
    more, and which the Muslims will not find
    again for all their searching,
Our noble friends have withdrawn their
    attention from it. The only guardian of the
    building is God.

The Lack of Holy Men

All the Sufi sanctuaries lie in ruins, those
    places of hope for the poor man and the king,
Where the paths of esoteric knowledge were open,
    on which the glances of the angels used to fall.
Where are those snares of divine longing?
Where are those holy men of God?

The Lack of Religious Experts

Where are those masters of the science of the
    Holy Law? Where are those expounders of
    religious Traditions?
Where are those fundamentalists and controversialists, where are those teachers of *hadith*
    [narratives of the Prophet] and Qur'anic
    interpretation?
In the assembly which was brilliantly lit
    throughout yesterday, the lamp does not even
    flicker anywhere now.

Khwaja Altaf Hussein Hali, *Hali's Musaddas: The Flow and Ebb of Islam*, translated from Urdu by Christopher Shackle and Javed Majeed (Delhi, India: Oxford University Press, 1997), pp. 167–177. First published in 1879. Introduction by Marcia K. Hermansen.

1. Aziz Ahmad, "Hali, Khwaja Altaf Hussain," in Bernard Lewis *et alia*, editors, *Encyclopedia of Islam*, 2d ed. (Leiden, Netherlands: E. J. Brill; London: Luzac, 1971), volume 3, pp. 93–94; Gail Minault, *Voices of Silence* (Delhi, India: Chanakya Publications, 1986); Frances W. Pritchett, *Nets of Awareness: Urdu Poetry and Its Critics* (Berkeley: University of California Press, 1994); Laurel Steele, "Hali and his Muqaddamah: The Creation of a Literary Attitude in Nineteenth Century India," *Annual of Urdu Studies*, volume 1, 1981, pp. 1–45.

Where are those schools of instruction in the
faith? Where are those stages of knowledge
and certitude?

Where are those pillars of the firmly fixed
Law? Where are those heirs of the trusty
Apostle?

The Community has no refuge of asylum left,
no judge or juristconsult, no mystic or
theologian.

The Lack of Religious Books

Where are those archives of religious books?
Where are those manifestations of divine
science?

Such a cold wind has blown upon this festive
gathering that the torches of divine light are
utterly extinguished.

No furnishings nor company are left, no flask
or instrument, no musician or cupbearer.

Those Who Claim Knowledge

Many people, making themselves out to be
well-wishers of the Community, and getting
the ignorant to acknowledge their excellence,

Keep continually going round from village to
village in turn, accumulating wealth.

These are the ones who are now acknowledged
as the leaders of Islam, these are the one who
now have the title of "heirs to the Prophet."

Those Who Claim to be Holy

Many people make themselves out to the
descendants of *pir*s [Sufi masters], without
having any excellence in their noble selves.

They take great pride merely in the fact that
their ancestors were the favorites of God.

As they go about, they work false wonders.
They eat by robbing their disciples.

These are the ones who journey on the mystic
way, whose station lies beyond the Holy
Law.

It is with them that revelation and the power of
miracles reach their apogee today.

It is in their power that the fate of God's
creatures lies.

It is these who are the objects of devotion now,
and these are their disciples.

These are the Junayds, these are the Bayazids now.[2]

Contemporary Theologians

To make speeches through which hate may be
inflamed, to compose writings through which
hearts may be wounded,

To despise God's sinful creatures, to brand
their Muslim brothers infidels,

This is the way of our theologians, this is the
method of our guides.

If someone goes to ask them about a problem,
he will come away with a heavy burden laid
upon him.

If, unfortunately, he has some doubt about the
matter, he will certainly be branded with the
title of "damned."

If he openly utters an objection, it will be
difficult for him to get away from there
unharmed.

Sometimes they make the veins in their neck
swell, sometimes they foam at the mouth.

Sometimes they call him "pig" and "dog,"
sometimes they raise their staff to strike him.

They (may the evil eye be far!) are the pillars of
our religion. They are the exemplars of the
gentleness of the trusted Apostle.

If a man wishes to be happy in their company,
it is a necessary condition that he be a
Muslim by community,

That he should have the mark of prostration
clearly visible upon his forehead, that there
should be no shortcoming in his observance
of the Law,

That his mustaches should not be too long, nor
his beard curled back, nor his trousers be cut
beyond their proper length,

2. [Junayd al-Baghdadi (Arabia, 10th century), *Shaykh*
Junayd (Iran, 15th century), Abu Yazid Bayazid al-Bastami
(Iran, 9th century), and *Pir* Roshan Bayazid Ansari (South
Asia, 16th century) were influential mystics.—Ed.]

That in all matters of belief he should be of the
same opinion as "His Reverence," that he
should speak with the same voice on every
principle and point of the Law,

That he should be most suspicious of his
master's opponents, and utter the most
fulsome praises of his disciples.

If he is not like this, he is an outcast from his
religion, unfit to associate with its revered
elders.

The commands of the Holy Law were so
agreeable that Jews and Christians were filled
with love for them.

The entire Qur'an is witness to their mildness.
The Prophet himself proclaimed, "Religion is
easy."

But here they have made them so difficult that
believers have come to consider them a
burden.

They have given believers no guidance in
morality, nor produced purity in their hearts.

But they have so increased external commandments that there is no escaping them even for
a moment.

They have turned the religion which was the
spring from which virtuous gentleness
flowed into the dirty water left from bathing
and ablutions.

In their hearts they continually bear hostility
toward those who truly inquire, thinking that
by relying upon the Traditions the Faith is
injured.

The whole basis of their practice lies in their
*fatwa*s [rulings]. Their every opinion is an
excellent substitute for the Qur'an.

Only the name of the Book and the Prophet's
example remain. They have no further use for
God and the Prophet.

Where Traditions differ among themselves, we
are never content with the straightforward
Tradition.

We consider the one which reason would never
regard as sound to be superior to every other
Tradition.

Whether great or small, all are caught up in
this, so weighed down has our understanding
become.

Polytheism and Claims to Monotheism

If a non-Muslim worships idols, he is an
infidel. Whoever attributes a son to God is an
infidel.

If someone bows down before fire as an act of
prostration, he is an infidel. If someone
believes in the power of the stars, he is an
infidel.

If for believers all paths are open— let them
worship with enthusiasm whatever they please.

Let those who so please turn the Prophet into
God. Let them exalt the *imam*s [founders of
legal schools] above the Prophet in rank.

Let them make offerings day and night at
shrines. Let them keep going to offer their
prayers to the martyrs.

Not the slightest injury will result to the belief
in God's oneness. Their Islam will not be
spoilt nor their faith leave them.

That religion, by which monotheism was spread
throughout the world, by which the truth was
made gloriously manifest in space and time,

In which no trace of polytheism, superstition or
idle fancy was left, that religion was changed
when it came to India.

That upon which Islam had always prided
itself, even that treasure was finally thrown
away by the Muslims.

Bigotry

Bigotry, which is the foe of humankind, which
has been the ruin of hundreds of prosperous
homes,

Which broke up Nimrod's [legendary Biblical
figure] merry feast, which offered Pharaoh
[the Egyptian ruler] up to the storm,

By whose ferment Abu Lahab [early enemy of
Islam] was destroyed, and which sank the
fleet of Abu Jahl [another early enemy of
Islam],

Appears here in a strange guise, under cover of
which its harmful effect is concealed.

The cup which is entirely filled with poison
appears to us to be the Water of Eternal Life.

We think bigotry to be a part of faith, and hell
  to be the highest heaven.

This is the teaching our preachers have given
  us: "No matter what task there be, religious
  or worldly,
It is bad to perform it in imitation of one's
  opponent." The mark of the real spirit of the
  True Faith is simply this:
"Think of everything in the opposite way to
  your opponent. Think of whatever he calls
  night as day.

"If you find his steps set on the straight road,
  then go off on a diversion from the direct
  route.
Endure whatever obstacles you may encounter
  upon it. No matter how much you suffer, let
  yourselves stumble on it.
If his craft gets safely out of the whirlpool,
  push your boat right into it.

"If your features are hideously transmogrified,
  if your conduct comes to resemble that of
  beasts,
If your nature completely alters, if your
  condition is utterly ruined,
Then consider that this too is a manifestation of
  God, that this too is a reflection of the light
  of faith.

"In manners no one resembles you, none can
  surpass you in morality.
No one can attain this same enjoyment in their
  food, nor discover the same elegance in
  dress.

In every branch of learning your attainments
  are plain. Even in your ignorance there is a
  certain grace.

"Do not think that anything of yours is bad. Go
  on loudly proclaiming what you have to say.
Since you stand in defense of Islam, you are
  free from any evil or sin.
Evil does not cause believers to suffer harm. Your
  sins are the same as the obedience of others.

"If you speak of your enemy, then mention him
  with vilification and abuse.
Never give ground unwittingly in this matter.
  You will see its results on the Day of
  Judgment.
It is as if you were freed from sins when you
  curse your adversaries."

When there is no love between Sunni and Shi'a
  [two major sects of Islam], no sense of
  community between Numani and Shafi'i [two
  legal schools in Sunni Islam],
No abatement of the hatred between Wahhabi
  [scripturalists] and Sufi [mystics], and when
  the Traditionalist curses his opponent,
There is such civil war being waged by the
  people of the qibla [the direction of prayer]
  that the whole world laughs at God's religion.

If anyone sets himself to the task of reform,
  consider him to be worse than Satan.
The path of anyone who seeks benefit from
  such a trouble-maker must have diverged
  from God.
Both destroy the Holy Law, and both, master
  and pupil, are accursed.

The Proposed Political, Legal, and Social Reforms

Chiragh 'Ali (North India, 1844–1895), a staunch supporter of Sayyid Ahmad Khan (chapter 40), was the Aligarh movement's most outspoken critic of traditional Islamic scholarship and legal stagnation. Of Kashmiri background, he grew up in North India. After his father died young, Chiragh 'Ali's family responsibilities, along with the turbulent events of the 1857 uprising, prevented him from pursuing formal higher education. Still, he was able to find work with the colonial regime in various revenue and judicial positions. In 1877, with the recommendation of Sir Sayyid, he entered the administration of the Nizam of Hyderabad, where he rose to the position of finance secretary. Chiragh 'Ali's writings often refuted missionary and Orientalist criticisms of Islam as being hostile to reason and incapable of reform. He argued, rather, that the Islamic legal system and schools were human institutions capable of modification. His position was that while the Qur'an taught religious doctrine and rules for morality, it did not support a detailed code of immutable civil law or dictate a specific political system. In his English-language writings, such as the passage that follows—and in his Urdu articles, many published in Sir Sayyid's journal, *Tahdhib al-Akhlaq* (*Cultivation of Morals*)—Chiragh 'Ali espoused a variety of modernist positions, including the importance of girls' education. His arguments on interpretation of *hadith* (narratives of the Prophet) and the possibility of *ijtihad* (rational interpretation) drew on the writings of Shah Wali Allah al-Dihlawi (Indian religious scholar, 1703–1762), a precursor to modernist Islamic thought in South Asia.[1]

"Let there be people among you who shall invite to good, and bid what is reasonable, and forbid what is wrong; these are the prosperous." (The Qur'an, Sura 3, Verse 100)

and are now published for the information of those European and Anglo-Indian writers who, I am sorry to remark, suffer under a delusion that Islam is incapable of any political, legal, or social reforms.

Introductory

The following pages were written on the perusal of an article entitled "Are Reforms Possible under Mussulman Rule?" by the Reverend Mr. Malcolm MacColl [1831–1907] in the *Contemporary Review* of August 1881, in the last quarter of the same year,

The British Empire, the Greatest Muhammadan Power

It is very unbecoming of English writers to be so ill-informed on a topic of vital interest to England. The British Empire is the greatest Muhammadan Power in the world, that is, the Queen of England, as Empress of India, rules over more Muhammadans than

Moulavi Cheragh Ali, *The Proposed Political, Legal, and Social Reforms in the Ottoman Empire and Other Mohammadan States* (Bombay, India: Printed at the Education Society's Press, Byculla, 1883), pp. i–lx. Introduction by Marcia K. Hermansen.

1. Munawwar Husain, *Maulavi Chiragh 'Ali ki 'Ilmi Khidmat (The Intellectual Contribution of Maulavi Chiragh 'Ali)* (Patna, India: Khuda Bakhsh Library, 1997); Peter

Hardy, *Muslims of British India* (Cambridge, England: Cambridge University Press, 1972), pp. 111–114; Aziz Ahmad, *Islamic Modernism in India and Pakistan, 1857–1964* (New York: Oxford University Press, 1967), pp. 57–64; Gail Minault, "Chiragh 'Ali," in John L. Esposito, ed., *Oxford Encyclopedia of the Modern Islamic World* (New York: Oxford University Press, 1995), volume 1, pp. 278–279.

any sovereign, not excepting His Imperial Majesty the [Ottoman] Sultan of Turkey.[2]

European Knowledge of Muhammadanism Always Superficial

The ideas that Islam is essentially rigid and inaccessible to change; that its laws, religious, political and social, are based on a set of specific precepts which can neither be added to, nor taken from, nor modified to suit altered circumstances; that its political system is theocratic; and that in short the Islamic code of law is unalterable and unchangeable, have taken a firm hold of the European mind, which is never at any trouble to be enlightened on the subject. The writers of Europe do not deeply search the foundations of Islam, in consequence of which their knowledge is not only superficial in the highest degree, but is often based on unreliable sources.

Islam Capable of Moral and Social Progress

I have endeavored to show in this book that Muhammadanism as taught by Muhammad, the Arabian Prophet, possesses sufficient elasticity to enable it to adapt itself to the social and political revolutions going on around it. The Muhammadan Common Law, or *shariʿa*, if it can be called a Common Law, as it does not contain any Statute Law, is by no means unchangeable or unalterable. The only law of Muhammad or Islam is the Qurʾan, and only the Qurʾan, which in comparison with the Muhammadan Common Law the Rev. MacColl himself admits to be a code of purity and mercy.[3]

Republican Character of the Muslim Law

The Muhammadan states are not theocratic in their system of government, and the Muhammadan law being based on the principles of democracy is on

this account a great check on Muslim tyrants. The first four or five caliphates [reigns of successors to Muhammad] were purely republican in all their features. The law, when originally framed, did not recognize the existence of a king, of a nobility, or even of a gentry in the sense in which the term was at first understood. The position of the early caliphs and their authority might be compared to that of the dictators of the ancient Republic of Rome, each successor being chosen from amongst the people by common consent. The government of Turkey does not and cannot claim or profess to be theocratic, as Mr. MacColl tries to prove.[4] Sir Henry Elliot [1817–1907], the British Ambassador at Constantinople, writes in his Dispatch of the 25th May 1876 regarding the *softa*s [seminary students], "Texts from the Qurʾan are circulated with a view to proving to the faithful that the form of government sanctioned by it is properly democratic."

The Several Schools of Muhammadan Jurisprudence

There have been several churches, or schools of jurisprudence, developed in accordance with the social and political changes going on around the Muhammadan world, with a view of adapting the law still further to the progressive needs and altered circumstances of the Muslim. But none of these schools was final, all of them being decidedly progressive; they were merely halting stages in the march of Muhammadan legislation.

The following are the founders of the schools of interpretation or the system of jurisprudence called *madhhab*:

Names of Founders (Dates of Death)

1. ʿAbdullah Ibn Masʿud (32 A.H.) [companion of the Prophet, died 652–653 A.D.]
2. ʿAbdullah ibn ʿUmar [ibn al-Khattab] (73 A.H.) [companion of the Prophet, died 693 A.D.]
3. ʿAʾisha [bint Abi Bakr], the widow of the Prophet (58 A.H.) [678 A.D.]
4. Mujahid [ibn Jabr al-Makki] (between 100 and 104 A.H.) [718–722 A.D.]
5. ʿUmar ibn ʿAbd al-ʿAziz (101 A.H.) [720 A.D.]

---

2. The number of Muhammadans in British India is estimated at 45,000,000, while there are only 16,168,000 Muhammadans of the Sultan in Europe, Asia, and Africa.

3. Reverend Mr. MacColl, "The Christian Subjects of the Porte," *Contemporary Review*, November 1876, p. 986.

4. *Ibidem*, p. 977.

6. Al-Sha'bi (103 or 104 A.H.) [728 A.D.]
7. 'Ata' [ibn Abi Rabah] (115 A.H.) [733 A.D.]
8. [Abu Muhammad Sulayman] al-A'mash (147 or 149 A.H.) [circa 765 A.D.]
9. *Imam* Abu Hanifa (150 A.H.) [767 A.D.]
10. [Abu 'Amr 'Abd al-Rahman] al-Awza'i (157 A.H.) [774 A.D.]
11. Sufyan al-Thawri (161 A.H.) [778 A.D.]
12. *Imam* Layth [ibn Sa'd] (175 A.H.) [791 A.D.]
13. *Imam* Malik [ibn Anas] (179 A.H.) [796 A.D.]
14. Sufyan ibn 'Uyayna (196 A.H.) [811 A.D.]
15. *Imam* [Abu 'Abdullah Muhammad] al-Shafi'i (204 A.H.) [820 A.D.]
16. Ishaq Abu Ya'qub Ibn Rahwayh (238 A.H.) [853 A.D.]
17. *Imam* Ahmad ibn Hanbal (241 A.H.) [855 A.D.]
18. *Imam* Dawud Abu Sulayman al-Zahiri (270 A.H.) [884 A.D.]
19. Muhammad ibn Jarir al-Tabari (310 A.H.) [923 A.D.]

The Change in Modern Circumstances Requires a Change in the Law

It might be supposed that as the growing needs of the Muslim Empire led to the formation of the several schools of jurisprudence, the various systems of interpretation of the Qur'an, and the different methods of testing and accepting the authority of the oral traditions; so now the requirements of modern social and political life, as well as the change of circumstances, as is to be perceived in Turkey and India, might be met by a new system of analogical reasonings and strict adherence to the principles of the Qur'an hitherto not regarded as the sole and all-sufficient guide. Legislation is a science experimental and inductive, not logical and deductive. The differences of climate, character, or history must be observed; the wants and wishes of men, their social and political circumstances must be taken into consideration, as it was done in the various stages of the first days of the growing Muslim Empire.

The Several Schools of Jurisprudence Based on the Above Principles

All the four *mujtahids*, or founders of the schools of Muhammadan jurisprudence now in force, and others whose schools have now become extinct, had adhered to the principles above referred to, which

were moreover local in their applications, and hence could not be binding either on the Muhammadans of India or those of Turkey.

Mr. Sell Quoted

The Reverend Mr. Edward Sell [1839–1932] writes: "The orthodox belief is, that since the time of the four *imams* [leaders; namely, Malik, Abu Hanifa, Ibn Hanbal, and Shafi'i, founders of the four major Sunni *madhhabs*] there has been no *mujtahid* who could do as they did. If circumstances should arise which absolutely require some decision to be arrived at, it must be given in full accordance with the *madhhab*, or school of interpretation, to which the person framing the decision belongs. This effectually prevents all change, and by excluding innovation, whether good or bad, keeps Islam stationary."[5]

Changes Not Prevented

There is no legal or religious authority for such an orthodox belief, or rather misbelief, nor can it be binding on Muslims in general. In the first place, the founders of the four schools of jurisprudence never claimed any authority for their system or legal decisions as being final. They could not dare do so. They were very far from imposing their analogical deductions or private judgments on their contemporaries, much less of making their system binding on the future generation of the wide-spreading Muslim Empire. In the second place, none of the *mujtahids*[6] or *muhaddiths* [scholars of *hadith*, sayings of the Prophet] would accord such a high position to any of the four *imams* or doctors of jurisprudence.

Muqallids

Muqallids[7] (those who follow blindly any of the four doctors or schools of jurisprudence, without having

---

5. The Reverend E. Sell, Fellow of the University of Madras, *The Faith of Islam* (1880), p. 23.
6. "*Mujtahid* is derived from *jahd*, same as *jihad* [holy struggle], meaning making efforts of mind to attain the right solution of legal questions.
7. The word is derived from *taqlid*, which means to put a collar round the neck.

any opinion, insight, discretion, or knowledge of their own) only entertain the belief that since the time of the four *mujtahid*s there has been no other *mujtahid* who can found a school of analogical deductions or a system of interpretation; they say, "we are shut up to following the four *imam*s," and "to follow any other than the four *imam*s is unlawful," as quoted by Mr. Sell from *Nihayat al-murad* [*The Ultimate Purpose*, by 'Abd al-Ghani Nabulusi, 1641–1731] and *Tafsir-i Ahmadi* [*The Ahmadi Exegesis*, by Shaykh Ahmad Mulla Jivan, 1637–1717]. Both these books have been the productions of the worst of *muqallid*s. Mr. Sell, without taking notice, perhaps, of the distinction between *mujtahid*s and *muqallid*s, quotes from the latter to show the authority of the four *imam*s, and at the same time the finality of their system of legislation and polity to be binding on the whole of the Muhammadan world, the non-*muqallid*s, the *mujtahid*s, and the scholars of *hadith*. No regard is, however, to be paid to the opinions and theories of the *muqallid*s.

Ijtihad (Elaboration of New Ideas) Not Extinct

The Hanbali school of jurisprudence, one of the four so-called orthodox systems, very emphatically asserts that there should be a *mujtahid* in each age. Now the *muqallid*s consider the *ijtihad* (the state of being a *mujtahid*) to have become extinct since the four *imam*s, and will not believe in the possibility of the appearance of any more *mujtahid*s; and their advocate, Mr. Sell, will be very much perplexed to discover the mistake of their delusive theory.

Bahr Al-'Ulum Quoted

I will, here, refer Mr. Sell to *Maulavi* 'Abd al-'Ali [al-Lakhnawi, circa 1731–1810], surnamed Bahr al-'Ulum (the ocean of sciences!), who spent the latter part of his life at Madras. In his commentary on the *Musallam al-thubut* [*The Sure Proof*, by Muhibb Allah Bihari, died 1707], named *Fawatih al-rahamut* [*Keys to the Realm of Mercy*], treating on the principles of the Muhammadan Common Law, the *maulavi* writes: "Some people consider that *ijtihad fi'l-madhhab*, relative independence in legislation [as long as one remains within the rulings of the same

madhhab, or legal school], was closed after the death of *Allama* ['Abdullah ibn Ahmad al-]Nasafi [died 1310], and *ijtihad mutlaq*, or absolute independence, had become extinct since the four *imam*s [founders of the four Sunni legal schools]. These men have gone so far as to make it incumbent on Muslims to follow one of these *imam*s. This is one of their many foolish ideas, which can have no authority for itself, nor should we pay any regard to what they say. They are among those in connection with whom the Prophetical *hadith* has that 'they award their decision without knowledge, they go astray, and mislead others. They have not understood that this assertion is a pretension to know the future which is only known to God.' Referring to Sura 34, Verse 31, which has '. . . but no soul knoweth what it shall have gotten on the morrow.'"

Characteristics of the Schools of Jurisprudence

The characteristics of each of the four orthodox schools now in force would show that they were never intended to be either divine or finite.

Hanafis. Imam Abu Hanifa made almost no use of traditions [*hadith*s] as a source of law, admitting only 18 of them as authoritative in his system. His jurisprudence was exclusively founded on private opinion and analogy, called *ra'i* and *qiyas* respectively. Taking these two principles for the basis, he and most of his disciples spun out a complete legal system. His own teaching was oral, and he compiled no book. All the maxims, theories, hypotheses, logical deductions, inferences, and developments worked out by his disciples and their disciples—of whom Abu Hanifa never dreamt—in their turn, go by his name, and authority. The disciple of Abu Hanifa named Abu Yusuf [Ya'qub al-Kufi, died 798] was far too prone to set aside traditions in his legal decisions and resolve points of law by means of rational deductions, which in fact destroyed the tradition or Common Law under the pretense of obeying it.

Malikis. The system of legislation adopted by *Imam* Malik was chiefly based on "the customs of Medina." It may be called strictly a Common Law comprising usages and practices of the people among whom he lived, and for whom he wrote the hitherto unwritten law. He utilized 300 traditions [*hadith*s] in his *Muwatta'* [*The Well-Trodden Path*]. It was, moreover, a system better adapted to the simple modes of Arabian life than the elaborate, artificial, and complicated one of the Hanafis. The system of *Imam* Malik, based, as it was, on the customs of Medina, was purely a local one. The precepts which sufficed for the primitive Arab city were not deemed efficient to cope with the wants of a vast concourse of human beings abroad. But by some chance, the system of *Imam* Malik prevailed chiefly throughout Spain and Northern Africa.

Shafi'is. Imam Shafi'i was an eclectic. He built up his system on the materials of Abu Hanifa and Malik. But he was the first person who composed a work on the principles of exegesis and jurisprudence, called *usul*.

Hanbalis. Imam Ahmad ibn Hanbal discarded altogether the principle of deductions or analogical judgments. In his *Musnad* [*hadith* collection], he embodied 30,000 traditions [*hadith*s]. His system was both in its theological and legal aspects, a reaction to the lax spirit of the age. The Hanafi court jurisconsults under the caliph Ma'mun [reigned 813–833], by the extreme elasticity which the principle of analogical deductions[8] afforded them, found no difficulty in making the moral doctrines of the Qur'an subservient to the most wanton excesses of arbitrary power, and pandering to the licentious passions of caliphs and *amir*s [rulers]. To check this great evil, *Imam* Ahmad had resort to the prophetical traditions which were current amongst the commonalty. Though most of these traditions were unauthentic fabrications, they contained the principles of the republican form of government, and hence were well suited to check the profligacies of despotic caliphs.

---

8. I have given an instance of such ridiculous deductions [later in] this work. There is another cited by Colonel [Robert Durie] Osborn [1835–1889] in *Islam under the Khalifs of Baghdad*, p. 28. "Thus," he writes, "there is a verse in the Second Sura [verse 22] which says, 'God has created the whole world for *you*.' According to the Hanafi jurists, this text is a deed of gift which annuls all other rights of property. The 'you' means, of course, the true believers; and the whole world has been created for their use and benefit. The whole earth they then classify under three heads: 1) land which never had an owner; 2) land which had an owner and has been abandoned; 3) *the persons and the property of the infidels*. From this third division the same legists deduce the legitimacy of slavery, piracy, and a state of perpetual war between the faithful and the unbelieving world." I have not come across such a fanciful corollary, and I do not think the persons and property of the non-Muslims can come under the divisions of the Earth. Perhaps Colonel Osborn was misinformed. [. . .]

Zahiris. I here take the opportunity of mentioning another orthodox system of jurisprudence founded by Dawud Abu Sulayman al-Zahiri, a native of Isfahan, generally known by his surname al-Zahiri, which means the exteriorist. He was so called because be founded his system of jurisprudence on the exterior or literal meaning of the Qur'anic texts and traditions. He thus rejected the authority of an *ijma'* (the general consent of the Muslims), and the *qiyas* or analogical judgments, the third and the fourth sources of Muhammadan jurisprudence. He was born in 201 or 202 A.H. and died in 270 A.H.[9] His system was a reaction to the Hanafi school, as he rejected both *ijma'* and *qiyas*. Another reaction was that of Ahmad bin Hanbal, who rejected the analogical reasoning, and held an *ijma'*, or the unanimous consent of the *mujtahid*s, at a certain time impossible. [Abu Muhammad 'Ali] Ibn Hazm [994–1064] and [Muhyi al-Din] Ibn 'Arabi [1165–1240], the two Spanish writers, as well as [Abu Ishaq Ibrahim ibn Sayyar al-]Nazzam (died 231) [845 A.D.] and [Muhammad] Ibn Habban (died 354) [965 A.D.], have likewise denounced the authority of an *ijma'* other than that of the Companions of the Prophet.

These Systems Not Finite in Their Nature

This account of some of the important and main schools of jurisprudence will be sufficient to prove that none of the systems was imposed as finite or divine, and that neither the founders of these sundry systems intended them to be so, nor wished their own to bear precedence over others. Every system was progressive, incomplete, changeable, and undergoing alterations and improvements. The logical deductions, analogical judgments, and capricious speculations which were adhered to for want of information in the beginning were wholly done away with in after days, in the system of legislation. Every tendency was centered in legislating with regard to the wants and wishes of the people, and to the changes in the political and social circumstances of the new [Islamic] Empire. Every new school of jurisprudence made legislation experimental and inductive, while the former systems of speculative

---

9. See Ibn Khallikan [1211–1282], *Biographical Dictionary*, translated by [Baron William] de Slane [1801–1878], volume 1, p. 502, note 1.

and deductive legislation were shelved into oblivion. Ahmad ibn Hanbal, the last of the four orthodox *imams*, wholly disregarded the fourth principle of Muhammadan legislation, that is, analogical reasoning or deductive judgment. About a century later, the Zahiri school set aside the third principle also, that is, the *ijma'* or the unanimous consent of the Doctors of Law in a certain epoch, as the former *ijma'*s on several points of legislation did not well suit the altered circumstances of later ages. Consequently, the legislation of the Muhammadan Common Law cannot be called immutable; on the contrary, it is changeable and progressive.

Review of the Sources of the Law

I have given a short sketch of the principal schools of Muhammadan jurisprudence in the foregoing pages. I will here review briefly the sources of its civil and canon law. There are three constituent elements of the Muhammadan Common Law: first, the Qur'an; second, the traditions from the Prophet and his Companions; third, the unanimous consent of the learned Muhammadans on a point of the civil or canon law not to be found in the two preceding sources; [and] last, the supplemental source, the *qiyas*, [an] analogy of the process of reasoning by which a rule of law is established from any of the three elements.

The Qur'an

The Qur'an does not profess to teach a social and political law, all its precepts and preachings being aimed at a complete regeneration of the Arabian community. It was neither the object of the Qur'an, the Muhammadan Revealed Law, to give particular and detailed instructions in the Civil Law, nor to lay down general principles of jurisprudence. Some points of the civil and political law which were the most corrupt and abused have been noticed in it, such as polygamy, divorce, concubinage, and slavery. In these as well as other denunciations against immoral practices, the Qur'an has checked and removed the gross levity of the age. A few judicious, reasonable, helpful, and harmless accommodations were allowed by the Qur'an to some of the civil and social institutions of the pagan and barbarous Arabs, owing to their weakness and immaturity. These accommodations were set aside in

their adult strength, or in other words when they had begun to emerge under its influence from their barbarism into a higher condition of amelioration.

The more important civil and political institutions of the Muhammadan Common Law based on the Qur'an are bare inferences and deductions from a single word or an isolated sentence. Slavish adherence to the letter, and taking not the least notice of the spirit of the Qur'an, is the sad characteristic of the Qur'anic interpretations and deductions of the Muhammadan doctors. It has been said there are about 200 out of 6,000 verses of the Qur'an on the civil, criminal, fiscal, political, devotional, and ceremonial (canon or ecclesiastical) law. Even this insignificant number of the *ayat ahkam* (law verses), a thirtieth part of the first source of the law, is not to be depended upon. These are no specific rules, and more than three-fourths of them, I believe, are mere letters, single words, or mutilated sentences from which fanciful deductions repugnant to reason, and not allowable by any law of sound interpretations, are drawn.[10]

For the purpose of legal and juridical interpretations of the Qur'an, apart from the doctrinal, moral, prophetical, and historical interpretations, the words, sentences, and their uses have been divided and subdivided into four symmetrical divisions as follows:

Words
　Khass (Special)
　'Amm (Collective or Common)
　Mushtarik (Complex)
　Mu'awwal (Required to be explained)
Sentences
　Zahir (Obvious)
　　Zahir (Obvious)
　　Nass (Manifest)
　　Mufassar (Explained)
　　Muhkam (Perspicacious)
　Khafi (Hidden)
　　Khafi (Hidden)
　　Mushkal (Ambiguous)
　　Mujmal (Compendious)
　　Mutashabih (Intricate or Allegorical)

10. Some of the Muhammadan doctors have exerted themselves in picking out the law verses, as they are so called, and in compiling separate treatises in which they have made an abstract of all such verses of the Qur'an. They have applied them to the different heads of the various branches of the canon and civil law, giving their fanciful processes of reasoning and the deductive system of jurisprudence.

Their Uses
   Haqiqat (Literal)
   Majaz (Figurative)
   Sarih (Clear)
   Kinaya (Metaphorical)
The Process of Reasoning
   'Ibarat (Plain Sentence)
   Isharat (Hint)
   Dalalat (Argument)
   Iqtida' (Requirement)

This will show that the 200 verses are not specific rules or particular teachings of the Qur'an on the civil law, most of the deductions being fortuitous interpretations.

In short the Qur'an does not interfere in political questions, nor does it lay down specific rules of conduct in the Civil Law. What it teaches is a revelation of certain doctrines of religion and certain general rules of morality. Under the latter head come all those civil institutions of the ancient Arabs, such as infanticide, polygamy, arbitrary divorce, concubinage, degradation of women, drunkenness, reckless gambling, extortionate usury, superstitious arts of divination, and other civil institutions which were combined with religious superstition and gross idolatry. These all have either been condemned, or ameliorated and reformed. These subjects are neither treated as civil in situations, nor have any specific rules been laid down for their conduct. But the Muhammadans have applied the precepts of the Qur'an to the institutions of their daily life to as great an extent as the Christians have done with regard to those of the Bible, and as much as circumstances permitted. There has been a tendency rather to expand than to contract the application of the Jewish law to the wants of modern society. In Christendom, theology has been severed from morals and politics only very lately. "The separation from morals was effected late in the seventeenth century; the separation from politics before the middle of the eighteenth century."[11] The enlightened Muhammadans of Turkey and India are in this nineteenth century striving to do the same, and this will, in no way, affect their religion. How futile is the remark of Sir W[illiam] Muir [1819–1905], who writes, "The Coran [Qur'an] has so encrusted the religion in a hard and unyielding casement of

ordinances and social laws, that if the shell be broken, the life is gone."[12]

The Traditions or Sunna

There is a vast ocean of traditions from the Prophet, his Companions and their successors, on the various subjects of the social, political, civil, and criminal law incorporated in the Muhammadan law books. In fact the Companions of the Prophet and their successors were averse to commit to writing the traditions concerning the private life and public teachings of the Prophet. But naturally the conversation of the followers of the Prophet was much about him. The Companions and their successors enthusiastically expatiated upon his acts and sayings, specially when the later generations had endowed him with supernatural powers, and the same was the case with the [Christian] Gospels. Consequently the traditions grew apace. The vast flood of traditions soon formed a chaotic sea. Truth and error, fact and fable, mingled together in an indistinguishable confusion. Every religious, social, and political system was defended, when necessary, to please a caliph or an *amir*, to serve his purpose, by an appeal to some oral traditions. The name of Muhammad was abused to support all manner of lies and absurdities, or to satisfy the passion, caprice, or arbitrary will of the despots, leaving out of consideration the creation of any standard of test.

It was too late when the loose and fabricated traditions had been indiscriminately mixed up with genuine traditions, that the private and individual zeal began to sift the mass of cumbrous traditions. The six standard collections of traditions[13] were compiled in the third century of the Muhammadan era, but the sifting was not based on any critical, historical, or rational principles. The mass of the existing traditions were made to pass a pseudocritical ordeal. It was not the subject matter of the tradition, nor its internal and historical evidence which tested the genuineness of a tradition, but the unimpeachable character of its

11. [Henry Thomas] Buckle [1821–1862], *History of Civilization in England* (London, 1878), volume 1, p. 425.

12. *The Early Caliphate and Rise of Islam*, being the Rede Lecture for 1881, by Sir William Muir, p. 26.

13. Muhammad ibn Isma'il Bukhari, died 256 A.H. [870 A.D.]; Muslim ibn al-Hajjaj Nishapuri, died 261 A.H. [875 A.D.]; Abu Da'ud al-Sijistani, died 275 A.H. [889 A.D.]; Abu 'Isa Muhammad Tirmidhi, died 279 A.H. [892 A.D.]; Abu 'Abd al-Rahman Nasa'i, died 303 A.H. [915 A.D.]; [Muhammad ibn Yazid] Ibn Majah al-Qazwini, died 273 A.H. [887 A.D.].

narrators and their unbroken links [back] to the time of the Prophet or his Companions, with two or three other minor observations and technicalities. The criterion of the subject matter, and the application of an intelligent and rational canon, was left to others. Hence the critics did not consider the traditions called *akhbar-i ahad* (single reports) to be binding on the conscience.

The European writers like Muir, Osborn, [Thomas Patrick] Hughes [1838–1911], and Sell, while describing the Muhammadan traditions, take no notice of the fact that almost all of them are not theoretically and conscientiously binding on the Muslims. This, in fact, demolishes the foundation of the Common Law. But the legists argue that though the traditions carry no authority with them as single reports, they are practically binding on the Muslim world. This is tantamount to our acting in accordance with the traditions even when our reason and conscience have no obligations to do so. The maxim of the critics who had collected and sifted the traditions—that in general, however sound and strong their *isnad* [chain of transmission] may be, they are not to be believed in and they do not convey a sure knowledge of what they relate—had in reality left no necessity for them to frame a criterion of truth to test a tradition on the ground of its intrinsic incredibility, or rational principles.

Now, though most of the Muhammadan civil and political as well as the canon laws are derived from traditions, it is apparent they cannot be unchangeable or immobile, from the simple fact that they are not based on sure and positive grounds. Muhammad had never enjoined his followers to collect the oral traditions and random reports of his public and private life, nor even did his Companions think of doing so. This circumstance establishes beyond all contradiction the fact that he did not interfere with the civil and political institutions of the country, except those which came in direct collision with his spiritual doctrines and moral reforms. This is certainly an incontrovertible proof that the civil and political system, founded on hazy traditions and uncertain reports, are in no way immutable or finite.

The Ijma'

The unanimous consent of all the learned men of the whole Muhammadan world at a certain time on a certain religious precept or practice for which there is no provision in the Qur'an or *sunna*, is called an *ijma'*. If any one of the constituent doctors dissents from the others, the *ijma'* is not considered conclusive or authoritative.

Shaykh Muhyi al-Din Ibn 'Arabi, a Spanish writer of great authority and sanctity (died in 638 A.H.); Dawud Abu Sulayman al-Zahiri, a learned doctor of Isfahan, and the founder of the Zahiri (Exteriorist) school of jurisprudence; Abu Hatim Muhammad ibn Habban al-Tamimi al-Basti, generally known as Ibn Habban (died 354 A.H.); Abu Muhammad 'Ali Ibn Hazm, also a Spanish theologian of great repute (died 400 A.H.); and, according to one report, *Imam* Ahmad ibn Hanbal (died 241 A.H.), denounce the authority of any *ijma'* other than that of the Companions of the Prophet; while Abu Ishaq Ibrahim ibn Sayyar al-Nazzam al-Balkhi, generally known as Nazzam (died 231 A.H.), and Ahmad ibn Hanbal, according to another report, deny the existence of any *ijma'*, whether of the Companions or other Muslims in general. *Imam* Malik, the famous legist and founder of the second school of jurisprudence, admitted the authority of the *ijma'* of the Medinites only, and not of any one else. In fact, his theory or system of legislation was based chiefly on the practices and usages of the people of Medina. *Imam* Shafi'i, the third of the orthodox *imam*s, and founder of the school of Muhammadan jurisprudence which bears his name, held that an *ijma'* (unanimous consent of all the learned Muslims of the whole Muslim world, at a certain time on a certain point of law) becomes binding on all, only on the expiration of the age in which they who had thus unanimously constituted the *ijma'* lived; provided that none of them had ever swerved from the opinions held by him at the time of the *ijma'*, as the dissentient voice of a single individual in his afterlife would dissolve the *ijma'* and nullify its authority.

The *ijma'* is either *'azimat* [a necessary practice], when all the learned men declare their consent to the law point or maxim agreed upon, or they commence practicing the same if it be practicable. It is called *rukhsat* [a rule of indulgence or dispensation] when it is tacitly permitted by those who do not give their consent thereto. Under this circumstance it is also called *suquti*, silent or mute, but *Imam* Shafi'i would not admit the latter as authoritative.

It is held by *Imam* Abu Hanifa that only that *ijma'* can be authoritative on a point of law in which there would have been no disagreement before the *ijma'* took place. Such is the report of [Abu'l-Hasan]

Karkhi [died 952]. *Imam* Muhammad [al-Shaybani, circa 750–805] does not agree with his master [Abu Hanifa] on this point, and Abu Yusuf had two verdicts of his own. In one of them he gives his consent to the sentiments expressed by his master, Abu Hanifa, and in the other with his fellow pupil, *Imam* Muhammad.

When at a certain period there were two parties differing from one another, it is not allowed at a subsequent period to dissent from both the previous opinions and constitute *ijma'* on a third. Such an *ijma'* is called *murakkab* [composite].

A report of *ijma'* having taken place must be communicated to posterity by a vast concourse of reporters in each age, so as to remove the doubt of its being spurious. The report of an *ijma'* communicated to us as related above is called *ijma' mutawatir* [consensus attested to by multiple sources], but if it is not reported in such a manner, it is styled *ijma' ahad* [a consensus verified on the basis of only one source]. The former is considered to be binding on the conscience as a true report necessitating implicit obedience, the latter cannot be obligatory, that is, we cannot believe it to be true, yet our compliance thereto is necessary.

This is then the theory of *ijma'*, the third principle of the Muhammadan Common Law or system of legislation. But its very foundation is shaken by the most eminent jurisconsults and legists who would not admit in the first place the existence of such an *ijma'*, as being practically impossible. In the second place they would not admit its authority except on the strength of the Prophet's Companions. In the third place some of them would not allow any *ijma'* whether it be derived from the Companions or from some other source. In the fourth place, supposing that such *ijma'*s have taken place and exercise universal authority, it is impossible that the transcriptions of their reports will successively reach us and will be binding on the conscience. It is absurd to believe in its decision, though we do not know certainly whether there was any *ijma'*, or not.

Mr. Sell has been apparently misinformed on the subject of *ijma'*, as it appears in his *The Faith of Islam*. His quotations bearing on the subject are all derived from secondary sources which ought not to be authoritative at all. He quotes from what he calls "a standard theological book much used in India," as follows: "*Ijma'* is this, that it is not lawful to follow any other than the four *imam*s" (page 19). He

writes further on without referring to any "standard theological work":[14] "The *ijma'* of the four *imam*s is a binding law on all Sunnis" (page 23). Now whether there was ever an *ijma'* as defined above to follow blindly these *imam*s, or these *imam*s ever constituted an *ijma'*, is to be decided. There is no proof for the former; as for the latter, it is unsatisfactory on the bare face of it, for the four *imam*s were not contemporaries of one another, how could they then effect an *ijma'*?

Qiyas

Qiyas is wrongly described by Mr. Sell as the fourth foundation of Islam.[15] The reverend gentleman has committed another great mistake in calling it a foundation of the faith.[16] Technically it means analogical reasonings based on the Qur'an, traditions, or *ijma'*. It is therefore not an independent source of law, [so that] the medium, or as it is called the *illat* (cause or motive [behind the ruling]), through a process of reasoning must be found in one of the three sources of law. All these analogical reasonings are doubtful in their origin, and cannot in any way carry weight of authority with them. Notwithstanding this, *qiyas* is the greatest source of the Muhammadan Civil Law. How can it then be called a final or immutable law?

The authority of *qiyas* as a source of law was denounced by Ibn Mas'ud, a companion of the Prophet (died 32 A.H.); by 'Amr al-Shubi, one of the successors of the companions at Kufa (died 109 A.H. [727 A.D.]); by [Abu Bakr] Muhammad ibn Sirin (died 110 A.H. [728 A.D.]); by Hasan al-Basri (died 110 A.H. [728 A.D.]); and by Ibrahim al-Nazzam (died 231 A.H.).[17] Dawud [Abu Sulayman] Isfahani, the founder of the Zahiri sect (died 270 A.H.) and his son Muhammad [Ibn Dawud ibn]'Ali (died 294 A.H. [909 A.D.]) well versed in jurisprudence, and Abu

14. This subject has nothing to do with the Muhammadan theological books. The subject falls within the province of jurisprudence. It is *fiqh* [jurisprudence] or *usul* [principles of jurisprudence] and is quite separate from theology, or *ilahiyat* or *aqa'id*. The four *imam*s are never called theologians, but they are mere legists or casuists.

15. *The Faith of Islam*, p. 27.

16. *Ibidem*.

17. See Ibn Hajar [al-'Asqalani, Egyptian religious scholar, 1372–1449] in *Fath al-bari* [*The Creator's Conquest*], a commentary on Bukhari quoting from Ibn 'Abd al-Barr [978–1070], ['Abdullah] Darimi [797–869], et cetera.

Bakr Ibn Abi 'Asim [al-Dahhak, 822–900], a juris-consult who flourished in the fourth century [tenth century A.D.], have also disapproved of *qiyas* or juris-prudential deductions, and have rejected that mode of proceeding.

Hafiz Abu Muhammad 'Ali Ibn Hazm, generally known as Ibn Hazm, a Spanish writer of great repute in Muhammadan theology and jurisprudence (died 400 A.H.), had written a treatise denouncing the va-lidity of *ra'i*, "opinion," of *qiyas*, "analogical deduc-tions," of *istihsan* [using discretion in preferring less obvious analogies], "a sub-division of *qiyas* as the source of law," of *dalil*, "the ascertainment of the causes or motives of the precepts" (and making ana-logical deductions therefrom), and *taqlid*, "the blind pursuit of one of the four schools of Muhammadan jurisprudence."

Some Chapters of the Civil Law Require Rewriting

There is no doubt that the several codes of Muham-madan jurisprudence were well suited to the then-existing state of life in each stage of its development, and even now where things have undergone no changes, they are sufficient enough for the purpose of good government and regulation of society. But there are certain points in which the Muhammadan Common Law is irreconcilable with the modern needs of Islam, whether in India or Turkey, and re-quires modifications. The several chapters of the Common Law, [such] as those on political institutes, slavery, concubinage, marriage, divorce, and the dis-abilities of non-Muslim fellow subjects are to be re-modeled and rewritten in accordance with the strict interpretations of the Qur'an, as I have shown in the following pages.

Equality between Fellow Subjects

Legal, political, and social equality on a much more liberal scale than hitherto granted by the several *khatt*s [decrees] and *firman*s [orders] of the [Otto-man] Turkish sultans[18] must be accorded in theory

18.   [The Tanzimat reforms of the nineteenth century granted certain citizenship rights to all Ottoman subjects.—Ed.]

as well as in practice even in the "*shara'i*" or reli-gious tribunals of Turkey. On the other hand, con-formity, in certain points, with foreign laws must be allowed to Muslims, living under the Christian rule, either in Russia, India, or Algiers. Political and so-cial equality must be freely and practically granted to the natives of British India. Political inequality, race distinctions, and social contempt evinced by Englishmen in India toward their fellow subjects, the Natives, is very degrading and discouraging.

Major [earlier referred to as Colonel] Osborn writes: "The experience of British rule in India shows that where the subtle and persuasive power of sym-pathy is wanting, where social equality does not or cannot exist, there the gulf which divides the con-queror from the conquered remains unfilled. Within the boundaries of Hindustan we have established peace and placed within the reach of her people the intellectual treasures which the happier West has accumulated, but we are farther than ever from win-ning their affections. Never, perhaps, did the people of India dislike the Englishman with a profounder dislike than at the present day. There are hundreds of educated Muhammadans and Hindoos in that country who are as clearly convinced as any Euro-pean of the falseness of their ancestral beliefs, the incompatibility of their old ways of life with intel-lectual and social progress. But such convictions do not detach them from the external profession of those beliefs, the diligent observance of those obsolete practices. They cling to them as a kind of protest against the conqueror. They prefer to bury themselves in the darkness, than be led toward the light by guides whom they abhor. And why is this? It is because the presence of the Englishman in India is a wound in-flicted on their self-respect, which never heals, which the experience of almost every day causes to bleed afresh. The Englishman does not mean to lacerate their feelings. He cannot help conveying in his speech, his manners, his actions, that calm, un-doubting conviction of immeasurable superiority with which he is inwardly possessed; his exclusive-ness is due, partly of course, to his insular rigidity, but far more to the constitution of native society, which renders free intercourse between the two races simply impossible. But, on the other hand, it is not strange that the native should be unable to make al-lowances for difficulties of this kind. He only sees an alien race settled in the land which his ancestors ruled, and conducting themselves as though they were beings made of a finer clay than the people whom they govern. He knows and feels that he cannot enter their presence without being reminded at every instant that he is regarded as an inferior. His inability to resent the tacit insult (for so he regards it), his powerlessness to free himself from the strong hand which holds him in his grasp, tend, of course, to intensify the bitterness of his hate. What we have done for India is to convert it into a gigantic model prison. The discipline we have established is admirable, but the people know they are prisoners, and they hate us as their jailers. And until a prison is found to be an effective school for the inculcation of virtue, and a jailer a successful evangelist, it is folly to expect the regeneration of India. Reports on her material and moral progress will, of course, continue to be written, but if we estimate the effects of British rule, not by trade statistics but by its results on the spirit of man, we shall find that the races of India have declined in courage and manliness, and all those qualities which produce a vigorous nation, in proportion to the period they have been subjected to the blighting influence of an alien despotism. There is no human power which can arrest the progress of decay in a people bereft of political freedom, except the restitution of that freedom. This sentence of doom glares forth from the records of all past history, like the writing of fire on the wall of Belshazzar's palace. It is a hallucination to suppose that British rule in India is a reversal of the inexorable decree."[19]

Who Can Effect the Proposed Reforms?

But now the question naturally comes up before us, Who can effect the proposed reforms mentioned above? I reply at once, His Imperial Majesty the [Ottoman] Sultan. He is competent enough to bring about any political, legal, or social reforms on the authority of the Qur'an, just as the former sultans introduced certain beneficial measures both in law and politics in direct contravention of the Hanafi school of the Common Law. He is the only legal authority on matters of innovation; being a successor to the successors of the Prophet, and the *amir al-mu'minin* [leader of the believers], the *saut al-hayy*, or the living voice of Islam. The first four caliphs,

no doubt, had an arbitrary power to legislate, and of their own authority (*ijtihad*) they modified at will the yet undeveloped *leges non scripta* [unwritten laws] of Islam. The imaginary caliph of the Quraysh [Muhammad's tribe], to be chosen by the Faithful and installed at Mecca to invite the *'ulama'* [religious scholars] of every land to a council at the time of pilgrimage for the purpose of appointing a new *mujtahid* with a view to propound certain modifications of the *shari'a*, necessary to the welfare of Islam, and deducible from traditions, as proposed by Mr. W[ilfrid S.] Blunt [1840–1922], is not required at all.[20]

It has been stated on high authority that all that is required for the reform of Turkey is that the *qanun*, or orders of the sultan, should take the place of the Hanafi Law. The sultan is competent enough to do so either as a sultan or a caliph. The idea that by so doing Islam would cease to be the state religion is groundless, for Islam, as a religion, is not a barrier to the good administration of the Turkish government. As a caliph, the sultan is not bound to maintain the Hanafi Law, which is said to suit ill the conditions of modern life. All the perfect caliphs [the first four successors of the Prophet] have existed before the compilation of the Hanafi Law, and during the subsequent caliphates, it was not fully and universally administered, there being different laws in different Muhammadan countries.

How to Begin the Proposed Reforms: To What Can We Make Appeal?

I do not agree with Colonel Osborn, who remarks that a religious revolution is required before the work of political reform can begin in a Muhammadan state. I will not repeat here my reasons, as I have already fully explained how the social, legal, and political reforms can be introduced in Muhammadan states. But I will briefly discuss here how it is to begin. To what can we appeal?

"There is not a crime or defect in the history of Islam," writes Major Osborn, "the counterpart of which is not to be found in the history of Christendom. Christians have mistaken a lifeless formalism for the vital element in religion; Christians have interpreted

---

19. Major R. D. Osborn, *Islam under the Arabs* (London, 1876), pp. 274–276.

20. Wilfrid S. Blunt, *The Future of Islam* (London, 1882), pp. 165–166.

the Gospel as giving a sanction for the worst cruelties of religious persecution; Christians have done their utmost to confine the intellect and the moral sense within limits defined by a human authority; but the strongest witness against all these errors has been Christ Himself. Every reformer who rose to protest against them could appeal to Him and His teaching as his authority and justification, But no Muslim can lift up his voice in condemnation of polygamy, slavery, murder, religious war, and religious persecution, without condemning the Prophet himself; and being thereby cut off from the body of the Faithful."[21]

I have protested against polygamy, slavery, and intolerance in this book, and have appealed to the Qur'an and the teachings of Muhammad. The subjects of murder, religious wars, and religious persecutions I have fully discussed in my other work, entitled *All the Wars of Muhammad Were Defensive*.[22] See also pages 13 to 16 of the first part of this book.

All the political, social, and legal reforms treated of in the following pages are based on the authority and justification of the Qur'an. The Muhammadans have interpreted the Qur'an as giving sanction to polygamy, arbitrary divorce, slavery, concubinage, and religious wars. But the strongest witness against all these errors is the Qur'an itself. For the Qur'anic injunctions against polygamy, arbitrary divorce, religious persecutions and wars, slavery, and concubinage, consult the following verses:

> Against polygamy, [Sura] 4, [Verses] 3 and 128.
> Against arbitrary divorce, [Sura] 2, [Verses] 226, 227, 229, 230, 237, 238; [Sura] 4, [Verses] 23–25, 38, 39, 127–129; [Sura] 33, [Verse] 48; [Sura] 58, [Verses] 2, 5; [Sura] 65, [Verses] 1, 2, 6.
> Against religious intolerance, [Sura] 109; [Sura] 88, [Verses] 21–24; [Sura] 50, [Verses] 45, 46; [Sura] 72, [Verses] 21–24; [Sura] 16, [Verses] 37, 84; [Sura] 29, [Verse] 17; [Sura] 18, [Verse] 40; [Sura] 42, [Verse] 47; [Sura] 2, [Verse] 257; [Sura] 44, [Verse] 12; [Sura] 3, [Verse] 19; [Sura] 24, [Verse] 53; [Sura] 9, [Verse] 6; [Sura] 5, [Verses] 93, 99; [Sura] 18, [Verse] 28; [Sura] 39, [Verses] 16, 17; [Sura] 6, [Verse] 107; [Sura] 10, [Verse] 99.
> Against slavery, [Sura] 90, [Verses] 8–15; [Sura] 2, [Verse] 172; [Sura] 24, [Verse] 33; [Sura] 5, [Verse] 91; [Sura] 47, [Verse] 4; [Sura] 9, [Verse] 60.

21. Robert Durie Osborn, Major in the Bengal Staff Corps, *Islam under the Khalifs of Baghdad* (London, 1777), p. 80.
22. Is being printed by Messrs. Thackers, Spink, and Company, Calcutta. [...]

Against concubinage, [Sura] 4, [Verses] 3, 29–32; [Sura] 24, [Verse] 32; [Sura] 5, [Verse] 7.

The last verse, as it has not been quoted in page 174 of this book, I take the opportunity of quoting here: " . . . And you are permitted to marry virtuous women who are believers, and virtuous women of those who have been given the Scriptures before you, when you have provided them their portions, living chastely with them without fornication, and not taking concubines."—*Rodwell's Translation* [by J. M. Rodwell, 1808–1900].

Mr. Stanley Lane-Poole [1854–1931] remarks in his introduction to [Edward W.] Lane's [1801–1876] selections from the Qur'an: "If Islam is to be a power for good in the future, it is imperatively necessary to cut off the social system from the religion. At the beginning, among a people who had advanced but a little way on the road of civilisation, the defects of the social system were not so apparent; but now, when Easterns are endeavouring to mix on equal terms with Europeans, and are trying to adopt the manners and customs of the West, it is clear that the condition of their women must be radically changed if any good is to come of the Europeanising tendency. The difficulty lies in the close connection between the religious and social ordinances in the Qur'an: the two are so intermingled that it is hard to see [how] they can be disentangled without destroying both. The theory of revelation would have to be modified. Muslims would have to give up their doctrine of the syllabic inspiration of the Qur'an, and exercise their moral sense in distinguishing between the particular and the general, the temporary and the permanent: they would have to recognize that there was much in Muhammad's teaching which, though useful at the time, is inapplicable to the present conditions of life; that his knowledge was often partial; and his judgment sometimes at fault; that the moral sense is capable of education as much as the intellect, and, therefore, that what was apparently moral and wise in the seventh century may quite possibly be immoral and suicidal in a society of the nineteenth century. Mohammad himself said, according to tradition, 'I am no more than a man: when I order you anything respecting religion, receive it; and when I order you about the affairs of the world, then I am nothing more than man.' And he seemed to foresee that the time would come when his minor regulations would call for revision: 'Ye are in an age,' he said, 'in which, if ye abandon one-tenth of what is ordered, ye will be ruined. After this, a time will come when he who shall observe one-tenth of what is now ordered will be redeemed.'"[23]

I have shown here as well as in the second part of this book that Islam as a religion is quite apart from inculcating a social system. The Muhammadan polity and social system have nothing to do with religion. Although Muhammadans in after days have tried to mix up their social system with the Qur'an, just as the Jews and Christians have done in applying the precepts of the Bible to the institutions of their daily life, they are not so intermingled that "it is hard to see [how] they can be disentangled without destroying both." In effecting the proposed reforms, it is not necessary to modify the theory of inspiration.

The political and social reforms which I have explained in the first and second parts of this book are neither casuistical deductions, nor fortuitous interpretations, nor analogical constructions of the Qur'an, but on the contrary, they are the plain teachings, self-indicating evident (*zahir*) meanings, *nass*, *mufassar*, or *muhkam* (obvious) injunctions of the Qur'an.

The Qur'an Not a Barrier to Spiritual Development or Political and Social Reforms

In short, the Qur'an or the teachings of Muhammad are neither barriers to spiritual development or freethinking on the part of Muhammadans, nor an obstacle to innovation in any sphere of life, whether political, social, intellectual, or moral. All efforts at spiritual and social development are encouraged as meritorious and hinted at in several verses of the Qur'an.

". . . Then give tidings to my servants who listen to the word[24] and follow the best thereof; they it is whom God guides, and they it is who are endowed with minds." Sura 29, Verse 19.

"And vie in haste for pardon from your Lord." [Sura] 3, [Verse] 127.

"Hasten emulously after good." [Sura] 2, [Verse] 143.

"Be emulous for good deed." [Sura] 5, [Verse] 33.

". . . And others by permission of God, outstrip in goodness, this is the great merit." [Sura] 35, [Verse] 29.

"These hasten after good, and are first to win it." [Sura] 23, [Verse] 63.

"And that there may be among you a people who invite to the Good, and enjoin the Just, and forbid the Wrong. These are they with whom shall be well." [Sura] 3, [Verse] 100.

These verses fully sanction the development of the Muslim mind in all spheres of life.

Church and State Not Combined Together

There is a tradition related by the *Imam* Muslim to the effect that Muhammad the Prophet while coming to Medina saw certain persons fecundating date trees.[25] He advised them to refrain from doing so. They acted accordingly, and the yield was meager that year. It being reported to him, he said, "He was merely a man. What he instructed them in their religion they must take, but when he ventured his opinion in other matters he was only a man."[26]

This shows that Muhammad never set up his own acts and words as an infallible or unchangeable rule of conduct in civil and political affairs, or, in other words, he never combined the church and state into one. The Arab proverb, "State and religion are twins," is a mere saying of the common people, and not a Muslim religious maxim. It is incorrect to suppose that the acts and sayings of the Prophet cover all law, whether political, civil, social, or moral.

Free Thinking Sanctioned by the Prophet

It has been narrated by Tirmidhi, Abu Da'ud, and Darimi that Muhammad, when deputing Mu'adh [ibn Jabal, died 627] to Yemen, had asked him how he

23. *Mishkat al-Masabih* [*The Lights of "The Lamps"*, by Muhammad Khatib al-Tibrizi, 14th century], volume 1, pp. 46, 51.

24. I have followed Professor [Edward Henry] Palmer's [1840–1882] translation. Mr. [George] Sale [circa 1697–1736] and the Reverend Rodwell translate "*my* word." The original text does not warrant the word "my."

25. "By means of the spadix of a male tree which is bruised or brayed and sprinkled upon the spadix of the female by inserting a stalk of the raceme of the male tree into the spadix of the female, after shaking off the pollen of the former upon the spadix of the female."—Lane's *Arabic Lexicon*, book 1, part 1, p. 5.

26. See *Mishkat al-Masabih*, chapter on *i'tisam bissunna* [adherence to tradition].

would judge the people. Mu'adh said, "I will judge them according to the Book of God." Then Muhammad asked again, "And if you do not find it in the Book of God?" The former returned, "I will judge according to the precedent of the Prophet," but he was once more questioned, "If there be no such precedent?" to which it was speedily replied, "I will make efforts to form my own judgment (*ijtahidu ra'i*)."[27] Muhammad thanked God for this judicious opinion of his delegate.

It is evident from this anecdote of Muhammad that he never intended his teachings to bear a despotic influence on the Muslim world, and become universal obstacles to all kinds of political and social reforms. He did not prevent any change from taking place, and never wished to keep Islam stationary. He did never intend to make legislation purely deductive; on the contrary, he made it inductive. Mu'adh was to rely on his own judgment, which makes legislation purely inductive. The tradition not only sanctions enlightened progress but encourages an intelligent and healthy growth of the mind, and leads to the search of new truths.

Regarding this tradition, Syed Ameer 'Ali [Indian reformer, 1849–1928; see chapter 43] says, "It was 'an age of active principles' which Mohammed ushered in,"[28] concerning which the Reverend Mr. Sell says: "It is true that *ijtihad* literally means 'great effort,' it is true that the Companions and *mujtahidin* [*mujtahids*] of the first class had the power of exercising their judgment in doubtful cases, and of deciding them according to their sense of the fitness of things, provided always that their decision contravened no law of the Qur'an or the *sunna*; but this in no way proves that Islam has any capacity for progress, or that 'an age of active principles' was ushered in by Muhammad, or that his 'words breathe energy and force, and infuse new life into the dormant heart of humanity.' For, though the term

'*ijtihad*' might, in reference to the men I have mentioned, be somewhat freely translated as 'one's own judgment,' it can have no such meaning now. It is a purely technical term, and its use and only use now is to express the referring of a difficult case to some analogy drawn from the Qur'an and the *sunna*."

Mr. Sell commits a palpable error in saying that the word "*ijtihad*," translated as "one's own judgment," "can have no such meaning now." His own words show that formerly, that is, in the time of Muhammad and up to the time it was restricted to a jurisprudential or legal technicality, centuries after Muhammad, it had the classical or literal meaning of "one's own judgment." We know that in the phraseology of the Muhammadan principles of jurisprudence, a science but of late origin, the word "*ijtihad*" is a purely technical term, and its use in that science is to express the referring of a difficult case to some analogy drawn from the Qur'an and the *sunna*. But such was not the case during Muhammad's time. In the classical Arabic it was, and is, used to mean making great efforts, and when the word "*ra'i*," or opinion, is suffixed to it, it means making effort to form a judgment. Mu'adh said, "*Ijtihadu ra'i*," that is, "I will make efforts to form my own judgment." But Mr. Sell considers that Mu'adh only used the word "*ijtihad*," which is now a purely conventional word among the jurists, as a technical term, but this is altogether an absurd supposition. In the first place, Mu'adh did not use the simple word "*ijtihad*," which is now restricted to a particular and technical meaning, but he prefixed it with the word "*ra'i*," my own judgment. Secondly, he did not and could not use it in its subsequent technical sense now in use, which got currency among the legists centuries after Mu'adh.

The Tradition Secures Us Enlightened Progress and Removes the Fetters of the Past

We lay no stress on the word *ijtihad*, [as] it simply signifies making effort, moral or mental, but we lay stress on the word "*ra'i*," opinion, judgment, and thought; and the tradition secures for us a wide field of spiritual development, moral growth, an intellectual and enlightened progress, and reformed legislation. It unfetters us from the four schools of jurisprudence, and encourages us to base all legislation on the living needs of the present, and not on the fossilized ideas of the past.

27. The *isnad* of the tradition by Tirmidhi is from Hannad [ibn al-Sari], from Waki' [ibn al-Jarrah], from Shu'ba [ibn al-Hajjaj], from Abi 'Awn, from Harith ibn al-'Amr, from the persons in the company of Mu'adh, and from Mu'adh himself. Another *isnad* is from Muhammad ibn Bishar, from Muhammad ibn Ja'far and 'Abd al-Rahman ibn Mahdi, from Shu'ba, from Abi 'Awn, from Harith ibn 'Awn, and Mughira ibn Shu'ba's nephew, from the people of Hims, from Mu'adh.

28. Syed Ameer 'Ali, Moulvi, M.A., LL.B., *A Critical Examination of the Life and Teachings of Mohammed* (London, 1873), p. 290.

Lecture on Islam

Sayyid Ahmad Khan (North India, 1817–1898) was the most prominent early leader of the modernization movement among Indian Muslims, noted especially for his advocacy of social and educational reforms. He came from a noble family and was brought up in his grandfather's house, as his father died young. He did not receive a traditional *madrasa* (seminary) education, but did study the Qur'an in Arabic and Persian classics. As an employee in the British colonial judiciary, he was greatly affected by the failed struggle for independence of 1857. Ahmad Khan became active in analyzing both the causes of the revolt and the reasons for what many perceived as the backwardness of Muslims in scientific and social fields. He concluded that the Muslims' needs could be addressed by a program of education that would incorporate both modern subjects and a respect for Islamic values. Therefore, in 1875, he established the Mohammadan Anglo-Oriental College at Aligarh in North India, offering English-medium higher education. His journal *Tahdhib al-Akhlaq* (*Refinement of Morals*) was a showcase of modernist thought, featuring his articles and those of like-minded supporters. Prevalent themes in his writings include "demythologized" Qur'anic interpretation, presenting the sacred texts as in harmony with science and reason, criticism of *hadith* (narratives of the Prophet), and calls for renewed *ijtihad* (religious interpretation). In the passage that follows, Sir Sayyid—he was knighted in 1888 by the British Empire—presented the case for renewed Islamic theology, capable of assuring an appropriately scientific and rational understanding of religious truth.[1]

[(i) No Claim to Authoritative Teaching]

My brothers in religion! You have come here today desiring that I may state before you my ideas about the religion of Islam. For that I am grateful to you. I have no objection to stating my ideas before friends who are eager to listen to them. Yet, first, I want to say this—I am an ignorant person, neither a *maulavi* [religious scholar], nor a *mufti* [religious official], nor a *qadi* [judge], nor a preacher. Also, I do not wish that anybody, even my closest friend, should [blindly] follow my ideas. I consider that no person, except the Messenger of God, has such a rank in matters relating to the things of heart and spirit—matters between God and His servants—as to make him wish that people should follow him [blindly]. This rank was that of the messengers, and finally, that of the Prophet of God, Muhammad Mustafa (the Chosen of God)—may God keep alive his religion that is from eternity to eternity—and, indeed, He will surely keep it alive; as it is without beginning, so it is without end. With Islam has arrived the end of prophethood.

But before I state my ideas, I should first like to explain my objective in presenting them. I think that there are in this world, since it was peopled and from the time God began regularly to send His prophets and messengers—from that time till today—there have [always] been and still are two kinds of people.

Sayyid Ahmad Khan, "Lecture on Islam," translated from Urdu by Christian W. Troll in *Sayyid Ahmad Khan: A Reinterpretation of Muslim Theology* (New Delhi, India: Vikas Publishing House, 1978), pp. 307–332. Lecture delivered in Lahore on February 2, 1884, before the Anjuman-i Himayat-i Islam (Islamic Protection Association). Introduction by Marcia K. Hermansen.

1. Altaf Hussain Hali, *Hayat-i Javid* (*Immortal Life*), translated by David J. Mathews (New Delhi, India: Rupa & Co., 1994); J. M. S. Baljon, *The Reforms and Religious Ideas of Sir Sayyid Ahmad Khan* (Lahore, Pakistan: Ashraf, 1958). B. A. Dar, *Religious Thought of Sayyid Ahmad Khan* (Lahore, Pakistan: Institute of Islamic Culture 1957); Hafeez Malik, *Sir Sayyid Ahmad Khan and Muslim Modernization in India and Pakistan* (New York: Columbia University Press, 1980). Christian W. Troll, *Sayyid Ahmad Khan: A Reinterpretation of Muslim Theology* (New Delhi, India: Vikas, 1978).

One group concerning whom God has said, "God guideth whom He will unto a straight path." [Qur'an, Sura 2, Verse 213] "Lo thou (O Muhammad) guidest not whom thou lovest, but God guideth whom He will." [Sura 28, Verse 56] "It may be that thou tormentest thyself (O Muhammad) because they believe not." [Sura 26, Verse 31] With regard to the second group He has said to His Messenger that you cannot guide those whom you desire to guide. Howsoever much you try—even if you torment your soul to death—they will not believe. These are the two groups of men which we find clearly depicted in the Glorious Qur'an. From there it becomes evident with regard to those who have believed formerly and those who believe now that God has made their natural constitution or their nature such that the disposition for belief or unbelief is in it. Because there can be no change in what is the nature of man. It is beyond the power of the person himself or any other person, and be he even a prophet, to change it.

[(ii) Unquestioned Belief and Critical Belief]

This occurs daily in all aspects of our life. In this world many things happen, the truth of which we cannot prove. But in the heart, from unknown causes, something arises by which their truth acquires full certainty. This applies exactly to Islam. Thousands, hundred thousands, even ten millions of men have passed or are alive now or lived at the very time of the Messenger of God whose heart accepted the instruction and who believed firmly in the truth of it, although they had no knowledge of the arguments for its truth. The only reason for this [their firm belief] was that God had made their heart in such a way that they would, even with a minimum of instruction, accept the straight path. Their heart accepted this guidance and they believed. (*Cheers.*) Thanks are due to God that at this moment, too, that His mercy is lavished over thousands, hundred thousands, and ten millions of Muslims. These people from their heart believe in Islam without knowing the proofs for its truth according to the principles of logic and philosophy. I am convinced that people who believe in Islam without the arguments and proofs of philosophy have a more solid faith than those who believe in Islam or hold it for certain on the basis of philosophical proofs and arguments. Because into their hearts no shade of

doubt and hesitation has found its way, there is no room for that in their heart. These people are the *ahl-i jannat* [people of paradise], who will go straight to heaven. (*Cheers.*)

I remember a story of my country. In our region there lives a tribe, the Ramghar [a branch of the Rajput, settled in the region of Gurgaon, Punjab], which at some time had become Muslim. Probably up to the time before *Maulavi* [Shah Muhammad] Isma'il [Shahid, religious reformer, 1789–1831], all the customs of the Hindus were practiced among them. They wore *dhotis* [loincloths] and shirts of the *ulte pardi* type [tunics cut to open on the left side, Hindu-style, rather than the right]. The *qadi* [Muslim judge] performed the marriage, and the Brahmin led the bride around the fire. Many other Hindu customs were common among them. One day a Muslim passed through one of their villages. He was thirsty and desired to drink water. He saw an earthen pot kept there, filled with water. Yet he had doubts whether this water belonged to Hindus or Muslims. The person he asked about it answered very harshly: "Are you blind? Don't you see on top of the earthen water jar the *kulhra* (that is an earthen cup for drinking water)?" As if this was a sign for being a Muslim—whereas all people [Muslims and Hindus] drink water from [such] a cup. He had answered harshly because the traveler had doubts about his being a Muslim, in spite of the presence of the [supposedly distinctive] Muslim sign.

My brothers! When these people were so ignorant, how could they know the tenets of Islam and the philosophical arguments for its truth? There was nothing on the basis of which they could call themselves Muslims, except the faith in God and His Messenger. But, I assure you, I consider their faith to be much more solid than my own faith. (Why should I mention somebody else's?)

My brothers! The faith of such people who have no doubt whatsoever, nor any uncertainty in their heart, is usually very solid and intense. They believe with the certainty of their heart in God and the Prophet and recognize as Muslim anyone who calls himself so. They do not need any logical proof or philosophical demonstration for knowing God and for believing in the Prophet. Whatever is stated to them as having been taught by God and the Messenger, be it irrational or unbelievable, be it true or false, they will believe in it. I consider such people the stars of firm belief, models of firm Islam and true Muslims.

But there is also the second group, which wants a proof for the truth of everything. People of that group desire that the tenets of Islam should be explained to them by philosophical argument, that the doubts of their hearts be removed so that their hearts may find satisfaction. They do not want that whilst in their heart they waver, they should confess [outwardly] by tongue, "Yes, yes"—for fear of the people and because of the pressure of society. These alone are the people we address and with whom we argue.

[(iii) A Precedent to the Present Situation]

At the time when the reign of the 'Abbasid caliphs [750–1258] flourished and the star of the Muslims was at its zenith, Greek philosophy and natural science had gained popularity among the Muslims, with the result that doubts arose among the people concerning many questions regarding Islam. Because the very people who acknowledged the tenets of philosophy and natural science to be true found a discrepancy between these and the contemporary teachings of Islam, as they had been elaborated by independent judgment, thus doubts about Islam arose among them. If one can rely on history, it emerges as an established fact that that period was one of hard attacks on Islam, and yet that Islam does not have to fear damage from the hardest attacks by its hardest enemies. All the 'ulama' [religious scholars] had to define Islam at that time. They made great efforts to protect Islam and to make it triumph. May God accept their efforts! They established three ways of protecting Islam. The first was to prove that tenets of Greek wisdom and philosophy which were against Islamic teachings were wrong. The second was to formulate such objections to the propositions of [Greek] wisdom and philosophy by which these tenets would themselves become doubtful. Third, to harmonize between the tenets of Islam and the tenets of wisdom and philosophy.

By pursuing this debate, a new science originated among Muslims which they call 'ilm al-kalam [the science of theological argumentation]. Till this day the books of this science are part and parcel of the learning and teaching of the 'ulama' of our religion, and they are quite proud of them. It was for this reason that many of the tenets of Greek philosophy and natural science of the third kind [that is, that which could be harmonized] were incorporated by the Muslims into their religious books and that, step by step, they began to be accepted like religious tenets, whereas in fact they are by no means connected with the religion of Islam. It is no easy task today to separate them from it. Therefore, I think that since Islam is in the same state, attacked in the same way as then, we must make, to the best of our ability, the same efforts our elders made in former times.

My friends! You know well that in our time a new wisdom and philosophy have spread. Their tenets are entirely different from those of the former wisdom and philosophy [of the Greeks]. They are as much in disagreement with the tenets of ordinary present-day Islam as the tenets of Greek wisdom and philosophy were with the tenets of customary Islam during their time. Moreover, an especially difficult problem is posed by the tenets of Greek natural science. The erroneousness of these tenets is by now an established fact. Yet the Muslim scholars of that time accepted them like religious tenets, as I have just explained, and this has made things even more difficult.

[(iv) Former Science and Modern Science]

My friends! Another problem is the big difference between critical research today [and its results] and the tenets of Greek wisdom of old, because the tenets of former wisdom were based on rational and analogical arguments, and not upon experience and observation. It was very easy for our forbears, whilst sitting in the rooms of mosques and monasteries, to disprove teachings arrived at by analogous reasoning and to refute rational teachings by rational demonstrations, and not to accept them. But today a new situation has arisen which is quite different from that [brought about] by the investigations of former philosophy and wisdom. Today doctrines are established by natural experiments [that is, experiments in natural science], and they are demonstrated before our eyes. These are not problems of the kind that could be solved by analogical arguments, or which can be contested by assertions and principles which the 'ulama' of former times have established. Take for instance the question of the piercing of the roof of heaven and the closing of [the doors of] heaven, which is a very big issue in the natural sciences of our tradition, and which has lived on in our learning and teaching. Closely connected with this question are also the principles of natural science which have been accepted in the religion of Islam. But of what use is this doctrine [of the piercing and closing of the cupola of heaven] now and what utility is there in studying and teaching it, since it has been established that the way in which former philosophers and 'ulama' decided upon the existence of heaven is wrong. What is needed now is to reflect upon what "heaven" means, and for this it is necessary to work out new principles and tenets instead of simply calling to memory the worn-out and obsolete doctrines. (*Cheers.*)

A very big issue with us was that of matter and form. If one accepted matter following [the understanding of] Greek philosophy, then the existence of a state after death, which is an important tenet of Islam, would be in vain. The long discussions of the philosophers of Islam concerning this issue were somehow fruitless and insufficient. In any case, present-day natural philosophy does not discuss "matter" at all. Rather, it is accepted that all bodies are composed of small elements. What is therefore the use of the debate on matter and form, a discussion which forms a part of our religious and worldly teaching? There are many other problems of this kind which could be stated as an example here.

My friends! Forgive me when I say that one highly necessary subject has been neglected by the 'ulama'. They did much to confront Greek wisdom and philosophy, but nothing or very little to satisfy the heart of the denier or doubter of Islam, by the way they would present to them the religion of Islam. It is neither sufficient for the firm believer, nor does it satisfy the mind of the doubter, to say simply that in Islam this has been taught in this way and has to be accepted. (*Cheers.*)

[(v) Need for a New 'Ilm al-Kalam]

In the same way, there are many other reasons for which in our time Muslims need to adopt new methods in controversy. The person who considers Islam to be true and believes firmly in it, that person's heart will testify that Islam alone is true—whatever changes may occur in logic, philosophy, and natural science, and however much the doctrines of Islam seem to be in contradiction with them. This attitude is sufficient for those who believe with a true and uncomplicated mind in Islam, but not for those who reject or doubt it. Furthermore, it is by no means a

work of proper protection to confess just by the tongue that Islam is true, and to do nothing to strengthen it in its confrontation with the modern propositions of wisdom and philosophy. Today we need, as in former days, a modern 'ilm al-kalam by which we either render futile the tenets of modern sciences or [show them to be] doubtful, or bring them into harmony with the doctrines of Islam.

I am not well acquainted with all the venerable persons present in this assembly; yet I am sure that quite a number of learned people are present in this gathering. I address myself to them with utmost sincerity—those of you who are able to make an all-out effort to harmonize the tenets of contemporary natural science and philosophy with the doctrines of Islam, or to prove the futility of the tenets of contemporary science and philosophy and yet fail to do so, are all sinners—and certainly so. If only two or three among them accomplish this task, then undoubtedly the collective duty will have been fulfilled. (*Cheers.*)

I happen to believe that there is nobody who is well acquainted with modern philosophy and modern natural science as they exist in the English language, and who at the same time believes in all the doctrines which are considered doctrines of Islam in present-day understanding. May the English-educated [literally English-reading] young men and students forgive me, but I have not yet seen anybody well acquainted with English and interested in the English sciences who believes with full certainty in the doctrines of Islam as they are current in our time. I am certain that as these sciences spread—and their spreading is inevitable and I myself after all, too, help and contribute toward spreading them—there will arise in the hearts of people an uneasiness and carelessness and even a positive disaffection toward Islam as it has been shaped in our time. At the same time, I believe firmly that this is not because of a defect in the original religion, but rather because of those errors which have been made, wilfully or not, to stain the face of Islam.

I am never entitled to claim that I could clean the black stains of these errors from the luminous face of Islam, or that I could take upon me the responsibility to undertake the work of protecting Islam. This is the duty and the privilege of other saintly and learned people. But since I have striven to spread among Muslims those sciences which, as I have just stated, are to a certain extent in discrepancy with contemporary Islam, it was my duty that, as far as it could be done by me, I should do, rightly or wrongly, whatever was in my power to protect Islam and to show forth to people the original luminous face of Islam. My conscience told me that if I failed to do so I should be a sinner before God. (*Cheers.*)

O my friends! I do not say that whatever I investigated is true. But once I had no other choice but to do whatever could be done by me, then I had certainly to do exactly what I did and what I am still doing. God knows my pure intention. If I have done wrong, may he forgive me who wants to and refuse to do so who does not want to. If I have done any good, then I do not want any reward from any human being. Therefore I do not fear people calling me *kafir* [non-Muslim] or *nechari* [naturist, meaning materialist], nor do I frown upon it. I shall not ask those people who slander me because of my efforts, and call me a *kafir*, to intercede for me either. My good or bad actions are with God. If I have made mistakes or shall make mistakes in the future, then I hope to God that He will have mercy on me. (*Cheers.*)

[(vi) Truth and the Plurality of Religions]

My friends! After this lengthy introduction I shall now state my ideas concerning Islam. Whatever I say here I shall certainly state in a free and frank manner. I shall not state my ideas precisely as a Muslim, because in the statement of a doctrine from the point of view of a Muslim, there is no need for this kind of untrammeled argumentation [based purely on reason]. At this moment I shall adopt a way of speaking which a third person would employ in explaining the principles and tenets of Islam to people who have doubts about Islam or its principles. Or I address myself to the English-educated young students whom modern philosophy and the modern natural sciences have thrown into doubt about the truths of the principles of Islam, or who have come to believe that they are wrong. The person that states Islam to be true must also state how he can prove the truth of Islam. When people want to corroborate or affirm the truth of their religion, be it Islam, Christianity, or Hinduism, they must first prove its truth. To argue that this and this person is without any doubt holy, and that we believe in the word of this holy person, is not sufficient for establishing the truth of that religion, because such a statement remains in the realm of mere

belief. Among all people who follow somebody, whether an avatar or a prophet or the God of the Christians, they all consider in the same way the one whom they follow as holy. All members of a religion hold the same firm belief in their religion as members of another religion in theirs. With what justification then can we call one religion true and the other false?

However, if we say that we possess a book sent by God, in which there is not even a suspicion of error, then another person can say, in a similar manner, that I too possess the book of God, and not the slightest doubt attaches to its truth. Given this state of affairs, one must offer the reason for preferring the one to the other, and one must be able to give a reason that satisfies, which is not based on some belief [only], as for instance the book sent to us after all is sent by God, whilst the one sent to the other is not.

If we put forward the miracles of our prophets to prove the truth of our religion, then apart from the difficulties which attach to the possibility and, further, to the proof of their occurrence, the followers of the other religion likewise will state similar miracles of their religious leaders. So what justification have we for acknowledging the miracles we put forward as trustworthy, and for declaring those which the other people put forward as false? All such arguments are based on beliefs [only]. Nobody can confute them, nor can anybody say that this belief is true and this one wrong. If one person holds such a belief, how can one expect the other person to adopt it? Therefore, in order to arrive at the truth, it is necessary that we discover a criterion and establish a touchstone which is related to all religions in the same manner, and by which we can prove our religion or belief to be true. (*Cheers.*)

[(vii) The Criterion for Establishing the True Religion]

Now I shall state this criterion which is related to the religions of the whole world in the same way. By this criterion I shall justify without any wavering what I acknowledge to be the original religion of Islam, which God and the Messenger have disclosed, not that religion which the *'ulama'* and blessed *maulavi*s and preachers have fashioned. I shall prove this religion to be true, and this will be the decisive difference between us [and] the followers of other religions.

No people, be they attached to a religion or not, can deny that God has created humans as a composition of various powers in such a way that they are able to do one or the other work. During this life, therefore, one has to adopt a mode of conduct that coordinates one's [exterior] forces and [interior] faculties toward the purpose for which they exist, and are created. Thus the only criterion for the truth of the religions which are present before us is whether the religion [in question] is in correspondence with the natural disposition of humankind, or with nature. If yes, then it is true, and such correspondence is a clear sign that this religion has been sent by that One which has created humankind. But if this religion is against the nature of humans and their natural constitution, and against their forces and faculties, and if it hinders humans from employing these profitably, then there can be no doubt that this religion is not sent by the One that created humankind, because everyone will agree that religion was made for humankind. You can turn this [around] and state to the same effect that humankind was created for religion.

So I have determined the following principle for discerning the truth of the religions, and also for testing the truth of Islam, that is, is the religion in question in correspondence with human nature or not, with the human nature that has been created into humankind or exists in humankind. And I have become certain that Islam is in correspondence with that nature. (*Cheers.*)

No doubt this should have been the work of outstanding thinkers and scholars. I do not possess the ability to achieve it. But for the reason I explained a few moments earlier, I embarked upon it to the best of my capability. I hold for certain that God has created us and sent us His guidance. This guidance corresponds fully to our natural constitution, to our nature, and this constitutes the proof for its truth. Because it would be highly irrational to maintain that God's work and God's word are different and unrelated to one another. All beings, including humans, are God's work, and religion is His word; the two cannot be in conflict. This criterion I have established for those who themselves in their heart want to settle the truth of any religion and desire to satisfy their minds, and also for those who are in doubt about Islam, or oppose it. To my mind there be no further additional criterion.

After determining this criterion, I clarified that Islam is in full accordance with nature. So I formulated that "Islam is nature and nature is Islam." This is a wholly correct proposition. Yet, unfortunately, there were people who deliberately accused me of being a naturist, or *nechari* in a different sense. They will have to answer for it before God. God is the Creator of all things, as He is the Creator of heaven and earth and what is in them, and of all creatures; so is He also the Creator of nature. What a tremendous slander is it, therefore, when opponents state that I call nature Creator or—God forbid—nature God. What I declare to be created, they accuse me of calling Creator. On that day when there will be the interrogation of our deeds, there will stand before God men with long full beards, with prayer marks on their foreheads, wearing their pajamas neatly above their ankles [sign of strict adherence to the details of religious law]. Men who buy lies for truth—they will be questioned. I leave them, who have made this false accusation, to God. No, I do not leave them to God; rather I forgive them on my part! (*Very loud cheers!*) I do not want to take revenge of any brother, of any fellow creature, neither in this world nor on the Day of Resurrection. I am an utter nothing. Yet I am a descendant of that Messenger who is the mercy of the two worlds [heaven and earth]. I shall walk on the path of my ancestor. And all people who have spoken ill of me and accused me falsely or will do so in the future—all of them I shall forgive. (*Cheers.*)

[(viii) This Path Is Not Entirely New in the History of Islam]

Can anybody say that the path I have outlined above is not apt to strengthen Islam? Can we not meet in this way the great philosophers, the natural scientists, and the atheists? Is our method in any way opposed to Islam? Here, too, I do not claim that the method I adopted is absolutely free from error. I am not infallible and do not claim to be so. I am an ignorant man. I have done this work, for which I am not qualified, out of love for Islam. No doubt it is a new path, and yet in it I have followed the ancient *'ulama'*. As they developed an *'ilm al-kalam* in a new fashion, so I, like them, have developed a new method to prove the same truth. We cannot exclude the possibility of a mistake. Yet future *'ulama'* will render it fully correct and will help Islam. In my view, Islam can be reaffirmed against doubters in this way, and not in any other. (*Cheers.*)

[(ix) Basic Islam: Unity]

Gentlemen, you have asked me to state what Islam is. In answer I say that Islam is [basically] the profession of the *tawhid* (unity) of God. By the firm belief in that unity, a person can be called a Muslim or Musalman [Urdu for Muslim]. The person who in truth acknowledges God, and firmly believes in His unity, is a Muslim. This is the first and foremost pillar of Islam, and all the other pillars are subordinate to it, and as deeply linked with it as in a genuine drug various ingredients are mixed up with the basic paste. Islam means to acknowledge God and to understand Him to be absolutely One and the Creator of everything, but not only to know and understand but rather to be certain of this, and a Muslim is the one who firmly believes in it. God Almighty, when mentioning in the Holy Qur'an the iteration of Christians and Jews, has said, "Nay, but whosoever surrendereth his purpose to God while doing good, his reward is with his Lord." [Sura 2, Verse 112] That is, those who believe in God direct their face towards Him and do good—their reward is with the Lord. God did not want anything from the "people of the book" except that they should acknowledge God and serve Him, when He said, "O people of the Scripture! Come to an agreement between us and you, that we shall worship none but God." [Sura 3, Verse 64] And in one place the Prophet of God said that "My prayer and my worship and my life and my death are for God." [See also Sura 6, Verse 126.] And after this he said, "I am the first of those who surrender (unto Him)." [Sura 6, Verse 163] [The prophets] Isma'il [Ishmael] and Ibrahim [Abraham] said this prayer: "Our Lord, make us submissive unto Thee and of our seed a nation submissive unto Thee." [Sura 2, Verse 129] The disciples of [the prophet] Jesus also, after believing in God, said: "Bear Thou witness that we have surrendered (unto Him)." [Sura 3, Verse 52] God said to Ibrahim, "Surrender!" and Ibrahim said: "I have surrendered to the Lord of the Worlds." [Sura 2, Verse 131] Ibrahim enjoined to his sons: "O my sons! Lo! God has chosen for you the (true) religion; therefore die not, save as men who have surrendered (unto Him)." [Sura 2, Verse 132] And in one place God has said, "Lo! Religion with God is surrender (al-Islam)." [Sura 3, Verse 19] Again, God has said: "Ibrahim was not a Jew; nor yet a Christian; but he was an upright man who had surrendered (to God), and he was not of the idolaters" [Sura 3, Verse 67]—that is, Ibrahim was not a Jew, nor a Christian, but rather a pure Muslim. Hence the truth of Islam, as

God revealed it, is to acknowledge God and firmly believe in Him.

One can have a firm belief in God and God's unity only when one has become absolutely certain about His essence and attributes, which are, in reality, one, and about His right to be worshiped, which is essential to Him. To believe in His essence means to believe that He exists as eternal essence without beginning or end, as One without associate. To believe in His attributes means to be certain that in no one else are attributes like His. The attributes like knowledge, mercy, and life, and so on, are related to God. With the notion of these, other attributes inevitably enter our mind because they are associated in the imagination. Now to acknowledge that the attributes of God are pure and unalloyed [by other attributes associated with them in our mind] means to believe firmly in the attributes of God. To believe in His right to be worshiped means that nothing but God deserves to be worshiped, that is, is worthy of worship. The person who in this way believes firmly in God is a Muslim. Not I, [but] God Himself says so.

[(x) . . . And Acknowledgment of the One Who Finally Preached Tawhid, Muhammad]

True, I shall certainly maintain that a person who acknowledges exclusively the One God [without recognizing Muhammad as His Prophet] is not a Muhammadan. The usage of the Qur'an is what I have stated, but in our time Muhammadan and Muslim are used synonymously. Therefore I consider it necessary to go to a certain extent into detail. For being a Muhammadan, it is necessary that we firmly believe also in the person who, in his bounty, has taught us *tawhid*, because of whom we know God and recognize His attributes. Our reason tells us that we cannot refuse to believe him as the guide through whom we received guidance. It was Muhammad the Messenger of God who guided us in Islam, the truth of which I have stated with such firmness. Therefore, to affirm him [Muhammad] as the Prophet sent by God is necessarily the second pillar of Islam, which cannot be separated from the first. It follows from this whole passage that the person who acknowledges God and accepts Him as One and without partner, and believes firmly in Him—yet does not affirm any prophet [before Muhammad] nor the Prophet [Muhammad]—such a person certainly cannot be considered a Muhammadan or a Muslim, the latter word taken here as a synonym of the first. Yet according to the principles of Islam, it is not correct to call such a person unbeliever in the sense of associationist [polytheist] or to refuse to call him a unitarian.

No doubt, to affirm the prophethood is the second pillar of Islam. From early on, it has been a moot point among the *'ulama'* whether those who acknowledge only the unity of God [that is, without believing in the prophets and Muhammad] will be in eternal hellfire or not. Some maintained they would, whereas others said they would reach salvation after punishment. Leave this discussion to the *'ulama'*, and let us stay with the saying of our Friend [the Prophet]: "Despite Abu Dharr [al-Ghifari, a devout companion of the Prophet, died 653], I did so."[2]

[(xi) The Religious Duties of Islam]

After the belief in the unity of God and the divine mission of the Prophet, there are further elements in Islam which God has established as religious duty, for instance ritual prayer, fasting, pilgrimage, almsgiving, and so on.

We consider those who do not perform these duties as sinners, and we regard the one who denies them like the one who denies the divine mission of the Prophet as not a Muhammadan or Muslim, both terms taken synonymously. With regard to such people's eternal punishment in hellfire, the same discussion arises which we mentioned in the context of those who proclaim only the unity of God [but do not believe in His messengers].

My friends! This is an important and extremely subtle discussion, and to cover it very much time is required. Because of [lack of] time we do good to keep it short. Likewise, the question of associationism [polytheism], which is the outright enemy of Islam and with which Islam cannot go together by any means, is also

2. [Possibly a reference to the *hadith* (tradition of the Prophet) related by Abu Dharr, in which Abu Dharr asked the Prophet several times whether those who commit illegal sexual intercourse and theft would be allowed into paradise if they die believing in God and monotheism. The Prophet answered in the affirmative: "Even if he had committed adultery and theft, despite Abu Dharr." See the *hadith* collections of Muslim ibn al-Hajjaj (821–875), volume 1, number 172; and Muhammad ibn Isma'il Bukhari (810–870), volume 7, number 717.—Ed.]

a big issue. Yet I shall explain it just a little bit here. God is one in essence and attributes, and nobody shares with Him in this unity. In the same way, therefore, those who consider the precepts of any person—except those of the Messenger—in religious matters as incumbent on themselves, they too, in a way, associate [others with God]. I call this associationism in prophethood. When accusing Jews and Christians of the same thing, God has said: "They have taken as lords beside God their rabbis and their monks." [Sura 9, Verse 31] Such a following [of the precepts of men, except the Prophet] leads finally to taking "lords beside God."

Do not imagine from what I have said that I hold a view opposed to the community of religious scholars. No, I consider them to be the crown of the Crown of the *umma* [Muslim community] and their *ijtihad* [independent judgment] and differences of opinion a source of mercy. Also, do not think that I denounce those who follow them blindly or that I detest *taqlid* [imitation of a religious scholar] as bad. But I certainly do think that some of the actions of those who follow blindly have reached the point where they—by their own mistake, not by virtue of following the community of religious scholars—have made the latter "lords beside God." And those people who are against this tenet of blind following and hold the doctrine of *'adam-i taqlid* [absence of *taqlid*] and who desire to try to implement this—these persons also I respect. I consider the objective of both groups to be one. Both desire to please God and the Messenger. (*Cheers.*) It is a pity that because of these two groups, mutual vexation and enmity have arisen. These are the evil inspirations of Satan, which are designed to split Islam and weaken its power. In truth Islam means to profess "*La ilaha illah Allah*" ["There is no god but God," the first part of the Islamic profession of faith], to believe this firmly and sincerely and to regard all who profess the word as brothers. To split the assembly of Islam by being opposed to one another is against the principles of Islam, and is ingratitude for the blessing God has bestowed upon us, which He has expressed in the words: "And He made friendship between your hearts." [Sura 3, Verse 103] (*Cheers.*)

[(xii) The Belief in the Prophethood of Muhammad, in the Modern Context]

Now I want to deal a little with those subjects that are related to the affirmation of the prophethood [of

Muhammad] and to those tenets of Islam that on first sight seem to be opposed to reason and science. A detailed treatment of these subjects would need a very long time and would probably not be finished in years. This is no matter of surprise. But it may not be out of place to succinctly deal with these subjects for the benefit of some English-educated young men, or for other people who desire to alter their outlook.

To be a Muhammadan, or (what is synonymous with it) to belong to the circle of Islam, demands belief not only in the unity of God but also in the divine mission of the Prophet, that is, in prophethood. Two things put the English-educated or liberal-minded young man into doubt. First, the belief in the prophethood; second, those tenets of Islam which seem to contradict contemporary wisdom and philosophy or reason, or which seem to be far removed from reason. The discussion of the prophethood along the principles of nature is a lengthy one. I am not going to open it up now. Instead I shall state a few points, as one does in a speech, concerning the truth of the prophethood of Muhammad—points which the heart can accept. Many great philosophers of the past and present, who have reached a very high rank in scholarship, and have written many excellent books, accept, nevertheless, the teaching of basic Islam and the principles upon which it is built. But leave them aside and examine yourself how excellent, solid, and unrivaled the principles of basic Islam are, omitting the independent judgments and complex problems of the jurisprudents, which do not correspond to the plain and simple principles of Islam. Even those who all their life have investigated into the essence of philosophy, wisdom, the natural sciences, and human nature—even such people would not be able to establish such principles. I therefore do not think it out of place to argue that a person who was born in a land full of sand and stones, who had become an orphan at a tender age, who had neither received training in a house of sciences nor heard the doctrines of Socrates, Hippocrates, or Plato [Greek philosophers, fifth–fourth century B.C.], nor sat at the feet of a teacher nor enjoyed the company of wise men, philosophers, or men of political and moral science, but who spent forty years of his life among uneducated and rude camel drivers, who for 40 years had seen nobody but a people addicted to idolatry, internecine warfare, and men and women who prided themselves on theft and fornication. Such a man, who all at once rose against all his own people and, al-

beit surrounded on four sides by idolatry, yet professed "*La ilaha illah Allah*"—who not only said it but made all his people say it, people who for centuries had worshiped Lat and Manat and 'Uzza [pre-Islamic Arab goddesses]; who eradicated from his people all this bad behavior and these immoral practices; who made them throw to ground and break their idols and exalted the name and worship of God throughout the entire peninsula, the peninsula which, after Ibrahim and Isma'il, had been sullied by a thousand acts of impurity. Who then restored to it its original purity and the great religion of Ibrahim? Who, I ask, after forty years, put light in man's heart, the light which has illuminated not only the Arab peninsula but the whole world?

After teaching the *shahada* [profession of faith], he gave the people precepts about the morals of religion. Could any philosopher have said more than what this illiterate man said? And not only did he pronounce these precepts, but rather, by the influence of his pure heart and tongue, he implanted them in the hearts of people. This work was such that it could not have been achieved by any philosopher or any powerful political ruler. What was the thing in this orphan child which demonstrated not only to the Arab peninsula but to the whole world the wonder of divinity?

O my friends! The most hardened materialist, irreligious persons, if they do not—God forbid—accept such a person as a prophet, surely they shall have, at least, to acknowledge that if after God there is any person as great, it is he alone. "My spirit a sacrifice to you, O Messenger of God!" [Arabic phrase] Thus whoever arrives at understanding the true nature of prophethood cannot but put faith in the prophethood of the Messenger of God. These few words about our affirmation of prophethood will be fully sufficient to satisfy the mind of a person who possesses a little intelligence and understanding.

[(xiii) Need to Clearly Distinguish Between the Doctrines of "Pure Islam" and Later Doctrinal Elaborations]

Now I have to say something about the doctrines of Islam. As you know very well, they are of two kinds. One, what is revealed explicitly; the other, what is arrived at by *ijtihad*—established by the *'ulama'* in the goodness of their heart and intention. If a doctrine of the second kind—that is, from those which are called *ijtihadiyat*—should be contrary to nature or human nature, then this does not bring any reflection upon Islam, because such a doctrine is the independent judgment of a human being or *mujtahid* [one who conducts *ijtihad*], and he is not preserved from negligence and error.

The leaders of the four *madhhab*s [the four main legal schools of Sunni Islam] have themselves accepted the saying: "The *mujtahid* may err and may be correct." It is therefore pointless in our context to discuss the *ijtihad* and *qiyas* doctrines [arrived at by analogous reasoning] of the *'ulama'*. They can be right or wrong. We are partisans of Islam and not of the opinion or independent judgment of every Tom, Dick, and Harry. If there is an error in these, this does not do any harm to Islam; and if they are correct, then there is no reason whatsoever for Islam to be proud of it. It is our task to establish the explicitly revealed doctrines as being in correspondence with human nature. Not by any traditional argument, nor by any proofs of the *mujtahid*s based on independent judgment, but by nature. We are prepared to prove these doctrines by the same science, through the study of which doubts have arisen in the hearts of those people. Whatever people may think about our claim—and although some people may consider it impossible to fulfill—we proclaim with a loud voice what is in our heart, and of what we are certain. In our understanding, no doctrine of "pure Islam," nor anything stated in the Glorious Qur'an, is contrary to any old or new science. Nor can any wisdom or any philosophy demolish it. (*Cheers.*)

[(xiv) The Miracle of the Qur'an]

I firmly believe that there is no religion, except Islam, which when compared with former or contemporary research, with philosophy and natural philosophy, emerges in all respects true and valid. Only that much holds true—that truth never changes. Yes, surely, when the style of philosophy changes, the principles of debate change, and there arises the need for new argument. For this reason the arguments formerly set up by our elders have lost their relevance in our time. We need therefore to adopt a new method of controversy. The Glorious Qur'an, which for 1,300 years has been firmly held to be *mu'jiz* [that is, disabling an opponent of the Prophet in a contest; in the follow-

ing: miraculous], I, too, accept it as such. Yet our elders had put forward only a superficial argument for its being miraculous, that is, the excellence of its pure language and speech. And this only because till today no human, no one, however fluent of speech, however eloquent, has managed to compose one or ten verses in the same fluency and eloquence, even when challenged in a public contest to do so. No doubt I, too, accept the Glorious Qur'an in the very same way as fluent and eloquent of speech. And why should I not, since I firmly believe that it is the word of God and dictated revelation. Its words are the very same that God put in the heart of the Messenger, and which reached from the tongue of the Messenger. I also accept that till today nothing comparable has been spoken by any human being. But I regard this proof to be weak, not solid, and I do not interpret the relevant passages of the Glorious Qur'an in this way. Further, even if this proof is a real proof, it cannot still be put forward in confrontation with nonbelievers. It will not satisfy their mind. I have another proof which I consider more solid than the one mentioned. What proof is this? The direction for man given in the Glorious Qur'an cannot surely be bettered by others. This I consider to be the miracle, rather the basic miracle of the Glorious Qur'an. The Glorious Qur'an "descended" at a period marked by ignorant, uninformed, and uneducated people. The Qur'an was at the same time guidance for the ignorant people of that period and guidance for the most highly educated people, then and in all ages to come. It was necessary that its precepts should be stated in such a way that both a Bedouin camel driver of the desert and an outstandingly wise man like Socrates or Hippocrates would likewise receive from them profit and guidance. The Glorious Qur'an is a word that possesses this quality. From it people of different degrees [of learning], or rather opposed qualities, would receive one and the same guidance. An ignorant Bedouin and a holy *maulavi* would both receive from its literal meanings the same guidance as a philosopher from the intended meanings of the same words, and the latter would not find one word [of it] opposed to nature or philosophy. Compose for me and show me any book in any language—French, Latin, Arabic, Persian, Sanskrit, and so on, or name me a book written formerly in these languages which contains the most exalted thoughts of philosophy and wisdom—and yet in extremely pleasant and fluent words and which is of equal use to both illiterate and learned, ignorant and philosopher, and which makes an equal impression on the hearts of all; you will find it utterly impossible. The Glorious Qur'an is the only book in which there are all these qualities, and this is the original, true, and real miracle of it. Its doctrines were true when the earth was regarded as immovable. In the same way today, when the sun is regarded as immovable and the earth as revolving round it, it is equally true and satisfies the mind. Jews, Christians, Chinese, and Hindus all have their books, which they regard as sacred. But tell me, which of these possesses the quality I have explained? In the Torah, it is stated that the sun halted for Joshua [Book of Joshua, Chapter 10, Verse 13]. If this was the case, when would the destruction of the whole world ever be accomplished? In contrast, the Glorious Qur'an refrains from preaching such things, and if it gives a counsel it is the following—"There is no altering (the laws of) God's creation." [Sura 30, Verse 30]

I firmly believe, although it is liable to be opposed as being a prediction, that if the wisdom and philosophy considered to be true today turn out tomorrow to be wrong, as has happened to Greek wisdom in our days, and should there be established as true totally new principles, still, I maintain, then also the Glorious Qur'an will prove to be true in the same way as it is true today. After reflection, it will be established that what was erroneous was so [on account of] the deficiency of our knowledge—the Qur'an, in contrast, is as true as ever. Our ancient exegetes have greatly stressed [the need] to harmonize the Qur'an with Greek wisdom and astronomy. But the people who reflect on the Qur'an in the light of God's guidance, understand that whatever might seem wrong in it was their error and not that of the Glorious Qur'an.

[(xv) Explicitly Revealed Precepts and Duties Elaborated by Rational Conclusions]

My brothers! My friends! This is an arduous road, not free from obstacles. But for people who claim to belong to the religion of Islam, it is necessary to reflect about it. What I am doing [here] should have been, in fact, the work of other people, not the work of an ignorant man like me. But when no one undertook it, there was an impulse in my heart and I responded to it. I understand that God put this impulse into my heart. If I did not try to the best of my ability, what answer was I to give to God? It is a pity that people did not understand my intention and objec-

tive, and that they opposed me on behalf of some really minor differences which are not even completely new [in the light of Islamic history], and made various false accusations against me. Yet reflect about the past conditions and study thoroughly the books of former 'ulama', and you will see what a contradiction there exists between principles that lead to kufr [disbelief] on the one side, and those on the other leading to Islam. One group professes the vision of God and says that it is explicitly revealed. Then there is a group of the very traditional Sunni scholars who profess God to have hands, feet, eyes, and a nose, who firmly believe that He resides on a throne, and who hold this to be explicitly revealed. Another group opposes this and regards it as kufr. If the former 'ulama', from early on, have differed to such an extent in basic matters, what then is my sin when I differ from doctrines formulated by those 'ulama' of old? In the end they, too, were human beings and not preserved and protected from error.

The undisputed and unequivocal, explicitly revealed precepts like prayer, fasting, pilgrimage, and almsgiving which God Almighty has declared in the Qur'an to be religious duty, I consider to be religious duties in the same way as does an ignorant Muslim. But when an opponent [of Islam] attacks them, it becomes unavoidable to discuss their inner reason and original meaning. When the question is raised what the washing of hands and face, that is ablution, has to do with worship, which after all relates to the heart or what "out of place" rinsing and washing of the mouth has to do with an accidental cause of ritual impurity, or what has prayer, which is a spiritual action, to do with standing, sitting, lowering of the head, and raising of the hips, then we shall, willy nilly, have to discuss the inner reason and original meaning of the "pillars" of prayer, and we will have to explain why ablution has been prescribed as a duty and why the constituent parts of prayer have been determined [by revelation]. To explain these things, proofs by simply adducing revealed texts without rational argument will not do, because the doubter in religion, or the religious, will not accept such. Rather, it will be necessary to explain them in a manner corresponding with reason, nature, or human nature, so that the mind of the other person will be satisfied. (Cheers.) Or do you think it will satisfy people who are an alien party to Islam to argue that this and nothing else is the precept, accept it as it stands?

[(xvi) The True Meaning of Islam as the Perfect Religion]

O my brothers! Certainty, which is another name for faith, does not originate from the mere saying of another person. If I, in this very situation here where a splendid hall is illuminated by chandeliers made of crystal, by glass shades and wall lamps, if I should state: in this hall is total darkness—and you, out of regard for me and my words, accept and repeat my words, saying that yes, it is darkness, will there, because of my saying so, be certainty in your hearts? Surely if you are reasonable and truly and sincerely consider me worthy of respect, and my words as deserving certain assent, then you will, no doubt, reflect and think about what is the meaning [here] of darkness. And when you have understood this, will there then be in your heart true certainty? My point is this, and I desire this from my Muslim brethren—don't call the Glorious Qur'an a miracle only by tongue, but acknowledge it as a miracle in your heart. For this reason, I have said that arguments should be put before them through which certainty will originate about the Qur'an being a miracle, or at least about its being true. Since I had exactly such certainty about the Qur'an, it was therefore my desire to demonstrate to the world, without fear and anxious thought, whether this agrees or disagrees with the opinion of the revered men and without fearing the *fatwa*s [religious rulings] of *kufr* by the contemporary *'ulama'*, that the Glorious Qur'an and Islam are likewise in accordance with the nature of humankind. I hope that my Muslim brethren, insofar as they are able, will correct whatever I have done, and if I have made mistakes will forgive, instead of regarding me the inventor of a sect or the founder of a new *madhhab*. I assure you that I affirm, as far as I can, all the doctrines of Islam which are authentic. Can you call this a new *madhhab*? It is my creed that the religion of Islam is the perfect and final religion. I am absolutely certain of the word of God which says that "this day I have perfected your religion for you and completed my favor unto you, and have chosen for you as religion al-Islam." [Sura 5, Verse 3] Yet if the exegetes—may God have mercy upon them—explain the meaning of this perfection—that God has made perfect religion by declaring this animal *halal* [lawful to eat] and that animal *haram* [unlawful]—then I oppose them, be they a Fakhr al-Din Razi [famous exegete and theologian, 1149–1209] or a *Mulla* [Abu'l-Hasan] 'Ali Nishapuri [died 1075],

or somebody greater than them. I propose humbly to these revered men, Sirs, if this is the meaning of the perfection of religion, then adieu. I maintain that this exegesis is wrong. The religion of Islam has been perfected by pronouncing the unity of God in a perfect way and by throwing light on every detail and principle of [this unity]. This alone is the perfection of religion, and because of this perfection Islam is the last religion and will stay on unchanged to the Day of Resurrection. Yes, til after Resurrection as well. (*Cheers.*)

[(xvii) Distinction between Fundamental and Nonfundamental Elements in the Religious Commandments]

Now I want to say something about various precepts mentioned in the Glorious Qur'an. Prayer, for instance—I understand that God has made prayer a duty, precisely with respect to the nature God has put into humankind, that is to say, in order that the memory of the One worshiped may stay in the heart, and that people may not forget their aim, and that they may express their heartfelt longing and submission before Him. This is the fundamental element of prayer, which God has made a duty. Yet in order to teach humankind how to perform this duty, he has fixed "pillars" for it that, in reality, are not a fundamental element of it. Rather, they are meant to protect the fundamental element, and as such cannot be separated from it. They have therefore become part of the fundamental element, and have become incumbent in the manner of the fundamental element. We easily arrive at the distinction [between fundamental and nonfundamental element] in the following way, when we consider that people can be excused from performing an element which is meant to protect the fundamental one. Given the case of excuse, the religious obligation of ablution, the obligation to stand, sit, prostrate, yes, even to recite aloud, can be waived. Yet, the attention toward God and the performance of sincere longing and submission, which is the fundamental element of prayer, cannot be waived as long as a person is conscious and breathes. Thus it is crystal-clear that those elements which can be waived in the end are not fundamental. Only that element is fundamental which cannot at any time, as long as a human is human, be waived. (*Cheers.*) Now, who can say that this mode of prayer is against nature or human nature? (*Cheers.*)

True, the question remains with regard to these fixed "pillars" of prayer—why have they been established and how do they accord with human nature? My [first] answer is yes, they do correspond to human nature. Yet here I shall answer in another, a philosophical way. If we were to determine some other "pillars" for the performance of this [fundamental] duty, then the same question that arises with regard to the determining of the now established "pillars" of prayer will arise, with regard to the proposed ones, and so on. And to raise an objection that refutes itself is unreasonable.

Of course, one must raise the point whether more excellent "pillars" of prayer could not have been established. But I am certain that no person could name other "pillars" better than these, in which all exoteric and esoteric, all inner and outer organs, all ways of respect and submission of body and soul find expression, and which impress man in accordance with the exigencies of nature.

[(xviii) Overall Objective: Restatement of Islam]

I have, in a succinct way, told you my thoughts concerning the religion of Islam. I have also explained to you why I have adopted this new way of reaffirming Islam and of [defending it in] debate. I have also pointed out why I felt it necessary to take a stand different from that of the former *'ulama'*. It would need much time to state on which issues the *'ulama'* differ among themselves, on which issues I have taken a stand different from theirs, on which of these latter issues some ancient *'ulama'* too had chosen the approach which is mine, and how many points there are on which I am on my own and all former *'ulama'* are against me. Yet now, after my statement here, I leave the critical assessment of the question whether what I have said is a reaffirmation of Islam or not— that, gentlemen, I leave to you.

To end, I want to say that the [kind of] reaffirmation of Islam I have adopted to my best knowledge has not come about for the reason that I am a Muslim, was born in a Muslim family, and therefore had willy nilly to reaffirm Islam. I do not think highly of that [kind of motivation]. That a person born in a certain religion should quietly walk in it is one thing, and to set out to reaffirm your religion another. The latter work does not become a man who has not reached full certainty about it. I have reflected a lot, with an open mind about Islam. After considerable reflection and thought I became deeply convinced that if there is any true religion, it is Islam alone, and I reaffirm Islam on the basis of this heartfelt certainty, not because I was born in a Muslim home and because I am Muslim. (*Very loud cheers.*)

Islam as a Moral and Political Ideal

Muhammad Iqbal (North India, 1877–1938) was a great poet in both the Persian and Urdu languages and a progressive thinker known as the intellectual father of Pakistan. Iqbal was born in Punjab and completed his early studies with a scholar who had been strongly influenced by Sayyid Ahmad Khan's (chapter 40) Aligarh movement. He later studied at Government College in Lahore, and then, after teaching Arabic and English at various Lahore colleges, went to Europe in 1905 for graduate study. He was awarded a doctorate in philosophy from Munich University in 1907, and also studied law in London and philosophy at Cambridge University. Upon his return to Punjab, he sporadically practiced law while earning fame as a poet and intellectual. He was knighted by the British in 1922 for his contributions to poetry, and was elected to the Punjab legislature in 1927. His presidential speech to the All-India Muslim League in 1930, arguing that the predominantly Muslim regions of North-West India should be governed autonomously under an Islamic system, is widely credited with inspiring the Pakistan movement. Major themes in Iqbal's poetry included the decline of Muslim creativity, influence, and authenticity. He sought to reverse this decline through the promotion of a dynamic and forward-looking sense of self, in contrast to the "ego" criticized in Islamic ethical and mystical literature. The selection presented here, written early in Iqbal's career, argued for the progressive and egalitarian nature of Islam, in both the ethical and political realms.[1]

There are three points of view from which a religious system can be approached: the standpoint of the teacher, that of the expounder, and that of the critical student. I do not pretend to be a teacher, whose thought and action are, or ought to be, in perfect harmony in so far as he endeavors to work out, in his own life, the ideals which he places before others, and thus influences his audience more by example than by precept. Nor do I claim the high office of an expounder, who brings to bear a subtle intellect upon his task, endeavors to explain all the various aspects of the principles he expounds, and works with certain presuppositions, the truth of which he never questions. The attitude of the mind which characterizes a critical student is fundamentally different from that of the teacher and the expounder. He approaches

the subject of his inquiry free from all presuppositions, and tries to understand the organic structure of a religious system, just as a biologist would study a form of life or a geologist a piece of mineral. His object is to apply methods of scientific research to religion, with a view to discover how the various elements in a given structure fit in with one another, how each factor functions individually, and how their relation with one another determines the functional value of the whole. He looks at the subject from the standpoint of history and raises certain fundamental questions with regard to the origin, growth, and formation of the system he proposes to understand. What are the historical forces, the operation of which evoked, as a necessary consequence, the phenomenon of a particular system? Why should a particular religious system be produced by a particular people?

Dr. *Shaikh* Muhammad Iqbal, "Islam as a Moral and Political Ideal," *Hindustan Review*, Allahabad, India, July 1909, pp. 29–38, and August 1909, pp. 166–171. Introduction by Marcia K. Hermansen.

1. Annemarie Schimmel, *Gabriel's Wing: A Study into the Religious Ideas of Sir Muhammad Iqbal* (Leiden, Netherlands: E. J. Brill, 1963); Annemarie Schimmel, "Ikbal, Muhammad," in Bernard Lewis *et alia*, editors, *Encyclope-dia of Islam*, 2d ed. (Leiden, Netherlands: E. J. Brill; London: Luzac, 1971), volume 3, pp. 1057–1059; Hafeez Malik, editor, *Iqbal, Poet-Philosopher of Pakistan* (New York: Columbia University Press, 1971); Hafeez Malik, "Iqbal, Muhammad," in John L. Esposito, editor, *Oxford Encyclopedia of the Modern Islamic World* (New York: Oxford University Press, 1995), volume 2, pp. 221–224.

What is the real significance of a religious system in the history of the people who produced it, and in the history of mankind as a whole? Are there any geographical causes which determine the original locality of a religion? How far does it reveal the inmost soul of a people, their social, moral, and political aspirations? What transformation, if any, has it worked in them? How far has it contributed toward the realization of the ultimate purpose revealed in the history of man? These are some of the questions which the critical student of religion endeavors to answer, in order to comprehend its structure and to estimate its ultimate worth as a civilizing agency among the forces of historical evolution.

I propose to look at Islam from the standpoint of the critical student. But I may state at the outset that I shall avoid the use of expressions current in popular Revelation Theology, since my method is essentially scientific and consequently necessitates the use of terms which can be interpreted in the light of everyday human experience. For instance, when I say that the religion of a people is the sum total of their life experience finding a definite expression through the medium of a great personality, I am only translating the fact of Revelation into the language of science. Similarly, interaction between individual and universal energy is only another expression for the feeling of prayer, which ought to be so described for purposes of scientific accuracy. It is because I want to approach my subject from a thoroughly human standpoint, and not because I doubt the fact of Divine Revelation as the final basis of all religion, that I prefer to employ expressions of a more scientific content. Islam is, moreover, the youngest of all religions, the last creation of humanity. Its founder stands out clear before us; he is truly a personage of history and lends himself freely even to the most searching criticism. Ingenious legend has weaved no screens round his figure; he is born in the broad daylight of history; we can thoroughly understand the inner spring of his actions; we can subject his mind to a keen psychological analysis. Let us then, for the time being, eliminate the supernatural element and try to understand the structure of Islam as we find it.

I have just indicated the way in which a critical student of religion approaches his subject. Now, it is not possible for me, in the short space at my disposal, to answer, with regard to Islam, all the questions which as a critical student of religion I ought to raise and answer in order to reveal the real meaning of this religious system. I shall not raise the question of the origin and the development of Islam. Nor shall I try to analyze the various currents of thought in the pre-Islamic Arabian society, which found a final focus in the utterances of the Prophet of Islam. I shall confine my attention to the Islamic ideal in its ethical and political aspects only.

To begin with, we have to recognize that every great religious system starts with certain propositions concerning the nature of man and the universe. The psychological implication of Buddhism, for instance, is the central fact of pain as a dominating element in the constitution of the universe. Man, regarded as an individuality, is helpless against the forces of pain, according to the teachings of Buddhism. There is an indissoluble relation between pain and the individual consciousness, which, as such, is nothing but a constant possibility of pain. Freedom from pain means freedom from individuality. Starting from the fact of pain, Buddhism is quite consistent in placing before man the ideal of self-destruction. Of the two terms in this relation, pain and the sense of personality, one (that is, pain) is ultimate; the other is a delusion from which it is possible to emancipate ourselves by ceasing to act on those lines of activity, which have a tendency to intensify the sense of personality. Salvation, then, according to Buddhism, is inaction; renunciation of self and unworldliness are the principal virtues. Similarly, Christianity, as a religious system, is based on the fact of sin. The world is regarded as evil and the taint of sin is regarded as hereditary to man, who, as an individuality, is insufficient and stands in need of some supernatural personality to intervene between him and his Creator. Christianity, unlike Buddhism, regards human personality as something real, but agrees with Buddhism in holding that man as a force against sin is insufficient. There is, however, a subtle difference in the agreement. We can, according to Christianity, get rid of sin by depending upon a Redeemer; we can free ourselves from pain, according to Buddhism, by letting this insufficient force dissipate or lose itself in the universal energy of nature. Both agree in the fact of insufficiency, and both agree in holding that this insufficiency is evil; but while the one makes up the deficiency by bringing in the force of a redeeming personality, the other prescribes its gradual reduction until it is annihilated altogether. Again, Zoroastrianism looks upon nature as a scene of endless struggle between the powers of evil and the powers of good, and recognizes in man the power to choose any course of action he likes. The universe, according to Zoroastrianism, is partly evil, partly good; man is neither wholly good nor wholly evil, but a combination of the two principles—light and darkness continually fighting against each other for universal supremacy. We see then that the fundamental presuppositions, with regard to the nature of the universe and man, in Buddhism, Christianity, and Zoroastrianism, respectively, are the following:

(1) There is pain in nature, and man regarded as an individual is evil (Buddhism).
(2) There is sin in nature, and the taint of sin is fatal to man (Christianity).
(3) There is struggle in nature; man is a mixture of the struggling forces and is free to range himself on the side of the powers of good, which will eventually prevail (Zoroastrianism).

The question now is, what is the Muslim view of the universe and man? What is the central idea in Islam which determines the structure of the entire system? We know that sin, pain, and sorrow are constantly mentioned in the Qur'an. The truth is that Islam looks upon the universe as a reality and consequently recognizes as reality all that is in it. Sin, pain, sorrow, struggle are certainly real, but Islam teaches that evil is not essential to the universe; the universe can be reformed; the elements of sin and evil can be gradually eliminated. All that is in the universe is God's, and the seemingly destructive forces of nature become sources of life, if properly controlled by man, who is endowed with the power to understand and to control them.

These and other similar teachings of the Qur'an, combined with the Qur'anic recognition of the reality of sin and sorrow, indicate that the Islamic view of the universe is neither optimistic nor pessimistic. Modern psychometry has given the final answer to the psychological implications of Buddhism. Pain is not an essential factor in the constitution of the universe, and pessimism is only a product of a hostile social environment. Islam believes in the efficacy of well-directed action; hence the standpoint of Islam must be described as melioristic—the ultimate presupposition and justification of all human effort at scientific discovery and social progress. Although Islam recognizes the fact of pain, sin, and struggle in nature, yet the principal fact which stands in the way of man's ethical progress is, according to Islam,

neither pain, nor sin, nor struggle. It is fear, to which man is a victim owing to his ignorance of the nature of his environment and want of absolute faith in God. The highest stage of man's ethical progress is reached when he becomes absolutely free from fear and grief.

The central proposition which regulates the structure of Islam, then, is that there is fear in nature, and the object of Islam is to free man from fear. This view of the universe indicates also the Islamic view of the metaphysical nature of man. If fear is the force which dominates man and counteracts his ethical progress, man must be regarded as a unit of force, an energy, a will, a germ of infinite power, the gradual unfoldment of which must be the object of all human activity. The essential nature of man, then, consists in will, not intellect or understanding.

With regard to the ethical nature of man, too, the teaching of Islam is different from those of other religious systems. And when God said to the angels, "I am going to make a Viceroy on the earth," they said: "Art Thou creating one who spills blood and disturbs the peace of the earth, and we glorify Thee and sing Thy praises?" God answered: "I know what you do not know." This verse of the Qur'an [Sura 2, Verse 30] read in the light of the famous tradition [*hadith*, or tradition of the Prophet] that every child is born a Muslim (peaceful), indicates that, according to the tenets of Islam, man is essentially good and peaceful—a view explained and defended, in our own times, by [Jean-Jacques] Rousseau [French philosopher, 1712–1778], the great father of modern political thought. The opposite view, the doctrine of the depravity of man held by the Church of Rome, leads to the most pernicious religious and political consequences. Since if man is elementally wicked, he must not be permitted to have his own way; his entire life must be controlled by external authority. This means priesthood in religion and autocracy in politics. The Middle Ages in the history of Europe drove this dogma of Romanism to its political and religious consequences, and the result was a form of society which required terrible revolutions to destroy it and to upset the basic presuppositions of its structure. [Martin] Luther [German founder of Protestant Christianity, 1483–1546], the enemy of despotism in religion, and Rousseau, the enemy of despotism in politics, must always be regarded as the emancipators of European humanity from the heavy fetters of Popedom and absolutism, and their religious and political thought must be understood as a virtual denial of the Church dogma of human depravity. The possibility of the elimination of sin and pain from the evolutionary process, and faith in the natural goodness of man, are the basic propositions of Islam, as of modern European civilization, which has, almost unconsciously, recognized the truth of these propositions in spite of the religious system with which it is associated. Ethically speaking, therefore, man is naturally good and peaceful. Metaphysically speaking, he is a unit of energy, which cannot bring out its dormant possibilities owing to its misconception of the nature of its environment. The ethical ideal of Islam is to disenthral man from fear, and thus to give him a sense of his personality, to make him conscious of himself as a source of power. This idea of man as an individuality of infinite power determines, according to the teachings of Islam, the worth of all human action. That which intensifies the sense of individuality in man is good, that which enfeebles it is bad. Virtue is power, force, strength; evil is weakness. Give man a keen sense of respect for his own personality, let him move fearless and free in the immensity of God's earth, and he will respect the personalities of others and become perfectly virtuous. It is not possible for me to show in the course of this paper how all the principal forms of vice can be reduced to fear. But we will now see the reason why certain forms of human activity, such as self-renunciation, poverty, slavish obedience which sometimes conceals itself under the beautiful name of humility and unworldliness—modes of activity which tend to weaken the force of human individuality—are regarded as virtues by Buddhism and Christianity, and altogether ignored by Islam. While the early Christians glorified in poverty and unworldliness, Islam looks upon poverty as a vice, and says: "Do not forget thy share in the world." [Qur'an, Sura 28, Verse 77] The highest virtue from the standpoint of Islam is righteousness, which is defined by the Qur'an in the following manner:

It is not righteousness that ye turn your faces in prayers towards east and west, but righteousness is of him who believeth in God and the last day and the angels and the scriptures and the prophets, who give the money for God's sake unto his kindred and unto orphans and the needy and to strangers and to those who ask for the redemption of captives, of those who are constant at prayer, and of those who perform their covenant when they have covenanted, and behave themselves patiently in adversity and in times of violence. [Sura 2, Verse 177]

It is, therefore, evident that Islam, so to speak, transmutes the moral values of the ancient world, and declares the preservation, intensification of the sense of human personality, to be the ultimate ground of all ethical activity. Man is a free responsible being; he is the maker of his own destiny; his salvation is his own business. There is no mediator between God and man. God is the birthright of every man. The Qur'an, therefore, while it looks upon Jesus Christ as the spirit of God, strongly protests against the Christian doctrine of Redemption, as well as the doctrine of an infallible visible head of the Church—doctrines which proceed upon the assumption of the insufficiency of human personality and tend to create in man a sense of dependence, which is regarded by Islam as a force obstructing the ethical progress of man. The law of Islam is almost unwilling to recognize illegitimacy, since the stigma of illegitimacy is a great blow to the healthy development of independence in man. Similarly, in order to give man an early sense of individuality, the law of Islam has laid down that a child is an absolutely free human being at the age of fifteen.

To this view of Muslim ethics, however, there can be one objection. If the development of human individuality is the principal concern of Islam, why should it tolerate the institution of slavery? The idea of free labor was foreign to the economic consciousness of the ancient world. Aristotle [Greek philosopher, 384–322 B.C.] looks upon it as a necessary factor in human society. The Prophet of Islam, being a link between the ancient and the modern world, declared the principle of equality and though, like every wise reformer, he slightly conceded to the social conditions around him in retaining the name slavery, he quietly took away the whole spirit of this institution. That slaves had equal opportunity with other Muhammadans is evidenced by the fact that some of the greatest Muslim warriors, kings, premiers, scholars, and jurists were slaves. During the days of the early caliphs, slavery by purchase was quite unknown; part of public revenue was set apart for purposes of manumission, and prisoners of war were either freely dismissed or freed on the payment of ransom. 'Umar [ibn al-Khattab, second caliph, 634–644] set all slaves at liberty after his conquest of Jerusalem. Slaves were also set at liberty as a penalty for culpable homicide and in expiation of a false oath taken by mistake. The Prophet's own treatment of slaves was extraordinarily liberal. The proud aristocratic Arab could not tolerate the social elevation of a slave, even when he was manumitted. The democratic ideal of perfect equality, which had found the most uncompromising expression in the Prophet's life, could only be brought home to an extremely aristocratic people by a very cautious handling of the situation. He brought about a marriage between an emancipated slave and a free Quraysh woman, a relative of his own [tribe]. This marriage was a blow to the aristocratic pride of this free Arab woman; she could not get on with her husband, and the result was a divorce, which made her the more helpless, since no respectable Arab would marry the divorced wife of a slave. The ever-watchful Prophet availed himself of this situation and turned it to account in his efforts at social reform. He married the woman himself, indicating thereby that not only a slave could marry a free woman, but also a woman divorced by him could become the wife of a man no less than the greatest Prophet of God. The significance of this marriage in the history of social reform in Arabia is, indeed, great. Whether prejudice, ignorance, or want of insight has blinded European critics of Islam to the real meaning of this union, it is difficult to guess.

In order to show the treatment of slaves by modern Muhammadans, I quote a passage from the English translation of the autobiography of the late *Amir* 'Abd al-Rahman of Afghanistan [reigned 1880–1901]: "For instance," says the amir, "Framurz Khan, a Chitrali slave, is my most trusted Commander-in-Chief at Herat, Nazir Muhammad Safar Khan, another Chitrali slave, is the most trusted official of my Court; he keeps my seal in his hand to put to any document and to my food and diet; in short he has the full confidence of my life, as well as my kingdom is in his hands. Parwana Khan, the late Deputy Commander-in-Chief, and Jan Muhammad Khan, the late Lord of Treasury, two of the highest officials of the kingdom in their lifetime, were both of them my slaves."

The truth is that the institution of slavery is a mere name in Islam, and the idea of individuality reveals itself as a guiding principle in the entire system of Muhammadan law and ethics.

Briefly speaking, then, a strong will in a strong body is the ethical ideal of Islam. But let me stop here for a moment and see whether we, Indian Musalmans [Muslims], are true to this ideal. Does the Indian Muslim possess a strong will in a strong body? Has he got the will to live? Has he got sufficient strength of character to oppose those forces which tend to disintegrate the social organism to which he belongs? I regret to answer my questions in the negative. The reader will understand that in the great struggle for existence it is not principally number which makes a social organism survive. Character is the ultimate equipment of man, not only in his efforts against a hostile natural environment, but also in his contest with kindred competitors after a fuller, richer, ampler life. The life-force of the Indian Muhammadan, however, has become woefully enfeebled. The decay of the religious spirit, combined with other causes of a political nature over which he had no control, has developed in him a habit of self-dwarfing, a sense of dependence, and, above all, that laziness of spirit which an enervated people call by the dignified name of "contentment" in order to conceal their own enfeeblement. Owing to his indifferent commercial morality, he fails in economic enterprise; for want of a true conception of national interest and a right appreciation of the present situation of his community among the communities of this country, he is working, in his private as well as public capacity, on lines which, I am afraid, must lead him to ruin. How often do we see that he shrinks from advocating a cause, the significance of which is truly national, simply because his standing aloof pleases an influential Hindu, through whose agency he hopes to secure a personal distinction? I unhesitatingly declare that I have greater respect for an illiterate shopkeeper, who earns his honest bread and has sufficient force in his arms to defend his wife and children in times of trouble, than the brainy graduate of high culture, whose low, timid voice betokens the dearth of soul in his body, who takes pride in his submissiveness, eats sparingly, complains of sleepless nights, and produces unhealthy children for his community, if he does produce any at all. I hope I shall not be offending the reader when I say that I have a certain amount of admiration for the devil. By refusing to prostrate himself before Adam, whom he honestly believed to be his inferior, he revealed a high sense of self-respect, a trait of character which, in my opinion, ought to redeem him from his spiritual deformity, just as the beautiful eyes of the toad redeem him from his physical repulsiveness. And I believe God punished him not because he refused to make himself low before the progenitor of an enfeebled humanity, but because he declined to give absolute obedience to the will of the Almighty Ruler of the Universe. The ideal of our educated young men is mostly [government] service, and service begets, specially in a country like India, that sense of dependence which undermines the force of human individuality. The poor among us have, of course, no capital; the middle class people cannot undertake joint economic enterprise owing to mutual mistrust; and the rich look upon trade as an occupation beneath their dignity. Truly, economic dependence is the prolific mother of all the various forms of vice. Even the vices of the Indian Muhammadan indicate the weakness of life-force in him. Physically, too, he has undergone dreadful deterioration. If one sees the pale, faded faces of Muhammadan boys in schools and colleges, one will find the painful verification of my statement. Power, energy, force, strength, yes physical strength, is the law of life. A strong man may rob others when he has got nothing in his own pocket; but a feeble person, he must die the death of a mean thing in the world's awful scene of continual warfare.

But how [to] improve this undesirable state of things? Education, we are told, will work the required transformation. I may say at once that I do not put much faith in education as a means of ethical training—I mean education as understood in this country. The ethical training of humanity is really the work of great personalities, who appear, from time to time, during the course of human history. Unfortunately, our present social environment is not favorable to the birth and growth of such personalities of ethical magnetism. An attempt to discover the reason of this dearth of personalities among us will necessitate a subtle analysis of all the visible and invisible forces which are now determining the course of our social evolution—an enquiry which I cannot undertake in this paper. But all unbiased persons will easily admit that such personalities are now rare among us. This being the case, education is the only thing to fall back upon. But what sort of education? There is no absolute truth in education, as there is none in philosophy or science. Knowledge for the sake of knowledge is a maxim of fools. Do we ever find a person rolling in his mind the undulatory [wave] theory of light simply because it is a fact of science? Education, like other things, ought to be determined by the needs of the learner. A form of education which has no direct bearing on the particular type of character which you want to develop is absolutely worthless. I grant that the present system of education in India gives us bread and butter. We manufacture a number of graduates, and then we have

to send titled mendicants to government to beg appointments for them. Well, if we succeed in securing a few appointments in the higher branches of service, what then? It is the masses who constitute the backbone of the nation; they ought to be better fed, better housed, and properly educated. Life is not bread and butter alone; it is something more; it is a healthy character reflecting the national ideal in all its aspects. And for a truly national character, you ought to have a truly national education. Can you expect free Muslim character in a young boy who is brought up in an aided [that is, Christian] school and in complete ignorance of his social and historical tradition? You administer to him doses of [Oliver] Cromwell's history [English republican leader, 1599–1658]; it is idle to expect that he will turn out a truly Muslim character. The knowledge of Cromwell's history will certainly create in him a great deal of admiration for that Puritan revolutionary; but it cannot create that healthy pride in his soul which is the very lifeblood of a truly national character. Our educated young man knows all about [the Duke of] Wellington [English military hero, 1769–1852] and [William] Gladstone [English prime minister, 1809–1898], [François Marie] Voltaire [French philosopher, 1694–1778] and Luther. He will tell you that Lord [Frederick] Roberts [English general, 1832–1914] worked in the South African War like a common soldier at the age of 80 [actually 68]; but how many of us know that Muhammad II [Mehmet Fatih, Ottoman caliph, 1432–1481] conquered Constantinople at the age of 22? How many of us have even the faintest notion of the influence of our Muslim civilization over the civilization of modern Europe! How many of us are [familiar] with the wonderful historical productions of Ibn Khaldun [Tunisian historian, 1332–1406] or the extraordinarily noble character of the great *Mir* 'Abd al-Qadir [ibn Muhyi al-Din] of Algeria [anticolonial leader, 1808–1883; see chapter 15]? A living nation is living because it never forgets its dead. I venture to say that the present system of education in this country is not at all suited to us as a people. It is not true to our genius as a nation, it tends to produce an un-Muslim type of character, it is not determined by our national requirements, it breaks entirely with our past, and it appears to proceed on the false assumption that the idea of education is the training of human intellect rather than human will. Nor is this superficial system true to the genius of the Hindus. Among them it appears to have produced a number of political idealists, whose false reading of history drives them to the upsetting of all conditions of political order and social peace. We spend an immense amount of money every year on the education of our children. Well, thanks to the King-Emperor [Edward VII of Great Britain, reigned 1901–1910], India is a free country; everybody is free to entertain any opinion he likes—I look upon it as a waste. In order to be truly ourselves, we ought to have our own schools, our own colleges, and our own universities, keeping alive our social and historical tradition, making us good and peaceful citizens and creating in us that free but law-abiding spirit which evolves out of itself the noblest types of political virtue. I am quite sensible of the difficulties that lie in our way; all that I can say is that if we cannot get over our difficulties, the world will soon get rid of us.

Having discussed in the last issue of this *Review* the ethical ideals of Islam, I now proceed to say a few words on the political aspect of the Islamic ideal. Before, however, I come to the subject, I wish to meet an objection against Islam so often brought forward by our European critics. It has been said that Islam is a religion which implies a state of war and can thrive only in a state of war. Now there can be no denying that war is an expression of the energy of a nation; a nation which cannot fight cannot hold its own in the strain and stress of selective competition which constitutes an indispensable condition of all human progress. Defensive war is certainly permitted by the Qur'an; but the doctrine of aggressive war against unbelievers is wholly unauthorized by the Holy Book of Islam. Here are the words of the [Qur'an]:

> Summon them to the way of thy Lord with wisdom and kindly warning, dispute them in the kindest manner. Say to those who have been given the book and to the ignorant: Do you accept Islam? Then, if they accept Islam, they are guided aright; but if they turn away, then thy duty is only preaching; and God's eye is on His servants. [Sura 3, Verse 20]

All the wars undertaken during the lifetime of the Prophet were defensive. His war against the Roman Empire in 628 A.D. began by a fatal breach of international law on the part of the government at Constantinople, who killed the innocent Arab envoy sent to their court. Even in defensive war [the Prophet] forbids wanton cruelty to the vanquished. I quote here the touching words which he addressed to his followers when they were starting for a fight:

> In avenging the injuries inflicted upon us, disturb not the harmless votaries of domestic seclusion, spare the weakness of the female sex, injure not the infant at the breast, or those who are ill in bed. Abstain from demolishing the dwellings of the unresisting inhabitants, destroy not the means of their subsistence, nor their fruit trees, and touch not the palm.

The history of Islam tells us that the expansion of Islam as a religion is in no way related to the political power of its followers. The greatest spiritual conquests of Islam were made during the days of our political decrepitude. When the rude barbarians of Mongolia drowned in blood the civilization of Baghdad in 1258 A.D., when the Muslim power fell in Spain and the followers of Islam were mercilessly killed or driven out of Cordova by Ferdinand [III, king of Castile and Leon, died 1252] in 1236, Islam had just secured a footing in Sumatra and was about to work the peaceful conversion of the Malay Archipelago. "In the hours of its political degradation," says Professor [Thomas Walker] Arnold [1864–1930], "Islam has achieved some of its most brilliant conquests. On two great historical occasions, infidel barbarians have set their foot on the necks of the followers of the Prophet, the Seljuk Turks in the eleventh and the Mongols in the thirteenth century, and in each case the conquerors have accepted the religion of the conquered." "We undoubtedly find," says the same learned scholar elsewhere, "that Islam gained its greatest and most lasting missionary triumphs in times and places in which its political power has been weakest, as in South India and Eastern Bengal."

The truth is that Islam is essentially a religion of peace. All forms of political and social disturbance are condemned by the Qur'an in the most uncompromising terms. I quote a few verses from the Qur'an:

> Eat and drink from what God has given you, and run not on the face of the earth in the manner of rebels. [Sura 2, Verse 60]

> And disturb not the peace of the earth after it has been reformed; this is good for you if you are believers. [Sura 7, Verse 85]

> And do good to others as God has done good to thee, and seek not the violation of peace in the earth, for

God does not love those who break the peace. [Sura 28, Verse 77]

That is the home in the next world which We build for those who do not mean rebellion and disturbance in the earth, and the end is for those who fear God. [Sura 28, Verse 83]

Those who rebelled in cities and enhanced disorder in them, God visited them with His whip of punishment. [Sura 89, Verses 11–13]

One sees from these verses how severely all forms of political and social disorder are denounced by the Qur'an. But the Qur'an is not satisfied with mere denunciation of the evil of *fasad* [corruption]. It goes to the very root of this evil. We know that both in ancient and modern times, secret meetings have been a constant source of political and social unrest. Here is what the Qur'an says about such conferences: "O believers, if you converse secretly—that is to say, hold secret conference—converse not for purpose of sin and rebellion." [Sura 58, Verse 9] The ideal of Islam is to secure social peace at any cost. All methods of violent change in society are condemned in the most unmistakable language. [Ibn Abi Randaqa Abu Bakr] Tartushi—a Muslim lawyer of Spain [circa 1059–1126]—is quite true to the spirit of Islam when he says: "Forty years of tyranny are better than one hour of anarchy." "Listen to him and obey him," says the Prophet of God in a tradition mentioned by [Muhammad ibn Isma'il] Bukhari [*hadith* collector, 810–870], "even if a Negro slave is appointed to rule over you." Muslim [ibn al-Hajjaj, *hadith* collector, 821–875] mentions another important tradition of the Prophet on the authority of 'Arfaja [ibn Harthama al-Bariki, a companion of the Prophet], who says: "I heard the Prophet of God say, 'When you have agreed to follow one man, then if another man comes forward intending to break your stick (weaken your strength) or to make you disperse in disunion, kill him.'"

Those among us who make it their business to differ from the general body of Muslims in political views ought to read this tradition carefully, and if they have any respect for the words of the Prophet, it is their duty to dissuade themselves from this mean traffic in political opinion which, though perhaps it brings a little personal gain to them, is exceedingly harmful to the interests of the community. My object, in citing these verses and traditions, is to educate political opinion on strictly Islamic lines. In this

country we are living under a Christian government. We must always keep before our eyes the example of those early Muhammadans who, persecuted by their own countrymen, had to leave their home and to settle in the Christian state of Abyssinia. How they behaved in that land must be our guiding principle in this country, where an overdose of Western ideas has taught people to criticize the existing government with a dangerous lack of historical perspective. And our relations with the Christians are determined for us by the Qur'an, which says:

And thou wilt find nearer to the friendship of the believers those men who call themselves Christians. This is because among them there are learned men and hermits, and they are never vain. [Sura 5, Verse 82]

Having thus established that Islam is a religion of peace, I now proceed to consider the purely political aspect of the Islamic ideal—the ideal of Islam as entertained by a corporate individuality. Given a settled society, what does Islam expect from its followers regarded as a community? What principles ought to guide them in the management of communal affairs? What must be their ultimate object, and how is it to be achieved? We know that Islam is something more than a creed, it is also a community, a nation. The membership of Islam as a community is not determined by birth, locality, or naturalization; it consists in the identity of belief. The expression "Indian Muhammadan," however convenient it may be, is a contradiction in terms, since Islam in its essence is above all conditions of time and space. Nationality with us is a pure idea; it has no geographical basis. But inasmuch as the average man demands a material center of nationality, the Muslim looks for it in the holy town of Mecca, so that the basis of Muslim nationality combines the real and the ideal, the concrete and the abstract. When, therefore, it is said that the interests of Islam are superior to those of the Muslim, it is meant that the interests of the individual as a unit are subordinate to the interests of the community as an external symbol of the Islamic principle. This is the only principle which limits the liberty of the individual, who is otherwise absolutely free. The best form of government for such a community would be democracy, the ideal of which is to let man develop all the possibilities of his nature by allowing him as much freedom as practicable. The caliph of Islam is not an infallible being; like other Muslims he is subject to the same law; he is elected by the people and is deposed by them if he goes contrary to the law. An ancestor of the present sultan of Turkey was sued in an ordinary law court by a mason, who succeeded in getting him fined by the town *qadi* [judge]. Democracy, then, is the most important aspect of Islam regarded as a political ideal. It must, however, be confessed that the Muslims, with their ideal of individual freedom, could do nothing for the political improvement of Asia. Their democracy lasted only thirty years and disappeared with their political expansion. Though the principle of election was not quite original in Asia (since the ancient Parthian Government was based on the same principle), yet somehow or other it was not suited to the nations of Asia in the early days of Islam. It was, however, reserved for a Western nation politically to vitalize the countries of Asia. Democracy has been the great mission of England in modern times, and English statesmen have boldly carried this principle to countries which have been, for centuries, groaning under the most atrocious forms of despotism. The British Empire is a vast political organism, the vitality of which consists in the gradual working out of this principle. The permanence of the British Empire as a civilizing factor in the political evolution of mankind is one of our greatest interests. This vast Empire has our fullest sympathy and respect, since it is one aspect of our political ideal that is being slowly worked out in it. England, in fact, is doing one of our own great duties, which unfavorable circumstances did not permit us to perform. It is not the number of Muhammadans which it protects, but the spirit of the British Empire that makes it the greatest Muhammadan Empire in the world.

To return now to the political constitution of the Muslim society. Just as there are two basic propositions underlying Muslim ethics, so there are two basic propositions underlying Muslim political constitution:

(1) The law of God is absolutely supreme. Authority, except as an interpreter of the law, has no place in the social structure of Islam. Islam has a horror of personal authority. We regard it as inimical to the unfoldment of human individuality. The Shi'is, of course, differ from the Sunnis in this respect. They hold that the caliph or *imam* [in Shi'i Islam, a divinely inspired descendant of the Prophet] is appointed by God and his interpretation of the law is final; he is infallible and his authority, therefore, is absolutely supreme. There is certainly a grain of truth in this view; since the principle of absolute authority has functioned usefully in the course of the history of mankind. But it must be admitted that the idea works well in the case of primitive societies and reveals its deficiency when applied to higher stages of civilization. Peoples grow out of it, as recent events [the Constitutional Revolution of 1906] have revealed in Persia, which is a Shi'i country, yet demands a fundamental structural change in her government in the introduction of the principle of election.

(2) The absolute equality of all the members of the community. There is no aristocracy in Islam. "The noblest among you," says the Prophet, "are those who fear God most." There is no privileged class, no priesthood, no caste system. Islam is a unity in which there is no distinction, and this unity is secured by making men believe in the two simple propositions—the unity of God and the mission of the Prophet—propositions which are certainly of a supernatural character, but which, based as they are on the general religious experience of mankind, are intensely true to the average human nature. Now, this principle of the equality of all believers made early Musalmans the greatest political power in the world. Islam worked as a leveling force; it gave the individual a sense of his inward power; it elevated those who were socially low. The elevation of the downtrodden was the chief secret of the Muslim political power in India. The result of the British rule in this country has been exactly the same; and if England continues true to this principle, it will ever remain a source of strength to her as it was to her predecessors.

But are we Indian Musalmans true to this principle in our social economy? Is the organic unity of Islam intact in this land? Religious adventurers set up different sects and fraternities, ever quarreling with one another; and then there are castes and subcastes like the Hindus! Surely we have out-Hindued the Hindu himself; we are suffering from a double caste system—the religious caste system, sectarianism, and the social caste system, which we have either learned or inherited from the Hindus. This is one of the quiet ways in which conquered nations revenge themselves on their conquerors. I condemn this accursed religious and social sectarianism; I condemn it in the name of God, in the name of humanity, in the name of Moses, in the name of Jesus Christ, and in the name of him—a thrill of emotion passes through the very fiber of my soul when I think of that exalted name—yes, in the name of him who brought the final message of freedom and equality to mankind. Islam is one and indivisible; it brooks no distinctions in it. There are no Wahhabis, Shi'is, Mirza'is, or Sunnis in Islam. Fight not for the interpretations of the truth, when the truth itself is in danger. It is foolish to complain of stumbling when you walk in the darkness of night. Let all come forward and contribute their respective shares in the great toil of the nation. Let the idols of class distinctions and sectarianism be smashed forever; let the Musalmans of the country be once more united into a great vital whole. How can we, in the presence of violent internal dispute, expect to succeed in persuading others to our way of thinking? The work of freeing humanity from superstition—the ultimate ideal of Islam as a community, for the realization of which we have done so little in this great land of myth and superstition—will ever remain undone if the emancipators themselves are becoming gradually enchained in the very fetters from which it is their mission to set others free.

Islam Is a Religion That
Respects Reason

Muhammad Abdul Khader Maulavi (Malabar, 1873–1932), commonly known as Wakkom Maulavi, was the seminal modernist reformer of the Mappila Muslims of south India. Educated at home in a strong intellectual environment maintained by his merchant father, he inherited the latter's wealth in 1902 but not his business acumen, and was poor at his death. During his lifetime he launched four journals. The first, *Swadeshabhimani* (*The Patriot*, 1905–1910), was closed down because of its daring attacks on the ruling political structures of the region. His other journals—*Muslim* (1906–1917); the short-lived *al-Islam* (1918, in Arabic-Malayalam); and *Deepika* (*The Torch*, 1931–1932)—centered on educational and theological reform. In addition, he was indefatigable in organizing local Muslim associations dedicated to secular education, including women's education. Influenced by Muhammad 'Abduh (see chapter 3), Muhammad Rashid Rida's journal *al-Manar* (*The Beacon*) (see chapter 6), and reformers of earlier centuries, Wakkom Maulavi launched his own call for return to what he considered genuine Islam, which included the centrality of the Qur'an and *tawhid* (unity), reinterpreted in the light of modern needs. This return involved the overcoming of ignorance, *taqlid* (imitation of past scholars), the veneration of saints, and other popular religious practices. He passed on his reformist vision to Mappila political and educational leaders of the following generation, and to progressive movements such as the Aikhya Sankam Society and the Mujahids. Criticized by some as a modernist "strayer," Wakkom Maulavi is praised by many as the father of the Mappila renaissance.[1]

Islam is a religion that is compatible with reason; that is, it has no principles that contradict reason. The detailed matters of a bygone era that are improbable and difficult to interpret rationally will be judged by reason to be invalid. The basic approach of the religion is this: If one perceives in the Qur'an and the *hadith* [narratives of the Prophet] some words with an apparent meaning that seems unlikely, one must conclude that another interpretation is intended, an interpretation that does not contradict reason. There are two opinions among the *'ulama'* [religious scholars] regarding such passages. The first holds that while such words must have a meaning that does not

conflict with reason, it may be hard for us to grasp their real significance, and we should leave the matter to God. That is the view of the early *'ulama'* (*salafiya* [pious early Muslims]). The opinion of later *'ulama'*, however, is this: Having first expounded the passage on the basis of correct linguistic principles, one must then determine a meaning that is not contrary to reason. In short, if one senses that there is a contradiction between reason and the customary view, in choosing between the alternatives stated above, one must allow reason to decide the issue.

As we have stated earlier, Islam establishes beliefs that have the quality of being fitting for a goal.

Wakkom Muhammad Abdul Khader Maulavi, "Islam Buddhiye Acarikkunna Matumakunnu" (Islam Is a Religion That Respects Reason), in *Wakkam Maulaviyute Tiranynyetutta Krtikul* (*Selected Writings of Wakkom Maulavi*) (Wakkom, India: Wakkom Maulavi Publications, 1979), pp. 133–135. First published in 1915. Translation from Malayalam and introduction by Roland E. Miller.

1. M. Muhammadukunnu, *Wakkom Maulavi* (Kottayam, India: National Book Stall, 1981); S. Sharafuddeen, *Vakkom Maulavi, A Study* (Trivandrum, India: Samkramana Pusthaka Chakram, 1983); M. Abdul Samad, *Islam in Kerala* (Kollam, India: Laurel Publications, 1998); Roland E. Miller, *The Mappila Muslims of Kerala*, rev. ed. (Madras, India: Orient Longman, 1992).

A faith that is based either on a guess or without an appropriate purpose is one that insults both the faith itself and the believers. [The Qur'an says:] "They have no certainty about that. They only follow a guess. Guesswork has no value for knowing the truth." (Sura 53, Verse 28)[2] Islam strongly criticizes the words and the actions of past ancestors who closed their eyes and believed and practiced without discriminating between good and evil. "And when it is said to them, 'Come and believe God and God's Messenger,' they say, 'We will follow only the religion of our forefathers.' What! Will they only follow that even if their forefathers knew nothing and had not found the way of truth?" [Sura 2, Verse 170] With great intentionality Islam teaches that we should both examine and consider this universe and its principles. Moreover, it praises those who think in this way. "Tell me what is in the heavens and the earth." (Qur'an) [Sura 2, Verse 33] "Do they not look and consider all the realities that God has created in the heavens and the earth?" (Sura 7, Verse 185) "For those who remember God, whether standing, sitting, or lying, in the creation of the heavens and the earth, and in the alternation of night and day, there are many signs." (Sura 3, Verse 190) [conflated with Verse 191] Islam sharply condemns ignorant people who do not use their reason to know the essential meaning of things. "They have hearts, but no knowledge; they have eyes but do not see. They have ears, but they do not hear. They are like animals. Worse than that, they have erred and gone astray." [Sura 7, Verse 179]

---

2. [Wakkom Maulavi's Qur'anic citations are free renderings in Malayalam.—Trans.]

The Spirit of Islam (1922)

Ameer 'Ali (Bengal, 1849–1928) was one of the most influential modernists and apologists of Muslim India. His fame was due in part to the fact that he wrote in English, explaining Muslim history to Western and Westernized intellectuals. Born to a Shi'i family in Chinsura, Bengal, Ameer 'Ali studied law in England, where he was called to the bar in 1873. He had a distinguished legal and judicial career in British India and served on the Bengal high court. After retiring in 1904, he moved to England, where he served as the first Indian member of the Judicial Council of the Privy Council in London. He took an interest in Islamic political causes as well, establishing the London branch of the All-India Muslim League in 1908 and writing to the Turkish government in 1923 to support the restoration of the Ottoman caliph's authority. The Turkish Parliament, however, viewed this as foreign interference and voted to abolish the caliphate permanently in 1924. In the following passage, selected from the revised edition of Ameer 'Ali's most well known work, The Spirit of Islam, 'Ali depicts Islamic rule as enlightened and progressive, at its best. One may note evidence of Ameer 'Ali's Shi'a background in his praise of the Prophet's family and his footnoting of Shi'i sources. However, scholars have also noted that Ameer 'Ali praises orthodox Sunni caliphs as well, and that he develops a political theory combining the "apostolic" Shi'i imamate and the "pontifical" Sunni caliphate.[1]

We have already referred to the Arabian Prophet's devotion to knowledge and science as distinguishing him from all other Teachers, and bringing him into the closest affinity with the modern world of thought. Medina, the seat of the theocratic commonwealth of Islam, had after the fall of Mecca become the center of attraction, not to the hosts of Arabia only, but also to inquirers from abroad. Here flocked the Persian, the Greek, the Syrian, the Iraqi, and African of diverse hues and nationalities from the north and the west. Some, no doubt, came from curiosity, but most came to seek knowledge and to listen to the words of the Prophet of Islam. He preached of the value of knowledge:

Acquire knowledge, because he who acquires it in the way of the Lord performs an act of piety; who speaks of it, praises the Lord; who seeks it, adores God; who dispenses instruction in it, bestows alms; and who imparts it to its fitting objects, performs an act of devotion to God. Knowledge enables its possessor to distinguish what is forbidden from what is not; it lights the way to Heaven; it is our friend in the desert, our society in solitude, our companion when bereft of friends; it guides us to happiness; it sustains us in misery; it is our Ornament in the company of friends; it serves as an armor against our enemies. With knowledge, the servant of God rises to the heights of goodness and to a noble position, associates with sovereigns in this world, and attains to the perfection of happiness in the next.[2]

Ameer Ali, *The Spirit of Islam*, Revised Edition (London, England: Christophers, 1922), pp. 360–373, 399–402. Introduction by Marcia K. Hermansen.

1. K. K. Aziz, *Ameer Ali: His Life and Work* (Lahore, Pakistan: Publishers United, 1968); Martin Forward, *The Failure of Islamic Modernism? Syed Ameer 'Ali's Interpretation of Islam* (Bern, Switzerland: Peter Lang, 1999); Gail Minault, "Ameer Ali, Syed," in John L. Esposito, editor, *Oxford Encyclopedia of the Modern Islamic World* (New York: Oxford University Press, 1995), volume 1, pp. 84–85; W. Cantwell Smith, "Amir 'Ali," in H. A. R. Gibb *et alia*,

editors, *Encyclopedia of Islam*, 2d ed. (Leiden, Netherlands: E. J. Brill; London: Luzac, 1960), pp. 442–443.

2. Tradition from the *Bihar al-anwar* [*Oceans of Light*] of Mulla Baqir ibn Muhammad Taqi al-Majlisi [1628–1699], volume 1, chapter on "Knowledge," handed down by the *Imam* Ja'far al-Sadiq [descendant of the Prophet, 699–765], also quoted from Mu'adh ibn Jabal [companion of the Prophet] in the *Mustatraf* [*Spiritual Discoveries*, by Muhammad Ibshihi, circa 1388–1446], chapter 4; also in the *Kashf al-zunun* [*Clarification of Uncertainties*] of Haji Khalifa [Katib Çelebi, 1609–1657], [Gustav] Flügel's edition [of 1835–1858], p. 44.

He would often say, "The ink of the scholar is more holy than the blood of the martyr," and repeatedly impress on his disciples the necessity of seeking for knowledge "even unto China."[3] "He who leaves his home in search of knowledge, walks in the path of God." "He who travels in search of knowledge, to him God shows the way to paradise."[4]

The Qur'an itself bears testimony to the supreme value of learning and science. Commenting on the Sura al-'Alaq,[5] [Abu'l-Qasim Mahmud al-]Zamakhshari [1075–1144] thus explains the meaning of the Qur'anic words:

> God taught human beings that which they did not know, and this testifieth to the greatness of His beneficence, for He has given to His servants knowledge of that which they did not know. And He has brought them out of the darkness of ignorance to the light of knowledge, and made them aware of the inestimable blessings of *the knowledge of writing*, for great benefits accrue therefrom which God alone compasseth; and without the knowledge of writing no other knowledge could be comprehended, nor the sciences placed within bounds, nor the history of the ancients be acquired and their sayings be recorded, nor the revealed books be written; and if that knowledge did not exist, the affairs of religion and the world, could not be regulated.

Up to the time of the Islamic Dispensation, the Arab world, properly so called, restricted within the peninsula of Arabia and some outlying tracts to the northwest and the northeast, had shown no signs of intellectual growth. Poetry, oratory, and judicial astrology formed the favorite objects of pursuit among the pre-Islamic Arabs. Science and literature possessed no votaries. But the words of the Prophet gave a new impulse to the awakened energies of the race. Even within his lifetime was formed the nucleus of an educational institution, which in after years grew into universities at Baghdad and Salerno, at Cairo and Cordova. Here preached the Master himself on the cultivation of a holy spirit: "One hour's meditation on the work of the Creator (in a devout spirit) is better than 70 years of prayer."[6] "To listen to the instruc-

tions of science and learning for one hour is more meritorious than attending the funerals of a thousand martyrs—more meritorious than standing up in prayer for a thousand nights"; "To the student who goes forth in quest of knowledge, God will allot a high place in the mansions of bliss ; every step he takes is blessed, and every lesson he receives has its reward"; "The seeker of knowledge will be greeted in Heaven with a welcome from the angels"; "To listen to the words of the learned, and to instil into the heart the lessons of science, is better than religious exercises, . . . better than emancipating a hundred slaves"; "Him who favors learning and the learned, God will favor in the next world"; "He who honors the learned honors me." 'Ali [ibn Abi Talib, caliph, 656–661] lectured on branches of learning most suited to the wants of the infant commonwealth. Among his recorded sayings are the following: "Eminence in science is the highest of honors"; "He dies not who gives life to learning"; "The greatest ornament of a man is erudition."

Naturally such sentiments on the part of the Master [Muhammad] and the chief of the Disciples ['Ali] gave rise to a liberal policy, and animated all classes with a desire for learning. The art of Kufic writing, which had just been acquired by a disciple at Hira, furthered the primitive development of the Muslims. It was, however, preeminently an age of earnestness and faith, marked by the uprise of the soul against the domination of aimless, lifeless philosophy. The practice of religion, the conservation of a devotional spirit, and the special cultivation of those branches of learning which were of practical value in the battle of everyday life, were the primary objects of the Muslim's attention.

The age of speculation was soon to commence; its germs were contained in the positive precepts of the Master; and even whilst he was working, the scholarly Disciple was thinking. The Master had himself declared that whosoever desired to realize the spirit of his teachings must listen to the words of the Scholar ['Ali].[7] Who more able to grasp the meaning of the Master's words than 'Ali, the beloved friend, the trusted Disciple, the devoted cousin and son? The gentle, calm teachings instilled in early life into the young mind bore their fruit.

In spite of the upheaval of the Arab race under the early caliphs, literature and arts were by no means

3. *Misbah al-shari'a* [*The Lamp of the Shari'a*, by Ja'far al-Sadiq].

4. *Jami' al-akhbar* [*Comprehensive Collection of the Reports*, by Muhammad Ibn Babawayh, 918–991].

5. Qur'an, Sura 96; see also other suras.

6. *Jami' al-akhbar*.

7. "I am the city of learning; 'Ali is its gate."

neglected in the metropolis of primitive Islam. 'Ali and ['Abdullah] Ibn 'Abbas [619–686], his cousin, gave public lectures on poetry, grammar, history, and mathematics; others taught the art of recitation or elocution; whilst some gave lessons in calligraphy—in ancient times an invaluable branch of knowledge.

On [caliph] 'Uthman's tragical death [in 656] the Scholar ['Ali] was called by the voice of the people to the helm of the state. During his retirement 'Ali had devoted himself to the study of the Master's precepts by the light of reason. "But for his assassination," to quote the language of a French historian, "the Muslim world might have witnessed the realization of the Prophet's teachings, in the actual amalgamation of Reason with Law and in the impersonation of the first principles of true philosophy in positive action." The same passionate devotion to knowledge and learning which distinguished Muhammad, breathed in every word of his Disciple. With a liberality of mind—far beyond that of the age in which he lived—was joined a sincere devoutness of spirit and earnestness of faith. His sermons, faithfully preserved by one of his descendants, and his litanies or psalms, portray a devout uplooking toward the Source of All Good, and an unbounded faith in humanity. The accession of the Umayyads [reigned 661–750] to the rulership of Islam was a blow to the progress of knowledge and liberalism in the Muslim world. Their stormy reigns left the nation little leisure to devote to the gentler pursuits of science; and to this, among the sovereigns, was joined a characteristic idolatry of the past. Their thoughts were engrossed by war and politics. During the comparatively long rule of a century, the House of Umayya produced only one man devoted to the cultivation of letters; and this man was Abu Hashim Khalid ibn Yazid [al-Umawi, circa 668–704], "the philosopher of the Marwanian family,"[8] as he has been called, who was set aside from the succession on account of his learning.

The jealous suspicion and the untiring animosity of the children of Abu Sufyan and Hind [early opponents of Islam, parents of the first Umayyad caliph] had obliged the descendants of the Prophet to live a life of humble retirement. "In the night of misery and unhappiness," they followed truly and faithfully the precepts of their ancestor, and found consolation in intellectual pursuits. Their ardent love of knowledge, their passionate devotion to the cause of humanity—their spirit looking upwards far above the literalness of common interpretations of the law—show the spirituality and expansiveness of Islam.[9] The definition by the *Imam* Ja'far al-Sadiq of sciences or knowledge gives some idea of their faith in the progress of man: "The enlightenment of the heart is its essence; Truth its principal object; Inspiration, its guide; Reason, its accepter; God, its inspirer; and the words of man its utterer."[10]

Surrounded by men whom love, devotion, and sympathy with their patience had gathered around them, the early descendants of the Prophet were naturally more or less influenced by the varied ideas of their followers. Yet their philosophy never sinks to that war of words without life and without earnestness which characterized the schools of Athens or Alexandria under the Ptolemies [Egyptian dynasty, 4th-1st centuries B.C.].

But though literature and philosophy were at a discount among the rulers, the example of the *Imam*s [divinely inspired descendants of the Prophet] naturally exercised no small influence on the intellectual activity of the Arabs and the subject races. Whilst the Umayyads discouraged the peaceful pursuits of the mind, the children of Fatima [daughter of the Prophet, circa 605–633], with remarkable liberalism, favored learning. They were not devoted to the past—the *salaf* [first generation of Muslims] was not their

---

8. *Makhaz-i 'ulum* [*Source of the Religious Sciences*] of *Maulavi* Sayyid Karamat 'Ali [Jawnpuri, 1796–1876]. This learned scholar was nearly 40 years curator of the Imambara at Houghly.

9. See the *hadith al-ihlilaj*, from the *Imam* 'Ali ibn Musa al-Riza [died 818], reported by Mufazzal ibn 'Umar Ju'fi [died 763], *Bihar al-anwar*. [The *hadith al-ihlilaj* is a Shi'i treatise on the existence and unity of God, attributed by the 150–volume *Bihar al-anwar* to Ja'far al-Sadiq. *Ihlilaj* is a small fruit with medicinal properties, myrobalan, that is repeatedly mentioned in illustrations in the treatise.—Ed.]

10. *Ta'rikh al-hukama'* [*History of the Wise Ones*], by Jamal al-Din ['Ali ibn Yusuf] al-Qifti [1172–1248], founded upon another work bearing the same name, by Shihab al-Din Suhrawardi [1154–1191]; Shihab al-Din was a Platonist—an Ishraqi [Illuminationist]—an idealist, and was condemned and put to death by the orthodox synod in the reign of Saladin's [1138–1193] son. Compare the first *khutba* [sermon] of the *Nahj al-Balagha* [*The Way of Eloquence*, attributed to 'Ali ibn Abi Talib], and the traditions [of the Prophet] on knowledge in the *Bihar al-anwar*.

guide. With the Master's precepts to light their path, they kept in view the development of humanity, and devoted themselves to the cultivation of science and learning in all its branches. Like the Master and the early caliphs, the "Philosophers of the House of Muhammad"[11] received with distinction the learned men whom the fanatical persecution of Justinian's [Byzantine emperor, 527–565] successors drove for refuge into foreign lands. The academies of philosophy and medicine founded by the Nestorians at Edessa and Nisibis, had been broken up; its professors and students were refugees in Persia and Arabia. Many betook themselves—as their predecessors had done before, in the time of the Prophet and the caliph Abu Bakr [reigned 632–634]—to Medina, which, after its sack by the Umayyads, had again gathered round Ja'far al-Sadiq a galaxy of talented scholars. The concourse of many and varied minds in the City of the Prophet gave an impetus to the cultivation of science and literature among the Muslims. From Medina a stream of unusual intellectual activity flowed toward Damascus. Situated on the northern confines of the Arabian desert, along the trade route from Mecca and Medina to Syria, Damascus had been associated from ancient times with the Umayyads; and the Syrian Arabs were closely allied by interest and kinship to the family whom they had assisted to elevate to the rulership of Islam. The Umayyads had naturally fixed upon this city as the seat of their empire; and though shunned with horror by the devout Muslims, it formed the gathering place for the representatives of the many races who had come under the sway of Islam. The controversies of Greek and Saracen furnished a strong incentive to the study of dialectics and Greek philosophy; and the invention of the diacritical and vowel points furthered the cultivation of grammar and philology. At this time flourished two Christian writers of note, who, fleeing before their orthodox persecutors, had taken shelter in Damascus. These were Johannes Damascenus [circa 675–749] and Theodorus Abucara [died circa 770]. Their polemical writings against the Muslims, their rationalistic and philosophical disputes with their own orthodox brethren, joined to the influence of the Medinite school, which flourished under Muhammad al-Baqir [died circa 732] and Ja'far al-Sadiq, soon led to the growth of philosophi-

11. *Makhaz-i 'ulum.*

cal tendencies among the Saracens. For centuries Greek philosophy had been known to the Persians and the Arabs; the Nestorians had spread themselves in the dominions of the Khosrows [pre-Islamic kings of Iran] since the beginning of Justinian's reign, but it was not until all the varied elements had been fused into an organic whole by Islam that Greek science and culture exercised any real effect on the intellectual development of Western Asia. It was toward the close of the Umayyad rule that several Muslim thinkers came into prominence, whose lectures on subjects then uppermost in the minds of the people attracted great attention. And their ideas and conceptions materially molded the thoughts of succeeding generations.

It was in the second century [8th century A.D.], however, that the literary and scientific activity of the Muslims commenced in earnest, and the chief impulse to this was given by the settlement of the Arabs in towns. Hitherto they had lived in camps isolated from the races they had subjugated. 'Uthman had laid a prohibition on their acquiring lands in the conquered countries, or contracting marriages with the subject nations. The object of this policy was apparent; it has its parallel in the history of all nations, ancient and modern. In British India and in French Algeria it is still in force, During the whole period of the Umayyad rule the Arabs had constituted the dominant element—the aristocratic military caste amongst their subjects. The majority of them were occupied in warlike pursuits. The gentler avocations of learning and science were left to the suspected Hashimis [descendants of Banu Hashim, the Prophet's clan] and the children of the *Ansar* [early Muslims of Medina, literally Helpers]—to the descendants of 'Ali, Abu Bakr, and 'Umar [ibn al-Khattab, caliph, 634–644]. The Arabs had carried with them into distant regions the system of clientage which had existed in Arabia, as it had existed among the Romans, from ancient times. Clientage afforded to the subjects protection and consideration, to the conquerors, the additional strength gained by numbers. Thus, both in the East and in the West, the leading families allied themselves with members of the prominent desert clans and became the *maulas* or clients, not freedmen, as has been incorrectly supposed, of their conquerors. To these clients, besides the Hashimites and the children of the *Ansar* and *Muhajirin* [early Muslims who had left Mecca for Medina with the Prophet], such as had survived the sack of Medina, was left scholarship and the cultivation of arts and sciences during the Umayyad rule. With the rise of the 'Abbasids [reigned 750–1258] commenced a new era. They rose to power with the assistance of the Persians; and they relied for the maintenance of their rule more upon the attachment of the general body of their subjects than the fickle affection of the military colonists of Arabia. Abu'l-'Abbas Saffah [died 754] held the reins of government for but two years. His brother and successor, [Abu Ja'far] al-Mansur [reigned 754–775], though cruel in his treatment of the Fatimids [Egyptian dynasty 909–1171], was a statesman of the first rank. He organized the state, established a standing army and a corps of police, and gave firmness and consistency to the system of administration. The Arabs had hitherto devoted themselves almost exclusively to the profession of arms; the method of government adopted by al-Mansur gave a new bent to their genius. They settled in cities, acquired landed properties, and devoted themselves to the cultivation of letters with the same ardor which they had displayed in the pursuit of war.

The rich and fertile valley of the Euphrates, watered by the two great rivers of Western Asia, has, from the most ancient times, been the seat of empire and the center of civilization. It was in this region that Babylon, Ctesiphon, and Seleucia had risen successively. Here existed at this epoch Basra and Kufa, with their unruly and volatile inhabitants. Basra and Kufa had, from the first conquest of the Muslims, formed important centers of commercial activity. The latter city was at one time the seat of government. To Basra and Kufa had come all the active spirits of the East, who either could not or would not go to the depraved capital of the Umayyads. For the 'Abbasids, Damascus had not only no attraction, but was a place of peril; and the uncertain and fickle temperament of the people of Basra and Kufa made those cities undesirable as the seat of government. Al-Mansur cast about for a site for his capital, and at last fixed upon the locality where Baghdad now stands—a six days' journey by river from Basra.

Baghdad is said to have been a summer retreat of Khosrow Anushirvan, the famous monarch of Persia [reigned 531–579], and derived from his reputation as a just ruler the name it bears—the "Garden of Justice." With the disappearance of the Persian monarchy had disappeared the famous Garden where the Lord of Asia dispensed justice to his multitudi-

nous subjects; tradition, however, had preserved the name. The beautiful site, central and salubrious, attracted the eyes of Mansur, and the glorious city of the caliphs arose, like the sea goddess issuing from the waves, under the magic wand of the foremost architects of the day.

The Baghdad of Mansur was founded in the year 145 of the *hijra* [Muhammad's departure from Mecca to Medina in 622 A.D.] on the western bank of the Tigris. Soon, however, another city—a new Baghdad—sprang up on the eastern bank under the auspices of the heir apparent, the Prince Imperial of the caliphate, who afterward assumed the title of al-Mahdi [reigned 775–785]. This new city vied in the splendor of its structures with the beauty and magnificence of the Mansuriyya [the city founded by Mansur]. In the days of its glory, before the destroying hordes of Genghis [Khan, died 1227] sweeping over Western Asia had engulfed in ruin every vestige of Saracenic civilization, Baghdad presented a beautiful and imposing appearance—a fit capital for the pontiffs of Islam.[12]

The beauty and splendor of the city, before its sack by the Mongols, have been immortalized in glowing lines by Anwari [Cental Asian poet, died circa 1190], most brilliant of panegyrists:[13]

> Blessed be the site of Baghdad, seat of learning and art—
> None can point in the world to a city equal to her,
> Her suburbs vie in beauty with the blue vault of heaven,
> Her climate in quality equals the life-giving breezes of heaven,
> Her stones in their brightness rival gems and rubies,
> Her soil in beneficence has the fragrance of the amber,
> The morning breeze has imparted to the earth the freshness of *Tuba* (the tree of Paradise),
> And the winds have concealed in her water the sweetness of *Kauthar* (the spring of Eden),
> The banks of the Tigris with their beautiful damsels surpass (the city of) Khullakh,[14]

---

12. For a description of Baghdad under the 'Abbasids, see [the author's] *Short History of the Saracens* (Macmillan [1899]), p. 444.

13. This English rendering gives an inadequate idea of the beauty of the original.

14. A city in Cathay famous for the beauty of its women.

The gardens filled with lovely nymphs equal
    Kashmir,
And thousands of gondolas on the water,
Dance and sparkle like sunbeams in the sky.

Its designation of the City of Peace, *Dar us-Salam*, was derived from a prophecy made by the astronomer-royal Nawbakht [died circa 776], that none of the caliphs would die within the walls of the city, and the strange fulfillment of this prognostication in the case of 37 pontiffs. The great number of holy men who have found their last resting place within or about its walls, and whose tombs are objects of veneration to all Muslims, gave to Baghdad the title of Bulwark of the Holy. Here are the mausoleums of the greatest *Imam*s and the most pious *Shaykh*s [Sufi leaders]. Here reposes the *Imam* Musa al-Kazim [died 818], and here lie buried Abu Hanifa [circa 699–767], the *Shaykh*s [Abu'l-Qasim] Junayd [died 910], [Abu Bakr] Shibli [861–946], and 'Abd al-Qadir Jilani [1077–1166], the chiefs of the Sufis.

In the midst of the monuments of the *Imam*s and *Shaykh*s stood those of the caliphs and their consorts. Of the numerous academies, colleges, and schools which filled the city, two institutions surpassed all others in importance by their wealth and the number of their students, These were the Nizamiyya and Mustansariyya; the first established in the first half of the fifth century of the *hijra* [11th century A.D.] by Nizam al-Mulk [1018–1092], the great vizier of Malik Shah, sultan of the Seljuks [reigned 1072–1092], and the second, built two centuries later, by the caliph al-Mustansir b'illah [reigned 1226–1242].

"It is a remarkable fact," says the historian of culture under the caliphs, "that the sovereign who makes us forget some of the darker sides of his nature by his moral and mental qualities, also gave the impetus to the great intellectual movement which now commenced in the Islamic world."[15] It was by Mansur's command that literary and scientific works in foreign languages were first translated into Arabic. Himself no mean scholar and mathematician, he had the famous collections of Indian fables

(the *Hitopadesa*), the Indian treatise on astronomy called the *Siddhanta*, several works of Aristotle [Greek philosopher, 384–322 B.C.], the *Almagest* of Claudius Ptolemy [astronomer, 2nd century], the books of Euclid [mathematician, 4th-3rd centuries B.C.], as well as other ancient Greek, Byzantine, Persian, and Syrian productions, translated into the language of the Arabs. Mas'udi [died 956] mentions that no sooner were these translations published than they were studied with much avidity. Mansur's successors were not only warm patrons of the learned, who flocked to the metropolis from all quarters, but were themselves assiduous cultivators of every branch of knowledge. Under them the intellectual development of the Saracens, in other words of the conglomerate races of the vast empire which constituted the caliphate, proceeded with wonderful rapidity.

Each great nation of the world has had its golden age. Athens had her Periclean era; Rome, her Augustan age; so, too, had the Islamic world its epoch of glory; and we may with justice look upon the period which elapsed from the accession of Mansur to the death of Mu'tadid b'illah [reigned 892–902], with only a brief intermission during the reign of Mutawakkil [847–861], as an epoch of equal if not superior greatness and magnificence. Under the first six 'Abbasid caliphs, but especially under Ma'mun [reigned 813–833], the Muslims formed the vanguard of civilization. The Saracenic race by its elastic genius as well as by its central position—with the priceless treasures of dying Greece and Rome on one side, and of Persia on the other, and India and China far away sleeping the sleep of ages—was pre-eminently fitted to become the teacher of mankind. Under the inspiring influences of the great Prophet, who gave them a code and a nationality, and assisted by their sovereigns, the Saracens caught up the lessons of wisdom from the East and the West, combined them with the teachings of the Master, and "started from soldiers into scholars." "The Arabs," says [Alexander von] Humboldt [German scientist, 1769–1859], "were admirably situated to act the part of mediators, and to influence the nations from the Euphrates to the Guadalquivir and mid-Africa. Their unexampled intellectual activity marks a distinct epoch in the history of the world."

Under the Umayyads we see the Muslims passing through a period of probation, preparing themselves for the great task they were called upon to

---

15. [Alfred von] Kremer [German Orientalist, 1828–1889], *Culturgeschichte des Orients unter den Chalifen* [*Cultural History of the Orient under the Caliphs*], volume 2, p. 412.

undertake. Under the 'Abbasids we find them the repositories of the knowledge of the world. Every part of the globe is ransacked by the agents of the caliphs for the hoarded wealth of antiquity; these are brought to the capital, and laid before an admiring and appreciating public. Schools and academies spring up in every direction; public libraries are established in every city free to every comer; the great philosophers of the ancient world are studied side by side with the Qur'an. Galen, Dioscorides, Themistius, Aristotle, Plato, Euclid, Ptolemy, and Apollonius [ancient Roman and Greek scientists and philosophers] receive their due meed of appreciation. The sovereigns themselves assist at literary meetings and philosophical disquisitions. For the first time in the history of humanity a religious and autocratic government is observed to ally itself with philosophy, preparing and participating in its triumphs.

Every city in the empire sought to outrival the other in the cultivation of the arts and sciences. And governors and provincial chiefs tried to emulate the sovereign. Traveling in search of knowledge was, according to the precept of the Master, a pious duty. From every part of the globe students and scholars flocked to Cordova, to Baghdad, and to Cairo to listen to the words of the Saracenic sages. Even Christians from remote corners of Europe attended Muslim colleges. Men who became in afterlife the heads of the Christian Church,[16] acquired their scholarship from Islamic teachers. The rise of Cairo under al-Mu'izz li-Din Allah [reigned 953–975] added a spirit of rivalry to the patronage of learning on the part of the caliphs of the houses of 'Abbas [the 'Abbasids, based in Damascus] and Fatima [the Fatimids, based in Cairo]. Al-Mu'izz was the Ma'mun of the West—the [Gaius] Maecenas [Roman patron of literature, circa 70–8 B.C.] of Muslim Africa, which then embraced the whole of the continent from the eastern confines of Egypt to the shores of the Atlantic and the borders of the Sahara. During the reign of al-Mu'izz and his first three successors, the arts and sciences flourished under the especial and loving protection of the sovereigns. The free university of Cairo, the *Dar al-Hikmat*—Scientific Institute—established by al-Mu'izz, "anticipated [17th-century English scientist Francis] Bacon's

ideal with a fact." The Idrisids [reigned 789–921] at Fez, and the Moorish sovereigns in Spain [reigned 756–1492], outvied each other in the cultivation of arts and letters. From the shores of the Atlantic eastward to the Indian Ocean, far away even to the Pacific, resounded the voice of philosophy and learning, under Muslim guidance and Muslim inspiration. And when the House of 'Abbas lost its grasp on the empire of the East, the chiefs who held the reins of government in the tracts which at one time were under the undivided temporal sway of the caliphs, extended the same protection to science and literature as the pontiffs from whom they still derived their title to sovereignty. This glorious period lasted, in spite of the triumph of patristicism and its unconcealed jealousy toward scientific and philosophical pursuits, until the fall of Baghdad before the Tatar hordes [in 1258]. But the wild savages who overturned the caliphate and destroyed civilization, as soon as they adopted Islam, became ardent protectors of learning!

What was the condition of learning and science in Christendom at this epoch? Under Constantine [Roman emperor, reigned 306–337] and his orthodox successors, the Aesclepions [hospitals] were closed forever; the public libraries established by the liberality of the pagan emperors were dispersed or destroyed; learning was "branded as magic or punished as treason"; and philosophy and science were exterminated. The ecclesiastical hatred against human learning had found expression in the patristic maxim, "Ignorance is the mother of devotion"; and Pope Gregory the Great [reigned 590–604], the founder of ecclesiastical supremacy, gave effect to this obscurantist dogma by expelling from Rome all scientific studies, and burning the Palatine Library founded by Augustus Caesar [reigned 32 B.C.– 14 A.D.]. He forbade the study of the ancient writers of Greece and Rome. He introduced and sanctified the mythologic Christianity which continued for centuries the predominating creed of Europe, with its worship of relics and the remains of saints. Science and literature were placed under the ban by orthodox Christianity, and they succeeded in emancipating themselves only when Free Thought had broken down the barriers raised by orthodoxy against the progress of the human mind.

'Abdullah al-Ma'mun has been deservedly styled the Augustus of the Arabs. "He was not ignorant that

---

16. Such as Gerbert [circa 945–1003], afterward Pope Sylvester II, who studied in Cordova.

they are the elect of God, his best and most useful servants, whose lives are devoted to the improvement of their rational faculties . . . that the teachers of wisdom are the true luminaries and legislators of the world."[17]

Ma'mun was followed by a brilliant succession of princes who continued his work. Under him and his successors, the principal distinguishing feature of the school of Baghdad was a true and strongly marked scientific spirit, which dominated over all its achievements. The deductive method, hitherto proudly regarded as the invention and sole monopoly of modern Europe, was perfectly understood by the Muslims. "Marching from the known to the unknown, the school of Baghdad rendered to itself an exact. account of the phenomena for the purpose of rising from the effect to the cause, accepting only what had been demonstrated by experience; such were the principles taught by the (Muslim) masters." "The Arabs of the ninth century," continues the author we are quoting, "were in the possession of that fecund method which was to become long afterwards, in the hands of the moderns, the instrument of their most beautiful discoveries." [. . .]

Islam inaugurated the reign of intellectual liberty. It has been truly remarked, that so long as Islam retained its pristine character, it proved itself the warm protector and promoter of knowledge and civilization—the zealous ally of intellectual freedom. The moment extraneous elements attached themselves to it, it lagged behind in the race of progress. But, to explain the stagnation of the Muslims in the present day, it is necessary to glance back for a moment at the events that transpired in Spain, in Africa, and in Asia between the twelfth and the seventeenth centuries. In the former country, Christianity destroyed the intellectual life of the people. The Muslims had turned Spain into a garden; the Christians converted it into a desert. The Muslims had covered the land with colleges and schools; the Christians transformed them into churches for the worship of saints and images. The literary and scientific treasures amassed by the Muslim sovereigns were consigned to the flames. The Muslim men, women, and children were ruthlessly butchered or burnt at the stake; the few who were spared were reduced to slavery. Those who fled were thrown on the shores of Africa helpless beggars. It would take the combined charity of Jesus and Muhammad to make Islam forget or forgive the terrible wrongs inflicted by the Christians of Spain upon the Andalusian Muslims. But the punishment was not long in coming. Before the world was a century old, Spain's fire had sunk into a heap of ashes!

In Western Africa, the triumph of Patristicism under the third Almohad sovereign[18] and the uprise of Berber fanaticism turned back the tide of progress, arrested the civilization of centuries, and converted the seats of learning and arts into centers of bigotry and ignorance. The settlement of the Corsairs on the Barbary coast and the anarchy which prevailed in Egypt under the later Mamluks [reigned 1254–1517], discouraged the cultivation of peaceful knowledge. In Asia the decadence of the Timurid dynasty [reigned 1370–1500], the eruption of the wild and fanatical Uzbeks, and the establishment of their power in [Samarqand,] the capital of [Amir] Timur [reigned 1370–1405], destroyed the intellectual vitality of the people. In Persia, under the Safavis [reigned 1501–1732], literature and science had begun to breathe once more; but this renaissance was only temporary, and with the irruption of the barbarous Ghilzais the renovated life of Iran came to an end. A deathlike gloom settled upon Central Asia, which still hangs heavy over these unhappy countries, and is slowly lifting in Afghanistan. Under Selim I [reigned 1512–1520], Sulayman [reigned 1520–1566] and the Murads [14th and 15th centuries], learning received support in the Ottoman

17. Abu'l-Faraj [Ibn al-Jawzi, 1126–1200].

18. On the decadence of the Fatimid power in Western Africa there arose a dynasty descended from a *marabout* or saint of the country, hence called Almoravid or al-Murabatiyya. To this family belonged Yusuf ibn Tashfin [reigned 1061–1106], the patron of [Abu Marwan] Ibn Zuhr [Andalusian physician, circa 1090–1162]. His son and successor was defeated and killed by 'Abd al-Mu'min [reigned 1130–1163], the founder of the dynasty of Almohads (al-Muwahidin, the Unitarians), who sacked and destroyed Morocco and Fez. They were akin to the Wahhabis and the Ikhwan [revivalist movements of the early 19th and 20th centuries] of Central Arabia, and probably not very different from the Mahdists [revivalist and anti-colonial movement, late 19th century] of Nubia [Sudan]. The first two sovereigns of this dynasty, 'Abd al-Mu'min and Yusuf, encouraged learning and arts; in the reign of Ya'qub al-Mansur [reigned 1184–1199], the third Almohad king, fanaticism became rampant.

dominions; but the Osmanlis were on the whole a military race. At first from ambition, afterward from sheer necessity and for self-preservation, they had been at war with a relentless foe, whose designs knew no slackening, whose purpose was inscrutable. That enemy has disappeared, but the nation has still to fight for its existence. Letters and arts, under such conditions, can make but little progress, Dealing with the charge of obscurantism, often leveled against Islam, M[onsieur Joseph-Arthur] Gobineau [French ethnologist, 1816–1882] makes the following pregnant observation:

> Imagine in any European country the absolute predominance of military and administrative despotism during a period of 250 years, as is the case in Turkey; conceive something approaching the warlike anarchy of Egypt under the domination of foreign slaves—Circassians, Georgians, Turks, and Albanians; picture to yourself an Afghan invasion, as in Persia after 1730, the tyranny of Nadir Shah [reigned 1736–1747], the cruelties and ravages that have marked the accession of the dynasty of the Qajars [reigned 1794–1924]—unite all these circumstances with their naturally concomitant causes, you will then understand what would have become of any European country although European, and it will not be necessary to look further for any explanation of the ruin of Oriental countries, nor to charge Islam with any unjust responsibility.

From the time of its birth in the seventh century up to the end of the seventeenth, not to descend later, Islam was animated by a scientific and literary spirit equal in force and energy to that which animates Europe of our own day. It carried the Muslims forward on a wave of progress, and enabled them to achieve a high degree of material and mental development. Since the eruption of the Goths and the Vandals, the progress of Europe has been on a continuous scale. No such calamity as has afflicted Asia, in the persons of the Tatars or the Uzbeks, has befallen Christendom since [Hun ruler] Attila's retreat from France [in 451]. Her wars, cruel and bitter, fierce and inhuman, have been waged on equal terms of humanity or inhumanity. Catholics and Protestants have burnt each other; but Europe has never witnessed, since the wholesale butcheries of the poor Spanish Moors, the terrible massacres committed by the Tatars in all the centers of civilization and culture, in which fell the gifted classes who formed the backbone of the nation.[19]

And now,

> The spider holds watch in the palace of Caesar,
> The owlet beats the drum on the tower of Afrasiyab.[20]

19. The sack of Baghdad by the Mongols exemplifies what happened in other cities, but in order to give a true conception of the fearful atrocities perpetrated by the savages, it requires to be painted by another [Edward] Gibbon [English historian, 1737–1794]. For three days the streets ran with blood, and the water of the Tigris was dyed red for miles along its course. The horrors of rapine, slaughter, and outraged humanity lasted for six weeks. The palaces, mosques, and mausoleums were destroyed by fire or leveled to the earth for their golden domes. The patients in the hospitals and the students and professors in the colleges were put to the sword. In the mausoleums the mortal remains of the *shaykh*s and pious *imam*s, and in the academies the immortal works of great and learned men, were consumed to ashes; books were thrown into the fire, or, where that was distant and the Tigris near, were buried in the waters of the latter. The accumulated treasures of five centuries were thus lost forever to humanity. The flower of the nation was completely destroyed. It was the custom of Hulagu [reigned 1256–1265], from policy and as a precaution, to carry along with his horde the princes and chiefs of the countries through which they swept. One of these princes was [Abu Bakr ibn] Sa'd ibn Zangi, the *atabek* [governor] of Fars [1226–1260]. The poet Sa'di [circa 1213–1292] had, it appears, accompanied his friend and patron. He was thus an eye-witness to the terrible state of Baghdad and its doomed inhabitants. In two pathetic couplets he has given expression to its magnitude and horrors:

> It is meet that heaven should rain tears of blood on earth
> At the destruction that has befallen the empire of Musta'sim, Commander of the Faithful [reigned 1242–1258].
> O Muhammad! If in the Day of Judgment you will raise your head above the earth,
> Raise your head and see the tribulation of the people now.

20. [The author's revised 1922 edition, excerpted here, omits a final sentence that appeared in earlier editions: "Perhaps the Muslims of India may, under the auspices of a great European power, restore to Western and Central Asia something of what their forefathers gave to Europe in the Middle Ages."—Ed.]

The Last Word

Abu'l-Kalam Azad (Bengal-India, 1888–1958) was the chief theoretician of the Khilafat movement for Islamic solidarity and a supporter of Indian independence. He was also an exegete of the Qur'an and a prominent literary figure—hence his sobriquet, "master of eloquence." Azad came from a scholarly family of Afghan descent that had migrated to Mecca, where Azad was born. When he was two, his family returned to India and settled in Calcutta, where he was educated at home following the traditional curriculum. In his late teens, Azad taught himself English and read the Bible and various books and newspapers, leading to a period of doubt and experimentation. He was dismayed by the disagreements among Muslims, and in the spirit of rejecting orthodoxy he adopted the pen name "Azad" (free). Later he returned to faith, but in the modernist spirit, influenced by the writings of Sayyid Jamal al-Din al-Afghani (chapter 11) and Egyptian reformers. Between 1912 and 1930, Azad edited the journals al-Hilal (The Crescent) and al-Balagh (The Message), the most important Muslim periodicals of the region. He joined the Indian independence movement, served as president of the All-India National Congress in 1940–1947, and remained an advocate for Hindu-Muslim amity for the rest of his life. When Pakistan was created, Azad remained in India, was appointed minister of education, and served as deputy leader of Congress. The present selection, a speech delivered on the occasion of one of Azad's many imprisonments by British colonial authorities, argues that Muslims must struggle for democratic self-rule.[1]

I had no intention to submit any oral or written statement. This [court] is a place where there is neither any hope for us, nor any demand nor even any complaint. This is only a turnpike without passing which we cannot reach our destination. For a short while therefore, even against our own will, we have to break our journey here. Otherwise we would have gone straight to jail.

This is the only reason why for the last two years I have always opposed the idea of noncooperators' taking any part in the proceedings of the court, although the All-India Congress Committee,[2] the Central Khilafat Committee,[3] and the Jamiat-ul-Ulema Hind[4] have given this permission that a written statement might be submitted for the information of the public, but personally I have always advised and preferred silence. I feel that a person who tenders the statement because he is not guilty, even though he does it with a view to give information to the public, is nevertheless not altogether free from suspicion. May be that a modest desire for acquittal and some unconscious weakness is working within him, while the path of noncooperation is clear and straight.

Abu'l-Kalam Azad, "Statement of Maulana Azad before the Presidency Magistrate," translated from Urdu by Durlab Singh, in *Famous Trials of Mahatma Gandhi, Jawaharlal Nehru, Maulana Abul Kalam Azad* (Lahore, Pakistan: Hero Publications, 1944), pp. 41–67. Statement delivered in Calcutta, India, January 11, 1922, and published the same year under the title *Qaul-i Faisal* (*The Last Word*). Introduction by Marcia K. Hermansen.

1. Ian Henderson Douglas, *Abul Kalam Azad: An Intellectual and Religious Biography* (Delhi, India: Oxford University Press, 1988); Mushirul Hasan, *Islam and Indian Nationalism: Reflections on Abu'l Kalam Azad* (New Delhi,

India: Manohar, 1992); 'Imadulhasan Azad Faruqi, *The Tarjuman al-Qur'an: A Critical Analysis of Maulana Abu'l Kalam Azad's Approach to the Understanding of the Qur'an* (New Delhi, India: Vikas, 1991).

2. [Azad had recently rejoined the Congress movement, founded in 1885, which was the primary pro-independence organization in British India.—Ed.]

3. [Azad was a leader of the Khilafat movement, founded in 1919, which was a South Asian effort to support the Ottoman caliphate and Muslim control over the holy sites of Arabia.—Ed.]

4. [The Jamiat-ul-Ulema Hind (Association of [Muslim] Religious Scholars of India) was founded in 1919.—Ed.]

Noncooperation is the result of utter disappointment with the existing conditions. And this despondency has led to determination for complete change. Noncooperation on the part of any man reveals his dissatisfaction with the justice of the government and shows his nonacceptance of force based on injustice, with the effect that he sees no other alternative except a change.

So if he is dejected to such a degree he sees no alternative except a change, how can he expect from that power that it will do justice to him.

Even if this reality is lost sight of, to expect acquittal in the present circumstances is not more than a vain desire. It will be as if a denial to one's own knowledge. With the exception of the government itself, no sensible man can expect justice from the law courts in the present state. Not because they are composed of such persons who do not like to do any justice, but because these are based on such a system of government where no magistrate can do justice to those criminals, with whom the government itself does not like to have fair play.

I want to make it clear here that noncooperation is directed only against the government, the system of the government, and principles of the present government, and never against individuals

History bears witness that, whenever the ruling powers took up arms against freedom and justice, the courtrooms were used as most simple and harmless weapons. The jurisdiction of courts is a force that can be utilized both for justice and injustice. In the hands of a just government, it becomes the best means of righteousness, but for the repressive and tyrannical government, no other weapon is more useful for vengeance and injustice than this.

Next to battlefields, courts have played the most prominent part in setting the example of injustice in the history of the world. From the holy founders of religions to the inventors and pioneers of science, there was no holy or righteous organization which was not produced before the courts like criminals.

The iniquities of courts of law constitute an endless list, and history has not yet finished singing the elegy of such miscarriages of injustice. In that list we observed a holy personage like Jesus, who had to stand in his time before a foreign court and was convicted even as the worst of criminals. We see also in the same list Socrates [Greek philosopher, 469–399 B.C.], who was sentenced to be poisoned for no other crime than that of being the most truthful person of

his age. We meet also the name of that great Florentine martyr to truth, the inventor Galileo [Italian astronomer, 1564–1642], who refused to belie his observations and researches merely because their avowal was a crime in the eyes of constituted authority. I have called Jesus a man, because to my belief he was a holy person who had brought the heavenly message of love and righteousness; but he was greater even than this in the eyes of millions of people. Consequently what a wonderful place this convict's dock is, where the most righteous as well as the most criminal people are made to stand.

When I ponder on the great and significant history of the convict's dock, and find that the honor of standing in that place belongs to me today, my soul becomes steeped in thankfulness and praise of God. And He alone sees the real joy and happiness of my mind. In this dock of the convicts I feel myself an object of envy for emperors. [. . .]

At any rate it was never my intention to present a statement; but on the 6th of January [1922], when I was produced before the court, I found that the Government was quite bewildered in the matter of securing punishment for me, although I am a man who, in accordance with his desires, must be given the maximum punishment.

First I was prosecuted under section 17/2 [of the] Criminal Amendment Act; but when such proof could not be produced as is considered absolutely necessary for proving the crime these days, the case under this section was withdrawn, although reluctantly. Then a case under section 124-A had been set up against me, but unfortunately that too was not enough for the purpose. [. . .]

Seeing this, my mind changed. I felt that the reason which was responsible for my withholding the statement, demanded that I should not remain silent, and the crime that the government have not been able to prove I should rather admit myself with my own pen. [. . .]

The bureaucracy in India is nothing more nor less than the domination which powerful individuals will always normally attain over a nation decaying by its own neglect and internal weakness. In the natural course of things, such dominant authority cannot possibly countenance any nationalistic awakening or agitation for progress, reform, or justice. And as such agitation would spell the inevitable downfall of its dominant power, it seeks to kill all agitation by declaring it a crime against constituted authority. No power would tamely submit to movements likely to bring its own decline, however much such decline might be in the ultimate interest of justice. This posture of affairs is merely a struggle for existence in which both sides fight desperately for their principles. An awakened nation aspires to attain what it considers its birthright, and the dominant authority would fain not budge an inch from its position of unquestioned way. The contention might be advanced that the latter party even likes its opponents [and] is not open to any blame, inasmuch as it is merely putting up a fight for its own survival, and it is quite an incidental matter that its existence happens to be inimical to perpetuation of justice. We cannot deny facts of human nature and its inseparable characteristics. Like good, evil also desires to live in this world and struggles for its own existence.

In India also such a struggle for the survival of the fittest has already commenced. Most certainly, therefore, nothing can be a higher crime against the domination of government, as at present established, than the agitation which seeks to terminate its unlimited authority in the name of liberty and justice. I fully admit that I am not only guilty of such agitation, but that I belong to that band of pioneers who originally sowed the seed of such agitation in the heart of their nation and dedicated their whole lives to the cherishing and breeding of this holy discontent. I am the first Muslim in India who invited his nation for the first time in 1912 to commit this crime, and within three years succeeded in bringing about a revolution in their slavish mentality. Hence, if the government regards me a criminal and consequently desires to award punishment, I earnestly acknowledge that it would not be an unexpected thing, and that I will have absolutely no grudge against that.

The Real Reason for My Arrest

After the 17th of November [1921], of all the things in the world which could be desired and wished [by the government] was that on 24th December [1921], when the Prince [of Wales, later Edward VIII, 1894–1972] comes to Calcutta, there should be no *hartal* [general strike], and the folly that had been committed by introducing the Criminal Amendment Act [of] 1918 could be accepted for one day at least. The government was of the opinion that my presence and that of Mr. C[hitta] R[anjan] Das [Bengali indepen-

dence leader, 1870–1925] stood in its way. Both of us therefore were arrested after some bewilderment and consultations. [. . .]

For the last two years I could not remain continuously in Calcutta. All of my time was spent either in the central activities of the Khilafat Committee or political tours of country. [. . .] But suddenly the news about the fresh repression of the Bengal Government and of the communiqué of the 18th [November 1921] reached me in Bombay, and it became impossible for me to remain outside Calcutta any more under these circumstances. I consulted [Mohandas] Gandhi [Indian independence movement leader, 1869–1948] as well. He was also of this opinion that I should cancel all programs and go to Calcutta. We were apprehensive lest the repression of the government should make the people uncontrolled and undisciplined.

I reached Calcutta on the 1st of December. I saw *repression* as well as *toleration*, both in their extremes.

I saw that the government, unnerved by the memorable *hartal* of the 17th [November 1921], had become like a man who loses all sense of proportion in anger and rage. All the national organizations of volunteers were declared unlawful under the Criminal Law Amendment Act of 1908. All the public gatherings were banned with one stroke of the pen. The discretion of the police was synonymous with law, and under the pretext of unlawful organizations it could do anything.

On the contrary, the people [acted] as if [they had] taken oaths for patience and perseverance, and determined neither to be violent under any provocations, nor to deter from their path.

Under these circumstances, the path of duty was clear before me. I saw two bitter realities naked before me. First, the entire machinery of the government had centered itself in Calcutta. The final decision for victory or defeat would, therefore, be in this very place. Second, we were struggling with full liberty up to this time; but the present circumstances had revealed that this too was not possible henceforth. Freedom of speech and freedom of assembly: these are the birthrights of a man. The suppression of these, in the words of famous philosopher [John Stuart] Mill [English philosopher, 1806–1873], are in no way less than "the massacre of humanity." But this suppression is being carried on without any hesitation. So I canceled all other programmes and decided to remain in Calcutta so long as one of the two things did not make its appearance—either the government withdrew its communiqué or arrested me. [. . .]

The fact is that the past few days provided both the realities simultaneously for the pages of history. If on one hand, all the artificial curtains were removed from the face of the government; on the other side, the national strength also manifested itself after passing through a hard ordeal. The world witnessed that, if the government is unbridled in violence and repression, patience and toleration are also gaining momentum every day in the country. Just as it has always been refuted, it can even be denied today; but it will be the most instructive story for history of tomorrow. It will guide the future as to how moral and passive resistance can defeat the repression and pride of material forces, and as to how it can be possible to face bloody weapons with sheer nonviolence and sacrifice. I at least do not know where among the two parties—in the government or the country—to seek the education of that great man who had brought the message of patience and godliness as against evil. I think the officials of bureaucracy will not be unaware of his name. His name was Christ.

The philosophy of history tells us that lack of wisdom and farsightedness always befriended the declining powers. The government imagined that they would suppress the Khilafat and Swarajya [self-rule] movements with violence and repression and the *hartal* of 24th [December 1921] would be warded off . . . but soon the government realized that repression let loose against national awakening is not likely to prove fatal. I confess that not only on these two occasions, but in my numerous speeches in the last two years, I have used such and even more strong and definite phrases. To say so is my imperative duty in my creed, and I cannot hesitate from performing my duty simply because it would be regarded a crime under section 124-A. I want to repeat this even now, and will go on repeating it so long as my tongue works. If I don't do it, I will be guilty of the worst crime before the Creator and His creation.

Certainly, I have said, "This government is a tyrant." But if I don't say so, what else should I say? I don't understand why I am expected not to call spade a spade. I refuse to call "white" a thing which is apparently black. The mildest and the softest words that I could use in this respect were these. I could not think of any other thing for such a crystal reality.

I have certainly been saying that there are only two paths before us: the government should restrain from doing injustice and jeopardizing our rights; and if it can't, it must be wiped out of existence. I don't comprehend what else could be said. A thing which is apparently an evil should either mend itself or end itself. When I am convinced of the evils of the government, then certainly I cannot pray for its long life.

Why is it that this has become an article of my faith as well as of millions of my countrymen? [. . .] Let me make it clear that this is my faith simply because I am an Indian; because I am a Muslim; because I am a man.

It is my belief that liberty is the natural and God-given gift of man. No man and no bureaucracy consisting of men has got the right to make the servants of God its own slaves. However attractive be the euphemism invented for "subjugation" and "slavery," still slavery is slavery, and it is opposed to the will and canons of God. I, therefore, consider it a bounden duty to liberate my country from its yoke.

The notorious fallacies of "reform" and "gradual transference of power" can produce no illusions and pitfalls; this is my unequivocal and definite faith. Liberty being the primary right of man, it is nobody's personal privilege to prescribe limits or apportion shares in the distribution of it. To say that a nation should get its liberty in graduated stages is the same as saying that an owner should by right receive his property only in bits, and a creditor his dues by installments. [. . .] Whatever philanthropic acts might be performed by a man who has usurped our property, his usurpation would still continue to be utterly illegal.

Evils cannot be classified into good and bad. All that is in fairness possible is to differentiate the varying degree. For instance, we can say "very heinous robbery" and "less heinous robbery," but who can speak of "good robbery" and "bad robbery"? I cannot, therefore, at all, conceive of any justification for such domination, because by its very nature it is an act of inequity.

Such is my duty as a man and as an Indian, and religious injunctions have imposed upon me the same duty. In fact, the greatest proof of the truth of my religion is that it is another name for the teaching of the rights of man. I am a Muslim, and by virtue of being a Muslim this has become my religious duty. Islam never accepts as valid a sovereignty which is personal or is constituted of a bureaucracy of a handful of paid executives. Islam constitutes a perfected system of freedom and democracy. It has been sent down to get back for the human race the liberty which has been snatched away from it. Monarchs, foreign dominations, selfish religious pontiffs, and powerful sections had alike misappropriated this liberty of man. They had been fondly nursing the belief that power and possession spell the highest right. The moment Islam appeared, it proclaimed that the highest right is not might but right itself. No one except God has got the right to make serfs and slaves of God's creatures. All men are equal, and their fundamental rights are on a par. He only is greater than others whose deeds are the most righteous of all. [. . .]

The sovereignty of the Prophet of Islam and of the caliphs was a perfected conception of democratic equality, and it could only take shape with the whole nation's will, unity, suffrage, and election. This is the reason why the sovereign or a president of a republic is like a designated caliph; caliphate literally means nothing more nor less than a representation, so that all the authority a caliph possesses consists in his representative character, and he possesses no domination beyond this representative authority.

If Islam defines it as a duty of Muhammadans to refuse to acknowledge the moral justification even of an Islamic government, if full play is not granted in it to the will and franchise of the nation, it is perfectly superfluous to add what under Islam would be the ruling given about a foreign bureaucracy. If today there was to be established in India an Islamic government, but if the system of that government was based upon personal monarchy or upon bureaucratic oligarchy, then to protest against the existence of such a government would still be my primary duty as a Muslim. I would still call the government oppressive and demand its replacement.

I frankly confess that this original conception of Islamic sovereignty could not be uniformly maintained in its primal purity on account of the selfishness and personal domineering of the later Muhammadan sovereigns. The mighty magnificence of the emperors of ancient Rome and of the shahs of Persia had attracted the Muslim sovereigns powerfully to the dubious glory of great monarchial empires. They began to prefer the majestic figures of [Julius] Caesar [Roman emperor, died 44 B.C.] or Khosrow [king of Iran, reigned 531–579] to the simple dignity of the original caliphs, clad often times in old tattered cloaks. No period of the dynasties and sovereignties of Islam has however failed to produce some true Muslim martyrs, who have made public declarations

of the tyrannies and transgressions of such monarchies, and joyfully and triumphantly suffered all miseries and hardships which inevitably confronted them in the thorny paths of duty.

To expect from a Muslim that he should not pronounce what is right is to ask him to retire from Islamic life. If you have no right to demand from a person to give up his religion, then certainly you cannot require a Muslim that he should not call tyranny a tyranny; because both the things are synonymous.

This is that vital organ of Islamic life which, if cut off, terminates the very existence of its best characteristics. [. . .] In the Qur'an—the Holy Book of Islam—the Muslims have been told that they are witnesses of truth in God's universe. [Sura 5, Verse 83, and other verses] In the capacity of a nation, this is their national character. [. . .]

Among the numerous sayings of the Prophet of Islam, one is this, "Pronounce what is good, restrain the evil. If you don't do it, evil men will dominate you and God's curse will overtake you. You will offer prayers, but they will not be accepted."

But how would this national duty be performed? Islam has indicated three different standards under three different conditions: "If anyone of you sees an evil, it is necessary that he should correct it with his own hands. If he has not the power to do it personally, he should proclaim it, and if he feels that he has not the power to pronounce it even, he should consider it evil in his heart at least. But this last degree is the weakest stage of religion." In India we have not the capacity to correct the evils of the government with our own hands, we have, therefore, adopted the second measure, that is, we pronounce its evils.

The Holy Prophet of Islam has preached the following doctrine to the Muslims. That man is blessed with the best of deaths who proclaims the truth in face of a tyrannical administration and is slaughtered in punishment of this deed. The scripture of Islam, the Holy Qur'an, defines the greatest attribute of the true Muslim to be that they fear not any being except God, and whatever they consider to be the truth, they fear not any authority in the public proclamation of such truth. [Sura 6, Verses 14–19, and other verses] The Qur'an further defines the national characteristics of the Muslims as follows: They are the witnesses to truth on God's earth! [Sura 5, Verse 83, and other verses] As long, therefore, as they continue to be Muslims, they cannot desist from giving this public evidence. In fact, it has designated Muslims as witnesses, that is, givers of the evidence of truth. When the Prophet of Islam extracted a promise of righteousness from any person, one of the clauses of such a bond used to be, "I will always proclaim the truth in whatever condition and wherever I may happen to be."

To those Muslims who have it in their religious duties that they should accept death rather than hesitate from telling what is true, a case under section 124-A can never be a very frightful thing, the maximum punishment under which is seven years. [. . .]

In the early Islamic days, Muslims were truthful to such an extent that an old woman could dare say to the caliph of the time in the open court, "If you fail to do justice your hair would be uprooted like anything."

But instead of instituting a case against her, he would thank God that such outspoken tongues were present in the nation. Exactly in the *jum'a* [Friday communal] prayers gathering, when the sultan would get up and say, "Hear and obey," a man would get up at once and say, "Neither will we hear nor obey." Why? "Because the cloak that you have got on your person is much more than your own share of cloth, and this is a breach of trust." On this the caliph would produce his son for his witness, who would declare that he had given his own share of cloth to his father, and this cloak was prepared with that.

This attitude of the nation was toward the caliph whose bravery and enterprise overthrew the thrones of Egypt and Iran. Nevertheless there was no 124-A in Islamic government. When the attitude of ours, the Muslims, toward our own national governments had been such, then what hope can the officers of an alien government expect from us? Is "the government established by law" in India more dear for us than the one established by *shari'a* [Islamic law]?

Is the kingdom of England and status of Lord [Rufus D. I.] Reading [British viceroy of India, 1921–1926] more respectable for us than the caliphate of 'Abd al-Malik [ibn Marwan, reigned 685–705] and status of Hajjaj ibn Yusuf ['Abd al-Malik's governor in the Hijaz, 697–714]? If we leave aside the great difference between "alien and non-Muslim" and "national and Muslim," even then what we have been saying for the governments of Hajjaj ibn Yusuf and Khalid [ibn 'Abdullah al-]Qasri [another Umayyad governor, died circa 743], we will repeat the same about the "Reading" and [Baron Frederic]

"Chelmsford" governments [viceroy of India, 1916–1921]. We had said to them, "Fear from God because the earth is loaded with your tyrannies." We repeat the same today. As a matter of fact, what we are doing today in India, on account of our weakness and helplessness, was in reality meant to be done toward the tyranny and repression of our own national administrators, and not towards alien rulers. Had the agents of British government understood this reality, they would have realized that the patience and toleration of Muslims has passed all limits. More than this, they cannot quit Islam for Britain.

Islam has pointed out two ways to face the tyranny of rulers, because conditions are different in both the cases. One tyranny is forcible possession by alien rulers, and one of course is of Muhammadan rulers themselves. For the first, Islam orders the use of sword. For the second, the commandment is that the sword may not be taken up, but as far as possible every Muslim should go on proclaiming the truth. In the first case, there will be executions at the hands of the enemies, while in the second place there will be untold suffering and punishments at the hands of the tyrants. Muslims should make sacrifices of both the kinds in both the cases, and the result of the both is success and victory. Consequently the Muslims have made both kinds of sacrifices in the last thirteen centuries. They have suffered martyrdoms at the hands of foreigners, and also shown patience and perseverance against their own. Just as in the first case their "war efforts" are without parallel, in the second case their "spirit of martyrdom" is unique.

The Muslims in India today have adopted the second course, although their fight is with the first category.

The time had come for them to take up "the war effort," but they have adopted the "martyrdom spirit." They have decided not to fight with weapons, but rather to remain nonviolent—that is, they will do the same as they had to do in the case of Muslim rulers. Undoubtedly, a particular state of India is responsible for their attitude. But the government should think what more the unfortunate Muslims can do. Unexpectedly, they are doing against the foreigners what they should have done in case of their own national rulers.

Truly, I have not the slightest grievance that a case has been set up against me with a view to give me punishment. But the revolution of circumstances is very painful for me that a Muslim is expected not to call tyranny a tyranny because he will be tried under section 124-A.

An outstanding object-lesson in speaking the truth which their national history presents to the Muslims is to be found in the order of an autocratic monarch by which each organ of a rebellious victim's body was to be cut off. The charge against the victim was that he had proclaimed the inequity of the tyrant. Firm as a rock, he stood and took the punishment in all its heinous stages, but his tongue, right on to the moment when it was severed, went on proclaiming that autocrat was tyrant. This is an incident of the reign of the emperor 'Abd al-Malik, whose domain extended from Syria to Sind. Can any one then attach any weight to a sentence under section 124-A as compared to this terrible penalty?

I confess that it is the moral decadence of Muslims and their renouncing the real Islamic life that is responsible for the bringing about of this fallen state. While I am penning these lines, I know there is still living in India many a Muslim who through his weakness pays homage to this very tyranny. But the failure of man to act up to the spirit of certain tenets cannot belie the intrinsic truth of those principles. The tenets of Islam are preserved make it permissible for Muslims to enjoy life at the expense of freedom. A true Muslim has either to immolate himself or to live as a free nation; no third course is open for him in Islam.

I declare that during the last two years not a single day has passed when I had not proclaimed the tyranny of the government with regard to "the khilafat [movement]" and "the Punjab affairs."[5] I admit having always said that a government which is bent upon exterminating the *khilafat* [caliphate] and is neither prepared to compensate nor is ashamed of the tyrannies of the Punjab—there can be no loyalty for such a government in the heart of any Indian.

On December 13, 1917, when I was interned in Ranchi, I wrote a detailed letter to Lord Chelmsford that if the British government, against their declared promises, ever takes possession of Islamic countries or the Islamic caliphate, the Indian Muslims would find themselves faced with only two alternatives. Either they should side with Islam or with the British government.

At last the same happened. The government broke their promises glaringly. Neither that promise was kept up which the government announced on January 2, 1914 [reference unclear], nor could it keep up the words which [David] Lloyd George [1863–1945], the prime minister of England, made in the course of a speech in the House of Commons on January 5, 1918.[6]

These things created a strange position for the Indian Muslims. The minimum that they could do according to the Islamic law was to withdraw their support and cooperation. [. . .] Muslims have come to believe that to obtain what is right and just, they must have *swaraj*.

My own declaration in this respect, however, is quite unequivocal. The present government is an unjust bureaucracy. It is absolutely opposed to the will and wishes of millions of people. It has always preferred prestige over justice and truth. It regards the barbaric massacre of Jallianwala [in 1919] as right; it considers it no injustice that men should be made to creep like animals; it allows the whipping of young students til they became unconscious, simply because they refused to salute the Union Jack [the British flag]; it does not resist from trampling over the Islamic caliphate, even after petitions of 30 corore [15 million] people; it considers no sin in breaking all its pledges and promises, and so on. [. . .] If I don't call such a government a "tyrant" and [tell it to] "Either mend yourself or end yourself," should I call it "just" and [tell it,] "Don't mend yourself, but live long," simply because tyranny is powerful and is equipped with prison houses?

Continuously in the last 12 years, I have been training my community and my country to demand their rights and their liberty. I was only eighteen years old when I first started speaking and writing on this theme. I have consecrated my whole being to it and sacrificed the best of my life, meaning the whole of my youth, to my infatuation with this ideal. For four years I have suffered internment, but during my internment even, I have never desisted from pursuing my work and inviting people to this national goal. This is the mission of my life; and if I live at all, I elect to live only for this single purpose. Even as the

5. [The Punjab affairs of 1919 involved British suppression of Indian civil disobedience, culminating in the shooting of thousands of peaceful protestors in Jallianwala Bagh, a public square in Amritsar, Punjab.—Ed.]

6. [Possibly a reference to Lloyd George's speech of March 14, 1917, urging import protection taxes for India as a "great act of justice" (*The Parliamentary Debates*, House of Commons, fifth series, volume 91, p. 1183).—Ed.]

Qur'an says, "my prayers and my observances and my life my death are all for my lord, the God of the Universe." [Sura 6, Verse 162]

How could I deny this "crime" [of sedition], when I am the first pioneer in this latest phase of that Islamic movement in India which has created a tremendous revolution in the political world of the Indian Muslims and has gradually elevated them to that pinnacle of national consciousness on which they are seen today. In 1912 I started an Urdu journal, the *al-Hilal* [*The Crescent*], which was the organ of this movement, and the object of the publication of which was mainly what I have declared above. It is an actual fact that within three years it had created a new atmosphere in the religious and the political life of the Muslims of India.

Previously, they were not only cut off from the political activities of their Hindu brothers, but were acting as weapons in the hands of the bureaucracy. The government's policy of divide and rule created a sort of apprehension in their mind that Hindus are larger in numbers; and if the country attains independence there will be Hindu *raj* [rule] in India. But *al-Hilal* persuaded the Muslims to have confidence in their faith, instead of numerical inferiority, and invited them to join hands with the Hindus fearlessly. [. . .] Bureaucracy could not tolerate such a movement for long. First of all, therefore, the security of *al-Hilal* was forfeited, and when the paper was restarted under the name of *al-Bilagh* [*The Message*], the government of India interned me in 1916. I must say that *al-Hilal* was out and out an invitation for "liberty or death." [. . .]

On the 1st of January, 1920, I was set at liberty after an internment of four years; and since that time up to the moment of my arrest, the whole of my time was spent in publicity and propaganda of these very ideals. On February 28th and 29th, 1920, a *khilafat* conference was held in the Town Hall of Calcutta, where the Muslims in utter disappointment made this announcement: "If the British government even now fails to accede to the demands of the *khilafat*, the Muslims in accordance with their religious injunctions will be compelled to cut off all loyal connection."

I was the president of that conference.

I had clearly explained in my long presidential address all the facts which are presented in these two speeches (on the basis of which I am being tried here).

In this address I had also made an explanation of that Islamic injunction under which the Muslims are required to noncooperate with the government, that is, withdraw their hand of help and cooperation.

It was here in this conference where that resolution was adopted, under which it was declared un-Islamic for any faithful Muslim to serve in the army. The Karachi case [conspiracy charges against seven Khilafat leaders] was launched on the basis of the same resolution. I have often pointed out in the press and in my numerous speeches that this resolution was first of all drafted by me, and it has been thrice adopted under my presidentship. So I am the proper person to deserve punishment in connection with this "crime." Also I have with certain more additions published this statement in a book form with its English translation, as a written record of my "offenses."

During the last two years, alone and with *Mahatma* Gandhi, I have undertaken several tours of the country. There is hardly any city where I have not delivered speeches again and again on "The Khilafat," "The Punjab," "The Swaraj," and "Non-Cooperation," and where I have not repeated all these things which are being shown in these two speeches.

In December 1920, a conference of the All-India Khilafat Committee was held side by side with the annual session of the Indian National Congress. In April 1921, a conference of the Jamiat-ul-Ulema came off in Bareilly; in October last, Uttar Pradesh Provincial Khilafat Conference took place in Agra; in November, the annual session of All-India Jamiat-ul-Ulema was held in Lahore. I was also the president of all these conferences, and whatever was said by all the speakers in all these conferences or by me in the presidential speeches contained all the things that are being shown in these two speeches. I must declare that they were more unambiguous and equivocal than these.

If the implications of my two speeches come under section 124-A, I must confess that I have committed this crime innumerable times. I will have to say that in the last two years I have done nothing except infringement of section 124-A.

In this war of liberty and justice I have adopted the path of nonviolent noncooperation. Opposed to us stands an authority armed with the complete equipment for oppression, excess, and bloodshed. But we place our reliance and trust, next to God, only upon our own limitless power of sacrifice and unshakable fortitude. Unlike *Mahatma* Gandhi, my belief is not that armed force should never be opposed by armed force. It is my belief that such opposing of violence with violence is fully in harmony with the natural laws of God in those circumstances under which Islam permits the use of such violence. But at the same time, for purposes of liberation of India and the present agitation, I entirely agree with all the arguments of *Mahatma* Gandhi, and I have complete confidence in his honesty. It is my definite conviction that India cannot attain success by means of arms, nor is it advisable for it to adopt that course. India can only triumph through nonviolent agitation, and India's triumph will be a memorable example of the victory of moral force.

What I have already said in the beginning, I repeat the same in the conclusion. All that the government is doing today with us is nothing extraordinary for which it should be condemned. Violence and oppression are always a second nature of foreign governments at the moment of national awakening, and we should not expect that human instinct will be changed for us.

This is a national weakness common to all individuals and organizations. How many men are there in the world who would return the thing that has come into their possession simply because they have no right over it? Then why should such a mercy be expected for a full-fledged continent? Power does not acknowledge a certain argument simply because it is reasonable and logical. It will not yield until a greater power makes its appearance and compels it to submit to all unreasonable and illogical demands.

We realize that if our passion for freedom and determination for demanding what is our right is true and strong, the very government which holds us as criminals today will be compelled to greet us tomorrow as victorious patriots.

I am charged with "sedition," but let me understand the meaning of "sedition." Is "sedition" that struggle for freedom which has not as yet been successful? If this is so, I confess frankly, but at the same time let me remind that this very thing is called patriotism when it is successful. The armed leaders of Ireland were regarded rebels up til yesterday [when Ireland achieved independence in 1921], but what title would Great Britain suggest for [Eamon] De Valera [1882–1975] and [Arthur] Griffith [1871–1922] today?

Consequently, what is happening today, its judgment would come tomorrow. Iniquity would be effaced, and justice would live behind. We have our faith in the decision of the future.

In any case it is natural to expect showers when there are clouds in the sky. We see that all the signs for the change of weather are visible. But pity is over those eyes who refuse to see the signs.

I had said in these very speeches, "The seed of liberty can never yield fruit unless fertilized by the water of oppression."

The government has begun fertilization.

I had also said, "Don't be sad over the arrest of Khilafat volunteers. If you really want justice and freedom, get ready for going to the jails."

I want to say something about the magistrate also. Let him award the maximum punishment that he can without hesitation. I will never have any complaint or grudge. I know it that unless the entire administration is changed the instruments will go on with their work.

I finish my statement in the words of Giordano Bruno [scientist, 1548–1600], the famous martyr of Italy, who was also made to stand before the court like me: "Give me the maximum punishment that can be awarded, without hesitation. I assure you that the pain that your heart will feel while writing the order, not a hundredth part of it will be felt by me while bearing the judgment."

Mr. Magistrate! I will not take any more time of the court now. It is an interesting and instructive chapter of history which both of us are engaged in preparing. The [defendant's] dock has fallen to our lot, and to yours the magisterial chair. I admit that this chair is as much necessary for this work as this dock. Let us come and finish our role in this memorable drama. The historian is eagerly awaiting it, and the future is looking forward to us. Allow us to occupy this dock repeatedly and continuously, and you may also go on writing the judgment again and again. For some time more, this work will continue till the gates of another's court are flung open. This will be the court of the Law of God. Time will act as its judge and pass the judgment. And this verdict will be final in all respects.

Back to the Qur'an

Muhammad Akram Khan (Bengal-Pakistan, 1868–1968) was a controversial reformer and journalist. Born near Calcutta, Khan began his higher education at an English-medium school, then transferred to a traditional seminary. He founded and edited numerous Urdu and Bengali journals, and was jailed in the 1920s for writing on anticolonial and pan-Islamic themes in his journal *Sebak* (*The Worshipper*). In the 1940s, he was provincial president of the Muslim League, which sought a Muslim homeland in South Asia, and he became national vice-president in 1947 just as the region was being partitioned, whereupon he moved from Calcutta, India, to Dhaka, East Pakistan (later Bangladesh). In addition to journalistic articles, Khan wrote several longer works, including a biography of the Prophet Muhammad and a commentary on the Qur'an. Khan is generally regarded as a modernist, though he was also a member of the *Ahl-i-Hadith* movement, which some scholars regard as neotraditionalist. He criticized Bengali Muslim scholars as too often guided by superstition and ignorance. Khan recommended reform of Muslim family law in South Asia, arguing that current practices ignored the rights afforded to women in Islam. Similarly, Khan opposed injunctions against music that he considered to be unsupported by the sacred sources. While he affirmed the importance of *hadith* (narratives of the Prophet) in juristic matters, he did not advocate the methods of jurisprudence of any one school. As demonstrated in the essay presented here, he was hostile toward scholars whose allegiance to a particular school, he argued, instigated sectarian conflicts.[1]

The *hajj* [pilgrimage] season has arrived—travelers are gathering from various parts of the Islamic world, and Mecca has taken on a unique beauty. In the sacred precincts, people gather for sunset and evening prayers, and they number not less than 100,000. I tried my best to find out what was going on in this great assemblage of Muslims. I intend to convey [to you] the results of my [research] efforts.

Nowadays, learned Muslims from various countries have begun to give lessons at the sacred precincts. Some give lessons on [Muhammad ibn Isma'il] al-Bukhari [the foremost compiler of *hadith*, 810–870]; some on the *Muwatta'* [*The Well-Trodden Path*, by Malik ibn Anas, 710–796]; some on jurisprudence, and some on rhetoric and grammar. Hun-dreds of Muslims gain great satisfaction from their lessons. But, sad to say, I believe I did not benefit nor gain any satisfaction from all the lessons I sat in on. The main reason I did not benefit from them is that all the teachers have a sectarian mentality—they waste all their brilliance pleading their respective beliefs most of the time.

In order to uproot division, the Ka'ba was made the *qibla* [direction of worship] of all the world's Muslims. In order to mute contemptible sectarianism, this great equalizing practice of the *hajj* [takes place], yet people sit in the shade of that Ka'ba making entrenched divisions among pilgrims permanent. The sight of it is disheartening to me. Once or twice I had discussions with teachers regarding

Maulana Akram Khan, "Bak tu di kuran" (Back to the Qur'an), in Abu Jafar, editor, *Maolana Akarama Kham* (*Maulana Akram Khan*) (Dhaka, Bangladesh: Isalamika Phaundesana Bamladesa, 1986), pp. 418–420. First published in 1929. Translation from Bengali and introduction by Sufia Uddin.

1. Abu Jafar, *Maulana Akram Khan, A Versatile Genius* (Dhaka, Bangladeh: Islamic Foundation Bangladesh, 1984);

Abu Jafar, editor, *Maolana Akarama Kham* (*Maulana Akram Khan*) (Dhaka, Bangladesh: Isalamika Phaundesana Bamladesa, 1986); Anisuzzaman, *Creativity, Reality, and Identity* (Dhaka, Bangladesh: International Centre for Bengal Studies, 1993); E. T. M. Atikura Rahamana, *Bamlara Rajanitite Maolana Mohammada Akarama Kham, 1905–1947* (*Bengalis in Politics: Maulana Muhammad Akram Khan, 1905–1947*) (Dhaka, Bangladesh: Bamla Ekademi, 1995).

this extremely insufferable situation, until the discussions transgressed into arguments.

However that it may be, after intensive investigation, nowhere in the sacred precincts did I find the teaching and the study of the Qur'an. As a result, I am deeply hurt. And so I tried to gain some peace of mind by expressing my pain (to a distinguished person [who would understand]). For a long time he looked at me, and said with a smile, "The abode of ill practice is right here [in the sacred precincts]."

Imploring him to speak straight to the point, below I recount a portion of what he said.

God in the Qur'an gives Muslims advice on justice (*'adl*). The word justice means "Each thing in its place"—everything should be placed in its appropriate station. To put anything above or below its rightful place is contrary to justice. So the opposite of justice is force and oppression, and the perpetrators of oppression will be destroyed. God, most high, conveys this [point] to Muslims over and over again in the Qur'an. If one discusses the Muslims' situation, one will learn that their national life is filled with this oppression. Today, they strongly express their wish not to put their relentless effort in the right place. They are always eager to place the official (*wali*) and religious leader (*imam*) in the Prophet's place, and the Prophet in God's place, and because it is false their religious practice is bound to fail. This fatal disease has infected the way of thinking in every stratum of the Muslim nation. Many among our intelligent leaders are aware of this disease, but they have done very little research into the root cause. In my opinion, the root cause is: Muslims lack justice [when it comes] to the Qur'an. Muslims do not put the Qur'an in its rightful place [of importance]. Not only that, they take the Qur'an

from its highest place and instead bring it down, placing *hadith* [narratives of the Prophet] first and jurisprudence second, above the Qur'an. For this reason we find that for the study of the Qur'an our students do not put in one hundredth of the toil they do for knowledge of the essence of Bukhari and *Hidaya* [*Guidance*, by Burhanuddin Marghinani, died circa 1197]. In Muslim society there is no lack of talented scholars and possessors of intelligence. However, all of their genius is directed to the writing of books with detailed explanations of jurisprudence and *hadith*, thus wasting all their talent. As for the necessity of writing exegeses of the Qur'an, there are very few among them who have done so. The rare [gems] are *Imam* Fakhr al-Din Razi [1149–1209] and *Imam* [Muhammad ibn 'Ali] Shaukani [circa 1760–1839]. Everyone is aware of the rarity of *Imam* Razi's *hadith*. Owing to the widespread neglect of exegesis of the Qur'an, up to this day Shaukani's exegesis has not yet been printed. As a result, knowledge of the Qur'an and its stories is overshadowed by the stories compiled in *Jaygun Hanifa* [a Bengali romance of the 18th century]. If you do not read *Hidaya* and Bukhari, you cannot become a *maulavi* [religious scholar]. But it is heart-rending to note that to be a *maulavi* does not require study of the Qur'an. In our society in the modern world, how many *maulavi*s are able to say with sincerity that their study of the Qur'an is a tenth of their study of jurisprudence, *hadith*, and the principles of jurisprudence? The last chance to remedy the situation is now. Without any fear or anxiety, social reformers have a duty to situate this society in truth, namely "to put the Qur'an in its established place—to you, God, we will again [acknowledge you] in your rightful place [of honor]."

SECTION 6

Southeast/East Asia

An Exposition concerning the Malays

The Singapore-based journal *al-Imam* (*The Leader*), which appeared from July 1906 to December 1908, was the first publication in Southeast Asia to carry the modernist Islamic message. Singapore was the logical confluence of such ideas as it served as the principal transition point for Southeast Asians on their way to and from West Asia. By 1906 a group of young men from various Southeast Asian communities joined together in Singapore to study Islam and promote religious reform, under the leadership of *Shaykh* Tahir Jalal al-Din "al-Azhari" (Minangkabau, West Sumatra, 1867–1957), who had studied at Mecca and Cairo and had met Muhammad 'Abduh (see chapter 3) and Muhammad Rashid Rida (see chapter 6). Among the activists of this circle was 'Abbas bin Muhammad Taha (Minangkabau, West Sumatra, born 1885), who spent much of his youth in Mecca, later translated educational works from Syria and Egypt, and assumed primary editorial control of *al-Imam* around 1907. This magazine mimicked, in form and content, the Egyptian magazine *al-Manar* (*The Beacon*). *Al-Imam* translated pieces from *al-Manar* and other Arab periodicals into Malay, but placed these borrowings in the context of Southeast Asian conditions, in particular the "decline of the Malays" as a dynamic race and the challenge to Muslims in the struggle for modern civilization. Many contributions, including the one presented here, were anonymous, and can best be attributed to the collective effort of the editors of *al-Imam*.[1]

Al-Imam has received what follows here below:

Say the truth even if it is bitter![2]

[Say it] too, even if with abusive or insulting words, so long as they are true, in order to awaken those with intellect. This is like a vile manure which gives life to plants and makes them fertile for the benefit of their fruits. Such then is more important than falsely praising or exalting someone.

The Exposition

For argument's sake let us hold an imaginary debate beginning with the premise that the word "Malay" is the name or title of a particular race of people of the East found in the long-famous "Malay Peninsula." The origin of this term "Malay," which consists of five letters, is derived from "Mala Layu" [a wilting blossom], the flower of a plant that blooms in the hope that it shall become a fruit which bears seeds that will spread or scatter and thus extend and reproduce [the flower]. One form of this flower is the gardenia. (The Malays say that this is most often planted around their homes.) Its color is white and its scent is fragrant. Yet if we sniff it, occasionally there are parasites within its leaves which can cause a lasting nasal infection. Have we ever taken such a

['Abbas bin Muhammad Taha], "Uraian Melayu" (An Exposition concerning the Malays), *Al-Imam* (*The Leader*), Singapore, August 29, 1908, pp. 100–103, and September 27, 1908, pp. 140–146. Translation from Malay by Abu Bakar Hamzah, *Al-Imam: Its Role in Malay Society, 1906–1908* (Kuala Lumpur, Malaysia: Media Cendekiawan, 1991), pp. 181–190. Editing and introduction by Michael F. Laffan.

1. Abu Bakar Hamzah, *Al-Imam: Its Role in Malay Society, 1906–1908*; William R. Roff, *The Origins of Malay Nationalism* (New Haven, Conn.: Yale University Press, 1967), pp. 56–90; Asyumardi Azra, "The Transmission of *al-Manar* Reformism to the Malay-Indonesian World: The Cases of *al-Imam* and *al-Munir*," *Studia Islamika*, volume 6, number 3, 1999, pp. 75–100; Michael F. Laffan, "The Umma Below the Winds: Mecca, Cairo, Reformist Islam and a Conceptualization of Indonesia," Ph.D. dissertation, University of Sydney, 2000, pp. 177–192.

2. [This popular Arabic expression paraphrases a *hadith*, or narrative of the Prophet.—Ed.]

withering bloom to fruition other than by deliberately collecting and implanting its seeds? So too is this Malay race of ours, which, day by day, grows weaker. And its language in particular has become corrupted.

The original form [of the word Malay] is m-l-a-y-u. The initial "m" stands for both *malas* [lazy] [and] *mulia* [honorable]. We may find [both] in the *Hikayat 'Abdullah* [*The Story of 'Abdullah*, the autobiography of colonial translator 'Abdullah bin 'Abdul Kadir Munshi, written in 1849], when Mr. [Thomas Stamford] Raffles [British colonial official and founder of modern Singapore, 1781–1826] instructed Sultan Husayn [nominal ruler of Singapore, 1819–1824] to engage in trade in order to enlarge his income. However, the latter demurred, as his honor as a sultan would be debased by so doing.

"L" is the second letter, standing for *lalai* [negligent], *lemah* [weak], and *lembut* [pliant]. Hence the Malay race is "negligent" in demanding its rights. And we can see this in the conduct of Sultan Husayn Shah of Singapore, which is at odds with that of the late and eminent Abu Bakar, who was sultan of Johore [reigned 1862–1895].[3] [The Malays] are "weak" because of their obstinacy and lack of initiative or learning or knowledge. The Chief of Semantan [Abdul Rahman Dato' Bahaman, born 1838] was said to be mighty and powerful, and to have made himself mighty by bathing in a cauldron of boiling oil. Nonetheless he was vanquished by British cannon and bayonets [during the rebellion of 1891–1895]. Look [too] in the *Hikayat Tanah Melayu* [*History of the Malay Land*, 16th–17th century] at the tale of the Malacca War [of 1511], which took place in the time of Sultan Mahmud Shah [died 1528, sultan of Malacca and founder of Johore]. There the Europeans used matchlocks with round bullets which they said pierced and killed. And this was despite the Malays' being "magically impervious" and armed with ancient magic daggers. [The Malays] are "negligent" as, when they are reminded to do good, they pay no heed. Thus are they!

Refer too to the [*Handbook of the*] *Federated Malay States and Pahang*, in which a Malay scribe, educated in the ways of the world, says: "Our Malay race is so pliant that it cannot be defeated by attacking its roots. Its tongue is so pliant that when [a Malay] studies Chinese with its 'choo-cheng sound' he can [replicate it]. So too with the 'soos-sis' of the English tongue. Yet this pliability goes right to the back-bone and the ribs, much like a plant that may be coiled or twisted but which does not have the rigidity to be used as the supporting pillar of a house. Such rigidity is recalled by the Malay expression 'Should the supports break, the pillar will remain.'"

The third letter, the tall [Arabic] letter "alif," denotes *ikhtiar* [initiative], *istiadat* [traditions], and *ahmak dengan tiada ihsan* [stupid without compassion]. *Asutan* [agitation], that is, with the *tiada aturan* [disorder] of Islam, is also one of its members. And the *anggota* [limbs] of the Malays are no different from those of the Chinese or [even] the Japanese, who defeated the six-foot-tall giants [that is, the Russians, who were defeated by the Japanese in 1904–1905].

The "initiative" of the Malay is employed solely for his self and his nature. [This nature is] covetous and greedy, as well as malicious, perhaps because [the Malay] is afraid that his neighbor might be equal to, or perhaps better than, him.[4] Not one book, whether on magical potions or worldly knowledge, will he receive unless it is accompanied by yellow rice, fried chicken, and a betel-plate filled with *rupiah*s [coins]. If he receives this, then he will use the book for instruction. However, he will not pursue that instruction to the end before breaking off because [he does not want to concede] that its knowledge exceeds his own, which he does not want to reveal [to his students]. (This strong pull of the *rupiah* is illustrated in 'Abdullah Munshi's story of the elephant trapper of Malacca.)[5] All [Malay] knowledge is wrapped in secrecy. Go, sir, to any Malay engineer who has taken instruction in metallurgy but has not yet completed that study (that is, he has not yet obtained a "degree" or "title"). Ask him about some facet of his learning, like, "Tell me how to go about cutting copper." And despite him knowing how, he will reply, "Alas, I have no idea." Because of this greed, malice, covetousness, dullness, and stupidity—which are deeply planted within his heart—the Malay has not yet been pulled from his roots.

---

3. [Abu Bakar was a favorite with *al-Imam* due to his efforts to open up and modernize Johore.—Ed.]

4. [This appears to be a reference to the station and economic prosperity of the Chinese, Indians, and Arabs of Southeast Asia.—Ed.]

5. [In this incident the elephant trapper refused to reveal his special knowledge other than by intimations or partial disclosure.—Ed.]

The "traditions" [of the Malays]. (These are illustrated by the stamp of 30 years ago which bore the image of a snarling tiger.) [These "traditions" are] exemplified by the imperative for commoners to prostrate themselves, anywhere or at anytime, should they encounter their king. Look in 'Abdullah Munshi's *Kisah Pelayaran Abdullah* [*The Voyage of 'Abdullah*, 1838]. The customs of old could not be changed. Commoners could not wear yellow for fear of being struck down by the divine power of the dead king (see Book Three, "The Way to Knowledge").

"Stupid without compassion." That is: to be angry without method whilst inflamed by the carnal passion of Satan. [This is shown] in the *Cerita Keturunan Melayu* [*Story of the Ancestry of the Malays*], wherein the [legendary] Sultan of Kota Tinggi cut open the stomach of [a royal woman called] Bani Laksamana, who, due to her craving of jackfruit, had transgressed royal prerogative by tasting but one pip. It was due to her transgression of "custom" that, at the instigation of a minister, she was sentenced to death.

"Agitation." Listen to the story of [15th century folk hero] Hang Tuah, who was despicably slandered despite having saved the king from shameful disgrace. Everything that I have related thus far has come from the [traditional Malay] stories and annals. And believe me, dear readers, that some might be thinking in their hearts that all this is in the distant past and has been long done with. In short, [they may say that] it is just "nonsense." Yet why did the English compose stories, which they included in school curricula as lessons for children to become attentive, thoughtful, and capable? In particular, there are the stories of the famous Admiral [Horatio] Nelson [1758–1805], and the military heroes Sir John Moore [1761–1809] and the Duke of Wellington [Arthur Wellesley, 1769–1852]. Then there are the men who are together responsible for the organization of the government, [Robert Cecil] Salisbury, [William] Gladstone, Mr. [William] Pitt, and so on [British prime ministers of the 19th centuries]. Is this not useful for school children to differentiate stupidity and idiocy from intelligence and wisdom through [the example of] such men? Hence these "young bamboos" will not grow wildly and selfishly. (Your excellency may well say that "Such is the way of things in great countries." Fine. But shouldn't we practice self-improvement by the use of a great mirror?) It is the blessing of the Islamic religion that has allowed the Malays to remain in existence. This lucky fate is due to the arrival of an Arab in Malacca—for which the Malays must give thanks—and not the Portuguese priest who has disturbed the religions of China and Buddhism, as we can now see.

The letter "y" stands for *yakin* [convinced faith]. Yet this is only enunciated by their lips and is not inscribed on their hearts. The letter "w," the last in the word "Malay," is found in the expression, *wa bi'llah al-tawfiq* [in God alone does success abide] for the Malay people, who, by sentiment and thought, are of the Islamic religion. On the other hand "w" can stand for the *waba' wa bala'* [disease and affliction] that will lay waste to them and herald their destruction.

The Aims [of This Exposition]

It can be seen that our current Malay writers mention, in various newspapers and histories, how all sorts of Malays—whether from the end of Salang to Tanjung Romania—are, metaphorically speaking, looking at great mirrors, including the Mikado Mutsuhito [Meiji, emperor of Japan, 1867–1912] and the ascent of the Japanese race. Or they look at the fall and weakness of China, the fading of Egypt, or the exceptions made by His Excellency the late Abu Bakar and his "modern" state of Johore, and its like.

What then is the reason? (Recall, dear reader, the third letter "alif" and the question of the Englishmen to his friend, the Malay engineer, and the resulting [answer].)

His late Excellency had erased all the despicable qualities of the Malays from his heart by cultivating the benefits of human civilization. This he realized by traveling, not just to England but to China, Japan, the Malay Peninsula, Java, the ports of the continent of Europe, Germany, Italy, Turkey, Austro-Hungary, and so forth. Outwardly he was just taking time on holiday, yet his heart was filled with the intention to work and strive for just such an elevation of the Malay people, even as the Japanese nation had done and the Chinese are now doing, rousing from their slumber. (All the peoples of the world know of the Malays, yet few have seen them. Just look at the English *Windsor Magazine*, edited by Sir Frank Swettenham [1850–1946]. Therein you will see a "sketch" or depiction by a European artist of the murder of Mr. [James] Birch [British colonial official, assassinated in 1875], showing the Malay wearing only a loincloth!)

It seems then that words of great experience, opinion, comprehension, and vision were formed on the heart of this blessed ruler [Abu Bakar] through his comparing and discerning the most attractive and fitting actions of the nations of the world. This was best exemplified by looking at the Japanese nation. Before defeating China [in 1894–1895], and then Russia, the Japanese were outwardly very polite, soft of speech and action. Yet in their hearts they said, "Curse you! Yet what can we do? Soon you will see the Japanese nation!" Compare the Japan of today with its freedom, sturdiness, civilized ways, knowledge, skill, and wisdom. (Refer to *al-Shams al-mushriqa* [*The Rising Sun*, by Egyptian nationalist Mustafa Kamil Pasha, 1874–1908; published in Arabic in 1904 and translated into Malay in 1906].)

Who then did all this? The people of the land, or Mutsuhito their leader? All of us [Malays] are no different from a class of children in a school.[6] (This school is a place where knowledge is acquired in order to produce a practical and humane person.) Meanwhile, the teacher is a knowledgeable person who teaches his pupils all sorts of knowledge and things that may be appropriate for the benefit of the children (even where [this contravenes] existing regulations). However, if the teacher's knowledge is weak, coupled with his being lazy, [then he will be] in the habit of nodding off at his desk, despite having just warned his students loudly, saying while tapping his cane, "All of you! Keep quiet! Copy two or three pages from this book." And he will do so constantly in order to take up time, lazily believing that [education is like watching] plants grow. And at the end of the day he will go straight home to await his monthly salary.

"You don't understand the attitude of our teacher," said one little boy in the fourth grade. "What knowledge and learning can we gain by just sitting down copying without studying anything else?" "He's right," said another, followed by two or three others. They were soon silenced by a bigger lad (who was a proud lad, jealous of his status as a favorite of the teacher—or perhaps that teacher was afraid of his brute strength), who said: "It's enough to copy. Don't dizzy yourselves standing at the blackboard, giving your-

selves a headache trying to figure out mathematical problems. The sooner we finish this work, the sooner we can play."

"But," said the little one, "I was sent to school by my parents [to learn] so that all the school fees are not paid in vain. And I want to gain skills and knowledge, for the wise man says, 'Knowledge is the sum of a man.'"

Another answers, "But I have seen that some great men with many stars on their chests have never attended school, even though schools existed then." "Be quiet!" says the big boy in a mockingly polite voice, while furtively dropping his slate (as one would drop a pebble concealed in the hand), so that it will crash on the floor, hoping to startle the teacher awake to beat the little ones. This is because he likes to watch his teacher enraged. "You like to think too much. Just get your pocket-money and buy some cake, then eat and drink as much as you like."

"But what if our school is inspected and we who sit in the highest class are found to be stupid? In the past our school had a good name, thanks to the efforts of our old teacher." "Just let it happen," says the big boy. "It won't be our fault. After the inspection this year we shall be free, and we won't be at school any more." Dear readers, shouldn't children in "standard" one, two, or three think this wrong for a school of good name in which they are to remain for several more years?

"What's this chatter?" yells the teacher who, woken by the noise made deliberately by the big boy, grabs his cane and menaces the little boys. "Sir!" says the big boy, seeking to kill two birds with one stone, "These boys were all accusing sir of being lazy and self-serving. They say that sir does not give lessons in anything else, that sir likes only ordering us to copy and that he likes to beat us."

"Sip-sip" goes the cane to the sound of the boys' cries as it strikes their backs. Look meanwhile at the face of the big boy watching them and thinking to himself: "Serves you right! Now as the cane snaps you understand. Do you still plan to go on with this?" And to himself he says, "Were he to beat me with a cane then I'd punch his face. And what would happen then if a visitor came by, or [even] an inspector? Doubtless the school would 'fall' and the teacher would be relieved of his post."

It is clear now that the protests and cries of those students are in vain. These school children are [like] all of us, inferior and average people calling upon our

---

6. [A variant of the Dutch word for "school" is used here, as distinct from traditional Islamic *madrasa* schools.—Ed.]

people to arise and emulate [civilized] humanity. [We do] not do this in order to be a burden or a load. Nor [do we do it] to cause aggravation in the papers that seek to protect or serve the "idol-kings" or "chess-kings." For what is all this noise made by the people of Trengganu in the papers saying this and that? As a matter of fact their "government"[7] is a "despotic monarchy." It would be different if they had a "parliament" under the direction of the people of that state. Then such things would be possible. More importantly, I feel that the Malays should remain Malays, not the "civilized" Malays who pretend to follow the new ways while, in fact, their Malayness is just a category or uniform. God alone knows the answer [a common Arabic expression]. The "responsibility" rests upon the teachers and leaders [of the Malays]. And here [just as in Egypt] the cries of Mustafa Kamil Pasha may be heard. He tried to help his oppressed people remove the ferocious British lion from their necks. However, there were those who thought him a fool pursuing a lost cause. Yet he, in fact, showed his love for his homeland, the land of his birth, attacked by people without any right to that place.

7. [This word and the following words in quotation marks are transliterations of English terms.—Ed.]

The Unity of Human Life

Achmad Dachlan (Java, 1868–1923) received a traditional education in Java, but was influenced by modernist teachings during his three years of study at Mecca. He spent much of his life as a teacher of religion in the new educational system promoted by the Dutch Administration. One of several reformers who held that secular education needed a leavening of Islamic teaching, he and his followers devised and used new teaching material in Dutch, Javanese, and Indonesian. Active in many of the leading organizations of the day—the cultural Budi Utomo (High Endeavor), the educational Jami'at Khair (Benevolent Association), and the political Sarekat Islam (Islamic Association)—he also founded his own organization, the Muhammadiyah, which became the largest modernist Muslim organization in Southeast Asia. The Muhammadiyah was originally concerned with Muslim education, but later expanded into the entire social welfare sector. Dachlan was an accomplished teacher and organizer, but he wrote very few essays. The text selected here appears to have been part of instructions to Muhammadiyah leaders, exhorting them to provide role models, overcome the force of local custom, gain more knowledge of true Islam, and make it accessible to their followers. The work is not marked by intellectual citations or even religious allusions, but uses Islamic language, such as happiness in the "Hereafter" and the reality of God. Despite Dachlan's opposition to Sufi mysticism, he consistently draws that tradition into his work, especially with his rejection of human desires and reference to the importance of human conscience.[1]

The binding role for human life consists of a knowledge that is too large for humans to consider. Therefore it is hoped that readers will give this lesson serious consideration, remember it, and read it slowly.

To manage one's life a person should use an instrument, that is, the Qur'an. Are there reasons for all people to have common feelings? [Of course there are!] First of all, human beings, regardless of ethnicity, actually come from one [set of] ancestors, that is, Adam and Eve. So all humans are related to each other, because they are from one blood. The second reason is to establish a peaceful and happy order of human life that is impossible to gain without having common feelings and unified hearts. This is undeniably true.

O leaders, please think! Since the era of the Prophet, his Companions, and early leaders of the Muslim community, up to the present, there has been no common feelings and unified hearts among human beings. Though there were very famous and educated individuals [throughout that history] and many worked for long periods, they failed to achieve commonality.

Kyai Haji Ahmad Dachlan, "Kesatuan Hidup Manusia" (The Unity of Human Life), in *Pesan-Pesan Dua Pemimpin Besar Islam Indonesia (The Messages of Two Great Leaders of Indonesian Islam)*, edited by Abdul Munir Malkan (Yogyakarta, Indonesia: Medio, 1986), pp. 7–15. Text delivered as a speech to Muhammadiyah leaders in 1923. Translation from Indonesian by Achmad Jainuri. Introduction by Howard M. Federspiel.

1. Alfian, *Muhammadiyah: The Political Behavior of a Muslim Modernist Organization Under Dutch Colonialism* (Yogyakarta, Indonesia: Gadjah Mada University Press, 1989); Abdul Mukti 'Ali, "Modern Islamic Thought in Indonesia," *Mizan (The Scales)*, volume 2, number 1, 1984, pp. 11–29; Howard M. Federspiel, "The Muhammadijah: A Study of an Orthodox Islamic Movement in Indonesia," *Indonesia*, number 10, October 1970, pp. 57–80; Achmad Jainuri, *Muhammadijah: Gerakan Reformasi Islam di Jawa pada Awal Abad Kedua Puluh (The Muhammadiyah: An Islamic Reform Movement in Twentieth Century Java)* (Surabaya, Indonesia: Bina Ilmu, 1981); James L. Peacock, *Purifying the Faith: The Muhammaijah Movement in Indonesian Islam* (Tempe, Ariz.: Arizona State University Program for Southeast Asian Studies, 1992).

O leaders, do not be surprised! Look to your right and to your left! Everything is in disorder, is it not? Remember, I do not simply look at one nation, but at all human beings. Even if we focus on a single nation, we see that there is no common intention and will. This is not safe, but just the opposite, it is dangerous. Why? First, we leaders are not in agreement [with one another]. We neglect each other; one denies the other's knowledge, although we are aware that human beings need that knowledge. Beyond the leaders' lack of sufficient knowledge, there is also narrow-mindedness, so that all things are decided without certainty, like groping in the dark. From such a condition, a great debate arises among the leaders themselves.

The second reason is that the leaders have not yet led their people by [their own] actual behavior, but only lead by use of vocal direction. They are still trying to understand themselves, and to spread their understanding to the people, but they have not [yet] related this understanding to their own action and to the behavior of others. Consequently, most leaders rely on their voice to spread their opinions, although their own behavior is very bad and has a negative impact. Clearly, they are captive to their own desires, without any understanding and self-awareness. For example, personal appetite drives them to be lazy and stingy, and these characteristics mark their leadership styles. That is the way personal appetite works negatively in human life.

The third reason is that the majority of leaders do not have a universal goal. [. . .] They relate only to their own group, not universal humanity. Actually, some of them just think about themselves, their own bodies, and their own life. If their bodies get what they need and are satiated, they feel they earned the reward from God, and they believe that they have reached their goal. This kind of thing is so common in our society that the organization and community [such leaders] provide are broken into many parts; even to the original condition before the leaders arrived. Their hearts are then so heavy [when they realize they have not succeeded].

The Road toward Unity

Leaders have understood the behavior, condition, and traditions held by the people they lead, so as to be able to proceed properly, that is, remembering "the conditions of their own bodies." Do not rush, be clear, and understand which conditions are acceptable and which ones to reject. Do not ever oppress and force people to speak and act against their will. By following these suggestions, conditions for effective communication will be established and proceed to the goal itself, that is, the unity of human hearts.

It is common in society that what is understood and done in accordance with the teacher's guidance, a friend's opinion, or personal preference will make an individual happy. The advice will be followed consistently, particularly when such advice was also followed by their forebears. That advice is considered as bringing happiness to those who believe and causing suffering to those who are in denial. O leaders, please look and see! Does this kind of thing occur only in our own Muslim community? Buddhists, Christians, and Jews are much the same, [I suspect,] much the same as among Muslims; isn't this true?

O leaders! Since "truth" is actually unified (*tawhidi*), the question is how we obtain "truth" in order not to be false before God Almighty.

People usually refuse a new way that is different from what they have been following, because they believe that the new way will cause unhappiness and suffering, even though, in reality, the new matter will actually bring happiness and pleasure. This refusal will always occur, unless the [presenters of the new] have the common interests of people at heart and work for the universal human future.

Is the traditional conduct, described above, right and good? Of course not, because such people only use local tradition as their legal reference, while this tradition should not be used as a determinant for "good," "bad," "right," and "wrong." The reference for those legal and ethical judgments is the holy heart.

This situation should be studied, perceived, and pondered, because, in essence, happiness and unhappiness are at stake. Therefore, I call on leaders to think together to bring human hearts together. If this cannot be realized, the leaders will need to start from themselves, by unifying their own hearts for the interest of all people [as a precursor to the effort in the wider community]. This is the real obligation for them.

O leaders! Let us come together in a common place to speak the truth—without division, but for all universally. Do not feel self-satisfied and indifferent, or else we will not discover the truth. After that, let us promote one mode of conduct, one vision, and one mission. In short, all human beings should be in agreement with united hearts, so that they will attain happiness and realize the ultimate purpose of life.

[One might ask] why people neglect or deny the truth? Actually, there are several reasons:

1. Stupidity, which is very common.
2. Disagreement with the person bringing the truth.
3. Holding to traditional ways from forebears.
4. Fear of being separated from relatives and friends.
5. Fear of losing honor, position, job status, pleasure, and the like.

There are a few things to remember:

1. People need religion.
2. Originally, religion shines, but later it appears to become dull. Truly, it is not religion that becomes dull, but the person who follows the religion.
3. People should follow the rules made in accordance with the edicts of religious scholars. One should never make decisions by oneself [in matters of religion].
4. People must ever seek new knowledge. They should never feel satisfied with their own knowledge, or ever refuse knowledge from others.
5. People need to apply the knowledge they have. Do not let knowledge go wasted.

The Creature of God

All God's creatures have destiny. Every destiny extends toward a goal. And truly there must be a road to that goal.

It is obvious that God creates time and the path by which the goal can be reached. If this is so, then the destiny of a creature can be attained by following its time and path. Indeed, every condition depends on God's will, and God has provided all the necessary conditions.

Humankind

Actually, humans want no destiny but safety and happiness in this world and in the Hereafter.

The path for achieving human destiny requires the use of common sense, that is, the common intellect. A good intellect is characterized by the ability to select with care and consideration, and to place [the decision] in a courageous heart after selecting it.

Intellect

The nature of intellect is to accept all knowledge. That knowledge becomes the passion of intellect, because the intellect is like a seed in the earth. In order for a seed to grow, the seed needs to be watered and have all its needs fulfilled. Similarly, the intellect will not grow properly without being showered by knowledge. And all of this is absolutely in accordance with God's will.

The Teaching of Logic

The teaching of logic is conducted through learning *'ilm manthiq*, the science of logic, which reflects reality. This science can be gained only through the learning and teaching process, because humans have no other way to know names and languages without teachers who got the knowledge from their teachers, and so on. The [dependence on such learning] indicates that human beings have no power to know the primary source of knowledge, except those who get guidance from God Almighty.

Human beings who obtain more than basic principles of knowledge are like the person who takes jewelry, makes a fastener, and then uses it as a decoration on an item of clothing. This means that a person who can speak clearly and straight to the point, is actually supported by the other knowledge he or she has.

So, it is not surprising that some people speak very well and to the point. What is especially good and helpful is when a person can accept or agree with another's good religious opinion and pass it on to others. People should not be considered weak if they do not add to the explanation that they received. Rather, they should be regarded as furthering wisdom.

The Perfection of Intellect

There are six conditions for maintaining the perfect intellect and keeping it functioning:

First of all, logic should base itself on love and affection. Without this selection of love and affection, a human will not reach ultimate wisdom. On the other hand, a person with no love and affection will only follow behavior that is guided by negative emotional power.

The second is one's struggle to gain the highest happiness in this world and the Hereafter. This takes serious effort, for it will not be attained without great effort, and even sacrifices of a spiritual, financial, emotional, and intellectual nature.

Third, the [intellectual] endeavor should be undertaken carefully, since "good" is often accompanied by "bad." Hence, sometimes, a person who seeks a good thing gains a bad thing that should be refused. This occurs especially when the seeker has no real knowledge on the matter, but simply follows the traditions of his community.

Next, the seeker should have good intentions with regard to the matter under consideration, so that good and strong motivation will keep his search on the right path.

Fifth, the seeker of intellectual activity should take care and give it full attention. This is very important, because humans have a natural inclination to forget and become careless.

Finally, the person undertaking the activity should apply it properly. Knowledge will not bring a valuable and meaningful result without being set in its proper place.

Human Needs

Every individual in this world has personal needs. In reality, no human being can exist properly without support from others. Accordingly, every human being should understand the relevance of such needs.

Actually, useful knowledge for the intellect and brain is needed by human beings even more than food is needed for the stomach to help grow physically. Actually, seeking riches in the world is not as demanding as seeking knowledge to improve the spiritual quality of one's own behavior. In reality, we can find that the number of people devoted to this [spiritual improvement] is fewer than those who are less devoted, and the number of people who understand in principle is greater than those who manifest understanding in real behavior. Therefore, even people with

perfect logic at their disposal need to understand by searching within.

The Person with Accomplished Intellect

If human intellect falls into danger, there is an instrument in the human body that can control [the intellect], that is, the holy heart that consistently loves spiritual serenity. It is an obligation that the person with the accomplished intellect should avoid any risk that would destroy the holiness of the heart.

The spiritual level of a good person is truly regulated by the holiness of one's heart. A person will not reach real happiness in this world and the Hereafter without having exhibited behavior with an ethical basis. Therefore, one who wants to be wise should follow the road of wise people, that is, by striving to defeat one's own personal desires. In this way, one will be able to behave in accordance with legal, ethical, and aesthetic values, and will have a great opportunity to attain real happiness in this world and the Hereafter, as well as promoting spiritual serenity.

Therefore, it is obvious that those who want the good life in this world and the Hereafter cannot attain it simply by following the desire for fun and pleasure, or by being envious of the aims of others. It is possible to attain enjoyment in this world, even in very negative ways. But for genuine happiness in the Hereafter, one must attach oneself to the positive ways mentioned earlier.

The Difference between "Smart" and "Stupid"

The words "smart" and "stupid" are contradictory in meaning. For some people, however, they can have similar meanings, that is, in actual life the smart and the stupid person both like what they agree with and hate what they dislike. [Hence, it is difficult to ascertain stupidity or smartness from those choices.] Moreover, some matters that smart people can resolve can also sometimes be resolved by stupid ones. Therefore, it is necessary that a person with an accomplished intellect be able to perceive the difference between smart and stupid people.

Actually, the difference between the smart and stupid person can be seen clearly when they appear together. In this situation, the smart man will look confident, while the stupid one looks shaky and uncertain.

Actually there are three differences between them. The first is that the smart person absolutely understands what will lead him to happiness or to suffering, while the stupid person does not.

The smart person will, of course, always try to seek the right road toward real happiness, and to avoid the situation that will lead to unhappiness or suffering. The smart person who neglects God's guidance and follows personal desires will gradually fall into danger and suffering.

Ijtihad and *Taqlid*

Syekh Ahmad Surkati (Sudan-Java, 1872–1943) was an educator, intellectual, and businessman. Originally from a pious family in the Sudan, he received a traditional Muslim education in Egypt and then studied extensively in Medina and Mecca; later he received a diploma from an institution in Istanbul. He lived in Malaya and Sumatra before being summoned to teach at the Arab Benevolent Society's school in Jakarta at the age of thirty-four. Later he was a leader of the Union for Reformation and Guidance, generally known as *al-Irsyad*, which promoted modernist Muslim teachings in the schools that it founded. Surkati's writings on Islam are reflective of those of Muhammad 'Abduh (chapter 3), and his work was highly regarded among the Muslim modernist community in Java of his day. Not being a *sayyid* (descendant of the Prophet), he was at odds with the *sayyid*-dominated Arab population that dominated the Arab community in Southeast Asia. Some of his writing concentrated on the equality found in Islam and the lack of religious justification for special status for those from the Prophet's Quraysh tribe, or for those descended from the Prophet. He was especially attacked by *sayyids* and Qurayshis, who regarded him as an upstart with poor breeding. Perhaps in defense, Surkati made far more use of Qur'anic verses in justifying his arguments than did other Southeast Asian modernists of the period. The work chosen here for translation centers on the essential difference between traditionalists and modernists in their examination of religious sources.[1]

Ijtihad means to expend effort and capacity in something which involves some difficulty. As a jurisprudential term it means to derive *shari'a* laws from logical proofs and detailed general principles, that is, the ability to go into further detail or to choose one of two laws laid down in writing by following one of the procedures for choosing between laws recognized by the foundations of jurisprudence, such as: that its narrators are more numerous, although equal in characteristics of justice and respect; that the chain of authorities of the *hadith* [tradition of the Prophet] is stronger; that it is a saying which has the potential for specific action; that it is more detailed; that it is more intelligible; that it is in the Qurayshi dialect; that it came after the *hijra* [the exodus of Muslims from Mecca in 622 that marks the beginning of the Islamic era]; that it is universal; that it

is derived from original law; that it is a plausible report; that it is consistent with another proof, or with the action of the people of Medina; that it is more secure in the area of rights; or better prevents the imposition of punishments; or lightens the burden of observing the precepts of religion and devotional observances, or is more apposite as a means; or better prevents harm; or better lifts restrictions; or it is more conducive to acceptance in the area of calling people to religion.

If all this is understood, then one knows that there can be no *ijtihad* when there is a clear text that is not contradicted by an equivalent one; nor where it is not known whether one of the laws falls under one of the principles of the *shari'a*—in the first case because the law is definite and there is no *ijtihad* in definite matters, and in the second case because something

Syekh Ahmad Surkati, *Al-Masa'il al-thalath* (*The Three Questions*) (Cairo, Egypt: Dar al-'Ulum li'l-Tiba'a, 1977), pp. 19–36. First published in 1925. Translation from Arabic by Natalie Mobini-Kesheh. Introduction by Howard M. Federspiel.

1. Natalie Mobini-Kesheh, *The Hadrami Awakening: Community and Identity in the Netherlands East Indies.*

1900–1942 (Ithaca, N.Y.: Cornell University Southeast Asia Program Publications, 2000), pp. 71–90; Deliar Noer, *The Modernist Muslim Movement in Indonesia, 1900–1942* (Singapore: Oxford University Press, 1973), pp. 61–69; "Syekh Ahmad Soorkati," *Ensiklopedi Islam* (*The Encyclopedia of Islam*) (Jakarta, Indonesia: Ichtiar Baru van Hoeve, 1993), volume 4, pp. 280–284.

is not lawful if it does not fall under one of the principles of the *shari'a*.

Thus adhering to that which is established by God and His Prophet, and making appeal to the Book of God and the *sunna* of His Prophet, this is Islam. In His word the most high: "So hold fast to the revelation given to you. You are truly on a straight path." [Sura 43, Verse 43] In His word the most high: "So, you and those who turned to God with you, should walk along the straight path, as you have been commanded, and do not transgress." [Sura 11, Verse 112] In His word the most high: "Follow the revelation given to you by your Lord, and do not follow any other lord apart than Him." [Sura 7, Verse 3] In His word the most high: "We have sent down to you the Book containing the truth, in whose light you should judge among the people as God has shown you." [Sura 4, Verse 105] In His word the most high: "Hold firmly to what We have given you, and remember what is therein, that you make take heed." [Sura 2, Verse 63] In His word the most high: "This is My straight path, so walk along, and do not follow other ways, lest you should turn away from the right one. All this has He commanded. You may perhaps take heed for yourselves." [Sura 6, Verse 153] In His word the most high: "Accept what the Messenger gives you, and refrain from what he forbids." [Sura 59, Verse 7]

As for *ijtihad* in religion—that is, expending effort and contemplating the Book of God and the *sunna* of His Prophet (peace be upon him), and adapting the established laws to them—this is an obligation on every rational person who understands the Arabic language and has knowledge of the scope of the law.

In His word the most high: "Give glad tidings to my creatures. Those who listen to the Word, and then follow the best it contains, are the ones who have been guided by God, and are people of wisdom." [Sura 39, Verses 17–18] "The best" means the most appropriate according to the situation, time, and place, and the strongest in its chain of transmission and as a proof, and the most logical. It is known that whosoever does not expend effort in contemplation and reflection is not able to distinguish between the good and the best. In His word the most high: "Hold fast to what We have given you, and remember what is therein, that you make take heed." [Sura 2, Verse 63]

Whosoever does not expend effort in reflection will not adhere strongly to what is in the Book, as God commands him, and will not bear its contents in mind. In His word the most high: "We have sent down a Book to you which is blessed, so that people may apply their minds to its revelations, and people of wisdom may reflect." [Sura 38, Verse 29] From this it is clear that God revealed the Book in order that we may reflect on its contents.

In His word the most high: "Do they not ponder on what the Qur'an says? Or have their hearts been sealed with locks?" [Sura 47, Verse 24] This is a stern reproach to whosoever turns away from the Qur'an and does not reflect on its contents. In His word the most high: "And hold on firmly together to the rope of God, and be not divided among yourselves." [Sura 3, Verse 103] It is inconceivable that people would cling to it and hold fast to its laws if they do not know what it contains. God has commanded that we have recourse to His Book and to the *sunna* of His Prophet when there are differences and contention. In His word the most high: "In whatever matter you disagree, the ultimate judgment rests with God." [Sura 42, Verse 10]

In His word the most high: "Should you disagree about something, refer it to God and the Messenger, if you believe in God and the Last Day. This is good for you and the best of settlements." [Sura 4, Verse 59] It is not possible for us to have recourse to the Book of God and the *sunna* of His Prophet unless we are familiar with them both and contemplate what they contain. In His word the most high: "Say, 'My way, and that of my followers, is to call you to God on evidence as clear as seeing with one's own eyes.'" [Sura 12, Verse 108] There is no doubt that whosoever does not know what the Prophet brought cannot invite people to God "on evidence as clear as the seeing with one's eyes,'" because seeing is the proof and evidence and there is no proof in the hand of the blind follower.

In His word the most high "We have surely sent apostles with clear signs, and sent with them the Book and the Balance [the scales of right and wrong], so that people may stand by justice." [Sura 57, Verse 25] There is no doubt that those who do not have the Book and the Balance in their hand cannot stand by justice, and that if by chance someday they may stand by justice, it is without seeing with their own eyes.

In His word the most high: "And We have indeed made the Qur'an easy to understand. So is there any one who will be warned?" [Sura 54, Verse 17] That is, whosoever searches for its meanings will be assisted. In His word the most high: "And we have revealed to you the Book as an exposition of every thing." [Sura 16, Verse 89] "Has the time not yet come when the hearts of believers should be moved by the thought of God and the truth that has been sent down, so that they should not be like those who received the Book before them but whose hearts were hardened after a lapse of time? [Sura 57, Verse 16] [. . .] How clear have We made Our signs for those who understand." [Sura 6, Verse 98]

As for those who engage in *taqlid*, following a particular person blindly in all matters of religion, in such a manner that they prefer what that person says over what is fixed in the Book and the *sunna*, on the pretext that that person knows more than others, or that he is acquainted with the proofs of religion, despite the fact that they themselves are rational and free to choose and able to comprehend evidence, this is prohibited by reason and by law, according to the text of the Book and the *sunna*, and according to the ways of the Companions of the Prophet and the succeeding generation and the renowned *imam*s [founders of the major legal schools in Sunni Islam]. God has told us that such individuals are more lost than cattle. For cattle are not given this capacity, while God has given the capacity to humans, but they do not use it. They refuse to be anything but cattle. In His word the most high in the Sura of the Wall Between Heaven and Hell: "Many of the *jinn*s [spirit beings] and human beings have We destined for Hell, who possess hearts but do not feel, have eyes but do not see, have ears but do not hear—like cattle, even worse than them, for they are unconcerned." [Sura 7, Verse 179]

Indeed God, the most glorious, has censured those who in past times engaged in *taqlid* of their forefathers and leaders in their religion, and who turned away from the divine proofs, and who relied on the baseless ideas that they inherited from their forefathers and ancestors. God relates to us their rebuke so that we will learn a lesson from their mistakes. In disgust and condemnation, in His word the most high in the Sura of the Cow: "When it is said to them: 'Follow what God has revealed,' they say: 'No, we shall follow only the ways of our fathers'—even though their fathers had no wisdom or guidance!" [Sura 2, Verse 170] In His word the most high in the Sura of The Feast: "When you say to them: 'Come to what God has revealed, and the Prophet,' they say: 'Sufficient to us is the faith that our fathers had fol-

lowed,' even though their fathers had no knowledge or guidance." [Sura 5, Verse 104] In His word the most high in the Sura of Luqman: "When you ask them to follow what God has revealed, they say: 'No. We shall follow what we found our ancestors following," Even though the devil were calling them to the torment of Hell!" [Sura 31, Verse 21] In His word the most high in the Sura of the Allied Troops: "And they will say: 'O our Lord, we obeyed our leaders and elders, but they only led us astray. O our Lord, give them a double punishment, and put a grievous curse upon them." [Sura 33, Verse 67–68] In His word the most high in the Sura of the Ornaments of Gold: "Thus, whenever We sent an admonisher to a people before you, the decadent among them said: 'We found our fathers following this way, and we are walking in their footsteps." [Sura 43, Verse 23] "He said: 'Even if I bring you better guidance than the one you found your fathers following?'" [Sura 43, Verse 24]

Whosoever opposes a verse of the Qur'an or the confirmed *sunna* of the Messenger of God (peace be upon him) is following the design of those who God rebukes in the Qur'an, and is deserving of the proper punishment, because all judgments and punishments and rewards and recompense are indeed in accordance with attributes and not with the essence of individuals. In His word the most high: "It is not dependent on your wishes, nor the wishes of the people of the Book, [but] whosoever does ill will be punished for it, and will find no protector or friend apart from God." [Sura 4, Verse 123] In His word the most high: "Are the unbelievers among you any better than they? Or is there immunity for you in the Scriptures?" [Sura 54, Verse 43] In His word the most high: "Or have you a Book in which you read that you can surely have whatever you choose?" [Sura 68, Verses 37–38] "This is the law of God that has prevailed among His creatures. [Sura 40, Verse 85] [. . .] You will not find any change in the law of God." [Sura 48, Verse 23]

[. . .] It is understood from all this that the blind *taqlid* that is taking place today is not permissible, except for the simple person who is possessed of no understanding or knowledge, and no inclination and no reason. *Ijtihad* in understanding the Book and the *sunna* is obligatory upon every person who possesses understanding, and whose circumstances afford the opportunity, in every time and place, to the best of one's ability. In the sense that we see it used today, *taqlid* is contrary to reason and humanity, contrary to the Book and the *sunna*, contrary to the consensus of the Companions of the Prophet, and contrary to the instructions of the *imam*s whom those practicing *taqlid* claim to be imitating. Its perpetrators who have the capacity to understand the Book of God and the *sunna* of His Messenger are sinners who fabricate a lie against God, who speak against God that which they do not know. In His word the most high: "Do not utter the lies your tongues make up: 'This is lawful, and this is forbidden,' in order to impute lies to God. For they who impute lies to God will not find fulfilment." [Sura 16, Verse 116] In His word the most high: "Tell them: 'My Lord has forbidden repugnant acts, whether open or disguised, sin and unjust oppression, associating others with God with which He has sent down no authority, and saying things of God of which you have no knowledge.'" [Sura 7, Verse 33] God said to His Prophet: "Do not follow that of which you have no knowledge. Verily the ear, the eye, the heart, each will be questioned [on Judgment Day]." [Sura 17, Verse 36]

Those who perform *taqlid* say: In the religion of God we do not use our ears, our eyes, or our hearts, nor do we pursue knowledge. Rather, we pursue the opinion of so-and-so and so-and-so. In His word the most high: "We have given examples of every kind for people, in this Qur'an, so that they may contemplate. every kind of Parable in order that they may receive admonition. A clear discourse which expounds all things without any crookedness, so that they may take heed for themselves." [Sura 39, Verses 27–28]

Those who perform *taqlid* say: The Qur'an is not comprehensible and our minds are not adequate to understand it. So they made it inaccessible in vaults and contented themselves with repetition of its sounds, without the reflection that God commanded. In this they follow the habits of those who preceded them. The example uttered by God in the Sura of the Congregation is applicable to them. In His word the most high: "The likeness of those who were charged with [the law of] the Torah, which they did not observe, is that of a donkey who carries a load of books [oblivious of what they contain]." [Sura 62, Verse 5]

God says to His servants: "So be not like those who became disunited and differed among themselves after clear proofs had come to them. For them is great suffering." [Sura 3, Verse 105] In His word the most high: "As for those who have created schisms in their order, and formed different sects, you have no concern with them." [Sura 6, Verse 159] In His word the most high: "And hold on firmly together to the rope of God, and be not divided among yourselves." [Sura 3, Verse 103] Those who perform *taqlid* say: Our divisions are a blessing. They say, we adhere to the words of so-and-so and so-and-so, irrespective of the Book of God, and we refer whatever causes contention among us to the words of whomever we have chosen to be our *imam*, irrespective of God and His Messenger, and whatever we have differences about, we seek judgment on it from so-and-so and so-and-so. Thus they are divided and scattered. Each party is delighted with what it has, and every group claims the superiority of what it has, without reason or proof or guidance or the luminous Book.

God revealed His Book to creation and He said in it: "Verily there are signs in this for people of understanding." [Sura 20, Verse 128] Those who perform *taqlid* say: We are not among those emdued with understanding. In His word the most high: "So take heed, O people with eyes!" [Sura 59, Verse 2] So they say: We are not among those with eyes to see. In His word the most high: "There are surely signs in these things for those who understand." [Sura 13, Verse 4] So they say, we are not among those who understand.

Indeed those who perform *taqlid* are not content to bear the shame of apathy and ignorance. They do not merely confess that they are not seekers of knowledge, or endowed with understanding and reason. They even seek shade under the shadow of apathy and laziness and happily endure the shame of resisting the Book of God and the *sunna* of His Messenger, peace be upon him. They put the Book of God behind their backs. On top of all this, they denounce the people of virtue and knowledge and reason, who hold fast to the Book and the *sunna*, and they accuse them of *bid'a* [innovation] and deviation. How strange that the blind denounce the seeing, the deaf denounce the hearing, the stupid protest against the intelligent, the wise, and the able, and the lost resent the rightly guided ones! By God, this is terrible news and an unjust verdict.

[. . .] Those who perform *taqlid* are generally divided into three groups.

First: those who have the capacity and opportunity to understand the proofs of God and His laws, but do not use their mind to understand the Book of God and the *sunna* of His Messenger. They do not reflect on them, nor do they want to listen to them. God refers to such people in the Sura of the Wall Between Heaven and Hell. In His word the most high: "Many of the *jinn*s and human beings have We destined for Hell, who possess hearts but do not feel, have eyes but do not see, have ears but do not hear— like cattle, even worse than them, for they are unconcerned." [Sura 7, Verse 179]

Second: those who do not have the capacity to understand arguments by themselves, or who lack the opportunity to undertake the obligation of contemplation and reflection on the Book and the *sunna* and to memorize what they say. Such people are commanded by the Lawgiver to ask the people of knowledge about the laws brought by God and His Messenger, in accordance with their need. In His word the most high: "If you do not know, then ask the keepers of the oracles of God." [Sura 16, Verse 43] In the words of the Prophet, peace be upon him: "Verily, the cure for incapacity is to ask." But he should not ask the knowledgeable person for his opinion. Rather, he should ask him about the laws he has memorized from God and His Messenger, and ask for his help in understanding whatever is difficult for him to understand.

Third: those who are simple and barely able to understand speech, and who cannot comprehend arguments. Such people have no alternative but to undertake absolute *taqlid*, because God does not expect from anyone more than they are capable of. But they are obliged at least to ask the knowledgeable person who they imitate whether the ruling he gives is based on his own opinion, in which case other opinions exist as well, or whether it is from God and His Messenger. They should not be fanatical toward a particular *imam* or religious official, because of the possibility that they may meet one later who is more knowledgeable or more correct than the one they met first. If they are fanatical toward a certain individual and prefer him above others without reason, or give preference to his opinion over the opinion of someone who is higher than him, then they are just following their own desire. Those who perform *taqlid* are not obliged to follow one school, as confirmed by Ibn Burhan [probably Burhanuddin Marghinani, died circa 1197], [Muhyi al-Din] al-Nawawi [1233–1277], Ahmad ibn Hanbal [780–855], and others, except that they should not switch from the sayings of the first religious authority they follow unless there is sound reason to do so.

[. . .] It is said that the prerequisites for a consummate *mujtahid* [religious scholar] are that he be knowledgeable about all that relates to the laws from the texts of the Book and the *sunna*. This refers to approximately 500 clear and manifest verses from the Book, according to [Abu Hamid Muhammad] al-Ghazzali [1058–1111] and [Muhyi al-Din] Ibn 'Arabi [1165–1240], and others, and similarly with *hadith*. In the opinion of *Imam* Ahmad [ibn Hanbal, 780–855], it relates to 1200 *hadith*. In fact it is even more than that, as al-Nawawi and others have said. It is not obligatory to memorize them or to keep them in one's mind, but rather what is intended is the ability to refer to them, and awareness of what is in the books. He should also be familiar with matters of consensus, so that he does not breach it. What is intended is the consensus of all the Companions or all the *mujtahid*s who meet the prerequisites in the age, not just the four well-known ones [that is, the founders of the four major Sunni legal schools].

In addition he should know the Arabic tongue and its principles of grammar, syntax, inflection, and rhetoric sufficiently well to interpret what is said in the Book and the *sunna*, if necessary in consultation with others. It is not an obligation to memorize, but rather the ability to consult and understand is sufficient. He should also be knowledgeable in the roots of jurisprudence and the verses of the Book and the *sunna* that abrogate others, and those that are abrogated. It is generally said that these [abrogated sources] are five verses from the Book and ten *hadith* from the *sunna*, but it is also said that the *hadith* number 25 and the verses are more than that. Furthermore, he should be knowledgeable of the circumstances of those who related the *hadith* and their terminology. The *mujtahid* does not need to perform *ijtihad* in all matters, but only those in which it is necessary, and only those matters in which he is able to perform *ijtihad*, for this is the truth.

Nobody says that a single *imam* is thoroughly familiar with everything that the Lawgiver has brought. Nor is there anyone who is able to master the *sunna* of the Messenger of God, peace be upon him. This is said by [Abu 'Abdullah Muhammad] Shafi'i [767–820], and it is the opinion of the majority as related by al-Safi al-Hindi ['Ala' al-Din al-Hindi al-Baqi al-Shafi'i, died 1315]. It is the favored opinion, as Ibn Daqiq al-'Aid [1228–1302] recalled. Al-Ghazzali agreed on this, and so did [Abu'l Qadir] al-Rafa'i [al-Qazwini, died 1226] and others.

The Book takes precedence over the *sunna* when there is contradiction, due to its greater constancy and the certainty of its correctness, and *sunna* with continuous succession takes precedence over that which is related by only one person. There are degrees in this which can be known from the books on *hadith*. Similarly, the consensus of the Companions takes precedence over those following them, because the latter are not based on the text. Then follows the consensus of the *mujtahid*s of a given era, but only those who have indicated their reasoning. Then follows analogy in accordance with the reason on which a judgment is based, and then there is basic freedom. If the *ijtihad*s of a *mujtahid* at different times contradict each other, or the *ijtihad*s of two *mujtahid*s on the same matter contradict each other, then truly the truth is with one of them, as Malik [ibn Anas, 710–796] and [Abu 'Abdullah Muhammad] al-Shafi'i [767–820], and Abu Hanifa [circa 699–767] say. The *mujtahid* is rewarded in any case, as confirmed in this *hadith* of the Prophet, peace be upon him: "If a judge performs *ijtihad* and he is correct, then he is due two rewards; and if he performs *ijtihad* and he is wrong, then he is due one reward."

The foregoing demonstrates that the *taqlid* which is criticized by God and His Messenger and the *imam*s, and which we criticize following them, is not criticized for deriving law based on reasoning from trustworthy authorities, nor for having a good opinion of the well-known *'ulama'* [religious scholars] with regard to what they quote to us from God and His Messenger, nor for following their guiding principle in the derivation of law, nor for respecting their consensus. Rather, the *taqlid* which is censured involves depending on a saying that one has no evidence for, or to refer to the saying of a particular *imam* in all religious rulings, in such manner that one rejects anything contrary to it and accepts anything in agreement with it, solely on the pretext that that *imam* is more knowledgeable than others, or that he memorized a *shari'a* reason for every ruling, even though it is not evident and one does not remember it oneself. There is no doubt that this pretext is baseless. It is not right for people to judge the learning of a knowledgeable person or his memorization of reasons for every ruling that he has made, unless they know the proofs put forward by others. This requires people to be more knowledgeable than them all, so that they are able to judge between them. There is no doubt that confirming one piece of reasoning is simpler and easier than giving preference to one *imam* over others. Indeed, every person who takes a confidant other than God, and declares permissible whatever he permits, and declares unlawful whatever he declares unlawful, without considering a *shari'a* reason, has taken a master as a deity other than God. The reasoning for this is His word the most high: "They consider their priests and their monks to be gods apart from God." [Sura 9, Verse 31]

According to the interpretation of the Messenger, peace be upon him, as related by 'Adi Ibn Hatim [companion of the Prophet, died circa 687]: "The Messenger of God, may God's blessing and peace be upon him, when he concluded this verse, said: 'They consider their priests and their monks to be gods apart from God.' I said, 'O Messenger of God, we have not taken priests.' And the Messenger said, 'Do they not permit to you what has been forbidden, and you permit it, and they forbid you from that which has been permitted, and you forbid it?' I said, 'Yes.' He said, 'So this is worshiping them.'"

This applies to those who perform *taqlid*, who understand reason but put forward the saying of the person they imitate, on the pretext that he knows more about the situation or is more knowledgeable or understands better the reasons in this matter.

[. . .] It is not our purpose, in opening the door of *ijtihad*, to confirm that it is permissible to breach the consensus put forward by the *imam*s, nor to invalidate what they said. The purpose is to confirm that it is obligatory to take from their words that which is confirmed by reason, and not that which has weak reasoning, and to confirm the prohibition on fanaticism and on the claim that truth or the predominance of reason is limited to only one of the schools of law. It is to urge people to adhere to the Book of God and the *sunna* of His Messenger, and to refer their disagreements to them both and to nothing else, as God instructs them.

Asian Dawn

Hadji Agus Salim (Sumatra-Java, 1884–1954) was a Muslim political activist, journalist, and intellectual. He was born in a state functionary's family, attended Dutch colonial schools, and was one of a few Indonesians to graduate from the technical school in Batavia. He worked with the Dutch consulate in Arabia for a time assisting stranded pilgrims and acting as a point of contact with Indonesian students studying there. Afterward he joined the *Sarekat Islam* (Islamic Association) political movement, serving as one of its primary leaders for twenty-five years, even representing it in the Dutch-run People's Council. He was an important journalist, and also sponsored the *Jong Islamieten Bond* (Young Muslims Union), an organization for Indonesian students in Dutch schools to learn and discuss Islamic teachings, which produced a generation of leaders for Muslim organizations. After independence in 1945, he was a cabinet member in the first Indonesian cabinet. Salim's writing centered on the political issues of the day, particularly the shortcomings of Dutch colonialism, the threat of communism, and the dangers of nationalism not based on Islam. He was an important spokesman for Islamic nationalism and attempted to promote Islamic unity within Indonesia and throughout the world. In the selections presented here, two newspaper articles, Salim described his movement's modernist reforms and criticized the Dutch for running a colonial system lacking the democratic process and human rights that were observed in the Netherlands itself.[1]

Economics, Social Concerns, and Politics

In general our people do not receive much formal education, and those that attend schools receive insufficient amounts of inadequate knowledge; they learn only to read and write at a basic level, but intellectual development and skills are not obtained at all. The traditional manner of gaining knowledge is lacking, nor does a modern means appear either. Also, not even the number of our people who have finished schools, from elementary to higher education, is known. Further, those people do not . . . obtain any knowledge of their own people, our origins and culture, and our social relationships. Rather, everything they study is alien. It is natural then that our people simply become imitators [of Western manners and ways of doing things], even though they are not able to examine the origins of the things which they imitate. In [Islamic] religious terms this is known as *taqlid* [imitation].

It is the nature of *taqlid* to misunderstand. The essence of a matter is not known, but only the superficial label or name. Such people have much in common with the parrot, the animal which is cleverly able to imitate several words, and make it appear that it has mastered the matter, while it is only coincidentally mastering the labels. Obviously, the parrot's mind cannot understand each word and the meanings conveyed.

Consequently, our people generally have limited perceptions of the three words written above: "eco-

Hadji Agus Salim, "Ekonomi, Sosial dan Politik" (Economics, Social Concerns, and Politics) and "Haji Agus Salim Berbahaya?" (Is Haji Agus Salim Dangerous?), *Fadjar Asia* (*Asian Dawn*), February 13–15, 1929, and February 20, 1930. Translation from Indonesian by Erni Haryanti Kahfi. Introduction by Howard M. Federspiel.

1. Erni Haryanti Kahfi, "Islam and Indonesian Nationalism: The Political Thought of Haji Agus Salim," *Studia Islamika*, volume 4, number 3, 1997, pp. 1–64; Deliar Noer,

The Modernist Muslim Movement in Indonesia, 1900–1942 (Singapore: Oxford University Press, 1973), pp. 120–275; G. F. Pijper, *Studien over de geschidenis van de Islam in Indonesia 1900–1950* (*Studies on the History of Islam in Indonesia, 1900–1950*) (Leiden, Netherlands: E. J. Brill, 1977), pp. 141–144; Takashi Shiraishi, *An Age in Motion: Popular Radicalism in Java, 1912–1926* (Ithaca, N.Y.: Cornell University Press, 1990).

nomics, social, and politics." This is because each word is understood in a particular and limited way. This happens not only among the uneducated or less educated, but also among the educated and the students who are now acknowledged as intelligentsia; almost all of them have limited understanding of the terms.

For example, "economics" is defined as a matter of property income; so a "bank," which is referred to as a "national bank," is regarded as the key to improving our economics, because the bank is continually referred to as the instrument for managing dividends or profit sharing among company partners.

There are people who regard "our economics" as related to a "financial company," who do not perceive that the Bank of the Netherlands is not really a national bank of the Dutch people. In the same way, the Bank of England is not a national bank of Englishmen, and the Banque de France is not a national bank of Frenchmen. Rather, within these three countries people understand that these banks are "capital companies," which draw together the assets of many people from wide economic groups and entrust it to a small group of capitalists who run the bank.

On the other hand, the efforts and actions of the P. S. I. [*Partai Sareikat Islam*, Islamic Union Party] are designed to hinder the loss of lands of native people due to them by the law of land ownership and at the same time demand the return of thousands of *bau* [a *bau* is 0.7 hectares, or 1.7 acres] of lands, from which millions of *rupiah*s are diverted. [. . .] This effort [and the benefit it entails] is not understood as a meaningful economic effort; actually, it deeply concerns the economics of our fellow countrymen.

Economics has great meaning to us. Although we have not yet achieved great success with our efforts, it is at least useful to liberate minds and understand that our economy has been surrendered and depends on the alien nation that rules us, that is, the Netherlands. At the same time, it is now generally accepted that there are two goals that should be achieved simultaneously, that is, to gain control of our own economics and to remove the power of foreign capital in our economics.

Among us are those who take great pride in the collection of national resources in a national bank. However, these people do not regard the effort of the P. S. I. in challenging land inheritance laws as an effort to maintain national capital, which demonstrates how unappreciated its value really is.

The P. S. I. opposition to usury can be regarded as having great meaning for our economics, especially for those who want to think and understand this. Although there is no [legal] prohibition for people to engage in usury, the opposition will raise the consciousness and hostility of native people against companies associated with usury, such as pawnshops and installment-loan establishments. This inner hostility will then become a fertile base for people to establish their own companies [not relying on usurious practice] to replace these offending companies.

The foregoing constitutes our explanation of our economic understanding and direction, which is broader than the narrow understanding of *taqlid*.

Regarding social perceptions, generally speaking, those who engage in *taqlid* also do not have a wide view. Social awareness is interpreted in a very narrow sense, that is, helping people overcome misery, especially through the use of hospitals, disease control, establishing poor houses and orphanages, giving assistance to the poor, and founding schools to overcome ignorance.

Therefore, an organization which undertakes three or four kinds of social work is given the designation of "social institution. . . ." As such institutions are currently defined in our motherland, social activities that take place in such institutions consist of relatively unimportant activities, often intended to promote [narrow] social relationships or colonialism.

Therefore, [those practicing *taqlid*] do not really perceive the meaning of the P. S. I.'s social movement in collecting *zakat* [alms tax], improving [Islamic] marriage procedures, and developing our own educational system, all of which are based on religion. The [effort here in structuring such institutions] is to assist in lessening difficulties among social classes caused by national identity or social hierarchies. Their ignorance centers on a lack of understanding concerning the meaning of "social" and "improvement," that is, by truly living in a social environment and confronting all the malfunctioning of social relationships. Actually, both confrontation and subsequent improvement has to spring from a [popularly established social] network that focuses on establishing households and education of children.

Consequently, the social activities mentioned earlier, which make things worse, [can be shifted] to strengthen social conditions that spring from the ruined social foundation of this colonial land.

However, we need not continue this explanation further. The foregoing is sufficient for those who want to continue musing on this matter.

Finally we come to politics.

Here the practitioners of *taqlid* believe that politics compels us to become involved in the political arena and to confront the power holders [that is, the Dutch]. This viewpoint maintains that a political party focuses its action on government and sovereignty, and [especially] on seizing sovereignty by force. This "blind and deaf" perception is accompanied by the corollary that if sufficient power is lacking to achieve this goal, it should be put aside. In its place, attention should be given to "economic development" or "social development" as an initial step.

They forget that in this colonial land, economic and social development are closely tied to the success of Dutch authority. As a result, every effort to imitate economic and social development [for ourselves], even though intended to be in competition with Dutch authority, actually strengthens the Dutch economic and social system itself. This can clearly be seen in the efforts among Protestants and Catholic missionaries, and the spread of Theosophist propaganda, all of which support colonialism. So it is evident that any association or institution that undertakes efforts in those fields will become part of the colonialist endeavor. Similarly, the competition among the various Dutch banks and large Dutch corporations strengthens an economic environment that serves as the foundation of present-day colonialism. Consequently, there is no doubt that every effort undertaken in the name of [Indonesian] nationalism is a part of that economic environment, which intensifies the strength of the [colonial] environment itself.

Actually, "Dutch control" rests on the prevailing laws and political authority that operate in this colonial land. Therefore, every [. . .] effort that recognizes such "control" and at the same time attempts to remove it through competition, then has to face the pitfalls of the law and the political authority behind it. As a result, any of our social and economic movements emphasizing our nationalistic cause have to be involved in politics in order not to be mere tools of the foreign colonial power.

This is our explanation, which must be acknowledged as correct and clear for any group that is thoughtful and intelligent, and which realizes that it needs to resist worldly temptation, such as profit or happiness, that may be associated with it. Surely this foregoing explanation illustrates that in this colonial land, economics, social welfare, and politics cannot be separated. Therefore, all Muslims in this colonial land would find these three aspects in the Islamic Union Party. This is because Islam as religion, the foundation of this party, carries the foundation for the regulation and improvement of every aspect of life, economics, social, and political, as well as others which exist and intermingle in human life.

Is H. A. Salim Dangerous?

When I was in the Netherlands I made connections to enhance our labor and nationalist movements here. I made an agreement with the Netherlands Vak Verbond (N. V. V.) [Netherlands Trade Federation]. This Netherlands labor organization, consisting of several related organizations with a total membership of 240,000 members, indicated that they would take an interest in and provide support for our labor movement here. They would help provide some things we don't have and strengthen other things we do have. In the election to the Second Chamber [of the Dutch parliament in 1929], the Social Democratic Party (S. D. A. P.), received more than 800,000 votes, out of total of 3,000,000 voters, which means that it was supported by almost a quarter of the population of Netherlands; it gained 24 seats in the parliament as a result. The party acknowledged the right of the Indonesian people to freedom in our own country, and I received assurances that the party would support our national movement to obtain that freedom.

Support from those two movements requires that such aid and assistance will not be given to those who oppose their own basic positions. Clearly the labor and national-political movements are adamantly opposed to the communist movement and Bolshevism affiliated with Moscow. For me, as it is certainly stated in [the platforms of the] Islamic Union Party itself, the movement is not in accord with the platform and thinking of the Moscow movement, so that condition is not a hindrance [to our cooperation with the Dutch organizations].

So it happened that when I departed from the Netherlands I reviewed the promises of the two Netherlands labor organizations in an article sent to the magazine *De Strijd* [the *Struggle*], that is an organ of the NVV, which is read by all 240,000 members of that organization. In the article I outlined the interests of our movement here, so that our actions in conducting such a movement would be known and appreciated by modern labor organizations in the Netherlands. Truly we must not only appreciate the readiness of prominent figures of these modern movements [to embrace our cause], but must also gain the attention and forbearance of their thousands of followers as well. I stated my view that the Dutch labor movements gave attention to conditions here [in the Indies], because the conditions here affect their own economic and political struggle against their enemies, that is, capitalists and imperialists in their own country and in the wider world. I stated my belief that as the Dutch laborers' understanding of our movement's origins becomes fuller, that they would be more aware how this colonial land, ruled by the Netherlands, is manipulated to generate excessive advantages to a small number of Dutch capitalists and bourgeois, that is, wealthy people and those who hold important positions. At the same time, Dutch laborers do not receive similar benefits, but rather, they get just the opposite. Because this colonial land exists, the wealthy and important officeholders do not need to develop industry and undertake land cultivation in their own country, as should have been done. These two empowered groups are content with investing capital in commerce, shipping, land cultivation, and mining connected with this colonial land. At the same time, the economic system of the Netherlands is not developed by these two influential classes. Consequently, we observe that Dutch laborers are no better off or better employed than other European laborers, such as those in Sweden, Norway, and Denmark, which do not have colonial lands. Also, there are a hundred thousand poor people in the Netherlands, who live in poverty and unemployment. The wealthy people and holders of high office, who are laborers' enemies in economics and politics, have gained in strength. While the Netherlands has maintained a democracy for hundreds of years, ultimate power is held by the reactionary conservatism of the wealthy and those high officeholders.

This is more or less my viewpoint, as published in the organ of the Dutch labor movement, which can be freely examined, but is not necessary to argue further [at this point]. Such a viewpoint will not quickly be absorbed into the minds and thinking of Dutch laborers, who for more than 300 years have been deceived by their own wealthy and officeholding countrymen.

On the other hand, this power elite feels that this situation is "dangerous" and very threatening. They are well aware that when the Dutch laborers open their eyes to the real situation, they will change their course, and with their own well-organized movements, will campaign vigorously to oppose, deny, and ultimately fight against the exploitation of this colonial land. They will regard it as a violation of the Dutch labor movement itself, one that has adversely affected its fate.

It is not surprising that the voice of Dutch bourgeois here, the newspaper *Soerabaiaas Handelsblad* [*Soerabaia Commercial Gazette*], is startled and behaves like a liar whose secrets have been exposed. It states its denials, like a liar who cannot deny the obvious, undeniable reality. Its fate is assured. It knows that its first and principal duty is to the Netherlands Administration here, which inherited this colonial land from a commercial association [the Dutch East India Company]. [The Administration's task] is nothing else than to continue the profit-making of commercial ventures as expressed through the policies of the kingdom of the Netherlands, which continues its support of the interests of private Dutch capital. With this viewpoint in mind, [the newspaper] seeks to mislead [its readers] concerning our movement's confrontation [with Dutch authorities], which is intended to defend our rights and our life in our [. . .] motherland. [. . .]

"This is dangerous," says the *Soerabaiaas Handelsblad*. "Obviously, no native politician can be called a 'politician,' since none of them has any other purpose than expressing hatred against the Netherlands." As for Hadji A. Salim, it is further said [the author is paraphrasing], it is difficult to fathom his essential goals, and possibly he has a little higher purpose than his politician cronies, but even he is no different, wanting freedom from the Netherlands. In addition, this *haji*—who uses the influence of his title [indicating that he has made the pilgrimage to Mecca]—is actually more dangerous, because his political education is more advanced, and recently his knowledge was sharpened by additional experience gained during his journey in the Netherlands. He has been able to connect himself with Dutch labor movements in the fields of mass organization and politics. Therefore he now passes information to the Dutch labor movements.

This is more or less the *Soerabaiaas Handelsblad*'s criticism as it was delivered. Indeed an honest person will only be appreciated by other honest people. A deceitful person will not be accomplished enough to appreciate the honesty of other people. Accordingly we are not surprised when the *Soerabaiaas Handelsblad* does not appreciate the honesty of our movement's direction. Freed from the Netherlands, [Indonesians] will be a free people, governing themselves in their own country!

There is one more question: "Does the Dutch East Indies government, which currently is the agent of the wealthy and the holders of important positions, want to press its authority without even considering the aspirations of Indonesians who belong to this motherland?" Or is the Dutch East Indies government a considerate government, exercising its power in accordance with the spirit of the times, that is, taking on the responsibility for preparing these people to develop their own independent talents, so that Indonesians can have their own independent country?

Only the base desires and vested interests of the wealthy and entrenched elite would want the conditions outlined in the first question. Unfortunately, during the present period, human integrity and the [humanistic] assumptions accepted by all of the world's considerate nations are given little attention, except by those who understand the second question.

It is a fact that *Soerabaiaas Handelsblad* is a representative of old-fashioned thinking. And so we cool our souls and wait for a later era when our attitude and cause will be proved to have been correct. To the writer of *Soerabaiaas Handelsblad* and the society it serves, we say, "Goodbye to your conservatism!"

Question and Answer

Ahmad Hassan (Singapore-Indonesia, 1888–1958) was a teacher, polemicist, and uncompromising modernist. He was of Tamil extraction, born in Singapore, given a basic Islamic instruction by his father, and thereafter largely self-taught. He was involved in cloth merchandising and newspaper work at Singapore, then migrated in his late thirties to Bandung in Indonesia, where he became involved with a religious study group called the *Persatuan Islam* (Islamic Union). He exercised a leadership role in this group, calling for fervent opposition to secular nationalism, traditionalist Islam, Christian missionary work, the Ahmadiyya movement (a heterodox sect of Islam), and the Dutch colonial regime. Ahmad Hassan held that Muslim traditionalism and the doctrine of unquestioning obedience to the old masters of religious law had allowed stagnation to stifle Islamic dynamism, and that this situation could be reversed only through open investigation of religious sources. He wrote extensively, helping to create a new Islamic literature in the Indonesian language, including a commentary on the Qur'an, several works on Muslim belief and a lengthy set of legal opinions that laid out the modernist position in Muslim practice. The works selected for translation here lay out his basic thinking regarding the traditionalist-modernist debate. Along with this, three legal opinions on the Friday sermon in Malay and the position of Arabs in Indonesian society are given to provide examples of his thinking and his use of Islamic sources.[1]

Unquestioning Acceptance of Religious Scholars

Question: Is it permitted for Muslims to put our trust in the *'ulama'* [religious scholars] and to engage in *taqlid* [imitation] of them?

Answer: These two questions are really the same—that is, in religious matters, can we obey the *'ulama'* without support from either the Qur'an or the *sunna* [divinely inspired precedent] of the Prophet? To answer this problem, we first need to understand the meaning of several terms: *ijtihad* [rational interpretation], *ittiba'* [critical acceptance], and *taqlid*, as well as those who engage in these practices: *mujtahid*, *muttabi'*, and *muqallid*.

Ijtihad originally meant "exertion" or "effort," and it is defined by the classical scholars as a con-

certed effort to discover a religious rule in the Qur'an and *sunna* and apply it to issues that are difficult to interpret, and are beyond the ordinary. Such answers require them to find answers from the Qur'an or *hadith* [narratives of the Prophet] by hard toil and [complex] analogy. A person able to undertake such open interpretation is called a *mujtahid*.

A *mujtahid* needs strong Arabic language skills in order to clearly understand the principles [he is to undercover], as well as knowing the language in general, even though he does not need to be an Arab himself. *Ijtihad* is certainly needed in temporal matters, particularly when new problems arise and the Qur'an and the *sunna* do not explicitly lay down the applicable rule. In such a case, the appropriate judge or leader of Muslim society should undertake investigation and comparison in the existing law with sub-

Ahmad Hassan, *Soal-Djawab* (*Question and Answer*) (Bandung, Indonesia: Diponegoro, 1968–1969), pp. 388–391, 203–205, 463–465, 383–384, 581. First published in 1931–1934. Translation from Indonesian by Akhmad Minhadji. Introduction by Howard M. Federspiel.

1. G. F. Pijper, *Studien over de geschiedenis van de Islam in Indonesia 1900–1950* (*Studies on the History of Islam in*

Indonesia, 1900–1950) (Leiden, Netherlands: E. J. Brill, 1977), pp. 120–134; Howard M. Federspiel, *The Persatuan Islam: Islamic Reform in Twentieth Century Indonesia* (Ithaca, N.Y.: Cornell University Modern Indonesia Project, 1971); Akhmad Minhadji, "Ahmad Hassan and Islamic Legal Reform in Indonesia (1887–1958)," Ph.D. dissertation, McGill University, 1995.

stantiation from the Qur'an and *hadith*. An example of this is found with the *zakat* [alm tax] levied on certain crops. In the earlier Islamic era [that is, the time of the Prophet Muhammad], Muslims paid the *zakat* in grain, and this *zakat* was given to the needy, used for the public service, or otherwise distributed. But now, here [in Indonesia] there is no such grain, but rather rice, so the *zakat* given to the needy and otherwise used consists of that. In this case analogy can be used.[2] Undertaking such investigation is lauded in religious teaching; indeed, it is even commanded for those who are qualified.

The basic meaning of *ittiba'*, as defined by most *'ulama'*, means accepting something based on the commands, prohibitions, and behavior of the Prophet, the behavior of his Companions, or discovery of commands, prohibitions, and behavior from one's own reading or from questioning religious scholars. [. . .]

The one who exercises *ittiba'* is called a *muttabi'*. Such people do not necessarily have to know Arabic, for they are only asked to understand the religious reason for their daily religious practices, and not to search exhaustively as the *mujtahid* does to make analogies, give legal opinions, and the like. In fact, there are only two ways to pursue a correct understanding of religious teaching: *ijtihad* and *ittiba'*. No other way is acceptable.

In the era of the Companions of the Prophet, only a few people were *mujtahid*s, while all the Companions were *muttabi'*s—but none of them were *muqallid*s, because if they were not familiar with the law they asked the Prophet or the [other] Companions concerning the matter.[3]

Moreover, a *muttabi'* who receives two different rules from two knowledgeable clerics on the same matter has to check carefully which one of them is stronger. It can happen, for instance, that one cleric says that there is a *hadith* of the Prophet which allows us to recite the opening sura of the Qur'an behind the prayer leader during the Friday congregational prayer, while another cleric states that a *hadith* forbids this to be done. In such a case, the *muttabi'* should carefully check each of the arguments to see

which one has greater strength. The *muttabi'* cannot say, "I cannot check which one of them is true because I am not a cleric." If that were true, anything would be possible!

The problem faced by the *muttabi'* is similar to that of counterfeit money. All people must make the effort to find out whether or not their money is counterfeit; no one can say that I cannot do such checking because I am not a banker. [. . .]

Taqlid literally means imitating, and it is commonly defined as imitating, copying, or accepting certain rules without arguments of the Qur'an and *sunna* of the Prophet. Someone who exercises *taqlid* is called a *muqallid*. Such unquestioning acceptance is forbidden by religion. God has decisively decreed this in the Qur'an: "Do not follow that of which you have no knowledge."(Sura 17, Verse 36) He also says: "In case you are unaware, enquire of those who are keepers of the oracles of God." (Sura 16, Verse 43) Asking the scholars of the Qur'an means inquiring about the principles in the Qur'an, not their speculation about the matter.

It is not only God who forbids this [unthinking] approach, but the very classical scholars whose lessons are accepted unquestioningly. *Imam* Hanafi [Abu Hanifa, circa 699–767], for example, forbade his fellow Muslims to engage in *taqlid*. His great student, Abu Yusuf, also reminded his colleagues of this danger. This was also true of [the other founders of the major Sunni legal traditions,] *Imam* Malik [ibn Anas, 710–796], *Imam* [Abu 'Abdullah Muhammad] al-Shafi'i [767–820], and most particularly *Imam* [Ahmad ibn] Hanbal [780–855], who said: "Do not engage in *taqlid*. Do not take my concepts, or Malik's concepts, or Shafi'i's concepts, but take and acknowledge the sources from which we draw our religious arguments."

For us, the attitude of the traditionalist Muslims who always practice *taqlid* is unreasonable, for they claim that they practice *taqlid* toward their religious teachers, while the religious teachers themselves, basing themselves on the Qur'an and His Prophet, clearly forbid such thinking. Do people who do not base their findings on the Qur'an and the Prophet, and also do not follow the findings of their earlier scholars, which are based on the Qur'an and the Prophet, have the rights to claim them as their religious leaders?

Moreover, people here [in Indonesia] assert that they are followers of the Shafi'i religious school, but

---

2. Analogy is the proper meaning here since *hadith* recorded by both [Muhammad ibn Isma'il] Bukhari [810–870] and Muslim [ibn al-Hajjaj, 821–875] say that "food" was given out and the term was for "food" in general.

3. But they did not ask for a mere opinion on the matter [but asked for the actual principle that applied].

they fail to present even a single argument of Shafi'i which supports the practice of *taqlid*. The religious teachers have always stated that to understand the Qur'an and *hadith* is difficult and requires learning that not everybody has. Consequently, they claim that it is enough for people of our time to follow what has already been said by our religious scholars, who take their concepts from the great and famous religious scholars of the early centuries of Islam. But against this clarification it can be stated that Muslims who can engage in *ijtihad* should do so, if necessary; and the rest should employ *ittiba'*. As for *taqlid*, it simply is not permitted.

The Language of the Friday Sermon

Question: Is there any religious argument that allows us to use a language other than Arabic during the Friday sermon?

Answer: There are quite a number of Qur'anic verses which encourage us to continually think and seek to understand our surroundings, to be smart and knowledgeable, and, at the same time, to condemn those who do the opposite. Also, there are also many *hadith* which promote the importance of reason and denounce foolishness.

It is said in the Qur'an: "Do they not ponder on what the Qur'an says? Or have their hearts been sealed with locks?" (Sura 47, Verse 24) "We have sent down a Book to you which is blessed, so that people may apply their minds to its revelations, and people of wisdom may reflect." (Sura 38, Verse 29) These two verses indicate clearly that the Qur'an is not to be recited without thinking about it and properly understanding its contents.

The same case can be made with the Friday sermon. If the Qur'an condemns those who read the Qur'an without understanding, is it possible to say that those who read and listen to the sermon without understanding its content will be included among those whom God respects? It is true that the Prophet delivered his sermons in Arabic; but he was an Arab who delivered his sermons in an Arab land, and those who listened to him were all Arabs. But this does not mean that the sermon cannot be delivered in another language. Those who can discern will understand that we are commanded to hear the sermon, not the Arab language, which, after all is a human construction,

not the method of delivery used by the sermon giver. It is more significant that most, if not all, sermon givers do not even understand the content of their sermons, [since they were written by others and merely recited by the sermon givers].

Is it not then foolish and unreasonable to say that our religion teaches us to deliver the sermon in Arabic before audiences that do not understand Arabic? If it were the case that on Friday it is necessary [from a religious perspective] to listen to Arabic recitation, clearly it would be better to simply listen to a recitation of the Qur'an. The main goal of the sermon is to give religious advice, reflection, and teaching, and no advice or reflection is possible if the hearer does not understand.

There is not a single mention in the Qur'an or the *sunna* that requires the sermon to use the Arabic language, nor is there any mention that a sermon cannot be delivered in a language used by the hearers of the sermon. If this were the case, then it would be necessary for all Muslims to know Arabic, and there is no mention of this either.

If some people strenuously insist that the sermon must be given in Arabic because the Prophet delivered his sermons in Arabic, then these people must also strongly insist that the marriage ceremony cannot be given in any language but Arabic, because the Prophet was married and married others using Arabic. Likewise they must equally say that any advice cannot be given in a language other than Arabic, because the Prophet always did so using Arabic.

[I am aware that if the sermon can be delivered in a language other than Arabic,] someone will then say that the same idea applies to the practice of our daily prayers, that is, that they can be translated as well. To this we firmly answer that the sermon must be differentiated from prayer. The purpose of a sermon is advice and reflection, and sermons are not always the same, because they vary according to time, place and necessity. Accordingly, such advice must be structured in a language understandable to the listeners, because, if it was composed in the Arabic language, listeners who did not understand Arabic would certainly not understand the advice. As to the texts read during the daily prayers, they were permanently established by the Prophet and do not ever change. [. . .]

Muslims should be aware that religious teachings are divided into two parts: that is, matters of worship and matters of general behavior. Anything included in worship must be undertaken according to the examples of the Prophet. This includes the prayers, [. . .] which must be recited in Arabic as the Prophet did during his lifetime. The recitations of the Prophet during prayer were always the same from one time to the next, and from one place to another; consequently the texts are permanent.

In the case of matters which did not involve prescribed worship, that is, matters relating to general practice, such as giving advice and personal prayers, the Prophet did not always do things in the same way, as he did in matters of prescribed worship. Consequently we are free to do that as well, and we are free to use any appropriate language in that effort.

It stands to reason that if advice and personal prayer must be given in Arabic, the conclusion is that all Muslims cannot use any language other than Arabic. This is surely not true. [Further,] if it is believed that the sermon is required as prescribed worship, then the substance of the sermon could not ever be changed, but must be recited following the Prophet's recitation, as exists in the case of formal prayer. But, if the view is taken that the matter involves practice, rather than prescribed worship, then there is no impediment or prohibition for the sermon to be in a language other than Arabic. Actually, the only purpose of the sermon is for advice.

Some traditionalist religious scholars contend that the sermon may not be given in any language but Arabic. The listeners either understand or not, the sermon giver either understands or not. [According to this view,] the sermon must be given in Arabic because the Prophet gave his sermons in Arabic. . . . [ellipses in original][4]

Actually, we would ask such religious scholars why they always give advice [outside of prescribed prayer] in languages other than Arabic, since the Prophet never once did so. If it were possible and an Islamic state came into existence, obviously it would be right and proper that all people would be required to speak Arabic, so that all the Muslim peoples of the world would do so, and communication between different groups would be facilitated. But at this time here [in Indonesia], if a person teaches only in Arabic, he will not succeed.

Boasting about Heredity and Tribal Importance

Question: According to Islamic law, what is the position of those who exhibit pride in or even boast about having descent from the Prophet, having a royal title, being an Arab, and so on?[5]

Answer: God has already ruled in the Qur'an: "Whichever of you has the most integrity has indeed greater honor with God." (Sura 49, Verse 13) And the Prophet, peace be upon him, has also said: "There is no difference between Arab and non-Arab, the best among them are those who are closer to God."

Based on the verse and the *hadith*, we can conclude that all human beings are the same. Their status is based on their own positive effort during their life, according to the rules of Islamic law. In another verse of the Qur'an, God has also clearly indicated, "The faithful are surely brothers." (Sura 49, Verse 10)

If there are those who are proud of being the family of the prophets, let them know that all of us spring from one tree, the prophet Adam. Further, if there are those who are proud of being an Arab, tell them that they are also a descendant of Jews, who come from the same roots. In addition, if someone is proud of being the descendant of royalty, we should say that royalty are also human beings like us. They became kings because they gained control, or even seized control, from earlier kings, always helped and supported by monarchists.

Moreover, our religion teaches us not to boast or demand that others respect us without good reason; but rather to work hard for the prosperity of society based on the rules laid down by God, whereby others will respect us. Consequently, we should not boast as being the descendant of this or that, an attitude condemned by religious teaching. There is an Arabic expression: "A branch not bearing fruit is cut down for firewood, even though it comes from a tree that bears fruit."

---

4. When these traditionalist religious scholars agree with the actions and words of the Prophet, they go directly to the *hadith* as the source of this agreement. But if they disagree, then they go to their earlier scholars, on the basis that they themselves are not "original" scholars and may not use *hadith* directly. This is certainly a satisfying way of doing things. [The author is being ironic.—Ed.]

5. [At the time, Arabs in Southeast Asia, particularly descendants of the Prophet, were considered of higher social status than Indonesians.—Trans.]

Marrying a Woman Who Is a Descendant of the Prophet

Question: Almost every day we read in the newspapers the problem of those descended from the Prophet. The question is this: Why can't a woman descended from the Prophet marry outside her own family? According to Islamic law, what is the rule for those who have such an idea?

Answer: The main sources of Islamic law, the Qur'an and the *sunna* of the Prophet, do not forbid or hinder, but rather allow a Muslim woman to marry any Muslim man from any ethnic group or nation. Those who forbid a certain marriage because of the different family background belong to the group which forbids something which was originally allowed by God. We can make allowances for those who do not know Islamic law, but for those who have such knowledge and still follow that concept, we should ask them: According to Islamic law, what is the rule for those who forbid something allowed by God?

Some Advice

Kyai Haji Muhammad Hasyim Asy'ari (Java, 1871–1947) is widely regarded in Indonesia as one of the most respected religious leaders of the twentieth century. Educated in his father's school in Java, with further studies at Mecca, he founded and taught at several *pesantren* (seminaries) in East Java and was a primary organizer of the *Nahdlatul Ulama* (Renaissance of the Religious Scholars) association in 1926, leading that organization until his death in 1945. He was active in nationalist politics, usually calling for greater unity among Muslims in the independence movement. Asy'ari was a transitional figure between traditionalism and modernism in Muslim religious thought. He held tightly to the importance of the traditional Muslim schools of law, stating that they held the vital truth about Islamic doctrine. At the same time, he left room for new interpretation by scholars who were appropriately trained and who stayed within traditional bounds. He introduced new teaching methods in his schools and encouraged his son and his favorite students to undertake further experimentation in subject matter and styles of teaching. He attempted to seek reconciliation with modernists, but was usually rebuffed by them; at the same time he apparently convinced many in the Muslim community at large of his sincerity. The selection chosen for translation, a 1935 speech delivered to the *Nahdlatul Ulama* organization Asy'ari helped to found, appeals for harmony between traditionalists and modernists. Asy'ari describes the Islamic community as all-inclusive and tolerant, though his opponents did not view him or his efforts as achieving these goals.[1]

In the name of God, the beneficent, the merciful.

From the lowest and the most contemptible servant of God, namely Muhammad Hasyim Asy'ari. May God forgive him, his parents, and the entire *umma* [Muslim community]. Amen.

To my respected Muslim brothers, *'ulama'* [religious scholars], and ordinary people. Peace, God's mercy and blessing be upon all of you.

The news has reached me that among you there is rage, slander, and conflict at present. I know the reasons for this condition. Surely this happens because they have changed and replaced God's book, the Qur'an, and the *hadith* [sayings] and *sunna* [practice] of the Prophet, even though God, the most merciful, has stated: "The faithful are surely brothers, so restore friendship among your brothers." [Qur'an, Sura 49, Verse 10]

Nowadays, some members of the *umma* regard their Muslim brothers as enemies and do not want to improve brotherhood, but rather to destroy it. The prophet has stated: "You should not be jealous of others; you should not divide people; you should not quarrel; all of you should be God's servants who are close to one another." [Unfortunately,] people nowadays are envious, angry, divided, quarrelsome, and hostile to each other.

O, you *'ulama'* who have fanatically supported narrow opinions! Abandon your fanaticism concern-

Kyai Haji Muhammad Hasyim Asy'ari, "Beberapa Nasehat Kyai Haji Muhammad Hasyim Asy'ari" (Some Advice of *Shaykh* Hasyim Asy'ari), in *Pesan-Pesan Dua Pemimpin Besar Islam Indonesia* (*The Messages of Two Great Leaders of Indonesian Islam*), edited by Abdul Munir Malkan (Yogyakarta, Indonesia: Medio, 1986), pp. 16–20. Text of a speech delivered in 1935. Translation from Indonesian by Lathiful Khuluq. Introduction by Howard M. Federspiel.

1. Harry J. Benda, *The Crescent and the Rising Sun* (The Hague, Netherlands: Van Hoeve, 1958), pp. 151 and forward; Aboebakar Atjeh, *Sejarah Hidup K.H.A. Wahid Hasjim dan*

Karangan Tersiar (*Biography of K.H.A. Wahid Hasjim and His Various Writings*) (Jakarta, Indonesia: Kementerian Agama, 1957); Lathiful Khuluq, "K.H. Hasyim Asy'ari's Contribution to Indonesian Independence," *Studia Islamika*, volume 5, number 1, 1998, pp. 46–67; Lathiful Khuluq, *Ajar Kebangunan Ulama: Biographi K.H. Hasyim Asy'ari* (*Training Religious Scholars: Biography of K.H. Hasyim Asy'ari*) (Yogyakarta, Indonesia: LkiS, 2000).

ing contentious matters, since even the greatest scholars held more than one opinion about them. One stated that every *ijtihad* [rational, in this case scholarly, interpretation] is correct, while the other mentioned that even though only one interpretation can be correct, those who engage in such interpretation can still be rewarded, even though the end product of thinking is incorrect.

I ask my brothers to leave behind their clique mentality and abandon passions that are destructive. Fight for Islam by giving all your strength, and overcome them who slander the Qur'an and the attributes of God. Fight against those who teach harmful knowledge and who harm faith. Indeed, it is an obligation [for Muslims] to fight against those people. So, let us, brothers, sacrifice ourselves to meet these obligations.

O, all believers!

Before you stand infidels who deny God. They fill every corner of the country. Who [among you] is ready to engage in dialogue with them and guide them to the right path?

O, *'ulama'*!

Your discipline is the application of religious thought, and in that effort there are those who are stubborn.

Brothers, indeed your obstinacy in religious knowledge and the quarreling among you to gain a particular view are not appreciated by God, the most high! And such obstinacy and quarreling are also not appreciated by the Prophet, peace be upon him. If you [follow such a path, indeed] your real motivation is fanaticism, conflict, and hatred for one another.

If *Imam* [Abu 'Abdullah Muhammad] Shafi'i [767–820], *Imam* Abu Hanifa [circa 699–767], *Imam* Malik [ibn Anas, 710–796], *Imam* Ahmad [ibn Hanbal, 780–855], [Abu'l-'Abbas] Ibn Hajar [al-Haytami, 1504–1567], and [Muhammad ibn Ahmad] Ramli [circa 1511–1595] were still alive, they would certainly condemn your behavior and distance themselves from you and from your behavior. All of you surely see the great number of ordinary people—only God the greatest knows their number—who do not perform prayer five times a day, whereas according to *Imam* Shafi'i, *Imam* Malik, and *Imam* Ahmad they will be punished [in the Hereafter for that failure] by having their throats cut. You certainly cannot deny this, for certainly you yourself see your neighbor who does not perform prayers, and there are even those

in our own group who, more and more, neglect their prayers and put them aside.

Then, what is the significance and the need of quarreling about trivial religious matters which are also disputed by the experts of Islamic jurisprudence? On the contrary, you do not differ concerning some specific matters which are certainly forbidden by all scholars, such as fornication, usury, drinking alcohol, and the like. There should be no argument here, except between *Imam* Shafi'i and *Shaykh* Ibn Hajar [on minor points of interpretation]. Such arguing only creates division in the unity of faith and destroys your brotherhood. It gives the ignorant power over you. It diminishes your authority in the eyes of the people, especially those of poor character. These foolish people will humiliate your honor by saying impolite and improper things about you.

These people have suffered ruin because of you *'ulama'*. And you yourselves have suffered great harm because of your own great sin [of quarreling with one another].

O, *'ulama'*!

If you see people doing good deeds based on the opinions of the great teachers of the past, or accepting their word as truth without examining original sources, even if the teacher's opinion is not really correct, then, even if you do not agree, do not insult such people, but guide them in a nice way! Certainly those who [insult others with such condemnation] violate God's commands and commit great sin. Those who do that destroy the integrity of a nation and close every door to [communal] well-being.

Further, God forbids His believing servants to be hostile toward one another. Rather, give others advice on the ill effects of improper thought and behavior, that is, how certain actions will lead to sad events and bad consequences. God stated: "And do not ever be hostile to one another because hostility will cause brittleness, and cause your authority to disappear."[2]

O, Muslims!

Indeed, current events can be used as an instructional device; and the lessons drawn from this source are far from insignificant. Wise people are able to make use of and take advantage of such everyday experiences and events, even more than the preaching of

---

2. [This may be a paraphrase of the Qur'an, Sura 3, Verse 103, or Sura 8, Verse 46.—Trans.]

some sermon givers and the advice of those [legalists] proffering it. Take events to heart that occur before our eyes each and every day. Do we not regret [certain] actions? Are we not be aware of drunkenness [in our midst]? Don't we make mistakes? And are we also aware of [instances of] our own success, based on helping one another and unity? These positive cases exist because of clean hearts and pure intentions. Or will we continue to be divided, to be hypocrites: outwardly pleasant, inwardly hostile, hearts full of hatred and legacies of deep resentment.

Indeed, our religion is one: Islam! Our legal allegiance is one: the Shafi'i [school of Islamic legal scholarship]! Our region is one: Java![3] And we are all Sunnis.

So I swear by God, in truth, that your feeling of hateful dissension is woefully apparent, and that this constitutes a great danger to our progress.

O, Muslims!

Fear God and return to the book of God, behave according to the way of the Prophet, and establish good models of conduct in order that you be successful, even as the early Muslims before us were successful. Fear God and help each other in matters of goodness and piety. Do not abet others in sin and abomination. God will reward you in His mercy and grace. And do not be like people who say, "We have heard," but actually are not listening.

May good will be with us from the beginning to the end [of this congress].

3. [Religious scholars of Asy'ari's generation used "Java" to refer to all of Indonesia, following the practice of the Arabs.—Trans.]

Imperatives for Encouraging Islamic Culture

Ya'qub Wang Jingzhai (China, 1879–1949) is known as one of the "Four Great *Akhond*s" (religious scholars) of modern China. A journalist, translator, and religious scholar, Wang made significant contributions to the modernization and rejuvenation of Chinese Islam. The son of a Hui (Chinese Muslim) *imam* (prayer leader) in the city of Tianjin, in eastern China, Wang received early training in Arabic and Persian, as well as the Confucian classics. At the age of twenty-six he began his own career as *imam*, serving in several Muslim communities in eastern China and Taiwan. He became increasingly involved in Chinese Islamic revivalist movements, and focused on reforming Islamic education in China. Wang was also an advocate of intensifying relations between China's Muslims and the rest of the Muslim world. He participated in the first modern wave of Chinese Muslim students to seek advanced education in the Middle East, studying at al-Azhar in the 1920s, and helped other Chinese to follow him. Upon his return, he established several journals dedicated to Chinese Islamic issues and translated the Qur'an, the first complete translation into Chinese, carried out during the 1930s under the sponsorship of a Chinese Muslim warlord. Wang also compiled several Arabic-Chinese dictionaries, Islamic manuals, and guidebooks in Chinese, and wrote a commentary on the Qur'an. In the article translated here, Wang promotes the compatibility of pan-Islamic identity with Hui nationalism, and Hui nationalism with Chinese nationalism, which was both spurred and threatened in the 1930s by Japanese invasions.[1]

The Chinese Hui [Muslim] Patriotic Committee has just issued a pronouncement: The Supreme Council on National Defense considers that China's and India's Islamic cultures are a main component of Eastern culture, and China's Muslims number nearly 40 million, second in the world.[2] In consideration of this fact, and the exigencies of the War of Resistance against Japan, and the fit between Islamic culture [and Chinese culture], the need for urgent contact between Chinese and Islamic cultures is self-evident. The Islamic religion's texts are mostly written in Arabic, and in the Near East the languages of the small ethnic groups are also basically Arabic. To make contact between China and Arabic cultures, as well as promote plans for cooperation among minority peoples in the East [that is, in China], research on the Arabic language must be deemed essential.

Ya'qub Wang Jingzhai, "Fazhan Yisilan wenhua zhi biyao" (Imperatives for Encouraging Islamic Culture), in Li Xinghua and Feng Jinyuan, editors, *Zhongguo Yisilan jiao shi cankao ziliao xuanbian, 1911–1949* (*Anthology of Reference Materials on the History of Chinese Islam, 1911–1949*) (Ningxia, China: Ningxia renmin chubanshe, 1985), volume 2, pp. 920–928. Text of a speech first published in 1939. Translation from Chinese by Howard L. Goodman. Introduction by Zvi A. Ben-Dor.

1. Ibrahim Ma Zhao-chun, "Islam in China: The Internal Dimension," *Journal [of the] Institute of Muslim Minority Affairs*, volume 7, number 2, 1986, pp. 373–383; Ma Shou-qian, "The Hui People's New Awakening from the End of the 19th Century to the Beginning of the 20th Century," in *The Legacy of Islam in China* (Cambridge, Mass.: Fairbank Center for East Asian Research, Harvard University, 1989), pp. 111–137; Qiu Shusen *et alia*, editors, *Zhongguo Huizu da cidian* (*Great Dictionary of the Chinese Hui Nation*) (Nanjing, China: Jiangsu guji chubanshe, 1992), pp. 962–963; Yang Keli *et alia*, editors, *Zhongguo Yisilan baikequan shu* (*Chinese Encyclopedia of Islam*) (Chengdu, China: Sichuan cishu chubanshe, 1994), pp. 580–581; Françoise Aubin, "Les traductions du Coran en chinois" (Translations of the Qur'an into Chinese), *Études orientales* (*Oriental Studies*), numbers 13–14, 1994, pp. 1–17.

2. [Reliable statistics are unavailable, but this estimate is most likely an exaggeration.—Ed.]

Consequently, an order has been given to the Provincial Administration to issue instructions to the Education Department to appoint two lecturers to initiate courses at the National University, one in Arabic and one in Islamic culture. The Education Department has also designated new positions at National Central University, Northeast Union University and Yunnan University. At present the search for teaching talent is taking place, and since the time frame is short, we must plan to address current realities. [The author's paraphrase of the pronouncement ends here.]

When this news was handed down, we who heard it were elated. Those of us who have hoped against hope [for such a policy] could now see it becoming reality. It is a step forward for the unity of minority peoples during this time of the Resistance. However, this is no more than a first step. As a result, from this day forward we will deepen the development of Islamic culture, and so we must create specialized Arabic universities. When I traveled in India, places such as Lahore, Lucknow, and Delhi had plans for a comprehensive university specializing in Arabic studies that would surpass Egypt's al-Azhar University in all respects. According to conversations with my Indian coreligionists, the northwest corner of India had several universities specializing in Arabic studies, all established by the English government, with considerable annual budgets paid by the English government. Our compatriots felt completely indebted to the English, who in this case exhibited virtuousness for their ardent improvement of the level of Arabic culture in India. In retrospect, everywhere that the English created Arabic studies universities, talent grew ever greater, to the point that they were keeping pace with students at Egypt's al-Azhar University. In the past several decades, Indian scholars of Arabic have edited more than 10,000 Arabic texts, which have found a strong market in the Muslim areas of the northwest Chinese provinces of Gansu, Ningxia, and Qinghai. Persian studies would be included in our proposed Arabic studies university, so that Persian publications from India would also find a market in China, and so on.

England's ambitions are considerable when it comes to its stance toward its colonies, as well they should be—in this case, India's encouragement of Islamic culture. Our own Chinese government also should pay attention to encouraging and expanding native Islamic culture.

Japan, basically a Buddhist nation, has never had any Muslims, and Islamic culture has never had the opportunity to develop in that country. Yet in the past several years Japan has followed in the footsteps of England and sought to use Islamic culture as a tool of government. On one hand they have constructed a Muslim mosque in Tokyo and printed a translation of the Qur'an; on the other hand they have groups of students at Egypt's al-Azhar University diligently studying Arabic and investigating Muslim culture. We can guess that their intent is to implement their doctrine of Greater Asia,[3] and after that to control all of Asia's Muslims while completely manipulating Islamic culture. This Japanese plan is surely a delusion, and our own government ought to think of an appropriate countermeasure. The decision of our Supreme Council on National Defense to set up two courses in Arabic and Islamic cultural studies in the three national universities is, in effect, a tacit and suitable counterbalance to this outlandishly bizarre tactic of the Japanese. In addition, in view of these unusual times, ethnic peoples [in China] should intensify their good-faith unity, practice frugality, and end idle pleasures, so that each of these peoples may develop a coherent stance toward the outside world. The most important points for anyone involved in Islamic culture are to increase unity and resist outside oppression; they should talk of faith, listen to their consciences, and be diligent and hardworking; they should not enter into useless and wasteful matters; they must discard superstition and stick to reason. In this way, in this time of the War of Resistance, we shall promote Islamic culture and respond appropriately [to the war], both internally and externally.

While tending carefully to the advance of Chinese Muslim culture, I am striving as well to introduce the history of Chinese Muslim culture to the reading public, and am especially keen on supporting the addition of the two courses in Arabic studies and Islamic culture.

The Evolution of Chinese Islamic Culture

The culture of Islam dates back more than a thousand years, and gradually developed into the glorious

3. [In the 1930s, Japan developed a strategy of Asian domination called the "Great East Asia Co-Prosperity Sphere."—Trans.]

manifestation that we see today. The first steps in investigating this cultural progress were due to the exertions of Western [that is, Middle Eastern] scholars. For a long time, we Eastern peoples merely inherited their achievements, rather than develop them spontaneously. The first writings to come to China were for the most part Persian, with Arabic secondmost. When we examine just who it was that carried Islam into our country, [we see that] the first were Persian merchants, and a number of years after them pilgrims to Mecca carried back with them Arabic manuscripts from the West. Various individual courses of study gradually became well established. After the lifting of maritime isolationist policies and the invention of printing, Arabic books from the West proliferated like bamboo shoots after a spring rain. An enormous amount was conveyed into China. Quite a few came into the interior of China from India and Egypt; those from Turkey were next in number, and Mecca and Syria next after that. Subsequently, when Chinese pilgrims visited Mecca, they did not escape the hardships of traveling on foot, but at least they did not have to double their chore by loading up with books to take back. This one point alone testifies to the difficulty China encountered when it first promoted Islamic culture in the Far East early on.

Although Arabic studies fall under the category of Western literature, the way Chinese people read Arabic is not the same as the way they read English, French, German, Russian, and so forth. A [Chinese] reader of English, French, and so on reads in the original script, and can figure out the general meaning by recognizing particular words. Arabic is not read in this way: reading is actually the recitation, over and over, of a Chinese translation of the original. Not only does [the reader] understand it completely, but those who do not read Arabic, on listening to the recitation, are also able to get a full understanding of its meaning. The first person to translate Arabic into spoken Chinese, setting aside the original text in order to go directly to the meaning, was the venerable teacher Xian Dahu of Xiaxi [Elias Hu Dengzhou, circa 1522–1597]. This gentleman's skill in spoken and literary Chinese was most refined. So as to accommodate native readers, he created a deep linkage between the two languages. It goes without saying that to meld together both cultures, Arabic and Chinese, was an admirable feat. In the Chinese literary world, this venerable man was

a talent of special note, and today's students of Arabic still preserve his method. The Chinese translations fully maintain the original language's structure: a word may be placed in front or at the end, but not one word is discarded. The translated works flow relatively easily in popular spoken language. People call this the *madrasa* [seminary][4] method.

Courses in Chinese Islamic Culture

To categorize the courses of study for Islamic culture, we would have: vocabulary, first-level grammar, advanced grammar, rhetoric, theology, law, Qur'anic interpretation, and Persian. With the above as a formal curriculum, we would attempt to order a sequence in the following way:

1. Vocabulary. Arabic vocabulary is essential. Beginning with the study of spelling, Chinese readers of Arabic are barely able to recognize constructions. And to make further steps towards progress, one must do so without instruction from teachers. Western words are difficult, and Arabic ones even more so. Thus I myself have said, "Even with ten years of Arabic studies, you still cannot enter its true depths." The hardest part of learning Arabic is vocabulary. In the first place, the word roots are too numerous; and second, the morphology of words is complex. We estimate that there are about 400,000 roots. Each one undergoes numerous changes. For example, such categories as verbs, adjectives, nouns, and legal terms all have their own individual established usages with barely a hair's difference among them. But in addition to that, we have further distinctions of "characteristic": singles, doubles, and plurals, which are different. There are only twenty-nine letters, and at the very most it takes fifty minutes to learn them well. It is simply that in the case of an individual word, it is not like in Chinese, where the meaning can be derived by resorting to the phonetic [element of the written character]—this being the point about the difficulty of [Arabic] study. Given that Arabic is so difficult, that is why Chinese scholars stay bound to the well-practiced formulation [of transmitting Arabic texts only in oral recitations]. But it would be a mistake to believe that the difficulty of

---

4. [The author uses the term *jingtang*, denoting the traditional Islamic school.—Trans.]

learning Arabic is an obstacle to [the development of] Hui [Islamic] culture.

2. First-level grammar. There are enough Arabic grammar texts to "exhaust an ox and fill up a whole house." Our forebears in the world of Arabic studies in China chose about five of these, that is, the Five Books, among which there are differences in content. They generally only discuss the overall features of grammar, and so we call this the "first level." It requires two years of work in a normal *madrasa* before the five books are thoroughly digested. It goes without saying, however, that talented and smart students must also have able instructors.

3. Advanced grammar. There are two books for this generally in use in China: *Dao wu luo mi su ba ha* [*The Lamp*, by Nasir ibn 'Abd al-Sayyid Mutarrizi, 1144–1213] and *Kafei jiejing* [*Commentary on Sufficient (Lessons in Solving Grammatical Problems)*, by Jami, 1414–1492]. The quickest it takes is three years in order to master these two works. At that point one could truly claim to write and speak. Yet, one would only get the broad outline and feel inadequate as far as the small details are concerned. At present, newly published grammars are simple and suitable, but given the Chinese preference for sticking with the old, they are not disposed to choosing such texts. The grammar texts to be selected at our three national universities will be a major issue. The older texts are certainly unsuitable, but the administrators of textbook acquisition, being circumspect and conscious of all details, must continue setting a standard for the distant future.

4. Rhetoric. In China this means the study of methods needed to relate any matter in a direct and graceful way, as well as skill in debating. In comparison with the study of Arabic vocabulary, the study of rhetoric is quite difficult. Thus for a long time now, one is as likely to find stars under the morning sun, as to find a Chinese Arabicist who writes Arabic on a par with those trained in the West. It is extremely difficult to explain the rules of prosody in simple terms, and this complex [system] is as old as Arabic writing itself. With effort, it is possible to gain some familiarity.

5. Theology. Islamic thought strives toward the recognition that there is a Creator. As such, it is scientific, not mythological. This is the single point of our theology. Scientists generally believe that whatever is religious is in all ways superstitious and mythological. In actuality, these two things are, simply, rejected by our religion, because Islam preaches that

culture emphasizes the rational. One cannot speak [of Islam] in the same breath as religious authorities who bully an ignorant populace. Take for instance such unverifiable [Chinese creation] stories like Pangu separating heaven [and earth] and Nüwa transforming minerals [into humans]. These stories are not in our religion, and we [Hui] do not believe in them. Islamic theology relied first on Holy Scripture (the Qur'an) and wise remarks (the traditions of Muhammad), which were then assisted by the reasoning of scholars. After that, Greek philosophy assumed prominence, and many sharp conflicts of logic arose vis-à-vis Islamic theology. When Arab theologians translated Greek philosophy into Arabic, they refuted the numerous points, one by one, where the philosophy conflicted with Islamic theology. Since then, Islamic theology has become mingled throughout with appropriate theoretics. Moreover, the rules of deduction and conclusion in formal logic are clearly those of a Creator.

This shows that Islam's belief in the True Creator—allusions to the Qur'an and the wise traditions notwithstanding—utilizes modern scientific methods. But more than this, physical aspects of things in the universe also confirm that the theology of Muslims is a complete science, and not superstition. The new signs emerging in profusion today are ironclad proof of our theological ideas. At present, people's desires carry them along with vapid fashions and decadent styles. We should employ Islamic theology to rectify [such practices]. There is nothing as wonderful as causing people to recognize the Creator and in time to know that it is the fear [of God] that binds their hearts.

6. Law. Most everyone knows that the whole of law is divided into the studies of Roman law and religious law. But few of our countrymen who practice Islam are also trained in law. In law, the focus worldwide is on civil law, criminal law, peacetime international law, wartime international law, agricultural law, mercantile law, and so on. All of these are covered in Islamic teaching, whose laws concerning inheritance are most appropriate to our country's present reality. All one need say, today, in taking up the matter of female inheritance, is that in ancient China women lacked inheritance rights because China's earliest institutions were based on clan-lineage law. Each lineage had large and small sublineages, and inheritance based on lineage status became common practice. Despite being blood offspring, women were denied inheritance rights. Law in Islamic teaching has no lineage-status inheritance and gives women the right to inherit, but only one-half of male inheritance. For example, person A has one son and two daughters. His inherited property would be dispersed half to the son and half to the two daughters together. In China, only since the first and ninth resolutions at the Kuomintang's Second National Congress [in 1926] has there been any policy for women's inheritance rights. Nevertheless, the principle of equal status between men and women has been firmly decided and implemented. With regard to the promotion [of gender equality], there is no better example than in the areas of the northeastern Hui, where disputes frequently arise that result in a year's worth of litigation. Last year our northeastern coreligionists invited me to translate "Islamic Laws of Female Inheritance" in order for those dealing with such matters to have something to rely on. I acted on their request, and after the draft was done I wanted to send it to experts in the legal world to examine carefully. This had not yet been realized when the Sino-Japanese clash arose [in 1937].

7. Qur'anic exegesis. The most important course of study in our *madrasa* is that of exegesis of Holy Scripture. There is quite a lot of such exegesis, and the one utilized in China is *Gezhui zhu* [*Commentary on Gezhui*]. Someone edited it long ago into four large volumes, and it was circulated for years. In recent years, the *madrasa*s emerging everywhere in the northeast have followed the trend in circulating the *Housaini jiezhu* [*Exegesis of Husayni*]. It is bound in one large volume in the Western style and contains the complete Persian commentary. Its predecessor, *Gezhui zhu*, also received two large additional commentaries explaining the *Gezhui zhu*, or exegeses of an exegesis. Here we see how Islamic culture advances.

8. Persian. Muslim culture in China got its start through importation by Persian traders, as already noted above. Chinese students of Arabic view the worth of Persian as on a par with Arabic, even though it is a subdiscipline. Lately, proponents of the New Learning have eliminated Persian courses, and this has concentrated the efforts of students onto Arabic. This way of seeing things certainly cannot be dismissed summarily. However, since our forebears built a whole course of study through great tribulation, my conscience could not bear the casual destruction of it all. Therefore, I feel a great urge to support Persian studies. The discipline of Persian studies in China has generally used *Shengui gezhi* [*Commen-*

taries on Hadith] (in two volumes); *Huayuan lu* [*The Rose Garden*, by Sa'di, 1184–1292] (a well-known book of ethics); the teachings of self-cultivation (for example, the whole category of *Guizhen yaodao* [*The Path of God's Bondsmen*, by Najm al-Din Razi Daya, 1177–1256]); and Qur'anic commentary (for example, *Zhaxidi* [reference unclear]). Supposing that Persian [studies] were to be eliminated, then this curriculum would disappear into oblivion. We should be very sorry for such a senseless abandonment. Persia (today referred to as Iran) is one of the ancient nations of the East. In the history of Eastern literature, for example in philosophy, missing material recorded in Chinese historical texts can be looked up in old Persian documents. In light of this, we must recognize that Persian has contributed to the development of Chinese culture, and we are obliged to preserve it. Those who take an interest in Muslim culture should not ignore this point.

With this eight-point curriculum, one might calculate that Persian and Arabic language studies would involve a total of 13 texts. It would take 15 years to graduate from a *madrasa*. Without this [curriculum], [a student's] learning would not be firmly grounded, and it would be difficult to teach others. Leaving aside the 13 course-books, there are also quite a few supplemental works, the most well-known of which is *Mogematai* [*Muhammadanism*, transliterated from Russian] compiled by Mr. Haleirenyi [reference unclear]. This is the one book for traditional Arabic. In its fifteen chapters we have the quintessence of Arabic literature, and in its profuseness it makes a grand overview. Coming next, such areas as logic, astronomy, ethics, and inheritance law were in earlier times all set out in supplemental courses. Today, though, they have become merely another "Guangling san."[5]

Scholars of Traditional and Modern Arabic Literature

In speaking generally of Chinese scholars of Arabic, the leading light since Master Hu [Dengzhou]

---

5. ["Guangling san" is the name of a lute tune played by Xi Kang as he was led to his execution in 262 A.D. It is said that he always refused to teach it, and the tune was no longer known after his death.—Trans.]

was Liu Zhi of Nanjing (known as Jiekang gong [1655–1745]), who wrote no fewer than seventy-odd works. Those three volumes most to be commended, by scholars of our religion and by others, are *Tianfang dianli* [*Ritual and Ceremony of Islam*], *Tianfang xingli* [*The Nature and Principle of Islam*], and *Zhisheng shilu* [*The True Record of the Most Wise*]. Aside from Master Jiekang, we should mention Mr. Ma Fuchu of Yunnan [Ma Dexin, circa 1794–1874] as an eminence in Muslim culture. His works include titles such as *Daoxing jiujing* [*Completing the Path of the Way*], *Sidian yaohui* [*Essentials of the Four Seasons*], and *Dahua zonggui* [*The Great Change Ultimately Returns*]. Next, we have Zhenhui Laoren [the Old Master of Islam, Wang Daiyu, circa 1584–1670]. This master wrote *Qingzhen daxue* [*The Great Learning of Islam*]. This list contains older compilations, each with its own special features, all of which enjoyed broad appeal for a long time. The confident style of writing, the thoroughness of the reasoning—these are decidedly things that the later generation of scholars cannot even hope to match.

Of today's scholars, one would have to place as number one Yang Jingxiu of Tianjin (known as Zhongming [1870–1952]). Mr. Yang has written such titles as *Sijiao yaokuo* [*The Essential Strictures of the Four Teachings*] and *Zhong-A chuhun* [*A Learner's Book in Arabic*] (an Arabic language text). This master has been a blessing for our studies in China, and his essays are distinctly unique. At present he lives in the former capital, without any contact, working on Chinese translations from the Qur'an. Whenever these get published, there is no telling what a blossoming of splendor this will be for modern Islamic culture. Li Yanxiang of Qian'an (known as Yuchen [1884–1937]), who unfortunately passed away last year, wrote, among other works, *Da hua lishi* [*A Chronicle of the Creation*] and *Shengyu lu* [*A Manual of Hadith*], which have become cherished reading for our colleagues all over China. At present, the most well known of the fresh new youth in China's world of Arabic studies include Ma Jian [1906–1978], a native of Yunnan who has studied in Egypt, and Na Zijia, as well as Hai Weiliang of Hunan. Ma has written such Chinese works as *Huijiao zhexue* [*The Theology of Islam*] and *Huijiao zhenxiang* [*The Truth of Islam*], and also has translated the *Analects of Confucius* into Arabic and published it in Egypt. Na has published a translation titled *Yisilan jiao* [*The Teachings of Islam*].

Although Mr. Hai has not offered his colleagues a monograph, his newspaper essays, which are found everywhere outside of China, make us realize that his aspirations are unusual, and such time as he returns to China he will be a startling force. These scholars are all men who are at home equally in Arabic and Chinese literature.

In the area of Persian specialists, we must place as our founding father the early Qing era Master Chang of Jining [Chang Zhimei, 1610–1670]. This gentleman's works include *Posi wenfa* [*Persian Grammar*], which has remained popular throughout the country to this day. All Chinese readers of Persian use the book as a key. One might say that Master Chang has been a harbinger of the true path.

In addition to the scholars mentioned above, Ma Wanfu of Gansu (Old Hajj Ma of Guoyuan [1849–1934]) certainly must be mentioned in the demolition of the old writings that is going on in the modern era of Muslim culture. Though he was not conversant in Chinese history and literature, he exerted great effort in the correction of old mistakes in our religion and the development of a new Muslim culture. The Shuaizhen [Righteous] Faction among the *akhond*s [religious scholars] of the northwest (their opponents being called the New Teaching) for the most part got its start with the school of the Old [Hajj]. Since its emergence, it has not distributed among the populace any translations; yet its main business thrives, and that achievement is enormous.

Arabic Students' Arduous Struggle to Gain Knowledge

The structure of Muslim culture in the two provinces of Gansu and Qinghai is flourishing: the quota of students remains steady at approximately 100. Next are the provinces of Ji, Lu, and Yu. It is a pity that the numbers of students there do not amount to even a quarter of those in the northwest. Yet if one considers their spirit of hard work and perseverance, they rate a notch higher than students in the northwest. For years, I personally observed the best students of the old *madrasa*s, and afterward I was director of instruction for more than twenty years. The hardship that I endured was too much even to recount. For some years I ate crude meals and tasteless rice; my clothing was a rough cotton shirt and trousers; I did my own cooking and cleaning. I went over my lessons in odd moments of spare time. I would finally get to sleep only in the very small hours of the night. There were no places and no money to buy the books needed for higher study, and we could only copy them out by hand on paper we made ourselves. The paper was thick, made by using fine fur or flour that had thickened. First we made a paste out of wheat flour, and when the paper took shape, some white wax was applied and the paper flattened with polished rocks, making it harder and more durable than today's heaviest foreign paper. In writing we used bamboo pens, which were shaped like today's metal-nib pens. When we finished writing, the stack of paper was sometimes two inches thick. We used wooden boards to press it together, then a sharp knife to trim the edges, and finally nailed together a binding by hand. It looked a bit like modern Western binding.

I have narrated these trivial matters here in order to show just how difficult was the quest for learning that our sort of *madrasa* student undertook. Also, I have sought to commend the appropriate place that the Chinese students of Arabic of old held among their professional peers, and moreover the very minor model [of ingenuity] that they supplied in the context of new technologies. It is regrettable that outsiders knowing anything of this are rare indeed, and if we look for the reason, we must find it in the fact that there is no communication between Chinese and Arabic cultures. We may attribute this lack of thorough communication to the fact that scholars on both sides have not linked hands. When our thoughts and recollections touch on these issues, how great a pity it all seems. However, readers of Arabic benefit greatly, if invisibly, from their study of Chinese. Those schools that we call specialist Arabic textschools must by their nature be referred to as Chinese-Arabic schools. This is simply because in so many places, those who have never learned to read Chinese characters usually recite in Chinese as they read Arabic. There is no greater example of a small fault that one may find in something otherwise fine—and that comes as a delight, too.

Conclusion

For Chinese Muslims personally, the culture of Islam has provided a basis for rugged and independent survival. It would seem that we have no need for

contact with the outside [Chinese society], and also that the outside world has no need of adding Arabic and Muslim cultural studies to the process of broadening and developing their own individual school programs. Be that as it may, a cool-headed look reveals that the national universities face several urgent practical necessities:

1. Because appointments of Arabic specialists are higher paying than those for learned leaders in Islamic culture, the national universities' interest in excellent youthful lecturers would bring about the needed speed [in promoting Arabic studies], and also would be decidedly practical.

2. Quite frankly, Islam is a social force that seeks peaceful ends through martial vigilance: in various matters it talks peace and presents an exterior of profound ceremoniousness. But once it encounters outside oppression, then it forms a mass resistance without a moment's thought. In Mecca some years ago, there was a large convention of pilgrims, whose numbers exceeded 200,000. In a swirl of quick-step motion they arrived at the starting point outside the city, and in stick shacks and frosty lodgings the world's Muslims nonetheless generated a solemn and orderly event. Other religions do not have such well-precedented social movements. One finds numerous rituals of this type in Islam, and this suffices as an explanation. Returning to the present, to add Islamic cultural studies courses in response to a general clamor will, in effect, be of some help in the current War of Resistance.

3. In all ways, the teachings of Islamic culture advance innate knowledge, preserve society, and stabilize the nation's educational profession. The Qur'an teaches us, "If you change your mind, then there must be a change in the Lord's relation to you." [This appears to be a paraphrase of Sura 13, Verse 11.] This is a famous passage that calls for men to correct their thinking, and not just change [to meet the situation]. Elsewhere it says, "You will not breed hatred in any place; the Lord does not take joy in hatred between men." [Sura 5, Verse 64] This serves to warn men not to destroy the social order. Elsewhere it says, "Obey . . . those in authority among you" [Sura 4, Verse 59]—here meaning submitting to the head of the nation. This phrase standing alone is very terse. For example, in today's case, when our state leaders authorize a national decree, we have the duty to uphold it without faltering. When people's minds are restless, the social order needs to be more strongly preserved, and the patriotic emotions of the

populace must be elevated. Adding Islamic culture [to the university curriculum] is a fitting response, and will supply no small aid to people's minds, to society, and to the nation.

4. Islamic law is well suited to matters concerning human emotion, not just matters of wrongdoing. Its greatest worth to society can be seen in the friction between the poor and wealthy classes. For example, if a person's yearly income yields 29 Chinese yuan in surplus, there might be 5 mao for the purpose of charity. The annual practice of individual donation at the end of Ramadan (about 2 mao each) is considered an entitlement for the poor. It is a good method for reconciling the poor and wealthy classes. . . . If we contemplate China's current situation, then by simply imitating this system, grants to the poor would provide appropriate consolation.

5. Islam's very nature is one of frugality and injunctions against luxury. For example, the matter of clothing: No textile that is excessively steep in price is permitted to be used (this refers not only to silk goods). And in all daily commodities, most of all

drinking water, waste is not allowed. Our Muslim brethren all have this habit as a result of the way they are raised. Even something as tiny as a grain of food, they do not dare to throw it away. Currently our country is in the midst of the War of Resistance, and so savings achieved among the rear guard are imperative. Because Islam is a social system that encourages savings, it ought to redouble its efforts, and do its best to be a model for all.

6. Islam prohibits waste and loss. Therefore in the matter of gambling—Islam has prohibited this from the start. As for laxness and vice, and other matters of shamelessness and moral failure, they are all strictly banned. Generally, when a society is infected with such evils, it cannot avoid producing unwholesome phenomena that influence the entire nation. This sort of thing would be a great trouble to the nation. People of character are greatly distressed when minor officials and wealthy householders are wanton and debauched. At this moment, our response is to promote Islam's ancient culture so as to keep such people at bay.

Glossary

'ajam, non-Arab

amir, ruler

bay or *bey*, nobleman or rich man

bid'a, unlawful innovation

falsafa, philosophy

faqih, jurisprudent

fatwa, religious ruling

fiqh, Islamic jurisprudence

hadith, tradition of the Prophet

haji or *hajji*, Muslim who has been on the *hajj*, the pilgrimage to Mecca

haram, religiously prohibited

hijab, modest dress, especially for women

hijra, migration of the Muslims from Mecca to Medina in the year 622, beginning the Islamic calendar

ifta', ruling

ijma', consensus

ijtihad, rational interpretation, literally the intellectual effort of trained Islamic scholars to arrive at legal rulings on matters not covered in the sacred sources

'ilm, science, knowledge

imam, religious leader

isnad, chain of transmission, or sources

ittiba', critical acceptance of precedent or authority

jihad, religious struggle

kafir, unbeliever

kalam, Islamic theology

khilafat, caliphate

kufr, disbelief

madhhab, one of the four main schools of Sunni Islamic law

madrasa, seminary

maktab, elementary school

maulavi, religious scholar

mufti, religious official or jurisconsult qualified to issue *ifta'*

mujtahid, religious scholar qualified to engage in *ijtihad*

mulla, religious scholar

muqallid, follower, one who engages in *taqlid*

pasha, nobleman

qadi, judge

qanun, law

qiyas, analogical reasoning

salaf, salafiyya, pious ancestors, the early Muslims

sayyid, descendant of the Prophet

shar', shari'a, Islamic law

shaykh, religious scholar or holy person

shura, consultation

softa, seminary student

sunna, practice of the Prophet

sura, chapter of the Qur'an

tanzimat, reforms intended to make government administration more orderly

taqlid, following precedent or authority

tawhid, divine unity

'ulama', religious scholars

umm, mother

umma, community, especially the community of Muslims

usul, principles

zahir, outward appearance

zakat, alms taxes, one of the five pillars of Islam

Index of Qur'anic Citations

Index of Personal Names